LeRoy & Ballard's

1572 Mellange de Chansons

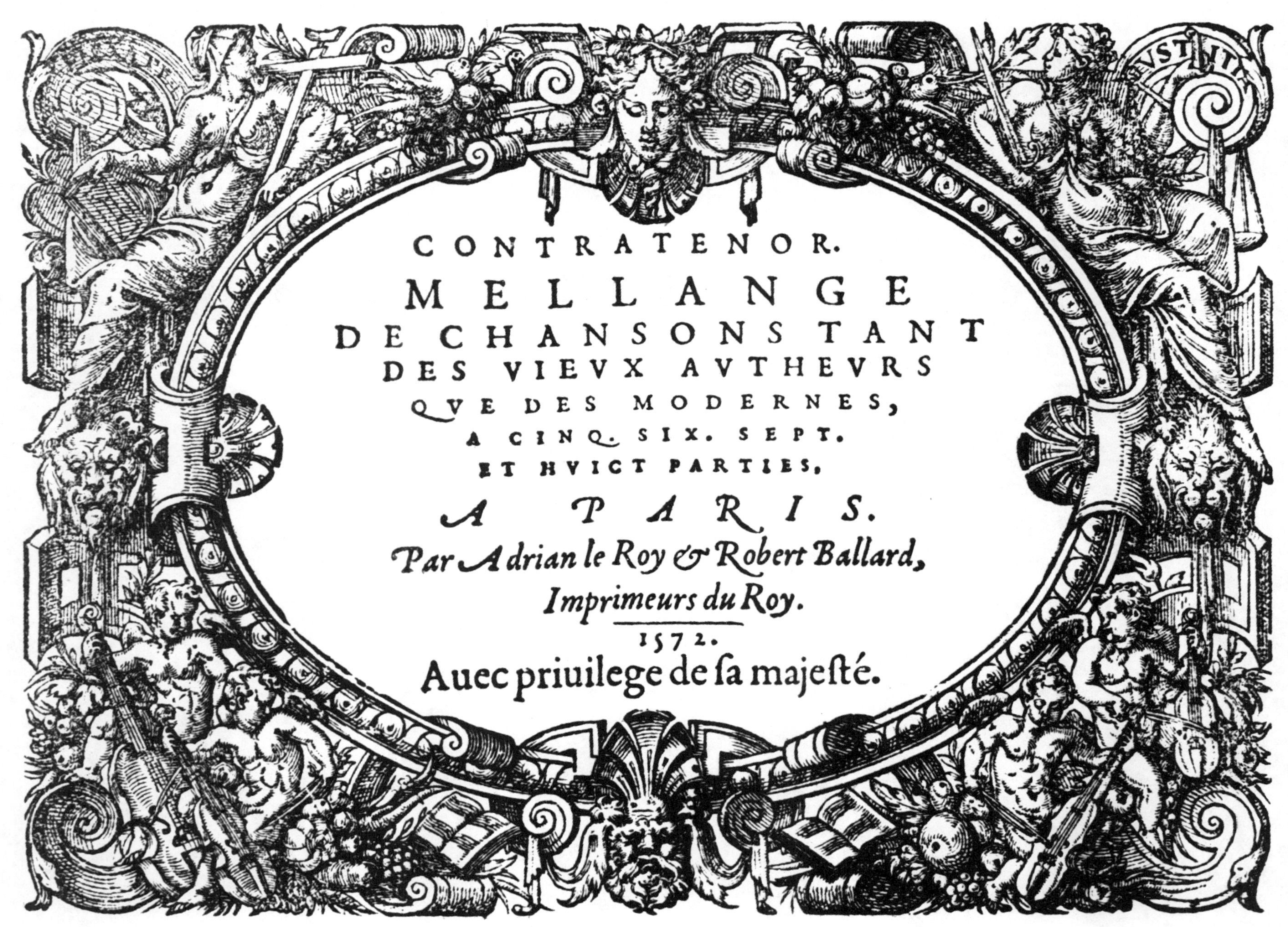

CONTRATENOR.
MELLANGE
DE CHANSONS TANT
DES VIEVX AVTHEVRS
QVE DES MODERNES,
A CINQ. SIX. SEPT.
ET HVICT PARTIES.
A PARIS.
Par Adrian le Roy & Robert Ballard,
Imprimeurs du Roy.
1572.
Auec priuilege de sa majesté.

LeRoy & Ballard's

1572 Mellange de Chansons

edited by Charles Jacobs

The Pennsylvania State University Press
University Park and London

For

Isabel Pope Conant

Distinguished Scholar,
inspiration to all in Hispanic studies
Valued Friend

Publication of this book was assisted by a grant from the Publications Program of the National Endowment for the Humanities, an independent Federal agency.

Library of Congress Cataloging in Publication Data

Mellange de chansons.
   LeRoy & Ballard's 1572 Mellange de chansons.

   Includes bibliography and indexes.
   1. Chansons, Polyphonic. I. Jacobs, Charles.
II. Adrian LeRoy & Robert Ballard (Firm)
III. Title. IV. Title: 1572 Mellange de chansons.
M1529.4.M44L4   81−83150
ISBN 0−271−00295−6   AACR2

Designed by Dolly Carr

Printed in the United States of America

Contents

List of the Music   7

List of Plates   11

Acknowledgements   13

Introduction   15

Mellange de Chansons   23
     Preface   25
     The Music   29

Critical Notes   587

Notes   625

Bibliography   633

Indexes   637
     Incipits   637
     Composers, poets   639

Plate Ia — *Mellange*, Tenor, fol. 77ᵛ

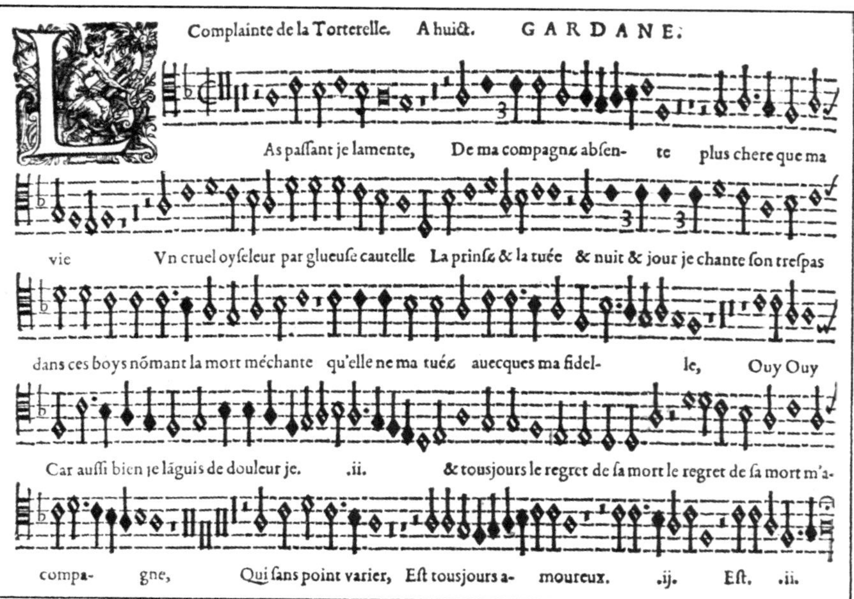

List of the Music

The form of the composer's name used is that most common in the source.

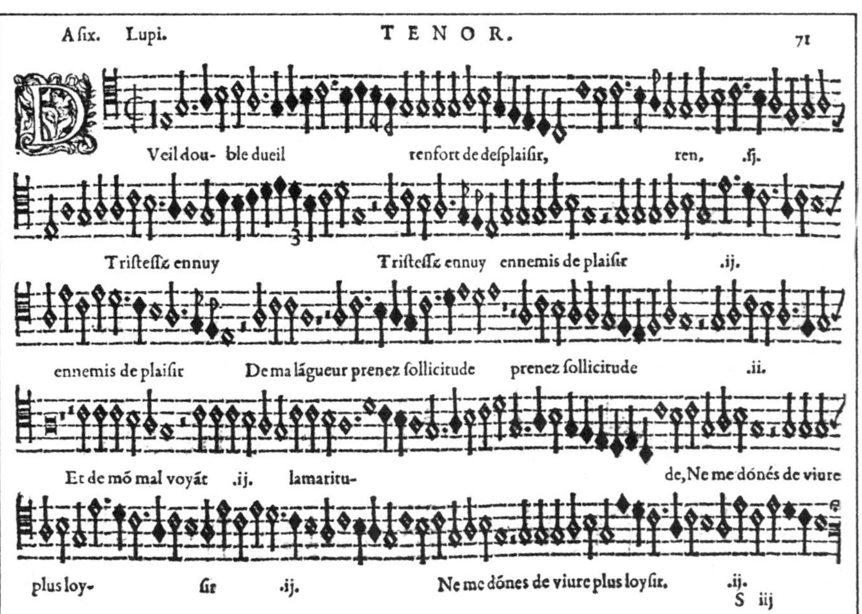

Plate Ib — *Mellange*, Tenor, fol. 71ʳ

1.	Vuillart, *Jouissance vous donneray* [C. Marot]	29
2.	Vuillart, *Helas ma mere*	32
3.	Vuillart, *Qui la dira*	36
4.	Mouton, *Ce que mon coeur pense*	38
5.	Mouton, *Le berger & la bergere*	41
6.	Richafort, *Cuidez vous que Dieu*	43
7.	Benedictus, *Je m'y levay par un matin*	45
8.	Arcadet, *Quand je me trouve*	48
9.	Vuildre, *Pour vous aymer*	50
10.	Vuildre, *Pour un plaisir*	52
11.	Vuildre, *Je me repens*	54
12.	Vuildre, *Ma bouche rit*	57
13.	Vuildre, *Je file quand Dieu*	59
14.	Monte, *Secourez moy ma dame* [C. Marot]	61
15.	Mouton, *Vray Dieu d'amours*	63
16.	Mouton, *La rousée du mois de may*	66
17.	Rousée, *Fortune, laisse moy la vie*	68
18.	Rore, *Susane un jour* [Guéroult]	71
19.	Strige, *Pour m'esloigner* [St. Gelais]	75
20.	Hauville, *Herbes & fleurs*	77
21.	Cornet, *Or me traictiez*	80
22.	LeJeune, *Allons, allons gay*	83
23.	Leschenet, *Puis que j'ay belle amye*	88
24.	LeJeune, *Quand vous seriés*	90
25.	Nicolas, *Je m'en vois au vert bois*	93
26.	Nicolas, *Susane un jour* [Guéroult]	97
27.	Nicolas, *Je ry & si ay larmes*	100
28.	Nicolas, *Tout ce qu'on peut*	103
29.	Nicolas, *A ce matin*	111

30. Nicolas, *Pour ton amour* [C. Marot]   114
31. Nicolas, *Il est bon enfant*   117
32. Richaffort, *Sy je m'y plain*   122
33. Vuillart, *Sonnez m'y donc*   124
34. Vuillard, *Puis que j'ay perdu ma maitresse*   128
35. Crequillon, *En languissant*   131
36. Crequillon, *Vivre en espoir*   135
37. Vuillard, *Aller m'y faut*   138
38. Maillard, *Force d'amour* [Ste. Marthe]   143
39. Nicolas, *N'aurai-je jamais mieux*   147
40. Maillard, *Helas ma fille, il te tuera*   151
41. Roussel, *Content ou non*   154
42. Vuillard, *Je l'ay aymée*   157
43. Vuildre, *Si de beaucoup*   161
44. Roussel, *Banny j'en suis*   163
45. Nicolas, *Avecques vous mon amour finira*   167
46. Goudimel, *Amour me tue* [Ronsard]   169
47. Crequillon, *Pis ne me peut venir*   173
48. Nicolas, *Sur tous regretz*   175
49. Farabosco, *Auprés de vous*   178
50. Josquin, *Je me complein*   181
51. Josquin, *Parfons regretz*   184
52. Vuillard, *Voulez ouir chansonnette*   188
53. Josquin, *N'est-ce pas un grand desplaisir*   192
54. Vuillard, *Mort ou mercy* [J. Marot]   194
55. Josquin, *Coeur langoureux*   198
56. Nicolas, *Las voulez vous*   201
57. Josquin, *Je ne me puis tenir d'aymer*   204
58. Godard, *Puis qu'ainsi est*   208
59. Vuillard, *Vous aurez tout ce qui est mien*   211
60. Crequillon, *A jamais croy*   214
61. Crequillon, *Content ou non*   218
62. Josquin, *Faute d'argent*   222
63. Nicolas, *Grace & Vertu*   226
64. Millot, *Le cors s'en va*   229
65. Millot, *Douce maitresse touche* [Ronsard]   233
66. Nicolas, *Force d'amour* [Ste. Marthe]   235
67. Nicolas, *Le coeur de vous* [C. Marot]   239
68. Benedictus, *Si je me plein*   242
69. Millot, *Revien vers moy* [Ronsard]   246
70. Gombert, *Le berger & la bergere*   249
71. Lupi, *Au joly bois*   253
72. Vuillard, *Sire don dieu*   257
73. Arcadet, *Si la beauté de ma dame*   261
74. Millot, *Susane un jour* [Guéroult]   263
75. Millot, *Si je trespasse* [Ronsard]   267
76. Millot, *Elle veut donc*   269
77. Millot, *Contentement combien*   272
78. Millot, *Sur la rousée*   275
79. LeBrun, *N'a vous point veu*   278
80. LeJeune, *Rossignol, mon mignon* [Ronsard]   282
81. Millot, *Le Rossignol sauvage*   289
82. Vuildre, *Un jeune moyne*   292
83. Vuildre, *Helas, ma dame*   294
84. Goudimel, *Allez, mes soupirs*   297

Plate IIa — *Mellange*, fol. 48ᵛ

85. Vuillard, *Je ne sçaurois*   301
86. Mouton, *Du bon du coeur*   304
87. Vuildre, *Une nonnain refaite* [C. Marot]   307
88. Vuildre, *Amour, partez*   312
89. Certon, *Regret, soucy, & peine*   314
90. Vuildre, *Je ne fay rien* [C. Marot]   317
91. Benedictus, *Arousez vo vi vo violette*   320
92. Richafort, *D'amour je suis desheritée*   324
93. Vuillard, *Baisés moy tant tant*   326
94. Crequillon, *Belle, donne moy*   330
95. Leschenet, *Est-il douleur cruelle*   333
96. Vuildre, *De vous servir*   338
97. Monte, *O triste ennuy*   340
98. Leschenet, *Gris & tanné*   348
99. LaRue, *Incessamment mon povre coeur*   352
100. Vuillard, *A la fontaine*   355
101. Vuillard, *Puis donc que ma maistresse*   359

102. Vuillard, *Or suis-je bien*   362
103. Vuillard, *En douleur & tristesse*   366
104. Vuillard, *Faute d'argent*   370
105. Vuillard, *Mon coeur, mon corps*   374
106. Vuillard, *Douleur me bat*   377
107. Vuillard, *Petite camusette*   380
108. Vuillard, *Vous ne l'aurez pas*   383
109. Vuillard, *Qui veut aymer*   387
110. Vuillard, *De retourner, mon amy*   389
111. Leschenet, *Je m'y plein fort*   392
112. Crequillon, *Sy me tenez tant*   395
113. Mouton, *Vray Dieu qu'amoureux*   398
114. Nicolas, *Vivés en paix*   401
115. Nicolas, *Dieu te gard, bergere*   404
116. Leschenet, *Le coeur est mien*   407
117. Leschenet, *Helas, pourquoy ne suis-je*   410
118. Gardane, *Je cerche autant amour*   414
119. Rousée, *La rousée du moys de may*   418
120. Moulu, *La rousée du moys de may*   420
121. Moulu, *En despit des faux médisans*   423
122. Nicolas, *Je recommence ma douleur*   426
123. Nicolas, *J'ay contenté ma volonté* [C. Marot]   430
124. Nicolas, *Voz huys sont ilz*   434
125. Nicolas, *Puis que j'ay belle amye*   438
126. Fourmentin, *Par trop amour*   441
127. Maillard, *Las, je languis*   445
128. Josquin, *Tenez moy en voz bras*   448
129. Josquin, *Allegez moy douce plaisant*   452
130. Nicolas, *Tout est vert*   454
131. LeJeune, *O pas en vain perdus* [Baïf]   459
132. LeJeune, *Je suis desheritée*   464
133. Lupi, *Dueil, double dueil*   466
134. LeJeune, *C'est une dure departie*   470
135. Clemens non papa, *C'est à grand tort*   474
136. Nicole, *Passa la nave mia* [Petrarch]   477
137. LeJeune, *Susanne un jour* [Guéroult]   485
138. Moulu, *J'ay mis mon coeur*   495
139. Gardane, *Fuyez de moy*   503

Plate IIb — *Mellange*, fol. 55ᵛ

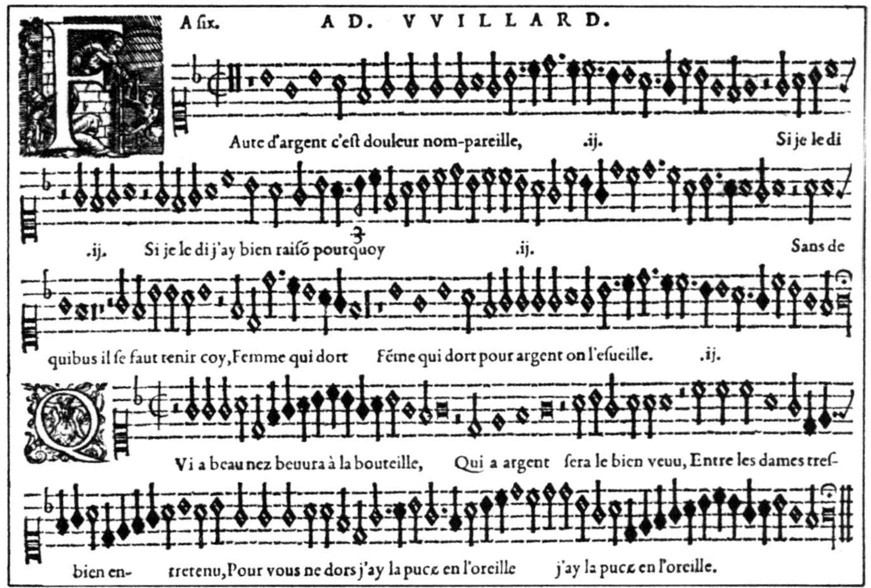

140. Crequillon, *Petite camusette* — 513
141. Certon, *Revien vers moy* [Ronsard] — 520
142. Vuildre, *Amy, souffrez* — 528
143. Clemens non papa, *Amour au coeur* [C. Marot] — 534
144. Gardane, *Complainte de la Torterelle (Que dis tu, que fais tu)* [Ronsard] — 540
145. Phinot, *Vivons m'amye* — 549
146. Phinot, *Qu'est-ce qu'amour* — 560
147. Phinot, *Par un traict d'or* [Forcadel] — 571
148. Verdelot, *Qui la dira* — 581

List of Plates

Plate III — *Mellange*, fol. [i^v]

Frontispiece — *Mellange*, Contratenor, fol. [i^r]	2
Ia — *Mellange*, Tenor, fol. 77^v	5
Ib — *Mellange*, Tenor, fol. 71^r	7
IIa — *Mellange*, fol. 48^v	8
IIb — *Mellange*, fol. 55^v	9
III — *Mellange*, fol. [i^v]	11
IVa and b — *Livre*, fols. [1^v] and [2^r]	12
IVc, d, and e — *Mellange*, fols. [ii^r]—[iii^r]	13-14
Va — *Livre*, fol. [60^v]	15
Vb — *Mellange*, fol. [84^v]	15
VIa and b — *Livre*, fols. 47^v and 48^r	16
VIc and d — *Mellange*, fols. 19^v and 20^r	17
VIIa — *Livre*, fol. 28^r	18
VIIb — *Mellange*, fol. 41^r	18
VIIIa — *Livre*, fol. 36^r	19
VIIIb — *Mellange*, fol. 48^r	19
IXa and b — *Livre*, fols. 19^v and 20^r	20
IXc and d — *Mellange*, fols. 49^v and 50^r	25
Xa — *Livre*, fol. 28^v	26
Xb — *Mellange*, fol. 52^v	26
XIa — *Livre*, fol. 44^r	27
XIb — *Mellange*, Contratenor, fol. 83^r	27

Plate IVa and b — *Livre*, fols. [1ᵛ] and [2ʳ]

PREFACE DE P. DE RONSARD
AV ROY FRANCOYS. II.

Ire, tout ainsi que par la pierre de touche, on a de coustume d'esprouuer l'or s'il est bon ou mauuais, Ainsi les anciens espreuuoyent par la Musique les esperits de ceux qui sont ge-nereux, magnanimes, & non foruoyans de leur premiere essence: & de ceux qui sont en-gourdiz, paresseux, & abastardiz en ce corps mortel, ne se souuenát de la celeste armonie du ciel, non plus qu'aux cópagnons D'Vlisse d'auoir esté hommes, apres que Circe les eut transformés en porceaux. Car celuy, Sire, lequel oyant l'accord de la Musique, ou la dou-ceur de la voix naturelle, ne s'en resiouyst point, ne s'en esmeut point, & de teste en piedz n'en tressault point, comme doucement raucy, & ie ne scay comment derobé hors de soy: c'est signe qu'il a l'ame tortue, vicieuse, & deprauée, & duquel il se fault dóner de garde, comme de celuy qui n'est point heureusement bien né. Car comment pourroit on accorder auec vn homme qui de son naturel hayt les accords? Celuy certes n'est pas digne de parti-ciper de la douce lumiere du soleil, qui ne fait honneur a la Musique, comme petite partie de celle, qui s'armonieusement (comme dit Platon) agitte tout ce grand vniuers. Au con-traire celuy qui luy porte hóneur & reuerence est ordinairement hóme de bien, il a l'ame saine & gaillarde, & de son naturel ayme les choses haultes, la philosophie, le maniment des affaires politiques, le trauail martial des guerres, & bref en tous offices honorables il fait tousiours apparoistre les estincelles de sa vertu. Or de declarer icy que c'est que Mu-sique, si elle est plus gouuernée de fureux que d'art, de ses concens, de ses tons, modulations, voix, interualles, sons, systemates, & cómuta-tions: de sa diuision en Armonique, laquelle pour sa difficulté ne fut iamais perfaittement en vsage: en Chromatique, laquelle pour sa lesquinet fut par les anciens barye des republiques, en Armonique, laquelle comme la plus aprochante de la melodie de ce grand vni-uers fust de tous approuuée. De parler de la Phrigienne, dorienne, lydienne: & cóme quelques peuples de Grece animez d'armonye, alloiét courageusement a la guerre, cóme noz soldatz asiourdhuy au son des trompettes & tabourins: cóme le Roy Alexandre oyant les cháps de Timothée, deuenoit furieux, & comme Agamemnon allant a Troye, laissa en sa maison tout expres ie ne scay quel Musicien Dorien, lequel par la vertu du pied Anapeste, moderoit les esfrenées passiós amoureuses de sa femme Clytemnestre, de l'amour delaquelle Aegiste tansfonmf, ne peut iamais auoir ioyssance, que premierement il n'eust fait meschanment mourir le Musicien. De vouloir encores deduire comme toutes choses sont composées d'accordz, de mesures, & do proportions, tant au ciel, en la mer, qu'en la terre, de vouloir discourir dauantage comme les plus honorables personnages des siecles passez, se sont tous curieusement sentiz espris des ardeurs de la Musique, tant Monarques, que Roys, Philosophes, gouuerneurs de prouinces, & cappitaines de renom. ie n'aurou iamais fait: dautant que la Mu-sique a tousiours esté le signe & la merque de ceux qui se sont móstrez vertueux, magnanimes & veritablement nez pour ne sentir rié

de vulgaire. Ie prédray seullemét pour exemple le feu Roy vostre pere, que Dieu absolue, lequel ce pendát qu'il a regné a fait apparoistre combien le ciel l'auoit liberallement enrichy de toutes graces, & de presens rares entre les Roys, lequel a surpassé soit en grandeur d'em-pire, soit en clemêce, en liberalité, bonté, pieté & religion, non seullement tous les princes ses predecesseurs, Mais tous ceux qui ont iamais vescu portant cet honorable tiltre de Roy: lequel pour descouurir les estincelles de sa bien-naissance, & pour móstrer qu'il estoit acóply de toutes vertuz, a tant honoré, aymé, & prisé la Musique, que tous ceux qui restent asiourdhuy en France bien affectiónez a cet art, ne le sont tant tous ensemble, que tout seul particulierement l'estoit. Vous aussi Sire, comme heritier & de son Royaume & de ses vertus, monstrez combien vous estes son filz, fauorisé du ciel, d'aymer sy parfaittemét telle science & ses accordz sans lesquelz chose de ce móde ne pourroit demourer en son entier. Or de vous conter icy d'Orphée, de Terpende, d'Eumolpe, d'Arion, ce sont histoires, desquelles ie ne veux empescher le papier, cóme choses a vous congneues. Seullement ie vous reciteray, que les plus magnanimes Roys faisoient ancienne-ment nourrir leurs enfans en la maison des Musiciens, cóme Peleus qui enuoya son filz Achille, & Æson son filz Iason, dedás l'Antre ve-nerable du Centaure Chiron, pour estre instruitz tát aux armes, qu'en la medecine, & en l'art de Musique: d'autát que ces trois mestiers meslez ensemble ne sont mal seans a la grádeur d'vn prince, & aduint d'Achille & de Iason, qui estoient princes de vostre age, vn sy recó médable exemple de vertu, que l'vn fut honoré par le diuin poëte Humere, cóme le seul autheur de la prinse de Troye, & l'autre celebré par Apolline Rhodien, comme le premier autheur d'auoir apris a la mer, de soufrir le fardeau incongnu des nauires: lequel ayant outre-passé les roches Symplegades, & donté la furie de la froide mer de Scytie, Finablemét sen retourna en son pays, enrichy de la noble toyson d'or. Donques, Sire, ces deux princes vous seront comme patrons de la vertu, & quand quelque foys vous serez lassé de voz plus vrgétes affaires, a leur imitation, vous adoucirez voz souciz par les accordz de la Musique, pour retourner apres plus fraiz & plus dispos a la charge royalle de vostre labeur. Il ne faut aussy que vostre Magesté s'esmerueille sy ce liure de meslanges (lequel vous est treshumblement dedié par voz treshumbles & tresobeissans seruiteurs & Imprimeurs Adrian le Roy, & Robert Ballard) est composé des plus vieilles chansons qui se puissent trouuer asiourdhuy, pource qu'on a tousiours estimé la Musique des anciens estre la plus diuine, d'autant qu'elle a esté composee en vn siecle plus heureux, & moins entaché des vices qui regnent en ce dernier age de fer. Aussy les diuines fureurs de Musique, de Poësie, & de paincture, ne viennent pas par degrez en perfection comme les autres sciences, Mais par boutées, & cóme es-clairs de feu, qui deca qui dela apparoissent en diuers pays, puis tout en vn coup se suanouyssent. Et pource, Sire, quád il se manifeste quel-que excellét ouurier en cet art, vous le deuez songneusemét garder, cóme chose d'autát excelléte, que raremét elle apparoist. Entre lesquels se sont depuis six ou sept vingtz ans esleuez, Iosquin des Prez, Hénuyer de nation, & ses disciples Mouton, Vuillard, Richaffort, Lonequin Maillard, Claudin, Moulu, Iaquet, Certon, Et de nostre temps Arcadet, lequel ne cede en la perfection de cet art, aux anciens, pour estre inspiré de son Apollon Charles Cardinal de Lorraine. Plusieurs autres choses se pourroient dire de la Musique, dont Plutarque & Boëce ont amplement fait mention. Mais ny la breueté de ce preface, ny la commodité du temps, ny la matiere ne me permect de vous en faire plus lóg discours, Supliát le Createur, Sire, d'augméter de plus en plus les vertuz de vostre Maiesté, & vous cótinuer en la bóne affection qu'il vous plaist de porter a la Musique, & a tous ceux qui s'estudient de faire reflorir souz vostre regne, les sciéces & les artz, qui florif-soient soubz l'empire de Cesar Auguste: duquel Auguste Dieu tout puissant vous vueille dóner les ans, les victoires, & la prosperité.

A ij

Acknowledgements

Plate IVc, d, and e — *Mellange*, fols. [ii^r]—[iii^r]

PREFACE DE P. DE RONSARD
AV ROY CHARLES IX.

S I R E, tout ainſi que par la pierre de touche, on eſprouue ſor ſil eſt bon ou mau-uais, Ainſi les anciens eſprouuoyent par la Muſique les eſprits de ceux qui ſont ge-nereux, magnanimes, & non foruoyás de leur premiere eſſence: & de ceux qui ſont engourdiz pareſſeux, & abaſtardiz en ce corps mortel, ne ſe ſouuenant de la celeſte armonie du ciel, non plus qu'aux compagnons D'vliſſe d'auoir eſté hommes, apres que Circe les eut tráſformés en porceaux. Car celuy, S I R E, lequel oyant vn doux accord d'inſtrumens ou la douceur de la voyx naturelle, ne ſ'en resjouiſt point, ne ſ'en eſmeut point & de teſte en piedz n'en treſſault point, comme doucement rauy, & ſi ne ſçay cóment derobé hors de ſoy: c'eſt ſigne qu'il à ſame tortue, vicieuſe, & deprauée, & duquel il ſe faut dóner garde, comme de celuy qui n'eſt point heureuſement né. Comment pourroit on accorder auec vn homme qui de ſon naturel hayt les accords? celuy n'eſt digne de voyr la douce lumiere du ſoleil, qui ne fait hon-neur a la Muſique, comme petite partie de celle, qui ſi armonieuſement (comme dit Platon) agitte tout ce grand vniuers. Au contraire celuy qui luy porte honneur & reuerence eſt ordinairement hóme de bien, il a ſame ſaine & gaillarde, & de ſon naturel ayme les choſes haultes, la philoſophie, le maniment des affaires politicques, le trauail des guerres, & bref en tous offices honorables il fait tousjours apparoiſtre les eſtincelles de ſa vertu. Or' de declarer icy que c'eſt que Muſique, ſi elle eſt plus gouuernée de fureur que d'art, de ſes concens, de ſes tons, modulations, voyx, intetualles, ſons, ſyſtemates, & cómutations: de ſa diuiſion en Enarmonique, laquelle pour ſa difficulté ne fut jamais perfaittement en vſage: en chromatique, laquelle pour ſa laſciueté fut par les anciens banye des re-publiques, en diatonique laquelle comme la plus aprochante de la melodie de ce grand vniuers fut de tous approuuée. De parler de la Phrigienne, dorienne, lydienne: & comme quelques peuples de Grece animez d'armonie, alloyent courageuſement a la guerre, cóme noz ſoldatz aujourdhuy au ſon des trompettes & tabourins: cóme le Roy Alexandre oyant les chams de Timothée, deue-noit furieux, & comme Agemennom allant a Troye, laiſſa en ſa maiſon tout expres je ne ſçay quel

In the preparation of this edition, I made use of the holdings of many libraries. The resources of the Isham Memorial Library, Harvard University, were of particular value and Mr. Larry Mowers, Assistant Curator of the collection, who extended innumerable courtesies, could not have been more helpful.

Colleagues responded graciously to queries directed to them. Professors Isabelle Cazeaux and Lawrence F. Bernstein were particularly kind and provided me with important bibliographical references. In addition, Professor Cazeaux read through many of my translations of the lyrics, making invaluable suggestions. Professor Bernstein went to considerable trouble to make photocopies of concordance materials for me and loaned me his personal microfilm of Munich, Bavarian State Library, Music MS 1508.

Professor William Shank, Graduate School Music Librarian, City University of New York, assisted unstintingly and with great imagination, making information and facilities easily accessible and thus minimizing consid-erably the work with which I had to occupy myself.

My heartfelt gratitude also is due to Professor Dr. hab. Stanisław Grzeszczuk, Director of the Jagiellonian University Library, Kraków, and Mr. Tadeusz Kondratowicz, Vice Consul, Consulate General of the People's Republic of Poland, New York, for their splendid cooperation in arranging for my use of a microfilm copy of the 1560 Livre de Meslanges *and ultimately for the extension of special permission for reproduction of parts of the 1560 source in this book.*

The edition undoubtedly would not have been realized at all without significant research assistance from the City University of New York. The State University of New York accorded additional valuable support.

The Kosciuszko Foundation, New York, generously provided me with a research grant for travel to Poland.

Special thanks go to Professors Denis Stevens and Richard Wexler for their early encouragement of this edition and useful advice.

Muſicien D'orien, lequel par la vertu du pied Anapeſte, modetoit les efrenées paſſiós amoureuſes de ſa femme Clytemneſtre, de l'amour de laquelle Ægiſte emflamé, ne peut jamais auoir joyſſance, que premierement il n'eut fait meſcháment mourir le Muſicien. De vouloir encores deduire cóme toutes choſes ſont compoſées d'accordz, de meſures, & de proportions, tant au ciel, en la mer, qu'en la terre, de vouloir diſcourir dauantage comme les plus honorables perſonnages des ſiecles paſſez ſe ſont curieuſemét ſentiz eſpris des ardeurs de la Muſique, tant monarques, Princes, Philoſophes, gouuerneurs de prouinces, & cappitaines de renom: je n'auroys jamais fait: d'autát que la Muſique à tousjours eſté le ſigne & la merque de ceux qui ſe ſont monſtrez vertueux, magnanimes & veritablement nez pour ne ſentir rien de vulgaire. Ie prédray ſeullement pour exemple le feu Roy votre Pere, que Dieu abſolue, lequel ce pendant qu'il a regné a fait apparoiſtre cóbien le ciel l'auoit liberallement enrichy de toutes graces, & de preſens rares entre les Roys lequel a ſurpaſſé ſoit en grandeur d'empire, ſoit en clemence, én liberalité, bonté, pieté & religion, non ſeullement tous les Princes ſes predeceſſeurs, Mais tous ceux qui ont jamais veſcu portant cet' honorable tiltre de Roy: lequel pour deſcouurir les eticelles de ſa-bié naiſſáce, & pour mótrer qu'il eſtoit acóply de toutes vertus, a tant honoré, aymé, & priſé la Muſique, que tous ceux qui reſtét aujourdhuy en Fráce bien affectionnez a cet art, ne le ſont tant tous enſemble, que tout ſeul particulierement l'eſtoit. Vous auſſi SIRE, cóme heritier & de ſon Royaume & de ſes vertus, móſtrez cóbien vous eſtes ſon filz fauoriſé du ciel, d'aymer ſi perfaittement telle ſçience & ſes accordz ſans leſquelz choſe de ce móde ne pourroit demourer en ſon entier. Or de vous cóter icy d'Orphée, de Terpádre, d'Eumolpe, d'Arion ce ſont hiſtoires, deſquelles je ne veux empeſcher le papier, cóme choſes a vous congneues. Seullement je vous reciteray que les plus magnanimes Roys faiſoyent anciennement nourrir leurs enfás en la maiſon des Muſiciens, cóme Peleus qui enuoya ſon filz Achille, & Æſon ſon filz Iaſon, dedás l'Antre venerable du Cétaure Chiron, pour eſtre inſtruitz tant aux armes, qu'en la medecine, & en l'art de Muſique: d'autant que ces trois meſtiers meſlez enſéble ne ſont mal ſeans a la grandeur d'un Prince, & aduint d'Achille & de Iaſon, qui eſtoyét princes de votre age, vn ſi recómandable exemple de vertu, que l'un fut honoré par le diuin poëte Homere, comme le ſeul autheur de la prinſe de

Troye: & l'autre celebré par Apolloine Rhodien, comme le premier autheur d'auoir apris a la mer, de ſoufrir le fardeau incongnu des nauires: lequel ayant outrepaſſé les roches Symplegades, & dóté la furie de la froide mer de Scytie, Finablemét ſ'en retourna en ſon pays, enrichy de la noble toyſon dor. Donques, SIRE, ces deux Princes vous ſeront cóme patrons de la vertu, & quand quelque foys vous ſerez laſſé de voz plus vrgentes affaires, à leur imitation, vous adoucirez voz ſouciz par les accordz de la Muſique, pour retourner plus fraiz & plus diſpos a la charge Royalle que ſi dextrement vous ſuportez. Il ne faut auſſi que votre Mageſté ſ'eſmerueille ſi ce liure de mellanges lequel vous eſt treshumblemét dedié par voz treshumbles & treſobeiſſás ſeruiteurs & Imprimeurs Adrian le Roy, & Robert Ballard, eſt compoſé des plus vieilles cháſſons qui ſe puiſſeht trouuer aujourdhuy, pource qu'on a tousjours eſtimé la Muſique des anciés eſtre la plus diuine, d'autát qu'elle a eſté compoſée en vn ſiecle plus heureux, & moins entaché des vices qui regnent en ce dernier age de fer. Auſſi les diuines fureurs de Muſique, de Poëſie, & de painéture, ne viennent pas par degrés en perfection comme les autres ſçiences, mais par boutées & comme eſclairs de feu, qui deça qui dela apparoiſſent en diuers pays, puis tout en vn coup ſeſuanouiſſent. Et pource, SIRE, quand il ſe manifeſte quelque excellent ouurier en cet art, vous le deuez ſongneuſemét garder, cóme choſe d'autát excellente, que rarement elle apparoiſt. Entre leſquelz ſe ſont depuis ſix ou ſept vingtz ans eſleuez, Ioſquin des prez, Hennuyer de nation, & ſes diſciples Mouton, Vuillard, Richaffort, Iancquin, Maillard, Claudin, Moulu, Iaquet, Certon, Arcadet. Et de preſent le plus que diuin Orlande, qui cóme vne mouche à miel a cueilly toutes les plus belles fleurs des antiens, & outre ſemble auoir ſeul deſrobé l'harmonie des cieux pour nous en reſiouir en la terre ſurpaſſant les antiens, & ſe faiſant la ſeule merueille de notre temps. Pluſieurs autres choſes ſe pourroyét dire de la Muſique, dont plutarque & Boëce ont amplement fait mention. Mais n'y la breueté de ce præface, ny la cómodité du temps, ny la matiere ne me permet de vous en faire plus long diſcours, Supliát le Createur, SIRE, d'augmenter de plus en plus les vertus de votre maieſté, & vous continuer en la bonne affection qu'il vous plaiſt porter a la Muſique, & à tous ceux qui ſ'eſtudient de faire reflorir ſoubz votre regne, les ſçiences & les artz qui floriſſoyent ſoubz l'empire de Ceſar Auguſte: duquel Auguſte Dieu tout puiſſant vous vueille donner les ans, les victoyres, & la proſperité.

Introduction

The LeRoy & Ballard *Mellange de Chansons, tant des vieux autheurs que des modernes* (Paris, 1572),[1] containing 148 chansons, is one of the most important sources of Renaissance secular music. It has been celebrated as "the [sixteenth] century's most brilliant showplace for chansons."[2]

The repertory of the *Mellange,* as suggested by its title, in effect provides a survey of the chanson literature from such late-fifteenth century figures as Josquin des Prez (ca. 1450–1521), Jean Mouton (ca. 1470–1522), and Pierre de LaRue (ca. 1470?–1518), to "modern" composers, born in the

Plate Va — *Livre*, fol. [60ᵛ]

Plate Vb — *Mellange*, fol. [84ᵛ]

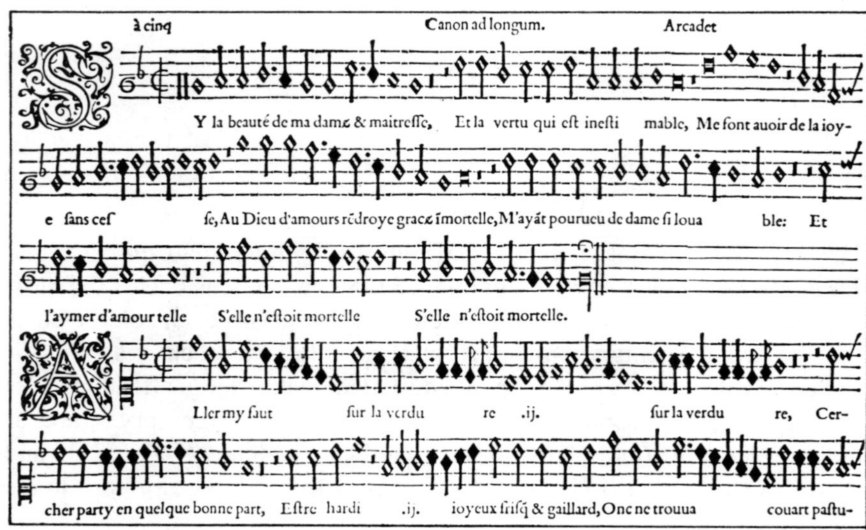

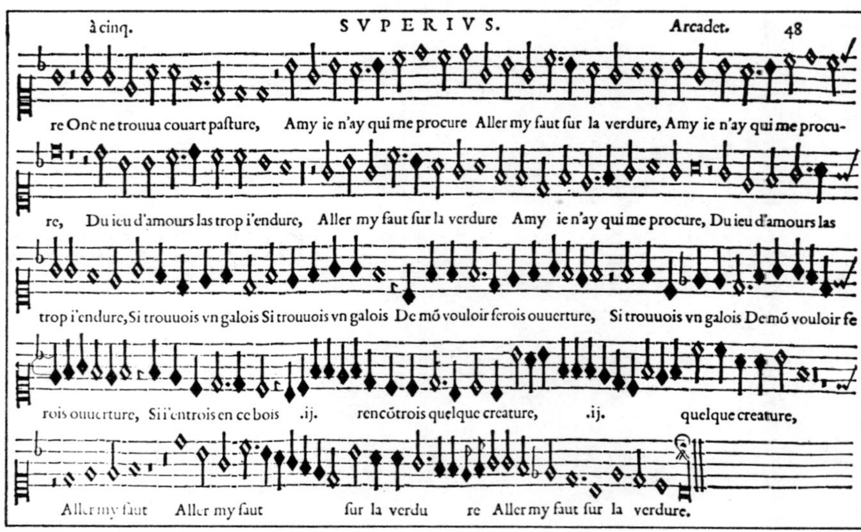

Plate VIa and b — *Livre*, fols. 47ᵛ and 48ʳ

following century, like Philippe de Monte (1521–1603) and Claude LeJeune (ca. 1525/30–1600). The collection is a principal source of the French secular music of Adrian Willaert (ca. 1480/90–1562). In company with these and other renowned masters, there is a host of composers in the *Mellange,* about whom little or nothing is known. As a consequence of its broad scope, the chansons of the *Mellange* run a stylistically wide gamut.

The omission from the pages of the *Mellange* of works by Claudin de Sermisy (ca. 1490–1562), Janequin (ca. 1500–ca. 1560), and Lassus (1532–94), doubtless the sixteenth century's most revered chanson composers, is conspicuous. Indeed, chansons by Lassus and Claudin had been included in the *Livre de Meslanges,*[3] issued by LeRoy & Ballard in 1560 and often regarded as an earlier edition of the 1572 *Mellange.* Since, however, Sermisy, Janequin, and Lassus enjoyed regular representation in contemporary publications by LeRoy & Ballard and other houses, their omission from the 1572 *Mellange* is not as odd as may at first glance seem. In the decade ending 1575, LeRoy & Ballard published no fewer than 22 collections wholly or largely devoted to Lassus's chansons;[4] the most significant of these is the monumental *Mellange d'Orlande de Lassus* (1570), containing over one hundred compositions, of which more than six dozen are

chansons. Perhaps the 1572 *Mellange* and the 1570 Lassus collection were intended by the publishers as companion volumes.

The popularity of the music contained in the *Mellange* was such in the sixteenth century that a very considerable number of its chansons were arranged for instrumental performance or appear in other musical contexts, i.e., as the basis for quite different compositions.[5]

The reading of the music in the *Mellange* is exceptionally reliable. Barring *contrafacta*, the search for which, in the absence of comprehensive thematic indices, would have been virtually futile, musical and textual concordances were sought. The lyrics — poetry — of the *Mellange* chansons were widely used throughout the chanson literature of the time. Musically, however, a number of the *Mellange* chansons appear unique to this source. Treatment of such matters as borrowings among chansons in this source or from chansons in other sources, the use of commonly inherited tunes — the *voix de ville* or *vaux de vire,* paraphrasing by one composer of another's music, and the modelling of music from still other music must be deferred as beyond the scope of this edition.

Considering how incomplete is the information available at present, it seems virtually pointless to undertake to establish the identity of the composer called simply "Nicolas" in the *Mellange*. Inasmuch as Nicolas, in Attaingnant's *Trente cincquiesme livre contenant XXIIII chansons nouvelles a quatre parties* (Paris, 1550),[6] is found in company of Nicolas Gombert and Nicolas de Marle, it seems unlikely he should be identified with either of them.[7] Indeed, the names, Nicolas and Gombert, appear separately in the *Mellange* itself for different music.[8] It has been suggested that Nicolas may be identified with Nicolas de LaGrotte;[9] but music by both LaGrotte and Nicolas is found in LeRoy & Ballard's *Livre d'Airs de Cour* (1571) and LeRoy's *A briefe and plaine Instruction* (London, J. Rowbothome, 1574).[10] A stronger possibility, in the opinion of this writer, is that in which the full name of Nicolas is suggested as Guillaume Nicolas,[11] a singer and chaplain in the French court chapel in Paris, ca. 1532–3.[12] Since no music definitely known to be by Guillaume Nicolas, however, is extant, all present consideration must be regarded as speculative.[13] On the basis of his personal prominence, the possibility cannot be disallowed that LeRoy & Ballard's colleague and rival, Nicolas DuChemin — a most celebrated Nicolas — was the Nicolas represented in the *Mellange*.[14] Indeed, an unusually high number — nine[15] — of the 21 chansons by Nicolas in the *Mellange* are, in themselves and in the collection as a whole, outstanding for their striking use of dissonance, perhaps denoting the effort of a man who, in writing "controversial music," could do so without undue concern for his musical reputation. The skill shown in the Nicolas chansons of the *Mellange*, however, makes it difficult to imagine that or to understand how their composer's musical prowess could have remained uncelebrated. The question of Nicolas' identity therefore clearly remains open.

It has been alleged that the *Mellange* is a later edition of LeRoy & Ballard's 1560 *Livre de Meslanges*.[16] The similarities between the two publications are obvious: a sharing of more than 80 chansons and, in effect, a common preface. Of the earlier collection's 120 chansons, 34 were omitted by LeRoy & Ballard for the 1572 publication, which includes 63 works not found in the 1560 volume.[17] The number of compositions shared by the two collections may in fact be somewhat smaller. "Aller m'y faut" (No. 37) is attributed to Willaert in the *Mellange* and to "Arcadet" (Arcadelt) in the *Livre*; "Je m'y levay par un matin" (No. 7) to Benedictus

Plate VIc and d — *Mellange*, fols. 19ᵛ and 20ʳ

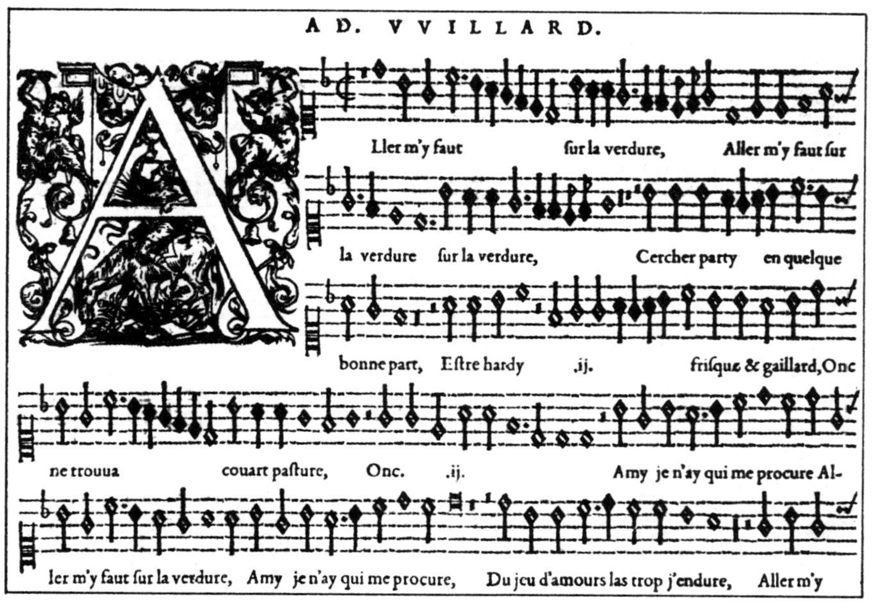

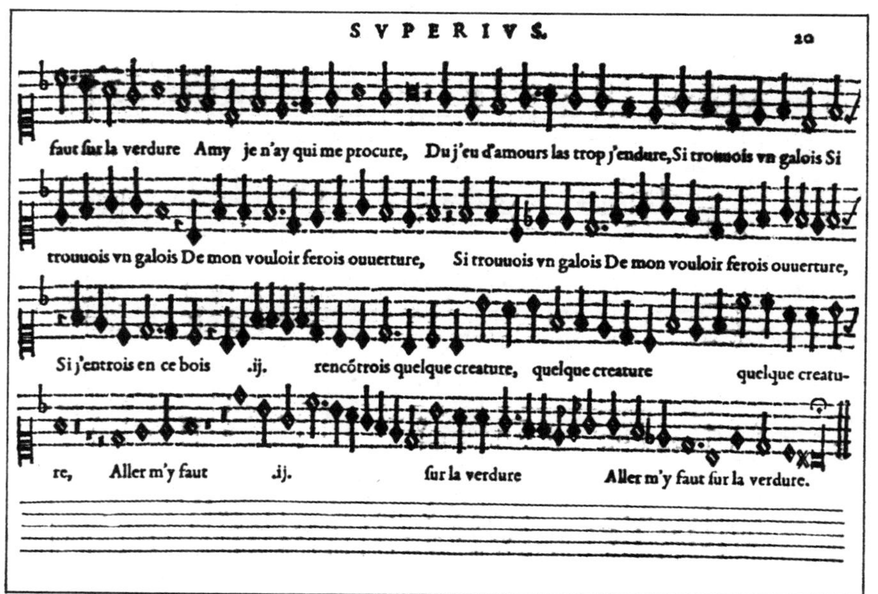

(Appenzeller) in the *Mellange,* to Verdelot in the *Livre*; "Secourez moy ma dame" (No. 14) to Monte in the *Mellange,* to "Orlande" (Lassus) in the *Livre.* In these chansons, the reading of the Superius part is nearly or exactly the same in the two collections. Yet, since Nicolas, to cite only a single example, in his "Le coeur de vous" (No. 67), employs a Superius essentially identical to Claudin's in the latter's setting of the same lyrics,[18] there is no way to ascertain if the above-mentioned three chansons attributed to six different composers are not in fact six different compositions, associated only by their Superius part.

When I began research for this edition of the *Mellange,* the surviving Superius partbook of the *Livre,* formerly in Berlin, was presumed lost, a casualty of World War II. Many people, the present writer included, were searching for missing sources that had been in Berlin. It was, however, in largest measure due to the efforts of the British ichthyologist, Peter Whitehead, that the vanished treasures at last reappeared.[19] At present, the 1560 *Livre* partbook is in the Jagiellonian University Library, Kraków,

where it, and many other primary source materials, may in fact ultimately remain, subject to negotiations between the governments of the Democratic Republic of Germany and Poland. Thanks to the courtesy of the Jagiellonian Library administration and appropriate Polish government officials in New York, I was able to consult the *Livre* Superius partbook in the preparation of this edition and to publish the pages from it I wished.

The notation employed in the *Mellange* is that generally known today as "white mensural notation." The occasional ligatures have been represented in the edition, as is customary, by horizontal brackets. A reduction by 2:1 of the rhythmic symbols was employed uniformly throughout the transcription. Barring, in accordance with the most prevalent signature, ¢, was provided in $\frac{2}{4}$ measures, except for music in triple meter. The editor used barlines through the staves, rather than between the staves, even for chansons in polyphonic style, since this, in his opinion, facilitates reading the music. Barlines, in this music, as of course in considerable music of later periods, should not be interpreted as rigidly indicating the presence of

Plate VIIa — *Livre,* fol. 28ʳ

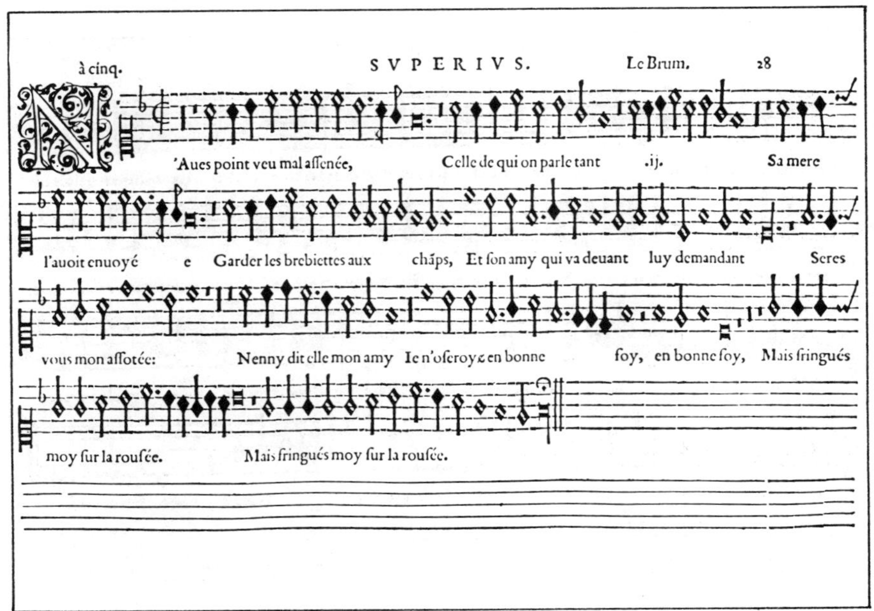

Plate VIIb — *Mellange,* fol. 41ʳ

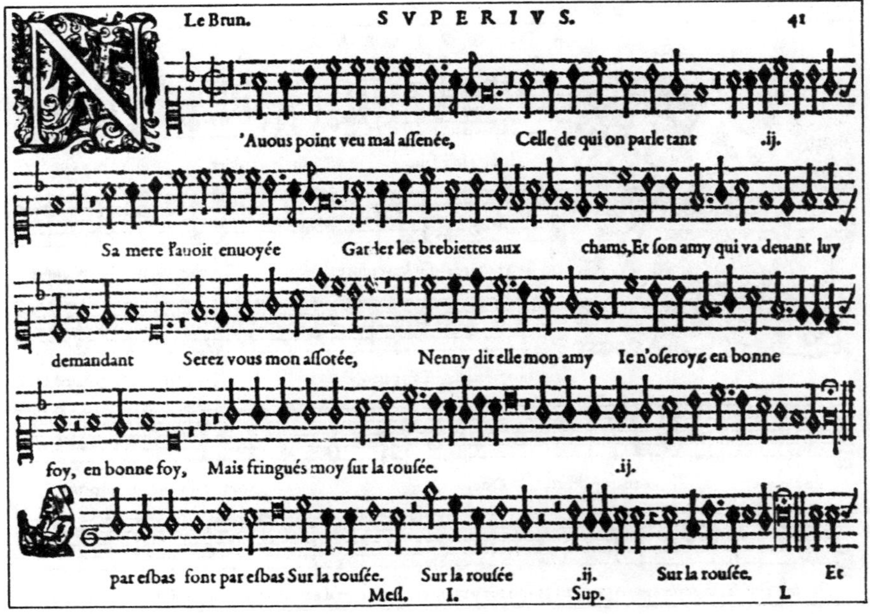

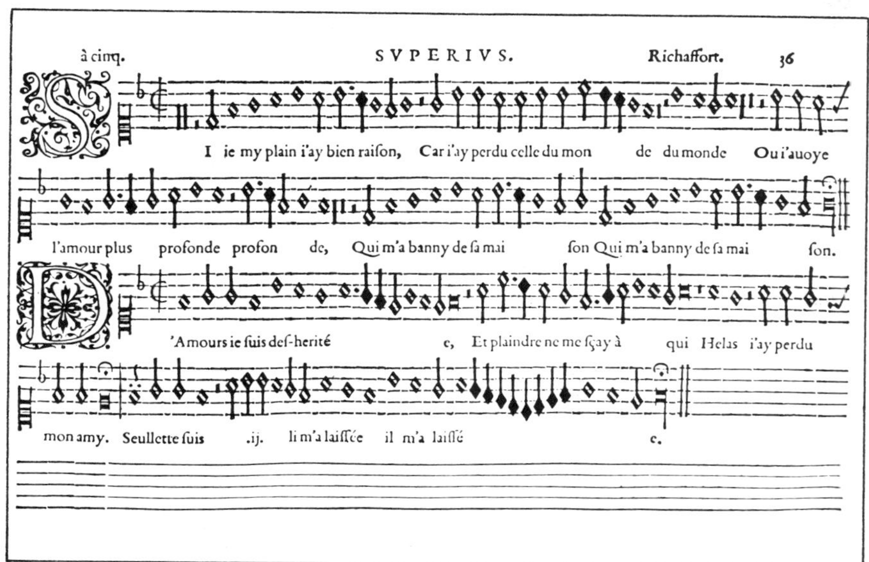

Plate VIIIa — *Livre*, fol. 36[r]

Plate VIIIb — *Mellange*, fol. 48[r]

an accented beat; ultimately, the musical sense of the performer must determine the phrasing of the music.[20]

Triple meter, indicated by the signature ₵3, is found in Nos. 2, 13, 72, and 93; in Nos. 109 and 123, music in triple meter is introduced simply by a "3". This does not seem to be an essential difference, since the triple meter occurs at the very beginning of the former compositions. In all cases, introduction of duple meter after music in triple meter is effectuated by use of ₵. In most of these chansons, normal white notation is used in the source in conjunction with the triple meter, leading to transcription in $\frac{3}{2}$. No. 13, on the other hand, is in coloration throughout and so was transcribed in $\frac{3}{4}$.[21]

Triplets, indicated simply by "3" and in normal white notation, are found repeatedly in the *Mellange* for isolated passages in individual voices: see Nos. 50, mm. 19–22 and 71 (Tenor);[22] 53, mm. 65–8 (Contratenor); 54, m. 28 (Contratenor); 55, mm. 27–8 (Contratenor); 104, m. 96 (Tenor); 111, mm. 70 (Tenor) and 78 (Contratenor); and 129, mm. 67–8 (Sexta). Triplets, again indicated only by "3" but involving coloration, are found in Nos. 54, m. 18 (Contratenor);[23] 104, m. 38 (Superius);[24] 133, mm. 30

(Tenor), 49–50 and 127–8 (Sexta), 109–10 (Contratenor);[23] 135, m. 37 (Contratenor);[23] 138, mm. 40–1 (Contratenor);[25] and 140, mm. 27 and 99 (Bassus).[24]

In No. 144,[26] the configuration of "minor coloration" — a black semibreve followed by a black minim — occurs, with the signature "3". If for no other reason, presence of the signature "3" permits interpretation of the rhythmic pattern as $\sqrt{3}$, rather than ♩ ♪ , the usual interpretation[27] of "minor coloration"; perhaps, owing to the employment here by the source of a signature, this notational peculiarity should not be regarded at all in No. 144 as "minor coloration."

Indeed, normal "minor coloration," i.e., without any signature, is found often in the *Mellange*. Theoretical information notwithstanding,[28] it was only with some misgiving that the editor transcribed the approximately two dozen examples of minor coloration in the *Mellange* in the usual way — as a dotted semiminim followed by a fusa or two semifusae: Nos. 31, mm. 52 (Contratenor)[29] and 109–10 (Bassus); 33, mm. 52 and 144–7 (Contratenor);[30] 46, m. 61 (Bassus); 48, m. 17 (Quinta); 50, mm. 97–8 and

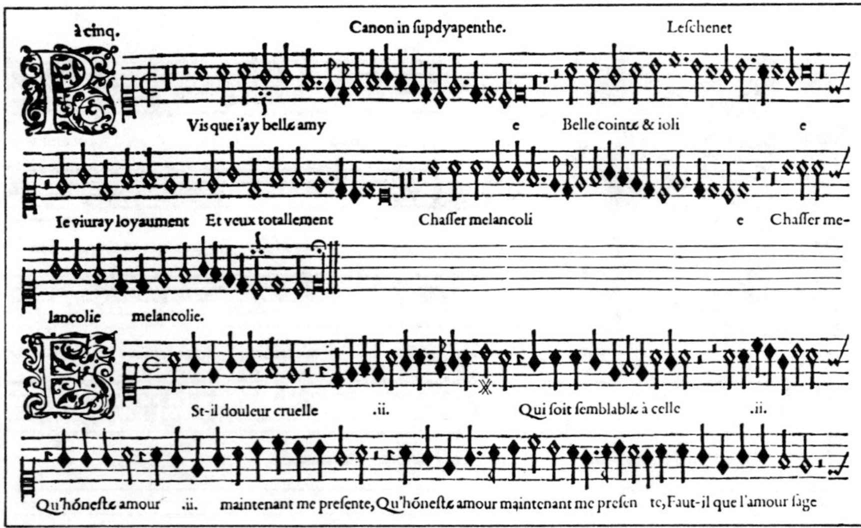

Plate IXa and b — *Livre*, fols. 19[v] and 20[r]

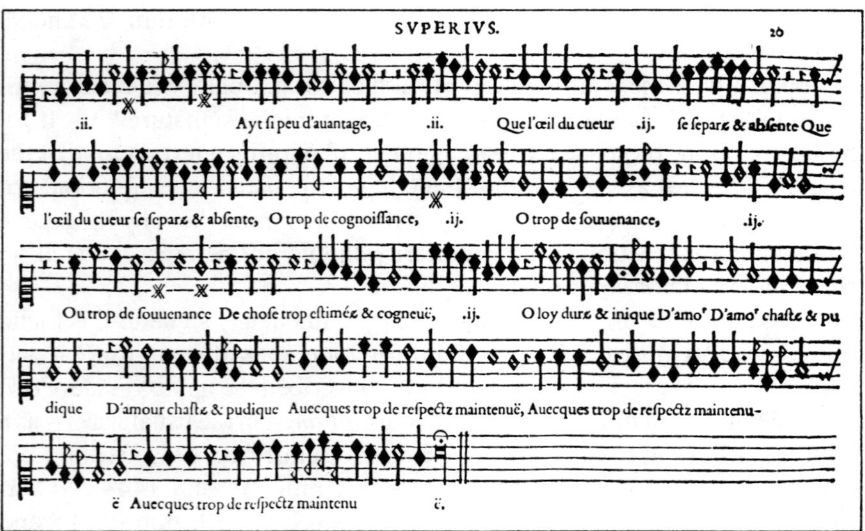

109—10 (Tenor);[31] 68, mm. 65—6, 79, and 116 (Contratenor);[32] 85, m. 119 (Contratenor); 104, mm. 92 and 100 (Tenor);[33] 114, m. 23 (Tenor); 122, m. 90 (Quinta); 133, mm. 47, 111,[34] 118—9, and 125 (Contratenor);[35] and 136, mm. 149—50 (Contratenor). But at No. 133, mm. 121—2 (Tenor), in both the *Mellange* and the concordance (see p. 619), a coloration group — black semibreve and black minim — is immediately followed in white notation by the rhythm it is held to represent, a dotted semiminim and fusa; and, at m. 127 (Tenor), minor coloration, also so given in the concordance, would concur rhythmically with the triplet in the Sexta but, interpreted as ♩ ♪, introduces rhythmic conflict.[36]

The use of coloration for hemiola patterns is also found in the *Mellange*, as follows: in Nos. 2, mm. 9—10 (Contratenor and Quinta);[37] 72 (shown by music rebarred in $\frac{3}{1}$ in the Superius and Tenor at the beginning of the work, and in the Superius and Quinta at the end);[38] and 93, mm. 18—9 and 96—7 (Tenor).

Underlay of the lyrics was realized, whenever possible, in accordance with information available concerning sixteenth-century practice[39] and in such a way that accentuation of the language regarded today as usual may be promoted. The source was only marginally helpful in this respect. In general, complete lines of lyrics are printed together at the beginnings of phrases of music to which they pertain or simply in a visually attractive way; placement of individual syllables was quite obviously left almost entirely to the performer's discretion. The meaning of the textual repeat signs employed in the *Mellange* is as often as not unclear; the signs themselves are frequently placed, again, in an attractive, if uninformative, way in the source.[40] Elision of syllables is shown in the *Mellange* by the letter "e", with a curved horizontal line through its middle.[41] Poetic rhyme scheme was occasionally violated in its musical setting; the editor has in all cases followed the source.[42] Syllabification, in the edition, conforms to modern practice. The source's rather sparse punctuation was augmented only when deemed absolutely essential. Original spelling has been retained, except in the case of unequivocal errors.

The *Mellange* lyrics cover a broad spectrum, including chansons with moralistic, humorous, and amorous texts. Major figures of French poetry, like Clément Marot and Ronsard, are liberally represented.[43] The sole Italian work in the volume, a madrigal by Vicentino, sets a sonnet by Petrarch.[44] The pronounced chromaticism of this madrigal forms only one example of textual illustration in the music of the *Mellange*; other examples are common, particularly for dramatic exclamations or in connection with the word "soupire" (to sigh).[45]

The usage of accidentals in this source, while not always entirely unambiguous, is generally unproblematical.[46]

Common dissonances in the *Mellange* are the *nota cambiata* formula, escaped note,[47] anticipation,[48] changing notes,[49] and $\frac{6}{4}$ triad or chord sonority.[50] Suspensions entered dissonantly[51] and ornamented resolutions of suspensions[52] also occur. The sonority of the seventh appears often and there are passages whose analysis is problematical for divers reasons, including concurrent use of different types of dissonance.[53] Many dissonances are mentioned in the commentary for the individual compositions in which they are found (see Critical Notes to this edition).

Cadential formulas common to the late sixteenth century are naturally found in the music of the *Mellange,* but both the "under third"[54] and "double leading-tone"[55] cadences appear, as well — the latter, however, very seldom.[56]

The *musica ficta* recommended for the music of this edition is cited, by individual work, in the Critical Notes.[57] The only accidentals editorially added above the notes to which they pertain are those removing presumed errors: improbable melodic motion by chromatic semitone, dissonant leaps, diminished triads or chords in root position,[58] and, occasionally, simultaneous cross-relations.[59] In the case of errors considered actual or definite, the accidentals have been inserted into the music in square brackets. This policy was adopted for two reasons: to provide the performer maximum permissible freedom and to minimize the effect of the many questions still unanswered regarding the application of *musica ficta.*

For example, application of the time-honored rule, "una nota supra la semper est canendum fa," is not entirely unequivocal: must the *nota* fall immediately, i.e., without interruption, to "la"?; in an ornamental passage, like B-A-B-C, should the initial note be lowered?; what is the effect of mode and tonality on application of the rule — should the rule be applied regardless?; should the extempore flat be applied, when the *nota* forms the dissonant member of a *nota cambiata* configuration? In his recommendation of *musica ficta,* the editor has suggested application of this rule only where the *nota* falls uninterruptedly to *la* and does not immediately appear in a rising position in a turn-like ornament.[60] He has applied the rule irrespective of mode or tonality, taking the note "A" always as forming *la.*[61] Where, as in numerous works in the *Mellange,* the source provides a signature of B♭ and many of those compositions may be considered as in Dorian transposed to G, E has been interpreted as forming the *nota* (hence becoming E♭) in the *hexachordum molle.*[62] The question of the interpretation of E as the *nota* where there is no B♭ signature is problematical, but the editor has suggested so treating a very few, in passages in which he felt an enterprising Renaissance performer might have decided to apply the appropriate solmization. The editor, despite personal inclination, has applied no *musica ficta,* when B functions as a *nota cambiata.*

Musica ficta has also been applied to fulfill the rule that the form of an imperfect consonance most proximate to a perfect consonance must appear in progressions from imperfect to perfect consonances. This rule has been applied occasionally where interchange of voices appears in the music.[63] When not provided by the source, a third in the final cadence of a work, through *musica ficta,* has been recommended as major.

Musica ficta has not been applied to dissonant notes, except if a dissonant note forms the *nota* falling to *la,* nor has it been applied when dissonance would thereby be produced. The editor applied *musica ficta* exceptionally, where an augumented fifth appears in a cadential formula.[64] Few other exceptions were made.[65] Cross-relations, on the other hand, were not considered impermissible products of the *musica ficta,*[66] since they occur very often in the *Mellange.*[67]

The 148 compositions comprising the *Mellange de Chansons* provide a rich, although necessarily incomplete, idea of secular musical life in sixteenth-century France. Their music represents a cross-section of Parisian musical taste at the time. Many chansons are constructed around canons.[68] Chordal passages abound and there are works strongly or wholly homophonic in character.[69] Sectional repetition is common.[70] But most of the music in the *Mellange,* as was common then, is simply freely imitative.[71]

Mellange de Chansons,
tant des vieux autheurs que des modernes

LeRoy & Ballard

Paris 1572

Preface

from P. de Ronsard to King Charles IX[1]

Sire, just as with touchstone, one[2] tests gold, [to see] if it is good or bad, so the ancients, through music, tested the spirits of those who are generous, magnanimous, and do not stray from their true nature, and of those who are torpid, lazy, and debased in this mortal body, no more remembering the celestial harmony of heaven than Ulysses' companions, after Circe had transformed them into pigs, [remembered] having been men. Because he, Sire, who, hearing a sweet accord of instruments[3] or the sweetness of the

Plate IXc and d — *Mellange*, fols. 49ᵛ and 50ʳ

natural voice, is neither gladdened nor excited, nor thrills from head to foot, as sweetly transported and in some mysterious way removed from himself — this is a sign he has a tormented, vicious, and depraved soul, and one should keep at a distance[4] from him, as from someone who is in no way fortunately born.[5] How could one be in harmony with a man who, by his nature, hates harmony?[6] He is not worthy to see[7] the sweet light of the sun, who does not honor music as a small part of that which so harmoniously (as Plato says) moves all this great universe. Conversely, he who manifests honor and reverence to it [music][8] is ordinarily a man of worth; his soul is healthy and gallant, and, by nature, he enjoys lofty things — philosophy, the conduct of political matters, the toil[9] of war; and, [in] brief, in all honorable affairs, he always makes apparent the brilliance of his virtue. But to make known here what music is — if it is governed more by madness than by art; [to make known] its concords, its tones, modulations, voices, intervals, sounds, systems, and transformations; its division into enharmonic[10] — which, for its difficulty, was never perfectly in use —, into chromatic — which, for its lasciviousness, was banished by the ancients from republics —, into diatonic[11] — which, as approaching most the melody of this great universe, was approved by all. To speak of the Phrygian, Dorian, Lydian; and how some peoples of Greece, animated by harmony, went courageously to war, as our soldiers today to the sound of trumpets and drums; how King Alexander, hearing the singing[12] of Timotheus, became furious; and how Agamemnon, going to Troy, deliberately left in his home I know not what Dorian musician, who, by virtue of the Anapestic foot, mitigated the wild amorous passions of his wife, Clytemnestra, inflamed by the love of whom Aegisthus, without having first put the musician wickedly to death, could never attain happiness. To wish, further, to deduce how all things — as much in the heavens, in the sea, as on earth — are composed of accords, measures, and proportions; to wish to discuss all the more how the most honorable personalities of past centuries — monarchs, princes,[13] philosophers, governors of provinces, and renowned captains — singularly were[14] deeply affected by the fervor of music; I should never have done; the more so, since music has always been the sign and mark of those who have shown themselves virtuous, magnanimous, and truly born to feel nothing vulgar. I shall take, for example, just the late King, your father,[15] may God absolve [him], who, during his reign, made apparent how much heaven had liberally favored him with all [the] graces and with gifts rare among kings; who surpassed, whether in

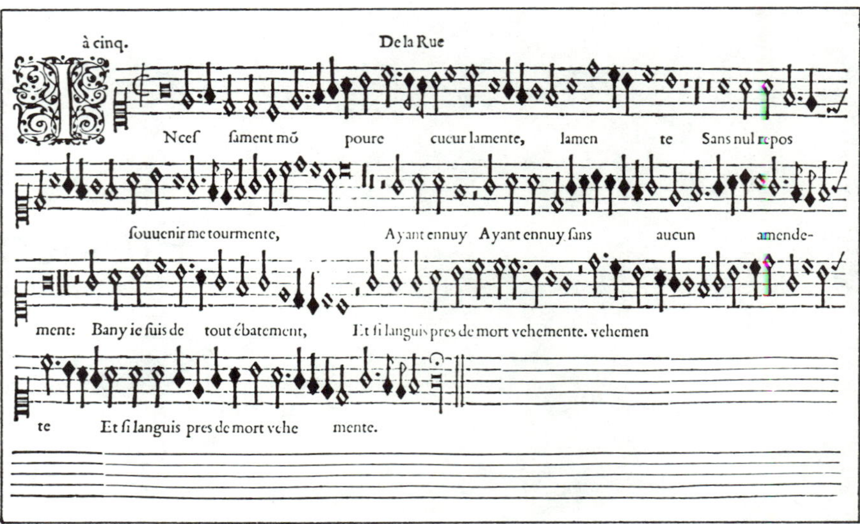

Plate Xa — *Livre*, fol. 28[v]

Plate Xb — *Mellange*, fol. 52[v]

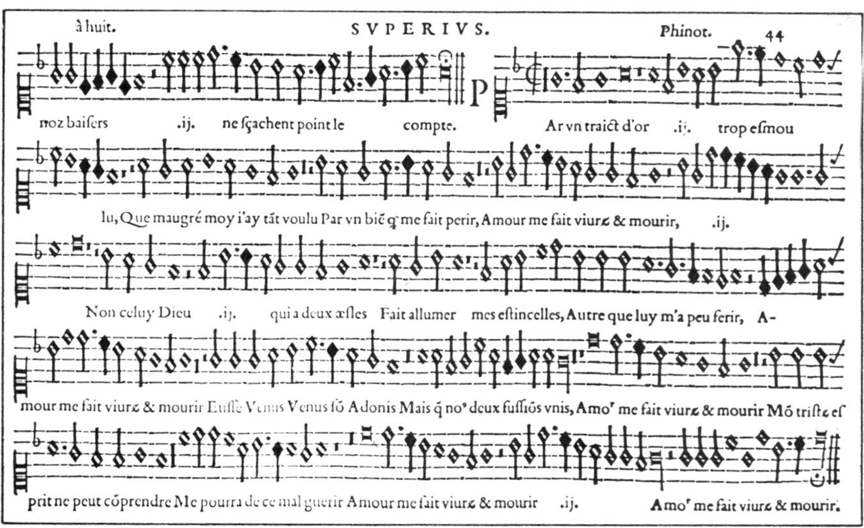

Plate XIa — *Livre*, fol. 44^r

Plate XIb — *Mellange*, Contratenor, fol. 83^r

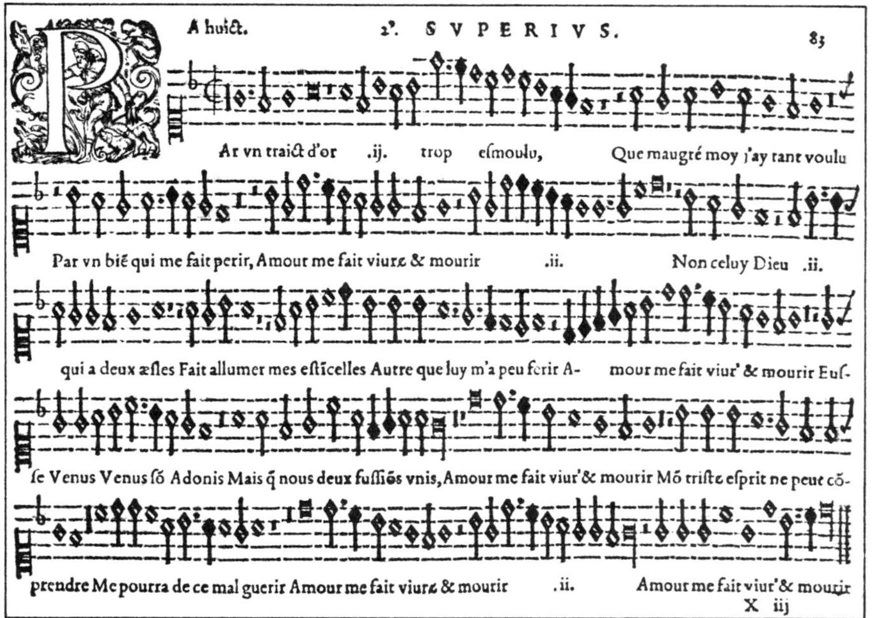

imperial grandeur or in clemency, liberality, goodness, piety, and religion, not only all the princes [who were] his predecessors but all those who have ever lived bearing that honorable title of king; who, to disclose the brilliance of his[16] high birth and to show that he was perfect in all virtues, so honored, loved, and prized music, that all those today in France who are very devoted to this art are not so much so, all together, as [he], all alone, [so] especially was. You, as well, Sire, as heir both[17] of his realm and of his virtues, how much you are his son, favored by heaven, by loving so completely such a science and its harmonies, without which nothing[18] of this world could remain whole. But to tell you here of Orpheus, Terpander,[19] Eumolpus,[20] Arion — these are stories, with which I do not wish to burden the paper, as things known to you. I shall only mention to you that the most magnanimous kings of ancient times had their children nurtured in the households of musicians, as Peleus, who sent his son Achilles, and Aeson, his son Jason, to the venerated cave of the centaur, Chiron, to be instructed as much in arms, as in medicine, and in the art of music, the more so, since these three callings combined are not unbecoming to the grandeur of a prince; and such a commendable example of virtue was provided[21] by Achilles, and by Jason, who were princes of your age,[22] that the one was honored by the divine poet, Homer, as the sole author of the capture[23] of Troy; and the other [was] celebrated by Apollonius of Rhodes as the first responsible for having taught the sea to suffer the unknown burden of ships, who, having passed beyond the Symplegades Rocks[24] and subdued the fury of the cold Scythian Sea, finally returned to his country, enriched by the noble golden fleece. Therefore, Sire, these two princes will be to you as patrons of virtue and when, sometime, you are fatigued by your most urgent affairs, in imitation of them, you will alleviate your cares with music's harmonies, so as to return[25] fresher and more disposed to the royal charge, which you carry so dexterously.[26] There is, in addition, no reason for your Majesty to be surprised if this *livre de mellanges*[27] — which you are most humbly dedicated by your most humble and most obedient servants and printers, Adrian LeRoy and Robert Ballard — is composed of the oldest *chansons* that can be found today, because the music of the old [masters] has always been considered to be the most divine, the more so, since it was composed in a century happier and less tainted by the vices which prevail in this vilest[28] Iron Age. For the divine transports of music, poetry, and painting do not arrive at perfection by degrees, like the other sciences; but by starts and like flashes of fire, some here, some there, [they] appear in different countries, then, all at once, vanish. And because, Sire, when some excellent craftsman in this art appears, you should carefully[29] watch over him, as something so excellent that it rarely appears. Among such men in the last six or seven score years are exalted Josquin des Prez, native of Hainaut, and his disciples, Mouton, Vuillard,[30] Richaffort, Janequin, Maillard, Claudin, Moulu, Jaquet, Certon,[31] Arcadet.[32] And at present, the more than divine Orlande,[33] who, like a bee, has culled all the most beautiful flowers of the old [composers] and, besides, seems alone to have stolen the harmony from the heavens, for us to delight in it on earth, surpassing the old [composers] and making himself the sole prodigy of our time.[34] Many other things could be said about music, of which Plutarch and Boethius have amply made mention. But neither the brevity of this preface, nor the convenience of time, nor the subject matter permits me to make a longer discourse to you.[35] Beseeching the Creator, Sire, to increase more and more Your Majesty's virtues and to continue you in the kind affection that it pleases[36] you to show to music and to all those who study in order to revive, under your reign, the sciences and arts which flourished under the empire of Caesar Augustus; [and as] with that Augustus, may omnipotent God grant you years, victories, and prosperity.[37]

The Music

1 Vuillart, *Jouissance vous donneray* [C. Marot]
Jou- is- san- ce vous don- ne- ray,
Jou- is- san- ce vous don-
Jou- is- san- ce vous don- ne- ray, Jou- is- san- ce vous don-
Jou- is- san- ce vous don-
Jou- is- san- ce, Jou- is- san- ce, Jou-

10
Jou- is- san- ce vous
ne- ray, Jou- is- san- ce vous don- ne- ray, Mon
ne- ray, vous don- ne- ray, Mon a- my & vous
ne- ray, Jou- is- san- ce vous don- ne- ray,
is- san- ce vous don- ne- ray, vous don- ne- ray,

19
don- ne- ray, Mon a- my & vous
a- my & vous me- ne- ray, Mon a- my & vous me- ne- ray, La
me- ne- ray, Mon a- my & vous
Mon a- my & vous me- ne- ray, Mon a-
Mon a- my & vous me- ne- ray,

39
ce, Vi- van- te ne vous
tend vo- tre es- pe- ran- ce, Vi- van- te
ran- ce, es- pe- ran- ce, Vi- van- te ne
ce, La ou pre- tend vo- tre es- pe- ran- ce, Vi-
vo- tre es- pe- ran- ce, Vi- van- te me,

29
me- ne- ray, La ou pre- tend vo- tre es- pe- ran-
ou pre- tend vo- tre es- pe- ran- ce, La ou pre-
me- ne- ray, La ou pre- tend vo- tre es- pe-
my & vous me- ne- ray, La ou pre- tend vo- tre es- pe- ran-
La ou pre- tend vo- tre es- pe- ran- ce,

48
lais- se- ray, ne vous lais- se-
ne vous lais- se- ray, Vi-
vous lais- se- ray, vous lais- se- ray, Vi- van- te
van- te ne vous lais- se- ray, ne vous lais- se-
Vi- van- te ne

ray, Vi- van- te ne vous lais-
van- te ne vous lais- se- ray, Vi- van-
ne vous lais- se- ray, Vi- van- te ne vous lais-
ray, Vi- van- te ne vous lais- se-
vous lais- se- ray, Vi- van- te ne vous lais se- ray,

te se- ray, L'es- prit en au- ra sou- ve- nan-
mor- te se- ray, L'es- prit en au- ra sou-
quand mor- te se- ray, L'es- prit en au- ra
mor- te se- ray, L'es- prit en au- ra sou-
quand mor- te se- ray, L'es- prit en au- ra,

se- ray, En- co- res quand mor-
te ne vous lais- se- ray, En- co- res quand
se- ray, En- co- res
ray, En- co- res quand mor- te se- ray,
En- co- res quand mor- te se- ray

ce, L'es- prit en au- ra sou- ve- nan- ce, L'es-
ve- nan- ce, L'es-
sou- ve- nan- ce, sou- ve- nan- ce,
ve- nan- ce, L'es- prit
L'es- prit en au- ra sou- ve- nan- ce, L'es- prit en

95
prit   en au-   ra sou- ve-   nan-
prit   en   au-   ra   sou-   ve-   nan- ce,
L'es- prit en au-   ra sou- ve- nan-   ce, sou-   ve-
en   au-   ra   sou- ve-   nan- ce,
au-   ra,   souve- nan-

He-las ma mere, he- las   ma- man,   He- las ma me- re les   dens, ma me-
He-las ma mere, he- las ma-man,   He- las ma mere, he- las ma-man, He- las,   He- las   ma
He-las ma mere, he- las ma-man,   He- las ma me- re les dens, He-
He- las ma mere, he- las   ma me- re les dens, He-
He- las   ma mere, he- las maman,   ma me- re les dens,

103
ce.
L'es- prit en au- ra sou- ve-   nan-   ce.
nan-   ce.
sou-   ve- nan-   ce.
ce,   sou- ve- nan-   ce.

9
re   les   dens, He- las ma me- re les   dens,   Les ca- qui- nes de der-
me- re les   dens, He- las, He- las ma me- re les   dens,   Les ca- qui- nes
las ma me- re les   dens, He- las ma me- re les   dens,
las   ma me- re les dens, He- las ma me- re les   dens, Les ca- qui- nes de der- rie-
ma me- re les   dens, He- las ma me- re les   dens,   Les ca- qui- nes de der-

19
rie- re, Font mal à ceux de de- vant,
de der- rie- re, Font mal à ceux de de- vant, L'au- tre jour mi
Les ca- qui- nes de der- rie- re, Font mal à ceux de de- vant,
re, Font mal à ceux de de- vant, L'au- tre jour mi che-
rie- re, Font mal à ceux de de- vant, L'au- tre jour, L'au-

30
L'au- tre jour mi che- mi- noi- e,
che- mi- noi- e, Mon che- min à saint Lau- rens, L'au- tre jour mi che- mi- noi- e, Mon che-
L'au- tre jour mi che- mi- noi- e, Mon che- min à saint Lau- rens,
mi- noi- e, à saint Lau- rens, Mon che- min à saint Lau-
tre jour mi che- mi- noi- e, Mon che- min à saint Lau- rens, Mon che- min à

43
Mon che- min à saint Lau- rens, Mon che- min à saint Lau- rens, Ren- con- tray u- ne ber-
min à saint Lau- rens, à saint Lau- rens, à saint Lau- rens, Ren- con- tray
à saint Lau- rens, à saint Lau- rens, Ren- con- tray u-
rens, à saint Lau- rens, à saint Lau- rens, Ren- con-
saint Lau- rens, à saint Lau- rens, à saint Lau- rens, Ren- con- tray,

56
ge- re, Qui cri- oit le mal des dens,
u- ne ber- ge- re, Qui cri- oit le mal des dens, Qui cri- oit le
ne ber- ge- re, Qui cri- oit le mal des
tray u- ne ber- ge- re, Qui cri- oit le mal des dens, Qui cri- oit le
Ren- con- tray u- ne ber- ge- re, Qui cri- oit le mal des dens, Qui cri- oit le

33

67
Qui cri- oit le mal des dens,   He- las ma mere, he- las ma- man,
mal des dens, Qui cri- oit le mal des dens, He- las ma mere, he- las ma- man,
dens, Qui cri- oit le mal des dens,   He- las ma mere, he- las ma- man, He- las ma mere, he-
mal des dens,   le mal   des dens,   He- las ma mere, he- las ma- man, He-
mal des dens,   He- las ma mere, he- las ma- man, [He- las   ma mere, he-

91
Les ca- qui- nes de der- rie- re, Font mal à ceux de de- vant,
dens,   Les ca- qui- nes de der- rie- re, Font mal à ceux de de- vant,
Les ca- qui- nes de der- rie- re, Font mal   à   ceux de de-
Les ca- qui- nes de der- rie- re,   Font mal à ceux de de- vant,
Les ca- qui- nes de der- rie-   re, Font mal à ceux de   de-

79
He- las ma me- re   les   dens,   ma me- re les dens,
He- las ma me- re   les dens,   He- las   ma   me-   re les
las ma- man,   He- las ma me- re les   dens,   He- las ma me- re les dens,
las ma me- re   les dens, He- las ma me- re les dens, les   dens,
las ma- man,]   He-   las ma me-   re les   dens,

102
Ren- con- tray u- ne ber- ge- re, Qui cry- oit le mal des
Ren- con- tray u- ne ber- ge- re,   Qui cry- oit le mal des dens,
vant,   Ren- con- tray u- ne ber- ge- re,   Qui cry- oit le mal des
Ren- con- tray u ne ber- ge- re,   Qui cry- oit le mal des dens, le
vant,   Ren- con- tray u- ne ber- ge- re,   Qui cry- oit le mal des

34

114
dens, Je luy pris à de- man- der, à de- man- der,
Je luy pris à de- man- der, à de- man- der,
dens, Je luy pris à de- man- der, Je luy pris à de- man- der, Bel- le qu'al- lés
mal des dens, Je luy pris à de- man- der, à de- man- der, Bel- le qu'al- lés
dens, Je luy pris à de- man- der, Bel- le qu'al- lés

137
He- las ma mere, he- las ma- man, He- las ma me- re les
las ma- man, He- las ma me- re les dens, ma
las ma- man, He- las ma mere, he- las ma- man, He- las ma me-
las ma mer[e], he- las ma- man, He- las les dens, he- las ma me- re les dens,
las ma- man, He- las ma mer[e], he- las ma- man,

126
Bel- les qu'al- lés vous cri- ant, Bel- le qu'al- lés vous cri- ant,
Bel- le qu'al- lés vous cri- ant, Bel- le qu'al- lés vous cri- ant, He- las ma mere, he-
vous cri- ant, Bel- le qu'al- lés vous cri- ant, He- las ma mere, he-
vous cri- ant, qu'al- lés vous cri- ant, Bel- le qu'al- lés vous cri- ant, He-
vous cri- ant, Bel- le qu'al- lés vous cri- ant, He- las ma mer[e], he-

147
dens, He- las ma me- re les dens.
me- re les dens, He- las ma me- re les dens.
re les dens, He- las ma me- re les dens.
he- las ma me- re les dens, ma me- re les dens.
He- las ma me- re les dens, He- las ma me- re les dens.

3 Vuillart, *Qui la dira*

38
pour mon a- my por- te,
Et la dou- leur, que pour mon a- my por- te,
que pour mon a- my por- te, que pour mon a- my
leur, que pour mon a- my por- te, que pour mon a- my

58
tien que tris- tes- se & lan- gueur, Je ne sou- tien que
Je ne sou- tien que tris- tes-
se & lan- gueur, Je ne sou- tien que
Je ne sou- tien que tris- tes- se & lan- gueur,
tien que tris- tes- se & lan- gueur, Je ne sou- tien que

47
que pour mon a- my por- te, Je ne sou- tien, Je ne sou-
que pour mon a- my por- te,
por- te, que pour mon a- my por- te, Je ne sou- tien que tris- tes-
a- my por- te,
por- te, Je ne sou- tien que tris- tes- se & lan- gueur, Je ne sou-

66
tris- tes- se & lan- gueur, J'ay- me- roie mieux, cer- tes en
se & lan- gueur, J'ay- me- roie
tris- tes- se & lan- gueur, J'ay- me- roie mieux cer- tes en es- tre
J'ay- me- roie mieux,
tris- tes- se & lan- gueur, J'ay- me- roie mieux, cer-

es- tre mor- te, J'ay- me- roye mieux,
mieux, cer- tes en es- tre mor- te, J'ay-
mor- te, J'ay- me- roye mieux, J'ay- me- roye mieux, cer-
cer- tes en es- tre mor- te, J'ay- me- roye
tes en es- tre mor- te, J'ay- me- roye mieux cer- tes en es- tre

Ce que mon coeur pen- se, Je ne le di pas
Ce que mon coeur pen- se, Je ne le di pas He-
Ce que, Je ne le di pas He-

cer- tes en es- tre mor- te, en es- tre mor- te.
me- roye mieux, cer- tes en es- tre mor- te.
tes en es- tre mor- te, en es- tre mor- te.
mieux, cer- tes en es- tre mor- te.
mor- te, cer- tes en es- tre mor- te.

Ce que mon coeur pen- se,
Ce que mon coeur pen- se, Je ne le di
He- las, Je ne le di pas He- las, Je ne le di pas
las, Je ne le di pas He- las, Je ne le di pas He-
las, Je ne le di pas He- las, Je ne le di pas,

Je ne le di pas He- las, Je ne le di pas He- las, Je
pas He- las, Je ne le di pas He- las, Je
Helas, Je ne le di pas He- las, Je ne
las, Je ne le dy pas He- las, Je ne le dy pas He- las, He-
Je ne le dy pas He- las,

Au jar- din, mon
pe- re, Un oy- seau y a,
Au jar- din, mon pe- re, Un oy- seau
din, mon pe- re, Un oy- seau
pe- re, Au jar- din, mon pe-

ne le di pas He- las,
ne le di pas He- las, Au jar- din, mon
le dy pas He- las, He- las, He- las,
las, He- las, He- las, Au jar-
He- las, He- las, He- las, Au jar- din, mon

pe- re, Au jar- din, mon pe- re, Un oy-seau y a,
Un oy- seau y a, [Un oy-seau y a,]
y a, Un oy- seau y a, Un oy- seau y a,
y a, Un oy- seau y a, Un oy- seau y a,
re, Un oy- seau y a, Un oy- seau y a,

61
Qui dit tous les jours, Qui s'en- vol- le- ra, He- las, He
Qui dit tous les jours, Qui dit tous les jours, Qui s'en- vo- le- ra, He- las,
Qui dit tous les jours, Qui dit tous les jours, Qui s'en- vo- le- ra, He- las,
Qui s'en-

85
las, Qui s'en- vo- le- ra:
las, Qui s'en- vo- le- ra, Ce que mon coeur pen- se, Je ne le di pas,
las, Qui s'en- vo- le- ra, He- las, He- las, Ce que mon coeur pen-
las, Qui s'en- vo- le- ra, He- las, Ce que mon coeur pen- se,
las, Qui s'en- vo- le- ra,

73
Qui dit tous les jours, Qui s'en- vol- le- ra, He-
las, Qui s'en- vo- le- ra: He-
Qui s'en- vo- le- ra: Qui s'en- vo- le- ra, He- las, Qui s'en- vo- le- ra, He-
Qui s'en- vo- le- ra, He- las, Qui s'en- vo- le- ra, He-
vo- le- ra, He- las, Qui s'en- vo- le- ra, Qui s'en- vo- le- ra, Qui s'en- vo- le- ra, He-

96
Ce que mon coeur pen- se, Je ne
Je ne le di pas He- las, Je ne le di pas He- las,
se, Je ne le di pas He- las, Je ne le di pas He- las,
Je ne le di pas He- las, Je ne le di pas He- las,
Je ne le di pas He- las, Je ne le di pas, Je ne

le di pas He- las, Je ne le di pas He- las, Je
He- las, Je ne le dis pas he- las, he- las, Je ne le dis
He- las, Je ne le dis pas he-
Je ne le di pas He- las, He- las, Je ne
le dis pas He- las, He- las, He- las, Je ne

Le ber- ger & la ber- ge- re,
Le ber- ger & la ber-
Le ber- ger & la ber- ge- re,
Le ber- ger & la ber- ge-
Le ber- ger

ne le di pas He- las.
pas he- las, je ne le dis pas, Je ne le dis pas He- las.
las, Je ne le dis pas he- las, Je ne le dis pas He- las.
le dis pas, Je ne le dis pas, Je ne le dis pas He- las.
le dis pas He- las, Je ne le dis pas He- las.

& la ber- ge- re, Bras à bras jou-
ge- re, & la ber- ge- re,
& la ber- ge- re, Bras à bras jou-
re, & la ber- ge- re,
& la ber- ge- re, & la ber- ge-

21
er s'en vont, Bras à bras jou- er s'en vont,
Bras à bras jou- er s'en vont, Bras à bras jou- er s'en vont,
er s'en vont, Bras à bras jou- er s'en vont, Je
Bras à bras jou- er s'en vont, Je
re, Bras à bras jou- er s'en vont, Bras à bras jou- er s'en vont,

45
nom, Et li- re lire li- ron: Et li- re lire li- ron:
nom, Et li- re lire li- ron: Et li- re lire li- ron:
nom, Et li- re lire li- ron: Je te prie
Et li- re lire li- ron: Je te prie (dit la ber- ge- re),
nom, Et li- re lire li- ron: Et li- re lire li- ron: Je te prie (dit

32
Je te prie (dit la ber- ge- re), Mon a- my dy moy ton
Je te prie (dit la ber- ge- re), Mon a- my dy moy ton
Je te prie (dit la ber- ge- re), Mon a- my dy moy ton
te prie (dit la ber- ge- re), Mon a- my dy moy ton nom,
Je te prie (dit la ber- ge- re), Mon a- my dy moy ton

58
Je te prie (dit la ber- ge- re), Mon a- my dy moy ton nom, Mon a- my
Je te prie (dit la ber- ge- re), Mon a- my dy moy ton nom,
(dit la ber- ge- re), Mon a- my dy moy ton nom,
Mon a- my dy moy ton nom, Le mi-
la ber- ge- re), Mon a- my dy moy ton nom, Le

6 Richafort, *Cuidez vous que Dieu*

ge- ment, lar- ge- ment,   Il à plus qu'il ne nous bai-
plus qu'il ne   nous bai-   lle, qu'il ne   nous bai-   lle,
lar- ge- ment, Il à plus qu'il ne nous bai- lle,   Il à plus qu'il ne   nous bai-
lar- ge- ment, Il à plus qu'il ne nous bai-   lle,
Il à plus qu'il ne   nous bai-   lle,   Et nous à tous

Jus- que au jour du ju- ge-   ment, du ju-
lle: Jus- que au jour du ju- ge- ment,
Jus- que au jour du ju- ge- ment, Jus- que au jour du ju- ge- ment,
ju- ge- ment, Jus- que au jour du ju- ge- ment, Jus- que au
Jus- que au jour du ju- ge- ment,   Jus- que au jour du

lle,   Et nous à tous mis en tai-   lle:
Et nous à tous mis en tai-
lle,   Et nous à tous mis en tai-   lle:
Et nous à tous mis en tai-   lle: Jus- que au jour du
mis en tai-   lle: Et nous à tous mis en tai-   lle:

ge-   ment, Com- pa- gnon ne vous en chai-
Com- pa- gnon ne
Jus- que au jour du ju- ge- ment, Com- pa- gnon ne vous en chai-   lle,
jour du ju- ge- ment, Com- pa- gnon ne vous en chai- lle,
ju- ge- ment, Com- pa- gnon ne vous en chai- lle,   Com- pa-

70
lle,
Com- pa-gnon ne vous en chai— lle, Le ter- me vaut
vous en chai— lle, Le ter- me vaut bien l'ar- gent,
Com- pa-
Com-pa-gnon ne vous en chai— lle,
Le ter- me vaut
Le ter- me vaut bien l'ar- gent,
Com-pa-gnon ne vous en chai—lle, Le ter- me vaut
gnon ne vous en chai—lle, Le ter- me vaut bien l'ar- gent,

Je m'y le- vay par un ma- tin,
Je m'y le- vay par un ma- tin,
Je m'y le- vay, Je m'y le- vay par un ma- tin,
Je
Je m'y le- vay, Je m'y le- vay, [Je m'y le-

84
bien l'ar- gent, Le ter- me vaut, Le ter- me vaut bien l'ar- gent.
gnon ne vous en chai— lle, Le ter- me vaut bien l'ar- gent.
bien l'ar- gent, Le ter- me vaut bien l'ar- gent, Le ter- me vaut bien l'ar- gent.
bien l'ar- gent, Le ter- me vaut bien l'ar- gent.
Com- pa- gnon ne vous en chai— lle, Le ter- me vaut bien l'ar- gent.

9
Jour n'es- toit my- e, [jour n'es- toit
Je m'y le- vay par un ma- tin, Jour n'es-
Je m'y le- vay par un ma- tin, Jour n'es- toit mi- e,
m'y le- vay par un ma- tin, Jour
vay,] Je m'y le- vay par un ma- tin, Jour n'es-

19
my- e,]
toit my- e, Jour n'es- toit my- e,
Jour n'es- toit mi- e, Je m'en al-
n'es- toit mi- e,
toit mi- e, Jour n'es- toit mi- e, Je

39
à l'huis m'a- my- e,
chan- ter à l'huis m'a- my- e, à l'huis m'a- my- e, Tout
ter, à l'huis m'a- my- e, à l'huis m'a- my- e, Tout aus- si
ter, à l'huis m'a- my- e,
droit chan- ter, à l'huis m'a- my- e, Tout aus- si tot qu'el-

29
Je m'en al- lay tout droit chan- ter,
Je m'en al- lay, Je m'en al- lay tout droit
lay, Je m'en al- lay tout droit chan- ter, Je m'en al- lay tout droit chan-
Je m'en al- lay tout droit chan-
m'en al- lay, Je m'en al- lay, [Je m'en al- lay,] Je m'en al- lay tout

51
Tout aus- si tot qu'el- le m'ou- it chan- ter,
aus- si tot qu'el- le m'ou- it chan- ter, El- le à pour
tot qu'el- le m'ou- it chan- ter, El- le à pour moy son huis fer- mé,
Tout aus- si tot qu'el- le m'ou-
le m'ou- it chan- ter, Tout aus- si tot, qu'el- le m'ou- it chan-

El- le à pour moy son huis fer- mé, son huis
moy son huis fer- mé, El-
El- le à pour moy son huis fer- mé, son huis
it chan- ter, El- le à pour moy son
ter, El- le à pour moy son huis

di- re, al- lez luy de- man- der, S'el- le à pour moy
lez luy de- man- der, al- lez, Al- lez luy di- re, al- lez luy de- man- der, S'elder, Al- lez luy di- re, al- lez luy de- man- der, S'el- le à
Al- lez luy di- re, al- lez luy de- man- der,
Al- lez luy di- re, al- lez luy de- man- der, S'el-

fer- mé, Al- lez luy
le à pour moy son huis fer- mé, Al- lez luy di- re, al-
fer- mé, Al- lez luy di- re, al- lez luy de- man-
huis fer- mé, son huis fer- mé,
fer- mé,

son huis fer- mé, son huis fer- mé.
le à pour moy son huis fer- mé.
pour moy son huis fer- mé.
S'el- le à pour moy son huis fer- mé.
le à pour moy son huis fer- mé.

Quand je me
Quand je me trou- ve au- pres de ma mai- tres- se, Et
Quand je me trou-
Quand je me trou- ve au- pres de ma mai- tres-
Quand je me trou- ve au- pres de ma mai- tres- se,

ne j'ap- pro- che, Et que ma bou- che à la sien- ne j'ap- pro- che, Tant
che, Et que ma bou- che à la sien- ne j'ap- pro- che, Tant ay de
pro- che, Et que ma bou- che à la sien- ne j'ap- pro- che, Tant ay de
Et que ma bou- che à la sien- ne j'ap- pro- che, Tant ay de
Et que ma bou- che à la sien- ne j'ap- pro- che, Tant ay de

trou- ve au- pres de ma mai- tres- se, Et que ma bou- che à la sien-
que ma bou- che à la sien- ne j'ap- pro-
ve au- pres de ma mai- tres- se, Et que ma bou- che à la sien- ne j'ap-
se, Et que ma bou- che à la sien- ne j'ap- pro- che,
Et que ma bou- che à la sien- ne j'ap- pro- che,

ay de joye & tant ay de li- es- se, Qu'en mon es- prit nul des- plai-
joye & tant ay, de li- es- se, Qu'en mon es- prit nul des-
joye & tant ay de li- es- se, Qu'en mon es- prit nul
joye & tant ay de li- es- se, Qu'en mon es- prit nul des- plai- sir
joye & tant ay de li- es- se, Qu'en mon es- prit nul des-

42
(sic)
sir n'ap- pro- che, Et si n'ay peur qu'il en vien- ne
plai- sir n'ap- pro- che, Et si n'ay peur qu'il en vien- ne
des- plai- sir n'ap-pro- che,
n'ap-pro- che, Et si n'ay peur qu'il en vien-
plai- sir n'ap- pro- che,

63
Mais je crain bien qu'en tel- le jou- is- san- ce,
se, Mais je crain bien qu'en tel- le jou- is- san- ce,
se, Mais je crain bien qu'en tel- le jou- is- san- ce, L'a- me ne fa- ce en el- le de- mou-
se, Mais je crain bien qu'en tel- le jou- is- san- ce, L'a- me ne fa-
se, Mais je crain bien qu'en tel- le jou- is- san- ce, L'a- me ne

52
re- pro- che, Pour- ce qu'el- le est,
re- pro- che, Pour- ce qu'el- le est de ver- tu la no- bles-
Pour- ce qu'el- le est de ver- tu la no- bles-
ne re- pro- che, Pour- ce qu'el- le est de ver- tu la no- bles-
Pour- ce qu'el- le est de ver- tu la no- bles-

74
L'a- me ne fa- ce en el- le de- mou- ran- ce,
L'a- me ne fa- ce en el- le de- mou-
ran- ce, L'a- me ne fa- ce en el- le de- mou- ran- ce, L'a-
ce en el- le de- mou- ran- ce, L'a- me ne
fa- ce en el- le de- mou- ran-

9 Vuildre, *Pour vous aymer*

* Flat indicated in the Livre.

re, Car pour cer- tain au- tre bien ne pro-
re, Car pour certain au- tre bien ne pro-
cu- re, Car pour cer- tain au- tre bien ne pro- cure, j'ay mis tou- te ma cu- re, Car pour cer- tain au-
cu- re, Car pour cer- tain au- tre bien ne

Vous sup- pli- ant que me fa- ciez sça- voir,
gra- ce a- voir, Vous sup- pli- ant que me fa-
ce a- voir, Vous sup- pli- ant que me fa- ciez sça- voir, que me
ce a- voir, Vous sup- pli- ant que me fa-
vo- tre gra- ce a- voir, Vous

cu- re, Fors seu- le- ment la vo- tre gra- ce a- voir,
cu- re, Fors seu- le- ment la vo- tre
re, Fors seu- le- ment, Fors seu- le- ment la vo- tre gra-
tre bien ne pro- cu- re, Fors seu- le- ment la vo- tre gra-
pro- cu- re, Fors seu- le- ment la vo- tre gra- ce a- voir, la

Si de m'a- mour vo- tre coeur au- ra cu- re, vo- tre coeur
ciez sça- voir, Si de m'a- mour, vo- tre coeur au- ra
fa- ciez sça- voir, Si de m'a- mour vo- tre coeur au-
ciez sça- voir, Si de m'a- mour vo- tre coeur, Si de m'a- mour vo-
sup- pli- ant que me fa- ciez sça- voir, Si de m'a- mour vo- tre coeur

au- ra cu- re, Si de m'a-mour vo- tre coeur au- ra cu- re,
cu- re, Si de m'a- mour, Si de m'a- mour, vo- tre coeur
ra cu- re, Si de m'a- mour
tre coeur au- ra cu- re, Si de m'a-mour vo- tre coeur,
au- ra cu- re, au- ra cu- re, Si de m'a-

Pour un plai- sir, que si peu du- re,
Pour un plai- sir, que si peu du- re, que si peu du- re, que
Pour un plai- sir que si peu du- re,
Pour un plai- sir que si peu du-
Pour

vo- tre coeur au- ra cu- re.
au- ra cu- re, vo- tre coeur au- ra cu- re.
vo- tre coeur au- ra cu- re, au- ra cu- re.
Si de m'a-mour vo- tre coeur au- ra cu- re, au- ra cu- re.
mour vo- tre coeur au- ra cu- re, au- ra cu- re.

Pour un plai- sir que si peu du- re, J'ay
si peu du- re, J'ay en-du- ré pei- ne & tra- vaux,
Pour un plai- sir que si peu du- re, J'ay en-du- ré pei- ne & tra-
re, Pour un plai- sir que si peu du- re, J'ay en- du- ré pei-
un plai- sir que si peu du- re, J'ay en- du- ré pei-

en- du- ré pei- ne & tra- vaux, J'en ay souf- fert dou- leur trop du- re,
peine & tra- vaux, J'en ay souf- fert dou- leur trop du- re, dou-
vaux, J'ay en- du- ré pei- ne & tra- vaux, J'en ay souf- fert dou- leur trop du- re,
ne & tra- vaux, J'en ay souf- fert dou- leur trop du- re, dou-
ne, J'ay en- du- ré pei- ne & tra- vaux, J'en

maux, J'en ay re- çeu cent mil- le maux, Or Dieu me doint bon- ne a- ven- tu- re,
J'en ay re- çeu cent mil- le maux, Or Dieu me doint bon- ne a- ven- tu-
çeu cent mil- le maux, Or Dieu me doint bon- ne a- ven-
ay re- çeu cent mil- le maux, Or Dieu me doint bon-
çeu cent mil- le maux, cent mil- le maux,

J'en ay souf- fert dou- leur trop du- re, J'en ay re- çeu cent mil- le
leur trop du- re, J'en ay re- çeu, J'en ay re- çeu cent mil- le maux,
trop du- re, J'en ay re- çeu cent mil- le maux, J'en ay re-
leur trop du- re, J'en ay re- çeu cent mil- le maux, J'en
ay souf- fert dou- leur trop du- re, J'en ay re- çeu cent mil- le maux, J'en ay re-

Or Dieu me doint bon- ne a- ven- tu- re, For- tu- ne à fait sur moy ses
re, Or Dieu me doint bon- ne a- ven- tu- re, For- tu- ne à fait
tu- re, For- tu- ne à fait sur moy, For- tu- ne à fait sur
ne a- ven- tu- re, Or Dieu me doint bon- ne a- ven- tu- re,
Or Dieu me doint bon- ne a- ven- tu- re, For- tu- ne à fait sur

sautz, For- tu- ne à fait sur moy ses sautz, For- tu- ne à fait sur moy ses
sur moy ses sautz, For- tu- ne à fait sur moy ses sautz, For- tu- ne à
moy ses sautz, For- tu- ne à fait sur moy ses sautz, For- tu- ne à
For- tu- ne à fait sur moy ses sautz, sur moy ses sautz,
moy ses sautz, For- tu- ne à fait sur moy ses sautz, For-

Je me re- pens d'a- voir ay-
Je me re- pens d'a- voir ay- mé, d'a- voir ay- mé,
Je me re- pens d'a- voir ay- mé, d'a- voir ay-

sautz, For- tu- ne à fait sur moy ses sautz.
fait sur moy ses sautz, For- tu- ne à fait sur moy ses sautz, For- tu- ne à fait sur moy ses sautz
fait sur moy ses sautz, For- tu- ne à fait sur moy ses sautz.
For- tu- ne à fait sur moy ses sautz, For- tu- ne à fait sur moy ses sautz.
tu- ne à fait sur moy ses sautz, For- tu- ne à fait sur moy ses sautz, sur moy ses sautz.

Je me re- pens d'a- voir ay- mé
mé, d'a- voir ay- mé, d'a- voir ay-
d'a- voir ay- mé, d'a- voir ay- mé, De
Je me re- pens d'a- voir ay- mé,
mé, d'a- voir ay- mé, De vray a-

18
De vray a- mour si loy- au- ment,
mé, De vray a- mour si loy-au- ment, De vray a-
vray a- mour si loy- au- ment, De vray
De vray a- mour si loy- au-
mour si loy- au- ment, De vray a- mour

38
Cel- le qui est sans loy- au- té, Et va- ri-
au- ment, Cel- le qui est sans loy- au- té, Cel- le qui est sans loy- au-
le qui est sans loy- au- té, sans loy-au- té, Et va- ri- an-
Cel- le qui est sans loy- au-
est sans loy- au- té, Cel- le qui est sans loy- au- té, Et

27
De vray a- mour si loy- au- ment,
mour si loy- au- ment, De vray a- mour si loy-
a- mour si loy- au- ment, si loy- au- ment, Cel-
ment, De vray a- mour si loy- au- ment,
si loy- au- ment, De vray a- mour si loy- au- ment, Cel- le qui

49
an- te com- me vent, com- me vent, Et va- ri-
té, sans loy- au- té, Et va- ri- an- te, Et
te com- me vent, com- me vent, com- me
té, Et va- ri- an- te com- me
va- ri- an- te com- me vent, Et va- ri- an- te com-

55

59
an- te com- me vent, com- me vent,
va- ri- an- te com- me vent,
vent, com- me vent, D'o- re- na- vant me gar- de-
vent, com- me vent, Et va- ri- an- te comme vent, com- me vent, D'o- re- na- vant me gar- de-

79
gar- de- ray, De trop ay- mer sou- dai- ne- ment,
gar- de- ray, De trop ay- mer sou- dai- ne- ment, De
gar- de- ray, De trop ay- mer sou- dai- ne- ment, De
me gar- de- ray, De trop ay- mer
De trop ay- mer sou- dai- ne- ment, De trop ay-

69
D'o- re- na- vant me gar- de- ray, me
D'o- re- na- vant me gar- de- ray, me gar- de- ray, me
ray, me gar- de- ray, me gar- de- ray, me
me vent, D'o- re- na- vant
ray, me gar- de- ray, me gar- de- ray,

90
De trop ay- mer sou- dai- ne- ment.
trop ay- mer sou- dai- ne- ment, De trop ay- mer sou- dai- ne- ment.
trop ay- mer sou- dai- ne- ment, De trop ay- mer sou- dai- ne- ment.
sou- dai- ne- ment, De trop ay- mer sou- dai- ne- ment.
mer sou- dai- ne- ment, De trop ay- mer, sou- dai- ne- ment, sou- dai- ne- ment.

Ma bou-che rit, & ma pen-sé-e pleu- re,
Ma bou-che rit, & ma pen-sé- e pleu- re, Mon oeil s'es-
Ma bou- che rit, & ma pen- sé-e pleu-re, Mon
Ma bou-che rit, & ma pen-sé- e pleu- re, Mon oeil
Ma bou-che rit, & ma pen-sé- e pleu- re, & ma pen-sé-

Qu'il eut le bien, qui sa san-té de-chas- se,
Qu'il eut le bien, qui sa san-té de- chas- se,
Qu'il eut le bien qui sa san-té de-chas- se, Et
eut le bien, Qu'il eut le bien qui sa san-té de-chas- se,
Qu'il eut le bien, qui sa san-té de-chas- se, qui sa san-té de-chas- se,

Mon oeil s'es- jou- ist & mon coeur mau-dit l'heu- re,
jou- ist, & mon coeur mau-dit l'heu- re,
oeil s'es- jou- ist & mon coeur mau- dit l'heu- re,
s'es- jou- ist & mon coeur mau- dit l'heu- re, Qu'il
pleu- re, Mon oeil s'es- jou- ist & mon coeur mau-dit l'heu- re,

Et le plai- sir que la mort tant pour-chas- se,
Et le plai- sir que la mort tant pour- chas- se,
le plai- sir, que la mort tant pour-chas- se, Sans
Et le plai- sir, que la mort tant pour-
Et le plai- sir, que la mort tant pour-

Sans re- con- fort, Sans re- con- fort qui m'ai- de ne
Sans re- con- fort, Sans re- con- fort qui m'ai-
re- con- fort qui m'ai- de ne se- queu- re, Sans re- con- fort qui
chas- se, Sans re- con- fort, qui m'ai- de ne se- queu- re,
chas- se, Sans re- con- fort, Sans re- con- fort qui m'ai- de ne se-

ma pen- sé- e pleu- re, Mon oeil s'es- jou- ist & mon coeur mau- dit l'heu-
pleu- re, Mon oeil s'es- jou- ist, & mon coeur mau- dit l'heu- re,
sé- e pleu- re, Mon oeil s'es- jou- ist & mon coeur mau- dit l'heu- re,
e pleu- re, Mon oeil s'es- jou- ist & mon coeur mau- dit l'heu- re,
pleu- re, & ma pen- sé- e pleu- re, Mon oeil s'es- jou- ist & mon coeur mau- dit l'heu-

se- queu- re, Ma bou- che rit, Ma bou- che rit, &
de ne se- queu- re, Ma bou- che rit, & ma pen- sé- e
m'ai- de ne se- queu- re, Ma bou- che rit, & ma pen-
ne se- queu- re, Ma bou- che rit, & ma pen- sé-
queu- re, Ma bou- che rit, & ma pen- sé- e

re, Mon oeil s'es- jou- ist & mon coeur mau- dit l'heu- re.
Mon oeil s'es- jou- ist, & mon coeur mau- dit l'heu- re, & mon coeur mau- dit l'heu- re.
Mon oeil s'es- jou- ist & mon coeur mau- dit l'heu- re.
Mon oeil s'es- jou- ist & mon coeur mau- dit l'heu- re. l'heu- re.
re, Mon oeil s'es- jou- ist, Mon oeil s'es- jou- ist & mon coeur mau- dit l'heu- re, l'heu- re.

13 Vuildre, *Je file quand Dieu*

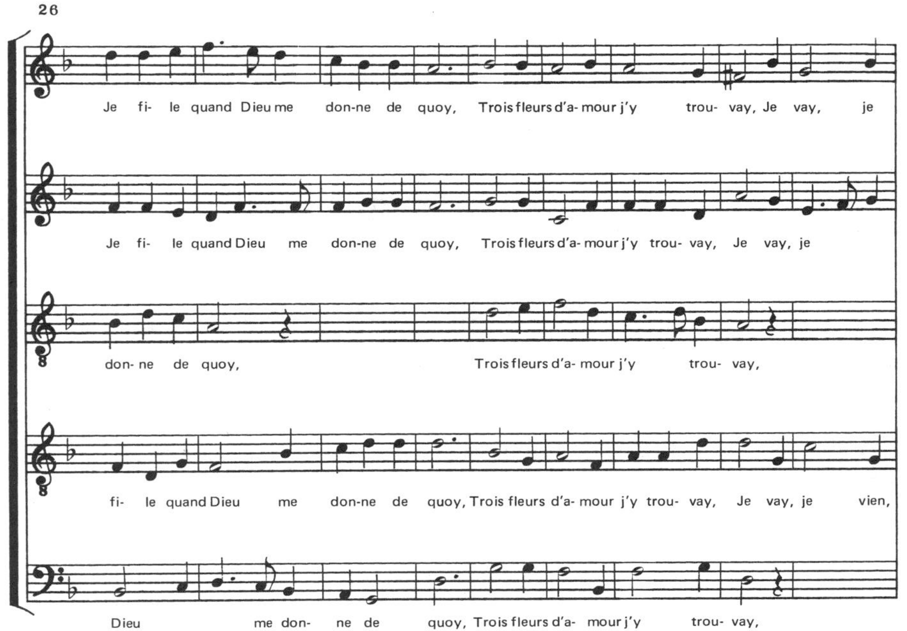

vien, Je tour-ne, je vi-re, je fer-re, je fi-le, je tons, je
vien, Je tour-ne, je vi-re, je fer-re, je fi-le, je tons, je
Je vay, je vien, Je tour-ne, je vi-re, je fer-re, je tai-lle,
Je vay, je vien, Je tour-ne, je vi-re, je fer-re, je tai-lle, je tons, je
Je vay, je vien, je tour-ne, je vi-re, je fer-re, je tai-lle,

four, Je gar-de mes ou-ai-lles du loup, Je fi-le ma que-nouille au
four, Je gar-de mes ou-ai-lles du loup, Je fi-le ma que-nouille au
four, Je gar-de mes ou-ai-lles du loup, Je fi-le ma que-nouille au
four,
four,

raiz, Je dan-se, je sau-te, je ris, je chan-te, je chauf-fe mon
raiz, Je dan-se, je sau-te, je ris, je chan-te, je chauf-fe mon
Je tons, je raiz, Je dan-se, je sau-te, je ris, je chan-te, je chauf-fe mon
raiz, je tons, je raiz, Je dan-se, je sau-te, je ris, je chan-te, je chauf-fe mon
je tons, je raiz, Je dan-se, je sau-te, je ris, je chan-te, je chauf-fe mon

voy, Je fi-le quand Dieu me don-ne de quoy, je fi-le ma que-nouille au voy, Je voy.
voy, Je fi-le quand Dieu me don-ne de quoy, je fi-le ma que-nouille au voy, Je voy.
voy, Je fi-le quand Dieu me don-ne de quoy, je fi-le ma que-nouille au voy, Je voy.
Je fi-le quand Dieu me don-ne de quoy, je fi-le ma que-nouille au voy, Je voy.
(sic)
1.
2.

14 Monte, *Secourez moy ma dame* [C. Marot]

*Flat indicated in the Livre.

15 Mouton, *Vray Dieu d'amours*

19
Qu'onc- q'en ma vi- e,
e,
e, la jour- né- e, Qu'onc-
jour- né- e,
di- te soit la jour- né- e, Qu'onc-q'en ma vi- e,
e, Qu'onc-q'en ma

38
Car main- te- nant, je suis la de- so- lé-
Car main- te- nant je suis la de- so- lé- e,
Car main- te- nant, je suis la de- so- lé-
nant, Car main- te- nant, je suis la de- so- lé- e,
Car main- te- nant, je suis, je

28
Qu'onc- q'en ma vi- e, a- mou- reu- se je fus,
q'en ma vi- e, a- mou- reu- se je fus,
Qu'onc- q'en ma vi- e a- mou- reu- se je fus,
Qu'onc- q'en ma vi- e a- mou- reu- se je fus, Car main- te-
vi- e, Qu'onc- q'en ma vi- e a- mou- reu- se je fus,

48
e, Seu- let- te suis
je suis la de- so- lé- e, Seu- let- te
e, Seu- let- te
je suis la de- so- lé- e, Seu- let- te suis
suis la de- so- lé- e, Seu- let- te

& si n'ay point d'a- my: Faut= il,
suis, & si n'ay point d'a- my: Faut= il,
suis & si n'ay point d'a- my: Faut= il,
& si n'ay point d'a- my: Faut=
suis & si n'ay point d'a- my[:] Faut= il, Faut= il qu'ain-

Seu- let- te suis & si n'ay point d'a- my, &
let- te suis, Seu- let- te suis, & si n'ay point d'a-
Seu- let- te suis & si n'ay point d'a- my,
te suis, Seu- let- te suis, & si n'ay point d'a- my, Seu- let- te
Seu- let- te suis, Seu- let- te suis, & si n'ay point d'a- my,

Faut= il qu'ain- si je soy- e,
Faut= il qu'ain- si je soy- e, Faut= il qu'ain-si je soy- e, Seu-
Faut= il qu'ain- si je soy- e, Faut= il qu'ain-si je soy- e,
il qu'ain-si je soy- e, Seu- let-
si je soy- e, qu'ain- si je soy- e,

si n'ay point d'a- my.
my, Seu- let- te suis, & si n'ay point d'a- my, & si n'ay point d'a- my.
Seu- let- te suis & si n'ay point d'a- my.
suis & si n'ay point d'a- my, & si n'ay point d'a- my.
Seu- let- te suis & si n'ay point d'a- my, & si n'ay point d'a- my.

16 Mouton, *La rousée du mois de may*

42
La rou- sée du mois de may, En un
La rou- sée du mois de may, En un jar- din m'en en-
vay, La rou- sée du mois de may, En un
le- vay, La rou- sée du mois de may,
sée du mois de may, du mois de may, La rou- sée du mois de may,

65
Dit- tes vous que je suis sot-
Dit- tes vous que je suis sot- te, que je
je suis sot- te, que je suis sot- te, Dit- tes vous que
Dit- tes vous que je suis sot- te, que je suis sot- te, Dit-
vous que je suis sot- te, Dit- tes vous que je suis

53
jar- din m'en en- tray, Dit- tes vous que je suis sot- te,
tray, En un jar- din m'en en- tray,
jar- din m'en en- tray, Dit- tes- vous que
En un jar- din m'en en- tray, Dit- tes vous que je suis sot- te,
En un jar- din m'en en- tray, Dit- tes

77
te, La rou- sée du mois de may, La rou- sée du mois de may, m'a
suis sot- te, La rou- sée du mois de may,
je suis sot- te, La rou- sée du mois de may, m'a gas-
tes vous que je suis sot- te, Dit- tes vous que je suis sot- te,
sot- te, La rou- sée du mois de may,

gas- té, m'a gas- té ma ver- te cot- te, m'a gas- té ma ver- te cot-
m'a gas- té ma ver- te cot- te, ma ver- te cot- te, m'a gas- té ma
té ma ver- te cot- te, m'a gas- té ma ver- te
m'a gas- té ma ver- te cot- te, m'a gas- té
m'a gas- té ma ver- te cot- te, ma ver- te cot-

Fortune, lais- se moy la vi-
For-
For- tu- ne, lais- se moy la vi-
For- tu- ne, lais- se moy la vi-
For-

te, ma ver- te cot- te.
ver- te cot- te, ma ver- te cot- te.
cot- te, m'a gas- té ma ver- te cot- te.
ma ver- te cot- te, ma ver- te cot- te.
te, M'a gas- té ma ver- te cot- te.

e, Tu me tour-men- te ru- de- ment, ru-
tu- ne, lais- se moy la vi- e,
e,
e,
Tu
tu- ne, lais- se moy la vi- e, Tu me tour-

20

de- ment, ru-
Tu me tour- men- te ru- de- ment,
Tu me tour- men- te ru- de- ment,
me tour- men- te ru- de- ment, Tu me tour- men- te
men- te ru- de- ment, Tu me tour- men- te ru- de-

40

de- ment, Lais- se moy
Lais- se moy vi- vre seu- le- ment,
de- ment, Lais- se moy vi- vre seu-
se moy vi- vre seu- le- ment, Lais- se moy
se moy vi- vre seu- le- ment, seu- le- ment,

30

de- ment, ru-
ment, Tu me tour- men- te ru- de- ment,
Tu me tour- men- te ru- de- ment, ru-
ru- de- ment, ru- de- ment, Lais-
ment, ru- de- ment, Lais-

51
(sic)

vi- vre seu- le- ment, seu- le- ment, Et je t'en pri- e, Et je t'en
Et je t'en pri- e, Et je t'en pri-
le- ment, Et je t'en pri- e,
viv- re seu- le- ment, Et je t'en pri- e, Et je t'en pri-
Lais- se moy vi- vre seu- le- ment, Et je t'en pri-

63
pri- e, Et je t'en pri- e,
e, Et je t'en pri- e,
Et je t'en pri- e, Et je t'en pri- e,
e, Et je t'en pri- e, Las, pour-quoy m'es=tu
e, Et je t'en pri- e, Las, pour-quoy m'es= tu

87
en- ne- mi- e, Ne se peut il,
ne- mi- e, Ne se peut il fai- re au-
Ne se peut il fai-
m'es= tu en- -ne- mi- e, Ne se peut il, Ne se peut
tu en- ne- mi- e, Ne se peut il fai- re au-tre- ment,

75
Las, pour-quoy m'es=tu en- ne- mi- e, Las, pour-quoy m'es= tu
Las, pour-quoy m'es= tu en- ne- mi- e, en-
Las, pour-quoy m'es= tu en- ne- mi- e,
en- ne- mi- e, Las, pour-quoy
en- ne- mi- e, Las, pour-quoy m'es=

98
Ne se peut il fai- re au-tre- ment, Ne se peut il fai- re au-tre- ment,
tre- ment, For-
re au- tre- ment, Ne se peut il fai- re au- tre- ment.
il fai- re au-tre- ment, Ne se peut il fai- re au- tre- ment,
Ne se peut il fai- re au-tre- ment,

18 Rore, *Susane un jour* [Guéroult]

20
vie- llars, con- voi- tans sa beau- té, Fut en son coeur
vie- llars, con- voi- tans sa beau- té, Fut en son
vie- llars, con- voi- tans sa beau- té,
vie- llars, con- voi- tans sa beau- té,
llars, con- voi- tans sa beau- té, Fut en son coeur,

41
te & des- con- for- té- e, Voy- ant l'ef- fort fait
e, tris- te & des- con- for- té- e, Voy- ant l'ef- fort fait
coeur tris- te & des- con- for- té- e, Voy- ant l'ef- fort fait
Voy- ant l'ef- fort fait
tris- te & des- con- for- té- e, Voy- ant l'ef- fort fait

30
tris- te, Fut en son coeur tris-
coeur, Fut en son coeur, tris- te & des- con- for- té-
Fut en son coeur tris- te, Fut en son
Fut en son coeur, tris- te & des- con- for- té- e,
Fut en son coeur tris- te & des- con- for- té- e,

53
à sa chas- te- té: El- le leur dit si par
à sa chas- te- té: El- le leur dit, si
à sa chas- te- té: El- le leur dit,
à sa chas- te- té: El- le leur dit si par des-
à sa chas- te- té: El- le leur dit si par des-

des- loy- au- té, De ce cors mien vous a- vez jou- is- san-
par des- loy- au- té, De ce cors mien vous a- vez jou- is- san-
si par des- loy- au- té, De ce cors mien vous a- vez jou- is- san-
loy- au- té, De ce cors mien vous a- vez jou- is- san-
loy- au- té, De ce cors mien vous a- vez jou- is- san-

tan- ce, Si je fay re- sis- tan- ce, Vous me fe- rez mou- rir
je fay re- sis- tan- ce, Vous me fe- rez mou- rir, mou- rir
tan- ce, Si je fay re- sis- tan- ce, Vous me fe- rez mou- rir
je fay re- sis- tan- ce, Vous me fe- rez mou- rir, mou- rir
Si je fay re- sis- tan- ce, Vous me fe- rez mou- rir, mou- rir

ce, C'est fait de moy, C'est fait de moy, Si je fay re- sis-
ce, C'est fait de moy, C'est fait de moy, Si
ce, C'est fait de moy, C'est fait de moy, Si je fay re- sis-
ce, C'est fait de moy, C'est fait de moy, Si
ce, C'est fait de moy, C'est fait de moy,

en des- hon- neur, Mais j'ay- me mieux, Mais j'ay- me mieux pe-
en des- hon- neur, Mais j'ay- me mieux, Mais j'ay- me mieux pe-
en des- hon- neur, Mais j'ay- me mieux pe- rir, pe- rir en
en des- hon- neur, Mais j'ay- me mieux, Mais j'ay- me mieux pe- rir,
en des- hon- neur, Mais j'ay- me mieux pe- rir

114
rir, Mais j'ay-me mieux pe- rir en in- no- cen- se,
rir, Mais j'ay- me mieux pe- rir en in- no- cen- se, Que
in- no- cen- se,
Mais j'ay-me mieux pe- rir en in- no- cen- se, Que
en in- no- cen- se,

134
par pe- ché le Sei- gneur, Que d'of- fen- ser
par pe- ché le Sei- gneur, Que d'of- fen- ser,
par pe- ché, le Sei- gneur, Que d'of- fen-
ser par pe- ché le Sei- gneur, Que d'of- fen- ser
par pe- ché le Sei- gneur, Que d'of- fen- ser

124
Que d'of- fen- ser par pe- ché le Sei- gneur, Que d'of- fen- ser
d'of- fen- ser par pe- ché le Sei- gneur, Que d'of- fen- ser
Que d'of- fen- ser
d'of- fen- ser par pe- ché le Sei- gneur, Que d'of- fen-
Que d'of- fen- ser

143
par pe- ché le Sei- gneur.
par pe- ché le Sei- gneur.
ser par pe- ché le Sei- gneur.
par pe- ché, le Sei- gneur.
par pe- ché le Sei- gneur.

19 Strige, *Pour m'esloigner* [St. Gelais]

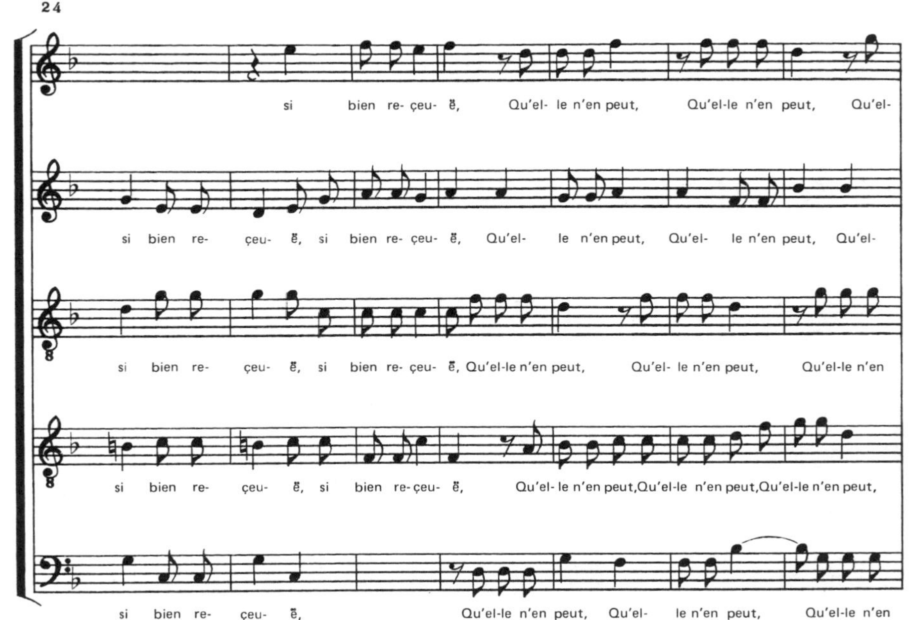

31
le n'en peut que par mort fai- re ys- su- e, Et ne croy point,
le n'en peut que par mort fai- re ys- su- e, Et ne croy point,
peut, que par mort fai- re ys- su- e, Et ne croy point, Et
que par mort fai- re ys- su- e, Et ne croy point, Et
peut que par mort fai- re ys- su- e, Et

45
meu- re, Si rien de nous, Si rien de nous, a- prés nous fait de-
le meu- re, Si rien de nous, Si rien de nous, a- prés nous fait de- meu-
le meu- re, Si rien de nous, Si rien de nous,
meu- re, Si rien de nous, Si rien de nous, a- prés nous fait de- meu-
le meu- re, Si rien de nous, a- prés nous fait de-

39
Et ne croy point, Et ne croy point qu'a- prés nous el- le
Et ne croy point, Et ne croy point, qu'a- prés nous el-
ne croy point, Et ne croy point, Et ne croy point qu'a- prés nous el-
ne croy point, Et ne croy point, qu'a- prés nous el- le
ne croy point, Et ne croy point, Et ne croy point, qu'a- prés nous el-

54
meu- re, a- prés nous fait de- meu- re.
re, a- prés nous fait de- meu- re, a- prés nous fait de- meu- re.
a- prés nous fait de- meu- re, a- prés nous fait de- meu- re.
re, a- prés nous fait de- meu- re, a- prés nous fait de- meu- re.
meu- re, a- prés nous fait de- meu- re.

Her- bes & fleurs & vous pres ver- doy- ans,
Her- bes & fleurs & vous pres ver- doy- ans,
Her- bes & fleurs & vous pres
Her- bes & fleurs & vous pres ver- doy-
Her- bes &

Ar- bres, buis- sons pe- tis & grans bo- ca- ges, Plei- nes & monts,
sons pe- tis & grans bo- ca- ges, Plei- nes
tis & grans bo- ca- ges, Ar- bres, buis- sons pe- tis &
Ar- bres, buis- sons pe- tis, pe- tis & grans bo- ca- ges, Plei-
ges, Ar- bres, buis- sons pe- tis & grans bo-

Ar- bres, buis- sons pe- tis & grans bo- ca- ges,
Ar- bres, buis- sons pe- tis & grans bo- ca- ges, Ar- bres, buis-
ver- doy- ans, Ar- bres, buis- sons pe-
ans, & vous pres ver- doy- ans, Ar- bres, buis- sons pe- tis,
fleurs & vous pres ver- doy- ans, Ar- bres, buis- sons pe- tis & grans bo- ca-

Plei- nes & monts, Plei- nes & monts & fleu-
& monts & fleu- ves un- doy- ans, Plei- nes & monts &
grans bo- ca- ges,
nes & monts, Plei- nes & monts, Plei- nes &
ca- ges, Plei- nes & monts & fleu- ves un- doy- ans,

31
ves un- doy- ans, Oy- seaux jo- lis, jo-
fleu- ves un- doy- ans, Oy- seaux jo- lis, jo- lis, qui
Plei- nes & monts & fleu- ves un- doy- ans,
monts & fleu- ves un- doy- ans, & fleu- ves un- doy- ans,
Plei- nes & monts & fleu- ves un- doy- ans, Oy-

45
voz ra- mai- ges, Al- lez pleu- rans, vo- tre dueil lan-
mai- ges, Al- lez pleu-rans vo- tre dueil lan- gou- reux,
Oy- seaux jo- lis, jo- lis, qui se- lon voz ra- mai- ges, Al-
lis, qui se- lon voz ra- mai- ges, Al- lez pleu- rans, vo- tre dueil
seaux jo- lis, jo- lis, qui se- lon voz ra- mai- ges, Al- lez pleu-

38
lis, qui se- lon voz ra- mai- ges, Oy- seaux jo- lis, qui se- lon
se- lon voz ra- mai- ges, Oy- seaux jo- lis, jo- lis, jo- lis, qui se- lon voz ra-
Oy- seaux jo- lis, jo- lis, qui se- lon voz ra- mai- ges,
Oy- seaux jo- lis, jo- lis, jo- lis, Oy- seaux jo- lis, jo- lis, jo-
seaux jo- lis, jo- lis, qui se- lon voz ra- mai- ges, Oy-

54
gou- reux, Si l'un de vous con-gnois-sez d'a- van-
Al- lez pleu- rans vo- tre dueil lan- gou- reux, Si l'un de
lez pleu- rans vo- tre dueil lan- gou- reux,
lan- gou- reux, Si l'un de vous con-
rans, vo- tre dueil lan- gou- reux,

64
tu- re, Si l'un de vous con- gnois- sez d'a- van-
vous con- gnois- sez d'a- van- tu- re, Si l'un de vous con- gnois- sez d'a- van-
Si l'un de vous con- gnois- sez d'a- van- tu- re,
gnois- sez d'a- van- tu- re, con- gnois- sez d'a- van-
Si l'un de vous con- gnois- sez d'a- van- tu- re,

80
me rend dou- lou- reux, qui me rend dou- lou- reux,
me rend do- lou- reux, qui me rend do- lou- reux, De-
qui me rend do- lou- reux, De- cla- rez luy la
me rend do- lou- reux, De- cla- rez luy la
qui me rend do- lou- reux, De- cla-

73
tu- re, Ce pe- tit, pe- tit Dieu, qui
tu- re, Ce pe- tit, pe- tit Dieu, Ce pe- tit, pe- tit Dieu, qui
Ce pe- tit, pe- tit Dieu, Ce pe- tit, pe- tit Dieu, Ce pe- tit, pe- tit Dieu,
tu- re, Ce pe- tit, pe- tit Dieu, Ce pe- tit, pe- tit Dieu, qui
Ce pe- tit, pe- tit Dieu, Ce pe- tit, pe- tit Dieu,

90
De- cla- rez luy la pei- ne que j'en-
cla- rez luy la pei- ne que j'en- du- re, la pei- ne que j'en-
pei- ne que j'en- du- re, la pei- ne que j'en- du-
pei- ne que j'en- du- re, De-
rez luy la pei- ne que j'en- du- re, la pei- ne

21 Cornet, *Or me traictiez*

20
tiez ain- si qu'il vous plai-
si qu'il vous plai- ra, Or me traic- tiez ain- si qu'il
traic- tiez ain- si qu'il vous plai- ra,
tez, Or me traic- tez ain- si qu'il vous plai-
plai- ra, Or me traic- tez ain- si qu'il vous plai-

36
rant, En en- du- rant mon coeur vous ser- vi- ra, Et
vous ser- vi- ra, En en- du- rant mon coeur vous ser- vi- ra,
mon coeur vous ser- vi- ra, En en- du- rant mon coeur
ser- vi- ra, En en- du- rant mon coeur vous ser- vi- ra, Et
rant mon coeur vous ser- vi- ra, mon coeur vous ser- vi- ra,

28
ra, En en- du- rant mon coeur vous ser- vi- ra, En en- du-
vous plai- ra, En en- du- rant mon coeur
En en- du- rant, En en- du- rant
ra, En en- du- rant mon coeur vous
ra, En en- du- rant,
En en- du-

45
ay- me mieux vous ser- vir, Et ay- me mieux,
Et ay- me mieux vous ser- vir en tris-
vous ser- vi- ra, Et ay-
ay- me mieux vous ser- vir en tris- tes-
Et ay- me mieux vous ser- vir en tris- tes- se,

Et ay- me mieux vous ser- vir en tris- tes-
tes- se, Et ay- me mieux vous ser- vir
me mieux, Et ay- me mieux vous ser- vir en tris
se, Et ay- me mieux, vous ser-
Et ay- me mieux vous ser- vir en tris- tes-

lleurs en joye & en li- es- se.
Qu'ay- mer ai- lleurs en joye & en li- es- se, Qu'ay- mer ai-
en li- es- se, & en li- es- se, Qu'ay- mer ai-
en li- es- se, Qu'ay- mer ai- lleurs en joye & en li-
& en li- es- se, Qu'ay- mer ai-

se, Qu'ay- mer ai-
en tris- tes- se, Qu'ay- mer ai- lleurs en joy- e,
tes- se, en tris- tes- se, Qu'ay- mer ai- lleurs en joye &
vir en tris- tes- se, Qu'ay- mer ai- lleurs en joye &
se, Qu'ay- mer ai- lleurs en joye

lleurs en joye & en li- es- se.
lleurs en joye & en li- es- se.
es- se, & en li- es- se.
lleurs en joye & en li- es- se.

22 LeJeune, *Allons, allons gay*

23
vous & moy, Mon pe- re à
moy, Mon pe- re à fait fai- re un cha- teau,
e- ment, vous & moy, Mon pe- re à fait, Mon pe- re à
ment, vous & moy, Mon pe- re à fait fai-
ment, vous & moy, Mon pe- re à fait fai- re un

36
fai- re un cha- teau, D'or & d'ar- gent sont les cre- neaux,
fai- r'un cha- teau, D'or & d'ar- gent sont les cre- neaux, gay- e-
fait fai- re un cha- teau, D'or & d'ar- gent sont les cre- neaux,
D'or & d'ar- gent sont les cre- neaux, gay- e- ment, ma
fai- re un cha- teau,

29
fait fai- re un cha- teau, Mon pe- re à fait
Mon pe- re à fait fai- re un cha- teau, à fait
fait fai- re un cha- teau, Mon pe- re à
re un cha- teau, Mon pe- re à fait fai- re un cha- teau,
cha- teau, Mon pe- re à fait fai- re un cha- teau, à fait

42
D'or & d'ar- gent sont les cre- neaux, gay- e-
ment, ma mi- gnon- ne, gay- e- ment, ma mi- gnon- ne,
gay- e- ment, ma mi- gnon- ne, D'or & d'ar- gent sont les cre-
mi- gnon- ne, D'or & d'ar- gent sont
D'or & d'ar- gent sont les cre- neaux, gay- e- ment, ma mi- gnon- ne,

48
ment, ma mi- gnon- ne, gay- e- ment, ma mi- gnon- ne, vous & moy,
ma mi- gnon- ne, gay- e- ment, ma mi- gnon- ne, vous & moy, Al- lons,
neaux, & d'ar- gent sont les cre- neaux, Al- lons, al- lons les cre- neaux,
les cre- neaux,
ma mi- gnon- ne, Al- lons, al- lons gay, gay- e-

60
moy, gay- e- ment, vous & moy,
e- ment, vous & moy,
gay- e- ment, vous & moy, D'or & d'ar-
ma mi- gnon- ne, vous & moy, gay- e- ment, vous & moy,
vous & moy,

54
Al- lons, al- lons gay, gay- e- ment, ma mi- gnon- ne, vous &
al- lons gay, gay- e- ment, ma mi- gnon- ne, gay-
gay, gay- e- ment, ma mi- gnon- ne, gay- e- ment, ma mi- gnon- ne,
Al- lons, al- lons gay- e- ment, ma mi- gnon- ne,
ment, ma mi- gnon- ne, vous & moy, gay- e- ment,

66
D'or & d'ar- gent sont les cre- neaux,
D'or & d'ar- gent sont les cre-
gent sont les cre- neaux, D'or & d'ar- gent sont
D'or & d'ar- gent sont les cre- neaux, D'or & d'ar-
D'or & d'ar- gent sont les cre- neaux, sont les cre-

85

72
D'or & d'ar-gent sont les cre-neaux, gay-e-ment, ma mi-gnon-
neaux, D'or & d'ar-gent sont les cre-
les cre-neaux, D'or & d'ar-gent sont les cre-neaux, Le
gent sont les cre-neaux, D'or & d'ar-gent sont les cre-
neaux, D'or & d'ar-gent sont les cre-neaux, sont les cre-neaux,

86
beau, gay-e-ment, ma mi-gnon-ne, Al-lons, al-lons gay,
gay-e-ment, ma mi-gnon-ne, ma mi-gnon-ne, Al-
ment, gay-e-ment, ma mi-gnon-ne, gay-e-ment, ma mi-gnon-ne, Al-lons, al-lons
gay-e-ment, gay-e-ment, ma mi-gnon-ne, Al-lons, al-lons gay, Al-
gay-e-ment, ma mi-gnon-ne, Al-lons,

79
ne, Le Roy n'en à point de si
neaux, Le Roy n'en à point de si beau, gay-e-ment, ma mi-gnon-ne,
Roy n'en à point de si beau, gay-e-ment, gay-e-
neaux, La Roy n'en à point de si beau,
Le Roy n'en à point de si beau,

92
Al-lons, al-lons gay, gay-e-ment, vous &
lons, al-lons gay, gay-e-ment, ma mi-gnon-ne, vous &
al-lons gay, gai-e-ment, gay-e-ment, vous & moy, Le
lons, al-lons gay, Al-lons, al-lons gay, gay-e-ment, vous &
al-lons gay, Al-lons, al-lons gay, gay-e-ment, gay-e-ment, vous &

97
moy, Le Roy n'en à point, Le Roy n'en à point de si beau, ma mi
moy, Le Roy n'en à point de si beau, gay- e- ment, ma
Roy n'en à point de si beau, gai- e- ment, vous & moy, gai- e- ment,
moy, Le Roy n'en à point de si beau, gai- e
moy,
gay- e- ment, ma mi

109
moy, Al- lons, al- lons gay, gay- e- ment, vous & moy, Al- lons,
ment, vous & moy, gai- e- ment, vous & moy, Al-
Al- lons, al- lons gay, gay- e- ment, vous & moy, ma mi
& moy, Al- lons,
Al- lons, al- lons gay, gay- e- ment, vous & moy, Al- lons, al- lons

103
gnon- ne, gai- e- ment, ma mi- gnon- ne, gay- e- ment, gay- e- ment, vous &
mi- gnon- ne, Al- lons, al- lons gay, gay- e- ment, gay- e
ma mi- gnon- ne, ma mi- gnon- ne, gay- e- ment, ma mi- gnon- ne,
ment, gay- e- ment, ma mi- gnon- ne, Al- lons, al- lons gay, gay- e- ment, vous
gnon- ne,

114
al- lons gay, Al- lons, al- lons gay, gay- e- ment, vous & moy.
lons, al- lons gay, gay- e- ment, vous & moy.
gnon- ne, gay- e- ment, ma mi- gnon- ne, vous & moy.
al- lons gay, gay- e- ment, vous & moy.
gay, gay- e- ment, gay- e- ment, gay- e- ment, vous & moy.

23 Leschenet, *Puis que j'ay belle amye*

loy- au- ment, Et veux to- tal- le-
Je vi- vray loy- au- ment, Et veux to- tal- le- ment,
Et veux to- tal- le- ment, to- tal- le- ment, Et
ment, Et veux to- tal- le- ment, Et veux to-
Et veux to- tal- le- ment, Et veux to-

ser me- lan- co- li- e,
Chas- ser me- lan- co- li- e,
e, Chas- ser me- lan- co-
e, Chas- ser me- lan- co- li- e, me- lan- co- li-
lan- co- li- e, Chas- ser me- lan- co- li-

ment, Chas-
veux to- tal- le- ment, to- tal- le- ment, Chas- ser me- lan- co- li-
tal- le- ment, Chas- ser me- lan- co- li-
tal- le- ment, Chas- se me- lan- co- li- e, Chas- ser me-

Chas- ser me- lan- co- li- e, me- lan- co- li- e.
Chas- ser me- lan- co- li- e, me- lan- co- li- e.
li- e, Chas- ser me- lan- co- li- e.
e, Chas- ser me- lan- co- li- e, Chas- ser me- lan- co- li- e.
e, Chas- ser me- lan- co- li- e.

Quand vous
Quand vous se- riés, Quand vous
Quand vous se- riés, Quand vous se- riés quel- que fi- lle d'un
Quand vous se- riés, Quand vous se- riés quel- que
Quand vous se- riés quel- que fi- lle d'un

fi- lle d'un Sci- the, En- cor' l'a-
riés, Quand vous se- riés quel- que fi- lle d'un Sci- the, En-
que fi- lle d'un Sci- the, En- cor' l'a- mour qui les Ti-
que fi- lle d'un Sci- the, En- cor' l'a- mour,
Sci- the, quel- que fi- lle d'un Sci- the, En- cor'

se- riés quel- que fi- lle d'un Sci- the, quel- que
se- riés quel- que fi- lle d'un Sci- the, Quand vous se-
Sci- the, quel- que fi- lle d'un Sci- the, Quand vous se- riés quel-
fi- lle d'un Sci- the, Quand vous se- riés quel-
Sci- the, Quand vous se- riés quel- que fi- lle d'un

mour qui les Ti- gres in- ci- te, qui
cor' l'a- mour qui les Ti- gres in- ci- te, En-
gres in- ci- te, qui les Ti- gres in-
En- cor' l'a- mour qui les Ti-
l'a- mour qui les Ti- gres in- ci- te, qui les Ti-

les Ti- gres in- ci- te, Vous for- ce- roit de mon mal se- cou-
cor' l'a- mour qui les Ti- gres in- ci- te, Vous for- ce- roit de mon mal
ci- te, qui les Ti- gres in- ci- te, Vous for- ce- roit, Vous
gres in- ci- te, qui les Ti- gres in- ci- te,
gres in- ci- te, qui les Ti- gres in- ci- te, Vous

for- ce- roit de mon mal se- cou- rir, Mais
mon mal se- cou- rir, Vous for- ce- roit de mon mal se- cou- rir,
roit de mon mal se- cou- rir, de mon mal se- cou- rir, Mais vous
vous for- ce- roit de mon mal se- cou- rir, Mais vous
de mon mal se- cou- rir, de mon mal se- cou- rir,

rir, Vous for- ce- roit, Vous
se- cou- rir, vous for- ce- roit de
for- ce- roit de mon mal se- cou- rir, Vous for- ce-
Vous for- ce- roit de mon mal se- cou- rir,
for- ce- roit de mon mal se- cou- rir,

vous trop plus qu'u- ne Ti- gres- se fie- re, qu'u-
Mais vous trop plus qu'u- ne Ti- gres- se fie- re,
trop plus qu'u- ne Ti- gres- se fie- re, qu'u- ne
trop plus, Mais vous trop plus qu'u- ne Ti- gres- se fie- re, Mais
Mais vous trop plus qu'u- ne Ti- gres- se fie- re,

73
ne Ti- gres- se fie- re,   Las   de
Mais vous trop plus q'u- ne Ti- gres- se fie- re,
Ti- gres- se fie- re, q'u- ne Ti- gres- se fie- re, Las
vous trop plus, q'u- ne Ti- gres- se   fie- re, Las de
q'u- ne Ti- gres- se, q'u- ne Ti- gres- se fie- re,

96
la meur- trie- re,   Et   ne
es- tes la meur- trie- re, Et ne vi- vés que de le voir mou- rir,   Et
es- tes la meur- trie- re, Et ne vi- vés que de le voir mou-
Et ne vi- vés que de le voir mou- rir, que de le voir mou-
es- tes la meur- trie- re, Et ne vi- vés que de le

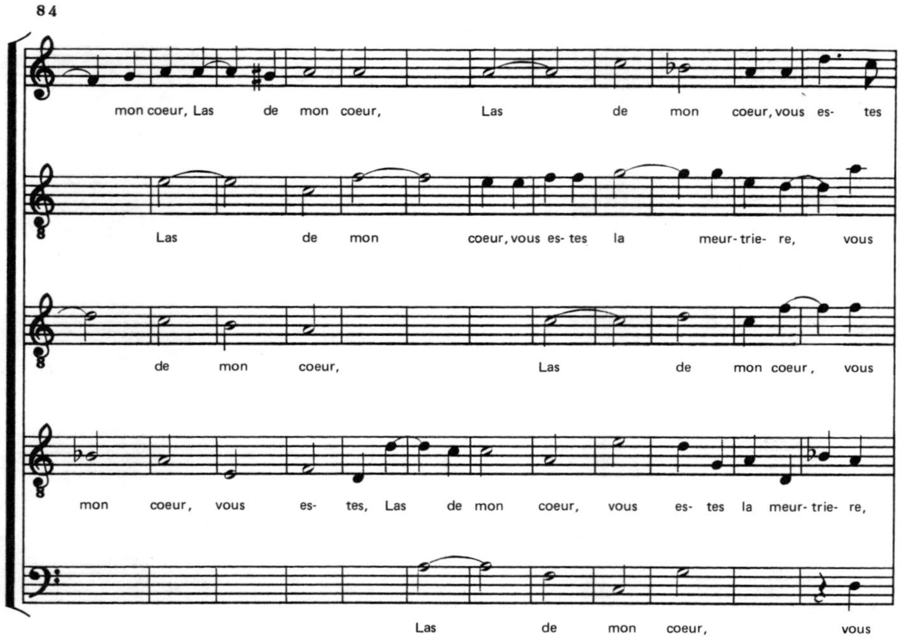
84
mon coeur, Las de mon coeur, Las de mon coeur, vous es- tes
Las   de mon coeur, vous es- tes la meur- trie- re, vous
de mon coeur, Las de mon coeur, vous
mon coeur, vous es- tes, Las de mon coeur, vous es- tes la meur- trie- re,
Las de mon coeur, vous

106
vi- vés que de le voir mou- rir, Et ne vi-
ne vi- vés que de le voir mou- rir, Et ne vi- vés, Et
rir, que de le voir mou- rir, Et ne vi- vés que de le voir mou-
rir, Et ne vi- vés, Et ne vi- vés que de le voir mou-
voir mou- rir, que de le voir mou- rir, Et ne vi- vés,

116
vés que de le voir mou- rir, Et ne vi- vés
ne vi- vés que de le voir mou- rir, que de le voir mou- rir,
rir, Et ne vi- vés que de le voir mou- rir, Et ne vi-
rir, Et ne vi- vés, Et ne vi- vés que de le
Et ne vi- vés que de le voir mou-

Je m'en vois au vert bois, Je
Je m'en vois au vert bois, au vert bois,
Je
Je m'en vois au vert bois ou- yr
Je m'en vois au vert bois,

126
que de le voir mou- rir.
Et ne vi- vés que de le voir mou- rir, le voir mou- rir.
vés que de le voir mou- rir, le voir mou- rir.
voir mou- rir, le voir mou- rir.
rir, le voir mou- rir, le voir mou- rir.

9
m'en vois au vert bois, ou- yr chan- ter l'oi- si-
Je m'en vois au vert bois, ou-
m'en vois au vert bois, Je m'en vois au vert bois ou- yr
chan- ter l'oi- si- llon, ou- yr chan- ter l'oi- si- llon,
ou- yr chan- ter l'oi- si- llon, l'oi- si-

llon, ou- yr chan- ter l'oi- si- llon,
yr chan- ter l'oi- si- llon, ou- yr chan- ter l'oi- si-
chan- ter l'oi- si- llon, l'oi- si- llon, Me di- sant,
Me di- sant, vous di- sant,
llon, ou- yr chan- ter l'oi- si- llon,

que c'es- toit pour Ma- ri- on, pour
on, pour Ma- ri- on, que c'es- toit pour Ma- ri- on,
toit pour Ma- ri- on, pour Ma- ri- on, que c'es- toit pour
que c'es- toit pour Ma- ri, Ma- ri- on,
que c'es- toit pour Ma- ri- on, que c'es- toit pour

Me di- sant, vous di- sant, que c'es- toit pour Ma- ri- on,
llon, Me di- sant, vous di- sant, que c'es- toit pour Ma- ri-
vous di- sant, Me di- sant, vous di- sant, que c'es-
Me di- sant, vous di- sant, Me di- sant, vous di- sant,
l'oi- si- llon, Me di- sant, vous di- sant,

Ma- ri- on, que c'es- toit pour Ma- ri- on,
que c'es- toit pour Ma- ri- on, Or y vont, vont
Ma- ri- on, pour Ma- ri- on, pour Ma- ri- on,
que c'es- toit pour Ma- ri- on, Or y vont, vont,
Ma- ri- on, que c'es- toit pour Ma- ri- on, pour Ma- ri- on,

48
Or y vont, vont,   Or y vont pas-
pas- tou- reaux & pas- tou- rel- les, Or y vont, Or y
Or y vont,
pas- tou- reaux & pas- tou- rel- les,
Or y vont, vont,

63
Et si font, font un bou- quet,
Et si font, font un bou- quet & puis s'en vont, un
tou- rel- les, Et si font, font
& pas- tou- rel- les, Et si font,
tou- rel- les, Et si font,

56
tou- reaux & pas- tou- rel- les,
vont, pas- tou- reaux & pas- tou- rel- les,
vont pas- tou- reaux, pas- tou- reaux & pas-
Or y vont, Or y vont, vont, pas- tou- reaux
Or y vont, vont, pas- tou- reaux & pas-

70
Et si font un bou- quet &
bou- quet & puis s'en vont,
un bou- quet & puis s'en vont, & puis s'en
font, un bou- quet, un bou-
un bou- quet & puis s'en vont,

puis s'en vont, & puis s'en vont un bou-quet
Et si font un bou-quet & puis s'en vont,
vont, un bou-quet & puis s'en vont, un bou-
quet & puis s'en vont, un bou-quet &
un bou-quet & puis s'en vont,

bois ou-yr chan-ter l'oi-si-llon, Je m'en vois au vert bois,
bois ou-yr chan-ter l'oi-si-llon, ou-yr chan-ter l'oi-
bois, ou-yr chan-ter l'oi-si-llon, ou-yr
bois, Je m'en vois au vert bois ou-yr chanter l'oi-si-llon, l'oi-
bois ou-yr chan-ter l'oi-si-llon, ou-yr chan-ter

& puis s'en vont, & puis s'en vont, Je m'en vois au vert
un bou-quet & puis s'en vont, Je m'en vois au vert
quet & puis s'en vont, & puis s'en vont, Je m'en vois au vert
puis s'en vont, un bou-quet & puis s'en vont, Je m'en vois au vert
un bou-quet & puis s'en vont, Je m'en vois au vert

me di-sant, vous di-sant que c'es-toit pour Ma-ri-on,
si-llon, me di-sant, vous di-sant, me di-sant,
chan-ter l'oi-si-llon, me di-sant, vous di-sant, me
si-llon, me di-sant, vous di-sant, me di-sant, vous di-sant,
l'oi-si-llon, l'oi-si-llon, me di-sant, vous di-sant

26 Nicolas, *Susane un jour* [Guéroult]

19
e, Par deux vie- llars, con- voi- tans sa beau-
e, Par deux, par deux vie- llars, par deux vie- llars, con- voi- tans sa beau-
e, Par deux vie- llars, Par deux vie- llars, con- voi- tans sa beau-
deux vie- llars con- voi- tans sa beau- té, sa beau- té, Fut
e, Par deux vie- llars, Par deux vie- llars con- voi- tans sa beau- té,

39
tris- te & des- con- for- té- e,
des- con- for- té- e, tris- te & des- con- for- té- e, Voy-
en son coeur tris- te & des- con- for- té- e, Voy- ant
te & des- con- for- té- e, tris- te & des- con- for- té- e, Voy-
Fut en son coeur tris- te & des- con- for- té- e, des- con- for- té- e, Voy-

29
té, Fut en son coeur, Fut en son coeur,
té, Fut en son coeur, Fut en son coeur tris- te &
té, Fut en son coeur, Fut en son coeur, Fut
en son coeur, Fut en son coeur, Fut en son coeur, Fut en son coeur tris-
Fut en son coeur tris- te, Fut en son coeur,

50
Voy- ant l'ef- fort, fait à sa chas- te- té,
ant, Voy- ant l'ef- fort, Voy- ant l'ef- fort fait à sa chas- te- té,
l'ef- fort, Voy- ant l'ef- fort fait à sa chas- te- té, fait à sa chas- te- té,
ant l'ef- fort, Voy- ant l'ef- fort, fait à sa chas- te- té,
ant l'ef- fort, Voy- ant l'ef- fort fait à sa chas- te- té, El-

El- le leur dit si par des-loy-au- té, De ce cors mien vous a- vez jou-is-san-
El- le leur dit, si par des- loy- au- té, De ce cors mien vous a- vez jou-is-san-
El- le leur dit si par des-loy- au- té, De ce corps mien vous a-vez jou-is-san-ce, vous a- vez
El- le leur dit si par des- loy-au- té, De ce corps mien vous a- vez
le leur dit si par des- loy- au- té, De ce corps mien vous a-vez jou-is- san- ce,

fay re- sis- tan- ce, Vous me fe- rez, Vous me fe- rez, Vous me fe- rez
je fay re- sis- tan- ce, Vous me fe- rez mou-rir en des- hon- neur, en des- hon- neur,
Si je fay re- sis- tan- ce, Vous me fe- rez, Vous me fe- rez mou-rir, mou- rir en
Si je fay re- sis- tan- ce, Vous me fe- rez mou-rir, Vous, Vous me fe-rez mou-
fay re- sis- tan- ce, Vous me fe- rez, Vous me fe- rez, Vous me fe- rez mou- rir en

ce, C'est fait, C'est fait de moy, Si je
ce, C'est fait de moy,C'est fait, C'est fait de moy, Si
jou- is- san- ce,C'est fait, C'est fait de moy, C'est fait de moy, fait,
jou-is-san- ce, C'est fait, C'est fait de moy,
C'est fait, C'est fait de moy, Si je

mou- rir en des- hon- neur, Mais j'ay-me mieux,
Vous me fe- rez mou-rir en des-hon- neur, Mais j'ay- me mieux pe- rir en in- no- cen-
des- hon- neur, mou-rir en des- hon- neur, Mais j'ay-me mieux pe- rir en in- no- cen-
rir en des- hon- neur, Mais j'ay-me mieux, pe- rir en in-no-cen-
des-hon- neur, Mais J'ay-me mieux pe- rir en in- no- cen-

27 Nicolas, *Je ry & si ay larmes*

16
(sic)
Je ry & si ay lar- mes a
Je ry & si ay lar- me[s] a
& si ay lar- mes a l'oeil, & si ay lar- mes a
si ay lar- mes a l'oeil, a l'oeil,
ry & si ay lar- mes a

32
Je chan- te sans a- voir plai- sir, Je
sans a- voir plai- sir, Je chan- te sans a-
sans a- voir plai- sir: Je chan- te sans a- voir plai- sir,
voir plai- sir: Je chan- te sans a- voir plai-
sans a- voir plai- sir: Je chan- te sans a

23
l'oeil, Je chan- te sans a- voir plai- sir:
l'oeil, Je chan- te sans a- voir plai- sir:
l'oeil, Je chan- te sans a- voir plai- sir: Je chan- te
Je chan- te sans a- voir plai- sir: Je chan- te sans a-
l'oeil, Je chan- te

42
dan- se au son de des- plai- sir, Je dan-
voir plai- si[r], sans a- voir plai- sir, Je dan- se au
Je chan- te sans a- voir plai- sir,
sir, Je chan- te sans a- voir plai- sir, Je dan- se au
voir plai- sir, Je dan- se au son, Je dan-

se au son de des- plai- sir, Je dan- se au
son de des- plai- sir, au son de des- plai- sir, Je
Je dan- se au son de des- plai- sir, au son de
son de des- plai- sir, de des- plai- sir, au son
se au son de des- plai- sir, de des- plai- sir,

m'es- bas, Je m'es- bas, Je m'es- bas,
m'es- bas, Je m'es- bas, Je m'es-
bas, Je m'es- bas, Je m'es- bas,
bas, Je m'es- bas, Je m'es-
Je m'es- bas, Je m'es- bas, Je

son de des- plai- sir, Je m'es- bas, Je
dan- se au son de des- plai- sir, Je m'es- bas, Je
des- plai- sir, Je m'es- bas, Je m'es-
de des- plai- sir, Je m'es- bas, Je m'es-
Je m'es- bas, Je m'es- bas,

Je m'es- bas & si n'ay que
bas, Je m'es- bas, Je m'es- bas & si
Je m'es- bas, Je m'es- bas,
bas & si, Je m'es- bas & si
m'es- bas, Je m'es- bas & si n'ay que

28 Nicolas, *Tout ce qu'on peut*

13
el- le voir, N'est que dou- ceur & a- my-
N'est que dou- ceur & a- my- tié, N'est que dou-ceur & a- my-
le voir, N'est que dou-ceur & a- my-
le voir, N'est que dou- ceur & a- my- tié, N'est
el- le voir, N'est

25
té, beau- té & un vou- loir,
Bon- té, beau- té & un vou- loir, Bon-
tié, Bon- té, beau- té & un
un vou- loir,
tié, Bon- té, beau- té & un

19
tié: N'est que dou- ceur, & a- my- tié, Bon-
tié, N'est que dou- ceur & a- my- tié,
tié, N'est que dou- ceur & a- my- tié, & a- my-
que dou- ceur & a- my- tié, & a- mi-

31
beau- té & un vou-
té, beau- té, beau- té & un vou- loir,
vou- loir, Bon- té, beau- té & un vou-
Bon- té, beau- té & un vou-
vou- loir, beau- té & un vou-

(sic)
loir, Tout plein d'a- mou- reu- se pi-
Tout plein d'a- mou- reu- se pi- tié: Tout plein d'a- mou- reu- se pi-
loir, Tout plein d'a- mou- reu- se pi- tié: Tout
loir, Tout plein d'a- mou- reu- se pi-
loir, Tout

(sic)
Mais je n'en suis e- di- fi- é,
Mais je n'en suis e- di- fi- é, Mais je n'en suis e-
Mais je n'en suis e-
Mais je n'en suis e- di- fi- é, Mais je n'en suis e-
Mais je n'en suis e-

tié: Tout plein d'a- mou- reu- se pi- tié:
tié: Tout plein d'a- mou- reu- se pi- tié:
plein d'a- mou- reu- se pi- tié: Tout plein d'a- mou- reu- se pi- tié:
tié: Tout plein d'a- mou- reu- se pi- tié:
plein d'a- mou- reu- se pi- tié: d'a- mou- reu- se pi- tié,

Mais je n'en suis e- di- fi- é,
di- fi- é, Mais je n'en suis e- di- fi- é, de rien
di- fi- é, Mais je n'en suis e- di- fi- é, de rien
di- fi- é, Mais je n'en suis e- di- fi- é,
di- fi- é, Mais je n'en suis e- di- fi- é,

58
de rien mieux, de rien mieux, Car le re- gard d'el-
mieux, de rien mieux, de rien mieux, Car le re-
mieux, de rien mieux, de rien mieux, Car le re- gard d'el-
de rien mieux, de rien mieux, Car le re- gard d'el-
de rien mieux, de rien mieux,

68
Que ne la puis di- re a moy-
en u- ne pei- ne tel- le, Que
pei- ne tel- le, Que ne la puis di- re a moy-
ne pei- ne tel- le, Que ne la puis di- re a moy-
u- ne pei- ne tel- le,

63
le, Me met en u- ne pei- ne tel- le,
gard d'el- le, Me met en u- ne pei- ne tel- le,
le, Car le re- gard d'el- le, Me met en u- ne
le, Car le re- gard d'el- le, Me met en u-
Car le re- gard d'el- le, Me met en

73
tié: Que ne la puis di- re a moy- tié:
ne la puis di- re a moy- tié: Que ne la puis di-
tié: Que ne la puis di- re a moy- tié: Que ne la puis di- re a moy-
tié: Que ne la puis di-
Que ne la puis di- re a moy- tié: Que ne la puis di-

78
Que ne la puis di- re a moy-
re a moy- tié: Que ne la puis di- re a moy- tié: a moy-
tié: Que ne la puis di- re a moy- tié:
re a moy- tié: Que ne la puis di- re a moy-
re a moy- tié: Que ne la puis di- re a moy-

87
Quand je la voy, je me tour- men-
men- te, Quand je la voy, je me tour- men-
voy, je me tour- men- te, Quand je la voy, je
voy, je me tour- men- te, je
men- te,

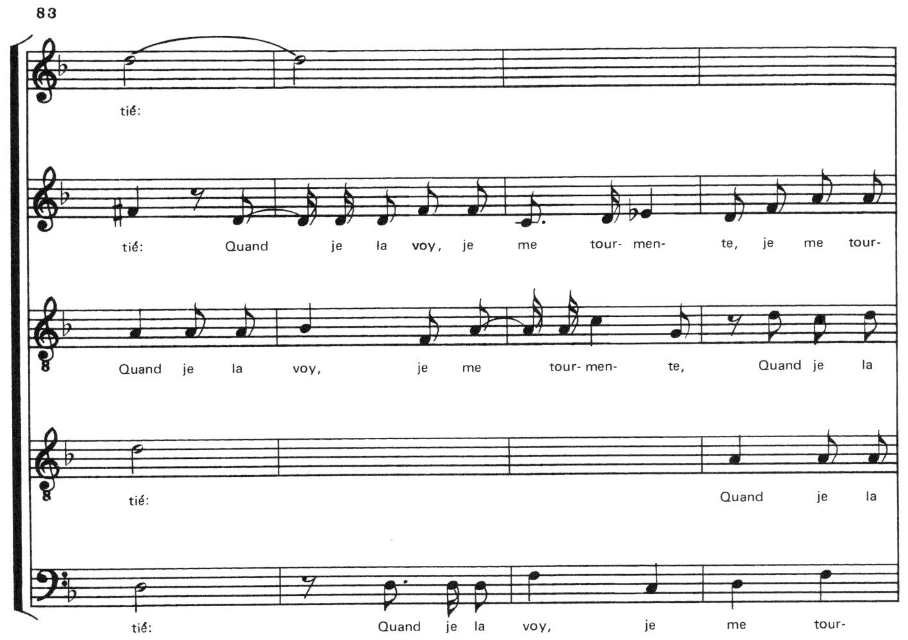

83
tié:
tié: Quand je la voy, je me tour- men- te, je me tour-
Quand je la voy, je me tour- men- te, Quand je la
tié: Quand je la
tié: Quand je la voy, je me tour-

92
te, Quand je la voy, je me tour- men- te, Si,
te, Si ne la voy, je me la- men- te,
me tour- men- te, Si ne la voy, je
me tour- men- te, Si ne la voy, Si ne la voy, je
Si ne la voy, je me la- men-

97
Si ne la voy, je me la- men- te, je
Si ne la voy, je me la- men- te, je
me la- men- te, Si ne la voy, je me la-
me la- men- te, Si ne la voy, je me
te,

108
te. Le doux n'est ja- mais sans l'a- mer,
te. Le doux n'est ja- mais sans l'a- mer, Le doux n'est ja- mais sans l'a-
te. Le doux n'est ja- mais sans l'a-
Le doux n'est ja- mais sans l'a- mer, Le doux n'est ja- mais sans l'a-
Le doux n'est ja- mais sans l'a-

102
me la- men- te, je me la- men-
me la- men- te, je me la- men- te, je me la- men-
men- te, je me la- men-
la- men- te, je me la- men- te.
je me la- men- te.

115
Le doux n'est ja- mais sans l'a- mer, Voi- la que c'est de
mer, Le doux n'est ja- mais sans l'a- mer, Voi- la que c'est de
mer, Le doux n'est ja- mais sans l'a- mer,
mer, Le doux, n'est ja- mais sans l'a- mer, Voi- la que c'est de
mer, Le doux n'est ja- mais sans l'a- mer,

trop ay- mer, Voi- la que
trop ay- mer, Voi- la
Voi- la que c'est de trop ay- mer,
trop ay- mer, Voi- la que c'est de trop ay- mer, Voi-
Voi- la que c'est de trop ay- mer,

Voi- la que c'est de trop ay- mer,
Voi- la, Voi- la que c'est de trop ay- mer,
que c'est de trop ay- mer, Le
la que c'est, Voi- la que c'est de trop ay- mer,
la que c'est de trop ay- mer,

c'est de trop ay- mer, Voi- la,
que c'est de trop ay- mer, Voi- la, Voi- la,
Voi- la que c'est, Voi- la
la que c'est de trop ay- mer, Voi- la que c'est, Voi-
Voi- la, Voi- la, Voi-

Le doux n'est ja- mais sans l'a- mer,
Le doux n'est ja- mais, ja- mais sans l'a- mer,
doux, Le doux n'est ja- mais sans l'a- mer,
Le doux n'est ja- mais sans l'a- mer,
Le

Le doux n'est ja- mais sans l'a- mer,
Le doux n'est ja- mais sans l'a- mer, Voi-
Le doux n'est ja- mais sans l'a- mer, Voi- la
Le doux n'est ja- mais sans l'a- mer, Voi- la que
doux n'est ja- mais, ja- mais sans l'a- mer, Voi-
que c'est de trop ay-
mer, Voi- la que c'est, Voi-
ay- mer, Voi- la que c'est, Voi- la
Voi- la que c'est de trop ay-
trop ay- mer, Voi- la, Voi-
Voi- la
la, Voi- la que c'est de trop ay-
que c'est, Voi- la que c'est de trop
c'est de trop ay- mer,
la que c'est de trop ay- mer, de
mer, de trop ay- mer.
la que c'est de trop ay- mer.
que c'est de trop ay- mer.
mer, de trop ay- mer.
la que c'est de trop ay- mer.

A ce ma- tin ce se- roit bon- nees- trei-
A ce ma- tin, ce se- roit bon- ne es- trei-
A ce ma- tin, ce se- roit, ce se- roit bon- ne es- trei-
A ce ma- tin, ce se- roit bon- ne es- trei- ne, De
A ce ma- tin, A ce ma- tin, ce se- roit bon- ne es- trei-

bon sa- lé, Et de bon vin, Et de bon vin, la grand' bou- tei-
bon sa- lé, Et de bon vin, Et de bon vin, la grand' bou-
bon sa- lé, Et de bon vin, Et de bon vin, la grand' bou-
Et de bon vin, Et de bon vin, la grand' bou- tei- lle plei- ne,
bon sa- lé, Et de bon vin, Et de bon vin, Et de bon vin, la grand' bou-

ne, De des- jeu- ner, De des- jeu- ner, De des- jeu- ner le bon jam-
ne, De des- jeu- ner, De des- jeu- ner, De des- jeu- ner le bon jam- bon, jam-
ne, De des- jeu- ner, De des- jeu- ner le bon jam- bon, De des- jeu- ner le bon jam-
des- jeu- ner, De des- jeu- ner le bon jam- bon sa- lé,
ne, De des- jeu- ner, De des- jeu- ner le bon jam- [bon], le bon

lle plei- ne, Car dou- ce- ment, Car dou- ce- ment, Car dou- ce- ment
tei- lle plei- ne, Car dou- ce- ment, Car dou- ce- ment, est de moy a- val- lé, est
tei- lle plei- ne, Car dou- ce- ment, Car dou- ce- ment, Car dou- ce- ment, Car dou- ce-
Car dou- ce- ment, Car dou- ce- ment, est de moy a- val-
tei- lle plei- ne, Car dou- ce- ment, Car dou- ce- ment, est de moy

est de moy a- val- lé, A- voir bon feu, Le pein blanc
de moy a- val- lé, A- voir bon feu, A- voir bon feu, Le pein blanc
ment, est de moy a- val- lé, A- voir bon feu, Le pein blanc cha- pe-
lé, A- voir bon feu, A- voir bon feu, Le pein blanc
est de moy a- val- lé, A- voir bon feu, Le pein

le au cors gent, Mais tou- te- fois a- voir beu & gal-
cors gent, Mais tou- te- fois a- voir, a- voir beu & gal- lé, a- voir beu & gal-
Mais tou- te- fois a- voir beu & gal- lé, a- voir beu & gal- lé, a- voir beu & gal-
cors gent, Mais tou- te- fois a- voir beu & gal- lé,
le au cors gent, Mais tou- te- fois a- voir beu & gal-

cha- pe- lé, Ac- com- pa- gné, Ac- com- pa- gné, de la bel-
cha- pe- lé, Ac- com- pa- gné, de la bel- le au cors gent, de la bel- le au
lé, Ac- com- pa- gné, Ac- com- pa- gné de la bel- le au corps gent,
cha- pe- lé, Ac- com- pa- gné, Ac- com- pa- gné, de la bel- le au
blanc cha- pe- lé, Ac- com- pa- gné, de la bel-

lé, Le prin- ci- pal c'est d'a- voir de l'ar- gent, Le
lé, Le prin- ci- pal c'est d'a- voir de l'ar- gent,
lé, Le prin- ci- pal c'est d'a- voir de l'ar- gent, Le prin- ci- pal c'est d'a- voir
Le prin- ci- pal c'est d'a- voir de l'ar- gent, c'est d'a- voir de l'ar- gent, Le
lé, Le prin- ci- pal c'est d'a- voir de l'ar- gent, Le prin-

49
prin- ci- pal c'est d'a-voir de l'ar- gent, Le prin- ci- pal c'est
Le prin- ci- pal c'est d'a-voir de l'ar- gent,
de l'ar- gent, c'est d'a-voir de l'ar- gent,
prin- ci- pal c'est d'a-voir de l'ar- gent, Le prin- ci- pal c'est
ci- pal c'est d'a- voir de l'ar- gent, Le prin- ci- pal,

62
voir de l'ar- gent.
pal c'est d'a- voir de l'ar- gent, c'est d'a-voir de l'ar- gent,
Le prin- ci- pal c'est d'a-voir de l'ar- gent, de l'ar- gent,
Le prin- ci- pal c'est d'a- voir de l'ar- gent, Le
d'a- voir de l'ar- gent, Le prin- ci- pal c'est d'a-voir de l'ar- gent, Le

55
d'a- voir de l'ar- gent, Le prin- ci- pal c'est d'a-voir, c'est d'a-
Le prin- ci- pal c'est d'a-voir de l'ar- gent, Le prin- ci-
Le prin- ci- pal c'est d'a-voir de l'ar- gent,
d'a- voir de l'ar- gent, Le prin- ci- pal c'est d'a-voir de l'ar- gent,
Le prin- ci- pal, Le prin- ci- pal c'est

68
Le prin- ci- pal c'est d'a- voir, c'est d'a- voir de l'ar- gent.
Le prin- ci- pal c'est d'a-voir de l'ar- gent.
prin- ci- pal c'est d'a- voir de l'ar- gent, c'est d'a- voir de l'ar- gent, c'est d'a-voir de l'ar- gent.
prin- ci- pal c'est d'a- voir de l'ar- gent, c'est d'a- voir de l'ar- gent.

30 Nicolas, *Pour ton amour* [C. Marot]

qui me tient, Que des-es- poir le cours du ciel re- tient, que des-es-poir,
me tient, Que des- es- poir le cours du ciel retient, Que des-es-
Que des- es- poir, Que des- es- poir le cours du ciel re- tient,
qui me tient, Que des- es- poir le cours du ciel re- tient, Que
tient, Que des- es- poir, Que des-es-poir

jour, A cel- le fin que le jour, A cel- le
fin, A cel- le fin que le jour,
cel- le fin, A cel- le fin que le jour ne s'ap- pro- che,
A cel- le fin, que le jour, que le jour
fin, A cel- le fin, A cel- le fin que le jour

que des- es- poir, A cel- le fin que le
poir, le cours du ciel re- tient, A cel- le
que des- es- poir le cours, le cours du ciel re- tient, A
des- es- poir, le cours du ciel re- tient, A cel- le fin,
Que des- es- poir le cours du ciel re- tient, A cel- le

fin que le jour, que le jour ne s'ap- pro-
que le jour ne s'ap- pro- che, que le jour ne s'ap-
que le jour, que le jour ne s'ap- pro-
ne s'ap- pro- che,
ne s'ap- pro- che, que le jour ne s'ap-

che, De l'at- ten- due & de- si- re ap- pro-
pro- che, De l'at- ten- due & de- si- re ap-
che, De l'at- ten- due & de- si- re ap- pro-
De l'at- ten- du- e,
pro- che,

de- si- re ap- pro- che, & de- si-
due & de- si- re ap- pro- che, & de- si- re ap-
pro- che, De l'at- ten- due & de- si- re ap-
che, De l'at- ten- due & de- si- re ap- pro- che, &
& de- si- re ap- pro- che, De l'at- ten- due

che, De l'at- ten- due &
pro- che, De l'at- ten-
che, De l'at- ten- due & de- si- re ap-
De l'at- ten- due & de- si- re ap- pro-
De l'at- ten- due & de- si- re ap- pro- che,

re ap- pro- che.
pro- che, & de- si- re ap- pro- che.
pro- che, & de- si- re ap- pro- che.
de- si- re ap- pro- che.
& de- si- re ap- pro- che, ap- pro- che.

31 Nicolas, *Il est bon enfant*

de mon pe- re, Au jar- din de mon
jar- din, Au jar- din de mon pe- re,
de mon pe- re, Au jar- din de mon
Au jar- din de mon pe- re, Au jar- din, Au jar- din
Au jar- din de mon pe-

pe- re, Au jar- din de mon
re, Au jar- din de mon pe- re, Au jar- din
re, Au jar- din de mon
jar- din de mon pe- re, de mon
Au jar- din de mon pe- re,

pe- re, Au jar- din de mon
Au jar- din de mon pe-
pe- re, Au jar- din de mon pe-
de mon pe- re, Au jar- din de mon pe- re, Au
re,

pe- re, Un blanc oy- seau y a,
de mon pe- re, un blanc oy- seau y
pe- re, un blanc oy- seau y
pe- re, un
Un blanc oy- seau, un blanc oy- seau y

un blanc oy- seau y a, un blanc oy- seau
a, un blanc oy- seau y a, un blanc oy-
a, un blanc oy- seau y a,
blanc oy- seau y a, un blanc oy-
a, un blanc oy- seau, un

Qui pleu- re & sou- pi- re, on ne sçait qu'il
Qui pleu- re & sou- pi- re,
sou- pi- re, Qui pleu- re & sou-
re & sou- pi- re, Qui pleu- re & sou-pi-
re & sou- pi- re, Qui pleu- re & sou-

y a,
seau y a, Qui pleu- re & sou- pi- re,
Qui pleu- re & sou- pi- re, Qui pleu- re &
seau y a, Qui pleu- re & sou- pi- re, Qui pleu-
blanc oy- seau y a, Qui pleu-

a, on ne sçait qu'il a, on ne sçait qu'il a,
Qui pleu- re & sou- pi- re, on ne sçait qu'il a,
pi- re, on ne sçait qu'il a, Qui pleu- re & sou-
re, on ne sçait qu'il a, on ne sçait qu'il a, on ne sçait qu'il
pi- re, on ne sçait qu'il a, on ne sçait qu'il a, on ne

on ne sçait qu'il a, on ne
on ne sçait qu'il a, on ne sçait qu'il a, on ne
pi- re, on ne sçait qu'il a, on ne
a, on ne sçait qu'il a, on ne sçait qu'il a,
sçait qu'il a, on ne sçait qu'il a, on ne sçait qu'il a, on ne

qu'il a, on ne sçait qu'il a,
ne sçait qu'il a, on ne sçait qu'il
on ne sçait qu'il a, on ne sçait
a, on ne sçait
a, on ne sçait qu'il

sçait qu'il a, on ne sçait
sçait qu'il a, on ne sçait qu'il a, on
sçait qu'il a, & on ne sçait qu'il a,
on ne sçait qu'il a, on ne sçait qu'il
sçait qu'il a, on ne sçait qu'il

on ne sçait qu'il a, Il est bon, Il est bon,
a, Il est bon,
qu'il a, Il est bon, Il est
qu'il a, Il est bon, Il est
a, on ne sçait qu'il a, Il est bon,

125
Il est bon en- fant, Il est bon, Il est bon
Il est bon en- fant, Il est bon en-
bon en- fant, Il est bon en- fant, Il est bon
bon en- fant, Il est bon en- fant, Il est
Il est bon en- fant,

142
en- fant, il n'y pen- se a nul mal, il
fant, il n'y pen- se a nul mal, il n'y pen- se a nul mal, Il est
se a nul mal, il n'y pen- se a nul mal, Il est
Il est bon en- fant, il n'y pen- se a nul mal,
se a nul mal, a nul mal, Il est bon en-

134
en- fant, il n'y pen- se a nul mal, Il est bon
fant, Il est bon en- fant, Il est bon en-
en- fant, il n'y pen- se a nul mal, il n'y pen-
bon en- fant, il n'y pen- se a nul mal,
Il est bon, Il est bon en- fant, il n'y pen-

151
n'y pen- se a nul mal, il n'y pen- se a nul mal.
bon en- fant, il n'y pen- se a nul mal.
bon en- fant, il n'y pen- se a nul mal.
Il est bon en- fant, il n'y pen- se a nul mal.
fant, il n'y pen- se a nul mal, a nul mal.

Sy je m'y plain j'ay bien rai-
Sy je m'y plain
Sy je m'y plain j'ay bien rai-
Sy je m'y plain j'ay bien rai-

son, Car j'ay per- du cel- le du mon- de,
j'ay per- du cel- le du mon- de, cel- le du mon-
le du mon- de, du mon-
son, Car j'ay per-
son, Car j'ay per- du cel- le du mon- de, cel-

Sy je m'y plain j'ay bien rai-
son, j'ay bien rai- son, Car
j'ay bien rai- son, Car j'ay per- du cel-
son, Si je m'y plain, j'ay bien rai-
son, j'ay bien rai-

du mon- de,
de, cel- le du mon- de, Ou j'a- voye l'a- mour,
de, Ou j'a- voye l'a-
du cel- le du mon- de, Ou j'a- voye l'a-
le du mon- de, Ou j'a- voye l'a-

36
Ou j'a- voye l'a- mour plus pro- fon- de,
l'a- mour plus pro- fon- de,
mour plus pro- fon- de, pro- fon- de,
mour, l'a- mour plus pro-
mour plus pro- fon- de, plus

55
Qui m'a ban- ny de sa mai- son, Qui m'a
son, de sa mai- son, Qui m'a ban- ny,
de sa mai- son, Qui m'a ban- ny de sa maison, Qui m'a ban- ny, de sa mai- son, de
son, Qui m'a ban- ny de sa

45
pro- fon- de,
l'a- mour plus pro- fon- de, Qui m'a ban- ny de sa mai-
Qui m'a ban- ny
fon- de, Qui m'a ban- ny de sa mai-
pro- fon- de, Qui m'a ban- ny de sa mai-

65
ban- ny de sa mai- son.
de sa mai- son, de sa mai- son.
son.
sa mai- son.
mai- son, de sa mai- son.

123

Son- nez m'y donc quand vous i- rez, Son- nez m'y
Son- nez m'y donc quand vous i- rez, Son- nez m'y donc quand vous
Son- nez m'y donc quand vous i- rez,
Son- nez m'y donc quand
Son- nez m'y donc quand vous i- rez, Son-

16
bi- et- tes, Sur l'her- be, Sur l'her- be, Sur
ner voz bre- bi- et- tes, Sur l'her- be,
Me- ner voz bre- bi- et- tes, Sur l'her- be,
Me- ner voz bre- bi-
et- tes, Me- ner voz bre- bi- et- tes,

8
donc quand vous i- rez, quand vous i- rez, Me- ner voz bre-
i- rez, quand vous i- rez, Me-
Son- nez m'y donc quand vous i- rez,
vous i- rez, Son- nez m'y donc quand vous i- rez,
nez m'y donc quand vous i- rez, Me- ner voz bre- bi-

24
l'her- be, En l'om-
Sur l'her- be, En l'om- bre d'un
Sur l'her- be,
et- tes, Sur l'her- be, sur l'her- be,
Sur l'her- be, sur l'her- be, En

32
bre d'un ar- bre vert, Au-
ar- bre vert, Au- prez
En l'om- bre d'un ar- bre vert, Au- prez d'u- ne es- glan- ti-
En l'om- bre d'un ar- bre vert,
l'om- bre d'un ar- bre vert, Au- prez d'u- ne es-

49
Trou- vay ber- gie- re a cou- vert, C'es- toit ma
gie- re a cou- vert, C'es- toit ma
Trou- vay ber- gie- re a cou- vert, C'es- toit ma va- len- ti- ne,
Trou- vay ber- gie- re a cou- vert, C'es- toit
vay ber- gie- re a cou- vert, Trou- vay ber- gie- re a cou-

40
prez d'u- n'es- glan- ti- ne, Au- prez d'u- n'es- glan- ti- ne,
d'u- ne es- glan- ti- ne, Trou- vay ber-
ne,
Au- prez d'u- ne es- glan- ti- ne,
glan- ti- ne, d'u- ne es- glan- ti- ne, Au- pres d'u- ne es- glan- ti- ne, Trou-

58
va- len- ti- ne, C'es- toit ma va- len- ti- ne,
va- len- ti- ne,
Qui fai- soit un cha-
ma va- len- ti- ne,
vert, C'es- toit ma va- len- ti- ne, ma va- len- ti- ne, Qui

66
Qui fai- soit un cha- pe- let, Tout de ro- se & de
Qui fai- soit un cha- pe- let, Tout de
pe- let, Tout de ro- se & de mu- guet,
Qui fai- soit un cha- pe- let, Tout de ro-
fai- soit, un cha- pe- let, Tout de

82
Tant jo- li- et est mon a- my, Qu'il m'a dit,
Tant jo- li- et est mon a- my, est mon a- my,
Tant jo- li- et est mon a- my,
jo- li- et est mon a- my, Tant jo- li-
Tant jo- li- et, Tant jo- li- et est mon a- my, Tant jo- li- et

74
mu- guet: Tant jo- li- et est mon a- my,
ro- se & de mu- guet, Tant jo- li- et est mon a- my,
Tant jo- li- et est mon a- my,
se & de mu- guet: Tant
ro- se & de mu- guet: Tant jo- li- et, Tant jo- li- et est mon a- my,

90
voz bre- bis vi- rez, Qu'il m'a dit, voz bre- bis vi-
Qu'il m'a dit, voz bre- bis vi- rez,
Qu'il m'a dit, voz bre- bis vi- rez, Qui
et est mon a- my, Qu'il m'a dit, voz bre- bis vi-
est mon a- my, Qu'il m'a dit, voz bre- bis vi- rez,

rez, Qui vont men-geant ma ger- be, Sur l'her- be, Sur
Qui vont men-geant ma ger- be, Sur l'her- be,
vont men-geant ma ger- be, Sur l'her- be, Qui
rez, Qui vont men-geant ma ger- be, Sur l'her- be,
Qui vont men-geant ma ger- be, Qui vont men- geant, Qui vont men-geant ma ger- be, Sur

be, Son- nez m'y donc quand vous i- rez, Son-
be, Son- nez m'y donc quand vous i- rez, Son- nez m'y donc
Son- nez m'y donc quand vous i- rez,
be, Son- nez m'y
ger- be, Son- nez m'y donc quand vous i- rez,

l'her- be, Qui vont men- geant ma ger- be, Sur l'her-
Sur l'her-
vont men-geant ma ger- be, Sur l'her- be,
Qui vont men-geant ma ger- be, Sur l'her-
l'her- be, Qui vont men- geant ma

nez m'y donc quand vous i- rez, quand vous i- rez, Me-
quand vous i- rez, quand vous i-
Son- nez m'y donc quand vous i- rez,
donc quand vous i- rez, Son- nez m'y donc quand
Son- nez m'y donc quand vous i- rez, Me- ner voz

133
ner voz bre- bi- et- tes, Sur l'her- be, Sur l'her- be,
rez, Me- ner voz bre- bi- et- tes, Sur l'her-
Me- ner voz bre- bi- et- tes, Sur l'her-
vous i- rez, Me- ner voz
bre- bi- et- tes, Me- ner voz bre- bi- et-

Puis que j'ay per- du ma mai- tres-
Puis que j'ay per- du ma mai- tres-
Puis que j'ay
Puis que j'ay per-

142
Sur l'her- be.
be, Sur l'her- be.
be, Sur l'her- be.
bre- bi- et- tes, Sur l'her- be, Sur l'her- be.
tes, Sur l'her- be, Sur l'her- be.

9
se, ma mai-
se, Puis que j'ay per- du ma mai-
Puis que j'ay per- du ma mai- trai-
per- du ma mai- tres- se, Puis que j'ay per- du
du ma mai- tres- se, ma mai- tres-

tres- se, Par for- tu- ne,
tres- se, Par for- tu- ne, Par for- tu- ne du-
se, Par for- tu- ne du- re & di- ver- se,
ma mai- tres- se,
se, Par for- tu- ne du- re & di- ver- se,

& di- ver-
se, Par for- tu- ne du- re & di- ver- se,
for- tu- ne, Par for- tu- ne du- re & di- ver-
Par for- tu- ne du- re & di- ver- se, De
Par for- tu- ne du- re & di- ver-

ne du- re & di- ver- se,
re & di- ver- se, & di- ver-
Par for- tu- ne, Par
Par for- tu- ne du- re & di- ver- se,
du- re & di- ver- se,

se, De quoy sers= je, De quoy sers= je plus
De quoy sers=je, plus en ce
se, De quoy sers= je plus en ce mon- de,
quoy sers= je, De quoy sers= je, plus en ce mon-
se, De quoy sers= je plus en ce mon-

54
en ce mon- de, Car
mon- de, De quoy sers= je plus en ce mon- de,
De quoy sers= je plus en ce mon-
de, De quoy sers= je plus en ce mon- de, Car
de, De quoy sers= je plus en ce mon- de,

74
de, Qui de la re- gre- ter ne ces- se, Qui
de, Car mon coeur en tout dueil a- bon-
de, Qui de la re- gre-
de, Qui de la re- gre- ter ne ces-
Qui de la re- gre- ter ne ces- se,

65
mon coeur en tout dueil a- bon-
Car mon coeur en tout dueil a- bon-
de, Car mon coeur en tout dueil a- bon-
mon coeur en tout dueil, Car mon coeur en tout dueil a- bon-
Car mon coeur en tout dueil a- bon- de,

83
de la re- gre- ter ne ces- se, ne
de, Qui de la re- gre- ter ne ces-
ter ne ces-
se, ne ces- se, Qui
Qui de la re- gre- ter ne ces-

91
ces-
se,
Qui
se,
Qui de la re- gre- ter ne ces-
de la re- gre- ter ne ces-
se,
Qui de la re- gre- ter ne ces-

En lan- guis- sant je con- sum- me mes jours, je
En lan- guis- sant je con- sum- me mes jours, En lan- guis-
En lan- guis- sant je con- sum-
En

99
se.
de la re- gre- ter ne ces- se.
se.
Qui de la re- gre- ter ne ces- se.
se,
Qui de la re- gre- ter ne ces- se.

11
con- sum- me mes jours,
sant je con- sum- me mes jours, En lan- guis- sant je con- sum-
me mes jours, Je con- sum- me mes jours, Je con- sum- me mes
En lan- guis- sant je con- sum- me mes jours, je
lan- guis- sant, je con- sum- me mes jours, En lan- guis- sant je con-

21
En lan- guis- sant je con- sum- me mes
me mes jours, je con- sum- me mes
jours, je con- sum- me mes jours,
con- sum- me mes jours, je con- sum- me mes
sum- me mes jours, je con- sum- me mes jours,

40
cours, En at- ten- dant se-
at- ten- dant se- cours, En at- ten- dant se- cours,
at- ten- dant se- cours, en at- ten- dant se-
En at- ten- dant se- cours, en at- ten- dant se-
ten- dant se- cours, Cours

30
jours, Nuit & jour suis en at- ten- dant se-
jours, Nuit & jour suis, Nuit & jour suis en at- ten- dant, En
Nuit & jour suis en at- ten- dant, Nuit & jour suis, En
jours, Nuit & jour suis en at- ten- dant, Nuit & jour suis,
je con- sum- me mes jours, Nuit & jour suis en at-

50
cours, Cours vit- te- ment al- le- gean- ce, m'a-
Cours
cours, Cours vit- te- ment al- le- gean- ce, m'a- my- e,
cours, Cours vit- te- ment al- le- gean- ce, m'a- my-
vit- te- ment al- le- gean- ce, m'a- my- e,

56
my- e, Cours vit- te- ment al-
vit- te- ment al- le- gean- ce, m'a- my-
Cours vit- te- ment al- le- gean- ce, m'a- my- e, al- le-
e, Cours vit- te- ment al- le- gean- ce, m'a- my-

68
m'a- my- e, Me se- cou- rir, Me se- cou- rir car
e, Me se- cou- rir, Me se- cou- rir, me se- cou- rir, me
e: Me se- cou- rir, Me se- cou-
ce, m'a- my- e,] Me se- cou- rir, Me se- cou- rir,
e, Me se- cou- rir, Me se- cou-

62
le- gean- ce, m'a- my- e, al- le- gean- ce,
e, Cours vit- te- ment al- le- gean- ce, m'a- my-
gean- ce, m'a- my-
e, [Cours vit- te- ment al- le- gean-
Cours vit- te- ment al- le- gean- ce, m'a- my-

78
d'au- tre n'ay en- vy- e: car d'au- tre n'ay
se- cou- rir, car d'au- tre n'ay en- vy- e: car d'au- tre n'ay en-
rir, car d'au- tre n'ay en- vy- e: Ou à la
Me se- cou- rir, car d'au- tre n'ay en- vy- e:
rir, car d'au- tre n'ay en- vy- e:

89
en- vy- e: car d'au- tre n'ay en- vy-
vy- e: Ou à la mort, Ou à la
mort, Ou à la mort je voy plus que le cours,
Ou à la mort, je voy plus que le cours, Ou
Ou à la mort, Ou à la mort,

106
plus que le cours, Ou à la mort je voy
mort je voy plus que le cours,
que le cours, Ou à la mort, je voy
que le cours, Ou à la mort, je
cours, je voy plus que le cours, Ou

99
e: Ou à la mort je voy
mort je voy plus que le cours, Ou à la
Ou à la mort je voy plus
à la mort je voy plus que le cours, je voy plus
Ou à la mort je voy plus que le

114
plus que le cours, je voy plus que le cours,
Ou à la mort, Ou à la mort je voy plus
plus que le cours, Ou à la mort,
voy plus que le cours,
à la mort, Ou à la mort, Ou

134

121
Ou à la mort je voy plus
que le cours, Ou à la mort je
je voy plus
je voy plus que le cours,
à la mort je voy plus que le cours, je

Vi- vre en es- poir me
Vi- vre en es- poir me con- vient de- sor-
Vi- vre en es- poir me con- vient de- sor-mais, Vi-

127
que le cours.
voy plus que le cours, Ou à la mort je voy plus que le cours.
que le cours.
Ou à la mort je voy plus que le cours.
voy plus que le cours, Ou à la mort je voy plus que le cours.

10
con- vient de- sor- mais,
mais, Vi- vre en es- poir me
vre en es- poir me con- vient de- sor-
Vi- vre en es-
Vi- vre en es- poir me con-

Vi- vre en es- poir me con- vient de- sor- mais, me
con- vient de- sor- mais, me con- vient de- sor-
mais, de- sor- mais, me con- vient de-
poir me con- vient de- sor- mais, Vi- vre en es- poir me con- vient de- sor-
vient de- sor- mais, Vi- vre en es- poir

de- sor- mais, Puis que vers moy ne
mais, Puis que vers moy ne se mon-
mais, Puis que vers moy ne se mon- tre re-
sor- mais, Puis que vers moy ne se mon- tre re- bel-
con- vient de- sor- mais, Puis que vers moy ne se mon- tre re-

con- vient de- sor- mais, Vi- vre en es- poir me con- vient
mais, de- sor- mais, me con- vient de- sor-
sor- mais, me con- vient de- sor-
mais, me con- vient de- sor- mais, me con- vient de-
me con- vient de- sor- mais, de- sor- mais, me

se mon- tre re- bel- le, ne se mon- tre re- bel-
tre re- bel- le, Puis que vers moy ne se mon- tre re- bel-
bel- le, Puis que vers moy ne se mon- tre re- bel- le,
le, Puis que vers moy ne se mon- tre re- bel- le, re- bel-
bel- le, Puis que vers moy ne se mon- tre re- bel-

60
le, Coeur, corps & bien, Coeur, corps & bien, tout j'a- ban- don- ne à
le, Coeur, corps & bien, tout j'a- ban- don- ne à el- le, à
Coeur, corps & biens tout j'a- ban- don- ne à el- le, Coeur, corps &
le, Coeur, corps & biens, tout j'a- ban- don- ne à elle, re- bel- le, Coeur, corps & biens tout j'a- ban- don- ne à

81
ja- mais, Car au- tre ay- mer ne re- quiers
Car au- tre ay- mer ne re- quiers à ja-
ja- mais, Car au- tre ay- mer ne re- quiers à
mer ne re- quiers à ja- mais, Car au- tre ay- mer ne re- quiers
mais, Car au- tre ay- mer ne re- quiers à ja- mais, à

71
el- le, Car au- tre ay- mer ne re- quiers à
el- le, Car au- tre ay- mer,
biens tout j'a- ban- don- ne à el- le, Car au- tre ay- mer ne re- quiers à
le, tout j'a- ban- don- ne à el- le, Car au- tre ay-
el- le, Car au- tre ay- mer ne re- quiers à ja-

91
à ja- mais, Car au- tre ay- mer ne
mais, ne re- quiers à ja- mais, Car au- tre ay- mer,
ja- mais, Car au- tre ay- mer ne re-
à ja- mais, ne re- quiers à ja- mais,
ja- mais, Car au- tre ay- mer ne re- quiers

re- quiers à ja- mais, Car
Car au- tre ay- mer ne re- quiers
quiers à ja- mais, ne re- quiers à
Car au- tre ay- mer ne re- quiers à ja- mais, ne
à ja- mais, Car au- tre ay- mer

Al- ler m'y faut sur la ver-
Al- ler m'y faut,
Al- ler m'y faut sur la ver- du-
Al- ler m'y faut sur la ver- du-
Al- ler m'y faut sur la ver-

au- tre ay- mer ne re- quiers à ja- mais.
à ja- mais, ne re- quiers à ja- mais.
ja- mais.
re- quiers à ja- mais, à ja- mais.
ne re- quiers à ja- mais, à ja- mais, ne re- quiers à ja- mais.

du- re, Al- ler m'y faut sur la ver- du- re,
Al- ler m'y faut sur la ver- du-
re, Al- ler m'y faut sur la ver- du- re, Al- ler m'y
re, Al- ler m'y faut sur la ver- du-
du- re, Al- ler m'y faut sur la ver- du-

16
sur la ver- du- re, Cer-
re, Cer- cher par- ty, Cer- cher par- ty en
faut sur la ver- du- re, Cer- cher par- ty en quel-
re, Cer- cher par- ty, Cer- cher par- ty, Cer- cher par-
re, Cer- cher par- ty en quel- que bon-ne part,

33
dy, Es- tre har- dy, fris- que & gai- llard, Onc ne trou- va
tre har- dy, Es- tre har- dy, fris- que & gai-llard, Onc
dy, fris- que & gai- llard, Onc ne trou- va co- vart
que & gai- llard, Onc ne trou- va
ne part, Es- tre har- dy, fris- que & gai-

24
cher par- ty en quel- que bon- ne part, Es- tre har-
quel- que bon- ne part, Cer- cher par- ty en quel- que bon- ne part, Es-
que bon- ne part, en quel-que bon- ne part, Es- tre har-
ty en quel- que bon- ne part, Es- tre har- dy, fris-
en quel- que bon-

42
co- vart pas- tu- re, Onc ne trou- va co-
ne trou- va co- vart pas- tu- re,
pas- tu- re, Onc ne trou-
co- vart pas- tu- re, Onc ne trou- va
llard, Onc ne trou- va co-

vart pas- tu- re, A- my, je n'ay qui me pro-
A- my, je n'ay qui me pro- cu-
va co- vart pas- tu- re, A- my, je n'ay qui me pro- cu-
co- vart pas- tu- re, A- my, je n'ay qui me pro-cu-
vart pas- tu- re,

me pro- cu- re, Du jeu d'a- mours, las,
qui me pro- cu- re, A- my, je n'ay qui me pro- cu- re,
cu- re, je n'ay qui me pro- cu- re, Du
n'ay, qui me pro- cu- re, qui me pro- cu- re,
me pro- cu- re, A- my, je n'ay qui me pro- cu- re, Du

cu- re, Al- ler m'y faut sur la ver- du- re, A- my, je n'ay qui
re, Al- ler m'y faut sur la ver- du- re, A- my, je n'ay
re, A- my, je n'ay qui me pro-
re, Al- ler m'y faut sur la ver- du- re, A- my, A- my, je
Al- ler m'y faut sur la ver- du- re, A- my, je n'ay qui

trop j'en- du- re, Al-
Du jeu d'a- mours, las, trop j'en- du- re, Al- ler m'y
jeu d'a- mours, Du jeu d'a- mours, las, trop j'en- du- re, Al- ler m'y
Du jeu d'a- mours, Du jeu d'a- mours, las, trop j'en- du- re, Al-
jeu d'a- mours, Du jeu d'a- mours, las, trop j'en- du- re, Al-

83
ler m'y faut sur la ver-du- re, A- my, je n'ay qui me pro- cu-
faut sur la ver- du- re, Du jeu d'a-
faut sur la ver-du- re, Al- ler m'y faut sur la ver-du- re,
ler m'y faut sur la ver-du- re, Al- ler m'y faut sur la ver-du-
ler m'y faut, Al- ler m'y faut sur la ver-du-

101
lois, Si trou-vois un ga- lois, De mon vou- loir fe- rois ou-ver-tu-
lois, Si trou- vois un ga- lois, De mon vou- loir fe- rois ou-
lois, Si trou-vois un ga- lois, De mon vou- loir fe- rois ou- ver-tu- re,
lois, Si trou- vois un ga- lois, De mon vou- loir, De mon vou- loir fe- rois
lois, Si trou-vois un ga- lois, De mon vou- loir, Si

92
re, Du jeu d'a- mours, las, trop j'en-du- re, Si trou-vois un ga-
mours, las, trop j'en-du- re,
Du jeu d'a- mours, Du jeu d'a- mours, las, trop j'en-du- re, Si trou-vois un ga-
re, Du jeu d'a- mours, Du jeu d'a- mours, las, trop j'en-du- re, Si trou-vois un ga-
re, Du jeu d'a- mours, Du jeu d'a- mours, las, trop j'en-du- re, Si trou-vois un ga-

107
re, Si trou-vois un ga- lois, De mon vou-loir fe- rois ou-ver-tu-
ver- tu- re, Si trou-vois un ga- lois,
Si trou-vois un ga- lois, De mon vou- loir fe-
ou- ver-tu- re, Si trou-vois un ga- lois, De mon vou-loir fe- rois ou-ver-
trou-vois un ga- lois, Si trou- vois un ga-lois, De mon vou-loir, De mon vou-

* Reading in the <u>Livre</u>:

137
Al- ler m'y faut sur la ver- du-
re, Al- ler m'y faut sur la ver- du- re,
ler m'y faut sur la ver- du- re, Al- ler m'y
re, Al- ler m'y faut sur la ver- du-
re, Al- ler m'y faut sur la ver- du-

For- ce d'a- mour, sou- vent me
For- ce d'a- mour, sou- vent me veut con- train-dre, sou- vent
For- ce d'a- mour, sou- vent me veut con-
For- ce d'a- mour, sou- vent me veut con- train- dre,
For- ce d'a- mour, sou-

144
re, Al- ler m'y faut sur la ver- du- re.
sur la ver- du- re.
faut sur la ver- du- re.
re, Al- ler m'y faut sur la ver- du- re.

10
veut con- train- dre,
me veut con-train- dre, Vous de- cla- rer mon coeur
train- dre, Vous de- cla- rer mon coeur, Vous
Vous de- cla- rer mon coeur
vent me veut con- train- dre, Vous de- cla-

19
Vous de- cla- rer mon coeur ap- per- te- ment, Mais
ap- per- te- ment, Mais
de- cla- rer mon coeur ap- per- te- ment, Mais le re- fus,
ap- per- te- ment, Mais le re- fus,
rer mon coeur ap- per- te- ment, Mais

37
à crain- dre,
à crain- dre, Jus- qu'à pre- sent m'a fait
dre, Jus- qu'à pre- sent m'a fait, Jus-
est à crain- dre, Jus- qu'à pre-
Jus- qu'à pre- sent m'a fait

28
le re- fus, qui tous- jours est
le re- fus, qui tous- jours est à crain- dre, qui tous- jours est
Mais le re- fus, qui tous- jours est à crain-
Mais le re- fus, qui tous- jours
le re- fus, qui tous- jours est à crain- dre,

45
Jus- qu'à pre- sent m'a fait em- pes- che- ment: Dont
em- pes- che- ment:
qu'à pre- sent m'a fait, em- pes- che- ment: Dont suis con-
sent m'a fait, em- pes- che- ment:
em- pes- che- ment, Dont suis con- traint,

54
suis con- traint en- du- rer dou- ce- ment, Dis- si- mu-
Dont suis con- traint en- du- rer dou- ce- ment, Dis- si- mu- lant
traint, en- du- rer dou- ce- ment, Dis- si- mu-
Dont suis con- traint, en- du- rer dou- ce- ment,
en- du- rer dou- ce- ment, Dis- si- mu- lant mon

73
le bien que je pour- suis, Le sou- ve- nir ren- for- ce mon
bien que je pour- suis, Le sou- ve- nir, ren- for- ce mon marle bien que je pour- suis, Le sou- ve- nir, ren-
D'au- tre cos- té, le bien que je pour- suis, Le sou- ve-
D'au- tre cos- té, le bien que je pour- suis, Le sou- ve- nir,

63
lant mon mal tant que je puis, D'au- tre cos- té
mon mal tant que je puis, D'au- tre cos- té, le
lant mon mal tant que je puis, D'au- tre cos- té,
Dis- si- mu- lant mon mal tant que je puis, D'au- tre cos- té,
mal tant que je puis, D'au- tre cos- té,

84
mar- ty- re: He- las!
ty- re: He- las! voy- és,
for- ce mon mar- ty- re: He- las voy- és, He- las! voy-
nir, ren- for- ce mon mar- ty- re: He-
ren- for- ce mon mar- ty- re: He- las! voy- és,

94
He- las! voy- és le tour- ment ou je suis,
He- las! voy- és, He- las! voy- és le tour- ment ou je suis, Je
és, He- las! voy- és le tour- ment ou je suis, Je
las! voy- és, He- las! voy- és le tour- ment ou je suis,
He- las! voy- és, Je veux par-

113
re, He- las!
di- re, He- las! voy- ez, He-
re, He- las! voy- és, He- las! voy- és,
puis un mot di- re, He- las! voy- és,
He- las! voy- és, He- las! voy-

104
Je veux par- ler & ne puis un mot di-
veux par- ler & ne puis un mot
veux par- ler, & ne puis un mot di-
Je veux par- ler, & ne puis un mot di- re, & ne
ler, & ne puis un mot di- re,

122
He- las! voy- és, le tour- ment ou je suis,
las! voy- és, He- las! voy- és, le tour- ment ou je suis, Je
He- las! voy- és, le tour- ment ou je suis, Je
He- las! voy- és, Je veux par-
és, He- las! voy- és, le tour- ment ou je suis,

Je veux par- ler & ne puis un mot di-
veux par- ler & ne puis un mot
veux par- ler, & ne puis un mot di-
ler, & ne puis un mot di- re, & ne

N'au- rai= je
N'au- rai= je ja- mais mieux que j'ay, N'au- rai= je ja- mais
N'au- rai= je ja- mais mieux que j'ay, N'au-
N'au- rai= je ja- mais mieux que j'ay, N'au- rai= je ja- mais mieux
N'au- rai= je

re.
di- re, & ne puis un mot di- re.
re.
& ne puis un mot di- re.
puis un mot di- re, un mot di- re.

(sic)
ja- mais mieux que j'ay,
mieux que j'ay, Suyi- e la ou je de- mour-
rai= je ja- mais mieux que j'ay, Suyi- e la ou
que j'ay, Ja- mais mieux que j'ay, Suyi-
ja- mais mieux que j'ay, Suyi- e la

15
Suyi- e la ou je
ray, Suyi- e la ou je de- mour- ray, la
je de- mour- ray, Suyi- e la ou je
e la ou je de- mour- ray, Suyi- e la ou,
ou je de- mour- ray, je de- mour- ray, Suyi-

27 (sic)
Vi- vrai= je tous- jours en souf- fran-
jours en souf- fran- ce, Vi- vrai= je tous-jours en souf-
vray= je tous- jours en souf- fran- ce, en souf- fran-
je, Vi- vray= je tous- jours en souf- fran- ce,
vray= je tous- jours en souf- fran- ce, en souf- fran-

21
de- mou- ray, je de- mou- ray,
ou je de- mour- ray, Vi- vrai= je tous-
de- mour- ray, Vi- vray= je tous- jours, Vi-
Suyi- e la ou je de- mour- ray, Vi- vrai=
e la ou je de- mour- ray, Vi-

33
fran- ce,
fran- ce, Vi- vrai= je tous- jours en souf- france, Vi- vrai= je tous- jours en souf- fran- ce,
Vi- vrai= je tous- jours en souf- fran- ce,
ce, en souf- fran- ce, Vi- vrai= je tous- jours en souf- fran-

N'au- rez vous de moy sou- ce, N'au- rez vous de moy sou- ve- nan- ce:
ce, N'au- rez vous de moy sou- ve- nan- ce:
ce, N'au- rez vous de moy sou- ve- nan- ce:
N'au- rez vous de moy sou- ve- nan- ce:
ce,
(sic)
Que je suis vo- tre & se- ray, & se- ray,
Que je suis vo- tre & se- ray,
je suis vo- tre & se-
je suis vo- tre & se- ray, Que je suis vo- tre
& se- ray, Que je suis
ve- nan- ce:
de moy sou- ve- nan- ce:
ce: Que
N'au- rez vous de moy sou- ve- nan- ce: Que
rez vous de moy sou- ve- nan- ce: Que je suis vo- tre
Que je suis vo- tre & se-
Que je suis vo- tre & se- ray, Que
ray, Que je suis vo- tre & se-
& se- ray, Que je suis vo- tre,
vo- tre & se- ray, Que je suis vo- tre & se-

149

59
ray,
je suis vo- tre & se- ray, Que je suis vo- tre &
ray, Que je suis vo- tre & se-
vo- tre & se- ray, Que
ray, vo- tre & se- ray, Que je suis vo- tre

70
& se- ray, Que je suis
& se- ray, Que je suis
Que je suis vo- tre & se-
ray, Que je suis vo-
Que je suis vo- tre & se- ray,

64
Que je suis vo- tre
se- ray, Que je suis vo- tre & se- ray,
ray, Que je suis vo- tre & se- ray,
je suis vo- tre & se-
& se- ray,

76
vo- tre & se- ray, & se- ray,
vo- tre & se- ray, Que
ray, Que je suis vo- tre & se-
tre & se- ray,
Que je suis vo-

80

Que je suis vo- tre & se-
je suis vo- tre & se- ray,
ray, Que je suis vo- tre
Que je suis vo- tre, Que je suis
tre & se- ray,

He- las, ma fi- lle, He- las, ma fi- lle, il te tue- ra,
He- las, ma fi- lle, il te tue- ra, De son grand
He- las, ma fi- lle, il te tue- ra, He- las, ma fi- lle, il te tue- ra, De
He- las, ma fi- lle, He- las, ma fi- lle, il te tue- ra,
He- las, ma fi- lle, He- las, ma fi- lle, il te tue- ra,

85

ray.
& se- ray, Que je suis vo- tre & se- ray.
& se- ray, Que je suis vo- tre & se- ray.
vo- tre & se- ray.
Que je suis vo- tre & se- ray.

9

De son grand cho-se qui re-mu- ë, re-mu- ë, re-mu- ë, re-
cho- se qui re-mu- ë, qui re- mu- ë, re-mu- ë, re-mu- ë,
son grand cho- se qui re-mu- ë, re-mu- ë, re-mu- ë, re- mu- ë,
De son grand cho- se qui re-mu- ë, re- mu- ë, re-mu- ë,
De son grand cho- se qui re-mu- ë, re- mu- ë, re-mu-

16
mu- ě, He- las, ma me- re, non fe- ra, As- sez suis for- te
He- las, ma me- re, He- las, ma me- re, non fe- ra,
He- las, ma me- re, non fe- ra, He- las, ma me- re, non fe- ra, As- sez suis for-
He- las, ma me- re, He- las, ma me- re, non fe- ra, As- sez suis
ě, He- las, ma me- re, He- las, ma me- re, non fe- ra, As- sez suis

34
Bois de- bout à grand sous- te- nu- ě, Fem- me à l'en- vers, Fem-
Bois de- bout à grand sous- te- nu- ě, Fem- me à l'en- vers,
de- bout à grand sous- te- nu- ě, Fem- me à l'en-
à grand sous- te- nu- ě, Fem- me à l'en- vers,
Bois de- bout, Bois de- bout à grand sous- te- nu- ě, Fem- me à l'en-

25
tou- te nu- ě: As- sez suis for- te tou- te nu- ě:
As- sez suis for- te tou- te nu- ě: As- sez suis for- te tou- te nu- ě:
te tou- te nu- ě: As- sez suis for- te tou- te nu- ě: Bois
for- te tou- te nu- ě: As- sez suis for- te tou- te nu- ě: Bois de- bout
for- te tou- te nu- ě: As- sez suis for- te tou- te nu- ě:

44
me à l'en- vers, Fem- me à l'en- vers por- te beau- coup, Il ne m'en chaut
Fem- me à l'en- vers por- te beau-
vers, Fem- me à l'en- vers por- te beau-
Fem- me à l'en- vers por- te beau- coup, Fem- me à l'en- vers por- te beau- coup, Il ne m'en
vers, Fem- me à l'en- vers por- te beau- coup,

53
pas,   Il ne m'en chaut   pas,   Il ne m'en chaut pas
coup,   Il ne m'en chaut pas s'il me tu- ë,   Il ne m'en chaut
coup,   Il ne m'en chaut pas s'il me tu- ë,   Il ne m'en chaut,   Il ne m'en chaut
chaut pas s'il me tu- ë,   Il ne m'en chaut pas s'il me tu- ë,
Il ne m'en pas s'il me tu- ë,   Il ne m'en pas s'il me tu- ë,
chaut   chaut

67
Mais que je meu- re   d'un beau coup,
que je meu- re   d'un beau coup,   Il ne m'en pas s'il me
chaut
coup, Mais que je meu- re,   d'un beau coup, Il ne m'en chaut pas,   Il ne m'en pas
chaut
Mais que je meu- re d'un beau   coup, Il ne m'en chaut pas,
d'un beau coup, Mais que je meu- re d'un beau   coup, Il ne m'en pas s'il me
chaut

58
s'il me tu- ë, s'il me tu- ë,   Mais que je meu- re,
chaut pas s'il me tu- ë,   Mais que je meu- re d'un beau coup,   Mais
[pas],   Mais que je meu- re,   Mais que je meu- re d'un
beau
Il ne m'en s'il me tu- ë,   Mais que je meu- re d'un beau coup,   meu- re,
chaut pas   Mais que je
Il ne m'en pas s'il me tu- ë,   Mais que je meu- re d'un beau coup,   Mais que je meu- re
chaut

74   (sic)
Il ne m'en chaut pas s'il me tu- ë,   Il ne m'en chaut pas s'il me tu-
tu- ë,   Il ne m'en chaut,   Il ne m'en chaut pas s'il me tu- ë, s'il me tu- ë,
s'il me tu- ë,   Il ne m'en chaut,   Il ne m'en chaut   [pas],   Mais
Il ne m'en pas s'il me tu- ë,   Il ne m'en pas s'il me tu-
chaut   chaut
tu- ë,   Il ne m'en chaut pas s'il me tu- ë,   Il ne m'en pas s'il me tu- ë,
chaut

153

80
ĕ, Mais que je meu-re d'un beau coup, Mais que je
Mais que je meu- re, Mais que je meu- re
que je meu- re, Mais que je meu- re d'un beau Mais meu- re, coup, que je
ĕ, Mais que je meu- re d'un beau coup, que je meu- re, Mais que je Mais
Mais que je meu- re d'un beau coup, Mais que je meu- re d'un beau coup, Mais

Con- tent ou non, il faut que je l'en- du- re,
Con- tent ou non, il faut que je l'en- du- re, Con-
Con- tent ou non, il faut que
Con-

88
meu- re d'un beau coup.
d'un beau coup, Mais que je Mais que je meu-re d'un beau coup. meu-re,
Mais que je meu- re d'un beau coup,Mais que je meu- re d'un beau coup.
meu- re d'un beau coup.
que je meu- re d'un beau coup, Mais que je meu-re d'un beau coup.

10
Con- tent ou non,
tent ou non, il faut que je l'en- du- re, l'en- du-
je l'en- du- re, il faut que je l'en- du-
Con- tent ou non, il faut que je l'en- du- re, Con-
tent ou non, il faut que je l'en- du-

19
Con- tent ou non, il faut que je l'en- du- re, il faut que je l'en-
re, Con- tent ou non, il faut que je l'en- du- re, il faut que
re, il faut que je l'en- du- re, il faut que
tent ou non, il faut que je l'en- du- re,
re,

38
& ma seu- le es- pe- ran- ce,
& ma seu- le es- pe- ran- ce, Ou- tre mon gré, &
& ma seu- le es- pe- ran- ce,
gré & ma seu- le es- pe- ran- ce, Ou- tre mon gré
Ou- tre mon gré

29
du- re, Ou- tre mon gré
je l'en- du- re, Ou- tre mon gré
je l'en- du- re, Ou- tre mon gré,
Ou- tre mon gré, Ou- tre mon gré, Ou- tre mon
du- re, Ou- tre mon gré,

47
Ou- tre mon gré & ma seu- le es- pe- ran-
ma seu- le es- pe- ran- ce, & ma seu- le es- pe- ran-
& ma seu- le es- pe- ran- ce,
& ma seu- le es- pe- ran- ce, & ma seu- le es- pe- ran-
& ma seu- le es- pe- ran- ce, & ma seu- le es- pe- ran- ce,

58
ce, Mais s'u- ne fois il vient, Mais s'u- ne fois il vient à ma puis-
ce, Mais s'u- ne fois il vient, à ma puis- san- ce, Mais
Mais s'u- ne fois il vient à ma puis- san- ce, Mais s'u- ne
ce, Mais s'u- ne fois il vient à ma puis- san- ce,
Mais s'u- ne fois il vient à ma puis- san- ce,

81
fin, Je met-tray fin à ce que trop me du- re, Je met-tray fin à ce que trop
Je met- tray fin, à ce que trop me du- re, Je met- tray fin à
Je met-tray fin à ce que trop me du- re, à
fin, Je met-tray fin à ce que trop me du- re, à
fin, à

69
san- ce, à ma puis- san- ce, Je met-tray fin, Je met- tray
s'u- ne fois il vient à ma puis- san- ce, à ma puis- san- ce, Je met- tray fin, Je met-tray fin,
fois il vient à ma puis- san- ce, Je met- tray fin,
Mais s'u- ne fois il vient à ma puis- san- ce, Je met-tray fin, Je met- tray
Mais s'u- ne fois il vient à ma puis- san- ce, Je met- tray

91
me du- re, Je met- tray fin, Je met- tray fin, Je met- tray
ce que trop me du- re, Je met- tray fin, Je met- tray fin, Je met- tray
ce que trop me du- re, Je met- tray fin, Je met- tray
ce que trop me du- re, Je met- tray fin, Je met- tray fin, Je met- tray
ce que trop me du- re, Je met- tray fin,

100
fin à ce que trop me du- re, Je met-tray fin à ce que trop me du-
fin, à ce que trop me du- re, Je met-tray fin à ce que trop me
fin à ce que trop me du- re, à ce que trop me
fin à ce que trop me du- re, à ce que trop me
à ce que trop me

Je l'ay ay-
Je l'ay ay- mé- e, Je l'ay
Je l'ay- ay- mé- e, Je l'ay ay- mé- e,

110
re.
du- re, Je met-tray fin à ce que trop me du- re.
du- re.
du- re, Je met-tray fin à ce que trop me du- re.
du- re, Je met-tray fin, à ce que trop me du- re.

10
Je l'ay ay- mé-
Je l'ay ay- mé-
mé- e, bien
ay- mé- e, Je l'ay ay- mé- e, Je l'ay ay-
Je l'ay ay- mé- e, Je

20
e,
bien sept ans & de- my,
bien
e,
bien sept ans
sept ans & de- my,
bien sept ans & de- my,
mé-
e, bien sept ans & de- my,
bien sept ans &
l'ay ay- mé-
e,
bien sept ans & de-

42
M'a- mour, mon as- so- té- e,
que
so- té-
e,
que mon coeur à choi-
so-
té- e,
que mon coeur à choi- si,
mon coeur à choi-
si,
que mon coeur à
mon as- so- té- e, M'a- mour, mon as- so- té-
e, que mon coeur

31
sept ans & de- my,
& de- my,
M'a-mour, mon as- so- té-
e, M'a- mour, mon as-
M'a- mour, mon as-
de- my,
M'a- mour, mon as- so- té-
e, que
my,
M'a-mour, mon as- so- té-
e,

53
mon coeur à choi- si,
si, que mon coeur à choi- si,
Cui- dant qu'el' fut m'a- my-
Cui- dant qu'el'
choi-
si,
Cui- dant qu'el' fut
m'a-
à choi- si,
Cui- dant qu'el' fut
m'a- my-
e,
Cui-

63
Cui- dant qu'elle fut   m'a- my-
e,   Cui- dant qu'el' fut   m'a- my-
fut   m'a- my-   e,
my-   e,   qu'el' fut m'a- my-
dant   qu'el' fut   m'a-   my-

83
Mais elle en à men- ty,   Un
Un au- tre par en-   vi
Un au- tre par en- vi- e,   Sy, d'el- le m'a ban-
à men- ty,   Un au- tre par en- vi
à   men-   ty,

72
e,   Mais elle en à men- ty,
e,   Mais elle en à men- ty,   Mais elle en à   men- ty,
Mais elle en à men- ty,   Mais elle en à men- ty,
e,   Mais elle en à men- ty,   Mais elle en
e,   Mais elle en à men- ty,   Mais elle en

92
au- tre par en- vi- e,   Sy, d'el- le m'a ban- ny,
e,   Sy, d'el- le m'a   ban-   ny,   He- las, he-
ny,   He-   las,
e,   Sy, d'el-   le m'a banny,   He- las, helas,
Sy, d'el-   le   m'a ban- ny,   He dieu, He-

102
He- las, he- las, he- las, he-
las, j'ay per- du mon sou- las, He dieu, he dieu,
he- las, He- las, he- las, j'ay per- du mon sou- las,
He- las, he- las, He- las, he- las, j'ay per- du mon sou-
las, He- las, he- las, j'ay per- du mon sou- las,

122
He dieu, he dieu, he my, j'ay per- du mon a- my,
my, He dieu, he dieu, he
mon a- my, He dieu, he dieu, he my, j'ay per- du mon
j'ay per- du mon a- my, j'ay
du mon a- my, He dieu, he my, j'ay per- du mon a-

113
las j'ay per- du mon sou- las,
he my, j'ay per- du mon a-
He dieu, he dieu, he my j'ay per- du
las, He dieu, he dieu he my,
He dieu, he dieu, he my, j'ay per- du mon a- my, j'ay per-

131
j'ay per- du mon a- my, j'ay per- du mon a- my.
my, j'ay per- du mon a- my, j'ay per- du mon a- my.
a- my, mon a- my.
per- du mon a- my, j'ay per- du mon a- my.
my, He dieu, he my, j'ay per- du mon a- my.

43 Vuildre, *Si de beaucoup*

35
(sic)
D'a- voir seul en vo- tre puis- san- ce,
D'a- voir seul en vo- tre puis- san-
en vo- tre puis- san- ce, Le bien en- tier & l'es- pe-
voir seul en vo- tre puis-san- ce, Le bien en- tier &
en vo- tre puis- san- ce, Le bien en- tier & l'es- pe-

55
tant de po- vres a- mou- reux, Que vo- tre hon-
po- vres a- mou- reux, a- mou- reux,
de po- vres a- mou- reux, De tant de po- vres a- mou- reux,
De tant de po- vres a- mou- reux, a- mou- reux,
de po- vres a- mou- reux,

45
Le bien en- tier & l'es- pe- ran- ce, De
ce, Le bien en- tier & l'es- pe- ran- ce, De tant de
ran- ce, Le bien en- tier & l'es- pe- ran- ce, De tant
l'es- pe- ran- ce, Le bien en- tier & l'es- pe- ran- ce,
ran- ce, & l'es- pe- ran- ce, De tant

64
nes- te jou- is- san- ce, D'at- ten- dans à fait mal-
Que vo- tre hon- nes- te jou- is- san- ce, D'at- ten- dans à fait mal-
Que vo- tre hon- nes- te jou- is- san- ce, D'at- ten- dans à fait
Que vo- tre hon- nes- te jou- is- san- ce, D'at- ten- dans
Que vo- tre hon- nes- te jou- is- san- ce, D'at-

72
heu- reux, Que vo- tre hon-nes- te jou- is- san- ce, D'at-
heu- reux, Que votre hon-nes- te jou- is- san- ce,
mal- heu- reux, Que vo-tre hon-nes- te jou-is-
à fait mal- heu- reux, Que vo-tre hon-nes-te
ten- dans à fait mal- heu- reux, Que vo-
tre hon-

Ban- ny j'en suis par faux sem- blant, par faux sem- blant,
Ban- ny j'en suis
Ban- ny j'en suis par faux sem-blant, par faux sem- blant,
Ban- ny j'en suis par faux sem- blant, Ban-
Ban-

81
ten- dans à fait mal-heu- reux.
D'at- ten- dans à fait mal-heu- reux.
san- ce, D'at-ten- dans à fait mal- heu- reux.
jou- is-san- ce, D'at- ten- dans à fait mal- heu- reux.
nes- te jou- is- san- ce, D'at-ten- dans à fait mal- heu- reux.

10
Ban- ny j'en suis par faux sem- blant, Mais pour nous
par faux sem- blant, Mais pour nous voir, Mais pour
Ban- ny j'en suis par faux sem- blant, Mais pour en- nous voir
ny j'en suis par faux sem- blant, Mais pour nous voir, Mais
ny j'en suis par faux sem- blant, par faux sem- blant, Mais pour nous voir, nous
Mais pour

20
voir en- cor' en- sem- ble, en- cor' en- sem- ble,   Faut que
voir en- cor' en- sem- ble en- cor' en- sem- ble,   Faut que me soy- ez res- sem-
cor' en- sem- ble,   en- cor' en- sem- ble,   Faut que me soy- ez res- sem-
pour en- cor' en- sem- ble,   en- cor' en- sem- ble,
nous voir
voir en- cor' en- sem- ble,   en- cor' en- sem- ble,   Faut que me soy- ez res- sem-

38
De fer- me- té car il me sem-   ble,   car il me sem-
Faut que me soy- ez res- sem- blant, De fer- me- té, car il me sem- ble, car il me sem-
soy- ez res- sem- blant,   De fer- me- té, De fer- me- té, car il me sem-
ez res- sem- blant, De fer- me- té car il me sem-   ble,
soy- ez res- sem- blant,   De fer- me- té, car il me sem-

28
me soy- ez res- sem- blant, res-   sem-   blant,
blant, Faut que me soy- ez res-   sem- blant, res- sem- blant,
blant,   Faut que me soy- ez res- sem- blant, Faut que me
Faut que me soy- ez res- sem- blant,   Faut que me soy-
blant,   Faut que me soy- ez res- sem- blant, Faut que me

49
ble, car il me sem-   ble, Que quand faux ra- port
ble, car il me sem-   ble, Que quand faux ra- port
ble,   Que quand faux ra- port,
car il me sem- ble, Que quand faux ra- port
ble,   Que quand faux ra- port, Que

des- as- sem- ble,
des- as- sem- ble, Les a- mans
Les a- mans qui sont as-
des- as- sem- ble, Les a- mans qui sont as-
quand faux ra- port des- as- sem- ble, Les a- mans qui sont

qui sont as- sem- blés, qui sont as- sem- blés,
blés, Les a- mans qui sont as- sem- blés,
a- mans qui sont as- sem- blés qui sont as- sem- blés, Si fer- me a-
Les a- mans qui sont as- sem- blés, Si fer- me a-
sont as- sem- blés, Si fer- me a-

Les a- mans qui sont as- sem- blés, Les a- mans
qui sont as- sem- blés, Les a- mans qui sont as- sem-
sem- blés, Les a- mans qui sont as- sem- blés, Les
sem- bles, qui sont as- sem- blés,
as- sem- blés, Les a- mans qui

Si fer- me a- mour, Si fer- me a- mour ne les r'as- sem- ble, Sans fin
Si fer- me a- mour, Si fer- ma a- mour ne les r'as- sem- ble,
mour, Si fer- me a- mour ne les r'as- sem- ble,
mour, Si fer- me a- mour, Sans
mour, Si fer- me a- mour ne les r'as- sem- ble,

92
se- ront des- as- sem- blés, Sans fin se- ront
Sans fin se- ront, Sans fin se- ront, Sans fin se- ront
Sans fin se- ront, Sans fin se- ront des- as-
fin se- ront, Sans fin se- ront des- as- sem- blés, Sans
Sans fin se- ront, Sans fin se- ront des-

111
ront des- as- sem- blés, Sans fin se- ront
se- ront, Sans fin se- ront, Sans fin se- ront
ront, Sans fin se- ront des- as- sem- bles, Sans
Sans fin se- ront, Sans fin se- ront des- as-

102
des- as- sem- blés, Sans fin se-
des- as- sem- blés, Sans fin se- ront des- as- sem- bles, Sans fin
sem- blés, Sans fin se- ront des- as- sem- blés, Sans fin se-
fin se- ront des- as- sem- blés,
as- sem- blés, se- ront des- as- sem- blés,

120
des- as- sem- blés.
des- as- sem- blés, Sans fin se- ront des- as- sem- blés.
fin se- ront des- as- sem- blés.
sem- blés, Sans fin se- ront des- as- sem- blés.
as- sem- blés, Sans fin se- ront des- as- sem- blés.

A- vec- ques vous, mon a- mour fi-
A- vec- ques vous, A- vec- ques vous, A- vec- ques vous mon a- mour
A- vec- ques vous, A- vec- ques vous,
A- vec- ques vous, A- vec- ques

15
vous mon a- mour fi- ni- ra, Puis
ques vous mon a- mour fi- ni- ra, Puis
A- vec- ques vous mon a- mour fi- ni- ra, Puis
vec- ques vous mon a- mour fi- ni- ra, Puis que mon coeur,
vec- ques vous mon a- mour fi- ni- ra, Puis

8
ni- ra, A- vec- ques
fi- ni- ra, mon a- mour fi- ni- ra, A- vec-
A- vec- ques vous, A- vec- ques vous,
vous, A- vec- ques vous mon a- mour fi- ni- ra, A-
vous, A- vec- ques vous, A- vec- que vous, A-

23
que mon coeur est en vous seu-
que mon coeur est en vous seu- le- ment, seu- le-
que mon coeur, Puis que mon coeur est en vous seu- le-
est en vous seu- le- ment, Plai-
que mon coeur, Puis que mon coeur est en vous seu- le-

30
le- ment, Plai- se vous donc a- voir,
ment, Plai- se vous donc a- voir, Plai- se vous donc
ment, Plai- se vous donc a- voir, Plai-
se vous donc a- voir, Plai- se vous donc a- voir, Plai- se vous donc
ment, Plai- se vous donc a- voir, a-

40
ment, Car le cors mort l'es-
con- ten- te- ment, Car le cors mort, Car
ten- te- ment, Car le cors mort, Car le cors
con- ten- te- ment, Car le cors mort, Car le
voir con- ten- te- ment, Car le cors mort, mort,

35
Plai- se vous donc a- voir con- ten- te-
a- voir, Plai- se vous donc a- voir, a- voir
se vous donc a- voir con- ten- te- ment, a- voir con-
a- voir con- ten- te- ment, a- voir con- te- ment, a- voir
voir, Plai- se vous donc a- voir, Plai- se vous donc a-

48
prit vous ser- vi- ra, l'es- prit vous ser- vi- ra, L'es-
le cors mort, l'es- prit vous ser- vi- ra, l'es- prit vous
mort, l'es- prit vous ser- vi- ra, l'es- prit vous ser- vi- ra, l'es-
cors mort, l'es- prit vous ser- vi- ra,
l'es- prit vous ser- vi-

prit vous ser- vi- ra, l'es- prit vous
ser- vi- ra, l'es- prit vous ser- vi- ra, l'es-
prit vous ser- vi- ra, l'es- prit vous ser- vi- ra,
l'es- prit vous ser- vi- ra, l'es- prit vous
ra, vous ser- vi- ra, Car le cors mort l'es- prit, l'es-

A- mour me tue & si je ne veux di- re,
A- mour me tue & si je ne veux di- re,
A- mour me tue & si je ne veux di- re, & si je ne veux di-
A-
A- mour me tue &

ser- vi- ra.
prit vous ser- vi- ra, l'es- prit vous ser- vi- ra.
l'es- prit vous ser- vi- ra.
ser- vi- ra, l'es- prit, l'es- prit vous ser- vi- ra.
prit vous ser- vi- ra, Car le cors mort l'es- prit vous ser- vi- ra.

A- mour me tue & si je ne veux di- re, A- mour me tue &
A- mour me tue & si je ne veux di- re, & si je ne di-
veux
re, A- mour me tue & si je ne veux di- re,
mour me tue & si je ne veux di- re, A- mour me
si je ne veux di- re, A- mour me tue & si je ne veux di-

17
si je ne veux di- re, A- mour me tue & si je ne veux di re, Le
re, A- mour me tue & si je ne veux di- re,
A- mour me tue & si je ne veux di- re, Le
tue & si je ne veux di- re, & si je ne veux di- re, Le
re, & si je ne veux di- re, Le

35
que ce m'est de mou- rir, Tant j'ay grand peur, Tant j'ay
rir, Tant j'ay grand peur, Tant j'ay grand peur,
de mou- rir, Tant j'ay grand peur, Tant j'ay grand
rir, que ce m'est de mou- rir, Tant j'ay grand
de mou- rir, Tant j'ay grand peur,

24
plai- sant mal que ce m'est de mou- rir, Le plai- sant mal
Le plai- sant mal que ce m'est de mou-
plai- sant mal que ce m'est de mou- rir, Le plai- sant mal que ce m'est
plai- sant mal que ce m'est de mou- rir, Le plai- sant mal que ce m'est de mou-
plai- sant mal que ce m'est de mou- rir, Le plai- sant mal que ce m'est

45
grand peur, qu'on vuei- lle se- cou- rir, qu'on vuei- lle se- cou- rir,
qu'on vuei- lle se- cou- rir, Le mal par qui dou- ce- ment je,
peur, qu'on vuei- lle se- cou- rir, Le mal par qui
peur, Tant j'ay grand peur, qu'on vuei- lle se- cou- rir, Le mal par qui dou-
Tant j'ay grand peur se- cou- rir, qu'on vuei- lle se- cou- rir, Le mal par qui
qu'on vuei- lle

54
Le mal par qui dou- ce- ment je, sou- pi- re, dou- ce- ment je,
sou- pi- re dou- ce-ment je, sou- pi- re dou- ce- ment je, sou- pi-
dou- ce- ment je, sou- pi- re dou- ce- ment je, sou-
ce- ment je, sou- pi- re dou- ce- ment je, sou- pi-
dou- ce- ment je, sou-pi- re dou- ce- ment je sou- pi-

70
Qu'a- vec le tems je me puis- se gue- rir, Qu'a- vec le
si- re, Qu'a- vec le tems je
si- re, Qu'a- vec le tems je me puis- se gue- rir, Qu'a- vec le
gueur de- si- re, Qu'a- vec le tems je me puis- se gue- rir, Qu'a- vec le
re, Qu'a- vec le tems je me puis- se gue- rir,

62
sou- pi- re, Il est bien vray, Il est bien vray,
re, Il est bien vray, Il est bien vray que ma lan- gueur de-
pi- re, Il est bien vray, Il est bien vray, que ma lan- gueur de-
re, Il est bien vray que ma lan-
re, Il est bien vray, que ma lan- gueur de- si-

77
tems je me puis- se gue- rir, Mais je ne veux,
me puis- se gue- rir, je me puis- se gue- rir, Mais je ne
tems je me puis- se gue- rir, je me puis- se gue- rir, Mais je ne veux
tems je me puis- se gue- rir, je me puis- se gue- rir, Mais je
je me puis- se gue- rir, Mais je ne

84
Mais je ne veux, ma- da- me, re- que- rir, Mais je
veux, Mais je ne veux, ma da- me, re- que-
Mais je ne veux, ma da- me,
ne veux, Mais je ne veux, ma da- me, re- que- rir, ma
veux, Mais je ne veux, ma da- me, re- que- rir, Mais

96
me plait mon mar- ty- re, Tant me plait
me plait mon mar- ty- re, Tant me plait mon mar- ty- re,
me plait mon mar- ty- re, Tant me plait mon mar- ty- re, Tant me
té, Tant me plait mon mar- ty- re, Tant me
Tant me plait mon mar- ty- re, Tant me plait

90
ne veux, ma da- me, re- que- rir, Pour ma san- té, Pour ma san- té, Tant
rir, ma da- me, re- que- rir, Pour ma san- té, Pour ma san- té, Tant
re- que rir, Pour ma san- té, Pour ma san- té, Tant
da- me, re- que- rir, Pour ma san- té, Pour ma san-
je ne veux, ma da- me, re- que- rir, Pour ma san- té,

103
mon mar- ty- re, Tant me plait mon mar- ty- re.
Tant me plait mon mar- ty- re.
plait mon mar- ty- re, Tant me plait mon mar- ty- re.
plait mon mar- ty- re, Tant me plait mon mar- ty- re.
mon mar- ty- re, Tant me plait mon mar- ty- re.

47 Crequillon, *Pis ne me peut venir*

17

9

25

34
de mer- cy, Et suis loin de mer-
de mer- cy, Et suis loin de mer- cy, Et suis loin de mer- cy,
de mer- cy, & suis loin de mer- cy, & suis loin de
Et suis loin de mer- cy, Et suis loin de mer- cy,
de mer- cy, Et suis loin de mer- cy, Et suis loin de mer-

54
ru- de- ment, Vo- tre coeur
ru- de- ment, Vo- tre coeur en- dur- cy, Me
ru- de- ment, Vo- tre coeur en- dur- cy, Me don- ne ce tour-
Vo- tre coeur en- dur- cy, Me don- ne ce tour-
Vo- tre coeur en- dur- cy, Me don- ne ce tour-

45
cy, Trait- té trop ru- de- ment, Trait- té trop
Trait- té trop ru- de- ment, Trait- té trop ru- de- ment, Trait- té trop
mer- cy, Trait- té trop ru- de- ment, Trait- té trop
Trait- té trop ru- de- ment, Trait- té trop ru- de- ment,
cy, Trait- té trop ru- de- ment, Trait- té trop ru- de- ment,

62
en- dur- cy, Me don- ne ce tour- ment,
don- ne ce tour- ment, Vo- tre coeur en- dur- cy me don-
ment, Me don- ne ce tour- ment, Vo- tre coeur en- dur- cy, Me
ment, Me don- ne ce tour- ment, Vo- tre coeur en- dur- cy
ment, Vo- tre coeur en- dur- cy, Me

Vo- tre coeur en- dur- cy, Me don- ne ce tour-
ne ce tour- ment, Me don- ne ce tour- ment, Vo-
don- ne ce tour- ment, Me don- ne ce tour-
me don- ne ce tour- ment, Me
don- ne ce tour- ment, Me don- ne ce tour- ment,

Sur tous re- gretz,
Sur tous re- gretz, Sur tous
Sur tous re- gretz, Sur tous re- gretz, Sur
Sur tous re- gretz, Sur tous re- gretz, Sur tous
Sur tous re- gretz, Sur

ment.
tre coeur en- dur- cy me don- ne ce tour- ment.
ment.
don- ne ce tour- ment.
Vo- tre coeur en- dur- cy, Me don- ne ce tour- ment.

Sur tous re- gretz, le mien plus pi- teux pleu-
re- gretz, le mien plus pi- teux pleu-
tous re- gretz le mien, plus pi- teux pleu- re,
re- gretz, le mien plus pi- teux pleu- re, plus pi- teux pleu- re,
tous re- gretz le mien plus pi- teux pleu- re, le

19
re,
Jet-
re,
le mien plus pi- teux pleu- re,
le mien plus pi- teux pleu- re, Jet- tans
le mien plus pi- teux pleu- re, Jet-
mien plus pi- teux pleu- re, Jet- tans

36
trans- per- sans mon las coeur,
coeur, trans- per- çans mon las coeur, Car j'ay per- du
per- sans mon las coeur, Car j'ay per- du
pirs, trans- per- sans mon las coeur, Car j'ay per- du,
pirs trans- per- sans mon las coeur, Car j'ay

27
tans sou- pirs,
Jet- tans sou- pirs, Jet- tans sou- pirs trans- per- sans mon las
sou- pirs, Jet- tans sou- pirs trans-
tans sou- pirs, Jet- tans sou- pirs, Jet- tans sou-
sou- pirs, Jet- tans sou-

45
Car j'ay per- du
l'a- mi- a- ble li- queur,
l'a- mi- a- ble li- queur, l'a- mi- a-
Car j'ay per- du l'a-
per- du, l'a- mi- a-

52
l'a- mi- a- ble li- queur, Que tant
Que tant je plein, Que tant je
ble li- queur, Que tant je plein, Que tant je
mi- a- ble li- queur, Que tant je plein, &
ble li- queur, Que tant je plein,

68
ple heu- re, Que tant
re, Que tant je plein, Que
re, Que tant je plein, Que
en am- ple heu- re, Que tant je plein,
re, Que tant je plein,

60
je plein, & plein- dray en am-
plein, & plein- dray en am- ple heu- re, & plein- dray en am- ple heu-
plein, & plein- dray en am- ple heu-
plein- dray en am- ple heu- re, & plein- dray
Que tant je plein & plein- dray en am- ple heu-

75
je plein, & plein- dray en
tant je plein, & plein- dray en am- ple heu- re, & plein- dray en
tant je plein, & plein- dray en am-
& plein- dray en am- ple heu- re, &
Que tant je plein & plein- dray en am-

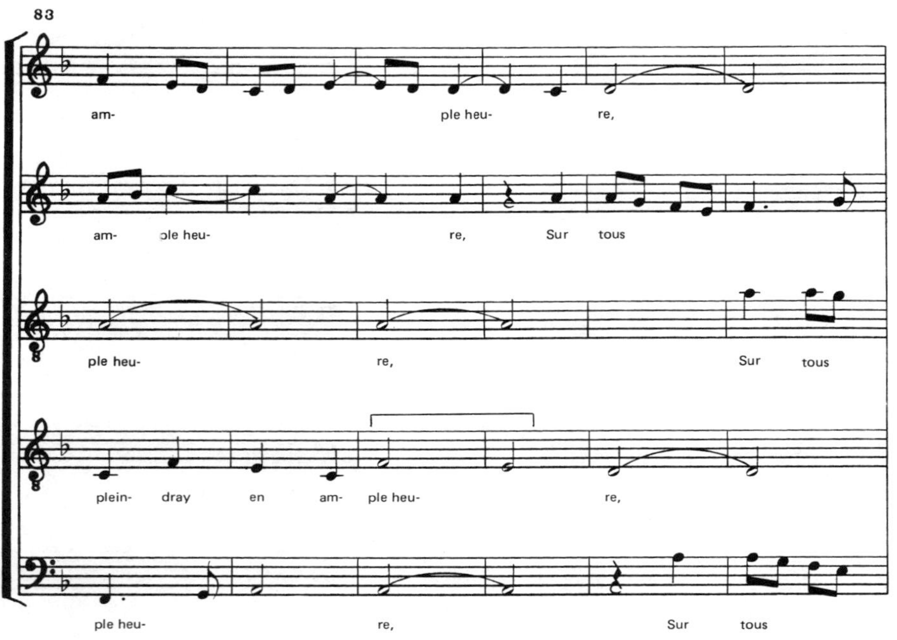
Au- prés de vous, se- cre- te- ment de- meu- re,
Au- prés de vous se- cre- te- ment de- meu- re, se-
Au- prés de
Au- prés de

se- cre- te- ment de- meu- re, se- cre- te- ment de- meu-
cre- te- ment de- meu- re, se- cre- te- ment de- meu- re, se- cre- te- ment,
Au- prés de vous, se-
vous se- cre- te- ment de- meu- re, se- cre- te- ment de-

Sur tous, Sur tous re- gretz.
re- gretz, Sur tous re- gretz.
re- gretz.
Sur tous re- gretz, Sur tous re- gretz.
re- gretz, Sur tous re- gretz.

14
re,   se- cre- te- ment de- meu-   re,
se-   cre- te- ment de- meu-   re, se- cre- te- ment de- meu- re,   Mon
cre- te- ment de- meu-   re,   se- cre- te- ment de- meu-
meu-   re,   se- cre- te- ment,   se- cre- te- ment de-meu-
ment de- meu-   re,   se- cre- te- ment de- meu-   re,

30
que nul   le   con- for-   te, Et si   lan- guit,
te, sans   que nul   le   con- for-   te, Et si lan- guit, Et si lan- guit, Et
te, sans   que nul   le   con- for-   te, Et si lan- guit,   Et   si
te, sans   que nul le   con- for-   te,   Et si lan- guit,
te, sans   que nul le con- for-   te,   Et

21
Mon   po- vre   coeur, Mon   po- vre   coeur,   sans
po-   vre   coeur, Mon   po- vre   coeur sans que nul,   le   con- for-
re,   Mon   po- vre   coeur sans   que   nul   le   con- for-
re,   Mon po- vre   coeur, Mon po- vre   coeur sans   que nul   le   con- for-
Mon   po-   vre   coeur,   sans   que nul   le con- for-

39
pour la   dou- leur qu'il por-   te,
si   lan- guit pour la   dou-   leur   qu'il por-   te, pour   la
lan- guit   pour   la   dou-   leur   qu'il por-   te,
Et   si   lan- guit pour la   dou-   leur   qu'il por-   te, pour la dou-
si   lan- guit,   pour   la   dou-

47
pour la dou- leur qu'il por- te,
dou- leur qu'il por- te, pour la dou- leur qu'il
pour la dou- leur qu'il por- te, pour la dou- leur, qu'il por-
leur qu'il por- te, pour la dou- leur qu'il
leur qu'il por- te, pour la dou- leur qu'il por-

65
qu'en ce tour- ment il meu- re, qu'en ce tour- ment il
meu- re, qu'en ce tour- ment il meu- re, Puis
ce tour- ment il meu- re, qu'en ce tour- ment
re, Puis que vou- lez, qu'en ce tour- ment il meu-
re, Puis que vou- lez, Puis que vou-

56
Puis que vou- lez,
por- te, Puis que vou- lez, Puis que vou- lez qu'en ce tour- ment il
te, Puis que vou- lez, Puis que vou- lez, Puis que vou- lez qu'en
por- te, Puis que vou- lez qu'en ce tour- ment il meu-
te, Puis que vou- lez qu'en ce tour- ment il meu-

74
meu- re, il meu- re, Puis que
que vou- lez qu'en ce tour- ment il meu- re, Puis que vou-
il meu- re, qu'en ce tour- ment il
re, qu'en ce tour- ment il meu- re,
lez qu'en ce tour- ment il meu- re, Puis que vou- lez,

vou- lez, qu'en ce tour- ment il
lez qu'en ce tour- ment il meu- re, qu'en ce tour-
meu- re, Puis que vou- lez, qu'en ce tour- ment il
qu'en ce tour- ment il meu- re, Puis que vou- lez,
Puis que vou- lez qu'en ce tour- ment il

Je me com- plein de mon
Je me com- plein, Je me com- plein, de mon a-
Je me com- plein de mon a- my, Je me com- plein de mon a-
Je me com- plein, de mon a-

meu- re, il meu- re.
ment il meu- re, il meu- re.
meu- re, il meu- re.
qu'en ce tour- ment il meu- re.
meu- re, il meu- re.

a- my, de mon a- my,
my, de mon a- my, de mon a- my,
my, de mon a- my, de mon a- my,
Je me com- plein de mon a- my,
my, de mon a- my, de mon a- my,

20
Qui me sou- loit tant ve- nir
De mon a- my,
de mon a- my, Qui me sou- loit tant ve-
de mon a- my, Qui
de mon a- my,

41
né- e, Or est
La fres- che ma- ti- né- e,
e, La fres- che ma- ti- né- e, Or est il
La fres- che ma- ti- né- e,
La fres- che ma- ti- né- e,

31
voir, La fres- che ma- ti-
Qui me sou- loit tant ve- nir voir,
nir voir, La fres- che ma- ti- né-
me sou- loit tant ve- nir voir,
Qui me sou- loit tant ve- nir voir,

52
il pri- me & s'est mi- di, & s'est mi- di,
Or est il pri- me & s'est mi- di, & s'est mi- di,
pri- me & s'est mi- di, & s'est mi- di, & s'est
Or est il pri- me & s'est mi-
Or est il pri- me & s'est mi- di, & s'est

62
Et si n'oy
Et si n'oy nou-		vel-le			de
mi-	di,		Et si		n'oy nou-		vel-	le
di,	& s'est		mi-	di,
mi-		di,				Et si		n'oy

80
s'a-	pro-			che la ves-				pré-
le	de		luy,	s'a-	pro-		che	la ves-
pro-che la ves- pré-
de	luy,				s'a-	pro-	che la		ves-	pré-

71
nou-	vel-	le de luy,
luy,		Et si n'oy nou-			vel-
de	luy, Et si n'oy nou-	vel-	le	de luy,	s'a-
Et si		n'oy nou-		vel- le
nou-	vel-	le de luy, Et si n'oy nou-		vel-	le

89
e,						s'a-
pré-
e,				s'a-	pro-	che la
pro-	che la	ves-			pré-	e.
e,	s'a-	pro-			che la	ves-

pro- che la ves- pré- e, La tri- co- ton, La tri- co-
e, la ves- pré- e, La tri- co- ton, La
ves- pré- e, La tri- co- ton, La tri- co-
pré- e, La tri- co- ton, La tri- co-

Par- fons re-
Par- fons re- gretz, Par-
Par- fons re- gretz, Par- fons re- gretz &

ton, la bel- le tri- co- té- e.
tri- co- ton, la bel- le tri- co- té- e.
ton, La tri- co- ton, La bel- le tri- co- té- e.
ton, La tri- co- ton, la bel- le tri- co- té- e.

gretz, & la- men- ta- ble joy- e, & la-
fons re- gretz, Par- fons re- gretz & la- men- ta- ble
la- men- ta- ble joy- e, & la- men-
Par- fons re-
Par- fons re- gretz, &

men- ta- ble joy- e, & la- men- ta- ble joy- e,
joy- e, & la- men- ta- ble joy-
ta- ble joy- e, & la- men- ta- ble
gretz, & la- men- ta- ble
la- men- ta- ble joy- e,

que je soy- e, quel- que part que je soy-
soy- e, quel- que part que je soy-
que je soy- e, quel- que part que je
moy, quel- que part que je
que part que je soy- e,

Ve- nez à moy, quel- que part
e, Ve- nez, Ve- nez à moy quel- que part que je
joy- e, Ve- nez à moy, quel- que part
joy- e, Ve- nez à
Ve- nez à moy, quel-

e, Et vous has- tez,
e, Et vous has- tez, sans
soy- e, Et vous has- tez sans point dis-
soy- e, Et
Et vous has- tez sans point

82
sans point dis- si-
point dis- si- mu- ler,
si- mu- ler, sans point dis- si- mu-
vous has- tez sans point dis- si-
dis- si- mu- ler,

80
mon coeur ex- e- cu- ter,
cu- ter,
ter, mon coeur ex- e- cu- ter,
pte- ment mon coeur ex- e- cu- ter,
cu- ter,

70
mu- ler, Pour prom- pte- ment,
Pour prom- pte- ment, mon coeur ex- e-
ler, Pour prom- pte- ment mon coeur ex- e- cu-
mu- ler, Pour prom-
Pour prom- pte- ment mon coeur ex- e-

88
Af- fin qu'en dueil & lar- mes il se noy- e,
Af- fin qu'en dueil, &
Af- fin qu'en dueil, &
Af- fin qu'en dueil &
Af- fin qu'en dueil & lar- mes il se noy- e,

99
lar- mes il se noy- e, Af- fin qu'en
lar- mes il se noy- e, Af-
lar- mes il se noy- e,
Af- fin qu'en

115
lar- mes il se noy- e, Af-
Af- fin qu'en
lar- mes il se noy- e, Af- fin qu'en
lar- mes il se noy- e.
Af- fin qu'en

107
Af- fin qu'en dueil & lar- mes il se noy- e.
dueil & lar- mes il se noy- e,
fin qu'en dueil, &
Af- fin qu'en dueil &
dueil & lar- mes il se noy- e,

123
fin qu'en dueil, & lar- mes il se noy- e.
dueil, & lar- mes il se noy- e.
dueil, & lar- mes il se noy- e.
dueil, & lar- mes il se noy- e.

187

52 Vuillard, *Voulez ouir chansonnette*

38
Qui dan- soient de- dans un pré, Qui dan-soient de-dans un pré,
dan- soient de- dans un pré, de- dans un pré,
de- dans un pré, A la plus bel- le des trois,
dan- soient de- dans un pré, de- dans un pré, A la plus bel-
dan- soient de- dans un pré, A la plus bel-

58
ter- re, Son psau- tier luy cheut en ter- re,
tier & ses heu- ret- tes, In jan voi- re,
Son psau- tier luy cheut en ter- re, In jan voi- re, In jan
ter- re, Son psau-tier luy cheut en ter- re, In
Son psau- tier luy cheut en ter- re, In jan, in jan, in jan voi- re,

48
A la plus bel- le des trois, Son psau- tier luy cheut en
A la plus bel- le des trois, Son psau- tier, Son psau-
A la plus bel- le des trois,
Son psau- tier luy cheut en
le des trois, A la plus bel- le des trois,

67
In jan voi- re, in jan, in
Son psau- tier luy cheut en ter- re, in jan voi- re,
voi- re, Son psau- tier luy cheut en ter- re, in jan voi- re,
jan voi- re, in
Son psau- tier luy cheut en ter- re, in jan, in jan, in jan

76
jan, in jan voi- re, Et
in jan, in jan, in jan voi- re, Et mon Dieu, s'a
in jan, in jan, in jan voi- re, in
jan, in jan, in jan voi- re, in jan voi- re, in jan, in jan, in jan
voi- re, in jan, in jan, in jan voi- re, in jan voi- re,

96
Que la ra- ci-
Je ne le sça- voi- e pas,
le sça- voi- e pas, Je ne le sça- voi- e
mon Dieu, s'a dit l'a- bes- se, Je ne le sça- voi- e pas,
Dieu, s'a dit l'a- bes- se, Je ne le sça- voi- e

86
mon Dieu, s'a dit l'a- bes- se, Je ne le sça- voi- e pas,
dit l'a- bes- se, Je ne le sça- voi- e pas,
jan voi- re, Et mon Dieu, s'a dit l'a- bes- se, Je ne
voi- re, Et mon Dieu, s'a dit l'a- bes- se, Et
in jan voi- re, Et mon

105
ne des dens, On l'a- lat cer- cher si bas, Que la ra- ci- ne des dens,
Que la ra- ci- ne des dens, On l'a- lat
pas, Que la ra- ci- ne des dens, Que la ra- ci- ne des dens, On
Que la ra- ci- ne des dens, Que la ra- ci- ne des dens, On
pas, Je ne le sça- voi- e pas,

115
On l'a- lat cer- cher si bas,   L'on vous
cer- cher si bas,   L'on vous rem- bour- ra voz bas,
l'a- lat cer- cher si bas,   L'on vous rem- bour- ra voz
l'a- lat cer- cher si bas,   L'on vous rem- bour- ra voz bas,
L'on vous rem- bour- ra voz bas,

133
rant la crou- pie- re,   In jan voi- re, in jan, in jan,
ser- rant la crou- pie- re,   In jan voi- re,   In jan voi- re,   in
ser- rant la crou- pie- re,   In jan voi- re,   in jan voi- re,
vous ser- rant la crou- pie- re,   In jan voi- re,   in jan
la crou- pie- re,   In jan voi- re,   in jan, in jan,

124
rem- bour- ra voz bas, L'on vous rem- bour- ra voz bas,   En vous ser-
L'on vous rem- bour- ra voz bas,   L'on vous rem- bour- ra voz bas, En vous
bas,   L'on vous rem- bour- ra voz bas,   En vous
L'on vous rem- bour- ra voz bas, L'on vous rem- bour- ra voz bas,   En
L'on vous rem- bour- ra voz bas,   En vous ser- rant

141
in jan voi- re, in jan voi- re,
jan voi- re, in jan, in jan voi- re, in
in jan, in jan, in jan voi- re,
voi- re, in jan, in jan, in jan voi- re, in
in jan voire, in jan voi- re, in jan

149
in jan voi- re,
jan voi- re, in jan, in jan voi- re, in
in jan, in jan, in jan voi- re,
jan, in jan voi- re, in jan, in jan, in jan
voi- re, in jan, in jan, in jan voi- re, in jan voi- re,

N'est= ce pas un grand des- plai- sir, un grand des-
N'est= ce pas un grand des-
N'est= ce pas un grand des-
N'est=
N'est= ce pas un grand des- plai- sir,

157
in jan voi- re.
jan, in jan, in jan voi- re, in jan, in jan, in jan voi- re.
in jan, in jan, in jan voi- re.
voi- re, in jan voi- re, in jan, in jan, in jan voi- re.
in jan voi- re, in jan, in jan voi- re, in jan voi- re.

10
plai- sir, un grand des- plai- sir, Quand je n'o- se pour mon
plai- sir, N'est=ce pas un grand des- plai- sir, Quand je n'o- se pour mon plai-
plai- sir, Quand je n'o- se pour mon
ce pas un grand des- plai- sir, Quand
N'est= ce pas un grand des- plai- sir, Quand

20
plai- sir, pour mon plai- sir, Pour mon bien & pour ma san-
sir, Quand je n'o- se pour mon plai- sir, Pour
plai- sir, Pour mon bien
je n'o- se pour mon plai- sir,

42
mien ma vo- lon- té, Fai- re du mien ma
mien ma vo- lon- té, Fai- re du mien ma vo- lon- té, Fai- re du mien ma vo- lon
ma vo- lon- té, Fai- re du mien ma
Fai- re du mien ma vo- lon- té,
Fai- re du mien ma vo- lon- té,

31
té, Pour mon bien & pour ma san- té, Fai- re du
mon bien & pour ma san- té, Pour mon bien & pour ma san- té, Fai- re du
& pour ma san- té, Fai- re du mien
Pour mon bien & pour ma san- té,
té, Pour mon bien & pour ma san- té,

53
vo- lon- té,
té, Et si n'ay point d'au- tre de- sir, Et si n'ay point d'au- tre
vo- lon- té, Et si n'ay point d'au- tre
Fai- re du mien ma vo- lon- té, Et
Fai- re du mien ma vo- lon- té, Et si n'ay point d'au- tre de-

Et si n'ay point d'au- tre de- sir, Et si n'ay point d'au- tre de-
de- sir, Et si n'ay point d'au- tre de- sir, Et si n'ay point d'au-
de- sir, Et si n'ay point d'au- tre
si n'ay point d'au- tre de- sir, Et
sir, Et si n'ay point d'au- tre de- sir,

Mort ou mer- cy, en lan- guis-
Mort ou mer- cy, en lan- guis- sant j'at- tens,
Mort ou mer- cy, en

sir, Et si n'ay point d'au- tre de- sir, Et si n'ay point d'au- tre de- sir.
tre de- sir, Et si n'ay point d'au- tre de- sir.
de- sir, Et si n'ay point d'au- tre de- sir.
si n'ay point d'au- tre de- sir.
Et si n'ay point d'au- tre de- sir, Et si n'ay point d'au- tre de- sir.

sant j'at- tens, en lan- guis- sant, en lan- guis- sant j'at-
Mort ou mer- cy en lan- guis- sant j'at- tens, en
Mort ou mer- cy, en lan- guis-
Mort
lan- guis- sant j'at- tens, Mort ou mer-

tens, en lan- guis- sant j'at-
lan- guis- sant j'at- tens, en lan- guis- sant j'at-
sant j'at- tens,
ou mer- cy, en lan- guis- sant j'at- tens,
cy, en lan- guis- sant j'at- tens, en lan- guis- sant

vein je pers mon tems, Rai- son, [Rai- son] le veut,
je pers mon tems, Rai- son le veut, Rai-
mon tems, Rai- son le veut, & con- seil
gnois- sant, qu'en vein je pers mon tems,
Rai- son le veut, Rai- son le veut, & con-

tens, Mais co- gnois- sant, qu'en
tens, Mais co- gnois- sant qu'en vein
Mais co- gnois- sant, qu'en vein je pers
Mais co-
j'at- tens, Mais co- gnois- sant qu'en vein je pers mon tems,

mais con- seil m'en en- hor- te, mais con- seil m'en en- hor-
son le veut, Rai- son le veut, & con- seil m'en en-
m'en en- hor- te, Rai- son le veut &
Rai- son le veut, & con- seil m'en en- hor- te,
seil m'en en- hor- te, & con- seil m'en en- hor- te, & con- seil m'en en-

60
te, mais con- seil m'en en- hor-
hor- te,
con- seil m'en en- hor- te,
Rai- son le veut & con- seil m'en en-
te, Rai- son le veut & con- seil m'en en-

78
te, De lais- ser tout, De lais- ser tout mais l'a- mour est si for-
mour est si for- te, mais l'a- mour est si for- te, mais l'a-
for- te, De lais- ser tout mais l'a- mour
De lais- ser tout mais l'a- mour est si for- te,
tout, De lais- ser tout mais l'a- mour est si for- te, De lais- ser tout, De

69
te, De lais- ser tout mais l'a- mour est si for-
De lais- ser tout, De lais- ser tout mais l'a-
De lais- ser tout mais l'a- mour est si
hor- te,
hor- te, De lais- ser tout, De lais- ser tout, De lais- ser

89
te, mais l'a- mour est si for- te, Que mes es-
mour est si for- te, mais l'a- mour est si for- te, Que
est si for- te, Que mes es-
De lais- ser tout mais l'a- mour est si for- te,
lais- ser tout, De lais- ser tout mais l'a- mour est si for- te,

98
prits, Que mes es- prits, ne
mes es- prits ne sont pas bien con- tens,
prits, Que mes es- prits ne sont pas
Que mes es- prits,
Que mes es- prits ne sont pas bien con- tens, Que mes es-
114
sont pas bien con- tens, con-
con- tens, ne sont
prits ne sont pas bien con- tens, Que
Que mes es- prits ne sont pas
mes es- prits, ne sont pas bien con-
106
sont pas bien con- tens, ne
Que mes es- prits ne sont pas bien
bien con- tens, Que mes es-
Que mes es- prits ne sont pas bien con- tens,
prits, ne sont pas bien con- tens, Que
121
tens.
pas bien con- tens.
mes es- prits ne sont pas bien con- tens.
bien con- tens.
tens, ne sont pas bien con- tens.

55 Josquin, *Coeur langoureux*

43
jou- is toy, Res- jou- is toy,
jou- is toy, Res- jou- is toy, Res- jou
sou- pi- rer, Res- jou- is toy, Res- jou
Res- jou-
pi- rer, Res- jou-

61
le mai- tres- se,
mai- tres- se, Car ta bel- le mai- tres- se,
tres- se, Car ta bel- le mai-
Car ta bel- le
le mai- tres- se, Car ta bel- le mai- tres- se,

52
Car ta bel-
is toy, Res- jou- is toy, Car ta bel- le
is toy, Res- jou- is toy, Car ta bel- le mai-
is toy, Res- jou- is toy,
is toy, Res- jou- is toy, Car ta bel-

70
Par sa pi- tié te veut don-
Par sa pi- tié,
tres- se, Par sa pi- tié,
mai- tres- se,
Par sa pi- tié te veut don- ner

81
ner lies- se,
Par sa pi- tié te veut don- ner
Par sa pi- tié, te veut don- ner
Par sa pi- tié te veut don- ner
lies- se, te veut don- ner lies-

99
Pour te re- con- for- ter.
ter, pour te re- con- for- ter, Pour te re- con- for- ter, Pour
ter, Pour te re- con- for- ter, Pour te re-
Joye & plai- sir pour te re- con- for- ter, Pour te re- conter, re- con- for- ter, Pour te re- con- for- ter,

90
Joye & plai- sir pour te re- con- for- ter,
lies- se, Joye & plai- sir pour te re- con- for-
lies- se, Joye & plai- sir pour te re- con- for-
lies- se,
se, Joye & plai- sir pour te re- con- for-

109
te re- con- for- ter, Pour te re- con- for- ter.
con- for- ter, Pour te re- con- for- ter.
for- ter.
Pour te re- con- for- ter.

56 Nicolas, *Las voulez vous*

34
que sou- pi- rer, Lais- sez chan-
Lais- sez chan- ter,
ne fait que sou- pi- rer, Lais- sez
fait que sou- pi- rer, Lais- sez chan-
sou- pi- rer, sou- pi- rer,

47
ter ce- luy qui se con- ten- te, Et me lais-
ce- luy qui se con- ten- te, Et me lais-
ter, ce- luy qui se con- ten- te, Et me lais- sez,
sez chan- ter ce- luy qui se con- ten- te, Et me lais- sez,
ter ce- luy qui se con- ten- te,

40
ter, Lais- sez chan- ter, Lais- sez chan-
Lais- sez lais- sez chan- ter, Lais- sez chan- ter,
chan- ter, Lais- sez chan-
ter, Lais- sez chan- ter, Lais- sez chan- ter, Lais-
Lais- sez chan- ter, Lais- sez chan-

55
sez, Et me lais- sez, Et
sez, Et me lais- sez, Et me lais- sez mon seul mal
Et me lais- sez, Et me lais- sez, Et me lais- sez mon seul mal
Et me lais- sez mon seul mal en- du- rer,
Et me lais- sez, Et me lais- sez,

62
me lais- sez mon seul mal en- du- rer, Et me lais- sez mon
en- du- rer, Et me lais- sez, Et
en- du- rer, mon seul mal en- du- rer, mon seul mal en- du-
Et me lais- sez, Et me lais- sez mon seul mal en- du-
Et me lais- sez, Et me lais- sez, lais- sez,

78
rer, Et me lais- sez, Et me
en- du- rer, Et me lais- sez mon seul mal en- du- rer,
rer, mon seul mal en- du- rer,
me lais- sez mon seul mal en- du- rer, Et
Et me lais- sez mon seul mal en- du- rer, Et

70
seul mal en- du- rer, Et me lais- sez, mon seul mal en- du-
me lais- sez mon seul mal en- du- rer, Et me lais- sez mon seul mal
rer, Et me lais- sez mon seul mal en- du-
rer, mon seul mal en- du- rer, Et
Et me lais- sez mon seul mal en- du- rer,

85
lais- sez, mon seul mal en- du- rer,
Et me lais- sez mon seul mal en- du- rer, Et
Et me lais- sez, mon seul mal en- du- rer,
me lais- sez, mon seul mal en- du- rer,
me lais- sez mon seul mal en- du- rer, mon

57 Josquin, *Je ne me puis tenir d'aymer*

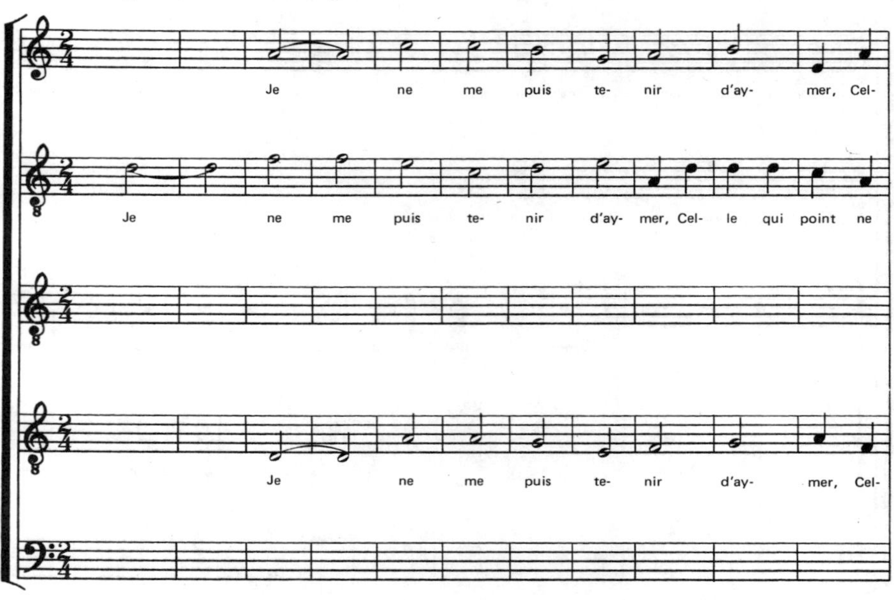

23
(sic)
mer,
Cel- le qui point ne m'ay-
mer,
Cel- le qui point ne
Je ne me puis te- nir d'ay- mer,
mer,
Cel- le qui point ne m'ay- me,
mer,
Cel- le qui point ne m'ay- me,

43
bien des- con- for- ter,
Je me doy bien des-
ne m'ay- me,
Je me doy bien des-
bien des- con- for- ter,
Je me doy bien des-
Je me doy bien des-

33
me,
Cel- le qui point ne m'ay- me,
Je me doy
m'ay- me,
Cel- le qui point
Cel- le qui point ne m'ay- me,
Cel- le qui point ne m'ay- me,
Je me doy

53
con- for- ter,
Car
con- for- ter,
Je me doy bien des- con- for-
Je me doy bien des- con- for-
con- for- ter,
Je me dois bien, des- con- for- ter,
con- for- ter,
Je me dois bien des- con- for-

63
j'ay per- du ma pei- ne:
ter, Car j'ay per- du ma pei-
ter, Car j'ay per- du ma pei- ne: Car
Car j'ay per- du ma pei- ne:
ter, Car

82
da- me sou- ve- rai- ne, Ma da- me sou- ve-
da- me sou- ve- rai- ne, Ma da- me sou- ve- rai- ne, Ma da- me sou- ve-
me sou- ve- rai- ne, Ma da- me sou- ve-
Ma da- me sou- ve- rai- ne, Ma da- me sou- ve-
Ma da- me sou- ve- rai- ne,

72
Ma da- me sou- ve- rai- ne, Ma
ne: Car j'ay per- du ma pei- ne: Ma
j'ay per- du ma pei- ne: Ma da-
Car j'ay per- du ma pei- ne: Ma da- me sou- ve- rai- ne,
j'ay per- du ma pei- ne: Ma da- me sou- ve- rai- ne,

94
rai- ne, Re- ce-
rai- ne, Re- ce- vez vo- tre a- my,
rai- ne, Re- ce- vez
rai- ne, Re- ce-
Re- ce- vez vo- tre a- my,

103
vez vo- tre a- my, Re- ce-
Re- ce- vez vo- tre a- my,
vo- tre a- my, Re- ce- vez vo- tre a- my,
vez vo- tre a- my, Par
Re- ce- vez vo- tre a- my,

122
votre bon- té plei- ne, Par vo- tre bon- té plei- ne, Ou
votre bon- té plei- ne, Par vo- tre bon- té plei- ne,
votre bon- té plei- ne, Ou
votre bon- té plei- ne, Par vo- tre bon- té plei- ne,
Par vo- tre bon- té plei- ne,

113
vez vo- tre a- my, Par vo- tre bon- té plei- ne, Par
Re- ce- vez vo- tre a- my, Par vo- tre bon- té plei- ne, Par
Re- ce- vez vo- tre a- my, Par
vo- tre bon- té plei- ne, Par vo- tre bon- té plei- ne, Par
Par vo- tre bon- té plei- ne,

131
mort est à de- my, Ou mort est à de- my,
Ou mort est à de- my,
mort est à de- my, Ou mort est à
Ou mort est à de- my, Ou mort est à de- my, Ou
Ou mort est à de- my, Ou mort

Ou mort est à de-
Ou mort est à de-
de- my, Ou mort est à de-
mort est à de- my, Ou mort est à de-
est à de- my, Ou mort est à de-

Puis qu'ain- si est que tous ceux qui ont vi-
Puis qu'ain-si est, que tous ceux qui ont vi- e,
Puis qu'ain- si
Puis qu'ain- si est, que
Puis qu'ain- si est, que tous ceux qui ont

my.
my, Ou mort est à de- my, Ou mort est à de- my.
my.
my, Ou mort est à de- my, Ou mort est à de- my.
my, Ou mort est à de- my, Ou mort est à de- my.

e, que tous ceux qui ont
que tous ceux qui ont vi- e, que tous ceux
est, que tous ceux qui ont vi- e,
tous ceux qui ont vi- e, que tous ceux
vi- e, que tous ceux qui ont vi-

19
vi- e, Pren- dront leur fin, Pren- dront leur
qui ont vi- e, Pren- dront leur fin, Pren- dront leur fin en ce mon- de ter-
que tous ceux qui ont vi- e,
qui ont vi- e, Pren- dront leur fin
e, Pren- dront leur fin, Pren- dront leur fin en ce mon- de ter-

39
de ter- res- tre, Et que par for- ce nous faut tous
de ter- res- tre, Et que par for- ce,
en ce mon- de ter- res- tre,
mon- de ter- res- tre, Et
de ter- res- tre, Et que par for- ce, Et

29
fin, en ce mon- de ter- res- tre, en ce mon-
res- tre, ter- res- tre, en ce mon-
Pren- dront leur fin en ce mon- de ter- res- tre,
en ce mon- de ter- res- tre, en ce
res- tre, en ce mon- de ter- res- tre, en ce mon-

48
en ter- re es- tre, Et que par for- ce nous faut tous en ter-
nous faut tous en ter- re es- tre, nous faut tous en ter-
Et que par for- ce nous faut tous en ter- re es-
que par for- ce nous faut tous en ter- re es- tre,
que par for- ce, Et que par for- ce nous faut tous en

58
re es- tre, nous faut tous en ter- re es-
re es- tre, nous faut tous en ter- re estre, nous faut tous en ter- re es- tre,
nous faut tous en ter- re es- tre,
ter- re es- tre, nous faut tous en ter- re es-

77
e, & n'en ay plus d'en- vi- e, & n'en ay
vi- e, & n'en ay plus d'en- vi- e, & n'en ay plus d'en- vi-
quit- te a- mour, & n'en ay plus d'en- vi-
& n'en ay plus d'en- vi- e, Je
vi- e, & n'en ay plus d'en- vi- e, & n'en ay plus d'en- vi-

67
tre, Je quit- te a- mour & n'en ay plus d'en- vi-
tre, Je quit- te a- mour, & n'en ay plus d'en-
Je quit- te a- mour, Je
Je quit- te a- mour, Je quit- te a- mour,
tre, Je quit- te a- mour, Je quit- te a- mour & n'en ay plus d'en-

87
plus d'en- vi- e, Je quit- te a- mour, & n'en ay plus d'en- vi-
e, Je quit- te a- mour, Je quit- te a- mour, & n'en ay plus d'en-
e, Je quit- te a- mour & n'en ay plus d'en-
quit- te a- mour & n'en ay plus d'en- vi- e,
e, Je quit- te a- mour, Je quit- te a- mour, & n'en ay plus d'en- vi-

e, Je quit-te a-mour, Je quit-te a-mour, & n'en ay plus d'en-
vi- e, Je quit-te a-mour, Je quit-te a-mour, Je quit-te a-mour, & n'en ay
vi- e, Je quit-te a-mour, & n'en ay plus
Je quit-te a-mour & n'en ay plus d'en-vi- e,
e, Je quit-te a-mour, Je quit-te a-mour, Je quit-te a-mour, & n'en ay

Vous au-rez tout ce qui est mien, tout ce
Vous au-rez tout ce qui est mien, Vous au-rez tout ce
Vous au-rez tout ce qui est
Vous au-rez tout ce qui est

vi- e, & n'en ay plus d'en- vi- e.
plus d'en-vi- e, & n'en ay plus d'en-vi- e, & n'en ay plus d'en- vy- e.
d'en-vi- e, & n'en ay plus d'en- vy- e.
& n'en ay plus d'en- vy- e.
plus d'en- vy- e, & n'en ay plus d'en- vy- e, & n'en ay plus d'en- vy- e.

qui est mien, Vous au-rez tout ce qui est
Vous au-rez tout ce qui est
qui est mien, Vous au-rez tout ce qui est
mien,
mien, tout ce qui est mien, Vous au- rez tout ce qui est

18
mien, Si je puis par au- cun
mien, ce qui est mien,
mien, Si je puis par au- cun moy- en, Si
Si je puis par
mien, Vous au- rez tout ce qui est mien, Si je puis par

33
ce, Ob- te- nir vo- tre bon- ne gra-
par au- cun moy- en, Ob- te- nir vo- tre bon- ne
par au- cun moy- en, Ob- te- nir vo- tre bon- ne
ce,
vo- tre bon- ne gra- ce,

26
moy- en, Ob- te- nir vo- tre bon- ne gra-
Si je puis
je puis par au- cun moy- en,
au- cun moy- en, Ob- te- nir vo- tre bon- ne gra-
au- cun moy- en, Ob- te- nir

41
ce, Car en ce mon- de ne
gra- ce,
gra- ce, Ob- te- nir vo- tre bon-
Car en ce mon- de, Car en ce mon-
Ob- te- nir vo- tre bon- ne gra- ce,

49
pour- chas- se, ne
Car en ce mon- de, Car en ce
ne gra- ce, Car en ce mon-
de ne pour- chas- se,

63
vrer au- tre bien, Ja- mais re-
Ja- mais re- cou- vrer au- tre
pour- chas- se,
Ja- mais re- cou- vrer
Car en ce mon-
ne pour- chas- se,

56
pour- chas- se, Ja- mais re- cou-
mon- de ne pour- chas- se,
de ne pour- chas- se, ne
Ja- mais re- cou- vrer au- tre bien,
de ne pour- chas- se, Car en ce mon- de

71
cou- vrer au- tre bien, Ja- mais re- cou- vrer au- tre
bien, Ja-
Ja- mais, re- cou- vrer
au- tre bien, Ja- mais re- cou- vrer au- tre
Ja- mais re- cou- vrer au- tre

78
bien, Ja- mais re- cou- vrer au- tre
mais re- cou- vrer au- tre bien, Ja- mais re- cou- vrer
au- tre bien, Ja- mais re- cou- vrer
bien, Ja-
bien, Ja- mais re- cou- vrer au-

A ja- mais croy qu'il en soit la pa- rei-
A ja- mais croy qu'il en soit la pa-
A ja- mais

86
bien, Ja- mais re- cou- vrer au- tre bien.
au- tre bien.
au- tre bien, Ja- mais re- cou- vrer au- tre bien, au- tre bien.
mais re- cou- vrer Ja- mais re- cou- vrer au- tre bien.
tre bien, Ja- mais re- cou- vrer au- tre bien.

10
lle, la pa- rei- lle, A ja- mais croy,
rei- lle, A ja- mais croy qu'il
A ja- mais croy qu'il en soit
croy qu'il en soit la pa- rei- lle, A ja- mais
A ja- mais croy qu'il en soit la pa- rei-

19
A ja- mais croy cu'il en soit la pa- rei-
en soit la pa- rei- lle, qu'il en soit la pa-
la pa- rei- lle, qu'il en
croy qu'il en soit la pa- rei- lle, la pa-
lle, A ja- mais croy qu'il en soit la pa-

35
A vous, da- me, A vous, da-
A vous, da- me, A vous, da-
A vous, da- me, de beau- té
beau- té l'ou- tre- pas- se,
beau- té l'ou- tre- pas- se, A vous, da-

27
lle,
rei- lle, A vous, da- me,
soit, la pa- rei- lle, A vous, da- me,
rei- lle, A vous, da- me, A vous, da- me, de
lle, A vous, da- me, de

43
me, de beau- té l'ou- tre-
me, A vous, da- me, de beau- té l'ou- tre-
l'ou- tre- pas- se, A vous, da- me, de
A vous, A vous, da- me, de beau- té l'ou-
me, de beau- té l'ou- tre- pas- se, A

50
pas- se, de beau- té l'ou- tre- pas-
pas- se, Tant
beau- té l'ou- tre- pas-
tre- pas- se, de beau- té l'ou- tre pas-
vous, da- me, de beau- té l'ou- tre- pas- se,

67
vei-
mon dor- mant je vei-
vous, qu'en mon dor- mant je vei-
vei- lle, qu'en mon dor- mant je vei-
lle, je vei- lle,

58
se, Tant pen- se à vous, qu'en mon dor- mant je
pen- se à vous, Tant pen- se à vous, qu'en
se, Tant pen- se à vous, Tant pen- se à
se, Tant pen- se à vous, qu'en mon dor- mant je vei-

75
lle, Brief, sans vous voir, Brief, sans vous voir,
lle, Brief, sans vous voir, à peu que ne tres- pas-
lle, Brief, sans vous voir, Brief, sans vous voir, Brief,
lle, Brief, sans vous voir, à
Brief, sans vous voir, à peu, Brief, sans vous voir,

83
à peu que ne tres- pas-
se,
à peu que ne tres-
sans vous voir
à peu que ne tres-
peu que ne tres- pas-
à peu que ne tres-

98
sans vous voir, à peu que ne tres- pas-
pas- se, à peu que ne
à peu que ne tres- pas-
Brief, sans vous voir, à peu que ne
sans vous voir, à peu que ne

90
se, Brief, sans vous voir, Brief,
pas- se, Brief, sans vous voir, à peu que ne tres-
pas- se, Brief, sans vous voir, Brief, sans vous voir,
se, à peu que ne tres- pas- se,
pas- se, tres- pas- se, Brief, sans vous voir, à peu, Brief,

106
se.
tres- pas- se, à peu que ne tres- pas- se.
se, à peu que ne tres- pas- se.
tres- pas- se.
tres- pas- se, que ne tres- pas- se.

217

Con- tent ou non il faut que je l'en-du-
Con- tent ou non il faut que je l'en-du-
Con- tent ou non il

Con- tent ou non il faut que je l'en-du-
re, il faut que je l'en-du-
que je l'en-du- re, il
re, il faut que je l'en-du-
re, il faut que je l'en-du- re, Con- tent ou non,

re, l'en- du- re,
re, il faut que je l'en-du-
Con- tent ou non il faut
faut que je l'en-du-
Con- tent ou non il faut que je l'en-du-

re, il faut que je l'en- du- re,
re, il faut que je l'en-du- re,
faut que je l'en-du- re, Puis
re, il faut que je l'en- du- re,
il faut que je l'en-du- re,

Puis que for- tu-
Puis que for- tu- ne, Puis que for-
que for- tu- ne,
Puis que for- tu- ne, Puis que for- tu- ne,
Puis que for- tu- ne, Puis que for-

si tres- per- se- & du- re, & du-
se & du- re, si tres- per- ver- se & du-
tres- per- ver- se & du- re, si tres- per-
du- re, si tres- per- ver- se & du- re, & du- re,
du- re, si tres- per- ver- se & du-

ne, Puis que for- tu- ne,
tu- ne, Puis que for- tu- ne, si tres- per- ver-
Puis que for- tu- ne, Puis que for- tu- ne, si
Puis que for- tu- ne, si tres- per- verse &
tu- ne, Puis que for- tu- ne, si tres- per- se &

re, Tant de lan- gueur si me faut en-
re, & du- re, Tant de lan- gueur si
ver- se & du- re, Tant
si tres- per- ver- se & du- re,
re, si tres- per- ver- se & du- re,

66
du- rer, si me faut en- du-
me faut en- du- rer, en- du-
de lan- gueur si me faut en- du- rer, faut en- du- rer, Tant
Tant de lan- gueur si me faut en du-

78
me faut en- du- rer, Tant de lan- gueur si me faut en-
rer, si me faut
rer, Tant de lan- gueur si me faut en- du- rer,
en- du- rer, si me faut
rer, Tant de lan- gueur si me faut en- du- rer, si me faut

72
rer, Tant de lan- gueur si
rer, Tant de lan- gueur si me faut en- du-
de lan- gueur si me faut en- du-
rer, Tant de lan- gueur si me faut
me faut en- du-

84
du- rer, Dont souf- fri- ray, Dont souf- fri-
en- du- rer, Dont souf- fri- ray, Dont souf- fri- ray, es-
Dont souf- fri- ray, es- pe- rant plus du- rer,
en- du- rer, Dont souf- fri- ray es- pe- rant plus du-
en- du- rer, Dont souf- fri- ray, es- pe- rant plus du- rer,

ray es- pe- rant plus du- rer, Dont souf- fri- ray,
pe- rant plus du- rer, es-
es- pe- rant plus du- rer, es- pe- rant plus du- rer, Dont
rer, Dont souf- fri- ray es- pe- rant plus du- rer,
Dont souf- fri- ray, Dont souf- fri-

plus du- rer.
ray es- pe- rant plus du-
du- rer, es- pe-
pe- rant plus du-
es- pe- rant plus du- rer,

Dont souf- fri- ray, Dont souf- fri- ray es- pe- rant
pe- rant plus du- rer, Dont souf- fri-
souf- fri- ray es- pe- rant plus
es- pe- rant plus du- rer, es-
ray, es- pe- rant plus du- rer,

rer, Dont souf- fri- ray es- pe- rant plus du- rer.
rant plus du- rer, es- pe- rant plus du- rer.
rer, es- pe- rant plus du- rer.
Dont souf- fri- ray es- pe- rant plus du- rer.

rei- lle, nom= pa- rei- lle,
c'est dou- leur nom= pa- rei- lle,
douleur nom- pa- rei- lle, c'est
Fau- te d'ar- gent, c'est dou- leur
rei- lle, c'est dou- leur

Fau- te d'ar- gent, c'est dou- leur nom= pa-
Fau- te d'ar- gent,
lle, c'est
rei- lle, Fau- te d'ar- gent, c'est dou- leur nom- pa-

c'est dou- leur nom= pa- rei- lle,
c'est dou- leur nom=pa- rei- lle,
dou- leur nom- pa- rei- lle, c'est dou- leur
nom- pa- rei- lle, c'est dou- leur nom- pa-
nom- pa- rei- lle, c'est dou- leur nom-pa-

36
c'est dou- leur nom= pa- rei- lle,
c'est dou- leur nom= pa- rei- lle,
nom- pa- rei- lle, c'est dou- leur nom- pa- rei-
rei- lle, c'est dou- leur nom- pa- rei-
rei- lle, c'est dou- leur nom- pa-

57
je sçay bien pour-
las! je sçay bien pour-
dy, Si je le dy, las! je sçay
Si je le dy,
Si je le dy,

46
Si je le dy, las! je sçay bien, las!
Si je le dy, Si je le dy,
lle, Si je le dy, Si je le dy, Si je le
lle, Si je le dy,
rei- lle, Si je le dy, Si je le dy, Si je le dy,

65
quoy, Sans de qui- bus,
quoy, Sans de qui- bus, il
bien pour- quoy, Sans de qui-
las! je sçay bien pour- quoy,
las! je sçay bien pour-

73
Sans de qui- bus, Sans de
se faut te- nir coy, il se faut te- nir coy,
bus, il se faut te- nir coy,
Sans de qui- bus, il se faut te- nir
quoy, Sans de qui-

90
Fem- me qui dort,
Fem-
dort, pour ar- gent on l'es- vei-
pour ar- gent on l'es- vei- lle, Fem- me qui dort, pour

81
qui- bus, il se faut te- nir coy,
il se faut te- nir coy, Fem- me qui
coy, il se faut te- nir coy,
bus, il se faut te- nir coy, Fem- me qui dort,

100
pour ar- gent on l'es- vei- lle,
me qui dort, pour ar- gent on l'es- vei-
lle, pour ar- gent on l'es- vei-
Fem- me qui
ar- gent on l'es- vei-

108
pour ar- gent,
pour ar- gent
lle,
pour ar- gent on l'es-
lle,
pour ar- gent on l'es- vei-
dort,
pour ar- gent on l'es- vei- lle,
lle,
pour ar- gent on l'es- vei- lle,

126
vei- lle,
pour ar- gent
lle,
pour ar- gent
on l'es- vei-
pour ar- gent on l'es- vei-
lle,
pour
pour ar- gent on l'es- vei- lle,
pour
pour ar- gent on l'es- vei- lle, pour ar- gent

116
on l'es- vei- lle,
pour ar- gent on l'es-
vei- lle,
pour ar- gent on l'es- vei-
lle,
pour ar- gent on l'es- vei- lle,
pour ar- gent on l'es- vei- lle,

135
on l'es- vei- lle.
lle.
ar- gent
on
l'es- vei- lle.
ar- gent
on
l'es- vei- lle.
on
l'es- vei- lle.

Gra- ce & ver- tu, bon- té, beau- té, no-
Gra- ce & ver- tu, bon- té, beau- té, no- bles-
Gra- ce & ver- tu, bon- té, beau- té,
Gra- ce & ver- tu, bon- té,
Gra- ce & ver- tu, bon- té,

à m'a- my- e, point ne le faut
Sont à m'a- my- e, point ne le faut ce- ler,
e, point ne le faut ce- ler, point ne
Sont à m'a- my- e, point ne le faut ce- ler, point
à m'a- my- e, point ne le faut ce-

bles- se, Sont
se, bon- té, beau- te, no- bles- se,
no- bles- se, Sont à m'a- my-
beau- té, no- bles- se,
beau- té, no- bles- se, Sont

ce- ler,
Trop me des- plait,
le faut ce- ler, Trop me des- plait d'en ou- ïr
ne le faut ce- ler, Trop me des- plait d'en ou- ïr mal parler, point ne le faut ce- ler, Trop me des- plait d'en ou- ïr

31
Trop me des- plait d'en ou- ïr mal par- ler, Trop me des-
me des- plait d'en ou- ïr mal par- ler, Trop me des- plait d'en ou- ïr
mal par- ler, Trop me des- plait d'en
ler, Trop me des- plait d'en ou- ïr mal par- ler,
mal par- ler, d'en ou- ïr mal par- ler, Trop me des-

48
luy qui l'hon- neur d'el- le bles-
hay ce- luy qui l'hon- neur d'el- le bles-
luy qui l'hon- neur d'el- le bles-
luy qui l'hon- neur d'el- le bles- se, qui
luy qui l'hon- neur d'el- le bles- se, qui l'hon- neur

40
plait d'en ou- ïr mal par- ler, Je hay ce-
mal par- ler, Je hay ce- luy, Je
ou- ïr mal par- ler, Je hay ce- luy, Je hay ce-
Je hay ce- luy, Je hay ce-
plait d'en ou- ïr mal par- ler, Je hay ce-

54
se,
se, qui l'hon- neur d'el- le
se, Je hay ce- luy qui l'hon- neur
l'hon- neur d'el- le bles- se, Je hay ce-
d'el- le bles- se, Je hay ce-

61
Je hay ce- luy qui l'hon- neur d'el-
bles- se, Je hay ce- luy qui l'hon- neur d'el- le
d'el- le bles- se, Je hay ce- luy, Je hay celuy, Je hay ce- luy qui l'hon- neur
luy, Je hay ce- luy qui l'hon- neur d'el- le
73
se.
se, Je hay ce- luy qui l'hon- neur
se, Je
Je hay ce- luy qui l'hon- neur d'el- le bles-
se, Je hay ce- luy qui l'hon- neur
67
le bles-
bles-
luy qui l'hon- neur d'el- le bles-
d'el- le bles- se,
bles- se, qui l'hon- neur d'el- le bles-
80
d'el- le bles- se.
hay ce- luy, qui l'hon- neur d'el- le bles- se.
se.
d'el- le bles- se.

Le cors s'en va, Le cors s'en
Le cors s'en va, Le cors s'en
Le cors s'en va,

15
Le cors s'en va, & le coeur vous de- meu- re,
le coeur vous de- meu- re, & le coeur vous
vous de- meu- re, & le coeur vous
va & le coeur vous de- meu- re, & le
le coeur vous de- meu- re,

8
va, Le cors s'en va,
va, Le cors s'en va, Le cors s'en va, &
Le cors s'en va, & le coeur
Le cors s'en va, Le cors s'en
Le cors s'en va, &

24
& le coeur vous de- meu- re, & le coeur
de- meu- re, & le coeur vous de- meu- re, &
de- meu- re, Le cors s'en va & le coeur
coeur vous de- meu- re, & le coeur vous de- meu- re, &
& le coeur vous

32
vous de- meu- re, Le- quel veut fair' a- vec vous sa de- meu-
le coeur vous de- meu- re, Le- quel veut fai- re a- vec vous sa de- meu-
vous. de- meu- re, Le- quel veut fai- re a- vec vous sa de- meu-
le coeur vous de- meu- re, Le- quel veut fai- re a- vec vous sa de- meu-
de- meu- re,

49
(sic)
loir ay- mer, Pour vous vou- loir ay- mer, tant &
ay- mer, Pour vous vou- loir ay- mer, tant
vous vo- loir ay- mer, Pour vous vou- loir ay- mer, tant
vou- loir ay- mer, tant & si fort, tant
Pour vous vou- loir, vous vou- loir ay- mer,

41
re, Pour vous vo- loir ay- mer, Pour vous vou-
re, Pour vous vo- loir ay- mer, Pour vous vou- loir
re, Pour vous vo- loir ay- mer, Pour
re, Pour vous vo- loir ay- mer, Pour vous
Pour vous vo- loir ay- mer, Pour vous vo- loir ay- mer,

57
si fort, tant & si fort, tant & si fort, tant & si fort, Qu'in-
& si fort, tant & si fort, tant & si fort, tant & si fort, tant & si
& si fort, tant & si fort, tant & si fort,
& si fort, tant & si fort, tant & si fort, tant & si fort, Qu'in-
tant & si fort, tant & si fort, Qu'in-

62
ces- sa- ment, Qu'in- ces- sa- ment, Qu'in- ces- sa- ment, Qu'in-ces-sa-ment,
fort, Qu'in- ces- sa- ment, Qu'in- ces- sa- ment, Qu'in-ces- sa- ment,Qu'in-ces-
Qu'in- ces-sa- ment, Qu'in- ces- sa- ment, Qu'in-ces- sa- ment,
ces- sa- ment, Qu'in-ces- sa- ment,Qu'in- ces- sa- ment, Qu'in- ces-sa- ment,
ces- sa- ment, Qu'in- ces- sa- ment, Qu'in- ces- sa- ment, Qu'in-ces-

77
tre en ef- fort,
tre en ef- fort, Pour vous ser- vir jus- ques à ce qu'il meu-
tre en ef- fort, Pour vous ser- vir jus- ques à ce qu'il meu-
tre en ef- fort, Pour vous ser- vir jus- ques à ce qu'il meu-
Pour vous ser- vir jus- ques à ce qu'il meu-

70
Qu'in-ces- sa- ment se veut met-tre en ef- fort, se veut met-
sa- ment, Qu'in-ces-sa- ment se veut met- tre en ef- fort, se veut met-
Qu'in- ces-sa- ment, se veut met-
Qu'in- ces-sa- ment se veut met- tre en ef- fort, se veut met-
sa- ment, se veut met- tre en ef- fort,

82
Pour vous ser- vir jus- ques à
re, Pour vous ser- vir jus- ques à ce qu'il meu- re,
re, Pour vous ser- vir, Pour vous ser- vir jus- ques à
re, Pour vous ser- vir jus- ques à ce qu'il
re, Pour vous ser- vir,

88
ce qu'il meu- re, Pour vous ser- vir, jus- ques
Pour vous ser- vir jus- ques à ce qu'il meu- re,
ce qu'il meu- re, Pour vous ser- vir,
meu- re, Pour vous ser- vir jus- ques à ce qu'il meu-
Pour vous ser- vir jus- ques à ce qu'il meu-

98
ser- vir, Pour vous ser- vir jus- ques à
vous ser- vir jus- ques à ce
Pour vous ser- vir, Pour vous ser- vir jus- ques à
re, Pour vous ser- vir, jus- ques à ce qu'il meu-
Pour vous ser- vir,

93
à ce qu'il meu- re, qu'il meu- re, Pour vous
jus- ques à ce qu'il meu- re, Pour
jus- ques à ce qu'il meu- re, Pour vous ser- vir,
re, jus- ques à ce qu'il meu-
re, jus- ques à ce qu'il meu- re,

104
ce qu'il meu- re, jus- ques à ce qu'il meu- re.
qu'il meu- re, jus- ques à ce qu'il meu- re.
ce qu'il meu- re, jus- ques à ce qu'il meu- re.
re, jus- ques à ce qu'il meu- re.
jus- ques à ce qu'il meu- re.

Dou- ce mai-tres- se, tou- che, Dou- ce
Dou- ce mai- tres- se, tou- che,
Dou- ce mai- tres- se, tou- che,
Dou- ce mai- tres- se, tou- che, Dou- ce mai-
Dou- ce

mal, pour sou- la- ger mon mal, Pour sou- la- ger mon
Pour sou- la- ger mon mal, Pour sou-
sou- la- ger mon mal, Pour sou- la- ger mon mal, Pour sou- la-
Pour sou- la- ger mon mal, Pour sou- la- ger,
ger mon mal, Pour sou- la- ger mon mal,

mai- tres- se, tou- che, Pour sou- la- ger mon
Dou- ce mai- tres- se, tou- che, Pour sou- la- ger mon mal,
Dou- ce mai- tres- se, tou- che, Pour sou- la- ger, Pour
tres- se, tou- che, Pour sou- la- ger mon mal,
mai- tres- se, tou- che, Pour sou- la-

mal, Pour sou- la- ger mon mal, Mes leu- res de ta
la- ger mon mal, Pour sou- la- ger mon mal, Mes leu- res de ta
ger mon mal, Pour sou- la- ger mon mal, Mes leu- res de ta bou-
Pour sou- la- ger mon mal, Mes leu- res de ta bou-
Pour sou- la- ger mon mal,

23
bou- che, Mes leu- res de ta bou- che, Mes leu- res de ta bou- che, Plus
bou- che, Mes leu- res de ta bou- che, Mes leu- res de ta bou- che, Plus
che, Mes leu- res de ta bou- che, Mes leu- res de ta bou- che,
che, Mes leu- res de ta bou- che, de ta bou- che,
Mes leu- res de ta bou- che, de ta bou- che, Plus

35
Plus rou- ge que co- rail, Plus rou-
rail, Plus rou- ge que
rail, Plus rou- ge que co- rail, plus rou- ge
plus rou- ge que co- rail,
rou- ge que co- rail, que co- rail,

29
rou- ge que co- rail, Plus rou- ge que co- rail, que co- rail,
rou- ge que co- rail, Plus rou- ge que co-
Plus rou- ge que co- rail, Plus rou- ge que co-
Plus rou- ge que co- rail, Plus rou- ge que co- rail, plus

39
ge que co- rail, plus rou- ge que co- rail.
co- rail, plus rou- ge que co- rail.
que co- rail, Plus rou- ge que co- rail, que co- rail.
Plus rou- ge que co- rail.

66 Nicolas, *Force d'amour* [Ste. Marthe]

31
re- fus, qui tous- jours est à crain-
re- fus, qui tous- jours, tous- jours est à crain- dre,
re- fus, qui tous- jours est à crain- dre,
re- fus qui tous- jours est à crain-
Mais le re- fus qui tous- jours est à crain-

49
fait em- pes- che- ment, Dont suis con- traint en- du- rer
ment, Dont suis con- traint en- du-
fait em- pes- che- ment, Dont suis con- traint, en- du- rer
fait em- pes- che- ment, Dont suis con- traint, en- du- rer dou- ce-
sent m'a fait em- pes- che- ment, Dont suis con- traint en- du- rer

40
dre, Jus- qu'à pre- sent m'a
Jus- qu'à pre- sent, Jus- qu'à pre- sent m'a fait em- pes- che-
Jus- qu'à pre- sent m'a fait em- pes- che- ment, m'a
dre, Jus- qu'à pre- sent m'a fait em- pes- che- ment, Jus- qu'à pre- sent
dre, Jus- qu'à pre- sent m'a fait em- pes- che- ment, Jus- qu'a pre-

58
dou- ce- ment, Dis- si- mu- lant mon mal
rer dou- ce- ment, Dis- si- mu- lant mon mal tant que
dou- ce- ment, Dis- si- mu- lant mon mal tant
ment, Dis- si- mu- lant mon mal, mon
dou- ce- ment, Dis- si- mu- lant mon

66
(sic)
tant que je puis, D'au- tre cos- té le bien que
je puis, D'au- tre cos- té, le bien que
que je puis, D'au- tre cos- té, le bien que je pour-
mal tant que je puis, D'au- tre cos- té le bien que
mal tant que je puis, D'au- tre cos- té,

84
ty- re, He-
re, ren- for- ce mon mar- ty- re, He-
ren- for- ce mon mar- ty- re, He- las! voy-
re, ren- for- ce mon mar- ty- re, He- las!
ty- re, mon mar- ty- re, He- las!

75
je pour- suis, Le sou- ve- nir ren- for- ce mon mar-
je pour- suis, Le sou- ve- nir ren- for- ce mon mar- ty-
suis, Le sou- ve- nir, Le sou- ve- nir ren- for- ce mon mar- ty- re,
je pour- suis, Le sou- ve- nir ren- for- ce mon mar- ty-
Le sou- ve- nir, ren- for- ce mon mar-

92
las! He- las, voy- ez le
las! He- las, voy- ez le tour- ment
ez, He- las, voy- ez le tour-
He- las, voy- ez, le tour- ment ou
He- las, He- las, voy- ez, voy- ez le

tour- ment ou je suis, Je veux par- ler &
ou je suis, Je veux par- ler & ne puis un
ment ou je suis, Je veux par- ler & ne puis un mot di-
je suis, Je veux par- ler & ne puis,
tour- ment ou je suis, Je veux par- ler & ne

re, He- las!
He- las, voy- ez, He- las, voy- ez, He-
He- las, voy- ez, He- las,
las, He- las, voy- ez le
re, He- las, He- las, He-

ne puis un mot di-
mot di- re, & ne puis un mot di- re,
re, & ne puis un mot, un mot di- re,
& ne puis un mot di- re, He-
puis un mot di- re, & ne puis un mot di-

He- las, voy- ez le tour- ment ou je suis,
las, voy- ez le tour- ment ou je suis, Je
voy- ez le tour- ment ou je suis,
tour- ment ou je suis, Je veux par-
las, voy- ez, voy- ez le tour- ment ou je suis, Je

67 Nicolas, *Le coeur de vous* [C. Marot]

16
bel- le, je me re- ti- re, Car sans
me re- ti- re, Car sans a- voir au- tre con- ten- te-
bel- le, je me re- ti- re, Car sans
pour le mieux, bel- le, je me re- ti- re, Car sans a- voir,
pour le mieux, bel- le, je me re- ti- re, Car sans a-

34
pour- rois, ser- vir si lon- gue-
ne pour- rois, ser- vir si lon- gue-
ser- vir si lon- gue- ment, ser- vir si lon- gue-
vir, Je ne pour- rois ser- vir si lon- gue-
ser- vir si lon- gue- ment, ser- vir si lon- gue-

25
a- voir, au- tre con- ten- te- ment, Je ne
ment, au- tre con- ten- te- ment, Je
a- voir au- tre con- ten- te- ment, Je ne pour- rois
a- voir au- tre con- ten- te- ment, Je ne pour- rois ser-
voir, Je ne pour- rois

41
ment, Ve- nons au point, Ve- nons au
ment, Ve- nons au point, Ve- nons au
ment, Ve- nons au point, Ve- nons au point, Ve- nons
ment, Ve- nons au point, au point, Ve- nons au point, au
ment, Ve- nons au point, Ve- nons au point, Ve- nons au point,

49
point, au point qu'on n'o- se di-
point, au point qu'on n'o- se di- re,
au point qu'on n'o- se di- re, qu'on n'o- se
point qu'on n'o- se di- re, qu'on n'o- se di- re,
au point qu'on n'o- se di-

64
au point, au point qu'on n'o- se di-
nons au point, au point qu'on n'o- se di-
nons au point qu'on n'o- se di- re, qu'on n'o-
au point qu'on n'o- se di- re, qu'on n'o- se di-
point, au point qu'on n'o- se di-

56
re, Ve- nons au point, Ve- nons
Ve- nons au point, Ve-
di- re, Ve- nons au point, Ve- nons au point, Ve-
Ve- nons au point, Ve- nons au point, au point, Ve- nons au point,
re, Ve- nons au point, Ve- nons au point, Ve- nons au

71
re.
re, Ve- nons au point, au point qu'on n'o- se di- re.
se di- re.
re, Ve- nons au point qu'on n'o- se di- re.
re, Ve- nons au point qu'on n'o- se di- re.

68 Benedictus, *Si je me plein*

36
tort, Et sans de- port
si m'a le che- min tort, Et sans de- port, Et
port, si m'a le che- min tort, Et sans de- port m'a
tort, si m'a le che-min tort, Et, sans de- port, m'a os-
faux ra- port si m'a le che- min tort, Et sans de- port,

55
port, Et le vray port
port, Et le vray port, Et
le vray port, Et le vray port
port, Et le vray port
Et le vray port, Et le vray

46
m'a os- té le sup-
sans de- port, m'a os- té le sup-
os- té le sup- port, Et
té le sup- port, ma os- té le sup-
m'a os- té le sup- port,

62
de mon bien & ma vi-
le vray port de mon bien &
de mon bien & ma
de mon bien, & ma vi-
port de mon bien, &

69
e, & ma vi- e,
ma vi- e, de mon bien & ma
vi- e, Ou
e, & ma vi- e, Ou ma
ma vi- e, Ou ma vie

87
as- sou- vi- e,
toit as- sou- vi- e, De tous sou- las de joye & de
vie es- toit as- sou- vi- e,
vi- e, De tous sou- las, de joye & de
De tous sou- las, De tous sou- las de joye

78
Ou ma vie es- toit
vi- e, Ou ma vie es-
ma vie es- toit as- sou- vi- e, Ou ma
vie es- toit as- sou- vi- e, as- sou-
es- toit as- sou- vi- e,

97
De tous sou- las,
con- fort, De tous sou- las, de joye
De tous sou- las de joye &
con- fort, De tous sou- las,
& de con- fort, De tous sou- las,

106
de joye & de con- fort,
& de con- fort, Con- fort
de con- fort, Con- fort n'ay
de joye & de con- fort,
de joye & de con-

124
Con- fort n'ay plus si= non la du- re
fort n'ay plus, Con- fort n'ay plus si= non la du-
plus si= non la du- re mort,
Con- fort n'ay plus, Con- fort n'ay plus si= non la du- re
Con- fort n'ay plus, Con- fort n'ay

115
Con- fort n'ay plus,
n'ay plus, Con- fort n'ay plus, Con-
plus, Con- fort n'ay
Con- fort n'ay plus si= non la du- re mort,
fort, Con- fort n'ay plus si= non la du- re mort,

133
mort, Que j'ay- me
re mort, Que j'ay- me mieux que
si= non la du- re mort, Que j'ay- me mieux,
mort, Que j'ay- me mieux, Que j'ay- me mieux, que
plus si= non la du- re mort, Que j'ay- me

141
mieux que la do- len-
la do- len- te vi- e, que
Que j'ay- me mieux, que la
la do- len- te vi- e, que la do-
mieux, que la do- len- te vi- e,

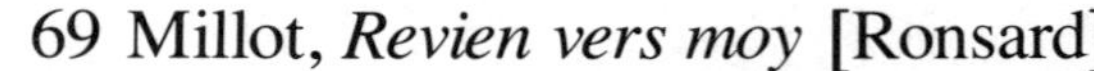

Re- vien vers moy, Re- vien
Re- vien vers moy,
Re- vien vers moy, Re-
Re- vien vers moy, Re- vien
Re- vien

148
te que vi- e.
la do- len- te vi- e.
do- len- te vi- e.
len- te vi-
que la do- len- te vi- e.

8
vers moy, Re- vien vers moy, qui suis tant
Re- vien vers moy, qui suis
vien vers moy, Re- vien vers moy, qui suis tant
vers moy, Re- vien vers moy, qui suis tant
vers moy, Re- vien vers moy,

16
de- so- lé- e, qui suis tant de- so- lé-
tant de- so- lé- e, qui suis tant de- so- lé- e, qui
de- so- lé- e, qui suis tant de- so-
de- so- lé- e, qui suis tant de- so- lé-
qui suis tant de- so- lé- e, qui

35
tu ver- ras, Et tu ver- ras,
tu ver- ras, Et tu ver- ras, L'en-nuy
ver- ras, Et tu ver- ras, L'en-nuy &
tu ver- ras, Et tu ver- ras, Et tu ver- ras, L'en- nuy,
Et tu ver- ras, Et tu ver- ras, L'en-

25
(sic)
e, qui suis tant de- so- lé- e, Et
suis tant de- so- lé- e, qui suis tant de- so- lé- e, Et
lé- e, qui suis tant de- so- lé- e, Et tu
e, qui suis tant de- so- lé- e, Et
suis tant de- so- lé- e, qui suis tant de- so- lé- e,

44
L'en- nuy & le tour- ment, & le tour-
& le tour- ment, L'en- nuy & le tour- ment, L'en-nuy & le tour-
le tour- ment, & le tour- ment, L'en-nuy & le tour-
L'en-nuy & le tour- ment, L'en- nuy, L'en-nuy & le tour- ment,
nuy & le tour- ment, L'en- nuy, L'en-nuy & le tour-

247

55
ment, L'en- nuy & le tour- ment,
ment, L'en- nuy & le tour- ment, Que j'ay
ment, L'en- nuy & le tour- ment, Que j'ay souf-
L'en- nuy & le tour- ment, Que j'ay
ment, L'en- nuy & le tour- ment, Que j'ay

74 (sic)
dant, Le tien re- tour, Le tien re- tour dont se- ray con- so-
tous- jours en at- ten- dant, Le tien re- tour, dont se- ray
jours en at- ten- dant, Le tien re- tour dont se- ray con-
tous- jours en at- ten- dant, Le tien re- tour dont se- ray con- so-
jours en at- ten- dant, Le tien re- tour,

64
Que j'ay souf- fert, tous- jours en at- ten-
souf- fert, Que j'ay souf- fert, tous- jours en at- ten- dant,
fert, Que j'ay souf- fert, tous- jours en at- ten- dant, tous-
souf- fert, tous- jours en at- ten- dant, tous- jours en at- ten- dant,
souf- fert tous- jours en at- ten- dant, tous-

83
lé- e, dont se- ray con- so- lé- e,
con- so- lé- e, con- so- lé- e, dont se- ray, dont se-
so- lé- e, dont se- ray con- so- lé- e, dont se- ray con-
lé- e, dont se- ray con- so- lé- e, dont se-
dont se- ray con- so- lé- e, dont se- ray

90
con- so- lé- e, Re- vien vers moy,
ray con- so- lé- e, Re- vien vers moy,
so- lé- e, Re- vien, Re- vien vers
ray con- so- lé- e, Re- vien vers moy,
con- so- lé- e, Re- vien,

Le ber- ger & la ber- ge- re, sont à
Le ber- ger & la ber- ge- re,
Le ber- ger & la ber- ge- re sont à l'om- bre d'un buis-
Le ber- ger &

99
Re- vien vers moy, Re- vien vers moy.
Re- vien vers moy, Re- vien vers moy.
moy, Re- vien, Re- vien vers moy.
Re- vien vers moy, Re- vien vers moy.
Re- vien vers moy, Re- vien vers moy.

7
l'om- bre d'un buis- son, sont à l'om- bre d'un buis-
sont à l'om- bre d'un buis- son,
son, sont à l'om- bre d'un buis- son, sont à
Le ber- ger &
la ber- ge- re sont à l'om- bre d'un buis- son,

13
son, sont à l'om- bre d'un buis- son,
sont à l'om- bre d'un buis- son, sont à l'om-
l'om- bre d'un buis- son, sont à l'om- bre d'un buis- son, sont à
la ber- ge- re, sont à l'om- bre d'un buis- son, sont à
sont à l'om- bre d'un buis- son,

28
sont si prés, Ilz sont si prés l'un de l'au- tre, Qu'à grand pei- ne
l'au- tre, Ilz sont si prés l'un de l'au-
Ilz sont si prés l'un de l'au- tre, Qu'à grand pei- ne les voit
Ilz sont si prés l'un de l'au- tre, l'un de l'au-
si prés l'un de l'au- tre, Qu'à grand

20
sont à l'om- bre d'un buis- son, Ilz
bre d'un buis- son, Ilz sont si prés l'un de
l'om- bre d'un buis- son, Ilz sont si prés l'un de l'au- tre,
l'om- bre d'un buis- son, sont à l'om- bre d'un buis-son,
sont à l'om- bre d'un buis- son, d'un buis- son, Ilz sont

34
les voit on, Qu'à grand pei- ne les voit on,
tre, Qu'à grand pei- ne les voit on, Qu'à grand pei-
on, Qu'à grand pei- ne les voit on, Qu'à grand pei- ne les voit
tre, Qu'à grand pei- ne les voit on, les voit on, Qu'à grand pei-
pei- ne les voit on, Qu'à grand pei- ne les voit on, les voit

250

40
Qu'à grand pei- ne les voit on, Qu'à grand pei- ne les voit
ne les voit on, Qu'à grand pei- ne les voit on, les
on, Qu'à grand pei- ne les voit on, Qu'à grand pei- ne les
ne les voit on, Qu'à grand pei- ne les voit on,
on, Qu'à grand pei-ne les voit on, Qu'à grand pei- ne

54
son mi- gnon, re- pre- nons no- tre a-
mi- gnon, re- pre- nons no- tre a- lei- ne,
gnon, re- pre- nons
pre- nons no- tre a- lei- ne,
re- pre- nons no- tre a- lei- ne, re- pre- nons no-

46
on, La da- me à dit à
voit on, La da- me à dit à son
voit on, La da- me à dit à son mi-
La da- me à dit à son mi- gnon, re-
les voit on,

62
lei- ne, re- pre- nons no- tre a- lei- ne, re- pre- nons
à son mi- gnon, re- pre-nons no- tre a- lei- ne, re- pre- nons, re-
no- tre a- lei- ne, re- pre- nons no- tre a- lei- ne,
re- pre- nons no- tre a- lei- ne,
tre a- lei- ne, re- pre-

70
no- tre a- lei- ne, Le loup, Le loup, Le
pre- nons no- tre a- lei- ne, Le loup, Le loup, Le
Le loup, Le loup, Le loup em-
re- pre- nons no- tre a- lei- ne, Le loup, Le loup,
nons no- tre a- lei- ne, Le loup, Le loup, Le

85
la lei- ne, Le loup,
vez, pour dieu sau- vez la lei- ne, Le loup,
sau- vez, pour dieu sau- vez la lei- ne, Le loup,
pa- gnon, pour dieu sau- vez la lei- ne, Le loup, Le
vez, pour dieu sau- vez la lei- ne, Le loup,

79
loup em- por- te mon mou- ton, mon com- pa- gnon, pour dieu, sau- vez
dieu, pour
loup em- por- te mon mou- ton, mon com- pa- gnon, pour dieu, sau-
por- te mon mou- ton, mon com- pa- gnon, pour dieu, pour dieu
Le loup, Le loup em- por- te mon mou- ton, mon com-
loup em- por- te mon mou- ton, mon com- pa- gnon, pour dieu, pour dieu sau-

92
Le loup em- por- te mon mou- ton, mon com- pa- gnon, pour dieu, pour dieu,
Le loup em- por- te, Le loup em- por- te,
Le loup em- por- te, Le loup em- por- te, pour
loup, Le loup, Le loup em- por- te mon mou-
Le loup em- por- te mon mou- ton, mon com- pa- gnon pour dieu

71 Lupi, *Au joly bois*

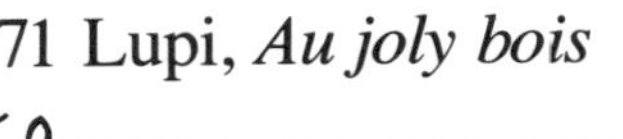

103

6

14
my je fuz trous- sé- e, De mon a- my je fuz trous- sé- e,
De mon a- my je fuz trous- sé-
mon a- my je fuz trous- sé-
De mon a- my je fuz trous- sé- e, De
De mon a- my fuz trous- sé- e, De mon a- my

32
a- voir re- gretz je n'ay cu- re,
D'en a- voir re- gretz
je n'ay
re- gretz je n'ay cu- re, je
D'en a- voir re- gretz je

23
De mon a- my je fuz trous- sé- e, D'en
e, fuz trous- sé- e,
e, D'en a- voir re- gretz
mon a- my je fuz trous- sé- e, D'en a- voir
fuz trous- sé- e, fus trous- sé- e,

39
D'en a- voir re- gretz je n'ay cu- re,
je n'ay cu- re,
cu- re,
n'ay cu- re, je n'ay cu- re, De
n'ay cu- re, D'en a- voir re- gretz je n'ay cu- re, De

48
De luy suis bien re- com- pen- sé- e,
De luy suis bien re- com- pen- sé- e,
luy suis bien re- com- pen- sé- e, De
luy suis bien re- com- pen- sé- e, De
luy suis bien, De luy suis bien re-

63
e, Car pour a- ba- tre la rou- sé- e,
la rou- sé- e, Car pour a- ba- tre
Car pour a- ba- tre la rou- sé- e, Car
sé- e, Car pour a- ba- tre la rou- sé- e,
ba- tre la rou- sé- e, Car pour a-

56
re- com- pen- sé- e, Car pour a- ba- tre la rou- sé-
Car pour a- ba- tre
luy suis bien re- com- pen- sé- e,
luy suis bien re- com- pen- sé- e, Car pour a- ba- tre la rou-
com- pen- sé- e, Car pour a-

68
En me fai- sant, le jo- ly som- bre
la rou- sé- e, En me fai- sant, le jo- ly som- bre
pour a- ba- tre la rou- sé- e, En me fai- sant le
En me fai- sant, le
ba- tre la rou- sé- e, En me fai- sant, le

74
saut, le jo- ly som- bre saut,
saut, le jo- ly som- bre saut,
jo- ly som- bre saut, le jo- ly som- bre saut, Il
jo- ly som- bre saut, le jo- ly som- bre saut, Il
jo- ly som- bre saut, le jo- ly som- bre saut, Il
85
a- bu- sé- e, Quant
e, Quant le bon
llard, Quant le bon
ne suis a- bu- sé- e, Quant le bon
point ne suis a- bu- sé- e, Quant le bon
79
Il est gai- llard, point ne suis
Il est gai- llard, point ne suis a- bu- sé-
est gai-
est gai- llard, point
est gai- llard, point ne suis a- bu- sé- e,
91
le bon vin point ne luy faut.
vin, point ne luy faut.
vin point ne luy faut.
vin point ne luy faut.
vin point ne luy faut.

72 Vuillard, *Sire don dieu*

257

25
tons,
Vou- lez vous que je vous di-
dent, quand ils gar- dent bre- bi- et- tes & mou- tons, Vou- lez vous que
ils gar- dent bre- bi- et- tes & mou- tons, Vou- lez vous que je
quand ils gar- dent bre- bi- et- tes & mou- tons,
gar- dent bre- bi- et- tes & mou- tons, Vou- lez vous que je vous di-

36
ge- re la chan- son, A un pe- tit feu d'es- pi- nes,
son, A un pe- tit feu d'es- pi- nes, La tres- bien chauf- foit son
pe- tit feu d'es- pi- nes, La tres- bien chauf- foit son fron,
son, A un pe- tit feu d'es- pi- nes,
A un pe- tit feu d'es- pi- nes, La tres- bien chauf- foit son fron,

31
e, Vou- lez vous que je vous di- e, De ber- ge- re la chan- son, De ber-
je vous di- e, De ber- ge- re la chan- son, la chan-
vous di- e, De ber- ge- re la chan- son, la chan- son, A un
Vou- lez vous que je vous di- e, De ber- ge- re la chan-
e, De ber- ge- re la chan- son,

41
La tres- bien chauf- foit son fron, Il à du poil sur la
fron, chauf- foit son fron, Il à du poil sur la
chauf- foit son fron, Il à du poil
La tres- bien chauf- foit son fron, Il à du poil sur la tes-
Il à du poil sur la tes- te l'or-

tes- te l'or- de bes- te, l'or- de bes- te, l'or- de bes- te,
tes- te l'or- de bes- te, l'or- de bes- te, l'or- de bes-
sur la tes- te l'or- de bes- te, l'or- de bes- te, La cho- se n'est
te l'or- de bes- te, l'or- de bes- te, l'or- de bes-
de bes- te, l'or- de bes- te, l'or- de bes- te, l'or- de bes- te, La

mon, Si- re don Dieu, tant ils sont ai- ses, Si- re don
mon, Si- re don Dieu, tant ils sont ai-
mon, Si- re don Dieu, Si- re don Dieu, Si- re don
Si- re don Dieu, tant ils sont ai- ses, Si- re
Si- re don Dieu, Si- re don

La cho- se n'est pas ho- nes- te, ce n'est mon, ce n'est
te, La cho- se n'est pas, La cho- se n'est pas ho- nes- te, ce n'est
pas hon- nes- te, La cho- se n'est pas ho- nes- te, ce n'est
te, La cho- se n'est pas hon- nes- te, ce n'est mon,
cho- se n'est pas hon- nes- te, ce n'est mon,

Dieu, tant ils sont ai- ses, Noz ber- ge- res,
ses, tant ils sont ai- se[s], Noz ber- ge- res, quand
Dieu, tant ils sont ai- ses, Noz ber- ge- res, Noz ber- ge-
don Dieu, tant ils sont ai- ses, Noz ber- ge-
Dieu, tant ils sont ai- ses, Noz ber- ge- res, Noz ber- ge-

quand ils gar- dent
ils gar- dent bre- bi- et- tes,
res, quand ils gar- dent bre- bi- et- tes & mou- tons, quand ils
res, quand ils gar- dent bre- bi- et- tes &
res, quand ils gar- dent bre- bi- et- tes & mou- tons,
bi- et- tes & mou-
mou- tons, quand ils gar- dent bre- bi-
mou- tons, quand
bi- et- tes & mou- tons, quand ils gar-
bre- bi- et- tes & mou- tons, quand ils gar- dent
bre- bi- et- tes & mou- tons, quand ils gar- dent bre-
quand ils gar- dent bre- bi- et- tes &
gar- dent bre- bi- et- tes &
mou- tons, bre-
quand ils gar- dent
tons.
et- tes & mou- tons.
ils gar- dent bre- bi- et- tes & mou- tons.
dent bre- bi- et- tes & mou- tons.
bre- bi- et- tes & mou- tons.

73 Arcadet, *Si la beauté de ma dame*

36
(sic)
se, Au Dieu d'a- mours ren-
ces- se, Au Dieu d'a- mours ren- droy' gra-
joy- e sans ces- se, Au Dieu d'a- mours, ren-
Au dieu d'a- mours ren- droye gra- ce im- mor- tel- le,
Au dieu d'a- mours ren-

53
gra- ce si lou- a- ble: Et l'ay- mer
de da- me si lou- a- ble, Et l'ay- mer d'a- mour tel- le, Et
da- me si lou- a- ble, Et l'ay- mer d'a- mour tel- le,
ble, Et l'ay- mer d'a- mour tel- le,
ble, Et l'ay- mer d'a- mour tel- le, Et l'ay- mer

44
droye gra- ce im- mor- tel- le, M'a- yant pour- veu de
c'im- mor- tel- le, M'a- yant pour- veu de da- me si lou- a- ble:
droye gra- ce im- mor- tel- le, M'a- yant pour- veu, de da- me, de
M'a- yant pour- veu de da- me si lou- a-
droye gra- ce im- mor- tel- le, M'a- yant pour- veu de da- me si lou- a-

62
d'a- mour tel- le, S'el- le n'es-
l'ay- mer d'a- mour tel- le, S'el- le n'es- toit mor- tel-
Et l'ay- mer d'a- mour tel- le, S'el- le n'es- toit mor- tel- le, S'el-
S'el- le n'es- toit mor- tel- le,
d'a- mour tel- le, S'el- le n'es-

toit mor- tel- le, S'el- le n'es-
le, S'el- le n'es- toit mor- tel- le, S'el- le n'es-
le n'es- toit mor- tel- le,
S'el- le n'es- toit mor- tel-
toit mor- tel- le, S'el- le n'es- toit mor- tel- le, S'el-

Su- sa- ne un jour, d'a- mour so- li- ci-
Su- sa- ne un jour, Su- sa- ne un jour d'a- mour so- li- ci-
Su- sa- ne un jour d'a- mour so- li- ci-
Su- sa- ne un jour d'a- mour so-
Su- sa- ne un jour d'a- mour so- li- ci-

toit mor- tel- le.
toit mor- tel- le, S'el- le n'es- toit mor- tel- le.
S'el- le n'es- toit mor- tel- le.
le.
le n'es- toit mor- tel- le, S'el- le n'es- toit mor- tel- le.

té- e, Su- sa- ne un jour d'a- mour so- li- ci- té-
té- e, Su- sa- ne un jour d'a- mour so- li- ci- té- e,
té- e, Su- sa- ne un jour, Su- sa- ne un jour, d'a- mour
li- ci- té- e, Su- sa- ne un jour, d'a- mour so-
té- e, d'a- mour so- li- ci- té- e, Su- sa- ne un jour d'a-

19
e, Par deux vie- llars, Par deux vie- llars con-
d'a- mour so- li- ci- té- e, Par deux vie- llars, Par deux vie- llars con-
so- li- ci- té- e, Par deux vie- llars, Par deux vie- llars con-
li- ci- té- e, Par deux vie- llars, Par deux vie- llars
mour so- li- ci- té- e, Par deux vie- llars, con-

37
des- con- for- té- e, Fut en son coeur tri- ste & des-
des- con- for- té- e, Fut en son coeur tris- te & des- con- for-
te & des- con- for- té- e, Fut en son coeur, Fut en son coeur,
te & des- con- for- té- e, Fut en son coeur,
des- con- for- té- e, tris- te & des- con- for- té- e, Fut en son

28
voi- tans sa beau- té, Fut en son coeur, tris- te &
voi- tans sa beau- té, Fut en son coeur, Fut en son coeur tris- te &
voi- tans sa beau- té, Fut en son coeur, Fut en son coeur tris-
con- voi- tans sa beau- té, Fut en son coeur tris-
voi- tans sa beau- té, Fut en son coeur tris- te &

47
con- for- té- e, Voy- ant l'ef- fort, Voy- ant l'ef-
té- e, tris- te & des- con- for- té- e, Voy- ant l'ef- fort, Voy- ant l'ef-
tris- te & des- con- for- té- e, Voy- ant l'ef- fort, Voy- ant l'ef-
tris- te & des- con- for- té- e, Voy- ant l'ef- fort, Voy- ant l'ef-
coeur tris- te & des- con- for- té- e, Voy- ant l'ef- fort,

57
fort fait à sa chas-te- té, El- le leur dit, El- le leur
fort fait à sa chas- te- té, El- le leur dit, El- le leur dit si
fort fait à sa chas- te- té, El- le leur dit, El- le
fort fait à sa chas-te-té, El- le leur dit,
fait à sa chas- te- té, El- le leur

78
mien, De ce cors mien, vous a- vez jou- is- san- ce, C'est fait
mien, De ce cors mien, vous a- vez jou- is- san- ce, C'est fait
mien, De ce cors mien vous a- vez jou- is- san- ce, C'est fait, C'est fait
mien vous a- vez jou- is- san- ce, C'est fait
De ce cors mien vous a- vez jou- is- san- ce, C'est fait

67
dit, si par des- loy- au- té, si par des- loy- au- té, De ce cors
par des- loy- au- té, si par des- loy- au- té, De ce cors
leur dit, si par des- loy- au- té, De ce cors mien, De ce cors
El- le leur dit si par des- loy- au- té, De ce cors mien, De ce cors
dit si par des- loy- au- té, De ce cors mien,

88
de moy, si je fay re- sis- ten- ce, Vous me fe- rez mou- rir en des-hon-
de moy, si je fay re- sis- ten- ce, Vous me fe- rez mou- rir en des-hon-
de moy, si je fay re- sis- ten- ce, Vous me fe- rez mou- rir,
de moy, si je fay re- sis- ten- ce, Vous me fe- rez mou- rir en des-hon-
de moy, si je fay re- sis- ten- ce, Vous me fe- rez mou- rir en des-hon-

100
neur, Vous me fe- rez mou- rir en des- hon- neur, Mais j'ay- me
neur, Vous me fe- rez mou- rir en des- hon-neur, Mais j'ay- me
Vous me fe- rez mou- rir en des- hon- neur, Mais j'ay- me mieux,
neur, Vous me fe- rez mou- rir en des- hon- neur, Mais j'ay- me
neur, Vous me fe- rez mou- rir, Mais j'ay- me mieux,

122
mieux pe- rir en in- no- cen- ce, Que d'of- fen-
rir en in- no- cen- ce, pe- rir en in- no- cen- ce,
j'ay- me mieux, pe- rir en in- no- cen- ce, Que d'of- fen-
Mais j'ay- me mieux, pe- rir en in- no- cen- ce,
cen- ce, Mais j'ay- me mieux pe- rir en in- no- cen- ce

111
mieux, pe- rir en in- no- cen- ce, Mais j'ay- me
mieux, Mais j'ay- me mieux pe- rir en in- no- cen- ce, Mais j'ay- me mieux pe-
Mais j'ay- me mieux pe- rir en in- no- cen- ce, Mais
mieux, Mais j'ay- me mieux pe- rir en in- no- cen- ce, Mais j'ay- me mieux,
Mais j'ay- me mieux pe- rir en in- no- cen- ce, pe- rir en in- no-

131
cer, Que d'of- fen- cer par pe- ché le Sei-
Que d'of- fen- cer, Que d'of- fen- cer par pe- ché le Sei-
cer, Que d'of- fen- cer par pe- ché le Sei-
Que d'of- fen- cer, Que d'of- fen- cer, Que
Que d'of- fen- cer,

75 Millot, *Si je trespasse* [Ronsard]

146 stave:

10 stave:

15
ma da- me, Je suis con-tent, Je suis con-tent, Je suis con-tent, Car je ne veux a-
da- me, Je suis con-tent, Je suis con-tent, Car je ne veux a-
bras, ma da- me, Je suis con-tent, Car je ne veux a-
da- me, Je suis con-tent, Je suis con-tent, Je suis con-tent, Car je ne veux a-
da- me, Je suis con-tent, Je suis con-tent, Car je ne veux a-

31
grand hon-neur au mon- de que me voir, En te bai-
voir, Plus grand hon-neur au mon- de que me voir, En te bai-
voir, Plus grand hon-neur au mon-de que me voir, En te bai-
voir, Plus grand hon- neur, Plus grand hon-neur au mon- de que me voir, En te bai-
voir, Plus grand hon-neur au mon- de que me voir,

25
voir, Plus grand hon- neur au mon-de que me voir, Plus
voir, Plus grand hon- neur au mon-de que me
voir, Plus grand hon- neur au mon-de que me voir, Plus grand hon- neur au mon-de que me
voir, Plus grand hon- neur au mon-de que me voir, Plus grand hon- neur au mon-de que me
voir, Plus grand hon- neur au mon-de que me

38
sant, dans ton sein ren- dre l'a- me, dans ton sein ren- dre
sant, En te bai- sant, dans ton sein ren- dre
sant, En te bai- sant dans ton sein ren- dre l'a- me, dans ton sein ren- dre
sant, En te bai- sant dans ton sein ren- dre l'a- me, dans ton sein,
En te bai- sant dans ton sein ren- dre l'a- me,

l'a- me, En te bai- sant, En te bai- sant, En te bai-
l'a- me, En te bai- sant, En te bai-
l'a- me, En te bai- sant, En te bai- sant, En te bai-
En te bai- sant, En te bai- sant,
En te bai- sant, En te bai-

El- le veut donc que d'el- le me con- ten- te, El-
El- le veut donc que
El- le veut donc que d'el- le me con- ten- te,
El- le veut donc que d'el- le me con-
El- le veut donc que d'el- le

sant dans ton sein ren- dre l'a- me, En me.
sant dans ton sein ren- dre l'a- me, En me.
sant dans ton sein ren- dre l'a- me, En me.
dans ton sein ren- dre l'a- me, En me.
sant dans ton sein ren- dre l'a- me, me.

le veut donc que d'el- le me con- ten- te, El- le veut donc que
d'el- le me con- ten- te, El le veut donc, El- le veut
El- le veut donc que d'el- le me con- ten- te, El-
ten- te, El- le veut donc que d'el- le me con- ten- te,
me con- ten- te, El- le veut donc que d'el- le me con-

10
d'el- le me con-ten- te, que d'el- le me con-ten- te, Et
donc que d'el- le me con- ten- te, me con- ten- te,
le veut donc que d'el- le me con-ten- te, me con- ten- te, Et
El- le veut donc que d'el- le me con-ten- te, Et
ten- te, El- le veut donc que d'el- le me con-ten- te,

26
cun al- le- ge- ment, Sans m'y don- ner au- cun al- le- ge-
ner au- cun al- le- ge- ment, Sans m'y don- ner au- cun al- le-
Sans m'y don- ner au- cun al- le- ge-
ner au- cun al- le- ge- ment, Sans m'y don- ner au- cun al- le- ge-
ner au- cun al- le- ge- ment, Sans m'y don- ner

16
que son bien & mon grand mal je sen- te, Sans m'y don- ner au-
Et que son bien & mon grand mal je sen- te, Sans m'y don-
que son bien, Et que son bien, & mon grand mal je sen- te,
que son bien, Et que son bien & mon grand mal je sen- te, Sans m'y don-
Et que son bien & mon grand mal je sen- te, Sans m'y don-

31
ment, Sans m'y don- ner, au- cun al- le- ge- ment, Et sans
ge- ment, Sans m'y don- ner au- cun al- le- ge- ment, Et sans es-
ment, Sans m'y don- ner au- cun al- le- ge- ment, Et sans es-
ment, Sans m'y don- ner, Sans m'y don- ner au- cun al- le- ge- ment,
au- cun al- le- ge- ment, Et sans es-

38
es- poir, Et sans es- poir d'en a- voir trait- te- ment,
poir, Et sans es- poir d'en a- voir trait- te- ment, For- ce se-
poir d'en a- voir trai- te- ment, d'en a- voir trai- te- ment,For- ce
Et sans es- poir, d'en a- voir trait- te- ment,For- ce se-
poir, Et sans es- poir d'en a- voir trai- te- ment,For- ce se-

53
te, For- ce se- ra,
te, que d'el- le je m'ab- sen- te, For- ce se-
te, que d'el le je m'ab- sen- te, For- ce se- ra que d'el-
te, que d'el- le je m'ab- sen- te, For- ce se-
que d'el- le je m'ab- sen- te, For- ce se-

46
For- ce se- ra que d'el- le je m'ab- sen- te, je m'ab- sen-
ra que d'el- le je m'ab- sen- te, que d'el- le je m'ab- sen-
se- ra, For- ce se- ra que d'el- le je m'ab- sen-
ra, For- ce se- ra que d'el- le je m'ab- sen-
ra,

59
For- ce se- ra que d'el- le je m'ab-
ra, For- ce se- ra que d'el- le
le je m'ab- sen- te, je m'ab- sen- te, For- ce se-
ra que d'el- le je m'ab- sen-

77 Millot, *Contentement combien*

sen- te, For- ce se- ra que d'el- le je m'ab- sen-
je m'ab- sen- te, For- ce se- ra que d'el- le je m'ab- sen- te,
ra que d'el- le je m'ab-sen- te, For- ce se- ra que d'el- le je m'ab-
que d'el- le je m'ab- sen- te, For- ce se- ra,
te, je m'ab- sen- te, For- ce se-

Con- ten- te- ment com- bien,
Con- ten- te- ment com- bien que
Con- ten- te- ment, com- bien que
Con- ten- te- ment, com- bien que soit grand'
Con- ten- te- ment com- bien que

te, que d'el- le je m'ab- sen- te.
For- ce se- ra que d'el- le je m'ab- sen- te.
sen- te, For- ce se- ra que d'el- le je m'ab- sen- te.
For- ce se- ra que d'el- le je m'ab- sen- te.
ra que d'el- le je m'ab- sen- te.

com- bien que soit grand' cho- se, com- bien que soit grand' cho-
soit grand' cho- se, com- bien, com- bien que soit grand cho- se,
soit grand' cho- se, com- bien que soit grand' cho- se, com-
cho- se, com- bien que soit grand' cho- se, com- bien que
soit grand' cho- se, com- bien que soit

se, Ne du-re pas la lon-gueur d'un seul jour, la
com-bien que soit grand cho-se, Ne du-re
bien que soit grand cho-se, Ne du-re pas la lon-gueur d'un seul
soit grand cho-se, Ne du-re pas la lon-gueur
grand cho-se, Ne du-re pas la lon-gueur d'un seul

pas la lon-gueur, Ne du-re pas la lon-gueur d'un seul jour, Rai-son, res-
lon-gueur d'un seul jour, Ne du-re pas la lon-gueur d'un seul jour, Rai-
du-re pas la lon-gueur d'un seul jour, la lon-gueur d'un seul jour, Rai-son, res-
jour, Ne du-re pas la lon-gueur d'un seul jour, Rai-son, res-
du-re pas, Ne du-re pas la lon-gueur d'un seul jour,

lon-gueur d'un seul jour, Ne du-re pas, Ne du-re
pas la lon-gueur d'un seul jour, Ne du-re pas, Ne du-re pas la
jour, Ne du-re pas la lon- gueur d'un seul jour, Ne
d'un seul jour, Ne du-re pas la lon-gueur d'un seul
jour, Ne du-re pas la lon-gueur d'un seul jour, Ne

sort, Rai-son, res-sort, l'ins-sa-ti-a-ble a-mour, l'in-sa-ti-a-ble a-
son, res-sort, l'ins-sa-ti-a-ble a-mour, l'in-sa-ti-a-ble a-
sort, Rai-son, res-sort, l'ins-sa-ti-a-ble a-mour, l'in-sa-ti-
sort, Rai-son, res-sort, l'ins-sa-ti-a-ble a-
Rai-son, res-sort, l'ins-sa-ti-a-ble a-mour,

35
mour, l'ins- sa- ti- a- ble a- mour, l'ins- sa- ti- a- ble a-
mour, l'ins- sa- ti- a- ble a- mour, l'ins- sa- ti- a- ble a-
a- ble a- mour, l'ins- sa- ti- a- ble a-
mour, l'ins- sa- ti- a- ble a- mour,
l'ins- sa- ti- a- ble a- mour, l'ins- sa- ti- a- ble a-

45
ller un coeur quand il re- po- se,
ller un coeur quand il re- po- se, Pour res- vei-
ller un coeur quand il re- po- se, Pour res- vei-
un coeur, quand il re- po- se,
res- vei- ller un coeur quand il re- po- se, Pour

40
mour, Pour res- vei- ller un coeur quand il re- po- se, Pour res- vei-
mour, Pour res- vei- ller un coeur quand il re- po- se, Pour res- vei-
mour, Pour res- vei- ller un coeur quand il re- po- se, Pour res- vei- ller, Pour res- vei-
Pour res- vei- ller un coeur quand il re- po- se, Pour res- vei- ller
mour, Pour res- vei- ller, Pour

50
Pour res- vei- ller un coeur quand il re- po- se.
ller, Pour res- vei- ller un coeur quand il re- po- se, quand il re- po- se.
ller un coeur quand il re- po- se, un coeur quand il re- po- se.
Pour res- vei- ller un coeur quand il re- po- se.
res- vei- ller, Pour res- vei- ller un coeur quand il re- po- se.

Sur la rou- sée m'y faut al- ler la ma- ti- né-
Sur la rou- sée m'y faut al- ler,
Sur la rou- sée m'y faut al-

15
sée m'y faut al- ler la ma- ti- né- e,
m'y faut al- ler la ma- ti- né- e, la ma- ti- né- e, Pour
ler la ma- ti- né- e, la ma- ti- né- e, Pour
Sur la rou- sée m'y faut al- ler la ma- ti- né- e,
e, la ma- ti- né- e, la ma- ti- né- e,

8
e, la ma- ti- né- e, la ma- ti- né- e, Sur la rou-
la ma- ti- né- e, la ma- ti- né- e, Sur la rou- sée
ler, la ma- ti- né- e, Sur la rou- sée m'y faut al-
Sur la rou- sée m'y faut al- ler, la ma- ti- né- e,

22
Pour le Ros- si- gnol es- cou- ter soubz la ra- mé- e, soubz la ra-
le Ros- si- gnol es- cou- ter, soubz la ra- mé- e, soubz
le Ros- si- gnol es- cou- ter, soubz la
Pour le Ros- si- gnol es- cou- ter soubz la ra- mé-
Pour le Ros- si- gnol es- cou- ter soubz la ra-

28
mé- e, soubz la ra- mé- e, soubz la ra- mé-
la ra- mé- e, soubz la ra- mé- e, soubz la ra- mé- e, soubz la
ra- mé- e, soubz la ra- mé- e, soubz la ra- mé- e, ra-
e, soubz la ra- mé- e, soubz la ra- mé- e, ra-
mé- e, soubz la ra- mé- e, soubz la ra-

42
man- dant, En luy de- man- dant, de- man- dant, En luy de- man-dant par es- bas
les bras, En luy de- man- dant par es- bas, par es-
par es- bas, En luy de- man-dant par es- bas, par es- bas,
luy de- man- dant par es- bas, En luy de- man-dant par es- bas u-
man- dant par es- bas, En luy de- man-dant par es- bas,

34
e, Te- nant sa da- me soubz les bras, En luy de-
ra- mé- e, Te- nant sa da- me, soubz
mé- e, Te- nant sa da- me soubz les bras, En luy de- man- dant
mé- e, Te- nant sa da- me soubz les bras, En
mé- e, Te- nant sa da- me soubz les bras, En luy de-

49
u- ne a- col- lé- e, u- ne a- col- lé- e,
bas, u- ne a- col- lé- e, u- ne a- col- lé- e, u-
u- ne a- col- lé- e, u- ne a- col- lé- e, u- ne a- col-
ne a- col- lé- e, u- ne a- col- lé- e, u- ne a- col-
u- ne a- col- lé- e, u- ne a- col- lé- e, u-

54
u- ne a- col- lé- e, Et puis la ren-ver- ser en bas, Et puis la
ne a- col- lé- e, Et puis la ren-ver- ser en bas, Et
e, u- ne a- col- lé- e, Et puis la ren-ver- ser en bas, Et puis la
lé- e, Et puis la ren-ver- ser en bas, Et
ne a- col- lé- e, Et puis la ren-ver- ser en bas,

67
Et puis la ren-ver- ser en bas, Com- me a-mou- reux font par es-
Et puis la ren-ver- ser en bas, Com- me a-mou- reux font par es-
ren- ver- ser en bas, Com- me a-mou-reux font par es- bas,
puis la ren- ver- ser en bas, Com- me a- mou- reux font par es-
puis la ren-ver- ser en bas, Com- me a- mou- reux font par es-

61
ren- ver- ser en bas, Com- me a-mou-reux font par es- bas, font par es- bas,
puis la ren- ver- ser en bas, Com- me a-mou-reux font par es- bas,
ren- ver- ser en bas, Com- me a-mou-reux font par es- bas, font par es- bas, Et puis la
puis la ren- ver- ser en bas, Com- me a-mou- reux font par es- bas, Et
Et

72
bas, font par es- bas, Sur la rou- sé-
bas, font par es- bas, Sur la rou- sé-
font par es- bas, Sur la rou- sé- e,
bas, font par es- bas, Sur
bas, font par es- bas, Sur la rou- sé- e,

79
e, Sur la rou- sé- e, Sur
e, Sur la rou- sé- e, Sur la rou- sé-
Sur la rou- sé- e, Sur la rou- sé- e, Sur la rou- sé-
la rou- sé- e, Sur la rou- sé- e, Sur la rou- sé-
Sur la rou- sé- e, Sur la rou- sé-

N'a vous point veu mal
N'a vous point veu mal as- se-
N'a vous point veu mal as- se- né- e,
N'a vous point
N'a vous point veu mal as- se- né- e,

84
la rou- sé- e, Sur la rou- sé- e, Et e.
e, Sur la rou- sé- e, Sur la rou- sé- e, e.
e, Sur la rou- sé- e, Sur la rou- sé- e, [Et] e.
e, Sur la rou- sé- e, [Et] e.
e, Sur la rou- sé- e, e.

8
as- se- né- e, Cel- le de
né- e, Cel- le de qui on
Cel- le de qui on par- le tant,
veu mal as- se- né- e, Cel- le de qui on par- le
Cel- le de qui on par- le tant,

16
qui on par- le tant, Cel- le de qui on par- le
par- le tant, Cel- le de qui on par- le tant,
Cel- le de qui on par- le tant,
tant, Cel- le de qui on par- le tant,
Cel- le de qui on par- le tant, on par- le

32
en- voy- é- e, Gar- der les
é- e, Gar- der les bre- biet-
Gar- der les bre- biet- tes aux chams,
l'a- voit en- voy- é- e, Gar- der les bre- biet- tes aux
Gar- der les bre- biet- tes aux chams,

24
tant, Sa me- re l'a- voit
Sa me- re l'a- voit en- voy-
Sa me- re l'a- voit en- voy- é- e,
Sa me- re l'a- voit en- voy- é- e, Sa me- re
tant, Sa me- re l'a- voit en- voy- é- e,

40
bre- biet- tes aux chams, Et son a- my qui va de-
tes aux chams, Gar- der les bre- biet- tes aux chams, Et son a- my qui va de- vant
Gar- der les bre- biet- tes aux chams, Et son a- my qui va de-
chams, Gar- der les bre- biet- tes aux chams, Et son a- my, Et
Et son a- my qui va de- vant,

50
vant luy de- man- dant,
luy de- man- dant, Et son a- my qui va de- vant, luy de- man-
vant, luy de- man- dant, luy de- man- dant,
son a- my qui va de- vant, Et son a- my qui va de- vant luy
Et son a- my qui va de- vant luy

70
Nen- ny, dit el- le, mon a- my,
mon as- so- té- e, Nen- ny, dit el- le, mon a- my,
Nen- ny, dit
vous mon as- so- té- e,

60
Se- rez vous mon as- so- té- e,
dant, Se- rez vous mon as- so- té- e, Se- rez vous
Se- rez vous mon as- so- té- e,
de- man- dant, Se- rez
de- man- dant, Se- rez vous mon as- so- té- e,

79
Je n'o- se- roye en
Nen- ny, dit el- le, mon a- my, Je n'o- se- roye en bon-
el- le, mon a- my, Je n'o- se- roye en
en bon- ne foy,
Nen- ny, dit el- le, mon a- my, Je n'o- se- roye en bon- ne

280

86
bon- ne foy, en bon- ne
ne foy, Je n'o- se- roye en
bon- ne foy, en bon- ne foy,
Je n'o- se- roye en bon- ne foy,
foy, en

99
moy sur la rou- sé- e,
e, Mais frin- gués moy sur la rou- sé-
e, Mais frin- gués moy sur la rou-
e, Mais frin- gués moy sur la rou- sé-
e, Mais frin- gués moy sur la rou-

92
foy, Mais frin- gués
bon- ne foy, Mais frin- gués moy sur la rou- sé-
Mais frin- gués moy sur la rou- sé-
en bon- ne foy, Mais frin- gués moy sur la rou- sé-
bon- ne foy, Mais frin- gués moy sur la rou- sé-

106
Mais frin- gués moy sur la rou- sé- e.
e.
sé- e, Sur la rou- sé- e.
e.
sé- e, sur la rou- sé- e.

80 LeJeune, *Rossignol, mon mignon* [Ronsard]

a tou gré vo-le-tant, a tou gré vo-lé, vo-le-
gré vo-le, vo-le, vo-le-tant, Et
gré vo-le-tant, a tou gré vo-le-tant,
gré vo-le-tant, tou gré vo-le-tant, vo-le, vo-le, vo-le-
a tou gré vo-le-tant, a tou gré vo-le, vo-le-

de moy qui vay chan-tant, Cel-le qui faut tous-
chan-tant, Cel-le qui faut tous-jours que
vy-de moy qui vay chan-tant, Cel-le qui
à l'en-vy-de moy qui vay chan-tant, Cel-le qui faut tous-jours que
vay chan-tant, Cel-le qui faut tous-jours, qui

tant, Et chan-tez à l'en-vy
chan-tez à l'en-vy, chan-tez à l'en-vy de moy qui vay
Et chan-tez à l'en-vy, Et chan-tez à l'en-
tant, Et chan-tez à l'en-vy, Et chan-tez
tant, Et chan-tez à l'en-vy-de moy qui

jours que dans la bou-che j'ay-e,
dans la bou-che j'ay-e, dans la bou-che j'ay-e,
faut tous-jours que dans la bou-che j'ay-e,
dans la bou-che j'ay-e, Nous sou-pi-rons tous
faut tous-jours que dans la bou-che j'ay-e, Nous sou-pi-

46
Nous sou- pi- rons tous deux,
Nous sou- pi- rons tous deux, ta dou- ce
Nous sou- pi- rons tous deux, ta dou- ce
deux, Nous sou- pi- rons tous deux,
rons tous deux, ta dou- ce

62
d'u- ne qui t'ay- me tant, Et moy tris- te je vay, Et
d'u- ne qui t'ay- me, qui t'ay- me tant, Et moy tris- te je vay, Et
ne qui t'ay- me tant, d'u- ne qui t'ay- me tant, Et moy tris- te, Et moy tris-
ne qui t'ay- me tant, d'u- ne qui t'ay- me tant, Et moy tris- te je vay, Et
ne qui t'ay- me tant, Et moy tris- te je vay, Et moy

53
ta dou- ce voix s'es- say- e, A son- ner l'a- mi- tié,
voix s'es- say- e, ta dou- ce voix s'es- say- e, A son- ner, A son- ner l'a- mi- tié,
voix s'es- say- e, ta dou- ce voix s'es- say- e, A son- ner l'a- mi- tié d'u-
ta dou- ce voix s'es- say- e, A son- ner l'a- mi- tié d'u-
voix s'es- say- e, A son- ner l'a- mi- tié d'u-

71
moy tris- te je vay la beau- té re- gre- tant, la
moy tris- te je vay la beau- té re- gre-
te je vay, la beau- té re- gre- tant, la beau- té
moy tris- te je vay, la beau- té re-
tris- te je vay la beau- té re- gre- tant,

80
beau- té re- gre- tant, Qui m'a fait dans le
tant, Qui m'a fait, Qui m'a fait dans le coeur, u- ne
re- gre- tant, Qui m'a fait dans le coeur,
gre- tant, Qui m'a fait dans le coeur u-
Qui m'a fait dans le coeur u- ne si ai- gre play- e,

97
Qui m'a fait dans le coeur u- ne si ai- gre play-
e, Qui m'a fait dans le coeur u- ne si ai- gre play-
e, Qui m'a fait dans le coeur u- ne si ai- gre play-
coeur u- ne si ai- gre play- e, si ai- gre play-
m'a fait dans le coeur u- ne si ai- gre play-

89
coeur u- ne si ai- gre play- e, u- ne si ai- gre play- e,
si ai- gre play- e, u- ne si ai- gre play-
Qui m'a fait dans le coeur, u- ne si ai- gre play-
ne si ai- gre play- e, Qui m'a fait dans le
Qui

105
e. Tou- te= fois Ros- si- gnol, Tou- te= fois
e. Tou- te- fois Ros- si- gnol, Ros- si- gnol, Tou-
e. Tou- te- fois Ros- si- gnol, Tou- te- fois Ros- si- gnol, Tou-
e. Tou- te- fois Ros- si- gnol,
e. Tou- te- fois Ros- si- gnol, Tou-

111
Ros- si- gnol, Tou- te= fois Ros- si- gnol, nous di-
te- fois Ros- si- gnol, nous di- fe- rons, nous dif-
te- fois Ros- si- gnol, nous di- fe- rons, nous dif-
Tou- te- fois Ros- si- gnol, nous dif- fe- rons
te- fois Ros- si- gnol, nous dif- fe- rons

125
mé, & je ne le suis point, & je ne
le suis point, & je ne le suis point,
je ne le suis point, & je ne le suis, &
mé, & je ne le suis point, & je ne
& je ne le suis point, & je ne le suis point, &

117
fe- rons d'un point, C'est que tu es ay- mé, c'est que tu es ay-
fe- rons d'un point, C'est que tu es ay- mé & je ne
fe- rons d'un point, C'est que tu es ay- mé &
d'un point, C'est que tu es ay- mé, C'est que tu es ay-
d'un point, C'est que tu es ay- mé, tu es ay- mé

130
le suis point, & je ne le suis point, Bien que tous deux ay-
& je ne le suis point, je ne le suis point, Bien que tous deux ay-
je ne le suis point, Bien que tous deux ay-
le suis point, & je ne le suis point, Bien que tous deux ay-
je ne le suis point, Bien que tous deux ay-

ons les Mu- si- ques pa- rei- lles, les Mu- si- ques pa- rei-
ons les Mu- si- ques pa- rei- lles, les Mu- si- ques pa- rei-
ons, les Mu- si- ques pa- rei-
ons les Mu- si- ques pa- rei- lles, les Mu- si- ques pa- rei-
ons les Mu- si- ques pa- rei- lles,

Mais la mien- ne qui prend, Mais la mien- ne qui prend
tes sons, Mais la mien- ne qui prend à des- pit, qui
la mien- ne qui prend, Mais la mien- ne qui prend, qui prend à
Mais la mien- ne qui prend, Mais la mien- ne qui prend,
la mien- ne qui prend, Mais la mien- ne qui prend à des- pit mes

lles, Car tu fles- chis ta voix au doux bruit de tes sons, au doux bruit de tes sons,
lles, Car tu fles- chis ta voix au doux bruit de tes sons, au doux bruit de
lles, Car tu fles- chis ta voix au doux bruit de tes sons, au doux bruit de tes sons, Mais
lles, Car tu fles- chis ta voix au doux bruit de tes sons, au doux bruit de tes sons,
Car tu fles- chis ta voix au doux bruit de tes sons, Mais

à des- pit mes chan- sons, Pour ne les es- cou- ter se
prend à des- pit mes chan- sons, Pour
des- pit mes chan- sons, à des- pit mes chan- sons, Pour ne les é- cou-
à des- pit mes chan- sons, Pour ne les é- cou-
chan- sons, à des- pit mes chan- sons,

168
bou- che les o- rei- lles, Pour ne les es- cou- ter se
ne les é- cou- ter se bou-che les o- rei- lles, Pour ne les
ter, Pour ne les é- cou- ter se bou- che les o- rei-
ter se bou- che les o- rei- lles, Pour ne les é- cou-
Pour ne les es- cou- ter se bou- che les o-

178
Pour ne les es- cou- ter, Pour ne les es- cou-
che les o- rei- lles, se
lles, Pour ne les é- cou- ter, Pour ne les é- cou- ter
ne les é- cou- ter se bou- che les o- rei- lles,
les o- rei- lles, Pour ne les é- cou- ter se

173
bou- che les o- rei- lles, Pour ne les es- cou- ter,
é- cou- ter se bou- che les o- rei- lles, se bou-
lles, Pour ne les é- cou- ter se bou- che les o- rei-
ter, Pour ne les é- cou- ter, Pour
rei- lles, Pour ne les es- cou- ter se bou- che

182
ter, se bou- che les o- rei- lles.
bou- che les o- rei- lles.
se bou- che les o- rei- lles.
se bou- che les o- rei- lles.
bou- che les o- rei- lles.

Le Ros- si- gnol sau- va- ge chan- ter jé
Le Ros- si- gnol sau- va- ge chan- ter jé l'oy tous- jours, Le Ros-
Le Ros- si- gnol sau-

ge chan- ter je l'oy tous- jours, chan- ter je l'oy tous- jours, Dans
Ros- si- gnol sau- va- ge, chan- ter je l'oy tous- jours, chan- ter je l'oy tous-
gnol sau- va- ge, Le Ros- si- gnol sau- va- ge chan- ter je l'oy tous- jours,
Le Ros- si- gnol sau- va- ge chan- ter je l'oy tous- jours, Dans un
gnol sau- va- ge chan- ter jé l'oy tous- jours, chan- ter je l'oy tous- jours, Dans

l'oy tous- jours, Le Ros- si- gnol sau- va- ge, Le Ros- si- gnol sau- va-
si- gnol sau- va- ge chan- ter jé l'oy tous- jours, Le
Le Ros- si- gnol sau- va- ge, chan- ter jé l'oy tous- jours, Le Ros- si-
va- ge chan- ter jé l'oy tous- jours, chan- ter je l'oy tous- jours, Le Ros- si- gnol,
Le Ros- si- gnol sau- va- ge, Le Ros- si-

un jo- ly bo- ca- ge, Dans un jo- ly bo- ca-
jours, Dans un jo- ly bo- ca- ge trai- tant de noz a-
Dans un jo- ly bo- ca- ge trai- tant de noz a- mours, Dans
jo- ly bo- ca- ge, Dans un jo- ly bo- ca- ge, trai- tant,
un jo- ly bo- ca- ge,

24
ge, trai-tant de noz a- mours, Dans un jo- ly bo-ca- ge, Dans
mours, Dans un jo- ly bo- ca- ge trai-tant de noz a-
un jo-ly bo- ca- ge trai-tant de noz a- mours, trai- tant de noz a-
Dans un jo- ly bo- ca- ge, trai- tant de noz
Dans un jo- ly bo-ca-

35
noz a- mours, trai- tant de noz a- mours, Et que dit ce
trai- tant de noz a- mours, trai- tant de noz a- mours, Et que dit ce beau mi-
noz a- mours, trai- tant de noz a- mours, Et que dit ce
tant de noz a- mours, trai- tant de noz a- mours, Et que dit ce
tant de noz a- mours, trai- tant de noz a- mours,

29
un jo- ly bo- ca- ge trai-tant de noz a- mours, trai- tant de
mours, Dans un jo- ly bo- ca- ge, trai-tant de noz a- mours,
mours, de noz a- mours, Dans un jo- ly bo- ca- ge trai- tant de
a- mours, Dans un jo- ly bo- ca- ge, Dans un jo- ly bo- ca- ge trai-
ge, Dans un jo- ly bo- ca- ge trai-tant de noz a- mours, trai-

42
beau mi- gnon, Il me dit, bon com-pa- gnon, Il me dit, Il me
gnon, ce beau mi- gnon, Et que dit ce beau mi- gnon, Il me dit,
beau mi- gnon, Et que dit ce beau mi- gnon, Il me dit,
beau mi- gnon, Il me dit, Il me dit, Il me dit, bon
Et que dit ce beau mi- gnon, Il me dit, Il me

47
dit, bon com- pa- gnon, Jet- te deux trais de tes yeux, Jet- te deux trais
Il me dit, bon com- pa- gnon, Jet- te deux trais de tes yeux, Jet- te deux trais
Il me dit, bon com- pa- gnon, Jet- te deux trais de tes yeux, Jet- te deux
com- pa- gnon, bon com- pa- gnon, Jet- te deux trais
dit, bon com- pa- gnon, bon com- pa- gnon, Jet- te deux trais de tes yeux,

62
A cel- le qu'ay- me le mieux, A cel- le qu'ay- me le mieux,
me le mieux, A cel- le qu'ay- me le mieux, Jet- te
qu'ay- me le mieux, A cel- le qu'ay- me le mieux,
me le mieux, A cel- le qu'ay- me le mieux, A cel- le qu'ay-me le
qu'ay- me le mieux, A cel- le qu'ay- me le mieux,

54
de tes yeux, Jet- te deux trais de tes yeux,
de tes yeux, Jet- te deux trais de tes yeux, A cel- le qu'ay-
trais de tes yeux, Jet- te deux trais de tes yeux, A cel- le
de tes yeux, Jet- te deux trais de tes yeux, A cel- le qu'ay-
Jet- te deux trais de tes yeux, A cel- le

68
Jet- te deux trais de tes yeux, A cel- le qu'ay- me le
deux trais de tes yeux, Jet- te deux trais de tes yeux, A cel-
Jet- te deux trais de tes yeux, A cel- le qu'ay- me le mieux,
mieux, Jet- te deux trais de tes yeux, A cel- le qu'ay-
Jet- te deux trais de tes yeux, A cel- le qu'ay- me le

82 Vuildre, *Un jeune moyne*

tré la non-net-te au cors gent, Se mit
da me bai-ser & ac-col-ler, En no
teurs sont de-ceus & gab-bez, En lieu
la non-net-te au | cors gent, Se mit à luy
bai-ser & ac-col-ler, En no-tre re-
sont de-ceus & gab-bez, En lieu de bien
gent, la non-net-te au cors gent, Se mit à luy de-man-der, S'el-le
rer, bai-ser & ac-col-ler, En no-tre re-li-gi-on, Brin-ba-
bez, sont de-ceus & gab-bez, En lieu de bien en-ton-ner, Vous fai-
non-net-te au cors gent, Se mit à luy de-man-der, S'el-le vou-loit brin-ba-
ser & ac-col-ler, En no-tre re-li-gi-on, Brin-ba-ler nous ap-pe-
de-ceus & gab-bez, En lieu de bien en-ton-ner, Vous fai-tes le lit bran-
gent, la non-net-te au cors gent, Se mit à luy de-man-der,
ler, bai-ser & ac-col-ler, En no-tre re-li-gi-on,
bez, sont de-ceus & gab-bez, En lieu de bien en-ton-ner,

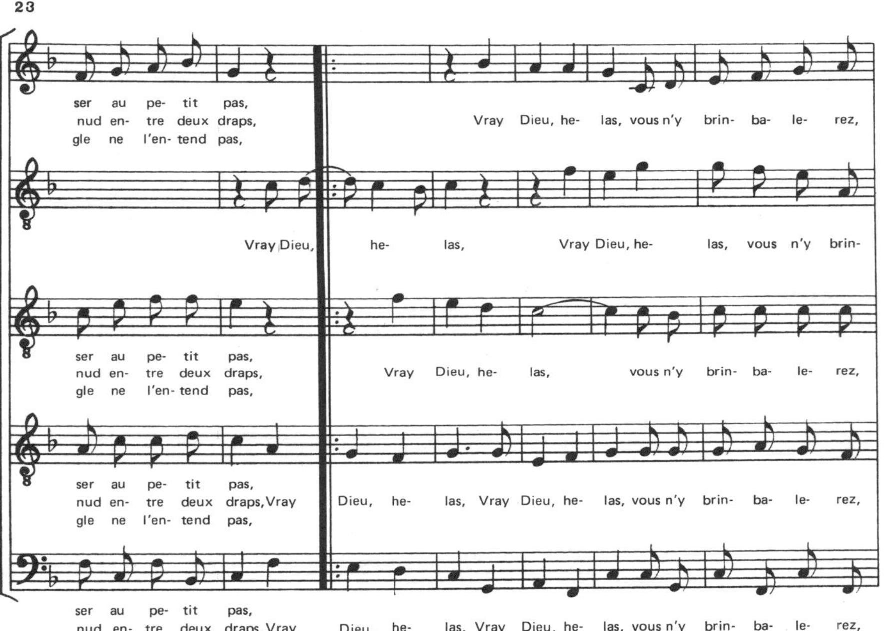

ser au pe-tit pas, Vray Dieu, he-las, vous n'y brin-ba-le-rez,
nud en-tre deux draps,
gle ne l'en-tend pas,
Vray Dieu, he-las, Vray Dieu, he-las, vous n'y brin-
ser au pe-tit pas, Vray Dieu, he-las, vous n'y brin-ba-le-rez,
nud en-tre deux draps,
gle ne l'en-tend pas,
ser au pe-tit pas, Vray Dieu, he-las, Vray Dieu, he-las, vous n'y brin-ba-le-rez,
nud en-tre deux draps, Vray
gle ne l'en-tend pas,
ser au pe-tit pas, Vray Dieu, he-las, Vray Dieu, he-las, vous n'y brin-ba-le-rez,

à luy de-man-der, S'el-le vou-loit brin-ba-ler, Ou dan-
tre re-li-gi-on, Brin-ba-ler nous ap-pe-lons, Nud à
de bien en-ton-ner, Vous fai-tes le lit bran-ler, La rei-
de-man-der, S'el-le vou-loit brin-ba-ler, Ou dan-ser au pe-tit pas,
li-gi-on, Brin-ba-ler nous ap-pe-lons, Nud à nud en-tre deux draps,
en-ton-ner, Vous fai-tes le lit bran-ler, La rei-gle ne l'en-tend pas,
vou-loit brin-ba-ler, S'el-le vou-loit brin-ba-ler, Ou dan-ser au pe-tit pas, Ou dan-
ler nous ap-pe-lons, Brin-ba-ler nous ap-pe-lons, Nud à nud en-tre deux draps, Nud à
tes le lit bran-ler, Vous fai-tes le lit bran-ler, La rei-gle ne l'en-tend pas, La rei-
ler, S'el-le vou-loit brin-ba-ler, Ou dan-ser au pe-tit pas, Ou dan-
lons, Brin-ba-ler nous ap-pe-lons, Nud à nud en-tre deux draps, Nud à
ler, Vous fai-tes le lit bran-ler, La rei-gle ne l'en-tend pas, La rei-
S'el-le vou-loit brin-ba-ler, Ou dan-ser au pe-tit pas, Ou dan-
Brin-ba-ler nous ap-pe-lons, Nud à nud en-tre deux draps, Nud à
Vous fai-tes le lit bran-ler, La rei-gle ne l'en-tend pas, La rei-

moy-ne, Vray Dieu, he-las, vous n'y brin-ba-le-rez pas, pas.
ba-le-rez, moy-ne, Vray Dieu, he-las, vous n'y brin-ba-le-rez pas, Vray Dieu, pas.
moy-ne, Vray Dieu, he-las, vous n'y brin-ba-le-rez pas, pas.
moy-ne, Vray Dieu, he-las, vous n'y brin-ba-le-rez pas, Vray pas.
moy-ne, Vray Dieu, he-las, vous n'y brin-ba-le-rez pas, Vray pas.

He- las, ma da- me, fai- tes luy quel- que bien, fai- tes luy quel- que
He- las, ma da- me, fai- tes luy quel- que bien, fai-
He- las, ma da- me, fai-

13
qui ne voit rien,
veu- gle qui ne voit rien,
gle, He- las, ma da- me, luy don- ne- rez vous rien, luy
ce po- vr'a- veu- gle, He- las, ma da- me, luy don- ne- rez vous
A ce po- vre a- veu- gle, He- las, ma

6
He- las, ma da- me, fai- tes luy quel- que bien, A ce po- vre a- veu- gle,
He- las, ma da- me, fai- tes luy que bien, A ce po- vre a-
quel-
bien, fai- tes luy quel- que bien, A ce po- vr'a- veu-
tes luy quel- que bien, fai- tes luy quel- que bien, A
tes luy quel- que bien, fai- tes luy quel- que bien,

19
He- las, ma da- me, fai- tes luy quel- que bien, A ce po- vre a- veu- gle, qui
He- las, ma da- me, fai- tes luy quel- que bien, A ce po- vre a- veu-
don- ne- rez vous rien, A ce po- vre a- veu- gle, A ce
rien, luy don- ne- rez vous rien, A ce po-
da- me, luy don- ne- rez vous rien, A ce po- vre a-

26
ne   voit   rien,   qui ne voit
gle,   qui   n'a   rien
po-vre a-veu-gle qui   ne voit rien,
vre a- veu-   gle,   qui ne   voit   rien, qui ne voit
veu-   gle,   qui ne   voit   rien, qui ne voit

41
cun bien fai- re,   au- cun bien   fai-   re,
fai- re,   au- cun bien fai- re,   Son pi-teux cri   tot
lez au-cun bien fai- re,   Son pi-teux cri tot fe-   riez
Son pi-teux cri   tot fe- riez tai-   re,   Son
Son pi-teux cri tot fe- riez tai-   re, tot

33
rien,   Sy luy vou- lez au-
sien,   Sy   luy vou- lez   au- cun bien
Sy luy vou-lez au- cun bien   fai- re, Sy luy vou-
rien, Sy luy vou- lez au-   cun bien fai-   re,
rien, Sy luy vou- lez au-   cun bien fai-   re,

48
Son pi- teux cri tot fe- riez tai-   re,
fe- riez tai- re,
tai-   re,   He- las, ma da- me, fai- tes luy quel-que bien,   fai-
pi- teux cri   tot fe- riez tai-   re,   He- las, ma da-   me, fai- tes luy quel-que
fe- riez tai-   re,   He- las, ma

55
He- las, ma da- me, fai- tes luy quel- que bien,
He- las, ma da- me, fai- tes luy quel- que
tes luy quel- que bien, fai- tes luy quel- que bien,
bien, fai- tes luy quel- que bien, fai- tes luy quel- que
da- me, fai- tes luy quel- que bien, fai- tes luy quel- que

67
He- las, ma da- me, luy don- ne- rez vous
He- las, ma da- me, luy
don- ne- rez vous rien, luy don- ne- rez vous
da- me, luy don- ne- rez vous rien, luy don- ne-
He- las, ma da- me, luy don- ne- rez

61
A ce po- vre a- veu- gle, qui ne voit rien,
bien, A ce po- vre a- veu- gle qui ne voit rien,
A ce po- vre a- veu- gle, He- las, ma da- me, luy
bien, A ce po- vre a- veu- gle, He- las, ma
bien, A ce po- vre a- veu- gle,

72
rien, A ce po- vre a- veu- gle, qui n'a rien
don- ne- rez vous rien, A ce po- vre a- veu- gle, qui
rien, A ce po- vre a- veu- gle, A ce po- vre a- veu- gle qui n'a
rez vous rien, A ce po- vre a- veu- gle qui
vous rien, A ce po- vre a- veu- gle,

84 Goudimel, *Allez, mes soupirs*

Al- lez, mes sou- pirs
a- mou- reux, Al- lez, mes sou- pirs
a- mou- reux, Al- lez, mes sou- pirs a-
sou- pirs a- mou- reux, Al- lez, mes
mes sou- pirs a- mou- reux, Al- lez,

lez à ce coeur froi- du- reux, Al-
ce coeur froi- du- reux, Al- lez à
Al- lez à ce coeur froi- du-
Al- lez à ce coeur froi- du- reux,
à ce coeur froi- du- reux, Al- lez

a- mou- reux, Al-
a- mou- reux, Al- lez à
mou- reux, a- mou- reux,
sou- pirs a- mou- reux, mes sou- pirs a- mou- reux,
mes sou- pirs a- mou- reux, Al- lez

lez à ce coeur froi- du- reux, Al- lez à ce coeur
ce coeur froi- du- reux, à ce coeur, à ce coeur froi-
reux, Al- lez à ce coeur froi- du- reux, à
Al- lez à ce coeur froi- du- reux, à ce coeur froi- du-
à ce coeur froi- du- reux,

45
froi- du- reux, Al- lez & rom- pez ces- te gla- ce,
du- reux, Al- lez & rom- pez ces te gla- ce,
ce coeur froi- du- reux, Al- lez & rom- pez
reux, Al- lez & rom- pez ces- te gla-
Al- lez & rom- pez ces- te gla- ce, Al- lez &

59
ce, Dont il fait rem- part à l'en- tour, Dont il fait rem-
gla- ce, Dont il fait rem- part à l'en- tour, Dont il fait
il fait rem-part à l'en- tour, Dont il fait rem-part à l'en- tour,
Dont il fait rem- part à l'en- tour,
ce, Dont il fait rem- part à l'en- tour, Dont

52
Al- lez & rom- pez ces- te gla- ce, & rom- pez ces- te gla-
Al- lez & rom- pez ces- te gla- ce, ces- te
ces- te gla- ce, Al- lez & rom- pez ces- te gla- ce, Dont
ce, Al- lez & rom- pez ces- te gla- ce, & rom- pez ces- te gla-
rom- pez ces- te gla- ce, & rom- pez ces-te gla-

69
part à l'en- tour,
rem- part à l'en- tour, Af-
Dont il fait rem- part à l'en- tour, Af-
Dont il fait rem- part à l'en-
il fait rem- part à l'en- tour, Af-

Af- fin que pi- tié à son tour, Af- fin que pi- tié
fin que pi- 'tié à son tour, Af- fin que pi- tié à
fin que pi- tié à son tour, Af- fin que pi- tié
tour, Af- fin que pi- tié à son tour, Af- fin que pi- tié
fin que pi- tié à son tour,
lar- mes es- chauf- fe la pla- ce,
lar- mes es- chauf- fe la pla- ce, es- chauf- fe la place, De lar- mes es- chauf- fe la pla- ce, De lar- mes es- chauf-
ce, De lar- mes es- chauf- fe la pla-
ce, De lar- mes es- chauf-
à son tour, De
son tour, De
à son tour, De lar- mes es- chauf- fe la pla-
à son tour, De lar- mes es- chauf- fe la pla-
De lar- mes es- chauf- fe la pla-
De lar- mes es- chauf- fe la pla- ce.
ce, De lar- mes es- chauf- fe la pla- ce.
fe la pla- ce, es- chauf- fe la pla- ce.
ce, De lar- mes es- chauf- fe la pla- ce.
fe la pla- ce, De lar- mes es- chauf- fe la pla- ce.

Je ne sçau-
Je ne sçau- rois, Je ne sçau-
Je ne sçau- rois, Je ne sçau-

17
sçau- rois chan- ter ne ri- re, chan-
ne ri- re,
Je ne sçau- rois, Je ne sçau- rois chan- ter
re, ne ri- re, chan- ter ne ri-
chan- ter ne ri- re, chan- ter

9
Je ne sçau- rois, Je ne
rois, Je ne sçau- rois chan- ter
rois, chan- ter ne ri-
rois, chan- ter ne ri- re,

26
ter ne ri- re, Tous mes plai-
Tous mes plai- sirs ne sont que pleurs,
ne ri- re, chan- ter ne ri-
re, Tous mes plai- sirs ne sont
ne ri- re, Tous mes plai- sirs ne sont que

35
sirs ne sont que pleurs, Tous mes plai- sirs
ne sont que pleurs, Tous mes plai- sirs ne sont que
re, Tous mes plai- sirs ne sont
que pleurs, ne sont que pleurs, ne sont
pleurs, Tous mes plai- sirs ne sont que pleurs,

53
a- mours, Voi- la pour- quoy, Voi-
a- mours, Puis que suis loin de mes a- mours,
pleurs, Puis que suis loin de mes a- mours,
suis loin de mes a- mours, de mes a- mours, Voi- la pour-
loin de mes a- mours, Puis que suis loin de mes a- mours, Voi-

44
ne sont que pleurs, Puis que suis loin de mes
pleurs, Puis que suis loin de mes
que pleurs, Tous mes plai- sirs ne sont que
pleurs, Puis que suis loin de mes a- mours,
Puis que suis loin de mes a- mours, Puis que suis

63
la pour- quoy mon coeur sou- pi- re,
Voi- la pour- quoy mon po- vre coeur sou- pi- re, M'a- mour &
Voi- la pour- quoy, Voi-la pour-quoy mon po- vre coeur sou- pi-
quoy, Voi- la pour- quoy, Voi- la pour-quoy mon po- vre coeur sou- pi-
la pour- quoy mon po- vre coeur sou- pi- re, Voi- la pour- quoy mon po- vre coeur sou-

M'a-mour & m'a-mi- et- te, Ma gen-te go-di- net-te, Ma da- me par
m'a-mi- et- te, Ma gen-te go- di- net- te, Ma da- me
re, M'a- mour & m'a-mi- et- te, Ma
re, M'a- mour & m'a-mi- et- te, Ma gen- te go- di-
pi- re, M'a- mour & m'a-mi- et- te,

bre seu- let- te, Pour mieux jou- ir de vous,
seu-let- te, Pour mieux jou- ir de vous, Sou- vent je
Sou- vent je vous sou- hait- te, En ma cham- bre seu- let- te,
te, Pour mieux jou- ir de vous, Sou- vent je vous sou-
te, En ma cham- bre seu- let- te, Pour mieux jou-

a- mours, Sou- vent je vous sou- hait- te, En ma cham-
par a- mours, Sou- vent je vous sou- hait- te, En ma cham- bre
gen- te go- di- net- te, Ma da- me par a- mours,
net- te, Sou- vent je vous sou- hait- te, En ma cham- bre seu- let-
Ma da- me par a- mours, Sou- vent je vous sou- hait-

Sou- vent je vous sou- hait- te, En ma cham-bre seul- let- te,
vous sou- hait- te, En ma cham- bre seul- let- te, Pour mieux jou- ir
Pour mieux jou- ir de vous, Sou- vent je vous sou-
hait- te, En ma cham- bre seul- let- te, Pour mieux jou-
ir de vous, Pour mieux jou- ir de vous, Pour

118
Pour mieux jou- ir de
de vous, Pour mieux jou- ir de
hait- te, En ma cham- bre seul- let- te,
ir de vous, Pour mieux jou- ir de
mieux jou- ir de vous, Pour mieux jou- ir de vous, Pour

Du
Du bon du coeur, ma che- re
Du bon du coeur, ma che- re da- me,

126
vous, Pour mieux jou- ir de vous.
vous, Pour mieux jou- ir de vous.
Pour mieux jou- ir de vous.
vous, Pour mieux jou- ir de vous.
mieux jou- ir de vous, Pour mieux jou- ir de vous.

11
bon du coeur,
da- me, Du bon du coeur, ma che-
Du bon
Du bon du coeur, ma che-
Du, Du bon du coeur, ma che-

20
Du bon du coeur, ma che- re
re da-
du coeur, ma che- re da- me, ma che- re dare da- me, ma che- re
re da- me, ma che-

38
vous sup- ply tres- hum- ble- ment, Que me
Je vous sup- ply tres- hum- ble- ment, Que me re-
tres- hum- ble- ment, Que me re- ce-
Que, Que me re- ce- vés dou-ce- ment,
vous sup- ply tres- hum- ble- ment, Que

28
da- me, Je vous ser- vi- ray loy- au-ment, Je
me, ma che- re da- me,
me, Je vous sup- ply tres- hum- ble- ment,
da- me, Je vous sup- ply tres- hum- ble- ment,
re da- me, Je

48
re- te- nés dou-
ce- vés dou- ce- ment, dou- ce-
vés dou- ce- ment, dou-
Que me re- ce- vés dou- ce- ment,
me re- ce- vés dou- ce- ment, Que

57
ce-
ment,
Pour vous ser- vir de
ment,
Pour vous ser- vir, Pour vous
ce-
ment,
Pour vous ser- vir,
Pour vous ser- vir, Pour vous ser-
me re- ce- vés dou- ce- ment, Pour vous ser- vir de corps & d'a-

75
Et si vous ju- re sur mon a-
me,
Et si vous ju- re sur mon a-
ju- re sur mon a- me,
me,
Que
Et si vous ju- re sur mon a-

66
cors & d'a- me,
ser- vir, de corps & d'a- me, de corps & d'a-
de corps & d'a- me, Et si vous
vir, de corps & d'a- me, de corps & d'a-
me,
de cors & d'a- me,

83
me,
Que vous ser- vi-
me,
Que vous ser-
Que vous ser- vi- ray loy-
vous ser- vi- ray loy- au- ment, Que vous ser- vi- ray
me, Que vous ser- vi- ray loy- au- ment,

87 Vuildre, *Une nonnain refaite* [C. Marot]

11
sé le mon- de, Se
voir lais- sé, Se re- pen- toit d'a- voir lais-
mon- de, le mon- de, Se re- pen- toit d'a- voir
re- pen- toit d'a- voir lais- sé, Se re- pen- toit d'a- voir
Se re- pen- toit d'a- voir lais- sé le mon-

22
Et je luy dy, m'a- mye, il ne faut point,
Et je luy dy, m'a- my- e, il
je luy dy, m'a- my- e, il ne faut point,
my- e, Et je luy dy, m'a- my-
Et je luy dy, m'a-

16
re- pen- toit d'a- voir lais- sé le mon- de,
sé, d'a- voir lais- sé le mon- de,
lais- sé le mon- de, Et
lais- sé le mon- de, Et je luy dy, m'a-
de, d'a- voir lais- sé le mon- de,

27
A- voir re- gret, à cho- se tant im- mun-
ne faut point, A- voir re- gret, à cho- se tant im- mun- de, tant im- mun-
A- voir re- gret à cho- se tant im- mun- de, a- voir re- gret
e, il ne faut point, A- voir re- gret, à cho- se tant
my- e, il ne faut point, A- voir re- gret, à

37
de, N'a- vez vous pas Je- sus- christ pur & mon-
de, N'a- vez vous pas Je- sus- christ pur & mon-
à cho- se tant im- mun- de, N'a- vez vous pas Je-
im- mun- de, N'a- vez vous pas Je- sus- christ
cho- se tant im- mun- de, N'a- vez vous pas Je- sus-

57
Au nom du- quel sont con- jointz voz es- pritz,
pris, Au nom du- quel sont con- jointz,
pris, Au nom du- quel sont con- jointz voz espris, Au nom du- quel sont con- jointz
fes- sion pris, Au nom du- quel sont con- jointz

46
de, Pour vo- tre es- poux en pro- fes- sion pris,
de, Pour vo- tre es- poux en pro- fes- sion
sus- christ pur & mon- de, Pour vo- tre es- poux en pro- fes- sion
pur & mon- de, Pour vo- tre es- poux en pro- fes- sion
christ pur & mon- de, Pour vo- tre es- poux en pro-

64
Au nom du- quel sont con- jointz voz es- pritz, Ouy,
Au nom du- quel sont con- jointz voz es- pritz,
pritz, Au nom du- quel sont con- jointz voz es- pritz,
voz es- pritz, Au nom du- quel sont con- jointz voz es- pritz,
voz es- pritz, Au nom du- quel sont con- jointz voz es- pritz,

72

dit el- le & ne le veux la- cher, Ouy, dit el- le & ne
Ouy, dit el-
Ouy, dit el- le & ne le veux la- cher,
Ouy, dit el- le & ne le veux la- cher, Ouy, dit el- le & ne le
Ouy, dit el- le & ne le veux la- cher,

83

es- poux des es- pritz,
christ est es- poux des es- pritz, Et je de- man- de un
Mais Je- sus- christ est es- poux des es- pritz, Et
cher, Mais Je- sus- christ est es- poux des es-
Mais Je- sus- christ est es- poux

77

le veux la- cher, Mais Je- sus- christ est
le & ne le veux la- cher, Mais Je- sus- christ, Mais Je- sus-
Ouy, dit el- le & ne le veux la- cher,
veux la-
Ouy, dit el- le & ne le veux la- cher,

88

Et je de- man- de un es- poux pour la chair,
es- poux, Et je de- man- de un es- poux, Et
je de- man- de un es- poux pour la chair, pour la chair,
pritz, Et je de- man- de un es- poux, Et
des es- pritz, Et je de- man- de un

94
Et je de- man- de un es- poux pour la
je de- man- de un es- poux pour la chair,
Et je de- man- de un es- poux pour la
je de- man- de un es- poux pour la chair, pour
es- poux pour la chair, Et je de- man-

105
poux pour la chair, Et
es- poux, Et je de- man- de un es- poux
chair, pour la chair, Et je de- man- de un es-
je de- man- de un es- poux, Et je de- man- de un es-
Et je de- man- de un es- poux pour

100
chair, Et je de- man- de un es-
Et je de- man- de un es- poux, Et je de- man- de un
chair, Et je de- man- de un es- poux pour la
la chair, Et
de un es- poux pour la chair,

110
je de- man- de un es- poux pour la chair.
pour la chair, pour la chair.
poux pour la chair.
poux pour la chair, un es- poux pour la chair.
la chair, Et je de- man- de un es- poux pour la chair.

A- mour, par- tez, je
A- mour, par- tez, je vous don- ne, je vous don-
A- mour, par- tez, je vous don-
A- mour, A- mour, par- tez, je
A- mour, par- tez, A- mour, par- tez,

15

se, Non pas pour mal, que mon coeur vous pro-
Non pas pour mal, que mon coeur vous pro- cu-
Non pas pour mal que mon coeur vous pro- cu-
pas pour mal, Non pas pour mal, que mon coeur
se, Non pas pour mal, que mon coeur vous pro- cu-

8

vous don- ne la chas-
ne la chas- se, je vous don- ne la chas- se,
ne la chas- se,
vous, je vous don- ne la chas- se, Non
je vous don- ne la chas-

23

cu- re, Mais faux sem-
re, Mais faux sem- blant qui met du tout sa cu- re,
re, Mais faux sem- blant qui met
vous pro- cu- re, Mais faux sem- blant, Mais
re, Mais faux sem- blant, qui

31
blant, qui met du tout sa cu- re,
Mais faux sem- blant qui met du tout sa cu- re,
du tout sa cu- re,
faux sem- blant qui met du tout sa cu- re, A
met du tout sa cu- re, du tout sa cu- re,
45
de ma gra- ce, vous
gra- ce, vous ba- nit de ma gra- re,
ba- nit de ma gra- ce,
vous ba- nit de ma gra- ce, vous ba- nit
ba- nit de ma gra- ce,
38
A de- ce- voir vous ba- nit
A de- ce- voir, vous ba- nit de ma
A de- ce- voir, A de- ce- voir vous
de- ce- voir vous ba- nit de ma gra- ce,
A de- ce- voir, vous
52
ba- nit de ma gra- ce.
ce, vous ba- nit de ma gra- ce.
vous ba- nit de ma gra- ce.
de ma gra- ce, de ma gra- ce.
vous ba- nit de ma gra- ce.

89 Certon, *Regret, soucy, & peine*

Regret, soucy, & peine,
Me font de vilains tours,
Si pitié n'est soudaine,
Tot finiray mes jours,

40
jours,					Tot fi- ni- ray mes
Tot fi- ni- ray mes jours, Tot fi- ni- ray mes jours, He- las, He- las,
Tot fi- ni- ray mes jours,		Tot fi- ni- ray mes jours,		He-
ni- ray mes jours,		Tot fi- ni- ray mes jours,		He- las,		He-
n'est sou- dai- ne, Tot fi- ni- ray mes jours, Tot fi- ni- ray mes jours,		He-

60
mours,					Qui me font tout ce-
mours, He- las,		He- las,		He- las, Qui me font tout
las, He- las, ce sont a- mours, Qui me font tout ce- cy,		Qui
He- las, ce sont a- mours,		Qui me font tout ce-
He- las, ce sont a- mours,		Qui me font tout

51
jours,		He- las, ce sont a- mours,		He- las, ce sont a-
He- las, ce sont a- mours,		He- las, He- las, ce sont a-
las, ce sont a- mours,		He- las, ce sont a- mours,		He-
las, ce sont a- mours, He- las, ce sont a- mours,		He- las,
las, ce sont a- mours,		He- las, ce sont a- mours,

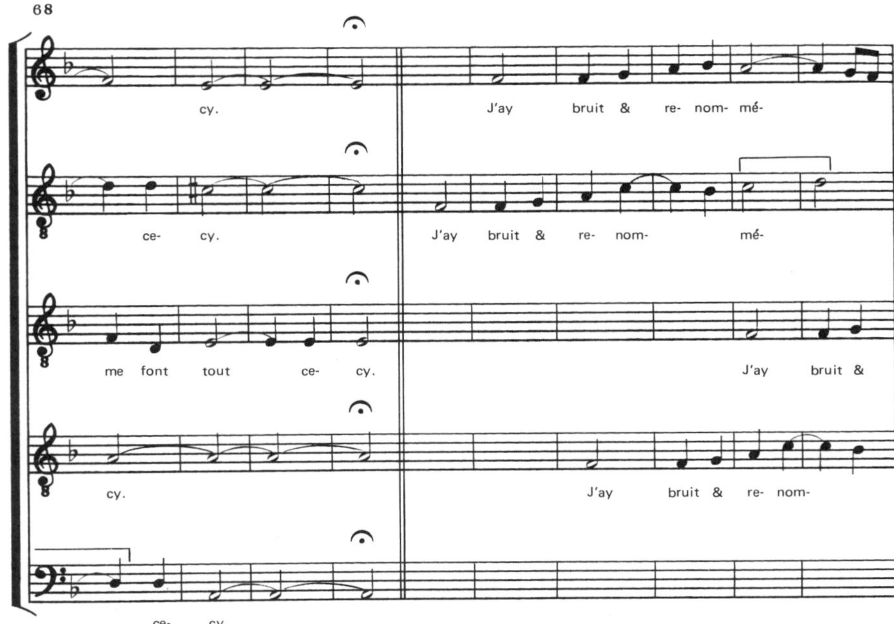

68
cy.				J'ay bruit & re- nom- mé-
ce- cy.				J'ay bruit & re- nom- mé-
me font tout ce- cy.				J'ay bruit &
cy.				J'ay bruit & re- nom-
ce- cy.

78
e, D'a- voir nou- vel a- my, D'a-
e, J'ay bruit & re- nom- mé- e,
re- nom- mé- e, D'a- voir nou- vel a- my,
mé- e, D'a- voir nou- vel, D'a- voir nou-
J'ay bruit & re- nom- mé- e,

95
J'ay bruit & re- nom- mé-
vel a- my, J'ay bruit & re- nom- mé- e,
J'ay bruit & re- nom- mé-
a- my, J'ay bruit &
a- my,

85
voir nou- vel a- my, D'a- voir nou- vel a- my,
D'a- voir nou- vel a- my, D'a- voir nou- vel a- my, nou-
D'a- voir nou- vel a- my, D'a- voir nou- vel a- my,
vel a- my, D'a- voir nou- vel a- my, D'a- voir nou- vel
J'ay bruit & re- nom- mé- e, D'a- voir nou- vel a- my, D'a- voir nou- vel

102
e, D'a- voir nou- vel a- my, D'a- voir nou-
e, J'ay bruit & re- nom- mé- e,
e, D'a- voir nou- vel, D'a- voir nou- vel a-
re- nom- mé- e, D'a- voir nou- vel a- my, D'a-
J'ay bruit & re- nom- mé- e, J'ay

90 Vuildre, *Je ne fay rien* [C. Marot]

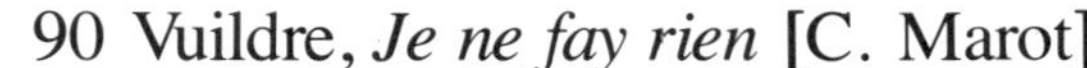

15
rir, Le don d'a- mou- reu- se li- es- se,
rir sans a- que- rir, Le don d'a- mou- reu- se li- es- se, Le don
rir, Le don d'a- mou- reu- se li- es- se,
que- rir, Le don d'a-
sans a- que- rir, Le

33
Las, ma mai- tres- se, dit- tes quand es- se,
tres- se, dit- tes quand es- se, dit- tes quand es- se,
ma mai- tres- se, dit- tes quand es- se, Qu'il
dit- tes quand es- se, Qu'il vous plai-
tres- se, dit- tes quand es- se, Qu'il vous plai-

24
Le don d'a- mou- reu- se li- es- se,
d'a- mou- reu- se li- es- se, Las, ma mai-
Le don d'a- mou- reu- se li- es- se, Las,
mou- reu- se li- es- se, Las, ma mai- tres- se,
don d'a- mou- reu- se li- es- se, Las, ma mai-

43
Qu'il vous plai- ra me se- cou- rir, Qu'il vous plai-
Qu'il vous plai- ra me se- cou- rir, Qu'il vous plai- ra me se-
vous plai- ra me se- cou- rir, Qu'il vous plai- ra me se- cou-
ra me se- cou- rir, Qu'il vous plai- ra me se- cou-
ra me se- cou- rir, Qu'il vous plai- ra me se- cou- rir,

51
ra me se- cou- rir, me se- cou-
cou- rir,
rir, Je ne fay rien que re- que-
rir, Qu'il vous plai- ra me se- cou- rir,
Qu'il vous plai- ra me se- cou- rir, Je ne fay rien que

66
que- rir, Je ne fay rien que re- cue-
que- rir, Je ne fay rien que re- que- rir sans ac- que-
rien que re- que- rir sans ac- que- rir,
Je ne fay rien que re- que- rir sans ac- que- rir,
Je ne fay rien que re- que- rir sans ac- que- rir,

58
rir, Je ne fay rien que re- que- rir sans ac-
Je ne fay rien que re- que- rir sans ac-
rir sans ac- que- rir, Je ne fay
Je ne fay rien que re- que- rir sans ac- que- rir,
re- que- rir sans ac- que- rir, sans ac- que- rir,

74
rir sans ac- que- rir.
rir, Je ne fay rien que re- que- rir sans ac- que- rir.
Je ne fay rien que re- que- rir sans ac- que- rir.
Je ne fay rien que re- que- rir sans ac- que- rir.
Je ne fay rien que re- que- rir sans ac- que- rir.

A- rou- sez vo vi vo vi, A- rou- sez vo vi- o- let-
A- rou- sez vo vi vo vi, A- rou-
A- rou- sez vo vi vo vi, A- rou- sez vo
A- rou- sez vo vi vo

vi- o- lier, A- rou- sez vo vi- o-
vi- o- let- te, A- rou-
vi vo vi, A- rou- sez vo vi- o- let- te, A- rou-
A- rou- sez vo vi- o- let- te,
sez vo vi vo vi- o- let- te,

A- rou- sez vo vi vo vi- o- let- te, A- rou- sez vo
te, A- rou- sez vo vi vo vi vo vi vo
sez vo vi- o- let- te, A- rou- sez vo
vi- o- let- te, A- rou- sez vo vi vo vi,
vi- o- let- te, A- rou-

let- te, A- rou- sez vo vi- o- lier, A- rou- sez vo vi- o-
sez vo vi vo vi- o- let- te, A- rou- sez vo vi- o-
sez vo vi- o- lier, A- rou- sez vo vi- o- let- te, A- rou-
A- rou- sez vo vi vo vi- o- lier, A- rou- sez vo
A- rou- sez vo vi vo vi,

let- te, A- rou- sez vo vi- o-
lier, A- rou- sez vo vi- o- lier, A- rou- sez vo vi vo vi- o-
sez vo vi vo vi, A- rou- sez vo
vi- o- lier, A- rou- sez vo vi vo vi- o-
A- rou- sez vo vi vo vi- o- lier,

Es- toit ay- mant par a- mou- ret- te,
nier, Es- toit ay- mant par a- mou- ret-
La fi- lle d'un jar- di- nier, Es- toit ay- mant par
nier, Es- toit ay- mant, par a- mou- ret- te, par a- mou-
La fi- lle d'un jar- di- nier, Es- toit ay- mant par

lier, La fi- lle d'un jar- di- nier,
lier, A- rou- sez vo vi- o- lier, La fi- lle d'un jar- di-
vi vo vi- o- let- te,
lier, La fi- lle d'un jar- di-

La fi- lle d'un jar- di- nier, Es- toit ay- mant par a- mou-
te, La fi- lle d'un jar- di- nier, Es- toit ay- mant par a- mou- ret-
a- mou- ret- te, par a- mou- ret- te, Son a- my,
ret- te, Son a-
a- mou- ret- te,

ret- te,
te, Son a- my luy don- ne un bai- ser,
Son a- my luy don- ne un bai- ser, Pre- ten- dant fai-
muy luy don- ne un bai- ser, Pre- ten- dant fai- re la cho- set-
Son a- my luy don- ne un bai- ser, Pre- ten- dant faire

te, Le jeu d'a- mours trop bien
te, Le jeu d'a- mours, trop bien luy
Le jeu d'a- mours trop bien luy hait- te,
te, trop bien luy hait-
bien luy hait- te,

Pre- ten- dant fai- re la cho- set-
Pre- ten- dant fai- re la cho- set-
re la cho- set- te,
te, Le jeu d'a- mours trop bien luy hait-
la cho- set- te, Le jeu d'a- mours trop

luy hait- te,
hait- te, trop bien luy hait- te,
Luy à dit, mon a- my
te, Luy à dit, mon a- my
Luy à dit, mon a- my cher,

88
Luy à dit, mon a- my cher, Luy à dit, mon a-
Luy à dit, mon a- my cher, Luy à dit, mon
cher, Luy à dit, mon a- my cher,
cher, Luy à dit, mon a- my cher,
mon a- my cher,

106
A- rou- sez vo vi- o- let- te, A- rou- sez vo vi- o-
cher, A- rou- sez vo vi vo vi- o-
sez vo vi- o- let- te, A- rou- sez vo vi- o- let- te, A- rou- sez vo
o- let- te, A- rou- sez vo vi vo
vi- o- let- te, A- rou-

98
my cher,
a- my cher, Luy à dit, mon a- my
A- rou- sez vo vi vo vi, A- rou-
A- rou- sez vo vi vo vi, A- rou- sez vo vi
A- rou- sez vo vi vo

113
lier, A- rou- sez vo vi- o- let- te, A- rou- sez vo vi-
let- te, A- rou- sez vo vi- o- lier, A- rou- sez vo vi- o- lier,
vi- o- lier, A- rou- sez vo vi vo vi,
vi- o- lier, A- rou- sez vo vi- o- lier, A- rou-
sez vo vi vo vi, A- rou- sez vo vi vo

119

o- let- te, A- rou-sez vo vi-
A- rou-sez vo vi vo vi- o- lier, A- rou-sez vo vi- o-
A- rou- sez vo vi vo vi,
sez vo vi vo vi- o- lier, A- rou-sez vo
vi- o- lier, A- rou-sez vo

D'a- mour je suis des- he- ri- té-
D'a- mour je suis des- he- ri- té-
D'a- mour je suis des- he- ri-
D'a- mour je

125

9

o- lier.
lier, A- rou-sez vo vi, A- rou-sez vo vi- o- lier, A- rou-sez vo vi- o- lier.
A- rou- sez vo vi vo vi- o- lier.
vi vo vi- o- lier.
vi vo vi, A- rou- sez vo vi- o- lier.

e, Et plain-dre ne me sçay
e, des- he- ri- té- e, Et plain-dre ne
té- e, Et plain-dre ne me sçay à qui,
suis des- he- ri- té- e, Et plain-dre ne
D'a- mour je suis des- he- ri- té- e, Et plain- dre

18
à qui, He- las, j'ay per- du
me sçay à qui, He- las j'ay per- du mon
He- las, He- las j'ay per- du
me sçay à qui, He- las, He- las j'ay per-
ne me sçay à qui, He- las, He- las, He- las, He- las j'ay

39
suis, il m'a lais- sé- e, il m'a lais- sé-
sé- e, il m'a lais-
suis, il m'a lais- sé- e,
suis, il m'a lais- sé- e, il m'a lais- sé- e, il m'a lais-
il m'a lais- sé- e, il m'a lais- sé-

28
mon a- my. Seu- let- te suis, Seu- let- te
a- my. Seu- let- te suis, il m'a lais-
mon a- my. Seu- let- te suis, Seu- let- te
du mon a- my. Seu- let- te suis, Seu- let- te
per- du mon a- my. Seu- let- te suis,

48
e, Seu- let- te suis,
sé- e, Seu- let- te suis,
il m'a lais- sé- e, Seu- let- te suis,
sé- e, Seu- let- te suis,
e, il m'a lais- sé- e, Seu- let- te suis,

Seu- let- te suis, il m'a lais- sé- e, il
il m'a lais- sé- e, il
Seu- let- te suis, il m'a lais-
Seu- let- te suis, il m'a lais- sé- e, il m'a lais-
il m'a lais- sé- e,

Bai- sés moy tant tant, frin- gués moy tant tant,
Bai- sés moy
Bai- sés moy tant tant, frin- gués moy tant tant,
Bai- sés moy tant, frin- gués moy tant tant tant,
Bai- sés moy tant tant, frin- gués moy tant tant tant tant,

m'a lais- sé- e.
m'a lais- sé- e.
sé- e, il m'a lais- sé- e.
sé- e, il m'a lais- sé- e.
il m'a lais- sé- e, il m'a lais- sé- e.

frin- gués moy tant tant, mon a- my, je vous
tant tant, frin- gués moy tant tant, mon a- my, je vous
frin- gués moy tant tant, mon a- my, je vous pri- e,
frin- gués moy tant, mon a- my, je vous pri- e, mon a-
frin- gués moy tant tant, mon a- my, je vous pri- e,

pri- e, Bai- sés moy tant tant, frin- gués moy tant
pri- e, Bai- sés moy tant, frin-gués moy tant tant, frin- gués
Bai- sés moy tant tant, frin- gués moy tant tant, Si se- ray
my, je vous pri- e, Bai- sés moy tant, frin-
Bai- sés moy tant tant, frin-gués moy tant tant, frin-gués moy tant

my- e, Si se- ray vo- tre a- my- e,
my- e, Si se- ray vo- tre a- my-
vo- tre a- my- e, Si se- ray vo- tre a-my- e, Au
Si se- ray vo- tre a- my- e,
vo- tre a- my- e, Au jo- ly

tant, Si se- ray vo-tre a-my- e, Si se- ray vo- tre a-
moy tant tant, Si se- ray vo-tre a-
vo- tre a-my- e, Si se- ray vo-tre a-my- e,
gués moy tant tant tant, Si se- ray vo- tre a-my- e,
tant, Si se- ray vo-tre a-my- e, Si se- ray

Au jo- ly bois je ren- con- tray m'a- my- e, je
e, Au jo- ly bois je ren- con- tray m'a- my-
jo- ly bois je ren- con- tray m'a- my- e, Au
Au jo- ly bois je ren- con- tray m'a- my- e, Au jo- ly
bois je ren-con- tray m'a- my- e, je ren- con- tray m'a- my-

36
ren- con- tray m'a- my- e, je ren- con- tray m'a- my- e, m'a-
e, je ren- con- tray m'a- my- e, je ren- con- tray m'a- my- e,
jo- ly bois je ren- con- tray m'a- my- e, je ren- con- tray m'a-
bois je ren- con- tray m'a- my- e, je ren- con- tray m'a- my- e,
e, je ren- con- tray m'a- my- e, je ren- con- tray

55
el- le fut res- jou- T-
T- e, el- le fut res- jou- T-
le fut res- jou- T- e, el- le fut res- jou- T-
Quand m'ap- per- çeut el- le fut res- jou- T-
e,

45
my- e, Quand m'ap- per- çeut,
Quand m'ap- per- çeut, Quand m'ap- per- çeut, el- le fut res- jou-
my- e, Quand m'ap- per- çeut, el- le fut res- jou- T- e, el-
Quand m'ap- per- çeut el- le fut res- jou- T- e,
m'a- my- e, Quand m'ap- per- çeut el- le fut res- jou- T-

63
e, El- le m'a
e, El- le m'a dit tout bas en sou- ri-
e, El- le m'a dit tout bas en sou- ri- ant, tout
e, El- le m'a dit tout bas en sou- ri- ant, el- le m'a
El- le m'a dit tout bas en sou- ri- ant, El- le m'a

dit tout bas en sou- ri- ant,   Bai- sés moy
ant,   tout bas en sou- ri- ant,
bas en sou- ri- ant,   tout bas   en sou- ri- ant,   Bai-
dit tout bas, tout bas en sou- ri- ant, tout bas   en sou- ri- ant,
dit tout   bas en sou- ri- ant,   tout bas en   sou- ri- ant,   Bai- sés

tant tant,   mon   a- my,   je vous   pri-   e, Bai-sés moy
tant,   mon   a- my,   je vous   pri-   e,   Bai- sés
a- my,   je   vous   pri-   e,   Bai- sés moy
my,   je vous   pri-   e,   mon   a- my,   je vous pri-
a- my,   je   vous   pri-   e,   Bai- sés moy

tant tant, frin- gués moy tant tant,   frin- gués moy
Bai- sés moy tant tant,   frin- gués moy   tant
sés moy   tant tant, frin- gués moy tant tant, frin- gués moy tant tant, mon
Bai- sés moy tant, frin-gués moy   tant tant   tant, frin- gués moy   tant,mon a-
moy tant   tant, frin-gués moy   tant   tant tant   tant, frin- gués moy   tant tant,   mon

tant tant,   frin- gués moy tant tant, Si se- ray vo- tre a- my- e, Si
moy tant, frin-gués moy   tant tant,   frin- gués moy   tant tant,   Si
tant tant,frin-   gués moy tant   tant, Si se- ray vo- tre a- my- e, Si se- ray vo- tre a-
e,   Bai- sés moy   tant, frin-   gués moy tant tant tant, Si   se- ray
tant tant, frin-gués moy   tant tant,   frin-gués moy tant   tant,   Si   se- ray vo- tre a- my-

94 Crequillon, *Belle, donne moy*

15
re- gard, Bel- le, don-
un re- gard, Bel- le,
re- gard, Bel- le, don- nez moy un re- gard,
un re- gard, Bel- le, don- nez
Bel- le, don- nez moy un re- gard,

28
l'oeil, Tant seu- le- ment du coin de l'oeil, Tant
Tant seu- le- ment du coin de
coin de l'oeil, du coin de l'oeil, Tant seu- le-
Tant seu- le- ment du coin de l'oeil, Tant seu- le- ment du coin de
Tant seu- le- ment du coin de l'oeil,

21
ne moy un re- gard, Tant seu- le- ment du coin de
don- nez moy un re- gard,
un re- gard, Tant seu- le- ment, Tant seu- le- ment du
moy, un re- gard,
Bel- le, don- nez moy un re- gard,

35
seu- le- ment du coin de l'oeil, Tant
l'oeil, Tant seu- le- ment du coin de l'oeil,
ment, Tant seu- le- ment du coin de l'oeil, du coin
l'oeil, Tant seu- le- ment du
Tant seu- le- ment du coin de l'oeil, Tant seu- le- ment

seu- le- ment du coin de l'oeil, Ce- la al- le- ge- ra
Ce- la al- le- ge- ra mon dueil, Ce- la al-
de l'oeil, du coin de l'oeil, Ce- la al- le- ge- ra mon dueil, al-
coin de l'oeil, du coin de l'oeil, Ce- la al- le-
du coin de l'oeil,

la al- le- ge- ra mon dueil, Ce- la al- le- ge- ra mon dueil,
dueil, Ce- la al- le- ge- ra mon
al- le- ge- ra mon dueil, al- le- ge- ra
dueil, al- le- ge- ra mon dueil, al- le- ge- ra mon dueil, Mais
dueil, Ce- la al- le- ge- ra mon dueil,

mon dueil, Ce-
le- ge- ra mon dueil, Ce- la al- le- ge- ra mon
le- ge- ra mon dueil, Ce- la al- le- ge- ra mon dueil,
ge- ra mon dueil, Ce- la al- le- ge- ra mon
Ce- la al- le- ge- ra mon dueil, Ce- la al- le- ge- ra mon

Mais qu'il vien- ne de bon- ne part, Mais qu'il
dueil, Mais qu'il vien- ne de bon- ne part, Mais qu'il vien- ne
mon dueil, Mais qu'il vien- ne de bon- ne part, de
qu'il vien- ne de bon- ne part, Mais qu'il vien- ne de bon-
Mais qu'il vien- ne de bon- ne part, de

95 Leschenet, *Est-il douleur cruelle*

* Accidental indicated in the <u>Livre.</u>

ge, Ayt si peu d'a- van- ta- ge, Ayt
ge, Ayt si peu d'a- van- ta- ge, Ayt si peu d'a-van-ta-
l'a- mour sa- ge, Ayt si peu d'a- van- ta- ge,
Ayt si peu d'a- van- ta- ge, Ayt si peu d'a- van-ta- ge,
sa- ge, Ayt si peu d'a- van- ta- ge, Ayt

se- pa- re & ab- sen- te, Que l'oeil du coeur se
coeur se se- pa- re & ab- sen- te, Que
l'oeil du coeur se se- pa- re & ab- sen- te,
Que l'oeil du coeur se se- pa- re &
re & ab- sen- te, Que l'oeil du

si peu d'a- van- ta- ge, Que l'oeil du coeur, Que l'oeil du coeur se
ge, Ayt si peu d'a- van- ta- ge, Que l'oeil du
Ayt si peu d'a- van- ta- ge, Que
Ayt si peu d'a- van- ta- ge, Que l'oeil du coeur,
si peu d'a- van- ta- ge, Que l'oeil du coeur se se- pa-

se- pa- re & ab- sen- te, O trop de co-gnois-san-
l'oeil du coeur se se- pa- re & ab- sen- te, O trop,
se se- pa- re & ab- sen- te, O trop de co-gnois-
ab- sen- te,
coeur se se- pa- re & ab- sen- te, O trop de

ce, O trop de co- gnois-san- ce, O trop de sou-ve- nan- ce,
O trop de co- gnois-san- ce,
san- ce, O trop de co- gnois- san- ce, O trop de
O trop de co- gnois- san- ce, O
co- gnois- san- ce, O trop de

O trop de sou- ve- nan- ce, O trop de
O trop de sou- ve- nan- ce,
sou- ve- nan- ce, O trop de sou- ve-
trop de co- gnois- san- ce, O trop de sou- ve- nan- ce,
co- gnois- san- ce, O trop de sou- ve- nan- ce, O trop de

sou- ve- nan- ce, De cho- se trop,
De cho- se trop, es- ti-
nan- ce, De cho- se trop es- ti- mée
De cho- se trop es- ti- mée & co- gneuë,
sou- ve- nan- ce, De cho- se trop es- ti-

es- ti- mée & co- gneuë, es- ti- mée & co- gneuë, O loy
mée & co- gneuë, es- ti- mée & co- gneuë, O
& co- gneuë,
es- ti- mée & co- gneuë,
mée & co- gneuë, O loy du- re &

71
du- re & i- ni- que, D'a- mour, D'a- mour chas- te & pu-
loy du- re & i- ni- que, D'a- mour
O loy du- re & i- ni- que, O loy du- re & i- ni- que,
O loy du- re & i- ni-
i- ni- que, D'a- mour chas- te & pu-

82
di- que, A- vec- ques trop de res- pectz main- te- nu-
pu- di- que, A- vec- ques trop de res- pectz, de res- pectz
A- vec- ques trop de res- pectz main- te- nu- ë,
te & pu- di- que, A- vec- ques trop, A- vec- ques trop de
di- que, A- vec- ques trop, A- vec- ques trop de

77
di- que, D'a- mour chas- te & pu-
chas- te & pu- di- que, D'a- mour chas- te &
D'a- mour chas- te & pu- di- que,
que, D'a- mour chas- te & pu- di- que, D'a- mour chas-
di- que, D'a- mour chas- te & pu-

87
ë, A- vec- ques trop, de res- pectz main- te- nu-
main- te- nu- ë, de res- pectz main- te- nu-
A- vec- ques trop de res- pectz main- te- nu- ë,
res- pectz, A- vec- ques trop de res- pectz
res- pectz main- te- nu- ë, A- vec- ques trop

92
ğ, A- vec- ques trop,
ğ, A- vec- ques trop de res- pectz
A- vec- ques trop de res- pectz
main- te- nu- ğ,
de res- pectz main- te- nu- ğ, de

De vous ser- vir, De vous ser- vir sur
De vous ser- vir, De vous ser- vir sur
De vous ser- vir, De vous ser- vir sur
De vous ser- vir, De vous ser- vir sur tou-
De vous ser- vir, De vous ser- vir sur

96
de res- pectz main- te- nu- ğ.
main- te- nu- ğ, de res-pectz main-te- nu- ğ.
main- te- nu- ğ.
de res- pectz main- te- nu- ğ, de res-pectz main- te- nu- ğ.
res- pectz main- te- nu- ğ, de res-pectz main-te- nu- ë.

9
tou- tes je pro- cu- re, Et nuit &
tou- tes je pro- cu- re, Et nuit &
tou- tes je pro- cu- re, Et nuit
tes je pro- cu- re, Et nuit &
tou- tes je pro- cu- re, Et nuit &

jour, Et nuit & jour mon coeur la- beu-
jour, Et nuit & jour mon pov- re coeur la- beu-
& jour, Et nuit & jour mon pov- re coeur la- beu- re, I-
jour, Et nuit & jour mon pov- re coeur la- beu-

en mon en- ten- de- ment, Com- ment
gi- nant en mon en- ten- de- ment, Com-ment pour-rois mon-
mon en- ten- de- ment, Com- ment pour- rois mon-strer e- vi-
de- ment, Com- ment pour-rois mon-
ten- de- ment, en mon en- ten- de- ment,

re, I- ma- gi- nant, I- ma- gi- nant,
re, I- ma- gi- nant, I- ma-
I- ma- gi- nant, I- ma- gi- nant, en
ma- gi- nant, I- ma- gi- nant en mon en- ten-
re, I- ma- gi- nant, I- ma- gi- nant en mon en-

pour- rois mon- strer e- vi- den- ment, La
strer e- vi- den- ment, La grand dou- leur
den- ment, La grand dou- leur que pour vous j'en-
strer, mon- strer e- vi- den- ment, La grand dou-
Com- ment pour- rois mon- strer e- vi- den- ment,

54
grand dou- leur, La grand dou- leur que pour vous j'en- du- re,
que pour vous j'en- du- re, La grand dou-
du- re, La grand dou- leur que pour vous j'en- du- re, La grand dou-leur que
leur, La grand dou- leur que pour vous j'en- du- re, La
La grand dou- leur que pour vous j'en- du- re, que pour vous j'en- du- re,

O tris- te en- nuy, O tris- te en- nuy, ô for-
O tris- te en- nuy, O tris- te en- nuy, ô
O tris- te en- nuy, O tris- te en- nuy, O tris- te en- nuy, ô
O tris- te en- nuy, O tris- te en- nuy, ô for- tu-
O tris- te en- nuy, ô for- tu- ne mes- chan- te,

65
La grand dou- leur, La grand dou- leur que pour vous j'en- du- re.
leur que pour vous j'en- du- re.
pour vous j'en- du- re, La grand dou- leur que pour vous j'en- du- re.
grand dou- leur, que pour vous j'en- du- re, j'en- du- re.
La grand dou- leur que pour vous j'en- du- re, que pour vous j'en- du- re.

9
tu- ne mes- chan- te, ô for- tu- ne mes- chan-
for- tu- ne mes- chan- te, ô for- tu- ne mes-chan-
for- tu- ne mes- chan- te, ô for- tu- ne mes- chan-
ne mes- chan- te, ô for- tu- ne mes- chan-
ô for- tu- ne mes- chan-

17
te,
Qui ne vo- lez à mon vueil as- pi- rer, Qui ne vo-
te, Qui ne vo- lez, Qui ne vo- lez à mon vueil as- pi- rer, Qui ne vo-
te, Qui ne vo- lez, Qui ne vo- lez à mon vueil as- pi- rer, Qui ne vo-
te, Qui ne vo- lez à mon vueil as- pi- rer,
te,
Qui ne vo- lez à

28
d'em- pi- rer, Quand le mal- heur ne fait que d'em- pi-
que d'em- pi- rer, Quand le mal- heur, ne fait
fait que d'em- pi- rer, Quand le mal- heur ne fait que d'em- pi-
d'em- pi- rer, Quand le mal- heur ne fait que d'em- pi- rer, ne
Quand le mal- heur ne fait que d'em- pi- rer, ne

22
lez à mon vueil as- pi- rer, Quand le mal- heur ne fait que
lez à mon vueil as- pi- rer, Quand le mal- heur ne fait
lez à mon vueil as- pi- rer, ne
lez à mon vueil as- pi- rer, Quand le mal- heur ne fait que
mon vueil as- pi- rer,

35
rer, que d'em- pi- rer, Las, vou- lez vous qu'u- ne per- son- ne
que d'em- pi- rer, Las, vou- lez vous qu'u- ne per- son- ne chan- te, Las,
rer, Las, Las,
fait que d'em- pi- rer, Las, Las, vou- lez
fait que d'em- pi- rer, Las, vou- lez vous, Las,

44
chan- te, Las, vou- lez vous, q'u- ne per-son- ne chan- te, Las, vou-lez
vou- lez vous q'u- ne per-son- ne chan- te, q'u- ne per-
vou- lez vous q'u- ne per- son- ne chan- te,
vous, q'u- ne per-son- ne chan- te,
vou- lez vous q'u- ne per- son- ne chan-

60
te. Voy- ant au vray tout mon heur ex- pi- rer,
chan- te. Voy- ant au vray tout mon heur ex- pi- rer,
chan- te. Voy- ant au vray, Voy- ant au vray tout
te. Voy- ant au vray tout mon heur
chan- te. Voy- ant au

52
vous q'u- ne per-son- ne chan- te, q'u- ne per-son- ne chan-
son- ne chan- te, q'u- ne per- son- ne
q'u- ne per-son- ne chan- te, q'u- ne per- son- ne
q'u- ne per-son- ne chan- te, q'u- ne per- son- ne chan-
te, q'u- ne per- son- ne chan- te, q'u- ne per-son- ne

69
Voy- ant au vray tout mon heur ex- pi- rer, tout mon heur
Voy- ant, Voy- ant au vray tout mon heur ex- pi- rer, Voy-ant au vray tout
mon heur ex- pi- rer, Voy- ant au vray,
ex- pi- rer, Voy- ant au vray tout mon heur ex-
vray tout mon heur ex- pi- rer, Voy- ant au vray tout mon heur

ex- pi- rer, tout mon heur ex- pi- rer, De lais- ser
mon heur ex- pi- rer, tout mon heur ex- pi- rer, De lais- ser veux, De lais- ser
tout mon heur ex- pi- rer, De lais- ser veux, De lais- ser
pi- rer, Voy- ant au vray tout mon heur ex- pi- rer,
ex- pi- rer, De lais- ser

tou- te cho- se plai- san- te, Et dy que joy- e,
veux tou- te cho- se plai- san- te, Et dy que joy- e, Et
veux tou- te cho- se plai- san- te, Et dy que joy- e, Et dy que
veux tou- te cho- se plai- san- te, Et dy que joy- e, Et dy que joye
veux tou- te cho- se plai- san- te, Et dy que

veux, De lais- ser veux tou- te cho- se plai- san- te, De lais- ser veux,
veux, De lais- ser veux tou- te cho- se plai- san- te, De lais- ser
veux, De lais- ser veux tou- te cho- se plai- san- te, De lais- ser
De lais- ser veux tou- te cho- se plai- san- te, De lais- ser
veux, De lais- ser

Et dy que joye à ce- luy n'est dui- san- te, A qui le
dy que joy- e à ce- luy n'est dui- san- te,
joye à ce- luy n'est dui- san- te, A qui le coeur,
à ce- luy n'est dui- san- te, A qui le
joye à ce- luy n'est dui- san- te, A qui le

101
coeur, A qui le coeur ne fait que sou-
A qui le coeur ne fait que sou- pi- rer,
A qui le coeur ne fait que sou- pi- rer, ne
coeur, A qui le coeur ne fait que sou- pi- rer, A
coeur, A qui le coeur, ne fait que sou- pi- rer,

118
si es- poir qui gui- de mon at- ten- te, Mais si es- poir qui gui-
si es- poir qui gui- de mon at- ten- te, Mais si es- poir qui gui-
si es- poir qui gui- de mon at- ten- te, Mais si es- poir qui gui-
si es- poir qui gui- de mon at- ten- te, Mais si es- poir qui gui-
Mais si es- poir qui gui-

109
pi- rer. Mais
A qui le coeur ne fait que sou- pi- rer. Mais
fait que sou- pi- rer. Mais
qui le coeur ne fait que sou- pi- rer. Mais
A qui le coeur ne fait que sou- pi- rer.

125
de mon at- ten- te, Me fait ce bien qu'a bon port
de mon at- ten- te, Me fait ce bien qu'a
de mon at- ten- te, Me fait ce bien qu'a bon port me ti- rer, qu'a
de mon àt- ten- te, Me fait ce bien qu'a bon port me ti- rer, qu'a
de mon at- ten- te, Me fait ce bien qu'a bon port me ti- rer,

132
me ti- rer, Je di- ray lors sans plus me mar- ti- rer,
bon port me ti- rer, Me fait ce bien qu'a bon port
bon port me ti- rer, Je di- ray lors sans plus me mar- ti- rer,
bon port me ti- rer, Je di- ray lors, Je di- ray lors sans plus me
Je di- ray lors, Je di- ray

150
Lais- sez chan- ter, Lais- sez chan-
chan- ter, Lais- sez chan- ter, Lais- sez chan-
sez chan- ter, Lais- sez chan- ter, Lais-
Lais- sez chan- ter, Lais- sez chan- ter
Lais- sez chan- ter,

141
Je di- ray lors sans plus me mar- ti- rer,
me ti- rer, Je di- ray lors sans plus me mar- ti- rer, Lais- sez
Je di- ray lors sans plus me mar- ti- rer, Lais-
mar- ti- rer, sans plus me mar- ti- rer, sans plus me mar- ti- rer,
lors sans plus me mar- ti- rer, sans plus me mar- ti- rer,

157
ter, Lais- sez chan- ter ce- luy qui
ter, Lais- sez chan- ter, ce- luy qui
sez chan- ter ce- luy qui se con-
ce- luy qui se con- ten- te, ce-
Lais- sez chan- ter, Lais- sez chan- ter ce-

164
se con- ten- te.
se con- ten- te.
ten- te, ce- luy qui se con- ten- te.
luy qui se con- ten- te.
luy qui se con- ten- te.
Lors l'en- vi- eux ne
Lors l'en- vi- eux ne pour-
Lors l'en- vi- eux ne pour- ra
Lors l'en- vi-
Lors l'en- vi- eux ne

182
men- te, Con- ten- te toy du grief qui
te, Con- ten- te toy du grief qui me tour-
ve- he- men- te, Con- ten- te toy du grief qui me
ve- he- men- te, Con- ten- te toy du grief qui me tour-
ve- he- men- te, Con- ten- te toy,

172
pour- ra plus du- rer, Ains s'es- cri- ra de voix bien ve- he-
ra plus du- rer, Ains s'es- cri- ra de voix bien ve- he- men-
plus du- rer, Ains s'es- cri- ra, Ains s'es- cri- ra de voix bien ve- he- men- te, bien
eux ne pour- ra plus du- rer, Ains s'es- cri- ra de voix bien
pour- ra plus du- rer, Ains s'es- cri- ra de voix bien

192
me tour- men- te, Con- ten- te toy du grief qui
men- te, Con- ten- te toy du grief qui me tour-
tour- men- te, Con- ten- te toy du grief qui
men- te, Con- ten- te toy du grief qui me tour-
Con- ten- te toy du grief qui me

201
me tour- men- te, du grief qui me tour- men- te, Et
men- te, Con- ten- te toy du grief qui me tour- men- te, Et me lais-
me tour- men- te, du grief qui me tour- men- te, Et
men- te, du grief qui me tour- men- te, Et
tour- men- te,

219
rer, Et me lais- sez, Et me lais- sez mon
Et me lais- sez mon seul mal en- du- rer, Et me lais- sez mon
du- rer, Et me lais- sez mon seul mal
du- rer, Et me lais- sez mon seul mal en- du- rer, Et me lais-
Et me lais- sez mon seul mal en- du- rer,

210
me lais- sez, mon seul mal en- du- rer, mon seul mal en- du-
sez, Et me lais- sez, mon seul mal en- du- rer,
me lais- sez, mon seul mal en- du- rer, mon seul mal en-
me lais- sez mon seul mal en- du- rer, mon seul mal en-
sez, Et me lais- sez mon seul mal en- du- rer, mon seul mal en- du- rer,

227
seul mal en- du- rer, mon seul mal en- du- rer.
seul mal en- du- rer, mon seul mal en- du- rer.
en- du- rer, Et me lais- sez mon seul mal en- du- rer.
sez mon seul mal, mon seul mal en- du- rer.
Et me lais- sez mon seul mal en- du- rer.

347

Gris & tan-
Gris
Gris & tan- né me faut por-
Gris & tan- né me faut

17
& tan- né me faut por- ter, Car
Gris & tan- né me faut por- ter, Car tan- né
ter, Car tan- né suis en es- pe-
faut por- ter, me faut por- ter, Car tan- né suis
faut por- ter, me faut por- ter, Car

8
né me faut por- ter, Gris
& tan- né me faut por- ter, me faut por- ter,
ter, Gris & tan- né me faut por-
por- ter, me faut por- ter, Gris & tan- né me
Gris & tan- né me faut por- ter, Gris & tan- né me

26
tan- né suis en es- pe- ran- ce, Car tan- né suis
suis en es- pe- ran- ce, Car tan- né suis en es- pe- ran- ce,
ran- ce, Car tan- né suis, Car
en es- pe- ran- ce, Car tan- né
tan- né suis en es- pe- ran- ce, Car tan- né suis

en es- pe- ran- ce,
en es- pe- ran- ce,
tan- né suis en es- pe- ran- ce, Et le jau- ne
suis, Et le jau- ne me faut lais-
en es- pe- ran- ce, Et le jau- ne me faut lais- ser,

Et le jau- ne me faut lais- ser,
ser, Et le jau- ne me faut lais- ser, Qu'a-
ne me faut lais- ser, me faut lais- ser, Qu'a- mour por-
faut lais- ser, Qu'a- mour por- te par
ne me faut lais- ser, me faut lais- ser,

Et le jau- ne me faut lais- ser,
Et le jau- ne me faut lais- ser, me faut lais-
me faut lais- ser, me faut lais- ser, Et le jau-
ser, Et le jau- ne me
Et le jau- ne me faut lais- ser, Et le jau-

Qu'a- mour porte par jou- is- san- ce, Qu'a- mour por- te par
mour por- te par jou- is- san- ce, Qu'a- mour por- te par jou- is- san- ce,
te par jou- is- san- ce, Qu'a- mour por-
jou- is- san- ce, Qu'a- mour por- te, Qu'a-
Qu'a- mour porte par jou- is- san- ce, Qu'a- mour por- te par jou-

73
jou- is- san- ce, Le noir se- ra si-
par jou- is- san- ce, Le noir se- ra si- gni- fi- an-
te, par jou- is- san- ce,
mour por- te par jou- is- san- ce, Le noir se- ra si- gni- fi- an-
is- san- ce, Le

92
an- ce, Le noir se- ra si- gni- fi- an-
gni- fi- an- ce, si- gni- fi- an-
Le noir se- ra si- gni- fi- an-
ce, si- gni- fi- an- ce, si- gni- fi- an-
ra si- gni- fi- an- ce,

83
gni- fi- an- ce, Le noir se- ra si- gni- fi-
ce, Le noir se- ra si-
Le noir se- ra si- gni- fi- an- ce,
ce, Le noir se- ra si- gni- fi- an-
noir se- ra si- gni- fi- an- ce, Le noir se-

101
ce, De vi- vreen dueil & en tris- tes-
ce, De vi- vreen dueil & en tris- tes- se, De
ce, De vi- vreen dueil & en tris-
ce, De vi- vreen dueil, De vi- vreen dueil & en tris-
De vi- vreen dueil & en tris- tes- se,

se, De vi- vre en dueil & en
vi- vre en dueil, & en tris-
tes- se, De vi- vre en dueil & en tris-
tes- se, De vi- vre en dueil & en tris- tes-
De vi- vre en dueil & en tris- tes- se,

lais- se, Puis qu'il con- vient que je vous
lais- se, Puis qu'il con- vient que je vous lais- se, que je vous
Puis qu'il con- vient, Puis qu'il con- vient que
se, Puis qu'il con- vient,
lais- se, Puis qu'il con- vient que je vous

tris- tes- se, Puis qu'il con- vient que je vous
tes- se, & en tris- tes- se, Puis qu'il con- vient que je vous
tes- se, Puis qu'il con- vient que je vous lais- se,
se, Puis qu'il con- vient que je vous lais-
& en tris- tes- se, Puis qu'il con- vient que je vous

lais- se.
lais- se, Puis qu'il con- vient que je vous lais- se.
je vous lais- se.
Puis qu'il con- vient que je vous lais- se.
lais- se, Puis qu'il con- vient que je vous lais- se.

16

99 LaRue, *Incessamment mon povre coeur*

* Reading in the <u>Livre</u>:

352

35
me tour- men- te,
sou- ve- nir me tour-men- te, Ay- ant en- nuy, Ay- ant en- nuy,
Ay- ant en- nuy, Ay- ant en- nuy, Ay- ant en-
pos, sou- ve- nir me tour- men- te,
te,

57
de- ment:
de- ment: Ba- ny je suis,
de- ment: Ba- ny je suis de
men- de- ment: Ba- ny je suis
Ba- ny je suis de tout es- ba- te-

46
Ay- ant en- nuy, Ay- ant en- nuy sans au- cun a- men-
sans au- cun a- men- de- ment: a- men-
nuy, sans au- cun a- men-
Ay- ant en- nuy, Ay- ant en- nuy sans au- cun a-
nuy, Ay- ant en- nuy sans au- cun a- men- de- ment:

65
Ba- ny je suis de tout es- ba-
de tout es- ba- te- ment, de tout es- ba-
tout es- ba- te- ment, Ba- ny je suis de tout
de tout es- ba- te- ment,
ment,

75
te- ment, Et si lan- guis pres de mort ve- he- men- te,
te- ment, Et si lan- guis, pres de mort
es- ba- te- ment, Et
Et si lan- guis pres de mort
Et si lan- guis pres de mort ve- he- men-

93
ve- he- men- te, pres de mort ve- he- men-
pres de mort ve- he- men-
te, Et si lan- guis pres de mort
Et si lan- guis pres de mort ve- he- men-
ve- he- men- te, ve- he- men-

85
Et si lan- guis pres de mort
ve- he- men- te, Et si lan guis,
si lan- guis pres de mort ve- he- men-
ve- he- men- te,
te, Et si lan- guis pres de mort

101
te.
te, ve- he- men- te.
ve- he- men- te.
te.
te.

A la fon- tai- ne du pray, Mar- got s'est
A la fon- tai- ne du pré, A la fon-
A la fon- tai- ne du pré, Mar- got s'est bai- gné-
A la fon- tai- ne du pré, A la
A la fon- tai- ne du
A la fon- tai- ne du pré,

gné- e, Mar- got s'est bai- gné- e, Son a-
ne du pré, Mar- got s'est bai- gné- e, Son
e, Mar- got s'est bai- gné- e,
gné- e, Mar- got s'est bai- gné- e, Mar- got s'est bai-
fon- tai- ne du pré, Mar- got s'est bai- gné- e,
Mar- got s'est bai- gné- e, Mar- got s'est bai- gné-

bai- gné- e, s'est bai-
tai- ne du pré, Mar- got s'est bai- gné- e, A la fon- tai-
e, Mar- got s'est bai- gné-
fon- tai- ne du pré, Mar- got s'est bai-
pré, Mar- got s'est bai- gné- e, A la
Mar- got s'est bai- gné- e,

my pas- soit par la, Son a- my pas- soit par
a- my pas- soit par la, Son a- my pas- soit par la,
Son a- my pas- soit par la, pas- soit par la,
gné- e, Son a- my pas- soit par la, Son a- my pas- soit par la, pas-
Son a- my pas- soit
e, Son a- my pas- soit par la, Son a- my pas- soit par la,

42
la, Son a- my pas- soit par la,
Son a- my pas- soit par la,
Son a- my pas- soit par la, Qui l'a re- gar- dé-
soit par la,
par la, Son a- my pas- soit par la, Son a- my pas- soit
Qui l'a re- gar- dé- e, hip,

62
l'a re- gar- dé- e, Qui
Qui l'a re- gar- dé- e, hip, Qui l'a re- gar- dé-
Qui l'a re- gar- dé- e, Qui
l'a re- gar- dé- e, Qui l'a re- gar- dé- e, hip, Qui l'a re- gar-
Qui l'a re- gar- dé- e, hip, Qui l'a re- gar- dé-
Qui l'a re- gar- dé- e, hip, Qui l'a re- gar- dé- e,

53
Qui l'a re- gar- dé- e, hip, Qui
Qui l'a re- gar- dé- e, hip,
e, Qui l'a re- gar- dé- e, Qui l'a re- gar- dé- e, hip,
Qui l'a re- gar- dé- e, hip, Qui
par la,
Qui l'a re- gar- dé- e,

73
l'a re- gar- dé- e, Qui l'a re-
e, Qui l'a re- gar- dé- e,
l'a re- gar dé- e, Qui l'a re- gar- dé-
dé- e, Qui l'a re- gar- dé-
e, Qui l'a re- gar- dé- e,
Qui l'a re- gar- dé- e, Qui l'a re-

81
gar- dé- e, Mar-
Bel- le, que fait- tes vous la, Mar- got,
e, Bel- le, que fait- tes vous
e, Bel- le,
Bel- le, que fait- tes vous la, Mar- got, Mar- gue- ri- te,
gar- dé- e, Bel- le, que fait- tes vous

101
Mar- got, Mar- gue- ri- te, J'ar- rou- se mon per- si-
te, J'ar- rou- se mon
Mar- got, Mar- gue- ri- te, Mar- gue- ri- te,
ri- te, Mar- got, Mar- gue- ri- te, J'ar- rou- se mon
te, Mar- got, Mar- gue- ri- te,
Mar- go, Mar- gue- ri- te, J'ar- rou- se mon

91
got, Mar- gue- ri- te, Bel- le, que fait- te vous la,
Mar- gue- ri- te, Mar- got, Mar- gue- ri-
la, que fait- tes vous la, Mar- got, Mar- gue- ri- te,
que fait- tes vous la, Mar- got, Mar- gue- ri- te, Mar- got, Mar- gue-
Mar- got, Mar- gue- ri-
la, Mar- got, Mar- gue- ri- te,

111
net, J'ar- rou- se mon per- si- net, Et
per- si- net, J'ar- rou- se mon per- si- net,
J'ar- rou- se mon per- si- net, Et ma ser- ri-
per- si- net, Et ma ser- ri- et- te, hip,
J'ar- rou- se mon per- si- net, Et ma ser- ri- et- te,
per- si- net, J'ar- rou- se mon per- si- net, Et ma ser- ri- et-

* Reading in the Livre:

121
ma ser- ri- et- te, hip,
Et ma ser- ri- et- te, Et ma ser- ri- et- te,
et- te, Et ma ser- ri- et- te, Et ma ser- ri- et- te,
Et ma ser- ri- et- te, Et
hip, Et ma ser- ri- et- te, Et ma
te,

132
Et ma ser- ri- et- te, hip, Et ma ser- ri- et- te,
Et ma ser- ri- et- te, Et
Et ma ser- ri- et- te, hip, Et ma ser- ri- et- te,
ma ser- ri- et- te, Et ma ser- ri- et- te, hip, Et ma ser- ri- et- te,
ser- ri- et- te,
ma ser- ri- et- te, Et

144
Et ma ser- ri-
ma ser- ri- et- te, hip, Et ma ser- ri- et- te,
Et ma ser- ri- et- te, hip, Et ma ser- ri- et-
Et ma ser-
Et ma ser- ri- et- te, hip, Et ma ser- ri- et- te,
ma ser- ri- et- te, hip, Et ma ser- ri- et- te, Et

152
et- te, hip, Et ma ser- ri- et- te.
Et ma ser- ri- et- te.
te, Et ma ser- ri- et- te.
ri- et- te, Et ma ser- ri- et- te.
Et ma ser- ri- et- te.
ma, Et ma ser- ri- et- te.

Puis donc que ma mais- tres- se, N'a
Puis donc que ma mais- tres-
Puis
Puis donc que ma mais- tres-
Puis

19
point pi- tié de moy, Il con- vient que je ces- se,
point pi- tié de moy, Il con- vient que je ces- se, De l'ay-
N'a point pi- tié de moy,
point pi- tié de moy, Il con- vient
point pi- tié de moy,
Il con- vient que je

8
point pi- tié de moy, N'a point pi- tié de moy, N'a
se, N'a point pi- tié de moy, N'a point pi- tié de moy, N'a point pi- tié de moy, N'a
donc que ma mais- tres- se, N'a point pi- tié de moy,
se, N'a point pi- tié de moy, N'a
donc que ma mais- tres- se, N'a point pi- tié de moy,

29
Il con- vient que
mer sur ma foy:
Il con- vient que je ces-
que je ces- se,
Il con- vient que je ces- se,
ces- se, De

36
je ces- se, De l'ay- mer
De l'ay- mer sur ma foy, De
se, De l'ay- mer sur
De l'ay- mer sur ma foy: De
De l'ay- mer sur ma foy:
l'ay- mer sur ma foy: De

54
Je ne plein point ma pei-
Je ne plein point ma
Je ne plein point ma pei-
ma pei- ne,
ne plein point ma pei- ne,
plein point ma pei- ne,

44
sur ma foy.
l'ay- mer sur ma foy,
ma foy, De l'ay- mer sur ma foy:
l'ay- mer sur ma foy, Je ne plein point
De l'ay- mer sur ma foy, Je
l'ay- mer sur ma foy, Je ne

63
(sic)
ne, Je ne plein point ma pei-
pei- ne, ma pei- ne, Je ne
ne, Je ne plein point ma pei-
Je ne plein point ma pei- ne,
Je ne plein point ma pei- ne, Je ne plein point ma
Je ne plein point ma

72
ne, Je ne plein point ma pei- ne, Je
plein point ma pei- ne, Je ne plein point ma peine, Je ne plein point ma pei-
Je ne plein point ma pei- ne, Je ne plein point ma pei-
pei- ne, Je ne plein point ma pei-
pei- ne,

90
coeur mon- stre qu'il ay- me, qu'il ay- me,
stre qu'il ay- me, Mon coeur mon-
Mon coeur mon- stre qu'il ay- me, mon coeur
Mon coeur mon- stre qu'il ay- me, Mon coeur mon- stre
Mon coeur mon- stre qu'il ay-
Mon coeur mon- stre qu'il ay-

82
ne plein point ma pei- ne, Mon
ne, Mon coeur mon-
ne, Je ne plein point ma pei- ne,
ne, Je ne plein point ma pei- ne, ma pei- ne,
ne,
Je ne plein point ma pei- ne,

98
stre qu'il ay- me, Mon coeur mon-stre qu'il ay- me, qu'il ay-
mon- stre qu'il ay- me,
qu'il ay- me, mon-stre
me, mon- stre qu'il ay- me, Mon coeur mon-stre
me, Mon coeur mon- stre qu'il ay- me, mon- stre qu'il

108
Mon coeur mon- stre qu'il ay- me, mon-
me,
Mon coeur mon- stre qu'il ay- me, Mon coeur mon-
qu'il ay- me, Mon coeur mon- stre qu'il ay-
qu'il ay- me, Mon
ay- me, Mon coeur mon-

Or suis= je bien, Or suis= je bien, Or
Or suis= je bien au pi-
Or suis= je bien au pi-

116
stre qu'il ay- me.
qu'il ay- me.
stre qu'il ay- me, mon- stre qu'il ay- me.
me.
coeur mon- stre qu'il ay- me, Mon coeur mon- stre qu'il ay- me.
stre qu'il ay- me, mon- stre qu'il ay- me.

10
Or
Or suis=
suis= je bien au pi- re, au
re, au pi- re, au pi-
Or suis= je bien au pi-
re, De mes mal- heu- reux jours, De mes mal- heu- reux jours, De

suis= je bien au pi- re, De
je bien au pi- re, De mes mal-
pi- re, De mes mal- heu- reux
re, De mes mal- heu- reux jours, De mes mal-
re, De mes mal- heu-
mes mal- heu- reux jours, De mes mal- heu-reux jours, De

Mon cas par trop s'em- pi- re,
Mon cas par trop s'em- pi- re, De mes mal-
pi- re, Mon cas par trop s'em- pi- re, Et
pi- re, Et me vient
par trop s'em- pi- re, Et me
trop s'em- pi- re, Et me vient au re- bours, Et

mes mal- heu- reux jours,
heu- reux jours,
jours, Mon cas par trop s'em-
heu- reux jours, Mon cas par trop s'em-
reux jours, Mon cas
mes mal- heu-reux jours, De mes mal- heu- reux jours, Mon cas par

Et me vient au
Et me vient au re-
me vient au re- bours, Et me vient au
au re- bours, Et me vient au re- bours,
vient au re- bours,
me vient au re- bours, Et me vient au re- bours, Et me vient au

re- bours,
bours,
re- bours, Et me vient au re- bours, Et tout ce- la me font a-
Et tout ce- la me font a- mours, me
Et tout ce- la me font
re- bours, Et tout ce- la me font a- mours, me font

en- du- rer grief mar- ty-
en- du- rer grief mar- ty-
font a- mours,
du- rer grief mar- ty- re, en-
ty- re,
grief mar- ty- re, en- du- rer grief mar- ty-

Et tout ce- la me font a- mours,
Et tout ce- la me font a- mours,
mours, Et tout ce- la me
font a- mours, me font a- mours, en-
a- mours, en- du- rer grief mar-
a- mours, en- du- rer

re, en- du- rer grief mar-
re, en- du- rer grief mar-
en- du- rer grief mar- ty- re, Si n'ay de
du- rer grief mar- ty- re, Si n'ay de
en- du- rer grief mar- ty- re,
re, en- du- rer grief mar- ty- re, en- du- rer grief mar-

ty- re,   Si
ty- re,   Si n'ay de
vous au- tre se- cours,   Si n'ay de vous au- tre se-
vous   au- tre   se-
Si n'ay de vous au- tre   se-   cours,
ty-   re, Si n'ay   de vous au- tre se-

For- ce se- ra,   que me re-
For- ce se- ra,   que me re-   ti-
For- ce se- ra,   For- ce se- ra,
ra que me re- ti-   re,   For- ce se-
ra,   que me re- ti-   re,   Force se- ra,   que me re- ti-   re,

n'ay de vous au- tre se- cours,   au-   tre se- cours,
vous au- tre se- cours,   au- tre   se-   cours,
cours,   Si n'ay de vous   au-   tre se-   cours,
cours,   For- ce se- ra, For- ce se-
au- tre   se-   cours,   For-   ce se-
cours,   Si n'ay de vous au- tre se-   cours,   For-

ti- re,   For- ce se- ra,   que me
re,   For- ce se- ra,   que me re-
For- ce se- ra,   que me re- ti-
ra   que me re- ti-   re,
ce se- ra,   que me re-   ti-   re,
For- ce se- ra,   que me re- ti-   re,   que

En dou- leur & tris- tes- se, Lan- gui- ray= je tous-
En dou- leur & tris- tes- se, Lan- gui- ray= je tous- jours, Lan- gui-
En
En dou- leur

jours, Lan- gui- ray= je tous- jours, Lan- gui- ray= je
ray= je tous- jours,
En dou- leur & tris- tes- se,
dou- leur & tris- tes- se, Lan- gui- ray= je tous-
En dou- leur
& tris- tes- se, Lan- gui- ray= je tous- jours, Lan-

tous- jours,
Lan- gui- ray= je tous-
Lan- gui- ray= je tous- jours,
Lan- gui- ray= je tous- jours,
jours, Lan- gui- ray= je tous-
& tris- tes- se, Lan- gui- ray= je
gui- ray= je tous- jours,

Si je pers ma mais- tres- se, Ma da- me, par
Si je pers ma mais- tres- se, Ma da- me, par a- mours, Ma
Si

jours, Lan- gui- ray= je tous- jours, tous- jours,
Lan- gui- ray= je tous- jours, tous- jours,
jours, Lan- gui- ray= je tous- jours,
tous- jours, Lan- gui- ray= je tous- jours,
Lan- gui- ray= je tous- jours,

a- mours, Ma da- me, par a- mours, Ma da- me, par
da- me, par a- mours,
Si je pers ma mais- tres- se,
Si je pers ma mais- tres- se, Ma da- me, par
Si
je pers ma mais- tres- se, Ma da- me, par a- mours,

60
a- mours, Ma da- me, par a-
Ma da- me, par a- mours,
Ma da- me, par a- mours,
a- mours, Ma da- me, par a-
je pers ma mais- tres- se, Ma da- me, par
Ma da- me, par a- mours,

70
mours, Ma da- me, par a- mours,
Ma da- me, par a- mours, par a- mours,
Ma da- me, par a- mours, a- mours,
mours, Ma da- me, par a- mours,
a- mours, Ma da- me, par a- mours,
Ma da- me, par a- mours,

81
M'a- mour luy ay don- né- e,
M'a- mour luy ay don-
M'a- mour luy ay don- né- e, luy
M'a- mour luy

91
M'a- mour luy ay don- né- e,
né- e, luy ay don- né- e,
M'a- mour luy ay don- né-
ay don- né- e, luy ay don- né- e,
M'a- mour
ay don- né- [e],

99
Ja- mais ne l'ou- bli-
M'a- mour luy ay don- né- e, Ja- mais ne
e, Ja- mais ne l'ou- bli-
M'a- mour luy ay don- né- e,
luy ay don-né- e,
M'a- mour, luy ay don- né-

117
Et en me- lan- co- li- e, Mes jours je
Et en me- lan- co- li- e,
Et en me- lan- co- li- e, Mes
ray, Et en me- lan- co- li- e,
ray, Et en me- lan- co- li- e,
ray, Ja- mais ne l'ou- bli- ray, Et en me- lan- co-

108
ray, Ja- mais ne l'ou- bli- ray,
l'ou- bli- ray,
ray, Ja- mais ne l'ou- bli- ray,
Ja- mais ne l'ou- bli- ray, Ja- mais ne l'ou- bli-
[e], Ja- mais ne l'ou- bli-

127
fi- ni- ray,
Mes jours je fi- ni- ray, Et en me-
jours je fi- ni- ray, Et
Mes jours je fi- ni- ray, Et en me-
Mes jours je fi- ni- ray,
li- e, Mes jours je fi- ni- ray, Mes

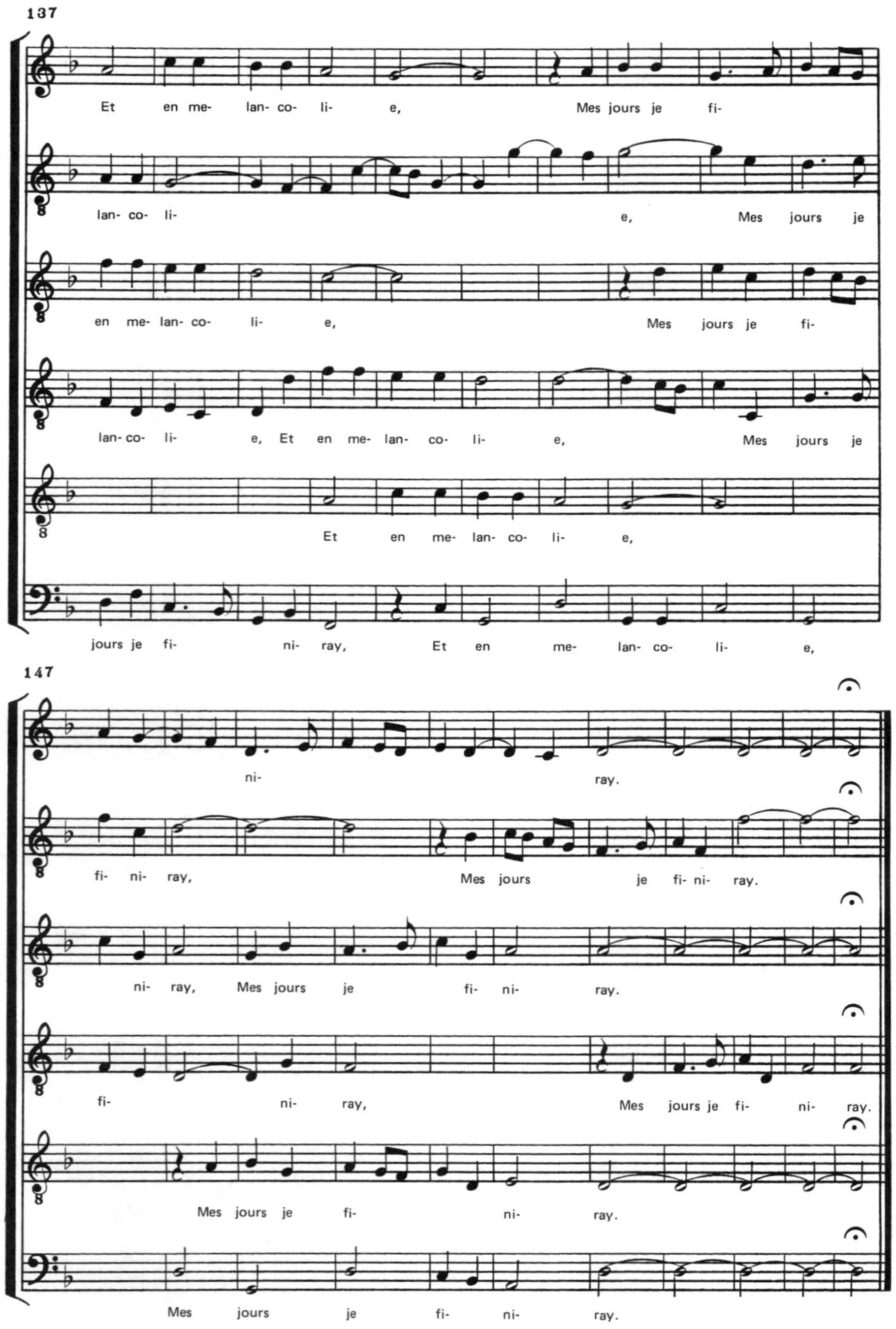

137

Et en me- lan-co- li- e, Mes jours je fi-
lan-co- li- e, Mes jours je
en me- lan-co- li- e, Mes jours je fi-
lan-co- li- e, Et en me- lan- co- li- e, Mes jours je
Et en me- lan-co- li- e,
jours je fi- ni- ray, Et en me- lan-co- li- e,

147

ni- ray.
fi- ni- ray, Mes jours je fi- ni- ray.
ni- ray, Mes jours je fi- ni- ray.
fi- ni- ray, Mes jours je fi- ni- ray.
Mes jours je fi- ni- ray.

11

20
c'est dou- leur nom= pa- rei- lle, Si je le di,
te d'ar- gent, c'est dou- leur nom=pa-rei- lle, Si je le di, Si
dou- leur nom= pa- rei- lle, Si je le
d'ar- gent, c'est dou- leur nom= pa- rei- lle,
pa- rei- lle, Si je le
nom= pa- rei- lle, Si

40
je le di, j'ay bien rai- son pour-
quoy, j'ay bien rai- son pour- quoy, j'ay bien rai-
quoy, j'ay bien rai- son pour-quoy, Sans de
bien rai- son pour- quoy, j'ay bien rai- son pour-quoy,
bien rai- son pour- quoy, j'ay bien rai- son pour-quoy, Sans de qui
j'ay bien rai- son pour- quoy,

29
3
Si je le di, Si je le di, j'ay bien rai- son pour-quoy, Si
je le di, Si je le di, j'ay bien rai- son pour
di, Si je le di, j'ay bien rai- son pour-
Si je le di, Si je le di, j'ay
di, Si je le di, j'ay bien rai- son pour- quoy, j'ay
je le di, Si je le di, j'ay bien rai- son pour-quoy,

51
quoy, Sans de qui- bus, il se faut
son pour- quoy, Sans de qui- bus, il se faut te-nir coy,
qui- bus, il se faut te- nir coy,
Sans de qui- bus, il se faut te- nir coy,
bus, il se faut te- nir coy, il se faut te-
Sans de qui- bus, il se faut te- nir

62
te- nir coy, Fem-me qui dort,
Fem- me qui dort,
nir coy, Fem- me qui dort pour ar- gent on l'es- vei-
coy, Fem- me qui dort pour ar- gent on l'es- vei-

84
pour ar- gent on l'es- vei- lle. Qui
ar- gent on l'es- vei- lle. Qui
dou- leur nom= pa- rei- lle. Qui
d'ar- gent c'est dou- leur nom= pa- rei- lle.
l'es- vei- lle. Qui
on l'es- vei- lle. Qui

73
Fem- me qui dort pour ar- gent on l'es- vei- lle, Fem- me qui dort
Fem- me qui dort pour ar- gent on l'es- vei- lle, pour
Fau- te d'ar- gent c'est
Fau- te
lle, pour ar- gent on l'es- vei- lle, pour ar- gent on
lle, pour ar- gent on l'es- vei- lle, pour ar- gent

91
a beau nez beu- vra à la bou- tei- lle,
[bev-?]
a beau nez, beu- vra à la bou- tei-
[bev-?]
a beau nez, beu- vra à la bou- tei- lle,
[bev-?]
Qui a beau nez, beu- vra à la bou- tei-
[bev-?]
a beau nez beu- vra à la bou- tei-
[bev-?]
a beau nez beu- vra à la bou- tei- lle, à la bou-
[bev-?]

99
Qui a ar- gent, se- ra le bien ve- nu, En-
lle, Qui a ar- gent se- ra le bien ve- nu, En-
Qui a ar- gent se- ra le bien ve- nu, En- tre les
lle, Qui a ar- gent se- ra le bien ve- nu,
lle, Qui a ar- gent se- ra le bien ve- nu, En- tre
tei- lle, Qui a ar- gent se- ra le bien ve- nu, se-

119
la pu- ce en l'o- rei- lle, j'ay la pu- ce en l'o-
j'ay la pu- ce en l'o- rei- lle, en l'o- rei- lle,
j'ay la pu- ce en l'o- rei- lle, Pour vous ne dors,
vous ne dors, j'ay la pu- ce en l'o- rei- lle, Pour
la pu- ce en l'o- rei- lle, Pour vous ne dors,
la pu- ce en l'o- rei- lle, Pour vous ne dors, j'ay

109
tre les da- mes tres- bien en- tre- te- nu, Pour vous ne dors, j'ay
tre les da- mes tres- bien en- tre- te- nu, Pour vous ne dors,
da- mes tres- bien en- tre- te- nu, Pour vous ne dors,
En- tre les da- mes tres- bien en- tre- te- nu, Pour
les da- mes tres- bien en- tre- te- nu, Pour vous ne dors, j'ay
ra le bien ve- nu, Pour vous ne dors, j'ay

128
rei- lle.
j'ay la pu- ce en l'o- rei- lle.
j'ay la pu- ce en l'o- rei- lle.
vous ne dors, j'ay la pu- ce en l'o- rei- lle.
j'ay la pu- ce en l'o- rei- lle.
la pu- ce en l'o- rei- lle.

373

105 Vuillard, *Mon coeur, mon corps*

Rien re- ser- vé, de bon coeur vous pre-
Rien re- ser- vé de bon coeur
vous pre- sen- te, Rien re- ser- vé, de bon coeur
de bon coeur vous pre- sen- te, Rien re- ser- vé de bon coeur vous pre-
de bon coeur vous pre- sen- te,
bon coeur vous pre- sen- te,

vous pre- sen- te, de bon coeur vous pre- sen- te, Or
Rien re- ser- vé de bon coeur vous pre- sen- te,
de bon coeur vous pre- sen- te, Or pen- sés
bon coeur vous pre- sen- te, de bon coeur vous pre- sen- te,
Or pen- sés
de bon coeur vous pre- sen- te, Or

sen- te, de bon coeur
vous pre- sen- te,
vous pre- sen- te, Rien re- ser- vé de bon coeur vous pre- sen- te, de
sen- te, Rien re- ser- vé de bon coeur vous pre- sen- te, de
Rien re- ser- vé de bon coeur vous pre- sen- te,
Rien re- ser- vé de bon coeur vous pre- sen- te,

pen- sés donc, quant grief- ve m'est l'at- ten- te, Or pen- sez
Or pen- sés donc,
donc quant grief- ve m'est l'at- ten- te, Or pen- sés donc quant grief- ve
Or pen- sés donc quant grief- ve m'est l'at- ten- te, Or
donc, quant grief- ve m'est l'at- ten- te, Or pen- sés
pen- sés donc, Or pen- sés

375

78
donc,
Or pen- sez donc quant
quant grief- ve m'est l'at- ten- te, Or pen- sez
m'est l'at- ten- te, Or pen- sez donc,
pen- sés donc, Or pen- sés donc
donc, quant grief- ve m'est l'at- ten- te,
donc quant grief- ve m'est l'at- ten- te, Or pen- sez

95
De voz deux yeux un doux re- gard a- voir, un
De voz deux yeux, un doux re-
doux re- gard a- voir, De voz deux yeux un doux re- gard
un doux re- gard a- voir, De voz deux yeux un doux re- gard a-
doux re- gard a- voir, De voz deux yeux, un
yeux un doux re- gard a- voir, De voz deux yeux, De voz deux yeux un

86
grief- ve m'est l'at- ten- te,
donc, quant grief- ve m'est l'at- ten- te,
quant grief- ve m'est l'at- ten- te, De voz deux yeux un
quant grief- ve m'est l'at- ten- te, De voz deux yeux,
De voz deux yeux, un
donc, quant grief- ve m'est l'at- ten- te, De voz deux yeux, De voz deux

105
doux re- gard a- voir.
gard a- voir.
a- voir.
voir, un doux re- gard a- voir.
doux re- gard a- voir.
doux re- gard a- voir, un doux re- gard a- voir.

Dou- leur me bat, Dou- leur me
Dou-
Dou- leur me bat, Dou- leur me bat, Dou-
Dou- leur me bat, Dou-
Dou- leur me bat, Dou-

22

le, & tris- tes- se m'af- fol- le,
le, A- mour me
le, m'af- fol- le, A- mour me
& tris- tes- se m'af- fol- le,
fol- le, & tris- tes- se m'af- fol- le,
fol- le, & tris- tes- se m'af- fol- le, A- mour me

11

bat, Dou- leur me bat, & tris- tes- se m'af- fol-
leur me bat, & tris- tes- se m'af- fol-
leur me bat, & tris- tes- se m'af- fol-
Dou- leur me bat,
leur me bat, Dou- leur me bat, & tris- tes- se m'af-
leur me bat, & tris- tes- se m'af-

33

A- mour me nuit,
nuit, & mal- heur me con- sol- le,
nuit, & mal- heur me con- sol- le, A- mour
A- mour me nuit, & mal- heur
A- mour me nuit, & mal- heur me con- sol-
nuit, A- mour me nuit, & mal- heur

& mal- heur me con- sol- le, Vou- loir me
Vou- loir
me nuit, & mal- heur me con- sol- le, Vou- loir me
me con- sol- le,
le, & mal- heur me con- sol- le, Vou- loir me
me con- sol- le, & mal-heur me con- sol- le,

me peut, Jou- ir ne puis, Jou- ir ne puis, du
puis, du grand bien qu'on me veut,
du grand bien qu'on me veut, Jou- ir ne puis, du grand bien
me peut, Jou- ir ne puis, du grand bien qu'on me
Jou- ir ne puis du grand bien qu'on me veut, Jou-
ne me peut, Jou- ir ne puis du

suit, Vou- loir me suit, mais ay- der ne me peut, ne
me suit, mais ay- der ne me peut, Jou- ir ne
suit, mais ay- der ne me peut, Jou- ir ne puis,
Vou- loir me suit, mais ay- der ne
suit, mais ay- der ne me peut, Vou- loir me suit, mais ay- der ne me peut,
Vou- loir me suit, Vou- loir me suit, mais ay- der

grand bien qu'on me veut, De vi- vre ain- si pour Dieu qu'on
De vi- vre ain- si, pour Dieu qu'on
qu'on me veut, De vi- vreain- si pour Dieu qu'on me de-
veut, De vi- vre ain-
ir ne puis du grand bien qu'on me veut, De vi- vre ain- si, pour Dieu
grand bien qu'on me veut, De vi- vre ain- si pour Dieu qu'on

89
me de- col- le, pour Dieu qu'on me de- col- le,
me de- col- le, pour Dieu qu'on me de-
col- le, De vi- vre ain- si pour Dieu qu'on me de-
si, pour Dieu qu'on me de- col- le,
qu'on me de- col- le, pour Dieu qu'on me de- col- le,
me de- col- le, qu'on me de- col- le, pour Dieu qu'on

113
vre ain- si, pour Dieu qu'on me de- col- le, pour Dieu qu'on
si, pour Dieu qu'on me de- col- le,
vi- vre ain- si pour Dieu qu'on me de- col- le, pour Dieu qu'on me de-
De vi- vre ain- si, pour Dieu qu'on me de-
vi- vre ain- si pour Dieu qu'on me de- col- le, pour Dieu qu'on
vi- vre ain- si pour Dieu qu'on me de- col- le, qu'on me de- col- le,

101
pour Dieu qu'on me de- col- le, De vi- vre ain- si, De vi-
col- le, De vi- vre ain-
col- le, De vi- vre ain- si, De vi- vre ain- si, De
pour Dieu qu'on me de- col- le,
pour Dieu qu'on me de- col- le, De vi- vre ain- si, De
me de- col- le, De vi- vre ain- si, De

125
me de- col- le, pour Dieu qu'on me de- col-
pour Dieu qu'on me de- col- le,
col- le, pour Dieu qu'on me de- col- le, pour Dieu qu'on me de-
col- le, pour Dieu qu'on me de- col-
me de- col- le, pour Dieu qu'on me de- col-
pour Dieu qu'on me de- col- le,

107 Vuillard, *Petite camusette*

A la
mis, A la mort m'a- vez mis,
mort m'a- vez mis,
mis, A la mort m'a- vez mis, A la mort
mis, A la mort m'a- vez mis,
la mort m'a- vez mis, A la

Ro- bin & Ma- ri- on, Ro- bin &
Ro- bin & Ma- ri- on, Ils
Ro- bin, Ro- bin & Ma- ri- on,
bin & Ma- ri- on, Ro- bin, Ro- bin & Ma- ri- on, Ils
& Ma- ri- on, Ils s'en vont bras à
bin & Ma- ri- on, Ils s'en vont bras à bras, Ils s'en vont bras à

mort m'a- vez mis, Ro- bin,
A la mort m'a- vez mis, Ro- bin,
A la mort m'a- vez mis, Ro- bin & Ma- ri- on,
m'a- vez mis, A la mort m'a- vez mis, Ro- bin, Ro-
A la mort m'a- vez mis, Ro- bin
mort m'a- vez mis, Ro- bin, Ro- bin & Ma- ri- on, Ro-

Ma- ri- on, Ils s'en vont bras à bras, Ils se
s'en vont bras à bras, bras à
Ils s'en vont bras
s'en vont bras à bras, Ils
bras, Ils se sont en- dor- mis,

60
sont en- dor- mis, Ils se sont en- dor-
bras, Ils se sont en- dor- mis,
à bras, Ils se sont en- dor-
s'en vont bras à bras, Ils se sont en- dor- mis, Ils se sont
en- dor- mis, Pe- ti- te,
Pe- ti- te, Pe-

81
ca- mu- set- te, A la
te ca- mu- set- te, A
Pe- ti- te ca- mu- set- te,
te, ca- mu- set- te, A
ti- te, Pe- ti- te ca- mu- set- te,
Pe- ti- te ca- mu- set- te, A

70
mis, Pe- ti- te
Ils se sont en- dor- mis, Pe- ti-
mis, en- dor- mis,
en- dor- mis, Pe- ti- te, Pe- ti- te ca- mu- set-
Pe-
ti- te ca- mu- set- te,

90
mort m'a- vés mis,
la mort m'a- vés mis, A la mort m'a-
A la mort m'a- vés mis,
la mort m'a- vés mis, A la
A la mort m'a- vés mis, A la mort
la mort m'a- vés mis, A la mort m'a- vés

108 Vuillard, *Vous ne l'aurez pas*

21
vez re- quis, Ce que m'a- vez
d'a-
Ce que m'a- vez
Vous ne l'au- rez pas si je puis,
ne l'au- rez pas si je puis, Ce que m'a- vez
si je puis,
si je puis, si je puis, je puis, Ce que

30
re- quis d'a- voir,
re- quis d'a- voir,
Ce que m'a- vez
re- quis d'a- voir, re- quis
Ce que m'a- vez re- quis d'a- voir,
m'a- vez re- quis d'a- voir, Ce que m'a-

39
Ce que m'a- vez re- quis d'a-
Ce que m'a- vez re- quis d'a-
re- quis d'a- voir,
d'a- voir, Ce que m'a- vez re-
Ce que m'a-
vez re- quis d'a- voir, Ce que m'a- vez

48
voir, Ce que m'a- vez re- quis d'a- voir, Et
voir, Et eus- siez vous
Ce que m'a- vez re- quis d'a- voir,
quis d'a- voir, Et eus- siez
vez re- quis d'a- voir,
re- quis d'a- voir, Ce que m'a- vez re- quis d'a- voir,

58
eus- siez vous au- tant d'a-	voir,	Et eus- siez vous
au-	tant d'a-	voir,
Et eus- siez vous	au-
vous au- tant d'a- voir, Et eus- siez vous au- tant d'a- voir, Et eus- siez vous au- tant d'a-
Et eus- siez vous	au- tant d'a-	voir,
Ce que m'a- vez re- quis d'a-	voir,	re-

68
au-	tant d'a- voir, Et eus-	siez vous	au-	tant	d'a-
Et eus- siez vous	au-	tant d'a-	voir,
tant	d'a- voir,	Et eus-siez
voir,	Et	eus-	siez vous au- tant d'a- voir,
Et eus- siez vous	au-	tant
quis d'a-	voir,	Et	eus-	siez vous au- tant	d'a-	voir, au-	tant d'a-

79
voir,	Qu'il en pour-roit	de-	dens	un	puis,
Qu'il en pour-roit de- dens	un
vous	au-	tant d'a- voir,
Qu'il	en pour- roit de- dens	un	puis,
d'a-	voir,	Qu'il
voir,	Et eus- siez vous	au-	tant	d'a-	voir, Qu'il en pour- roit de-

90
Qu'il en pour- roit	de-	dens	un	puis,	Qu'il en pour- roit
puis,	Qu'il en pour- roit de- dens	un	puis,
Qu'il	en pour- roit de- dens	un	puis,	Qu'il
Qu'il	en pour- roit de- dens	un puis,	Qu'il en pour- roit	de-
en pour- roit de- dens	un	puis,	Qu'il en pour- roit de- dens	un
dens	un	puis,	Qu'il en pour- roit de- dens	un

103
de- dens un puis, Qu'il en pour- roit de- dens un
Qu'il en pour- roit de- dens un puis,
en pour- roit de- dens un puis,
dens un puis, Qu'il en pour- roit de- dens
puis, Qu'il en pour-roit de-
puis, Qu'il en pour- roit de- dens
113
puis, de- dens un puis, Qu'il en pour- roit de-
Qu'il en pour-
Qu'il en pour- roit de- dens un puis,
un puis, Qu'il en pour-roit de- dens un puis, de-
dens un puis,
un puis, Qu'il en pour- roit de- dens un puis, Qu'il en
122
dens un puis, Qu'il en pour- roit de- dens un puis, de-
roit de- dens un puis,
Qu'il en pour-
dens un puis, Qu'il en pour- roit de- dens un puis,
Qu'il en pour- roit de- dens un puis,
pour- roit de- dens un puis, Qu'il en pour- roit
130
dens un puis.
de- dens un puis.
roit de- dens un puis.
de- dens un puis.
de- dens un puis.
de- dens un puis.

Qui veut ay- mer il faut es- tre joy- eux,
Qui veut ay- mer, il faut es- tre joy-
Qui veut ay- mer il faut es- tre joy- eux,
Qui veut ay- mer
Qui veut ay- mer, Qui veut ay- mer il faut es- tre
Qui veut ay- mer, Qui veut ay- mer il

rai- ne,
sou- ve- rai- ne, sa da- me sou- ve- rai-
da- me sou- ve- rai- ne, Et al- ler voir sa da- me
Et al- ler voir sa da- me sou- ve- rai-
sou- ve- rai- ne, Et al- ler voir sa da- me sou-
Et al- ler voir sa da- me sou- ve- rai- ne,

Et al- ler voir sa da- me sou- ve-
eux, Et al- ler voir sa da- me
il faut es- tre joy- eux, Et al- ler voir sa
il faut es- tre joy- eux,
joy- eux, joy- eux, Et al- ler voir sa da- me
faut es- tre joy- eux, Et al- ler voir sa da- me,

Deux ou trois fois ou qua- tre la se- mai- ne,
ne, Deux ou trois fois ou qua- tre la se- mai- ne,
sou- ve- rai- ne, Deux ou trois fois ou qua- tre la se- mai- ne, Deux
ne, Deux ou trois fois
ve- rai- ne, Deux ou trois fois,
Deux ou trois fois ou qua- tre la se- mai- ne,

39
Deux ou trois fois ou qua- tre la se- mai-
ou qua- tre la se- mai- ne, ou qua- tre la se-
ou trois fois ou qua- tre la se- mai- ne, ou qua- tre la se-
ou qua- tre la se- mai- ne,
Deux ou trois fois ou qua- tre la se- mai- ne, ou qua- tre
ou qua- tre la se- mai- ne,

57
Pour en a- voir un bai- ser
la se- mai- ne, Pour en a- voir,
la se- mai- ne, Pour en a- voir un bai- ser
Pour en a- voir, Pour en a- voir, Pour en a-
voir un bai- ser gra- ti- eux, un bai- ser gra- ti- eux, Pour en a- voir,

48
ne,
mai- ne, Deux ou trois fois ou qua- tre
mai- ne, ou qua- tre
Deux ou trois fois ou qua- tre la se- mai- ne,
la se- mai- ne, ou qua- tre la se- mai- ne,
Deux ou trois fois ou qua- tre la se- mai- ne, Pour en a-

66
gra- ti- eux,
un bai- ser gra- ti- eux, Pour en a-
gra- ti- eux, un bai- ser gra- ti- eux, Pour en
Pour en a- voir un bai- ser gra- ti- eux,
voir un bai- ser gra- ti- eux, Pour en a-
Pour en a- voir un bai- ser gra- ti- eux,

388

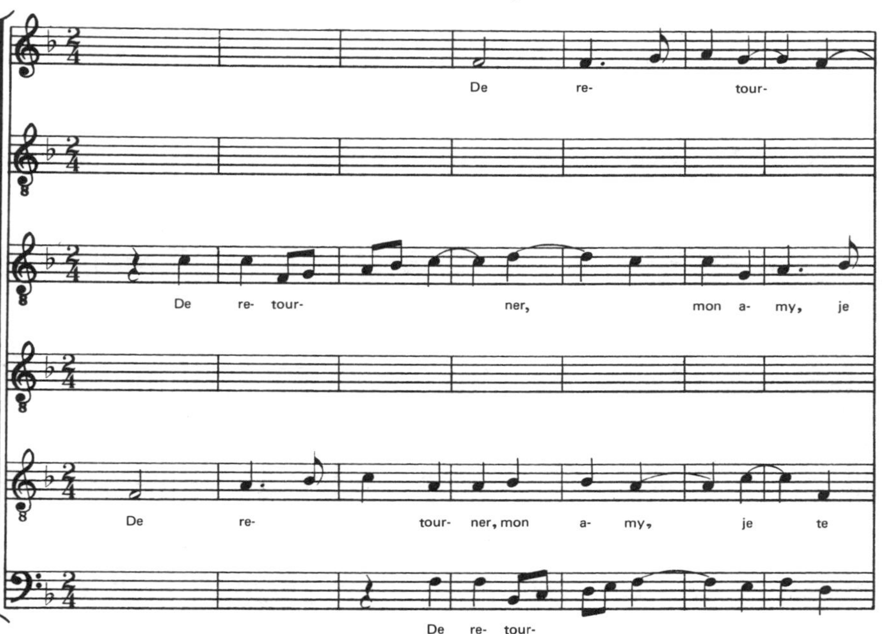

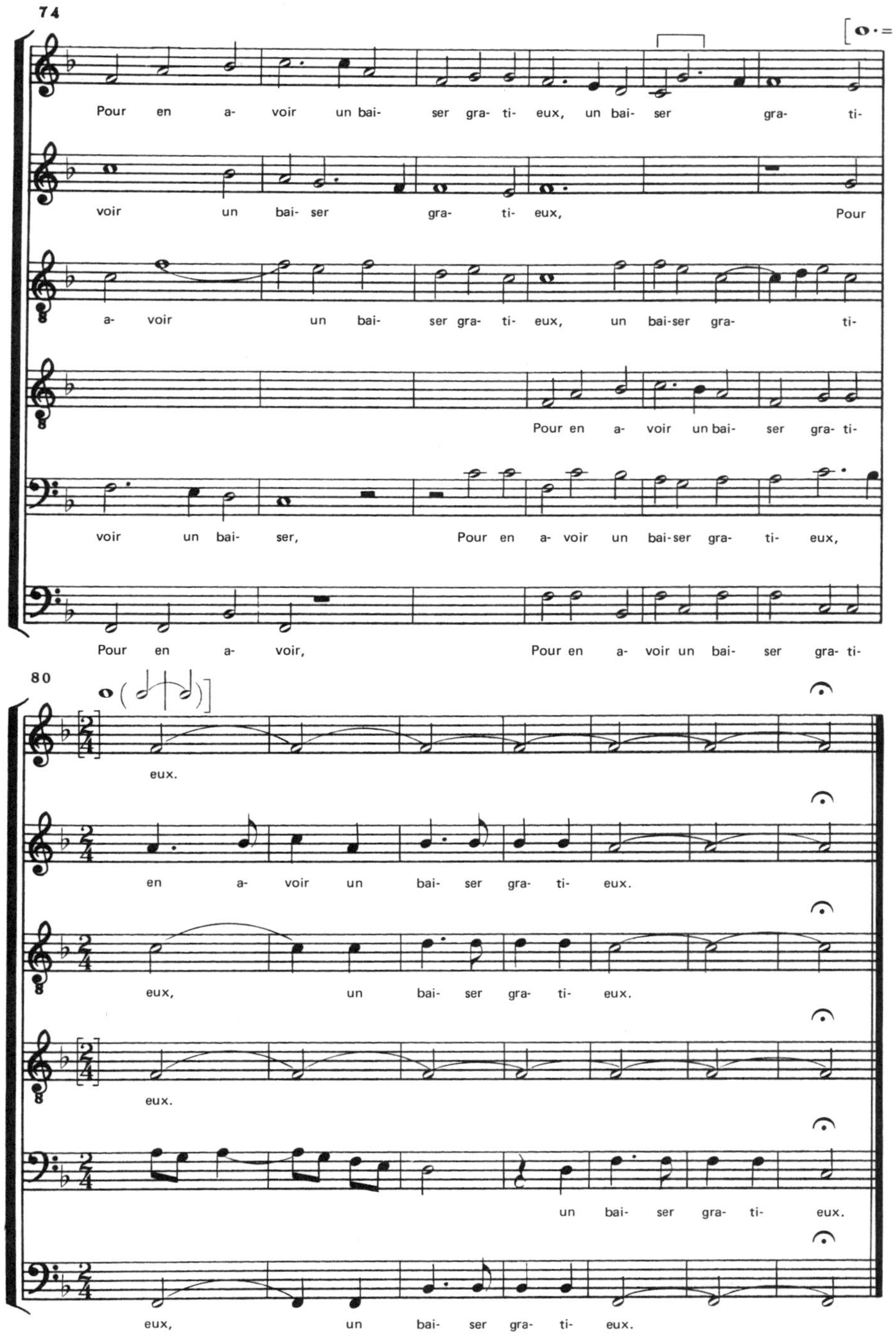
74
Pour en a- voir un bai- ser gra- ti- eux, un bai- ser gra- ti-
voir un bai- ser gra- ti- eux, Pour
a- voir un bai- ser gra- ti- eux, un bai-ser gra- ti-
Pour en a- voir un bai- ser gra- ti-
voir un bai- ser, Pour en a- voir un bai-ser gra- ti- eux,
Pour en a- voir, Pour en a- voir un bai- ser gra- ti-
80
eux.
en a- voir un bai- ser gra- ti- eux.
eux, un bai- ser gra- ti- eux.
eux.
un bai- ser gra- ti- eux.
eux, un bai- ser gra- ti- eux.

110 Vuillard, *De retourner, mon amy*

De re- tour-
De re- tour- ner, mon a- my, je
De re- tour- ner, mon a- my, je te
De re- tour-
8
ner, mon a- my, je te pri-
De re- tour- ner, mon
te pri- e, mon a- my, je te pri-
De re- tour- ner, mon a- my, je te pri-
pri- e, mon a- my, je te pri- e, je
ner, De re- tour-

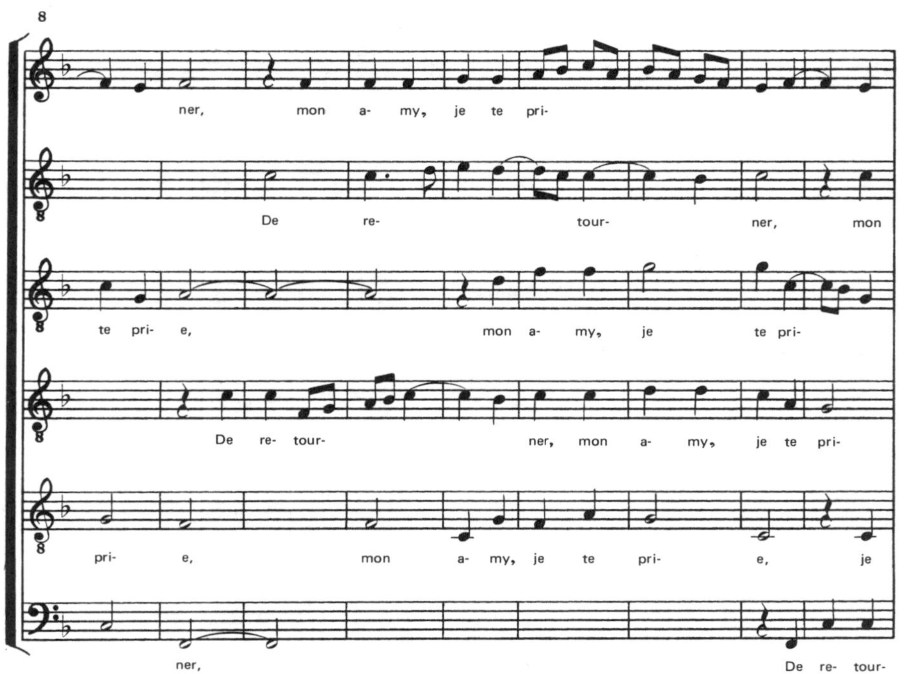

17
e,
Pour con-
a- my, je te pri-
e,
e, De re- tour- ner, mon a- my, je te pri- e, Pour con- ten-
e,
mon a- my, je te pri- e, Pour con- ten- ter,
te pri-
e,
Pour con- ten-
ter l'es-
ner,
mon a- my, je te pri-
e,
Pour con-
37
e,
Car sans ce- la ai- se ne
prit de ton a- my-
e,
e, Pour con- ten- ter l'es- prit de ton a- my- e, Car sans ce- la ai-
e,
l'es- prit de ton a- my-
e,
Car sans ce- la,
prit de ton a- my-
e,
Car sans ce- la, ai- se ne
ter,
l'es-
prit de ton a- my-
e, Car sans ce- la, Car sans ce- la ai-

26
ten-
ter, l'es- prit de ton a- my-
Pour con-
ten-
ter, l'es-
ter l'es- prit de ton a- my-
e,
l'es- prit de ton
a- my-
Pour con- ten-
ter l'es- prit de ton a- my-
prit de ton a- my-
e,
l'es-
prit de ton a- my-
e, l'es-
ten-
ter,
Pour con- ten-
48
puis a-
voir,
Car sans ce- la ai- se ne
Car sans ce- la ai- se ne puis a-
voir,
se ne puis a- voir, ai- se ne
puis a-
voir, Car sans ce- la ai-
ai-
se ne puis a-
voir,
Car sans ce- la ai- se ne puis a- voir, Car
puis a- voir,
ai- se ne puis a- voir,
Car sans ce- la,
Car sans ce- la,
se ne puis a- voir,
ai- se ne puis a- voir,
Car sans ce- la ai- se ne puis a- voir,

61
puis a- voir, Tris- te vi- vray, je le te
Car sans ce- la ai- se ne puis a- voir,
se ne puis a- voir, ai- se ne puis a- voir, Tris- te vi- vray, je
sans ce- la, ai- se ne puis a- voir, Tris- te vi-
ai- se ne puis a- voir, Tris- te vi- vray, Tris- te vi-
Car sans ce- la, ai- se ne puis a- voir, Tris- te vi- vray,
72
fay sça- voir, Si ne te
Tris- te vi- vray, je le te fay sça- voir,
le te fay sça- voir, Tris- te vi- vray, je le te fay sça- voir, Si ne te voy,
vray, je le te fay sça- voir, Tris- te vi- vray, je le te fay sça- voir, Si ne te voy
vray, je le te fay sça- voir, Tris- te vi- vray, je le te fay sça- voir, Si ne te voy car j'en ay
Tris- te vi- vray, Tris- te vi- vray, je le te fay sça- voir, Si ne te

84
voy car j'en ay grand en- vy- e,
Si ne te voy car j'en ay gran- d'en-
Si ne te voy car j'en ay grand en- vy- e, Si ne te voy car
car j'en ay gran- d'en- vy- e, Si ne te voy, Si ne te
gran- d'en- vy- e, Si ne te voy
voy car j'en ay gran- d'en- vy- e, Si ne te
93
Si ne te voy car
vy- e,
j'en ay grand en- vy- e, Si ne te voy, Si
voy, Si ne te voy car j'en ay gran- d'en-
car j'en ay gran- d'en- vy- e, Si ne te voy, SI
voy car j'en ay gran- d'en- vy- e, Si ne te voy car

111 Leschenet, *Je m'y plein fort*

19
C'est un bru- va-
jus, qu'a- mours m'ont ru- é jus, C'est un bru- va-
fort qu'a- mours m'ont ru- é jus,
é jus, m'ont ru- é jus, C'est un bru-
jus, C'est un bru- va- ge a- mer plus que ver-
Je m'y plein fort qu'a- mours m'ont ru- é jus, C'est

37
vous con- seille a tous, &
Je vous con- seille a tous,
ge a- mer plus que ver- jus, Je vous con- seille a
bru- va- ge a- mer plus que ver- jus, Je vous con- seille a tous, & si ne
ge a- mer plus que ver- jus, Je vous con- seille a tous, & si
Je vous con- seille a tous, &

28
ge a- mer plus que ver- jus, Je
ge a- mer, C'est un bru- va- ge a- mer plus que ver- jus,
C'est un bru- va-
va- ge a- mer plus que ver- jus, C'est un
jus, C'est un bru- va-
un bru- va- ge a- mer plus que ver- jus, plus que ver- jus,

48
si ne suis pas sa- ge, Que d'ay- mer par a-
& si ne suis pas sa- ge, & si ne suis,
tous, & si ne
suis pas sa- ge, & si ne suis pas sa-
ne suis pas sa- ge, & si
si ne suis pas sa- ge,

57
mours, e-
pas sa- ge, Que d'ay- mer par a- mours, e- vi- tiez
suis pas sa- ge, Que d'ay- mer par a- mours,
ge, Que d'ay-mer par a- mours, Que d'ay- mer par a- mours,
ne suis pas sa- ge,Que d'ay- mer par a- mours,
Que d'ay- mer par a- mours, e- vi- tiez le pas-

74
e- vi- tiez le pas- sa- ge,
le pas- sa- ge, e- vi- tiez
vi- tiez le pas- sa-
3
e- vi- tiez le pas- sa-
e- vi- tiez le pas- sa-
ge,

66
vi- tiez le pas- sa- ge,
le pas- sa- ge, e- vi- tiez
e-
e- vi- tiez le pas- sa- ge,
3
e- vi- tiez le pas- sa- ge,
sa- ge, e- vi- tiez le pa- sa-

81
e- vi- tiez le pas- sa- ge.
le pas- sa- ge.
ge.
ge, e- vi- tiez le pas- sa- ge.
ge, e- vi- tiez le pas- sa- ge.
e- vi- tiez le pas- sa- ge.

112 Crequillon, *Sy me tenez tant*

38

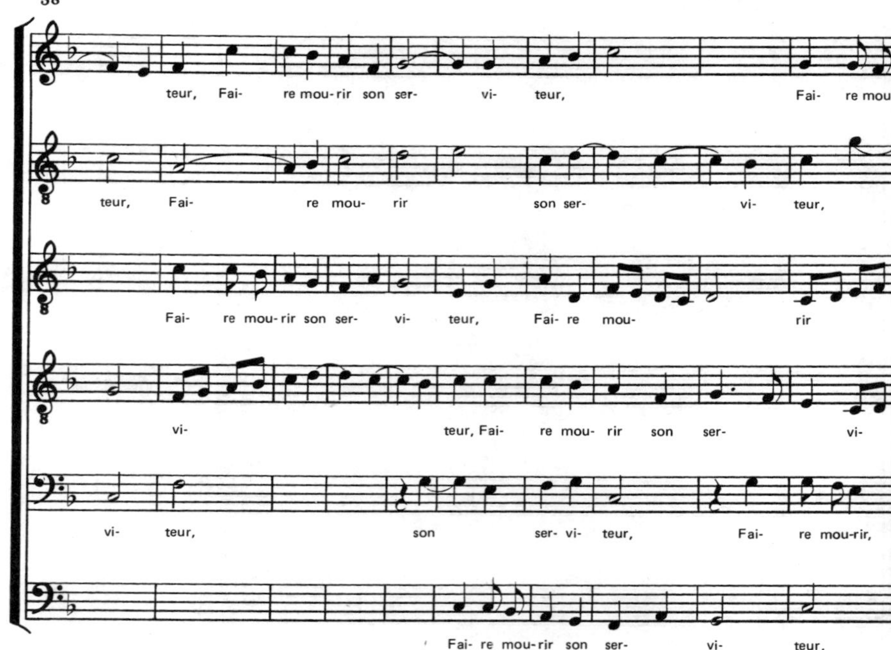

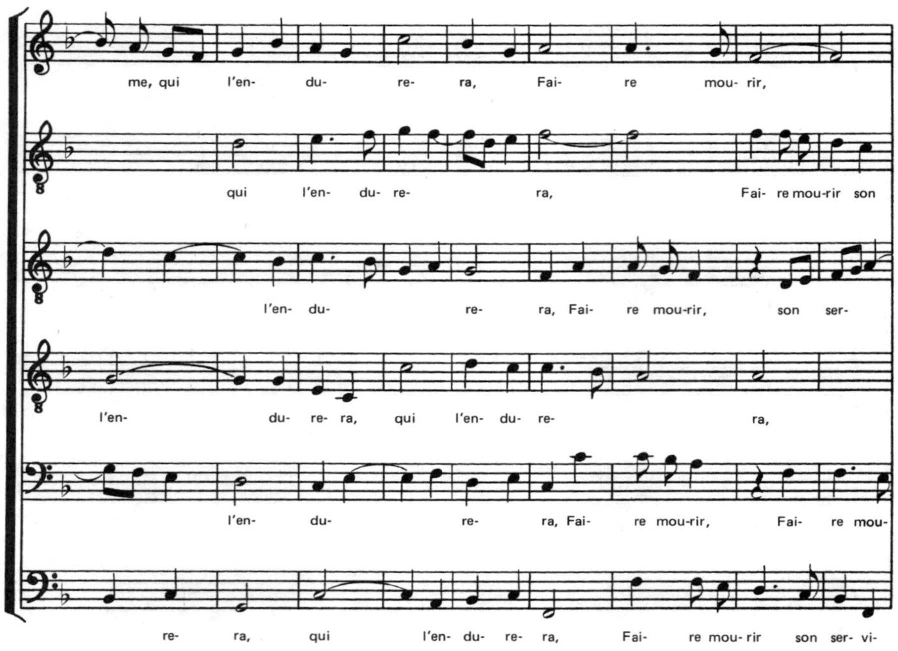
me, qui l'en- du- re- ra, Fai- re mou- rir,
qui l'en- du- re- ra, Fai- re mou- rir son
l'en- du- re- ra, Fai- re mou- rir, son ser-
l'en- du- re- ra, qui l'en- du- re- ra,
l'en- du- re- ra, Fai- re mou- rir, Fai- re mou-
re- ra, qui l'en- du- re- ra, Fai- re mou- rir son ser- vi-

47

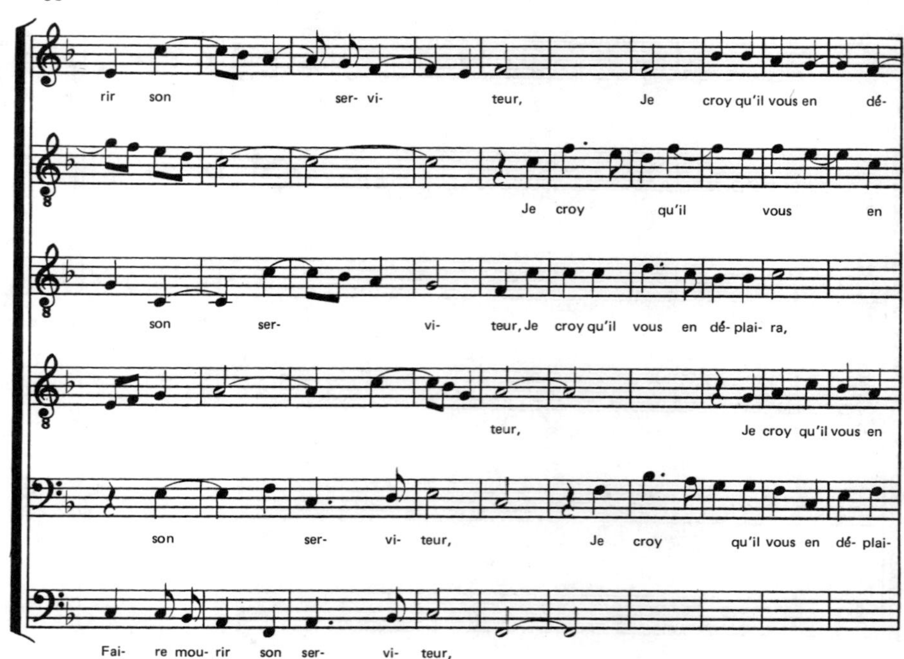

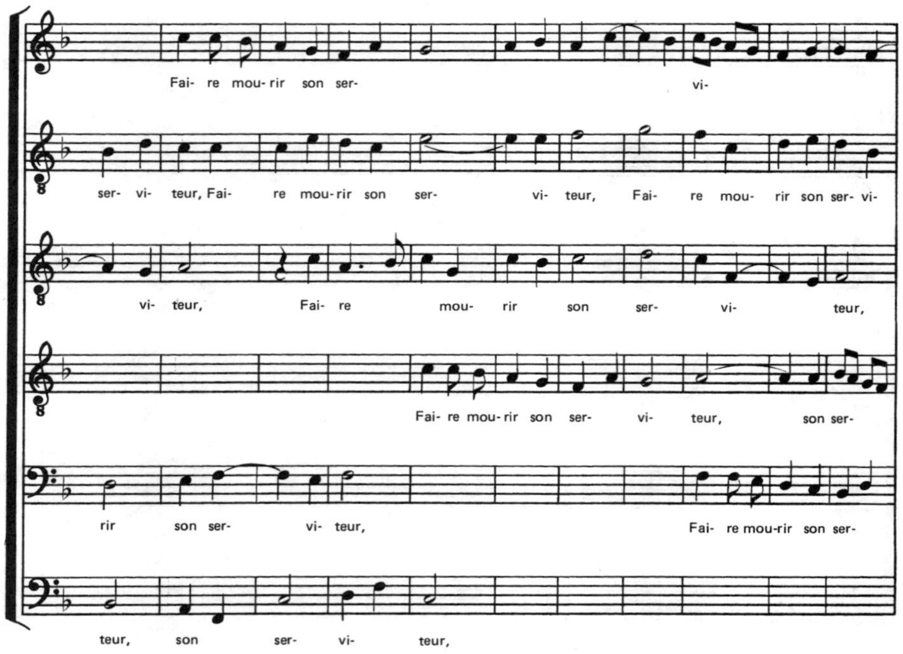
Fai- re mou- rir son ser- vi-
ser- vi- teur, Fai- re mou- rir son ser- vi- teur, Fai- re mou- rir son ser- vi-
vi- teur, Fai- re mou- rir son ser- vi- teur,
Fai- re mou- rir son ser- vi- teur, son ser-
rir son ser- vi- teur, Fai- re mou- rir son ser-
teur, son ser- vi- teur,

58

teur, Fai- re mou- rir son ser- vi- teur, Fai- re mou-
teur, Fai- re mou- rir son ser- vi- teur,
Fai- re mou- rir son ser- vi- teur, Fai- re mou- rir
vi- teur, Fai- re mou- rir son ser- vi-
vi- teur, son ser- vi- teur, Fai- re mou- rir,
Fai- re mou- rir son ser- vi- teur,

68

rir son ser- vi- teur, Je croy qu'il vous en dé-
Je croy qu'il vous en
son ser- vi- teur, Je croy qu'il vous en dé- plai- ra,
teur, Je croy qu'il vous en
son ser- vi- teur, Je croy qu'il vous en dé- plai-
Fai- re mou- rir son ser- vi- teur,

78
plai- ra, vous en dé- plai- ra, A tout le moins
dé- plai- ra, A tout le moins,
Je croy qu'il vous en dé- plai- ra, A tout le
dé- plai- ra, qu'il vous en dé- plai- ra, A tout le moins il lan- gui- ra,
ra, qu'il vous en dé- plai- ra, A tout le moins il lan- gui-
Je croy qu'il vous en dé- plai- ra, A tout le moins il lan- gui-

96
gui- ra, Pour le mal qu'il en- du-
gui- ra, Pour le mal qu'il en- du-
ra, Pour le mal qu'il en- du- re,
il lan- gui- ra, Pour le mal qu'il en- du- re,
ra, Pour le mal qu'il en-
gui- ra, Pour le mal qu'il en- du- re,

87
il lan- gui- ra, A tout le moins il lan- gui- ra, il lan-
A tout le moins il lan- gui- ra, il lan- gui- ra, A tout le moins il lan-
moins il lan- gui- ra, A tout le moins il lan- gui-
A tout le moins il lan- gui- ra, A tout le moins
ra, il lan- gui- ra, A tout le moins il lan- gui-
ra, A tout le moins il lan- gui- ra, A tout le moins il lan-

106
re, Mais vo- tre a- mour le gue- ri- ra, le gue- ri- ra, Car
re, Pour le mal qu'il en- du- re, Mais vo- tre a-
Mais vo- tre a- mour le gue- ri- ra,
Mais vo- tre a- mour, Mais vo- tre a- mour le gue-
du- re, Mais vo- tre a- mour le gue- ri- ra, Car d'au- tre ay-
Mais vo- tre a- mour le gue- ri- ra, Mais vo- tre a- mour le gue- ri- ra,

114
d'au-tre ay-mer n'a cu- re, Car d'au-tre ay-mer n'a cu- re, Car
mour le gue- ri- ra, Car d'au-tre ay-mer n'a cu- re,
Car d'au-tre ay-mer n'a cu- re, Car d'au-tre ay- mer n'a cu-
ri- ra, le gue- ri- ra, Car d'au-tre ay-
mer n'a cu- re, Car d'au-tre ay-mer n'a cu- re, Car
Car d'au- tre ay- mer n'a cu- re,

Vray
Vray Dieu qu'a- mou- reux ont de pei- ne,
Vray Dieu qu'a-
Vray Dieu qu'a- mou- reux ont de pei- ne,
Vray Dieu qu'a- mou- reux ont de pei- ne,

127
d'au-tre ay-mer n'a cu- re.
n'a cu- re, Car d'au-tre ay-mer n'a cu- re.
re, Car d'au-tre ay-mer n'a cu- re.
mer n'a cu- re.
d'au-tre ay-mer n'a cu- re, n'a cu- re.
Car d'au- tre ay-mer n'a cu- re.

10
Vray Dieu qu'a-mou- reux ont de pei- ne,
Dieu qu'a- mou- reux ont de pei- ne,
Cer- tes j'ay- me- roys mieux
mou- reux ont de pei- ne,
Cer- tes j'ay- me- roys mieux
Cer- tes j'ay- me- roys mieux

20
Cer- tes j'ay- me- roys mieux la mort,
Cer- tes j'ay- me- roys mieux la mort,
la mort, Je n'ay sur
Cer- tes j'ay- me- roys mieux la mort,
la mort, Je n'ay sur moy ny
la mort, Je n'ay sur moy

40
Qui ne se sen- te du re-
ne, Qui ne se sen- te
ne se sen- te du re- mort:
Qui ne se sen- te
Qui ne se sen- te du re- mort:
ne se sen- te du re- mort:

29
Je n'ay sur moy ny nerf, ny vai- ne,
Je n'ay sur moy ny nerf, ny vai-
moy ny nerf, ny vai- ne, Qui
Je n'ay sur moy ny nerf, ny vai- ne,
nerf ny vai- ne,
ny nerf, ny vai- ne, Qui

49
mort: Qui ne se sen- te du re- mort:
du re- mort: du re- mort:
Je m'y plein fort, las, ay je tort,
du re- mort: Qui ne se sen- te du re- mort:
Qui ne se sen- te du re- mort:
Je m'y plein

58
Je m'y plein fort, las, ay= je tort, L'on
Je m'y plein fort, las, ay= je tort,
Je m'y plein fort, las, ay= je tort,
Je m'y plein fort, las, ay= je tort,
Je m'y plein fort, las, ay= je tort,
fort, las, ay= je tort, Je m'y plein fort, las, ay= je tort, L'on

78
En- co- res dit on que j'ay tort,
En- co- res dit on que j'ay tort,
me, En- co- res dit on que
tort, L'on m'os- te ce que mon
ay- me, En- co- res dit on
En- co- res dit on que j'ay tort,

68
m'os- te ce que mon coeur ay- me,
L'on m'os- te ce que mon coeur ay- me,
L'on m'os- te ce que mon coeur ay-
Je m'y plein fort, las, ay= je
L'on m'os- te ce que mon coeur
m'os- te ce que mon coeur ay- me,

87
En- co- res dit on, En- co- res dit on, En-
En- co- res dit on, En- co- res dit on, En-
j'ay tort, En- co- res dit on, En- co- res dit on, En-
coeur ay- me, En- co- res dit on, En- co- res dit on, que
que j'ay tort, En- co- res dit on, En- co- res dit on, En-
En- co- res dit on, En- co- res dit on, En-

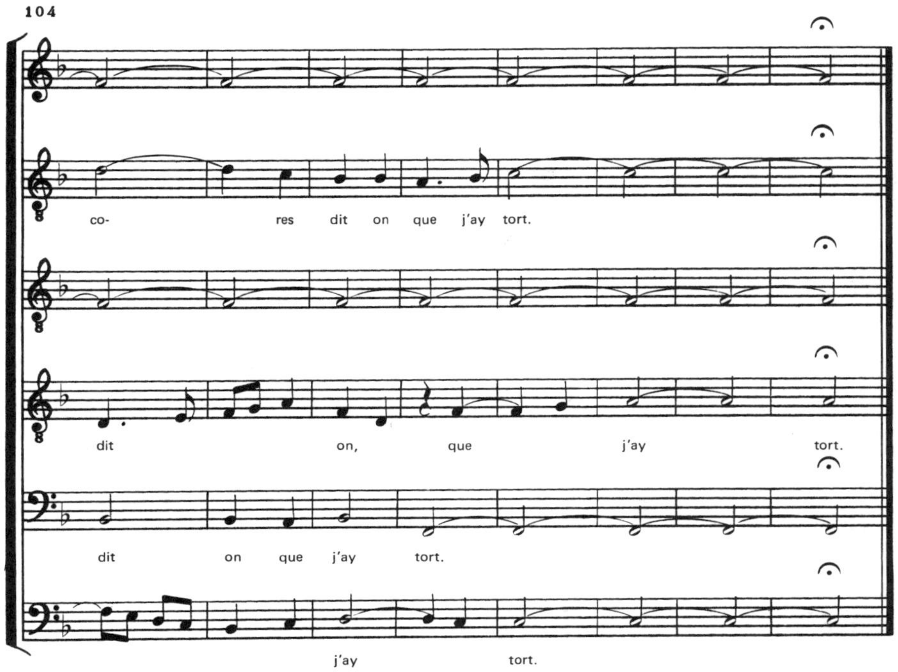

114 Nicolas, *Vivés en paix*

20
tous loy- aux a- mou- reux,
loy- aux a- mou- reux,
a- mou- reux, Lais- sez sou- ci, tout dueil &
Lais- sez sou- ci, tout
loy- aux a- mou- reux, Lais- sez sou-
vés en paix tous loy- aux a- mou- reux, Lais- sez sou- ci tout

37
plai- san- ce, Ay- ant d'a- mour la
ce, Ay- ant d'a- mour la plei- ne
ce, Ay- ant d'a- mour la plei- ne jou- is-
Ay- ant d'a- mour la plei- ne jou- is- san- ce,
ant d'a- mour la plei- ne jou- is- san- ce,
des- plai- san- ce, Ay- ant d'a- mour,

29
Lais- sez sou- ci, tout dueil & des-
Lais- sez sou- ci, tout dueil & des- plai- san-
des- plai- san-
dueil & des- plai- san- ce,
ci, & des- plai- san- ce, Ay-
dueil & des- plai- san- ce, tout dueil &

46
plei- ne jou- is- san- ce,
jou- is- san- ce,
san- ce, jou- is- san-
mau-
Ay- ant d'a- mour la plei- ne jou- is-
Ay- ant d'a- mour la plei- ne jou- is- san-

54
mau- gré qu'en
mau- gré qu'en ayent,
ce, mau- gré qu'en ayent, tous ces faux
gré qu'en ayent, tous ces faux en- vy- eux,
san- ce, mau- gré qu'en ayent, mau- gré qu'en ayent
ce, mau- gré qu'en ayent tous ces faux en- vy- eux, mau-

69
mau- gré qu'en ayent,
mau- gré qu'en ayent, tous
ces faux en- vy-
tous ces faux en- vy- eux,
vy- eux, tous ces faux
ayent tous ces faux en- vy- eux, mau- gré qu'en

62
ayent, tous ces faux en- vy- eux,
tous ces faux en- vy- eux,
en- vy- eux, mau- gré qu'en ayent, tous
mau- gré qu'en ayent,
tous ces faux en- vy- eux, tous ces faux en-
gré qu'en ayent tous ces faux en- vy- eux, mau- gré qu'en

75
tous ces faux en- vy- eux.
ces faux en- vy- eux.
eux, mau- gré qu'en ayent tous ces faux en vy- eux.
tous ces faux en- vy- eux.
en- vy- eux, tous ces faux en- vy- eux.
ayent tous ces faux en- vy- eux.

Dieu te gard, Dieu te gard,
Dieu te gard, Dieu te gard,
Dieu te gard, Dieu te gard, Dieu
Dieu te gard, Dieu te gard, Dieu te
12
Dieu te gard, ber- ge- re, Gar- dant tes mou-
ge- re, Gar-dant tes mou- tons, don don,
Gar- dant tes mou- tons, don don, don don,
tons, don don, Gar- dant tes mou- tons, don
Gar-dant tes mou- tons, don don, Gar- dant tes mou- tons, don
tes mou- tons, Gar- dant tes mou- tons, don

6
Dieu te gard, ber-
ber- ge- re, Gar-dant tes mou- tons, don don,
Dieu te gard, ber- ge- re, Gar- dant tes mou-
te gard, ber- ge- re, Gar- dant tes mou- tons,
gard, ber- ge- re, Gar-dant tes mou- tons, Gar- dant
19
(sic)
tons, don don, Ta bel- le ma- nie-
Ta bel- le ma- nie- re, M'a- mour je te
Ta bel- le ma- nie- re, M'a-mour je te don don,
don, Ta bel- le ma- nie- re, M'a- mour je te
don, Ta bel- le ma- nie- re, M'a-mour je te
don, Ta bel- le ma- nie- re, M'a- mour

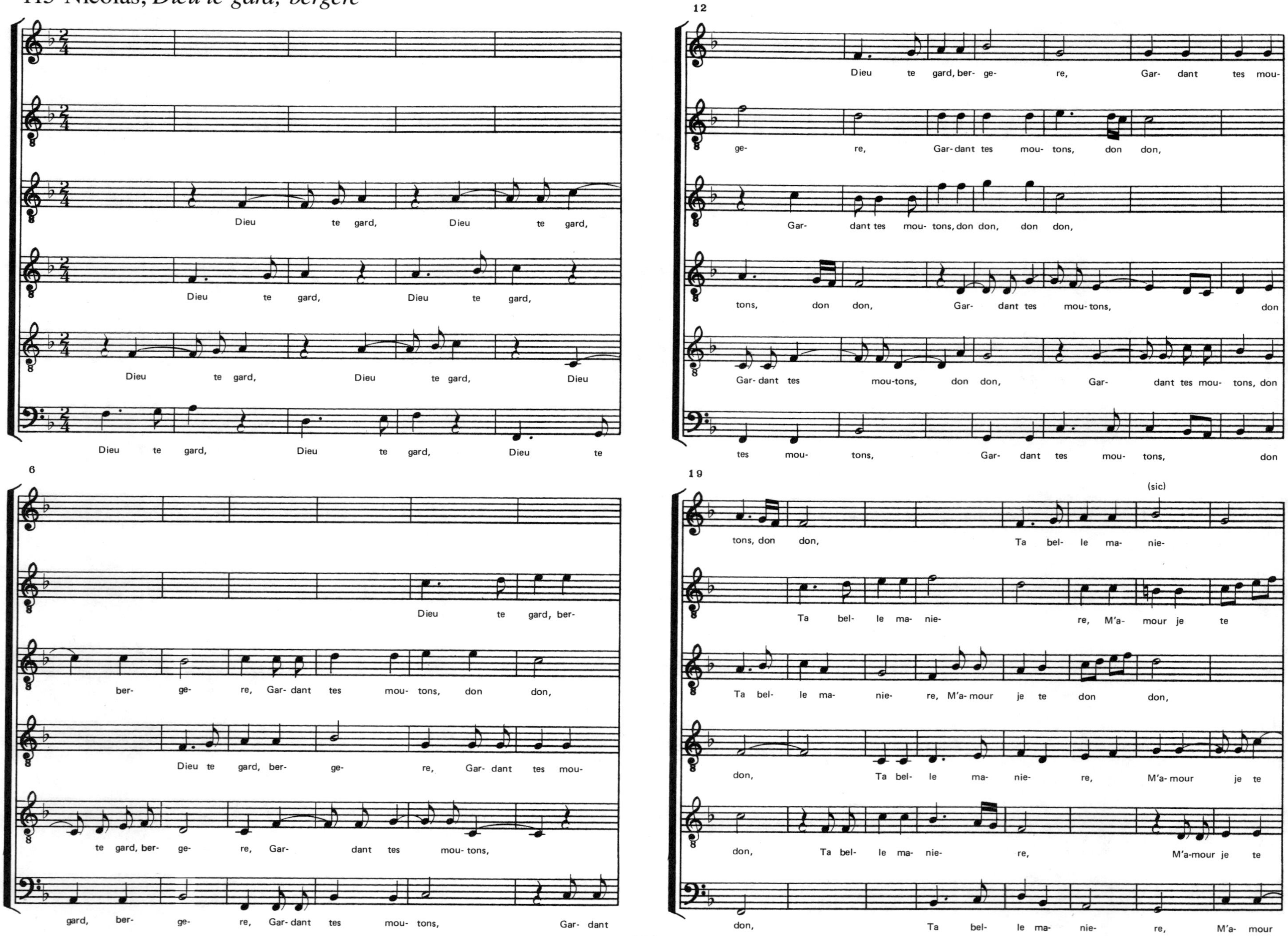

re, M'a- mour je te don don, M'a- mour je te don
don, M'a- mour je te don & don don
M'a- mour je te don don don, M'a- mour je te don don
don, M'a- mour je te don, M'a- mour
je te don, M'a- mour je te don &

tu point veu, mon oy- seau sau- va- ge,
mon oy- seau sau- va- ge, De- puis
va- ge, Ne l'as= tu point veu mon oy- seau sau- va
mon oy- seau sau- va- ge, De- puis le ma-
ge, mon oy- seau sau- va- ge,
tu point veu, mon oy- seau sau- va- ge,

don, don don don, Ne l'as=
don, Ne l'as= tu point veu,
don, Ne l'as= tu point veu, mon oy- seau sau-
je te don don don, Ne l'as= tu point veu,
Ne l'as= tu point veu, mon oy- seau sau- va-
don don don don don, Ne l'as= tu point veu, Ne l'as=

De- puis le ma- tin, il est au ri-
le ma- tin, il est au ri- va- ge,
ge, De- puis le ma- tin il est au ri- va
tin, il est au ri- va- ge,
De- puis le ma- tin, il est au ri- va-
De- puis le ma- tin, il est au ri- va-

405

va- ge, Mon oy- seau sau- va- ge,
Mon oy- seau sau- va- ge, mon jo- ly fau- con, don
ge, Mon oy- seau sau- va- ge, mon jo- ly fau-
Mon oy- seau sau- va- ge, mon jo- ly fau- con, don don, mon jo-
ge, Mon oy- seau sau- va- ge,
ge, Mon oy- seau sau- va- ge, mon jo- ly fau-

(sic) (sic)
la be- cas- se, con- nins de sai- son, don,
con- nins de sai- son, don don, con- nins de sai- son
son, don don, don don don,
son, don don, con- nins de sai- son, don don, don
con- nins de sai- son, con- nins de sai- son, don
de sai- son, don don don don don don, don don don don don

mon jo- ly fau- con, don don, Qui prent
don, Qui prent la be- cas- se
con, don don, Qui prent la be- cas- se con- nins de sai-
ly fau- con, don don, Qui prent la be- cas- se con- nins de sai-
mon jo- ly fau- con, don don, Qui prent la be- cas- se,
con, don don, Qui prent la be- cas- se con- nins

con- nins de sai- son, don don don don.
& don don don.
con- nins de sai- son, don don, con- nins de sai- son, don don.
don don don, con- nins de sai- son, don don.
don, don don don don.
don don don, don don don don don don don.

116 Leschenet, *Le coeur est mien*

32
en un lieu,
en un lieu, Fors en un lieu ou il fait sa de-
pris, Fors en un lieu ou il fait sa de- meu- re,
pris, Fors en
lieu ou il fait sa de- meu- re,
pris, Fors en un lieu ou il fait

48
re, Et y se- ra,
sa de- meu- re, Et y se- ra jus- ques à ce qu'il
lieu ou il fait sa de- meu- re, Et y se- ra jus- ques à ce qu'il
meu- re, Et y se-
ou il fait sa de- meu- re, Et y se- ra,
il fait sa de- meu- re, Et y se- ra jus- ques à

38
ou il fait sa de- meu-
meu- re, ou il fait sa de- meu- re,
ou il fait sa de- meu- re, Fors en un
un lieu, ou il fait sa de-
Fors en un lieu ou il fait sa de- meu- re,
sa de- meu- re, ou

58
jus- ques à ce qu'il meu- re,
meu- re, jus- ques à ce qu'il meu- re,
meu- re, jus- ques à ce qu'il meu-
ra, jus- ques à ce qu'il
jus- ques à ce qu'il meu-
ce qu'il meu- re, jus- ques à ce qu'il meu- re, jus- ques à

Car de long tems,
jus- ques à ce qu'il meu- re, Car de long tems l'a
re, Car de long
meu- re,
re, Car de long tems, Car de long
ce qu'il meu- re, Car de long tems, Car de long

tre- pris,
ain- si en- tre-
pris, Car de long
l'a ain- si en- tre- pris,
l'a ain- si en- tre- pris,
pris, l'a ain- si en- tre- pris, Car

l'a ain- si en-
ain- si en- tre- pris, l'a
tems l'a ain- si en- tre-
Car de long tems,
Car de long tems l'a ain- si en- tre- pris,
tems l'a ain- si en- tre-

Car de long tems, l'a
pris, Car de long tems l'a ain- si en- tre-
tems, Car de long tems l'a ain-
Car de long tems,
Car de long tems, Car de long tems l'a
de long tems, Car de long tems

98
ain- si en- tre- pris,
pris, l'a ain- si en- tre-
si en- tre- pris,
l'a ain- si
ain- si en- tre- pris, Car de long tems l'a
l'a ain- si en- tre- pris, l'a ain-

He- las, pour- quoy ne suis=
He- las, pour- quoy ne suis= je
He- las, pour-
He- las, pour- quoy ne suis= je ma- ri- é- e,

106
Car de long tems, l'a ain- si en- tre- pris.
pris.
Car de long tems l'a ain- si en- tre- pris.
en- tre- pris.
ain- si en- tre- pris, l'a ain- si en- tre- pris.
si en- tre- pris, l'a ain- si en- tre- pris.

10
je ma- ri- é- e, Je vis en
He- las, pour- quoy ne suis=
ma- ri- é- e, He- las, pour- quoy, He- las, pour-
quoy ne suis= je ma- ri- é- e
ne suis= je ma- ri- é- e,
He- las, pour- quoy ne suis= je ma- ri- é- e,

dueil, en pleurs,
je ma- ri- é- e,
quoy ne suis= je ma- ri- é- e, Je vis en dueil, en pleurs,
e, Je vis
Je vis en dueil, Je vis en dueil, Je
Je vis en dueil, en pleurs, en pleurs, Je

es- moy, & en es-
en pleurs,
pleurs, & en es- moy,
& en
en es- moy, & en
es- moy, & en es- moy,

Je vis en dueil, en pleurs & en
Je vis en dueil,
Je vis en dueil, Je vis en dueil, en
en dueil, en pleurs,
vis en dueil, en pleurs, &
vis en dueil, en pleurs & en es- moy & en

moy, & en es- moy, Vrais
& en es- moy,
& en es- moy,
es- moy, Vrais
es- moy, Vrais a- mou- reux,
& en es- moy,

52
a- mou- reux, Vrais a- mou- reux,
Vrais a- mou- reux, Vrais a- mou-
Vrais a- mou- reux, Vrais a- mou- reux, Vrais a- mou-
a- mou- reux, Vrais a- mou- reux,
Vrais a- mou- reux, Vrais a- mou-
Vrais a- mou- reux, Vrais a- mou- reux, Vrais a-

71
tié de moy, Et quel- que jour, Et
és pi- tié de moy,
moy, ay- és pi- tié de moy, Et quel- que jour,
Et quel- que jour, Et quel- que jour,
ay- és pi- tié de moy, Et quel- que jour, Et quel- que
Et quel- que jour, Et

62
Vrais a- mou- reux, ay- és pi- tié de moy, ay- és pi-
reux, ay-
reux, ay- és pi- tié de
ay- és pi- tié de moy,
reux, Vrais a- mou- reux, ay- és pi- tié de moy,
mou- reux, ay- és pi- tié de moy, ay- és pi- tié,

78
quel- que jour, vous di- ray ma pen- sé-
Et quel- que jour, Et quel- que jour, vous
vous di- ray ma pen- sé- e, Et quel- que jour,
vous di- ray ma pen- sé- e,
jour, Et quel- que jour
quel- que jour vous di- ray ma pen- sé- e, Et

e,
Et quel- que jour, Et
di- ray ma pen- sé- e,
vous di- ray ma pen- sé- e, Et quel- que jour,
Et quel- que jour, Et quel- que jour,
vous di- ray ma pen- sé- e, Et quel- que
quel- que jour, Et quel- que jour, Et

e,
Et quel- que jour, Et quel- que
di- ray ma pen- sé- e.
vous di- ray ma pen- sé- e, Et quel- que jour vous
vous di- ray ma pen- sé- e.
Et quel- que jour, vous di- ray ma pen-
vous di- ray ma pen- sé- e, vous

quel- que jour, vous di- ray ma pen- sé-
Et quel- que jour, Et quel- que jour, vous
vous di- ray ma pen- sé- e, Et quel- que jour
vous di- ray ma pen- sé- e,
jour, Et quel- que jour,
quel- que jour vous di- ray ma pen- sé- e,

jour, vous di- ray ma pen- sé- e.
di- ray ma pen- sé- e.
sé- e,
di- ray ma pen- sé- e.

Je cer- che au- tant a- mour & le de- si- re,
[cher-]
Je cer- che au- tant a- mour & le de-
[cher-]
Je cer- che au- tant a- mour & le de- si- re, & le de-
[cher-]
Je cer- che au- tant a- mour &
[cher-]
Je cer- che au- tant a- mour, Je cer- che au- tant a-
[cher-]
Je cer- che au- tant a- mour & le de- si-
[cher-]

18

le de- si- re, Com- me au- tre- foys,
de- si- re, Com- me au- tre- foys, je l'ay vou-
re, Com- me au- tre- foys, Com- me au- tre-
le de- si- re, Com- me au- tre- foys, Com- me au-
Com- me au- tre- foys je l'ay vou- lu fu- ir, je
le de- si- re, Com- me au- tre- foys, Com-

10

& le de- si- re, &
si- re, & le
re, & le de- si-
le de- si- re, & le de- si- re, &
mour & le de- si- re, & le de- si- re,
re, & le de- si- re, &

27

je l'ay vou- lu fu- ir,
lu fu- ir, je l'ay
foys je l'ay vou- lu fu- ir, Com- me au- tre- foys,
foys je l'ay vou- lu fu- ir, Com-
l'ay vou- lu fu- ir, je l'ay
me au- tre- foys je l'ay vou- lu fu- ir,

35
Je cer- che au- tant en de- si- rant
vou- lu fu- ir, Je cer- che au-
je l'ay vou- lu fu- ir, Je cer- che au-tant en de- si- rant jou-
me au- tre- foys je l'ay vou- lu fu- ir, Je cer- che au-tant en de- si- rant
vou- lu fu- ir,
Com- me au-tre- foys je l'ay vou- lu fu- ir, Je cer- che au-tant en de- si-

54
Com- me au- tre- foys, je n'eus- se o- sé
me au-tre- foys, Com- me au- tre- foys,
me au-tre- foys, Com- me au- tre- foys je n'eus-se o- sé le di- re,
Com- me au- tre- foys, je n'eus- se o-
tre- foys, Com- me au-tre- foys je n'eus- se o- sé le di- re, je
Com- me au-tre- foys je n'eus-se o- sé le di- re, je n'eus-

44
jou- ir, en de- si- rant jou- ir,
tant en de- si- rant jou- ir, en de- si- rant jou- ir, Com-
ir, en de- si- rant, en de- si- rant jou- ir, Com-
jou- ir, en de- si- rant jou- ir, Com-me au-tre- foys,
Je cer- che au- tant en de- si- rant jou- ir, Com- me au-
rant jou- ir, en de- si- rant jou- ir, Com-me au-tre- foys,

62
le di- re, Trou-
je n'eus- se o- sé le di-
je n'eus- se o- sé le di-
sé le di- re, Trou-
n'eus- se o- sé le di-
se o- sé le di- re, je n'eus- se o- sé le di- re, Trou-

69
ver ne puis, au- tre a-mour sans le di- re, Trou- ver ne puis au-
re, Trou- ver ne puis, au- tre a- mour sans le
re, Trou- ver ne puis au- tre a-mour sans le di- re, au- tre a-mour sans le
ver ne puis, Trou- ver ne puis, au- tre a- mour sans le dire, Trou- ver ne puis au- tre a- mour sans le di- re, au- tre a- mour
ver ne puis, au- tre a-mour sans le di- re, au-

89
Le mien pre- mier, & o- bli- gé
o- bli- gé de- voir,
gé de- voir, Qui rend heu- reux & con- tent mon sça- voir,
& o- bli- gé de- voir, & o- bli- gé
gé de- voir, & o- bli- gé de-
bli- gé de- voir, & o- bli- gé

80
tre a- mour sans le di- re, Le mien pre- mier,
di- re, Le mien pre- mier, &
di- re, Le mien pre- mier & o- bli-
re, sans le di- re, Le mien pre- mier,
sans le di- re, Le mien pre- mier & o- bli-
tre a- mour sans le di- re, Le mien pre- mier, & o-

98
de- voir, Qui rend heu- reux, & con- tent mon
Qui rend heu- reux & con- tent mon sça- voir, &
Qui rend heu- reux & con- tent mon sça- voir, & con- tent mon
de- voir, Qui rend heu- reux & con- tent
voir, Qui rend heu- reux & con- tent mon sça- voir, & con- tent mon sça-
de- voir, Qui rend heu- reux & con- tent mon sça- voir,

416

108
sça- voir, Sans plus cer- cher, ce- la
con- tent mon sça- voir, Sans plus cer- cher, Sans plus cer- cher,
sça- voir, Sans plus cer- cher, ce- la me doit
mon sça- voir, Sans plus cer- cher, ce-
voir, Sans plus cer- cher, ce- la
Sans plus cer- cher, ce- la

124
Qui rend heu- reux & con- tent mon sça- voir,
fi- re, Qui rend heu- reux & con- tent mon sça-
fi- re, Qui rend heu- reux, & con- tent mon sça-
Qui rend heu- reux, Qui rend heu- reux, & con- tent mon sça-
re, Qui rend heu- reux & con- tent mon sça- voir,
re, Qui rend heu- reux & con- tent mon sça- voir,

116
me doit suf- fi- re,
ce- la me doit suf-
suf- fi- re, ce- la me doit suf-
la me doit suf- fi- re,
me doit suf- fi- re, ce- la me doit suf- fi-
me doit suf- fi- re, me doit suf- fi-

133
Sans plus cer- cher, Sans plus cer- cher, ce- la me doit
voir, Sans plus cer- cher, Sans plus cer- cher,
voir, Sans plus cer- cher, ce- la me doit suf-
voir, Sans plus cer- cher, ce- la me doit
Sans plus cer- cher, Sans plus cer- cher, ce- la me doit suf- fi- re,
Sans plus cer- cher, ce- la, ce- la me

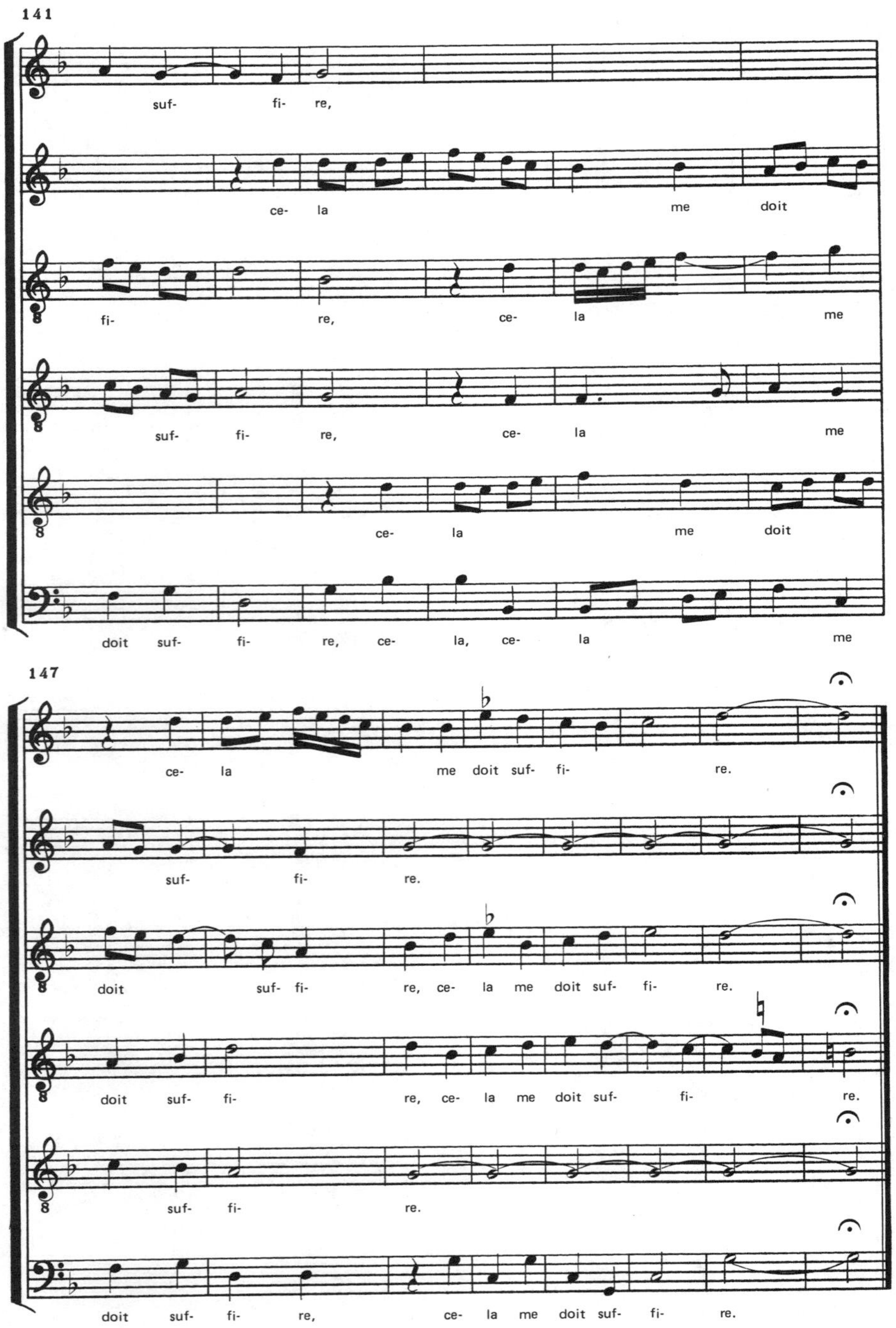
141
suf- fi- re,
ce- la me doit
fi- re, ce- la me
suf- fi- re, ce- la me
ce- la me doit
doit suf- fi- re, ce- la, ce- la me
147
ce- la me doit suf- fi- re.
suf- fi- re.
doit suf- fi- re, ce- la me doit suf- fi- re.
doit suf- fi- re, ce- la me doit suf- fi- re.
suf- fi- re.
doit suf- fi- re, ce- la me doit suf- fi- re.

119 Rousée, *La rousée du moys de may*

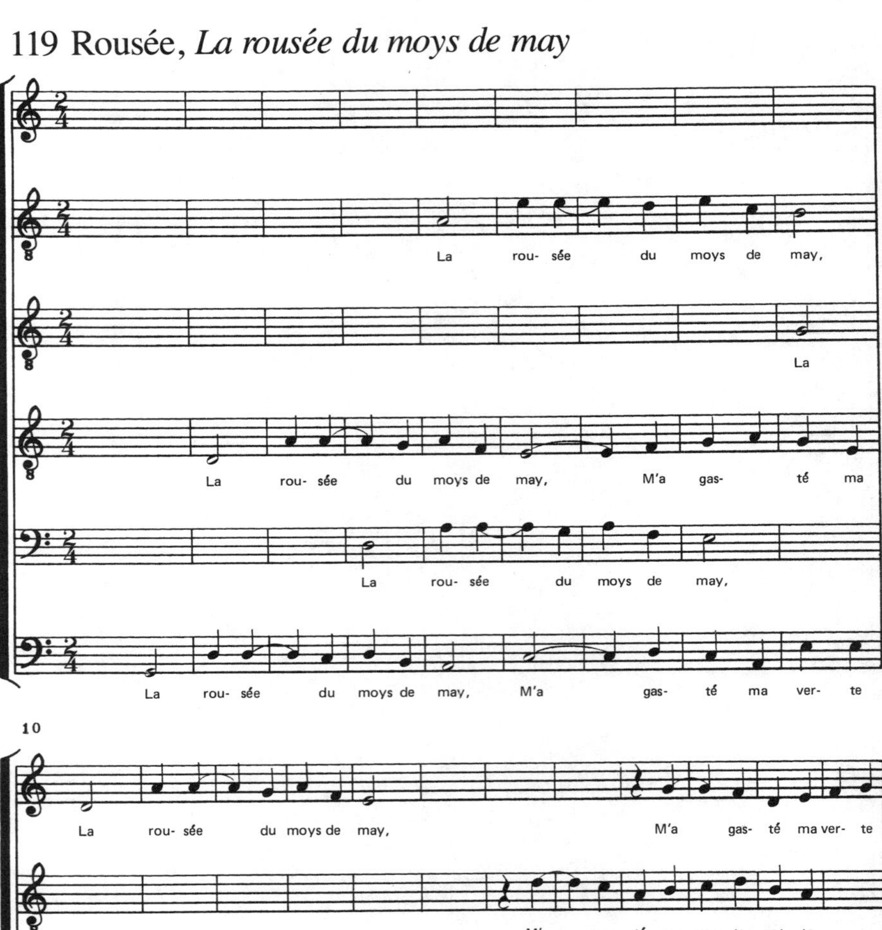

La rou- sée du moys de may,
La
La rou- sée du moys de may, M'a gas- té ma
La rou- sée du moys de may,
La rou- sée du moys de may, M'a gas- té ma ver- te
10
La rou- sée du moys de may, M'a gas- té ma ver- te
M'a gas- té ma ver- te cot- te,
rou- sée du moys de may, M'a gas- té ma ver- te cot- te, ma ver- te
ver- te cot- te, M'a gas- té, M'a gas- té ma
M'a gas- té ma ver- te cot- te,
cot- te, M'a gas- té ma ver- te cot- te, M'a gas- té ma

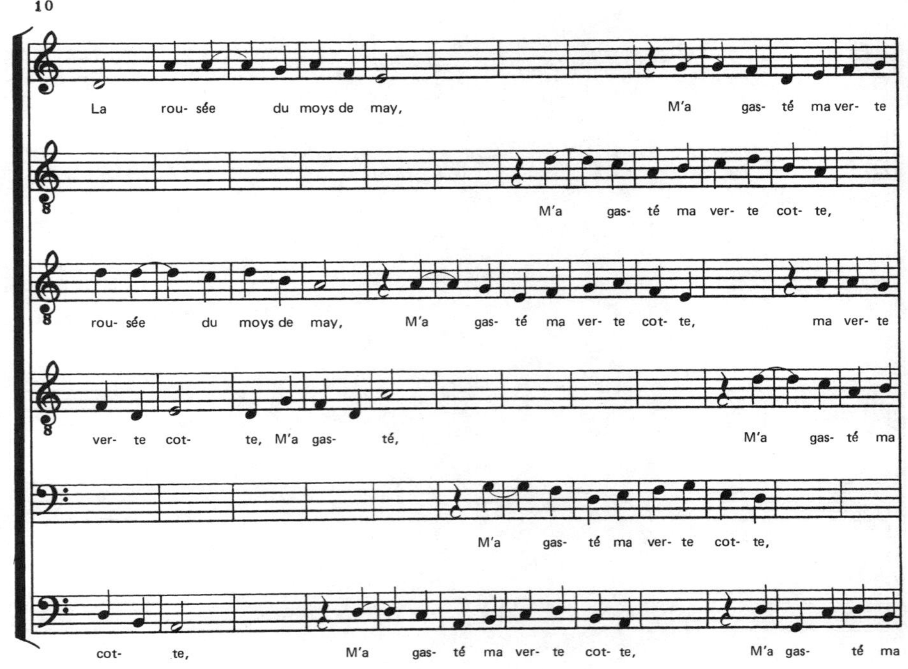

22
cot- te, M'a gas- té ma ver- te cot- te, Par un ma- tin
Par un ma- tin
cot- te, M'a gas- té ma ver- te cot- te,
ver- te cos- te, M'a gas- té ma ver- te cos- te,
Par un ma- tin m'y le-
ver- te cos- te, Par un ma- tin m'y

45
En un jar- din m'en en- tray,
En un jar- din m'en en- tray, Dit-
din m'en en- tray, En un jar- din m'en en- tray,
En un jar- din m'en en- tray, Dit- tes vous que
un jar- din m'en en- tray, Dit- tes
en- tray, En un jar- din m'en en- tray, Dit- tes vous que je suis

33
m'y le- vay, La rou- sée du moys de may,
m'y le- vay,
Par un ma- tin m'y le- vay, La rou- sée du moys de may, En un jar-
Par un ma- tin m'y le- vay,
vay, En
le- vay, La rou- sé' du moys de may, En un jar- din m'en

57
Dit- tes vous que je suis sot- te,
tes vous que je suis sot- te, La rou- sée du moys de
Dit- tes vous que je suis sot- te,
je suis sot- te, que je suis sot- te, La rou- sé' du moys de may, M'a gas- té
vous que je suis sot- te, La rou- sé' du moys de may,
sot- te, La rou- sé' du moys de may, M'a gas- té ma

La rou- sée du moys de may, M'a gas- té ma
may, M'a gas- té ma ver- te cot-
La rou- sée du moys de may, M'a gas- té ma ver- te cot- te, ma
ma ver- te cot- te, M'a gas- té, M'a gas-
M'a gas- té ma ver- te cot-
ver- te cot- te, M'a gas- té ma ver- te cot- te, ma ver- te

La rou- sée du moys de may, du
La rou- sée du moys de may, La
La rou- sée
La rou- sée du moys

ver- te cot- te, M'a gas- té ma ver- te cot- te.
te.
ver- te cot- te, M'a gas- té ma ver- te cot- te.
té ma ver- te cot- te, M'a gas- té ma ver- te cot- te.
te.
cot- te, ma ver- te cot- te.

moys de may,
La rou- sée du moys de may,
rou- sée du moys de may, M'a
du moys de may, M'a gas-
La rou- sée du moys de may,
de may, M'a gas- té ma

M'a gas- té ma ver- te cot-
M'a gas- té ma ver- te cot- te,
gas- té ma ver- te cot- te, M'a gas- té ma
té ma ver- te cot- te, M'a gas- té ma ver- te
M'a gas- té ma ver- te cot- te,
ver- te cot- te, M'a gas- té ma ver- te cot-

Par un ma- tin m'y le- vay,
Par un ma- tin m'y le- vay,
gas- té ma ver- te cot- te, Par un
m'y le- vay, La rou- sée du moys
ma- tin m'y le- vay, Par un ma- tin
un ma- tin m'y le- vay, La rou- sée

te, M'a gas- té ma ver- te cot- te,
M'a gas- té ma ver- te cot- te,
ver- te cot- te, M'a gas- té ma ver- te cot- te, M'a
cot- te, Par un ma- tin
M'a gas- té ma ver- te cot- te, Par un
te, M'a gas- té ma ver- te cot- te, Par

La rou- sée du moys de may,
La rou- sée du moys de may,
ma- tin m'y le- vay, La rou-
de may, En un jar-
m'y le- vay, La rou- sée du moys
du moys de may, En un jar- din m'en en- tray,

En un jar- din m'en en- tray, m'en en- tray
En un jar- din m'en en- tray,
sée du moys de may, du moys de may, En un jar- din
din m'en en- tray, Dit- tes vous que je suis
de may, En un jar- din m'en en- tray,
Dit- tes vous que je suis sot-

sée du moys de may, La rou- sée du moys de
je suis sot- te, La rou- sée du
La rou- sée du moys de may, du moys de
La rou- sée du moys de may,
suis sot- te, La rou- sé- e, du moys de
La rou- sée du moys de may,

Dit- tes vous que je suis sot- te, La rou-
Dit- tes vous que je suis sot- te, Dit- tes vous que
m'en en- tray, Dit- tes vous que je suis sot- te,
sot- te, Dit- tes vous que je suis sot- te,
Dit- tes vous que je suis sot- te, Dit- tes vous que je
te, Dit- tes vous que je suis sot- te,

may, du moys de may, M'a gas-
moys de may, M'a gas- té ma
may, M'a gas- té ma ver- te cot- te,
M'a gas- té ma ver- te cot- te,
may, M'a gas- té ma ver- te
M'a gas- té ma ver- te cot- te,

121 Moulu, *En despit des faux médisans*

23
bel- le a- my- e,   Si au- cuns en sont
le a- my- e,   Si au- cuns en   sont mal
u-   ne bel- le a- my-   e,   Si   au- cuns en
J'ay ac- quis u-   ne bel- le a- my-   e,
my-   e,   Si
J'ay ac- quis u-   ne bel- le a- my-   e,
(sic)

44
qu'on en di-   e,   En par- le qui par- ler vou-
quoy qu'on en di-   e, En par- le qui   par- ler vou- dra,
chaut quoy qu'on en di-   e,   En par- le qui
Il   ne m'en chaut quoy qu'on en di-   e,
Il   ne m'en chaut quoy qu'on   en di- e,
chaut quoy qu'on en di-   e,   En

33
mal   di- sans,   Il ne m'en chaut quoy
di-   sans,   Il ne m'en chaut
sont mal di- sans,   Il ne m'en
Si   au- cuns en   sont mal di-   sans,
au- cuns en   sont mal   di-   sans,
Si   au- cuns en   sont mal   di-   sans, Il ne m'en

55
dra,   En par- le qui par- ler vou-
En par- le qui par- ler   vou- dra,
par- ler vou- dra,   Haut & bas en
En   par- le qui   par- ler vou- dra,
En   par- le   qui par- ler vou- dra, En par- le qui   par- ler vou- dra,
par- le qui par- ler   vou- dra,

dra, Haut & bas en tous lieux,
Haut & bas en tous lieux, Haut & bas en tous lieux,
tous lieux, C'est grand fo- lie
Haut & bas en tous lieux,
Haut & bas en tous lieux, C'est grand' fo-
Haut & bas en tous lieux, Haut & bas en tous lieux, C'est

Car pour ce- la ne se per-
à eux, Car pour ce- la ne se per-
la ne se per- dra,
Car pour ce- la ne se per- dra,
L'a-
la ne se per- dra,

C'est grand fo- lie à eux,
C'est grand fo- lie à eux, Car pour ce-
C'est grand' fo- lie à eux,
lie à eux, C'est grand' fo- lie à eux,
grand' fo- lie à eux, C'est grand' fo- lie à eux, Car pour ce-

dra,
dra, L'a- mour d'en-
L'a- mour d'en- tre nous deux,
L'a- mour
mour d'en- tre nous deux, L'a- mour d'en- tre nous
L'a- mour d'en- tre nous deux, L'a- mour d'en-

103
L'a- mour d'en- tre nous
tre nous deux, L'a- mour d'en- tre nous deux,
L'a- mour d'en- tre nous
d'en- tre nous deux,
deux, L'a- mour d'en- tre nous deux, L'a-
tre nous deux, L'a- mour d'en- tre nous

Je re- com- men- ce ma dou- leur,
Je re- com- men-ce ma dou- leur,
Je re- com- men- ce ma dou- leur,
Je re- com- men- ce ma dou-
Je re- com-
Je re- com- men- ce ma dou- leur,

110
deux, L'a- mour d'en- tre nous deux.
L'a- mour d'en- tre nous deux, L'a-mour d'en- tre nous deux.
deux, L'a- mour d'en- tre nous deux.
L'a- mour d'en- tre nous deux.
mour d'en- tre nous deux, L'a-mour d'en- tre nous deux.
deux, L'a- mour d'en- tre nous deux, d'en- tre nous deux.

11
Je re- com- men- ce ma dou- leur,
Je re- com- men-ce ma dou- leur, Je re- com-
Je re- com- men- ce
leur, Je re- com- men- ce ma dou- leur,
men- ce ma dou- leur, Je re- com- men- ce ma dou-
Je re- com- men- ce ma dou-

Je re-com-men- ce ma dou-
men-ce ma dou-leur, Je re-com-men- ce ma dou-leur,
ma dou-leur, Je re- com-men- ce
Je re-com-men-ce ma dou-leur, Je re- com-men-ce ma
leur, Je re-com-men- ce ma dou- leur,
leur, Je re- com- men- ce ma dou-

leur, Et pleins, & pleurs,
Et pleins,& pleurs, Et pleins, & pleurs, en grand me-
ma dou- leur, En pleins, & pleurs,
douleur, Et pleins, & pleurs, Et pleins, &
Et pleins, & pleurs, Et pleins, & pleurs, Et pleins, &
leur, Et pleins, & pleurs, Et pleins, & pleurs,

Et pleins, & pleurs, en grand me- lan-co- li- e, en
lan-co-li-e, en grand me-lan-co-li-e, en grand me-lan-co- li- e,
En pleins, & pleurs, en grand me- lan-co- li- e, en
pleurs, en grand me- lan-co- li- e, en
pleurs, en grand me- lan-co- li- e, en grand me- lan-co- li- e,
Et pleins, & pleurs, en grand me- lan-co- li- e,

(sic)
grand me- lan-co- li- e, en grand me- lan-co- li- e,
en grand me- lan-co- li- e, Mau- di- te soit en-
grand me- lan-co- li- e, Mau- di-te soit en- vy-
grand me- lan-co- li- e, Mau- di-
en grand me- lan-co- li- e,
en grand me- lan-co- li-

61
Mau- di- te soit en- vy- e,
vy- e, Par qui suis en dou- leur, Par
e, Par qui suis en dou- leur,
te soit en- vy- e, Par qui,
Mau- di- te soit en-
e, Mau- di- te soit en- vy- e, Par

79
leur, El- le m'os- te m'a- my- e, El- le m'os- te m'a- my-
leur, El- le m'os- te m'a- my- e, Ce m'est un
El- le m'os- te m'a- my-
leur, El- le m'os- te m'a- my-
m'os- te m'a- my- e, El- le m'os- te m'a- my-
leur,

70
Par qui suis en dou-
qui, suis en dou- leur, Par qui suis en dou-
Par qui suis en dou- leur, suis en dou- leur,
Par qui suis en dou- leur, Par qui suis en dou-
vy- e, Par qui suis en dou- leur, El- le
qui, Par qui, Par qui suis en dou- leur, suis en dou-

89
e, Ce m'est un
grand, Ce m'est un grand mal- heur,
e, Ce m'est un grand mal- heur,
e, Je re- com- men- ce
e, Ce m'est un grand mal- heur, Je re- com-
Ce m'est un grand mal- heur,

grand mal- heur,
Je re- com- men- ce ma dou-
Je re- com- men- ce ma dou- leur,
ma dou- leur, Je re- com-
men- ce ma dou- leur, Je re- com- men- ce
Ce m'est un grand mal- heur,

Je re- com- men-
leur, Je re- com- men- ce ma dou- leur, Je re- com- men-
Je re- com- men- ce ma dou- leur, Je re- com- men- ce
men- ce ma dou- leur,
ma dou- leur, Je re- com- men- ce ma dou- leur,
Je re- com- men- ce ma dou- leur, Je

ce ma dou- leur.
ce ma dou- leur, Je re- comma dou- leur, Je re- com- men- ce ma
Je re- com- men- ce ma dou- leur,
re- com- men- ce ma dou- leur, Je

men- ce, Je re- com- men- ce ma dou- leur.
dou- leur, Je re- com- men- ce ma dou- leur.
Je re- com- men- ce ma dou- leur.
Je re- com- men- ce ma dou- leur.
re- com- men- ce ma dou- leur.

123 Nicolas, *J'ay contenté ma volonté* [C. Marot]

té di- ver- se- ment, Di- ver- se- ment, J'ay
té, di- ver-
mour trait- té, di- ver- se- ment, di- ver- se-
Car j'ay es- té d'a- mour trait- té di- ver-
Car j'ay es- té d'a- mour trait- té di- ver- se- ment,
Car j'ay es- té d'a- mour trait- té di- ver-

J'ay eu tour- ment,bon trait- te- ment, J'ay
ment, bon trait- te-
tour- ment, bon trait- te- ment,
bon trait- te- ment, J'ay eu tour- ment, bon trait- te- ment,
J'ay eu tour- ment, bon trait- te-
J'ay eu tour- ment, bon trait- te-

J'ay eu tour- ment,bon trait- te- ment,
se- ment, J'ay eu tour- ment,bon trait- te-
ment, J'ay eu
se- ment, J'ay eu tour- ment,
J'ay eu tour- ment,bon trait- te- ment,
se- ment, J'ay eu tour- ment,

eu dou- ceur & cru- au- té,
ment, J'ay eu dou- ceur,
J'ay eu dou- ceur, J'ay eu dou-
J'ay eu dou- ceur & cru- au-
ment, J'ay eu dou- ceur & cru- au-
ment,

(sic)
(sic)
J'ay eu dou- ceur
J'ay eu dou- ceur & cru- au- té,
ceur & cru- au- té,
té, J'ay eu dou- ceur & cru- au- té,
té, J'ay eu dou-
J'ay eu dou- ceur & cru- au-

[○· = ○ (♩♪)]
pleins fors seul- le- ment, D'a- voir ay- mé si loy- au- ment,
Et ne me pleins fors seul- le- ment, D'a- voir ay- mé si loy- au- ment,
Et ne me pleins fors seul- le- ment, D'a- voir ay- mé si loy- au- ment,
ne me pleins fors seul- le- ment, D'a- voir ay- mé si loy- au- ment, Cel-
Et ne me pleins fors seul- le- ment, D'a- voir ay- mé si loy- au-
Et ne me pleins fors seul- le- ment, D'a- voir ay- mé si loy- au- ment,

[○ (♩♩♩) = ○·]
& cru- au- té, Et ne me
J'ay eu dou- ceur, & cru- au- té,
J'ay eu tour- ment & cru- au- té,
& cru- au- té, & cru- au- té, Et
ceur, J'ay eu dou- ceur & cru- au- té,
té, J'ay eu dou- ceur & cru- au- té,

Cel- le qui est, Cel- le qui
Cel- le qui est,
Cel- le qui est, Cel- le qui est sans loy- au-
le qui est, Cel- le qui est sans loy-
ment, qui est, Cel- le
Cel- le qui, Cel- le qui est, sans loy-

106
est,
sans loy-
té, Cel- le qui est sans loy- au-
au- té, Cel- le qui est sans
qui est sans loy- au- té, sans
au- té, Cel- le qui est,
120
le qui est, sans loy- au-
au- té, Cel- le qui
loy- au- té, sans
qui est sans loy-
au-
est sans loy-
113
(sic)
sans loy- au- té, Cel-
au- té, Cel- le qui est sans loy-
té, Cel- le qui est sans
loy- au- té, Cel- le
loy- au- té, Cel- le qui est, sans loy-
sans loy- au- té, Cel- le qui
125
té, sans loy- au- té.
est sans loy- au- té.
loy- au- té, sans loy- au- té.
au- té.
té.
au- té.
433

124 Nicolas, *Voz huys sont ilz*

39
més vous, fi- llet- te, Dor-més vous, Dor- més
moy si m'ay- més, Dor- més vous, Fi- llet- te, Dor- més
Dor- més vous, Fi- llet- te, Dor-més vous, Fi-
les moy si m'ay- més, Dor-més vous, Dor-més vous, Fi- llet- te, Dor- més
les moy si m'ay- més, Dor- més vous,
rés les moy si m'ay-més, Dor- més vous, Fi- llet- te,

60
Fi- llet- te, vous dor- més,
Fi- llet- te, vous dor- més, Dor- més vous seul- let-
més, Fi- llet- te, vous dor- més, Dor- més vous
Fi- llet- te, vous dor- més,
llet- te, vous dor- més, Fi- llet- te, vous dor- més,
més, Dor- més vous, Dor- més vous seul-

50
vous seul- let- te, Fi- llet- te, vous dor- més,
vous, Fi- llet- te, Fi- llet- te, vous dor- més,
llet- te, Fi- llet- te, vous dor- més, Fi- llet- te, vous dor-
vous, Fi- llet- te, Fi- llet- te, vous dor- més,
Fi- llet- te, vous dor- més, vous dor- més, Fi-
Fi- llet- te, vous dor- més, Fi- llet- te, vous dor-

69
(sic)
Dor- més vous seul- let- te, Dor- més vous seul-
te, Dor- més vous seul- let- te, Dor- més vous
seul- let- te, Dor- més vous seul- let- te,
Dor- més vous seul- let- te, Dor- més vous seul- let-
Dor- més vous seul- let- te,
let- te, Dor- més

let- te,
seul- let- te, Car
Car pour vous sont
te, Car pour vous sont con-
Car pour vous sont con-sum-més,
vous seul- let- te, Car

més, Fi- llet- te, vous dor- més,
Fi- llet- te, vous dor- mez, Fi- llet- te, vous
llet- te, vous dor- més, Fi- llet- te, vous dor- més, vous
més, Fi- llet- te, vous dor- més, Fi- llet- te,
llet- te, vous dor- més, Fi- llet- te, vous dor- més, vous
més, Fi- llet- te, vous dor- més,

Car pour vous sont con-sum-
pour vous sont con-sum-més, Fi- llet- te, vous dor- més,
con-sum- més, Car pour vous sont con-sum-més, Fi-
sum- més, Car pour vous sont con- sum- més, Fi- llet- te, vous dor-
Fi- llet- te, vous dor- més, Fi- llet- te, vous dor- més, Fi-
pour vous, Car pour vous sont con-sum- més, Fi- llet- te, vous dor-

Mes sens d'a-mours en-flam-
dor- mez, vous dor- més, Mes sens d'a-mours en-flam-
dor- mez, Fi- llet- te, vous dor- més, Mes sens d'a-mours en-flam-
vous dor- mez, vous dor- més,
dor- mez, vous dor- mez,
Fi- llet- te, vous dor- mez,

115
més,   Dor- més vous, fi- llet-
més,   Dor- més vous, fi- llet-
més,   Dor- més vous, fi- llet- te,
Mes   sens d'a- mours en- flam- més, Dor- més vous,
Mes   sens d'a- mours en- flam- més,
Mes   sens d'a- mours en- flam- més,

134
vous dor- més, Dor- més vous seul- let- te,
Dor- més vous seul- let- te,
vous dor- més, Dor- més vous seul- let-
llet- te vous dor- més, Dor- més vous seul- let-
vous dor- més, Dor- més vous seul- let-
Dor- més vous seul- let- te,

125
te, Dor- més vous, fi- llet- te, Fi- llet- te,
te, Dor- més vous, fi- llet- te,
Dor- més vous, Dor- més vous, fi- llet- te, Fi- llet- te,
Dor- més vous, fi- llet- te, vous dor- més, fi-
Dor- més vous, fi- llet- te, Fi- llet- te,
fi- llet- te, vous dor- més,

143
Dor- més vous, Dor- més vous seul let-
Dor- més vous seul- let- te,
te, Dor- més vous seul-
te, seul- let- te, Dor- més vous seul- let- te,
te, Dor- més vous seul- let-
Dor- més vous seul- let- te,

125 Nicolas, *Puis que j'ay belle amye*

e,
El-
e, a- my- e,
my- e, El- le est coin- te &
bel- le a- my- e, El- le est coin-
bel- le a-my- e, El- le est coin- te & jo-
que j'ay bel- le a- my- e,

El- le est coin- te & jo- li-
e,
le est coin- te & jo- li- e,
El- le est coin- te & jo- li- e,
te & jo- li- e, El- le est coin- te & jo- li-
El- le est coin- te & jo- li-

le est coin- te & jo- li- e,
El- le est coin- te & jo- li-
jo- li- e, El-
te & jo- li- e, El- le est coin- te & jo- li- e,
li- e, El- le est coin- te & jo- li- e, El- le est coin-
El- le est coin- te & jo- li- e, El- le est coin- te & jo- li- e,

e, J'ay- me- ray loy- au- ment, Et
J'ay- me- ray loy- au- ment, Et veux to- tal- le- ment,
J'ay- me- ray loy- au- ment, Et veux to- tal- le-
J'ay- me- ray loy- au- ment, Et veux to- tal- le- ment,
e, J'ay- me- ray loy- au- ment,
e, J'ay- me- ray loy- au- ment, Et

55
veux to- tal- le- ment,
Chas- ser, Chas- ser,
ment, Chas-ser,
Chas- ser, Chas- ser, Chas- ser me- lan-co- li-
Et veux to- tal- le- ment, Chas- ser, Chas- ser, Chas- ser me-lan
veux to- tal- le- ment, chas-ser, Chas- ser, Chas-ser me- lan- co-

71
Chas- ser me- lan- co-
me- lan- co- li- e,
Chas- ser me- lan- co- li-
lan- co- li- e, me- lan- co- li-
e, Chas- ser me- lan-co- li-
lan- co- li- e, me- lan- co- li-

63
Chas- ser,
Chas- ser me- lan- co- li- e,
e, Chas-ser me-
co- li-
li- e, Chas- ser me-

79
li- e,
Chas- ser me- lan- co- li- e, Chas- ser me-lan- co- li-
e,
e,
Chas- ser me- lan- co- li-
e, Chas- ser me-lan- co- li-

89
Chas- ser me- lan- co-
e, me- lan- co- li-
Chas- ser me- lan- co-
Chas- ser me- lan- co- li- e,
e, Chas- ser me- lan- co- li-
e, Chas- ser me- lan- co- li- e, Chas- ser me-

99
li- e.
e, Chas- ser me- lan- co- li- e.
li- e, Chas- ser me- lan- co- li- e.
me- lan- co- li- e.
e, Chas- ser me- lan- co- li- e.
lan- co- li- e, Chas- ser me- lan- co- li- e.

Par trop a- mour me pour- chas- se de pres,
Par trop a- mour me pour- chas- se
Par trop a-
Par trop a- mour me pour- chas- se de
Par trop a- mour me
Par trop a- mour me pour- chas- se de pres,

10
Par trop a- mour, Par trop a- mour,
de pres, Par trop a- mour me pour- chas- se
mour me pour- chas- se de pres, me pour- chas- se
pres, me pour- chas- se de pres, me
pour- chas- se de pres, me pour- chas- se de pres, me pour- chas-
Par trop a- mour me pour- chas- se de pres,

me pour-chas- se de pres,
de pres, me pour-chas- se de pres, me pour-chas- se
de pres, me pour-chas- se de pres, me pour-chas
pour-chas- se de pres, me pour-chas- se
se de pres, me pour-chas- se
me pour-chas- se de pres, me pour-chas- se de pres,

se, & ver- tu me de-lais- se, De ses ray-
de- lais- se, De ses ray- ons me don-ne as- saux,
ver- tu me de- lais- se, De ses ray- ons me don-
se, & ver- tu me de- lais- se,
& ver- tu me de- lais- se,
se, De ses ray- ons me

Mais le pou- voir, Mais le pou- voir & ver- tu me de- lais-
de pres, Mais le pou- voir, Mais le pou- voir & ver- tu me
se de pres, Mais le pou- voir, Mais le pou- voir, &
de pres, Mais le pou- voir, & ver- tu me de- lais-
Mais le pou- voir, & ver- tu me de- lais-

ons me don-ne as- saux ex- pres: De ses ray- ons,
De ses ray- ons me don- ne as- saux ex- pres: De
ne as- saux ex- pres: as- saux ex- pres: me don-
De ses ray- ons me don-ne as- saux ex- pres:
De ses ray- ons me don- ne as- saux ex- pres: me
don- ne as- saux ex- pres: De ses ray-

442

61
De ses ray- ons, me don-ne as-saux ex-
ses ray- ons me don-ne as-saux ex- pres, me don- ne as-saux ex-
ne as- saux ex- pres: me don-ne as- saux ex- pres: me
me don- ne as- saux ex- pres: me don- ne as-saux
don-ne as- saux ex- pres: me don-ne as- saux ex- pres,
ons me don-ne as-saux ex- pres: me don- ne as- saux ex- pres: me don-ne as-saux

84
pres le bles- se, de par trop pres le bles- se, Y four-nis-
de par trop pres le bles- se, Y four-nis-sant, Y
par trop pres le bles- se, de par trop pres le bles- se,
de par trop pres le bles- se, Y
de par trop pres le bles- se,
trop pres le bles- se, Y four-nis-

72
pres: Ce- la mon coeur, Ce- la mon coeur de par trop
pres: me don- ne as- saux ex- pres: Ce- la mon coeur, Ce- la mon coeur,
don-ne as-saux ex- pres, Ce- la mon coeur, de
ex- pres, me don-ne as-saux ex- pres, Ce- la mon coeur, Ce- la mon coeur,
me don-ne as- saux ex- pres, Ce- la mon coeur,
ex- pres: Ce- la mon coeur, de par

95
sant, me vient u- ne foi- bles- se, Qui de por- ter,
four- nis- sant me vient u- ne foi- bles- se, Qui de- por- ter me
Y four-nis- sant me vient u- ne foi- bles- se, Qui
four-nis- sant, me vient u- ne foi- bles- [se,]
Y four-nis- sant me vient u- ne foi- bles- se,
sant me vient u- ne foi- bles- se, Qui de- por- ter me

Qui de- por- ter me fait de la pour- sui-
fait, Qui de- por- ter me fait, de la pour- sui- te,
de por- ter me fait, de la pour- sui-
Qui de- por- ter me fait de la pour- sui- te,
Qui de- por- ter me fait, de
fait, de la pour- sui-

n'est en moy n'y no- bles- se, n'est en moy n'y no- bles- se, A- dieu, vous
tu, n'est en moy n'y no- bles- se, A- dieu, vous
no- bles- se, A- dieu, vous
n'est en moy n'y no- bles- se,
en moy n'y no- bles- se, A- dieu, vous
en moy n'y no- bles- se, n'y no- bles- se,

te, de la pour- sui- te, Puis que ver- tu, Puis que ver- tu,
de la pour- sui- te, Puis que ver- tu, Puis que ver-
te, Puis que ver- tu n'est en moy n'y
de la pour- sui- te, Puis que ver- tu,
la pour- sui- te, Puis que ver- tu n'est
te, Puis que ver- tu, n'est

dis, A- dieu, vous dis, a- mour, je pren la fui- te, A-
dis, je pren la fui- te, A-
dis, A- dieu, vous dis, a- mour, je pren la fui- te,
A- dieu, vous dis, a- mour, je pren la fui- te, A-
dis, je pren la fui- te, A-
A- dieu, vous dis, a- mour, je pren la fui- te, A- dieu,

127 Maillard, *Las, je languis*

23
quoy, Vi- vant en dueil, Vi- vant en dueil,
quoy, Vi- vant en dueil, Vi- vant en
vant en dueil, Vi- vant en dueil, &
Vi- vant en dueil, Vi- vant en dueil,
en dueil, Vi- vant en dueil, & en me-
Vi- vant en dueil, Vi- vant en dueil, Vi- vant en dueil,

45
& en me- lan- co- li- e, Par- quoy
en me- lan- co- li- e, Par-
co- li- e, Par- quoy je dy, Par-
Par- quoy je dy, Par- quoy
e, Par- quoy je dy,
lan- co- li- e, Par- quoy je dy,

34
dueil, & en me- lan- co- li- e, &
en me- lan- co- li- e, & en me- lan-
& en me- lan- co- li- e,
lan- co- li- e, & en me- lan- co- li-
& en me- lan- co- li- e, & en me-

55
je dy & ju- re sur ma foy, Par- quoy je dy & ju- re sur
quoy je dy, & ju- re sur ma foy, &
quoy je dy & ju- re sur ma foy, & ju- re
je dy, & ju- re sur ma foy,
& ju- re sur ma foy, & ju- re sur ma
& ju- re sur ma foy, & ju- re sur

67
ma foy, Qu'il est bien fol,
ju- re sur ma foy, Qu'il
sur ma foy, Qu'il est bien fol, Qu'il
Qu'il est bien fol, Qu'il est bien
foy, Qu'il est bien fol,
ma foy, Qu'il est bien fol, Qu'il est bien fol,

88
mour se fi- e,
e, qui en a- mour se fi- e,
e, qui en a- mour se fi- e, Qu'il
en a- mour se fi- e, Qu'il est bien fol,
qui en a- mour se fi- e, Qu'il est bien
e, qui en a- mour se fi-

77
Qu'il est bien fol, Qu'il est bien fol qui en a-
est bien fol, qui en a- mour se fi-
est bien fol, qui en a- mour se fi-
fol, qui en a- mour se fi- e, qui
qui en a- mour se fi- e,
Qu'il est bien fol, qui en a- mour se fi-

99
Qu'il est bien fol, Qu'il est bien fol,
Qu'il est bien fol, qui en a-
est bien fol, qui en a- mour se fi- e,
Qu'il est bien fol, qui en a-
fol, qui en a- mour se fi- e,
e, Qu'il est bien fol, qui en a- mour

109
qui en a- mour se fi-
mour se fi- e, qui en a- mour se
qui en a- mour se fi- e,
mour se fi- e, qui en a- mour se
qui en a- mour se fi- e, qui
se fi- e, qui en a- mour se fi-
Te- nez moy
Te- nez moy en voz bras, mon a-
Te- nez moy en voz bras,
Te- nez moy en voz bras,
Te- nez moy en voz bras, mon
118
e.
fi- e.
qui en a- mour se fi- e.
fi- e, qui en a- mour se fi- e.
en a- mour se fi- e.
e, qui en a- mour se fi- e.
10
en voz bras,
my, je suis ma- la- de, mon
Te- nez moy en
mon a- my, je suis
je suis ma-
a- my, je suis ma- la- de,

mon a- my, je suis ma-
a- my, je suis ma- la- de,
voz bras,
ma- la- de, mon a- my, je suis
la- de,
mon a- my, je suis ma- la-

mour, me
Vo- tre a- mour, me gue- ri- ra,
moy en voz bras, Vo- tre a- mour
suis ma- la- de,
de, Vo- tre a- mour me
Vo- tre a- mour me gue- ri- ra,

la- de, Vo- tre a-
mon a- my, je suis ma- la- de,
mon a- my, je suis ma- la- de, Te- nez
ma- la- de, mon a- my, je
mon a- my, je suis ma- la-
de,

gue- ri- ra,
me gue- ri- ra, C'est à Pa- ris
me gue- ri- ra,
Vo- tre a- mour me gue- ri- ra, C'est à Pa- ris
gue- ri- ra, C'est à Pa- ris, ou
C'est à Pa- ris, ou par-

C'est à Pa- ris, ou par-
ou par- de- la, U- ne cle- re fon- tai-
C'est à Pa- ris, ou
ou par- de- la, U- ne cle- re fon- tai- ne y
par- de- la, C'est à Pa- ris, ou
de- la, U- ne cle- re fon- tai- ne y a,
de- la, U- ne cle- re fon- tai-
ne y a, U- ne cle- re fon- tai- ne y a,
par- de- la, U- ne cle- re fon-
a, U- ne cle- re fon- tai- ne y a,
par- de- la, U- ne cle- re fon-
U- ne cle- re fon- tai- ne y a,
ne y a, Te-
fon- tai- ne y a, Te- nez moy en voz bras,
tai- ne y a,
Te- nez moy en voz bras, Te- nez moy en
tai- ne y a, Te- nez moy en
Te- nez moy en voz bras, Mon a- my,
nez moy en voz bras,
Mon a- my, je suis ma- la- de,
Te- nez moy
voz bras, Te- nez moy
voz bras, je suis
Mon a- my, je suis ma- la- de,

Mon a- my, je suis
Te- nez moy, en voz bras,
en voz bras, Mon a- my, je suis
ma- la- de,
Mon a- my, je suis ma-

tre a- mour, me
me gue- ri- ra, me gue- ri-
nez moy en voz bras, Vo- tre a-
suis ma- la- de,
de, Vo- tre a- mour
Vo- tre a- mour me gue- ri-

ma- la- de, Vo-
Vo- tre a- mour me gue- ri- ra,
Mon a- my, je suis ma- la- de, Te-
ma- la- de, Mon a- my, je
Mon a- my, je suis ma- la-
de,

gue- ri- ra.
ra, Vo- tre a- mour me gue- ri- ra.
mour me gue- ri- ra.
Vo- tre a- mour me gue- ri- ra.
me gue- ri- ra.
ra, me gue- ri- ra.

129 Josquin, *Allegez moy douce plaisant*

tes mes dou- leurs, de tou- tes mes
de tou- tes mes
le- gez moy, de tou- tes mes
Al- le- gez moy de tou- tes mes dou- leurs,
Al- le- gez moy de tou- tes mes dou- leurs,
le- gez moy de tou- tes mes dou- leurs,

Vo- tre beau- té, me
Vo- tre beau- té, me
beau- té, Vo- tre beau-
Vo- tre beau- té, Vo-
tre beau- té, Vo- tre beau- té,
tre beau- té, Vo- tre beau- té,

dou- leurs, Vo- tre beau- té,
dou- leurs, Vo- tre beau- té,
dou- leurs, Vo- tre beau- té, Vo- tre
de tou- tes mes dou- leurs,
de tou- tes mes dou- leurs, Vo- tre beau- té, Vo-
de tou- tes mes dou- leurs, Vo- tre beau- té, Vo-

tient en a- mou- ret- te, Des- soubz la bou- di-
tient en a- mou- ret- te,
té, me tient en a- mou- ret-
tre beau- té, me tient en a- mou- ret-
me tient en a- mou- ret-
me tient en a- mou- ret- te,

78

net- te,
Des- soubz la bou- di- net- te, Des-
te, Des-
te, Des- soubz la bou- di- net- te.
te, Des- soubz la bou- di- net- te, Des-
Des- soubz la bou- di- net- te, Des-

84

Des- soubz la bou- di- net- te.
soubz la bou- di- net- te.
soubz la bou- di- net- te.
soubz la bou- di- net- te.
soubz la bou- di- net- te.
(sic)   (sic)

9

17
vert en no mai- son, mis- ton- don la mis-ton-dai- ne don,
mis- ton- don la mis- ton- dai- ne don, En
mis- ton-don, mis- ton-don, mis- ton-
son, mis-ton-don la mis-ton-dai- ne don,
la don la mis-ton-dai- ne don,
mis-ton- dai- ne don, don la mis- ton- don,

26
En re- ve- nant de Ly-
re- ve-nant de Ly- on, En re-ve-nant de Ly- on,
don, En re- ve- nant de Ly- on, En re- ve- nant
En re- ve- nant de Ly- on, En re-
En re- ve- nant de Ly- on, En re- ve- nant de Ly- on,
En re- ve- nant de Ly- on,

35
on, En re- ve- nant de Ly- on,
Ren- con- tray un va- le- ton,
de Ly- on, de Ly- on, Ren- con-tray
ve- nant de Ly- on, Ren- con-
En re- ve- nant de Ly- on don don, Ren- con- tray un va- le- ton,
En re- ve- nant de Ly- on don don, Ren- con- tray un va- le- ton, Ren-con-

45
Ren- con-tray un va- le- ton,
Ren- con- tray un va- le- ton, mis-ton-don la
un va- le- ton, Ren- con- tray un
tray un va- le- ton, mis- ton-
Ren- con-tray un va- le- ton, mis-
tray un va- le- ton, Ren- con- tray un va- le- ton,

54
mis- ton- don la mis- ton- dai- ne, mis- ton- don la mis- ton-
mis- ton- dai- ne, la mis- ton- dai- ne, la mis- ton-
va- le- ton, mis- ton- don la mis- ton- dai- ne,
don la mis- ton- dai- ne, mis- ton- don la mis- ton- dai- ne,
ton- don la mis- ton- dai- ne, mis- ton- don la mis- ton- dai- ne, la mis- ton-
mis- ton- don la mis- ton- dai- ne, la mis- ton-

72
son, mis- ton- don la mis- ton- dai- ne don,
mis- ton- don la mis- ton- dai- ne don,
mis- ton- don la mis- ton- dai- ne,
mis- ton- don la mis- ton- dai- ne don,
ton- dai- ne don la mis- ton- don, Il m'a
Tout est vert en no mai- son, mis- ton- don la

64
dai- ne, Tout est vert en no mai-
dai- ne, Tout est vert en no mai- son, mis- ton- don la mis- ton- dai- ne,
Tout est vert en no mai- son, mis- ton- don,
Tout est vert en no mai- son,
dai- ne, Tout est vert en no mai- son, mis-
dai- ne don, Tout est vert en no mai- son,

79
Il m'a de- man-
Il m'a de- man- dé mon nom, Il m'a de- man- dé mon nom,
Il m'a de- man- dé mon nom, Il m'a de- man- dé mon nom, mis-
Il m'a de- man- dé mon nom,
de- man- dé mon nom, Il m'a de- man- dé mon nom, mis- ton- don,
mis- ton- dai- ne don, Il m'a de- man- dé mon nom, Il m'a

89
dé mon nom, Il m'a de-man-dé mon nom, Ja- que-
Il m'a de-man-dé mon nom, mis-ton-don, mis-ton- don don don,
ton-don, Il m'a de-man-dé mon nom,
Il m'a de-man-dé mon nom, Ja- que- lin- ne m'ap- pe- l'on,
Il m'a de-man-dé mon nom, Ja- que-li- ne m'appe-l'on,
de-man- dé mon nom, Il m'a de-man-dé mon nom, Ja- que-li- ne m'ap-

107
don, mis-ton- don la mis- ton-
mis-ton- don la mis-ton- dai- ne,
mis-ton- don la mis-ton- dai- ne, mis-
mis-ton- don la mis- ton- dai- ne,
mis-ton- don la mis- ton- dai- ne, mis-ton-
mis-ton- don la mis-ton- dai- ne, mis-ton-don la mis- ton-

98
lin- ne m'ap- pe- l'on, Ja- que-lin ne m'ap-pe-l'on mis-ton-
Ja- que-li- ne m'appe-l'on, mis-ton- don, mis-ton-don, mis-ton-don,
Ja- que-li- ne m'app-pe-l'on, mis- ton-don,
Ja- que- lin- ne m'ap-pe- l'on mis-ton-don,
mis- ton- don, Ja- que-li- ne m'ap-pe-l'on, mis-ton-don,
pe-l'on, mis-ton- don, mis-ton- don,

117
dai- ne, mis- ton-don la mis- ton-dai- ne,
mis- ton-don la mis- ton- dai- ne, la mis- ton-dai- ne,
ton-don la mis-ton- dai- ne, la mis- ton-dai- ne,
mis- ton- don la mis- ton-dai- ne,
don la mis- ton-dai- ne, mis-ton- don la mis-ton-dai- ne, la mis-ton-dai- ne don,
dai- ne, mis- ton-don la mis- ton-dai- ne, la mis- ton-dai- ne

127
Tout est vert,
Tout est vert, Tout est vert, Tout est vert en no mai- son,
Tout est vert, Tout est vert en no mai- son,
Tout est vert,
tout est vert, tout est vert en no mai- son,
don, Tout est vert, tout est

143
mis- ton- don la mis- ton- dai- ne don.
don, mis- ton-don la mis- ton- dai- ne don, mis- ton- don, mis-
mis- ton- don, don, mis- ton- don, mis- ton- don,
ton- don la mis-ton- dai- ne don, mis- ton- don, don, don,
ton- don, mis-ton- don, mis- ton- don, mis- ton-
la mis-ton-dai- ne don, mis- ton- don, mis- ton- don, mis-

135
Tout est vert en no mai- son,
en no mai- son, mis- ton- don, mis- ton-
mis- ton- don la mis- ton- dai- ne don, mis- ton- don,
Tout est vert en no mai- son, mis-
en no mai- son, mis- ton- don, mis- ton- don, mis-
vert en no mai- son, tout est vert en no mai- son, mis- ton- don

151
ton- don don don, mis- ton- don.
mis- ton- don, mis- ton- don, mis- ton- don.
mis- ton- don, mis- ton- don, mis- ton- don.
don, mis- ton- don, mis- ton- don don, don.
ton- don, mis- ton- don don.

131 LeJeune, *O pas en vain perdus* [Bäif]

41
tei- nes, O sou- las peu cer- tains,
O sou- las peu cer- tains, Tris- tes- ses,
tei- nes, O sou- las peu cer- tains, O sou- las peu cer- tains, Tris-
fon- tei- nes, O sou- las peu cer- tains, Tris- tes- ses trop
deux fon- tei- nes, O sou- las peu cer- tains, Tris- tes- ses trop
O sou- las peu cer- tains, Tris- tes-

59
O pour si che- re foy, O gra- ces,
tes- ses trop cer- tai- nes, trop a- veu- gle ri- gueur, ô
ses trop cer- tai- nes, trop a- veu- glé ri- gueur, O gra- ces, ô
trop cer- tai- nes, O pour si che- re foy, O gra- ces, ô
tai- nes, trop cer- tai- nes, trop a- veu- glé ri- gueur, ô
trop cer- tai- nes, O pour si che- re foy, O gra- ces,

50
Tris- tes- ses trop cer- tai- nes,
Tris- tes- ses trop cer- tai- nes, Tris-
tes- ses trop cer- tai- nes, trop cer- tai- nes, Tris- tes-
cer- tai- nes, Tris- tes- ses, Tris- tes- ses
cer- tai- nes, Tris- tes- ses trop cer-
ses trop cer- tai- nes, Tris- tes- ses

70
dont la bel- le vi- gueur, en vi- gueur
beau- tez, dont la bel- le vi-
beau- tez, dont la bel- le vi- gueur, dont la bel- le vi-
beau- tez, dont la bel- le vi- gueur, en vi- gueur
beau- tez, dont la bel- le vi- gueur
dont la bel- le vi-

78
en- tre- tient, Tous- jours fres- ches mes pei-
gueur, en vi- gueur en- tre- tient, Tous- jours fres- ches mes
gueur, en vi- gueur en- tre- tient, Tous- jours fres- ches mes
en- tre- tient, Tous- jours fres- ches mes pei- nes,
en vi- gueur en- tre- tient, Tous- jours fres- ches mes
gueur, en vi- gueur en- tre- tient, Tous- jours fres- ches mes

86
nes, O, sou- pirs, ô re- gretz, O prés, cam- pa- gnes,
pei- nes, ô sou- haits, O, sou- pirs, ô pen- sers, O prés, cam- pa- gnes,
pei- nes, O, sou- pirs, ô pen- sers, ô re- gretz, O,
ô sou- haits, O, sou- pirs, ô pen- sers, ô re- gretz, O prés, cam- pa- gnes,
pei- nes, ô sou- haits, O, sou- pirs, ô pen- sers,
pei- nes, O, sou- pirs, ô re- gretz,

98
eaux, O Dé- es- ses, ô dieux de la ter- re & de l'on-
eaux, O Dé- es- ses, ô dieux de la ter- re & de l'on-
ro- chers, ô fo- restz, O Dé- es- ses, ô dieux,
eaux, O Dé- es- ses, ô dieux, ô dieux,
O ro- chers, ô fo- restz, O Dé- es- ses, ô dieux de la ter- re & de l'on-
O ro- chers, ô fo- restz, O Dé- es- ses, ô dieux,

109
de, O ciel, ô ter- re, ô mer,
de, O ciel, ô ter- re, ô mer, ô Dieu qui luys le
de la ter- re & de l'on- de, O ciel, ô ter- re, ô mer, O Dieu qui luys le
de la ter- re & de l'on- de, O ciel, ô ter- re, ô mer,
de, de la ter- re & de l'on- de, O ciel, ô ter- re, ô mer, O Dieu,
de la ter- re & de l'on- de, O ciel, ô ter- re, ô mer, O Dieu qui luys le

461

121
Dé- es- se qui la nuit, Voy- es vous
jour, Voy- es vous au- tre a- mour,
jour, Dé- es- se qui la nuit, Voy- es vous au- tre a- mour, Qui
Dé- es- se qui la nuit, Voy- es vous au- tre a-
Dé- es- se qui la nuit, Voy- es vous au-
jour, Voy- es vous au- tre a-

140
Tant de tris- tes- se a- bon- de,
de tris- tes- se a- bon- de, Tant de tris-
de tris- tes- se a- bon- de, Tant de tris- tes- se a-
qu'en ay- mant, Tant de tris- tes- se a- bon- de, Qui fa- ce qu'en ay- mant, Tant
Qui fa- ce qu'en ay- mant, Tant de tris- tes- se a- bon- de,
tes- se a- bon- de, Tant de tris- tes- se a- bon- de, Qui fa- ce

131
au- tre a- mour, Qui fa- ce qu'en ay- mant,
Qui fa- ce qu'en ay- mant, Tant
fa- ce qu'en ay- mant, Tant de tris- tes- se a- bon- de, Tant
mour, Voy- es vous au- tre a- mour, Qui fa- ce qu'en ay- mant, Qui fa- ce
tre a- mour, Qui fa- ce qu'en ay- mant,
mour, Qui fa- ce qu'en ay- mant, Tant de tris-

150
Tant de tris- tes- se a- bon- de, Qui
tes- se a- bon- de, Tant de tris- tes- se a- bon-
bon- de, Tant de tris- tes- se a- bon-
de tris- tes- se a- bon- de, Qui fa- ce qu'en ay-
Tant de tris- tes- se a- bon- de, Qui
qu'en ay- mant, Tant de tris- tes- se a- bon-

157
fa- ce qu'en ay- mant, Tant de tris-
de, Qui fa- ce qu'en ay- mant, Tant
de, Qui fa- ce qu'en ay- mant, Qui fa- ce qu'en ay-
mant, Tant de tris- tes- se a- bon- de, Tant de
fa- ce qu'en ay- mant, Qui
de, Qui fa- ce qu'en ay- mant, Tant de tris- tes- se a-

174
tes- se a- bon- de, Tant de tris- tes- se a- bon-
Tant de tris- tes- se a- bon- de,
de tris- tes- se a- bon- de, Qui fa- ce
bon- de, Tant de tris- tes- se a- bon-
Tant de tris- tes- se a- bon- de,
qu'en ay- mant, Tant de tris- tes- se a-

165
tes- se a- bon- de, Tant de tris-
de tris- tes- se a- bon- de,
mant, Tant de tris- tes- se a- bon- de, Qui fa- ce qu'en ay- mant, Tant
tris- tes- se a- bon- de, Tant de tris- tes- se a-
fa- ce qu'en ay- mant, Tant de tris- tes- se a- bon- de,
bon- de, Tant de tris- tes- se a- bon- de, Qui fa- ce

180
de.
Tant de tris- tes- se a- bon- de.
qu'en ay- mant, Tant de tris- tes- se a- bon- de.
de.
Tant de tris- tes- se a- bon- de.
bon- de, Tant de tris- tes- se a- bon- de.

Je suis des- he- ri- té- e
Je suis des- he- ri- té- e, Puis que j'ay per- du mon
Je suis des- he- ri- té- e, Puis que j'ay per- du
Je suis des- he- ri- té- e, Puis que j'ay per-

21
Seu- let- te il m'a lais- sé- e, Plei-
que j'ay per- du mon a- my, Seu- let- te il m'a lais-
my, Seu- let- te il m'a lais- sé- e, Plei- ne de
mon a- my, Seu- let- te il m'a lais- sé- e, Plei- ne de
que j'ay per- du mon a- my, Seu- let- te il m'a lais-
du mon a- my, Seu- let- te il m'a lais- sé- e,

10
e, Puis que j'ay per- du mon a- my,
Je suis des- he- ri- té- e, Puis
a- my, Je suis des- he- ri- té- e, Puis que j'ay per- du mon a-
Je suis des- he- ri- té- e, Puis que j'ay per- du
mon a- my, Puis que j'ay per- du mon a- my, Puis
du mon a- my, Puis que j'ay per-

32
ne de dueil & de sou- cy, Ros-
sé- e, Plei- ne de dueil & de sou- cy,
dueil, Plei- ne de dueil & de sou- cy, Ros- si- gnol du boys jo-
dueil & de sou- cy, Plei- ne de dueil & de sou- cy,
sé- e, Plei- ne de dueil & de sou- cy, Ros- si- gnol du
Plei- ne de dueil, Plei- ne de dueil & de sou- cy, Ros-

43
si- gnol du boys jo- ly, Sans plus fai- re
Ros- si- gnol du boys jo- ly,
ly, du boys jo- ly, Ros- si- gnol du boys jo- ly, Sans plus
Ros- si- gnol du boys, du boys jo- ly, du boys jo- ly, Sans
boys jo- ly, Ros- si- gnol du boys jo- ly, Sans plus fai- re de- meu- ré-
si- gnol du boys, du boys jo- ly, Sans plus fai- re

65
di- re à mon a- my, Que pour luy suis tour- men-
Va t'en di- re à mon a-
t'en di- re à mon a- my, Va t'en, Va t'en di- re à mon a-
a- my, Va t'en di- re à mon a- my, Que pour luy suis tour-
Va t'en di- re à mon a- my, Que pour luy suis
my, Va t'en, Va t'en di- re à mon a- my,

54
de- meu- ré- e, Va t'en
Sans plus fai- re de- meu- ré- e,
fai- re de- meu- ré- e, Sans plus fai- re de- meu- ré- e, Va t'en, Va
plus fai- re de- meu- ré- e, Va t'en di- re à mon a- my, Va t'en di- re à mon
e, Sans plus fai- re de- meu- ré- e, Va t'en di- re à mon a- my,
de- meu- ré- e, Va t'en, Va t'en di- re à mon a-

74
té- e, Que
my, Que pour luy suis tour- men- té-
my, Que pour luy suis, Que pour luy suis,
men- té- e, Que pour luy suis,
tour- men- té- e, Que pour luy suis tour- men-
Que pour luy suis tour- men- té- e, Que

133 Lupi, *Dueil, double dueil*

16
des-
des- plai- sir,
des-
plai- sir,
ren-
des- plai- sir, ren-
plai- sir, ren- fort de des- plai- sir, Tris-
plai- sir, Tris- tes- s'en-
ren- fort de des-
fort de des- plai- sir, ren- fort de des- plai- sir,
fort de des- plai- sir, Tris- tes-

33
nuy,
en- ne- mis de plai- sir,
ne- mis
de plai- sir, en- ne- mis
en- ne- mis de plai- sir, Tris-
Tris- tes- se, en- nuy, en- ne- mis de plai- sir, Tris- tes- se, en-
se, en- nuy, en- ne- mis de plai- sir,
tes- se, en- nuy, en- ne- mis de plai- sir, en- ne- mis

24
Tris- tes- se, en-
tes- se, en- nuy, en- nuy, en-
nuy, Tris- tes- s'en- nuy, Tris- tes- se, en- nuy,
plai- sir, Tris- tes- se, en- nuy,
Tris- tes- s'en- nuy, Tris- tes- s'en- nuy, Tris- tes-
s'en- nuy, Tris- tes- s'en- nuy, Tris-

42
en- ne- mis de
de plai- sir, en- ne- mis de plai-
tes- se, en- nuy, en- ne- mis de
nuy, en- ne- mis de plai- sir, en- ne- mis de
en- ne- mis de plai- sir, en- ne- mis de
de plai- sir, en- ne- mis de

50
plai- sir, De ma lan- gueur,
sir, De ma lan- gueur, De ma lan- gueur,
plai- sir, De ma lan- gueur, De ma lan- gueur, De ma lan- gueur,
plai- sir, De ma lan- gueur, pre- nez sol-
plai- sir, De ma lan- gueur, De ma lan- gueur, De ma lan- gueur,
plai- sir, De ma lan- gueur, De ma lan- gueur, pre-

68
de, Et de mon mal voy-
de, Et de mon mal voy-
pre- nez sol- li- ci- tu- de, Et de mon mal
de, sol- li- ci- tu- de, Et
pre- nez sol- li- ci- tu- de, Et de mon mal voy-
pre- nez sol- li- ci- tu- de, Et

59
pre- nez sol- li- ci- tu-
pre- nez sol- li- ci- tu-
De ma lan- gueur,
li- ci- tu- de, pre- nez sol- li- ci- tu-
pre- nez sol- li- ci- tu- de,
nez sol- li- ci- tu- de,

78
ant, Et de mon mal voy- ant l'a- ma- ri- tu-
ant, Et de mon mal voy- ant, l'a- ma- ri- tu-
voy- ant, Et de mon mal voy- ant l'a- ma-
de mon mal voy- ant, Et de mon mal voy- ant l'a- ma- ri- tu-
ant, Et de mon mal voy- ant, l'a- ma- ri- tu-
de mon mal voy- ant, Et de mon mal voy- ant, l'a-

de,

Ne

de,

Ne me don-

ri- tu-

de,

Ne

de,

Ne me don-

de, l'a- ma- ri- tu-

de,

Ne

ma- ri- tu-

de, l'a- ma- ri- tu- de,

de vi- vre plus loy- sir,

nés de vi- vre plus loy- sir,

nés de vi- vre plus loy- sir, Ne me don-

loy- sir, Ne me don- nés de vi- vre plus

plus loy- sir, de vi- vre plus loy- sir,

Ne me don- nés de vi- vre plus loy-

me don- nés, de vi- vre plus loy- sir, Ne me don- nés

nés, de vi- vre plus loy- sir, Ne me don- nés, Ne me don-

me don- nés, de vi- vre plus loy- sir, Ne me don-

de, Ne me don- nés, de vi- vre plus

me don- nés, de vi- vre plus loy- sir, de vi- vre

Ne me don- nés, de vi- vre plus loy- sir,

Ne me don- nes, de vi- vre plus loy- sir, Ne

sir, Ne me don- nes, de vi- vre plus loy-

nes, de vi- vre plus loy- sir, ne me don-

loy- sir, Ne me don- nes, de vi- vre plus

Ne me don- nes, de vi- vre plus loy- sir,

sir, Ne me don- nes, de vi- vre plus loy-

me don- nes de vi-
sir, Ne me don- nes de vi-
nes de vi- vre plus
loy- sir, de
de vi- vre plus loy- sir,
sir,

C'est u- ne du- re
C'est u- ne du- re de- par- ti- e, u-
C'est u- ne du- re de- par- ti- e, C'est u- ne
C'est u- ne
C'est u- ne du- re de- par- ti- e,
C'est u- ne du- re de- par- ti- e,

vre plus loy- sir.
vre plus loy- sir.
loy- sir, de vi- vre plus loy- sir.
vi- vre plus loy- sir.
Ne me don- nes de vi- vre plus loy- sir.
vi- vre plus loy- sir, de vi- vre plus loy- sir.

de par- ti- e, De ce- luy ou j'ay mis mon coeur,
ne du- re de- par- ti- e, De ce- luy
du- re de- par- ti- e, De ce- luy ou j'ay mis mon
du- re de- par- ti- e, De ce- luy
De ce- luy ou j'ay mis mon coeur,
De ce- luy ou j'ay

18
Dont m'en i- ray, dont m'en i- ray, dont
ou j'ay mis mon coeur, Dont m'en i- ray u-
coeur, ou j'ay mis mon coeur, Dont m'en i- ray u- ser ma vi-
ou j'ay mis mon coeur, Dont m'en i- ray u- ser ma
Dont m'en i- ray u- ser ma vi- e,
mis mon coeur, Dont m'en i- ray u- ser ma vi-

35
A l'her- mi- ta- ge de lan- gueur, Et
ta- ge de lan- gueur, Et tous les jours, Et
ta- ge de lan- gueur, Et tous les jours, Et
de lan- gueur, A l'her- mi- ta- ge de lan- gueur, Et tous les jours,
A l'her- mi- ta- ge de lan- gueur, Et
ta- ge de lan- gueur, de lan- gueur, Et tous les jours,

27
m'en i- ray u- ser ma vi- e,
ser ma vi- e, m'en i- ray u- ser ma vi- e, A l'her- mi-
e, Dont m'en i- ray u- ser ma vi- e, A l'her- mi-
vi- e, A l'her- mi- ta- ge
Dont m'en i- ray u- ser ma vi- e,
e, A l'her- mi-

44
tous les jours au ma- ti- net, Et tous les jours au
Et tous les jours au ma- ti- net,
tous les jours au ma- ti- net, au ma- ti- net, Et
Et tous les jours au ma- ti- net, Et tous les jours
tous les jours, Et tous les jours au ma- ti- net, au
Et tous les jours au ma- ti- net, Et

51
ma- ti- net, J'y- ray chan-
J'y- ray chan- ter sur
tous les jours au ma- ti- net, J'y- ray chan- ter sur
au ma- ti- net, au ma- ti- net, J'y-
ma- ti- net, au ma- ti- net, J'y- ray chan- ter,
tous les jours au ma- ti- net, J'y- ray chan- ter,

64
vert d'un buis- son- net, La pei- ne
Sous le cou- vert d'un buis- son- net,
buis- son- net, Sous le cou- vert d'un buis- son- net,
le cou- vert d'un buis- son- net, Sous le cou- vert d'un buis- son- net,
vert d'un buis- son- net, Sous le cou- vert d'un buis- son- net,
Sous le cou- vert d'un buis- son- net, La

57
ter sur la ver- du- re, Sous le cou-
la ver- du- re, Sous le cou- vert d'un buis- son- net,
la ver- du- re, Sous le cou- vert d'un
ray chan- ter sur la ver- du- re, Sous
sur la ver- du- re, Sous le cou- vert, Sous le cou-
chan- ter sur la ver- du- re,

73
que pour luy j'en- du- re, pour luy j'en-
La pei- ne que pour
La pei- ne que pour luy j'en- du- re, La pei- ne
La pei- ne que pour luy, La pei- ne que pour luy j'en- du- re, La
La pei- ne que pour luy j'en- du- re, que
pei- ne que pour luy j'en- du- re,

81
du- re, pour luy j'en- du-
luy j'en- du- re,
que pour luy, pour luy j'en-du- re, que pour luy j'en- du- re, La
pei- ne que pour luy j'en- du- re, pour luy j'en-du- re, pour
pour luy j'en- du- re, pour luy j'en- du-
La pei- ne que pour luy j'en- du-

96
du- re, La
luy j'en- du- re, pour luy j'en- du-
La pei- ne que pour luy j'en- du- re,
que pour luy j'en- du- re, pour luy j'en- du-
re, que pour luy j'en- du-
pei- ne que pour luy j'en- du- re,

89
re,
La pei- ne que pour luy j'en-
que pour luy j'en- du- re, La pei- ne que pour
pei- ne que pour luy j'en- du- re,
luy j'en- du- re, La pei- ne
re, pour luy j'en- du- re, pour luy j'en- du-
re, La pei- ne que pour luy, La

102
pei- ne que pour luy j'en- du- re, pour
re,
La pei- ne
La pei- ne que pour luy j'en- du- re, La
re, La pei- ne que pour luy, La pei- ne que pour luy j'en-
re, La pei- ne que pour luy j'en- du-
La pei- ne que pour luy j'en- du- re,

luy j'en- du- re, La pei- ne
que pour luy j'en- du- re.
pei- ne que pour luy, pour luy j'en- du- re, La
du- re, La pei- ne que pour luy j'en- du- re.
re, que pour luy j'en- du- re, La pei-
La pei- ne que pour luy,

C'est à grand tort,
C'est à grand tort, C'est à grand
C'est à grand tort, C'est à grand tort, C'est
C'est à grand tort, C'est à
C'est à grand tort, C'est à grand

que pour luy j'en- du- re.
pei- ne que pour luy j'en- du- re.
ne que pour luy j'en- du- re.
que pour luy j'en- du- re.

que moy pou- ret- te en-
tort que moy pou- ret- te en- du- re,
à grand tort, que moy pou- ret- te en- du-
grand tort que moy pou- ret- te en- du-
tort, que moy pou- ret- te en- du- re,
que moy pou- ret- te, que moy pou-

18
du- re, Et que je suis si tres- cour- te,
Et que je suis si tres- cour- te
[re,] Et que je suis, si tres- cour- te te- nu-
re, Et que je suis si tres- cour- te te- nu-
Et que je suis si tres- cour- te te- nu- e, Et
ret- te en- du- re, Et que je suis si tres- cour- te te- nu-

38
e, Plus mal- heu- reu- se, n'y
reu- se, n'y a des- soubz la nu-
e, Plus mal- heu- reu- se n'y a des- soubz la nu- e, n'y
te te- nu- e, Plus mal- heu- reu- se n'y a des- soubz la nu- e, Plus
te te- nu- e, Plus mal- heu- reu- se n'y a des- soubz la nu- e,
Plus mal- heu- reu- se, n'y a des- soubz la nu- e, n'y

28
Et que je suis si tres- cour- te te- nu-
te- nu- e, si tres- cour- te te- nu- e, Plus mal- heu-
e, si tres- cour- te te- nu- e, si tres- cour- te te- nu-
e, si tres- cour- te te- nu- e, si tres- cour-
que je suis si tres- cour- te te- nu- e, si tres- cour-
e, te- nu- e, te- nu- e,

49
(sic)
a des- soubz la nu- e, A l'en- du-
e, A l'en- du- rer, A
a des- soubz la nu- e, A l'en- du- rer, A
mal- heu- reu- se n'y a des- soubz la nu- e, A l'en- du-
n'y a des- soubz la nu- e, A l'en- du-
a des- soubz la nu- e, A l'en- du- rer,

57
rer, A l'en- du- rer, la pei- ne m'est trop du-
l'en- du- rer, la pei- ne m'est trop
l'en- du- rer, A l'en- du- rer la pei- ne m'est trop
rer, A l'en- du- rer la pei- ne m'est trop
rer, A l'en- du- rer, la pei- ne m'est trop
A l'en- du- rer, la pei- ne m'est,
76
l'en- du- rer, la pei- ne m'est
du- rer, A l'en- du- rer, la pei- ne m'est trop du-
A l'en- du- rer, A l'en- du- rer la pei- ne m'est trop
rer, A l'en- du- rer, la pei- ne m'est trop du-
A l'en- du- rer, la pei- ne m'est,
rer, A l'en- du- rer, la pei- ne m'est trop
67
re, A l'en- du- rer, A
du- re, A l'en-
du- re, A l'en- du- rer,
du- re, A l'en- du-
du- re, trop du- re, A l'en- du- rer,
la pei- ne m'est trop du- re, A l'en- du-
86
trop du- re.
re, la pei- ne m'est trop du- re.
du- re, la pei- ne m'est trop du- re.
re.
La pei- ne m'est trop du- re, La pei- ne m'est trop du- re.
du- re, la pei- ne m'est trop du- re.

Pas- sa la na- ve mi-
Pas- sa la na- ve mi- a,
Pas- sa la na- ve mi- a, cal-
Pas- sa la na- ve mi-
Pas- sa la na- ve mi- a, cal-
Pas- sa la na- ve mi- a,

19
me- za not- t'il ver- no,
per a- spro mar, per a- spro mar a me- za not- t'il ver-
not- t'il ver- no, in- fra Scil-
not- t'il ver- no, per a- spro mar a me- za not- t'il ver- no,
mar a me- za not- t'il ver- no, per a- spro mar a me- za not- t'il ver-
per a- spro mar a me- za not- t'il ver-

10
a, cal- ma d'o- bli- o, per a- spro mar a
cal- ma d'o- bli- o, cal- ma d'o- bli- o,
ma d'o- bli- o, per a- spro mar a me- za
a, cal- ma d'o- bli- o, per a- spro mar a me- za
ma d'o- bli- o, per a- spro
cal- ma d'o- bli- o,

29
in- fra Scil- l'e Ca- rib- di, in- fra Scil-
no, in- fra Scil- l'e Ca- rib- di,
l'e Ca- rib- di, in- fra Scil- l'e Ca-
in- fra Scil- l'e Ca- rib-
no, in- fra Scil- l'e Ca-
no, in- fra Scil- l'e Ca- rib- di,

l'e Ca- rib- di, & al go- ver- no, sie-
& al go- ver- no, sie- d'il si-
rib- di, & al go- ver- no, &
di, & al go- ver- no,
rib- di, & al go- ver-
& al go- ver- no, & al go-
o, an- z'il ne- mi-
sie- d'il si- gnor an-
an- z'il ne- mi- co mi- o, sie- d'il si- gnor an-
co mi- o, an- z'il ne- mi-
mi- co mi- o,
an- z'il ne- mi- co mi- o,
d'il si- gnor an- z'il ne- mi- co mi-
gnor, sie- d'il si- gnor,
al go- ver- no sie- d'il si- gnor
sie- d'il si- gnor an- z'il ne- mi-
no sie- d'il si- gnor, an- z'il ne-
ver- no, sie- d'il si- gnor
co mi- o,
z'il ne- mi- co mi- o, A
z'il ne- mi- co mi- o, A cia- scun rem',
co mi- o, A cia- scun
A cia- scun re- m'un pen-
A cia- scun re-

A cia- scun re- m'un pen- sier prom- pt'e
[pron-?]
cia- scun re- m'un pen- sier prom- pt'e ri-
[pron-?]
un pen- sier prom- pt'e ri- o,
[pron-?]
re- m'un pen- sier prom- pt'e ri- o, che
[pron-?]
sier prom- pt'e ri- o,
[pron-?]
m'un pen- sier prom- pt'e ri- o, che
[pron-?]

ch'ab- bi a scher- no, che la tem- pe— st'e'l fin par
che la tem- pe- st'e'l fin par ch'ab- bi a scher- no,
che la tem- pest', e'l fin par ch'ab-
st'e'l fin par ch'ab- bi a scher- no, che la tem-
la tem- pe— st'e'l fin par ch'ab- bi a scher- no, che
la tem- pe— st'e'l fin par ch'ab- bi a scher- no,

ri- o, che la tem- pe- st'e'l fin par
o, che la tem- pe- st'e'l fin par ch'ab- bi a scher- no,
che la tem- pe- st'e'l fin par ch'ab- bi a scher- no, che la tem- pe-
la tem- pe- st'e'l fin par ch'ab- bi a scher- no, che la tem- pe-
che la tem- pe- st'e'l fin, la tem- pe- st'e'l fin, che
la tem- pe- st'e'l fin par ch'ab- bi a scher- no, che

ch'ab- bi a scher- no,
la ve- la rom- p'un ven- to hu-
bi a scher- no, la ve- la rom- p'un ven- to hu-
pe— st'e'l fin par ch'ab- bi a scher- no, la ve- la
la tem- pe- st'e'l fin par ch'ab- bi a scher- no, la ve- la rom-
par ch'ab- bi a scher- no, la

82
la ve- la rom- p'un ven- to hu- mi d'e- ter-
mi d'e- ter- no, la ve- la rom- p'un
mi d'e- ter- no, un ven- to hu- mi- d'e- ter- no,
rom- p'un ven- to hu- mi d'e- ter- no, la
p'un ven- to hu- mi d'e- ter- no, la ve- la rom- p'un
ve- la rom- p'un ven- to hu- mi- d'e- ter- no, la

98
ran- ze, & di de- si- o, & di de- si-
spe- ran- ze, e di de- si-
ran- ze, di so- spir di spe- ran- ze, &
di spe- ran- ze, e di de- si-
ran- ze, e di de- si- o, e di de- si-
di spe- ran- ze, e di de- si- o,

89
no, hu- mi- d'e- ter- no, di so- spir, di spe-
ven- to, hu- mi- d'e- ter- no, di so- spir, di
di so- spir, di spe-
ve- la rom- p'un ven- to hu- mi- d'e- ter- no, di so- spir,
ven- to hu- mi- d'e- ter- no, di so- spir, di spe-
ve- la rom- p'un ven- to hu- mi- d'e- ter- no, di so- spir,

107
o, di so- spir di spe- ran-
o, di so- spir di spe- ran- ze
di de- si- o, di so- spir di spe- ran- ze
o,
o, di so-
di so- spir, di spe- ran- ze di de-

114
ze e di de- si- o.
di de- si- o, di spe- ran- ze di de- si- o.
di de- si- o, di spe- ran- ze di de- si- o.
di so- spir di spe- ran- ze di de- si- o.
di spe- ran- ze di de- si- o.
si- o, di spe- ran- ze di de- si- o.

122
Piog-
Piog- gia di la- gri- mar, neb- bia di sde- gni,
Piog- gia di la- gri- mar, neb- bia di
Piog- gia di la-
Piog- gia di la- gri-

132
Piog- gia di la- gri- mar,
gia di la- gri- mar, neb- bia di
Piog- gia di la- gri- mar, neb- bia di sde-
gri- mar, neb- bia di sde-
sde- gni, Piog- gia di la-
mar, neb- bia di sde- gni,

140
neb- bia di sde- gni, ba- gn'e ra- len- ta
sde- gni, ba- gn'e ra- len- ta le gia stan-
gni, ba- gn'e ra- len- ta le gia stan-
gni, neb- bia di sde- gni,
gri- mar, neb- bia di sde- gni ba- gn'e ra- len-
neb- bia di sde- gni,

148
le gia stan- che sar- te,
che sar- te, ba- gn'e ra-
che sar- te,
ba- gn'e ra- len- ta
ta le gia stan- che sar- te, ba-
ba- gn'e ra- len- ta le gia

162
tor- to, con i- gno- ran- ti'a- tor-
son d'er- ror con i- gno- ran- ti'a- tor- to,
ran- ti'a- tor- to, Ce- lan- s'i duoi miei
ror con i- gno- ran- ti'a- tor- to, Ce-
che son d'er- ror con i- gno- ran- ti'a- tor- to,
tor- to, con i- gno- ran- ti'a- tor-

155
che son d'er- ror con i- gno- ran- ti'a-
len- ta le gia stan che sar- te, che
che son d'er- ror con i- gno-
le gia stan che sar- te, che son d'er-
gn'e ra- len- ta le gia stan che sar- te,
stan- che sar- te che son d'er- ror con i- gno- ran- ti'a-

170
to, Ce- lan- s'i duoi miei dol- ci u- sa-
Ce- lan- s'i duoi miei dol- ci u- sa- ti se- gni, Ce-
dol- ci u- sa- ti se- gni, miei dol- ci u- sa- ti
lan- s'i duoi miei dol- ci u- sa- ti se- gni, miei dol- ci u-
Ce- lan- s'i duoi miei dol- ci u- sa- ti se- gni,
to, Ce- lan- s'i duoi miei dol- ci u- sa- ti se- gni,

178
ti se- gni, miei dol- ci u- sa- ti
lan- s'i duoi miei dol- ci u- sa- ti se- gni, miei dol- ci u-
se- gni, Ce- lan- s'i duoi miei dol- ci u- sa- ti se-
sa- ti se- gni, Ce- lan- s'i duoi miei dol-
Ce- lan- s'i duoi miei dol- ci u-
miei dol- ci u- sa- ti se- gni,

196
mor- ta fra l'on- de e la ra- gion
de, e la ra- gion, e la ra-
fra l'on- de e la ra- gion e l'ar- te, e
la ra- gion e l'ar- te, la ra-
la ra- gion e l'ar- te,
e la ra- gion, e

185
se- gni, mor- ta fra l'on- de,
sa- ti se- gni, mor- ta fra l'on-
gni, duoi miei dol- ci u- sa- ti se- gni, mor- ta
ci u- sa- ti se- gni, mor- ta fra l'on- de e
sa- ti se- gni, mor- ta fra l'on- de e
mor- ta fra l'on- de,

202
e l'ar- te, mor- ta fra l'on- de e
gion e l'ar- te, mor- ta fra l'on-
l'ar- te, mor- ta fra l'on- de, mor-
gion e l'ar- te, mor- ta
mor- ta fra l'on- de e la ra- gion
l'ar- te, mor- ta fra l'on- de e la ra-

483

210
la ra- gion e l'ar- te,
de e la ra- gion e l'ar- te, tal
ta fra l'on- de [e] la ra- gion e l'ar- te,
fra l'on- de e la ra- gion e l'ar-
e l'ar- te, tal ch'i'n- con- min- cio
gion e l'ar- te, tal ch'i'n- con- min-

222
spe- rar del por- to, tal ch'i'n- con-
to, tal ch'i'n- con- min- cio di- spe-
to, [a] di- spe- rar del por- to, tal ch'i'n- con-
ch'i'n- con- min- cio di- spe- rar del por- to,
to, tal ch'i'n- con- min- cio di- spe- rar
tal che, tal ch'i'n- con- min- cio di- spe-

217
tal ch'i'n- con- min- cio, di-
ch'i'n- con- min- cio di- spe- rar del por-
tal ch'i'n- con- min- cio di- spe- rar del porte, tal
di- spe- rar del por-
cio di- spe- rar del por- to,

229
min- cio di- spe- rar del por- to.
rar del por- to, a di- spe- rar del por- to.
min- cio, [a] di- spe- rar del por- to.
tal ch'i'n- con- min- cio di- spe- rar del por- to.
del por- to.
rar del por- to, a di- spe- rar del por- to.

137 LeJeune, *Susanne un jour* [Guéroult]

li- ci- té- e, Par deux vie- llars con- voi- tans sa beau- té, con- voi- tans sa beau- té,
jour, d'a- mour so- li- ci- té- e, Par deux vie- llars
té- e, d'a- mour so- li- ci- té- e, Par deux vie- llars, Par deux vie- llars con- voi- tans sa beau-
e, Par deux vie- llars, Par deux vie- llars con- voi- tans sa beau- té,
mour so- li- ci- té- e, Par deux vie- llars con- voi- tans sa beau-
jour, d'a- mour so- li- ci- té- e, Par deux vie- llars, Par deux vie- llars con- voi- tans sa beau- té, Par
mour so- li- ci- té- e, Par deux vie- llars, Par

Fut en son coeur, Fut en son coeur, tris- te & des- con- for- té-
con- voi- tans sa beau- té, Fut en son coeur,
té, con- voi- tans sa beau- té, Fut en son coeur, tris- te & des- con- for- té- e,
con- voi- tans sa beau- té, Fut en son coeur, Fut en son coeur tris- te & des- con- for- té-
té, Fut en son coeur, tris- te & des-
deux vie- llars con- voi- tans sa beau- té, Fut en son coeur, Fut en son coeur, Fut en son coeur,
deux vie- llars con- voi- tans sa beau- té, Fut en son coeur, Fut en son coeur, tris- te & des-

e, Voy- ant l'ef- fort, fait à sa chas- te- té, El-
tris- te & des- con- for- té- e, Voy- ant l'ef- fort fait à sa chas- te- té,
tris- te & des- con- for- té- e, Voy- ant l'ef- fort fait à sa chas- te- té, El- le leur dit, El-
e, Voy- ant l'ef- fort fait à sa chas- te- té, Voy- ant l'ef- fort fait à sa chas- te- té,
con- for- té- e, Voy- ant l'ef- fort fait à sa chas- te- té, El- le
tris- te & des- con- for- té- e, Voy- ant l'ef- fort, Voy- ant l'ef- fort fait à sa chas- te- té, El- le leur dit,
con- for- té- e, tris- te & des- con- for- té- e, Voy- ant l'ef- fort fait à sa chas- te- té, El-

le leur dit si par des- loy- au- té, El- le leur dit si par des- loy- au- té,
El- le leur dit si par des- loy- au- té,
le leur dit si par des- loy- au- té, El- le leur dit si par des- loy- au- té, De
El- le leur dit, si par des- loy- au- té, si par des- loy- au- té, des- loy-
leur dit si par des- loy- au- té, De ce cors
si par des- loy- au- té, De ce cors mien vous
le leur dit, El- le leur dit si par des- loy- au- té,

De ce cors mien, De ce cors mien vous a- vez jou- is- san- ce,
De ce cors mien vous a- vez jou- is- san- ce, C'est
ce cors mien vous a- vez jou- is- san- ce, C'est fait, C'est fait
au- té, De ce cors mien vous a- vez jou- is- san- ce, C'est fait
mien vous a- vez jou- is- san- ce, C'est fait de moy,
a- vez jou- is- san- ce, C'est fait, c'est fait de moy, C'est
De ce cors mien vous a- vez jou- is- san- ce, C'est fait de

C'est fait de moy, si je fay re- sis- tan- ce, Vous
fait de moy, si je fay re- sis- tan- ce,
de moy, si je fay re- sis- tan- ce, si je fay re- sis- tan- ce, Vous me fe- rez,
de moy, C'est fait de moy, si je fay re- sis- tan- ce, Vous
si je fay re- sis- tan- ce, Vous me fe- rez mou-
fait de moy si je fay re- sis- tan- ce, Vous me fe- rez mou- rir en
moy, C'est fait de moy si je fay re- sis- tan- ce, Vous me fe- rez

me fe- rez, Vous me fe- rez mou- rir en des- hon- neur, Mais
Vous me fe- rez mou- rir en des- hon- neur, Mais j'ay- me mieux,
Vous me fe- rez mou- rir en des- hon- neur, Mais j'ay- me mieux pe- rir
me fe- rez mou- rir en des- hon- neur, Vous me fe- rez mou- rir en des- hon- neur,
rir en des- hon- neur, Mais j'ay- me mieux,
des- hon- neur, mou- rir en des- hon- neur, Mais j'ay- me
mou- rir, Vous me fe- rez mou- rir en des- hon- neur, Mais j'ay- me mieux,

j'ay- me mieux pe- rir en in- no- cen- ce: Que d'of- fen- cer par pe- ché
pe- rir en in- no- cen- ce, Que
en in- no- cen- ce: pe- rir en in- no- cen- ce: Que d'of- fen- cer par pe- ché le
Mais j'ay- me mieux, pe- rir en in- no- cen- ce: Que d'of- fen- cer,
pe- rir en in- no- cen- ce: Que d'of- fen- cer par pe- ché
mieux, pe- rir en in- no- cen- ce:
pe- rir en in- no- cen- ce: Que d'of- fen- cer par pe- ché

le Sei- gneur, Que d'of- fen- cer, Que d'of- fen- cer par pe- ché le Sei- gneur.
d'of- fen- cer par pe- ché le Sei- gneur, Que d'of- fen- cer par pe- ché le Sei- gneur.
Sei- gneur, Que d'of- fen- cer par pe- ché le Sei- gneur.
Que d'of- fen- cer par pe- ché le Sei- gneur, Que d'of- fen- cer par pe- ché le Sei- gneur.
le Sei- gneur, Que d'of- fen- cer par pe- ché le Sei- gneur.
Que d'of- fen- cer par pe- ché le Sei- gneur, Que d'of- fen- cer par pe- ché le Sei- gneur.
le Sei- gneur, Que d'of- fen- cer par pe- ché le Sei- gneur, par pe- ché le Sei- gneur.

138 Moulu, *J'ay mis mon coeur*

seul- le- ment, Si tres= a- vant, qu'il ne s'en peut sor-
le- ment, Si tres= a- vant,
seul- le- ment, Si tres= a- vant, qu'il ne s'en peut sor- tir,
un lieu seul- le- ment, Si tres= a- vant, Si tres= a- vant, Si tres= a- vant, qu'il
ment, Si tres= a- vant,
Si tres= a- vant, Si
seul- le- ment, Si tres= a- vant, qu'il ne s'en peut sor- tir,

tir, Tant, Tant plus j'y pen-
qui ne s'en peut sor- tir, Tant, Tant
qu'il ne s'en peut sor- tir, Tant plus j'y pen- se,
ne s'en peut sor- tir, sor- tir, Tant plus j'y pen-
qu'il ne s'en peut sor- tir, Tant, Tant plus j'y
tres= a- vant qu'il ne s'en peut sor- tir, Tant plus j'y pen- se, &
Tant plus j'y pen-

se, & plus ay de sou- cy, Las,
plus y pen- se, & plus ay de sou- cy, Las,
& plus, ay de sou- cy, Las, je ne puis, Las,
se, & plus ay de sou- cy, Las, je ne puis,
pen- se, & plus ay de sou- cy, Las,
plus ay de sou- cy, de sou- cy,
se, & plus ay de sou- cy, Las, je ne puis, Las,

je ne puis, vi- vre joy- eu- se-
je ne puis, vi- vre joy- eu- se- ment,
je ne puis, vi- vre joy- eu- se- ment, Las,
vi- vre joy- eu- se- ment, vi- vre joy- eu- se-
je ne puis, vi- vre joy- eu- se- ment,
Las, je ne puis, vi- vre joy- eu- se- ment,
je ne puis, vi- vre joy- eu- se- ment, Las,

ment, Las, je ne puis vi- vre joy- eu- se- ment, vi- vre joy-
Las, je ne puis, vi- vre joy- eu-
je ne puis, Las, je ne [puis, Las, je ne] puis, vi- vre joy- eu- se- ment, vi- vre joy- eu- se- ment,
ment, Las, je ne puis vi- vre joy- eu- se- ment, Las, je ne puis, vi-
Las, je ne puis, vi- vre joy- eu- se-
Las, je ne puis, Las, je ne puis, vi- vre joy- eu- se-
je ne puis, Las, je ne puis, vi- vre joy- eu- se- ment, joy-

eu- se- ment, Las, je ne puis vi- vre joy- eu- se- ment,
se- ment, Las, je ne puis,
Las, je ne puis, Las, je ne [puis, Las, je ne] puis, vi- vre joy- eu- se-
vre joy- eu- se- ment, Las, je ne puis vi- vre joy- eu- se- ment, Las, je ne
ment, Las, je ne puis, vi-
ment, Las, je ne puis, Las, je ne puis vi- vre joy- eu- se-
eu- se- ment, Las, je ne puis, Las, je ne puis,

vi- vre joy- eu- se- ment.
vi- vre joy- eu- se- ment, joy- eu- se- ment.
ment, joy- eu- se- ment, vi- vre joy- eu- se- ment.
puis, vi- vre joy- eu- se- ment, vi- vre joy- eu- se- ment.
vre joy- eu- se- ment, joy- eu- se- ment.
ment, vi- vre joy- eu- se- ment.
Las, je ne puis vi- vre joy- eu- se- ment, joy- eu- se- ment.

139 Gardane, *Fuyez de moy*

Fuy- ez de moy, ô tra- vail a- mou- reux, Et vo- tre bien,   Et vo- tre bien
tra- vail a-   mou- reux,   Et vo- tre bien soit ma dou- leur cru- el-   le,
moy,   ô tra- vail a-   mou- reux,   Et vo- tre bien,   Et vo- tre bien soit ma dou- leur   cru-
a-   mou-   reux,   Et vo- tre bien soit   ma dou- leur cru- el-   le,
tra- vail a-   mou- reux,   Et vo-   tre bien soit ma dou- leur cru- el-   le,   Et vo-   tre bien soit ma dou- leur cru-
ô tra- vail a- mou-   reux,   Et vo- tre bien   soit ma dou- leur   cru-   el-   le,
a-   mou-   reux, ô tra- vail a-   mou-   reux,   Et vo-   tre bien   soit ma dou- leur   cru-

soit ma dou- leur cru- el- le, Et vo- tre bien soit ma dou- leur cru- el- le, Beau- té, tre- sor
Et vo- tre bien, Et vo- tre bien soit ma dou- leur cru- el- le, Beau- té, tre- sor, & chant ar-
el- le, cru- el- le, Et vo- tre bien soit ma dou- leur cru- el- le, Beau- té, tre- sor & chant ar-
Et vo- tre bien soit ma dou- leur cru- el- le, soit ma dou- leur cru- el- le, Beau- té, tre- sor,
el- le, soit ma dou- leur cru- el- le, Beau- té, tre- sor, & chant ar-
Et vo- tre bien soit ma dou- leur cru- el- le, Beau- té, tre- sor,
el- le, Et vo- tre bien soit ma dou- leur cru- el- le, Beau- té, tre- sor & chant ar-

& chant ar- mo- ni- eux, Et tout plai- sir, Et tout plai- sir, que mon coeur es- tin- cel- le, Et tout plai- sir que mon coeur
mo- ni- eux, ar- mo- ni- eux, Et tout plai- sir, Et tout plai- sir, que mon coeur es- tin- cel- le, que
mo- ni- eux, Et tout plai- sir, Et tout plai- sir que mon coeur es- tin- cel- le, que mon coeur
& chant ar- mo- ni- eux, Et tout plai- sir, Et tout plai- sir que mon coeur es- tin- cel- le, Et
mo- ni- eux, Et tout plai- sir, Et tout plai- sir, que mon coeur es- tin-
& chant ar- mo- ni- eux, Et tout plai- sir, Et tout plai- sir, que mon coeur es- tin- cel- le,
mo- ni- eux, & chant ar- mo- ni- eux, Et tout plai- sir, Et tout plai- sir, que mon coeur es- tin- cel- le, que

es- tin- cel- le: J'ay tout vain- cu, J'ay tout vain- cu, cui- dant com- plai- re à el- le, cui- dant com-
mon coeur es- tin- cel- le, J'ay tout vain- cu, cui- dant com- plai- re à el- le, cui- dant com- plai- re à el-
es- tin- cel- le, J'ay tout vain- cu, J'ay tout vain- cu, cui- dant com- plai- re à el- le, cui- dant, cui-
tout plai- sir que mon coeur es- tin- cel- le, J'ay tout vain- cu, J'ay tout vain- cu, cui- dant com-
cel- le, que mon coeur es- tin- cel- le, J'ay tout vain- cu, cui- dant com- plai- re à el- le,
que mon coeur es- tin- cel- le, J'ay tout vain- cu cui- dant, cui- dant com- plai- re à el- le, cui-
mon coeur es- tin- cel- le, J'ay tout vain- cu, cui- dant com- plai- re à el- le, cui- dant com- plai- re à

plai- re à el- le, Fors qu'à a- mour, car la vou- lant ser-
le, Fors qu'à a- mour, car la vou- lant ser- vir, car
dant com- plai- re à el- le, Fors qu'à a- mour, Fors qu'à a- mour, car la vou- lant ser-
plai- re à el- le, cui- dant com- plai- re à el- le, Fors qu'à a- mour, car la vou- lant ser- vir, car
cui- dant, cui- dant com- plai- re à el- le, Fors qu'à a- mour car la vou- lant ser- vir, car la vou-
dant com- plai- re à el- le, Fors qu'à a- mour, car la vou- lant ser- vir,
el- le, Fors qu'à a- mour, car la vou- lant ser- vir, car la vou- lant ser- vir,

vir, Me suis li- é, Me suis li- é, de pen- sée
la vou- lant ser- vir, Me suis li- é, Me suis li- é,
vir, car la vou- lant ser- vir, Me suis li- é, Me suis li- é de pen- sée im- mor- tel- le,
la vou- lant ser- vir, Me suis li- é, Me suis li- é, de pen- sée
lant ser- vir, Me suis li- é, Me suis li- é, de pen- sée im- mor- tel- le,
car la vou- lant ser- vir, Me suis li- é, Me suis li- é, de pen- sée
Me suis li- é, Me suis li- é, de pen- sée im- mor- tel- le, de

99
im- mor- tel- le, de pen- sée im- mor- tel- le, Qui à la mort,
de pen- sée im- mor- tel- le, im- mor- tel- le, Qui à la mort sou- dain
de pen- sée im- mor- tel- le, Qui à la mort sou- dain me va of- frir,
im- mor- tel- le, de pen- sée im- mor- tel- le, Qui à la mort sou- dain me
de pen- sée im- mor- tel- le, Qui à la mort sou- dain me va of- frir, Qui à
im- mor- tel- le, de pen- sée im- mor- tel- le, Qui à la
pen- sée im- mor- tel- le, Qui à la mort sou- dain me va of- frir,

Qui à la mort sou- dain me va of- frir, Qui à la mort, Qui à la
me va of- frir, Qui à la mort sou- dain me va of- frir, Qui à la mort,
Qui à la mort sou- dain me va of- frir, Qui à la mort, sou- dain me
va of- frir, Qui à la mort sou- dain me va of- frir, Qui à la mort,
la mort, Qui à la mort sou- dain me va of- frir, Qui à la mort sou- dain me
mort sou- dain me va of- frir, Qui à la mort sou- dain me va of- frir,
Qui à la mort, Qui à la mort sou- dain me va of- frir, sou- dain me va of- frir,

mort sou- dain me va of- frir, Qui à la mort sou- dain me va of- frir.
Qui à la mort sou- dain me va of- frir, Qui à la mort sou- dain me va of- frir.
va of- frir, Qui à la mort sou- dain me va of- frir.
va of- frir, Qui à la mort sou- dain me va of- frir, Qui à la mort sou- dain me va of- frir.
va of- frir, Qui à la mort sou- dain me va of- frir.
Qui à la mort, Qui à la mort sou- dain me va of- frir, sou- dain me va of- frir.
Qui à la mort, sou- dain me va of- frir, Qui à la mort sou- dain, sou- dain me va of- frir.

Pe- ti- te ca- mu- set- te, Pe- ti- te ca-
Pe- ti- te ca- mu- set- te, A la mort m'a- vez mis,
Pe- ti- te ca- mu-
Pe- ti- te ca- mu- set- te, A la mort
Pe- ti- te ca- mu- set- te,
Pe-
Pe- ti- te ca- mu- set- te, A la mort m'a- vez

mu- set- te, A la mort m'a- vez
A la mort m'a- vez mis, A la mort m'a- vez mis, Pe- ti- te
set- te, A la mort m'a- vez mis,
m'a- vez mis, Pe- ti- te ca- mu- set- te, A la mort m'a- vés
A la mort m'a- vez mis,
ti- te ca- mu- set- te, A la mort m'a- vez
mis, Pe- ti- te ca- mu- set- te, A la mort m'a- vés

mis,   Ro- bin & Ma-   ri- on, Ils s'en vont bras à bras,   Ils se sont
ca-   mu- set-   te,   Ils s'en vont bras à bras,   Ils
Ro- bin,   Ro- bin & Ma-   ri- on,
mis,   A la mort m'a- vés mis,   Ro- bin & Ma- ri- on, Ils s'en vont
Ro- bin,   Ro- bin & Ma-   ri- on,   Ils
mis,   Ro- bin,   Ro- bin & Ma-
mis,   Ro- bin & Ma- ri- on,   Ro- bin & Ma- ri- on, Ils s'en vont bras à bras,

en- dor- mis, Ils se sont en- dor- mis, Ils se sont en- dor- mis, Ils se sont en- dor-
se sont en- dor- mis, Ils se sont en- dor- mis,
Ils se sont en- dor- mis,
bras à bras, Ils se sont en- dor- mis, Ils se sont en- dor- mis, Ils se sont
se sont en- dor- mis,
ri- on, Ils se sont en- dor- mis,
Ils s'en vont bras à bras, Ils se sont en- dor- mis, Pe- ti- te,

mis, Pe- ti- te ca- mu- set- te, Pe- ti- te ca- mu- set-
Pe- ti- te ca- mu- set- te, A la mort m'a- vés mis, A la
Pe- ti- te ca- mu- set- te,
en- dor- mis, Pe- ti- te ca- mu- set- te, A la mort m'a- vés mis,
Pe- ti- te ca- mu- set- te,
Pe- ti- te ca-
Pe- ti- te ca- mu- set- te, A la mort m'a- vés

te, A la mort m'a- vés mis, A la mort m'a-
mort m'a- vés mis, A la mort m'a- vés mis, Pe- ti- te ca- mu- set-
A la mort m'a- vés mis,
Pe- ti- te ca- mu- set- te, A la mort m'a- vés mis, A
A la mort m'a- vés mis, Pe- ti- te ca-
mu- set- te, A la mort m'a- vés mis,
mis, Pe- ti- te ca- mu- set- te, A la mort

vés mis, A la mort m'a- vés mis, Pe- ti- te.
te, à la mort m'a- vés mis, Pe- ti- te ca- mu- set- te.
Pe- ti- te ca- mu- set- te.
la mort m'a- vés mis, Pe- ti- te ca- mu- set- te.
mu- set- te, Pe- ti- te ca- mu- set- te.
Pe- ti- te ca- mu- set- te.
m'a- vés mis, A la mort m'a- vés mis, Pe- ti- te.

141 Certon, *Revien vers moy* [Ronsard]

moy, Re- vien, qui suis tant de- so- lé- e,
moy, Re- vien vers moy,
vien vers moy, Re- vien vers moy, qui suis tant de- so- lé-
vers moy, Re- vien vers moy, qui suis tant de- so- lé- e, qui
moy, qui suis tant de- so- lé- e, qui suis,
Re- vien vers moy, qui suis tant
Re- vien vers moy, Re- vien vers moy, qui suis tant de- so- lé-

qui suis tant de- so- lé- e, qui suis tant de- so-
qui suis tant de- so- lé- e, qui
e, qui suis tant de- so- lé- e, qui suis tant de- so- lé- e,
suis tant de- so- lé- e,
qui suis tant de- so- lé- e, qui suis tant de- so- lé- e,
de- so- lé- e, qui suis tant de- so- lé- e,
e, qui suis tant de- so- lé-

lé- e, Et tu ver- ras l'en- nuy, Et tu ver- ras l'en- nuy,
suis tant de- so- lé- e, Et tu ver- ras,
qui suis tant de- so- lé- e, Et tu ver- ras, l'en-
qui suis tant de- so- lé- e, tant de- so- lé- e, Et tu ver- ras, l'en- nuy &
qui suis tant de- so- lé- e, l'en- nuy & le
Et tu ver- ras, l'en- nuy & le
e, qui suis tant de- so- lé- e, Et tu ver- ras, Et tu ver- ras,

Et tu ver- ras l'en- nuy & le tour- ment, l'en- nuy & le tour- ment, Que j'ay
l'en- nuy & le tour- ment, l'en- nuy & le tour- ment,
nuy & le tour- ment, l'en- nuy & le tour- ment,
le tour- ment, l'en- nuy & le tour- ment, Que j'ay souf-
tour- ment, l'en- nuy & le tour- ment, Que
tour- ment, l'en- nuy & le tour- ment, Que j'ay
l'en- nuy, l'en- nuy & le tour- ment, l'en- nuy & le tour- ment,

souf- fert, tous- jours en at- ten- dant, tous- jours en at- ten- dant,
Que j'ay souf- fert, tous- jours en
Que j'ay souf- fert, tous- jours en at- ten- dant, tous- jours en at-
fert, tous- jours en at- ten- dant,
j'ay souf- fert, tous- jours en at- ten- dant,
souf- fert, tous- jours en at- ten- dant, en at- ten- dant,
Que j'ay souf- fert, tous- jours en

tous- jours en at- ten- dant, tous- jours en at- ten- dant, Le tien re-
at- ten- dant, en at- ten- dant, Le tien re- tour dont
ten- dant, Le tien re- tour,
Le tien re- tour, dont se- ray con- so- lé- e,
tous- jours en at- ten- dant, Le tien re- tour dont se- ray con- so-
Le tien re- tour dont se- ray con- so- lé- e,
at- ten- dant, tous- jours en at- ten- dant, tous- jours en at- ten- dant, Le tien re- tour dont se- ray con- so-

tour, dont se- ray con- so- lé- e.
se- ray con- so- lé- e, dont se- ray con- so- lé- e.
Le tien re- tour, Le tien re- tour dont se- ray con- so- lé- e, dont se- ray ray con- so- lé- e.
dont se- ray con- so- lé- e, dont se- ray con- so- lé- e.
lé- e, dont se- ray con- so- lé- e, dont se- ray con- so- lé- e, dont se- ray con- so- lé- e.
dont se- ray con- so- lé- e.
lé- e, dont se- ray con- so- lé- e, dont se- ray con- so- lé- e.

142 Vuildre, *Amy, souffrez*

je vous ay- me, Et ne me te- nez la
ay- me, Et ne me te- nez la ri- gueur,
me, que je vous ay- me, Et ne me te- nez la ri- gueur, Et
me, Et
vous ay- me, A- my, souf- frez que je vous ay- me,
je vous ay- me, Et ne me te- nez la ri- gueur, Et
je vous ay- me, Et ne me te- nez la ri- gueur, Et

ri- gueur, Et ne me te- nez la ri- gueur, De
Et ne me te- nez la ri- gueur, De me di- re, que vo- tre
ne me te- nez la ri- gueur, De me di- re que vo- tre
ne me te- nez la ri- gueur,
Et ne me te- nez la ri- gueur, Et ne me te- nez la ri- gueur, De me di- re
ne me te- nez la ri- gueur, De me di- re que
ne me te- nez la ri- gueur, Et ne me te- nez la ri- gueur, De me di- re

me di- re que vo- tre coeur, Souf- fre pour moy, Souf- fre pour
coeur, que vo- tre coeur, que vo- tre coeur, Souf- fre pour moy, Souf- fre pour
coeur, que vo- tre coeur, Souf- fre pour moy, Souf- fre pour moy,
De me di- re que vo- tre coeur, Souf- fre pour moy, Souf- fre pour
que vo- tre coeur, Souf- fre pour moy, Souf- fre pour moy, Souf- fre pour
vo- tre coeur, que vo- tre coeur, Souf- fre pour moy, Souf- fre pour moy,
que vo- tre coeur, Souf- fre pour moy, Souf- fre pour moy,

moy dou- leur ex- tre- me, dou- leur ex- tre- me, Souf- fre pour
moy, dou- leur ex- tre- me, Souf- fre pour moy, Souf- fre pour
dou- leur ex- tre- me, dou- leur ex- tre- me, Souf- fre pour moy,
moy dou- leur ex- tre- me, Souf- fre pour
moy, souf- fre pour moy dou- leur ex- tre- me, Souf- fre pour
dou- leur ex- tre- me, dou- leur ex- tre- me, Souf- fre pour moy,
Souf- fre pour moy dou- leur ex- tre- me, Souf- fre pour moy,

moy, Souf- fre pour moy dou- leur ex- tre- me, dou- leur ex- tre- me.
moy, Souf- fre pour moy, dou- leur ex- tre- me, dou- leur ex- tre- me.
Souf- fre pour moy, dou- leur ex- tre- me, dou- leur ex- tre- me, ex- tre- me.
moy, Souf- fre pour moy dou- leur ex- tre- me.
moy, Souf- fre pour moy, Souf- fre pour moy dou- leur ex- tre- me, ex- tre- me.
Souf- fre pour moy, dou- leur ex- tre- me, dou- leur ex- tre- me.
Souf- fre pour moy, Souf- fre pour moy dou- leur ex- tre- me, dou- leur ex- tre- me.

143 Clemens non papa, *Amour au coeur* [C. Marot]

ay- mer je ne puis, Quand on ne m'ay- me point,
Mais ay- mer je ne puis, Quand on ne m'ay-
bien ay- mé je suis, Mais ay- mer je ne puis, Quand
Mais ay- mer je ne puis, Quand on ne m'ay- me point, Quand on ne
Mais ay- mer je ne puis, Mais ay- mer je ne puis, Quand
je ne puis, Mais ay- mer je ne puis, Quand on ne m'ay- me point,
Mais ay- mer je ne puis, Quand on ne m'ay- me point, Quand on ne m'ay- me
ay- mer je ne puis, Quand on ne m'ay- me point, Quand on ne m'ay- me point, Quand

Quand on ne m'ay- me point, Cha- cun soit ad- ver-
me point, Cha- cun soit ad- ver- ty,
on ne m'ay- me point, Quand on ne m'ay- me point, Cha- cun soit ad- ver- ty,
m'ay- me point, Cha- cun soit ad- ver- ty de fai- re com- me moy, de
on ne m'ay- me point, Quand on ne m'ay- me point, Cha-
Mais ay- mer je ne puis, Quand on ne m'ay- me point, Cha- cun soit ad-
point, Quand on ne m'ay- me point, Quand on ne m'ay- me point, Cha- cun soit
on ne m'ay- me point, Quand on ne m'ay- me point, Cha- cun soit ad- ver- ty,

ty, de fai- re com- me moy, de fai- re com- me moy, de fai- re com-
Cha- cun soit ad- ver- ty, de fai- re com- me moy, de fai- re com- me moy, de
Cha- cun soit ad- ver- ty de fai- re com- me moy, de fai- re com- me moy, de fai- re com- me moy, de fai- re
fai- re com- me moy, de fai- re com- me moy, de fai- re com- me moy, de fai- re com- me moy,
cun soit ad- ver- ty, de fai- re com- me moy, de fai- re com- me moy, de
ver- ty, Cha- cun soit ad- ver- ty, de fai- re com- me moy, de fai- re com-
ad- ver- ty, de fai- re com- me moy, de fai- re com- me moy, de fai- re
Cha- cun soit ad- ver- ty, de fai- re com- me moy, de fai- re com- me moy,

me moy, de fai- re com-me moy, Car d'ay-mer sans par- ty, Car d'ay-mer sans par- ty, C'est un trop grand es-
fai- re com-me moy, de fai- re com-me moy, Car d'ay-mer sans par- ty, C'est un trop grand es- moy, C'est un trop
com- me moy, Car d'ay-mer sans par- ty, Car d'ay-mer sans par- ty, C'est un trop grand es-
de fai- re com-me moy, Car d'ay-mer sans par- ty, C'est un trop grand es- moy, C'est
fai- re com- me moy, com-me moy, Car d'ay-mer sans par- ty, Car d'ay-mer sans par- ty, C'est un trop grand es- moy, C'est un trop grand es-
me moy, de fai- re com-me moy, Car d'ay-mer sans par- ty, Car d'ay-mer sans par- ty, Car d'ay-mer sans par- ty, C'est un trop grand es-
com- me moy, de fai- re com- me moy, Car d'ay-mer sans par- ty, C'est un trop grand es-
de fai- re com-me moy, Car d'ay-mer sans par- ty, C'est, C'est un trop grand es- moy, C'est

moy, trop grand es- moy, C'est un trop grand es- moy, C'est un trop grand es- moy, trop grand es- moy.
grand es- moy, C'est un trop grand es- moy, C'est un trop grand es- moy.
moy, C'est un trop grand es- moy, C'est un trop grand es- moy, C'est un trop grand es- moy, C'est un trop grand es- moy.
un trop grand es- moy, C'est un trop grand es- moy, C'est un trop grand es- moy, C'est un trop grand es- moy, C'est un trop grand, C'est un trop grand es- moy.
moy, C'est un trop grand es- moy, C'est un trop grand es- moy, C'est un trop grand es- moy, C'est un trop grand es- moy, trop grand es- moy.
moy, C'est un trop grand es- moy, C'est un trop grand es- moy.
moy, C'est un trop grand es- moy, C'est un trop grand es- moy, C'est un trop grand es- moy, C'est un trop grand, C'est un trop grand es- moy, C'est un trop grand es- moy.
un trop grand es- moy, C'est un trop grand es- moy, C'est un trop grand es- moy, C'est un trop grand es- moy, C'est un trop grand es- moy.

144 Gardane, *Complainte de la Torterelle (Que dis tu, que fais tu)* [Ronsard]

He pour-quoy,di le moy,
te, De ma com- pa- gne ab- sen- te plus che- re que ma vi- e, plus che- re que ma vi-
He pour- quoy, dy= le moy,
te, De ma com- pa- gne ab- sen- te, plus che- re que ma vi- e, plus che- re que ma
He pour- quoy, dy= le moy,
te, De ma com- pa- gne ab- sen- te, plus che- re que ma vi-
He pour- quoy, di le moy,
te, De ma com- pa- gne ab- sen- te, plus che- re, plus che- re que ma vi-

En quel- le part est el- le?
e, Un cru- el oy- se- leur, par glu- eu- se cau- tel- le, La pri- se & la tu- ée, & nuit & jour je chan-
En quel- le part est el- le?
vi- e, Un cru- el oy- se- leur par glu- eu- se cau- tel- le, La prin- se & la tu- é- e, & nuit & jour je chan-
En quel- le part est el- le?
e, Un cru- el oy- se- leur par glu- eu- se cau- tel- le, La prin- se & la tu- é- e, & nuit & jour je chan-
En quel- le part est el- le?
e, & nuit & jour je chan-

te son tres- pas dans ces boys, nom- mant la mort mé- chan- te qu'el- le ne m'a tu- ée a- vec- ques ma fi- del-
te son tres- pas dans ces boys, nom- mant la mort mé- chan- te, qu'el- le ne ma tu- ée a- vec- ques ma fi- del-
te son tres- pas dans ces boys, nom- mant la mort mé- chan- te, qu'el- le ne ma tu- ée a- vec- ques ma fi- del-
te son tres- pas dans ces boys, nom- mant la mort mé- chan- te, qu'el- le ne m'a tu- ée a- vec- ques ma fi- del-

78
Vou- drois= tu bien mou- rir, a- vec- ques ta com- pa- gne,
le, Ou- y, car aus- si bien je lan-guis de dou- leur, car
Vou- droys tu bien mou- rir, a- vec- ques ta com- pa- gne,
le, Ou- y, Car aus- si bien je lan-guis de dou- leur, je
Vou- droys tu bien mou- rir a- vec- ques ta com- pa- gne,
le, Ou- y, Ou- y, Car aus- si bien je lan- guis de dou-leur, je
Vou- drois= tu bien mou- rir, a- vec- ques ta com- pa- gne,
le, Ou- y, car aus- si bien je lan-guis de dou-

aus- si bien je lan- guis de dou- leur, & tous- jours le re- gret de sa mort, le re- gret de sa mort m'ac- com- pa-
lan- guis de dou- leur, & tous- jours le re- gret, & tous- jours le re- gret de sa mort m'ac- com- pa-
lan- guis de dou- leur, & tous- jours le re- gret de sa mort, le re- gret de sa mort m'a- com- pa-
leur, je lan- guis de dou- leur, & tous- jours le re- gret de sa mort, de sa mort m'ac- com- pa-

O gen- tilz oy- se- letz que vous es- tes heu- reux, D'ay- mer si con-stam- ment, Qu'heu- reux est vo- tre coeur,
gne,
O gen- tilz oy- se- letz que vous es- tes heu- reux, D'ay-mer si con-stam- ment, Qu'heu- reux est vo- tre coeur, Qui
gne,
O gen- tilz oy- se- letz que vous es- tes heu- reux, D'ay- mer, D'ay-mer si con- stam-ment, Qu'heu-reux est vo- tre coeur, Qu'heu-reux est
gne,
O gen- tilz oy- se- letz, que vous es- tes heu- reux, D'ay- mer, D'ay- mer si con- stam-ment, Qu'heu- reux est
gne,

Qui sans point va- ri- er, Est tous- jours a- mou- reux, Qui
Qui sans point va- ri- er,
sans point va- ri- er, Est tous- jours a- mou- reux, Est tous- jours a- mou- reux, Qui sans
Qui sans point va- ri- er,
vo- tre coeur, Qui sans point va- ri- er, Est tous- jours a- mou- reux, Qui sans point va- ri-
Qui sans point va- ri- er,
vo- tre coeur, Qui sans point va- ri- er, Qui sans point va- ri- er, Est tous- jours a- mou- reux, Qui sans point va- ri- er,
Qui sans point va- ri- er,

150
sans point va- ri- er, est tous- jours a- mou- reux, est tous- jours a- mou-reux.
Est tous- jours a- mou- reux, a- mou- reux, Est tous-jours a- mou-reux.
point va- ri- er, Est tous- jours a- mou- reux, Est tous- jours a- mou- reux, a- mou-reux.
Est tous- jours a- mou- reux, Qui sans point va- ri- er, Est tous- jours a- mou-reux.
er, Est tous- jours a- mou- reux, Est tous- jours a- mou- reux.
Est tous- jours a- mou- reux, Est tous- jours a- mou- reux, Est tous- jours a- mou- reux.
Est tous- jours a- mou- reux, Est tous- jours a- mou- reux.
Est tous- jours a- mou- reux, Est tous- jours a- mou- reux, Est tous- jours a- mou- reux.

145 Phinot, *Vivons m'amye*

my- e & l'a- mour pour-sui- vons, & l'a- mour pour- sui- vons,
m'a- my- e & l'a- mour pour-sui- vons, Sans
& l'a- mour pour- sui- vons, & l'a- mour pour- sui- vons, Sans
pour- sui- vons, & l'a- mour, & l'a- mour pour- sui- vons,
Vi- vons, m'a- my- e & l'a- mour pour-sui- vons, Sans fai- re
m'a- my- e, & l'a- mour pour-sui- vons, pour- sui- vons, Sans
e & l'a- mour pour- sui- vons & l'a- mour pour- sui- vons,
& l'a- mour pour-sui- vons, & l'a- mour pour-sui- vons, Sans

Sans fai- re cas, des pro- pos in- u- ti- les, De ces vie- llars fa- cheux, fa-
fai- re cas des pro- pos in- u- ti- les, De ces vie- llars, fa- cheux & dif- fi-
fai- re cas, des pro- pos in- u- ti- les, De ces vie- llars fa- cheux, fa- cheux & dif- fi- ci-
Sans fai- re cas, des pro- pos in- u- ti- les, De ces vie- llars fa- cheux, fa-
cas des pro- pos in- u- ti- les, De ces vie- llars fa- cheux, fa- cheux & dif- fi- ci-
fai- re cas, des pro- pos in- u- ti- les, De ces vie- llars fa- cheux, fa- cheux
Sans fai- re cas, des pro- pos in- u- ti- les, De ces vie- llars fa- cheux, fa-
fai- re cas des pro- pos in- u- ti- les, De ces vie- llars, fa- cheux & dif- fi- ci-

49
cheux & dif- fi- ci- les, Trom- pons le tems, pen- sant que nous de- vons, A- pres ce peu qu'a
ci- les, fa- cheux & dif- fi- ci- les, Trom- pons le tems, pen- sant que nous de- vons,
les, fa- cheux & dif- fi- ci- les, Trom- pons le tems, pen- sant que nous de- vons,
cheux & di- fi- ci- les, Trom- pons le tems, pen- sant que nous de- vons, A- pres ce peu qu'à
les, fa- cheux & di- fi- ci- les, Trom- pons le tems, pen- sant que nous de- vons,
& di- fi- ci- les, Trom- pons le tems, pen- sant que nous de- vons, A- pres ce peu qu'à
cheux & dif- fi- ci- les, Trom- pons le tems, pen- sant que nous de- vons, A- pres ce peu qu'à
les, De ces vie- llars fa- cheux & di- fi- ci- les, Trom- pons le tems, pen- sant que nous de- vons,

vi- vre nous a- vons, Don- ne moy donc, Don- ne moy donc, ma mi- gnon- ne,un bai-
Un long som- meil dor- mir & re- po- ser, Don- ne moy donc,
Un long som- meil dor- mir & re- po- ser, Don- ne moy donc,
vi- vre nous a- vons, Don- ne moy donc, Don- ne moy donc, ma mi- gnon- ne,un
Un long som- meil dor- mir & re- po- ser, Don- ne moy donc,
vi- vre nous a- vons, Don- ne moy donc, Don- ne moy donc, ma mi- gnon- ne,un bai-
vi- vre nous a- vons, Don- ne moy donc, Don- ne moy donc, ma mi- gnon- ne,un bai-
Un long som- meil dor- mir & re- po- ser, Don- ne moy donc,

ser, Puis cent, puis mil- le, & puis re- com- men-çons, Ces douz bai-
ma mi- gnon- ne,un bai- ser, Puis cent, puis mil- le, & puis re- com- men- çons,
ma mi- gnon- ne,un bai- ser, Puis cent, puis mil- le, & puis re- com- men- çons,
bai- ser, Puis cent, puis mil- le, & puis re- com- men-çons, Ces doux bai-
ma mi- gnon- ne,un bai- ser, Puis cent, puis mil- le, & puis re- com- men- çons,
ser, Puis cent, puis mil- le, & puis re- com- men- çons, Ces doux bai-
ser, Puis cent, puis mil- le, & puis re- com- men-çons, Ces doux bai-
ma mi- gnon- ne,un bai- ser, Puis cent, puis mil- le, & puis re- com- men- çons,

sers, Ces douz bai- sers, Ces doux bai- sers de mil- le au- tre fa- çons,
Ces doux bai- sers, Ces doux bai- sers de mil- le au- tre fa- çons, Les re- dou- blans,
Ces douz bai- sers, Ces douz bai- sers de mil- le au- tre fa- çons, Les re- dou- blans
sers, Ces doux bai- sers, de mil- le au- tre fa- çons,
Ces douz bai- sers, Ces douz bai- sers de mil- le au- tre fa- çons, Les re- dou-
sers, Ces doux bai- sers, de mil- le au- tre fa- çons, de mil- le au- tre fa- çons,
sers, Ces douz bai- sers, Ces douz bai- sers de mil- le au- tre fa- çons,
Ces doux bai- sers, Ces doux bai- sers de mil- le au- tre fa- çons, Les re- dou-

Les re- dou- blans d'u- ne sor- te si promp- te, Les re- dou-blans d'u- ne sor-
d'u- ne sor- te si prom- te, Les re- dou- blans d'u- ne sor- te si prom- te, d'u- ne sor- te si prom- te, d'u- ne
d'u- ne sor- te si prom- te, Les re- dou- blans d'u- ne sor- te si prom- te, d'u- ne sor-
Les re- dou- blans d'u- ne sor- te si promp- te, Les re- dou- blans, d'u- ne sor- te si
blans d'u- ne sor- te si prom- te, Les re- dou- blans d'u- ne sor- te si prom- te, d'u-
Les re- dou- blans d'u- ne sor- te si prom- te, Les re- dou-blans d'u- ne
Les re- dou- blans d'u- ne sor- te si prom- te, Les re- dou- blans d'u-
blans d'u- ne sor- te si prom- te, Les re- dou-blans d'u- ne sor- te si prom- te,d'u- ne sor-

te si promp- te, Que ces ja- loux, & en- vy- eux glou- tons, & en- vy- eux glou- tons, De noz bai- sers,
sor- te si prom- te, que ces ja- loux, & en- vy- eux glou- tons, De noz bai- sers, De
te si prom- te, Que ces ja- loux, & en- vy- eux glou- tons, De noz bai- sers, De
promp- te, que ces ja- loux, & en- vy- eux glou- tons, & en- vy- eux glou- tons, De noz bai-
ne sor- te si prom- te, Que ces ja- loux, & en- vy- eux glou- tons, De noz bai- sers, De
sor- te si prom- te, que ces ja- loux, & en- vy- eux glou- tons, & en- vy- eux glou- tons, De noz bai- sers
ne sor- te si prom- te, Que ces fa- cheux, & en- vy- eux glou- tons, & en- vy- eux glou- tons, De noz bai- sers,
te si prom- te, que ces ja- loux, & en- vy- eux glou- tons, De noz bai- sers, De

De noz bai- sers ne sça- chent point le comp- te, & en- vy- eux glou- tons,
noz bai- sers ne sça- chent point le con- te, ne sça- chent point le con- te, ces en- vy- eux glou- tons, De noz bai-
noz bai- sers ne sça- chent point le con- te, ne sça- chent point le con- te, ces en- vy- eux glou- tons, De noz bai-
sers, De noz bai- sers, ne sça- chent point le comp- te, ces en- vy- eux glou- tons,
noz bai- sers ne sça- chent point le con- te, ne sça- chent point le con- te, ces en- vy- eux glou- tons, De noz bai-
ne sça- chent point le con- te, De noz bai- sers, ne sça- chent point le con- te, ne sça- chent point le con- te,
De noz bai- sers ne sça- chent point le con- te, ces en- vy- eux glou- tons,
noz bai- sers ne sça- chent point le con- te, ne sça- chent point le con- te, ces en- vy- eux glou- tons, De noz bai-

De noz bai- sers, De noz bai- sers, De noz bai- sers ne sça- chent point le comp- te.
sers, De noz bai- sers, De noz bai- sers ne sça- chent point le con- te.
sers, De noz bai- sers, De noz bai- sers ne sça- chent point le con- te.
De noz bai- sers, De noz bai- sers, ne sça- chent point le comp- te.
sers, De noz bai- sers, De noz bai- sers ne sça- chent point le con- te.
De noz bai- sers, De noz bai- sers, ne sça- chent point le con- te.
De noz bai- sers, De noz bai- sers ne sça- chent point le con- te.
sers, De noz bai- sers, De noz bai- sers ne sça- chent point le con- te.

Qu'est= ce qu'a- mour, Qu'est= ce qu'a- mour, rien que vi- vre sans vi- e,
Qu'est= ce qu'a- mour, Qu'est= ce qu'a- mour, mou- rir
Qu'est= ce qu'a- mour, Qu'est= ce qu'a- mour, Qu'est= ce qu'a- mour, mou- rir
Qu'est= ce qu'a- mour, Qu'est= ce qu'a- mour, rien que vi- vre sans vi- e,
Qu'est= ce qu'a- mour, Qu'est= ce qu'a- mour, rien que vi- vre sans vi- e,
Qu'est= ce qu'a- mour, Qu'est= ce qu'a- mour, Qu'est=ce qu'a- mour, mou- rir
Qu'est= ce qu'a- mour, Qu'est= ce qu'a- mour, rien que vi- vre sans vi- e,
Qu'est= ce qu'a- mour, Qu'est= ce qu'a- mour, mou- rir

Re- pos plein de tra- vaux, Fin de tous biens, com-
sans mort, c'est vo- lup- té de dou- leur as- sou- vi- e, Fin de tous
sans mort, c'est vo- lup- té de dou- leur as- sou- vi- e, Fin de tous
Re- pos plein de tra- vaux, Fin de tous biens,
Re- pos plein de tra- vaux, Fin de tous biens, Fin de tous
sans mort, c'est vo- lup- té de dou- leur as- sou- vi- e, Fin de tous
Re- pos plein de tra- vaux, Fin de tous biens, com-
sans mort, c'est vo- lup- té de dou- leur as- sou- vi- e, Fin de tous

men- ce- ment de maux, Fin de tous biens,com- men- ce- ment de maux, Fin de tous biens, com-
biens, com- men- ce- ment de maux, Fin de tous biens,com- men- ce- ment de maux,
biens, com- men- ce- ment de maux, com- men- ce- ment de maux, Fin
com- men- ce- ment de maux, com- men- ce- ment, com- men- ce- ment de maux, Qu'est= ce qu'a- mour, Fin
biens, com- men- ce- ment de maux, Fin de tous biens,com- men- ce- ment de maux, Fin de tous biens,
biens, com- men- ce- ment de maux, Fin de tous biens,com- men- ce- ment de maux,
men- ce- ment de maux, com- men- ce- ment de maux, com- men-
biens, com- men- ce- ment de maux, com- men- ce- ment de maux,

men- ce- ment de maux, Qu'est= ce qu'a- mour, con- train- te vo- lon- tai- re, Re- pos
com- men- ce- ment de maux, Qu'est= ce qu'a- mour, Re- pos pe- neux,
de tous biens, com- men- ce- ment de maux, Qu'est= ce qu'a- mour, Re- pos pe- neux[, Re-
de tous biens, com- men- ce- ment de maux, Qu'est- ce qu'a- mour, con- train- te vo- lon- tai- re, Re- pos pe-
com- men- ce- ment de maux, Qu'est= ce qu'a- mour, con- train- te vo- lon- tai- re, Re- pos pe-
com- men- ce- ment de maux, Qu'est= ce qu'a- mour, Re- pos pe- neux,
ce- ment de maux, Qu'est= ce qu'a- mour, con- train- te vo- lon- tai- re, Re- pos pe-
com- men- ce- ment de maux, Qu'est= ce qu'a- mour, Re- pos pe-

pe- neux, Tra- vail oy- sif, Mort sans dou- leur,
& fran- che ser- vi- tu- de, li- ber- té tri- bu- tai- re, Tra-
pos pe- neux] & fran- che ser- vi- tu- de, Li- ber- té tri- bu- tai- re, Tra-
neux, Mort sans dou- leur, Tra- vail oy- sif,
neux, Mort sans dou- leur, Tra- vail oy- sif, Soing
& fran- che ser- vi- tu- de, Mort sans dou- leur, Li- ber- té tri- bu- tai- re, Tra- vail
neux, Mort sans dou- leur, Tra- vail oy- sif,
neux, & fran- che ser- vi- tu- de, li- ber- té tri- bu- tai- re, Tra-

Soing sans so- li- ci- tu- de, Soing sans so- li- ci- tu- de, Qu'est= ce qu'a- mour,
vail oy- sif, Soing sans so- li- ci- tu- de, Soing sans so- li- ci- tu- de, Pas-
vail oy- sif, Soing sans so- li- ci- tu- de, Soing sans so- li- ci- tu- de, Pas-
Soing sans so- li- ci- tu- de, Soing sans so- li- ci- tu- de, Qu'est= ce qu'a-mour,
sans so- li- ci- tu- de, Soing sans so- li- ci- tu- de, Qu'est= ce qu'a- mour,
oy- sif, Soing sans so- li- ci- tu- de, Soing sans so- li- ci- tu- de, Qu'est=ce qu'a- mour, Pas- sion de-
Soing sans so- li- ci- tu- de, Soing sans so- li- ci- tu- de, Qu'est= ce qu'a- mour,
vail oy- sif, Soing sans so- li- ci- tu- de, Soing sans so- li- ci- tu- de, Pas-

Fiel a- dou- cy, miel con- fit en a- mer, Ri- gueur be- ni- gne, Et lan- gueur ac- cep-
sion de- lec- ta- ble, Fiel a- dou- ci, Miel con- fit en a- mer, Ri- gueur be- ni- gne,
sion de- lec- ta- ble, Fiel a- dou- ci, Miel con- fit en a- mer, Ri- gueur be- ni- gne,
Fiel a- dou- cy, Miel con- fit en a- mer, en a- mer, Ri- gueur be- ni- gne, Et lan- gueur ac- cep-
Fiel a- dou- cy, miel con- fit en a- mer, Ri- gueur be- ni- gne, Et lan- gueur ac- cep-
lec- ta- ble, Fiel a- dou- ci, Miel con- fit en a- mer, Ri- gueur be- ni- gne,
Fiel a- dou- cy, miel con- fit en a- mer, Ri- gueur be- ni- gne, Et lan- gueur ac- cep-
sion de- lec- ta- ble, Fiel a- dou- ci, Miel con- fit en a- mer, Ri- gueur be- ni- gne,

ta- ble, Pro- pos con- stans, com- me va- gues en mer, va- gues
Pro- pos con- stans com- me va- gues en mer, com- me va- gues
Pro- pos con- stans com- me va- gues en mer, va- gues en
ta- ble, Pro- pos con- stans, con- stans, com- me va- gues en mer, A-
ta- ble, Pro- pos con- stans, Pro- pos con- stans com- me va- gues en mer, com- me va-
Pro- pos con- stans, com- me va- gues en mer, com- me va- gues
ta- ble, Pro- pos con- stans, con- stans, com- me va- gues en mer, va- gues
Pro- pos con- stans, com- me va- gues en mer, com- me va- gues

en mer, A- mour, tous- jours com- men- ce par au- da- ce, Par crain- te & foy,
en mer, A- mour, & par tra- vail ac- quiert per- se- ve- ran- ce, Par
mer, A- mour, & par tra- vail ac- quiert per- se- ve- ran- ce, Par
mour, A- mour, tous- jours com- men- ce par au- da- ce, Par crain- te & foy
gues en mer, A- mour, tous- jours com- men- ce par au- da- ce, Par crain- te &
en mer, A- mour, & par tra- vail ac- quiert per- se- ve- ran- ce, Par
en mer, A- mour, tous- jours com- men- ce par au- da- ce, Par crain-
en mer, A- mour, & par tra- vail ac- quiert per- se- ve- ran- ce, Par

re- tient son ef- fi- ca- ce, Se- cret par- ler le tient en
crain- te & foy, re- tient son ef- fi- ca- ce, Se- cret par- ler le tient en as- seu
crain- te & foy re- tient son ef- fi- ca- ce, Se- cret par- ler le tient en
re- tient son ef- fi- ca- ce, Se- cret par- ler, le tient en
foy re- tient son ef- fi- ca- ce, Se- cret par- ler, le tient en
crain- te & foy re- tient son ef- fi- ca- ce, Se- cret par- ler le
te & foy, re- tient son ef- fi- ca- ce, Se- cret par- ler, le tient en as-
crain- te & foy, re- tient son ef- fi- ca- ce, Se- cret par- ler le tient en

as- seu- ran- ce, Se- cret par- ler, le tient en as- seu- ran- ce.
ran- ce, Se- cret par- ler le tient en as- seu- ran- ce.
as- seu- ran- ce, Se- cret par- ler le tient en as- seu- ran- ce.
as- seu- ran- ce, Se- cret par- ler, le tient en as- seu- ran- ce.
as- seu- ran- ce, Se- cret par- ler, le tient en as- seu- ran- ce.
tient en as- seu- ran- ce, Se- cret par- ler le tient en as- seu- ran- ce.
seu- ran- ce, Se- cret par- ler, le tient en as- seu- ran- ce.
as- seu- ran- ce, Se- cret par- ler le tient en as- seu- ran- ce.

147 Phinot, *Par un traict d'or* [Forcadel]

16
mou- lu, Que mau- gré moy, j'ay tant vou-
es- mou- lu, Que mau- gré moy j'ay tant vou- lu,
trop es- mou- lu, Que mau- gré moy j'ay tant vou- lu,
lu, Que mau- gré moi, Que mau- gré moi j'ay tant vou-
lu, Que mau- gré moi, mau- gré moi, j'ay tant vou-
es- mou- lu, Que mau- gré moy j'ay tant vou- lu,
lu, Que mau- gré moy, Que mau- gré moy j'ay tant vou-
trop es- mou- lu, Que mau- gré moy j'ay tant vou- lu,

lu, Par un bien qui me fait pe- rir, A- mour me fait vi- vr'& mou- rir,
Par un bien qui me fait pe- rir, A- mour me fait vi- vre & mou- rir, A- mour me fait
Par un bien qui me fait pe- rir, A- mour me fait vi- vre & mou- rir, A- mour
lu, Par un bien qui me fait pe- rir, A- mour me fait vi- vr'& mou- rir,
lu, Par un bien qui me fait pe- rir, A- mour me fait vi- vr'& mou- rir,
Par un bien qui me fait pe- rir, A- mour me fait vi- vre & mou- rir, A- mour me
lu, Par un bien qui me fait pe- rir, A- mour me fait vi- vr'& mou- rir,
Par un bien qui me fait pe- rir; A- mour me fait vi- vre & mou- rir, A- mour me

A- mour, A- mour me fait vi- vr'& mou- rir, Non ce- luy Dieu, Fait al- lu-
vi- vre & mou- rir, Non ce- luy Dieu, Non ce- luy Dieu qui a deux ae- sles,
me fait vi- vre & mou- rir, Non ce- luy Dieu, Non ce- luy Dieu qui a deux ae- sles,
A- mour me fait vi- vr'& mou- rir, Non ce- luy Dieu, Fait al- lu-
A- mour me fait vi- vr'& mou- rir, Non ce- luy Dieu, Fait al-
fait vi- vre & mou- rir, Non ce- luy Dieu, Non ce- luy Dieu qui a deux ae- sles,
A- mour me fait vi- vr'& mou- rir, Non ce- luy Dieu, Fait al- lu-
fait vi- vre & mou- rir, Non ce- luy Dieu, Non ce- luy Dieu qui a deux ae- sles,

mer, Fait al- lu- mer mes es- tin- cel- les, Au- tre que luy m'a peu fe-
Fait al- lu- mer, mes es- tin- cel- les, Au- tre que luy m'a peu fe- rir, A- mour me
Fait al- lu- mer, Au- tre que luy m'a peu fe- rir,
mer, Fait al- lu- mer mes es- tin- cel- les, Au- tre que luy m'a peu
lu- mer, Fait al- lu- mer mes es- tin- cel- les, Fait al- lu- mer mes es- tin- cel- les, Au- tre que luy m'a peu
Fait al- lu- mer mes es- tin- cel- les, Au- tre que luy m'a peu fe- rir,
mer, Fait al- lu- mer mes es- tin- cel- les, Au- tre que luy m'a peu
Fait al- lu- mer, mes es- tin- cel- les, Au- tre que luy m'a peu fe- rir,

80
rir, A- mour me fait vi- vr'& mou- rir, Eus- se Ve- nus son A- do- nis, Mais
fait vi- vr'& mou- rir, Eus- se Ve- nus, Ve- nus son A- do- nis, Mais que nous deux
A- mour me fait vi- vr'& mou- rir, Eus- se Ve- nus, Ve- nus son A- do- nis, Mais que nous
fe- rir, A- mour me fait vi- vr'& mou- rir, Eus- se Ve- nus, Ve- nus son A- do- nis,
fe- rir, A- mour me fait vi- vr'& mou- rir, Eus- se Ve- nus son A- do- nis, Mais
A- mour me fait vi- vr'& mou- rir, vi- vr'& mou- rir, Eus- se Ve- nus, Ve- nus son A- do- nis, Mais que nous
fe- rir, A- mour me fait vi- vr'& mou- rir, Eus- se Ve- nus son A- do- nis, Mais
A- mour me fait vi- vr'& mou- rir, Eus- se Ve- nus, Ve- nus son A- do- nis, Mais que nous

que nous deux fus- sions u- nis, Plus beau n'en vou-drois ac- que- rir, A- mour me
fus- sions u- nis, A- mour me fait vi- vr'& mou- rir,
deux fus- sions u- nis, A- mour me fait vi- vre & mou- rir,
Mais que nous deux fus- sions u- nis, Plus beau n'en vou-drois ac- que- rir, A- mour me
que nous deux, fus- sions u- nis, Plus beau n'en vou-drois ac- que- rir, A- mour me
deux fus- sions u- nis, A- mour me fait vi- vr'& mou- rir,
que nous deux fus- sions u- nis, Plus beau n'en vou-drois ac- que- rir, A- mour me
deux fus- sions u- nis, A- mour me fait vi- vre & mou- rir,

fait vi- vr'& mou- rir, Si mort quand me vien- dra sur- pren- dre,
Mon tris- te es- prit ne peut com- pren- dre, Me pour- ra de ce mal gue-
Mon tris- te es- prit ne peut com- pren- dre, Me pour- ra de ce mal
fait vi- vre & mou- rir, Si mort quand me vien- dra sur- pren- dre,
fait vi- vr'& mou- rir, Si mort quand me vien- dra sur- pren- dre,
Mon tris- t'es- prit ne peut com- pren- dre, Me pour- ra de ce
fait vi- vr'& mou- rir, Si mort quand me vien- dra sur- pren- dre,
Mon tris- te es- prit ne peut com- pren- dre, Me pour- ra de ce mal

Me pour- ra de ce mal gue- rir, A- mour me fait vi- vre & mou- rir, A-
rir, A- mour me fait vi- vre & mou- rir, A- mour me fait vi-
gue- rir, A- mour me fait vi- vre & mou- rir, A- mour me fait vi-
Me pour- ra de ce mal gue- rir, A- mour me fait vi- vr'& mou- rir,
Me pour- ra de ce mal gue- rir, A- mour me fait vi- vr'& mou- rir,
mal gue- rir, A- mour me fait vi- vre & mou- rir, A- mour me fait vi-
Me pour- ra de ce mal gue- rir, A- mour me fait vi- vre & mou- rir,
gue- rir, A- mour me fait vi- vre & mou- rir, A- mour me fait vi-

148
mour me fait vi- vre & mou- rir, A- mour me fait vi- vre & mou- rir.
vre & mou- rir, A- mour me fait vi- vr'& mou- rir.
vre & mou- rir, A- mour me fait vi- vre & mou- rir.
A- mour me fait vi- vr'& mou- rir, A- mour me fait vi- vr'& mou- rir.
A- mour me fait vi- vr'& mou- rir, A- mour me fait vi- vr'& mou- rir.
vre & mou- rir, A- mour me fait vi- vre & mou- rir.
A- mour me fait vi- vre & mou- rir, A- mour me fait vi- vre & mou- rir.
vre & mou- rir, A- mour me fait vi- vre & mou- rir.

148 Verdelot, *Qui la dira*

17
la dou- leur, que pour mon a- my por- te, que pour mon a- my por- te,
coeur, Et la dou- leur, que pour mon a- my por- te, que pour mon
la dou- leur, que pour mon a- my por- te, que pour mon a- my por- te,
Et la dou- leur, que pour mon a- my por- te, que pour mon
la dou- leur, que pour mon a- my por- te, que pour mon a- my por- te,
Et la dou- leur, que pour mon a- my por- te, que pour mon a- my
la dou- leur, que pour mon a- my por- te, que pour mon a- my por- te,
coeur, Et la dou- leur, que pour mon a- my por- te, que pour mon

Je ne sou- tien que tris- tes- se & lan- gueur, Je ne sou- tien que tris- tes- se & lan- gueur,
a- my por- te, Je ne sou- tien que tris- tes- se & lan- gueur, Je ne sou- tien que tris- tes- se & lan- gueur,
Je ne sou- tien que tris- tes- se & lan- gueur, Je ne sou- tien que tris- tes- se & lan- gueur,
a- my por- te, Je ne sou- tien que tris- tes- se & lan- gueur, Je ne sou- tien que tris- tes- se & lan- gueur,
Je ne sou- tien que tris- tes- se & lan- gueur, Je ne sou- tien que tris- tes- se & lan- gueur,
por- te, Je ne sou- tien que tris- tes- se & lan- gueur, Je ne sou- tien que tris- tes- se & lan-
Je ne sou- tien que tris- tes- se & lan- gueur, Je ne sou- tien que tris- tes- se & lan- gueur,
a- my por- te, Je ne sou- tien que tris- tes- se & lan- gueur, Je ne sou- tien que tris- tes- se &

J'ay- me- roye mieux, J'ay- me- roye mieux, cer- tes en es- tre mor-
J'ay- me- roye mieux, J'ay- me- roye mieux, cer-
J'ay- me- roye mieux, J'ay- me- roye mieux, cer- tes en es- tre mor-
J'ay- me- roye mieux, J'ay- me- roye mieux, cer-
J'ay- me- roye mieux, J'ay- me- roye mieux, cer- tes en es- tre mor-
gueur, J'ay- me- roye mieux, J'ay- me- roye mieux,
J'ay- me- roye mieux, J'ay- me- roye mieux, cer- tes en es- tre mor-
lan- gueur, J'ay- me- roye mieux, J'ay- me- roye mieux,

77
te,   cer- tes en es-   tre mor-   te,   cer-   tes en es- tre mor-   te.
tes en es-   tre mor-   te,   cer- tes en es-   tre mor-   te.
te,   cer- tes en es-   tre mor-   te,   en es-   tre mor-   te.
tes en es-   tre mor-   te,   cer- tes en es-   tre mor-   te.
te,   cer-   tes en es-   tre mor-   te.
cer-   tes en es-   tre mor-   te,   cer- tes en es-   tre mor-   te.
te, cer- tes en   es-   tre mor-   te, cer- tes en es-   tre mor-   te, cer- tes en es-   tre mor-   te.
cer-   tes en   es-   tre mor-   te, cer- tes en es-   tre mor-   te, cer- tes en es-   tre mor-   te.

Critical Notes

The following abbreviations are employed in the Critical Notes to this edition:

br.	— breve	5^a	— Quinta
Bs.	— Bassus	rhy.	— rhythmic
bt.	— beat(s)	S.	— Superius
CT.	— Contratenor	sbr.	— semibreve, wholenote
dt.	— dotted	6^a	— Sexta
fu.	— fusa, eighth note	sfu.	— semifusa, sixteenth note
li.	— ligature	smi.	— semiminim, quarter note
m. (mm.)	— measure(s)	T.	— Tenor
mi.	— minim, half note	v. (vv.)	— voice(s)
n. (nn.)	— note(s)		

Foliation given for Nos. 1-136 is from the Superius partbook, but there is exact correspondence among the *Mellange* partbooks, except for the Sexta. The last contains only music for Nos. 100–42, excluding entirely the chansons in eight parts. For the seven- and eight-part chansons, foliation for each part is given as necessary, when not uniform, as in the preceding compositions. Position of the parts, given horizontally for each work and determined by general range, should be read as from highest to lowest; the Superius always forms the uppermost part in the score of this edition, as the Bassus (= Bassus I) or Bassus II the lowermost. Labelling of the parts herein follows source designations.

1. Ad. Vuillart[1] [Willaert], *Jouissance vous donneray* (fol. 1[r]) [C. Marot]

Lyrics: I shall delight you, my friend, and guide you,
  Your hopes affirm the way,
  Alive [I] shall not leave you,
  Even when [I] am dead,
  Your spirit will remember.

Parts: S., CT., T., 5^a, Bs.
Concordances: Le sixiesme livre contenant trente et une chansons nouvelles a cincq et a six parties. (Antwerp, T. Susato, 1545; = RISM 1545[14]), fol. 2[r];[2] *Livre,*[3] fol. 2[v].[4]

Musica Ficta: mm. 2 (b♭), 4 (c♯′, b♭), 6 (b♭), 8 (c♯′), 10 (B♭), 12 (c♯), 14 (b♭), 15 (c♯′), 25 (g♯′), 36 (b♭′), 38 (g♯′), 41 (b♭, e♭), 42 (e♭′), 44 (c♯′, twice), 49 (c♯), 56 (c♯′), 60 (b♭), 61 (b♭, twice), 66 (g♯′), 70 (B♭), 74 (b♭), 75 (b♭′), 80 (b♭), 84 (b♭′), 86 (g♯′), 88 (b♭), 89 (b♭), 92 (c♯′), 93 (b♭), 95 (f♯), 97 (c♯), 101 (b♭), 104 (c♯′).
Remarks: At m. 65, consecutive harmonic dissonances occur.

2. Ad. Vuillart [Willaert], *Helas ma mere* (fol. 1ᵛ)

Lyrics: Alas, Mother, alas, *maman,*
Alas, Mother, for my teeth,
The chattering teeth behind,
Hurt those in front,
The other day [on] my way,
My road to Saint Laurens,
[I] met a shepherdess,
Who was suffering from toothache,
I asked her,
Beautiful, why are you suffering,
Alas, Mother, alas, maman,
Alas, Mother, for my teeth.

Parts: S., CT., T., 5ᵃ, Bs.
Concordances: Livre, fol. 3ʳ.[5]
Errors: mm. 26ff, "Lautre" (not "L'autre"); mm. 48 and 51, 5ᵃ, and 48 and 50, Bs., "L'aurens" (not "Laurens").
Musica Ficta: mm. 1 (c♯′), 10 (g♯′), 11 (c♯′), 12 (c♯′), 13 (b♭ in 5ᵃ; c♯′, twice), 21 (b♭), 25 (c♯′), 28 (b♭), 30 (c♯′), 31 (g♯), 33 (b♭), 34 (b♭), 37 (B♭), 42 (b♭′), 43 (b♭), 48 (g♯, twice, and f♯), 51 (g♯′), 53 (c♯′), 55 (f♯′), 61 (b♭′), 62-3 (g♯′, twice), 66 (b♭), 67 (g♯), 68 (c♯′), 70-1 (g♯, twice), 73 (c♯′), 81 (g♯′), 83 (c♯′), 84 (g♯′), 87 (b♭), 88 (b♭), 89 (c♯′), 97 (b♭), 101 (c♯′), 103 (b♭), 108 (f♯), 109 (g♯), 111 (b♭′), 113 (g♯′), 122 (b♭′), 126 (B♭), 128 (b♭′), 129 (b♭), 143 (g♯′), 145 (c♯′), 146 (g♯′), 147 (c♯′, f♯), 148 (b♭), 150 (c♯), 151 (B♭), 152 (c♯′, f♯), 153 (c♯′), 154 (b♭), 155 (c♯′).

3. Ad. Vuillart [Willaert], *Qui la dira* (fol. 2ʳ)

Lyrics: Who will tell her [of] my heartache,
And the pain that I bear for my friend,
I sustain only sadness and lassitude,
I would love better, certainly, in being dead.

Parts: S., CT., 5ᵃ, T., Bs.

Concordances: Munich, Bavarian State Library, Music MS 1508, No. 86;[6] *Livre,* fol. 3ᵛ; modern edition: *Antonio Valente: Intavolatura de Cimbalo (Naples, 1576)* (ed. C. Jacobs, 1973), 157.[7]
Errors: mm. 68ff, the final "e" of "J'aymeroie" is not elided.
Musica Ficta: mm. 4 (c♯), 5 (b♭), 8 (b♭, twice), 9 (b♭), 21 (c♯′), 24 (b♭), 26 (g♯), 28 (b♭′), 30 (g♯′), 31 (b♭), 39 (b♭′), 42 (b♭), 47 (b♭), 50 (b♭′), 51 (c♯), 52 (g♯′), 54 (c♯), 56 (b♭), 59 (b♭), 60 (g♯), 63 (b♭), 71 (B♭), 72 (f♯), 75 (f♯), 76 (b♭), 77 (c♯′), 78 (f♯), 79 (g♯), 82 (B♭), 83 (f♯), 86 (f♯), 87 (b♭′), 88 (c♯′), 89 (f♯′, twice), 90 (b♭).

4. Mouton, *Ce que mon coeur pense* (fol. 2ᵛ)

Lyrics: What my heart thinks,
I shall not say, Alas,
In the garden, Father,
There is a bird,
Which sings every day,
Which will fly away, Alas,
What my heart thinks,
I shall not say, Alas.

Parts: S., CT., T., 5ᵃ, Bs.
Concordances: Livre, fol. 32ᵛ.
Errors: m. 76, Bs., second n. reads A (not d).
Musica Ficta: mm. 9 (c♯′), 12 (e♭, B♭), 15 (c♯′), 17 (e♭, B♭), 20 (c♯′), 23 (f♯′), 24 (c♯′), 28 (c♯′), 36 (c♯′), 46 (b♭), 48 (b♭), 49 (g♯), 50 (b♭′), 55 (b♭′), 58 (b♭′), 62 (c♯′), 64 (c♯′), 74 (c♯), 75 (c♯′), 77 (B♭), 88 (c♯′, twice), 90 (c♯′), 100 (e♭), 101 (e♭, B♭), 110 (c♯′), 117 (f♯), 118 (c♯′), 121 (c♯′), 127 (f♯).
Remarks: m. 76, T., flat only indicated for initial n.

5. Mouton, *Le berger & la bergere* (fol. 3ʳ)

Lyrics: The shepherd and the shepherdess,
Arm in arm to play, they went,
I prithee (said the shepherdess),
My friend, tell me your name,
and *lire, lire, liron:*[8]
I prithee (said the shepherdess),
My friend, tell me your name,
Her darling replied to her,
By Jove, my name is Fourbifron,
And polish me it,[9] then.[10]

Parts: S., CT., T., 5ᵃ, Bs.
Concordances: Livre, fol. 33ᵛ.
Errors: mm. 33ff and 53ff, the final "e" of "prie" is not elided; ditto, mm. 47ff, the final "e" of the second "lire"; m. 53, Bs., 2nd n. reads G; mm. 82ff, "bieu" (not "bleu").
Musica Ficta: mm. 6 (b♭), 7 (c♯), 12 (c♯), 15 (b♭), 18 (Bs., 1st n., B♭), 20 (b♭), 21 (b♭, twice), 22 (b♭), 24 (b♭), 25 (B♭), 26 (b♭), 29 (b♭'), 30 (g♯'), 33 (b♭), 38 (b♭), 42 (c♯'), 47 (c♯'), 50 (c♯'), 52 (b♭), 53 (c♯'), 56 (b♭), 59 (e♭), 60 (b♭), 66 (b♭), 67 (g♯), 68 (b♭'), 69 (g♯'), 72 (b♭), 73 (e♭), 76 (b♭), 77 (c♯), 80 (b♭'), 83 (g♯), 89 (c♯'), 92 (B♭), 95 (B♭), 96 (f♯), 98 (F♯), 99 (b♭, twice).

6. Richafort,[11] *Cuidez vous que Dieu* (fol. 3ᵛ)

Lyrics: Do you believe that God may fail to be generous to us,
　　　He has more than He gives us,
　　　And we all are to be taken to task,
　　　Until Judgment Day,
　　　Companion,[12] don't you care about it [?]
　　　The term [of suffering] is worth the payment.

Parts: S., 5ᵃ, CT., T., Bs.
Concordances: Vingt et six chansons musicales & nouvelles a cincq parties (Antwerp, T. Susato, 1543; = RISM [1543]₁₅), fol. 10ʳ; *Livre,* fol. 35ᵛ.[13]
Errors: "faille" is syllabified "fail-le" (only in S.).[14]
Musica Ficta: mm. 5 (b♭'), 12 (b♭), 13 (e♭), 14 (e♭, twice), 15 (b♭), 21 (T., b♭), 22 (c♯'), 28 (e♭'), 30 (b♭), 34 (b♭'), 38 (b♭'), 43 (b♭'), 47 (b♭), 51 (b♭), 56 (b♭), 59 (b♭'), 67 (b♭'), 74 (b♭), 75 (e♭), 76 (e♭, twice), 77 (b♭), 83 (T., b♭), 84 (c♯'), 87 (f♯'), 90 (b♭), 93 (B♭), 94 (c♯'), 95 (f♯).
Remarks: Note *appoggiature* in mm. 43 (e') and 61 (d).

7. Benedictus [Appenzeller],[15] *Je m'y levay par un matin* (fol. 4ʳ)

Lyrics: I got up one morning,
　　　The day was not [far] advanced,
　　　I betook myself straight on to sing at the door [of] my friend,
　　　Just as soon as she heard me singing,
　　　She closed her door to me,
　　　Go, speak to her, ask her,
　　　If she has her door closed for me.

Parts: S., CT., T., 5ᵃ, Bs.
Concordances: As for No. 6 (RISM [1543]₁₅), fol. 5ᵛ; *Livre,* fol. 40ʳ.
Errors: mm. 2ff, "my" (not "m'y", as in *table*).

Musica Ficta: mm. 19 (B♭), 20 (e♭', b♭), 23 (f♯, twice), 26 (f♯), 45 (B♭, e♭'), 46 (b♭), 47 (c♯'), 65 (b♭), 66 (b♭), 67 (c♯'), 72 (c♯'), 74 (B♭, b♭), 76 (B♭), 77 (c♯), 84 (c♯'), 93 (e♭', b♭), 94 (B♭), 97 (B♭, b♭), 100 (b♭, c♯').
Remarks: At m. 86, Bs., the second syllable of "dire," in contradistinction to the other vv., is not elided. In the concordance, the last three mm. lack f♯; instead, b♭ is given therein for m. 102.

8. Arcadet [Arcadelt], *Quand je me trouve* (fol. 4ᵛ)

Lyrics: When I find myself close to my mistress,
　　　And when I bring my mouth to hers,
　　　There is so much joy and there is so much merriment,
　　　That nothing unpleasant can enter my spirit,
　　　And if there is only fear that a reproach may come,
　　　Because she is noble in virtue,
　　　But I truly believe that in such joy,
　　　My soul only in her finds its dwelling.

Parts: S., CT., T., 5ᵃ, Bs.
Concordances: Livre, fol. 48ᵛ;[16] modern edition: *Jacobus Arcadelt: Opera Omnia* (= *Corpus Mensurabilis Musicae,* 31; ed. A. Seay), IX (1968), 105.
Errors: mm. 13ff, CT., T., 5ᵃ, the second time "sienne" appears, the second syllable is elided; mm. 37ff, "Q'uen" (not "Qu'en").[17]
Musica Ficta: mm. 4 (e♭', twice), 6 (f♯), 7 (b♭), 11 (f♯'), 20 (c♯'), 22 (b♭), 37 (c♯'), 38 (c♯'), 39 (c♯', twice), 41 (b♭'), 46 (c♯'), 49 (c♯'), 51 (b♭), 52 (c♯'), 56 (c♯'), 70 (g♯'), 71 (b♭), 74 (b♭), 76 (b♭'), 78 (b♭), 80 (b♭), 81 (e♭'), 82 (c♯'), 83 (b♭), 84 (g♯, thrice, and f♯), 85 (b♭), 88 (b♭), 90 (b♭'), 93 (b♭), 97 (b♭), 98 (c♯').
Remarks: m. 95, Bs., flat only indicated for initial n. At m. 51, a simultaneous cross-relation occurs.

9. Phl. Vuildre [Wilder], *Pour vous aymer* (fol. 5ʳ)

Lyrics: To love you, I have directed all my attention,
　　　Because, for certain, such good fortune I won't [again] obtain,
　　　But only to have your favor,
　　　Entreating you to make me know,
　　　If your heart will care for my love.[18]

Parts: S., CT., T., 5ᵃ, Bs.
Musica Ficta: mm. 5 (b♭), 8 (c♯'), 9 (b♭), 13 (B♭), 14 (c♯', twice), 15 (f♯'), 22 (c♯'), 27 (b♭'), 42 (b♭'), 48 (b♭, twice), 49 (b♭'), 52 (b♭, c♯'), 55 (b♭), 58 (g♯, twice, and f♯), 59 (b♭'), 62 (g♯', twice, and f♯'), 66 (c♯'), 70 (c♯', twice), 72 (g♯,

twice, and f♯), 73 (b♭'), 76 (g♯', twice, and f♯'), 79 (f♯), 80 (c♯'), 84 (c♯', twice), 87 (CT., b♭), 88 (b♭).
Remarks: At m. 3, CT., sharp only indicated for the initial n. affected. The following dissonances occur in this work: mm. 3–4 (CT.), a melodic diminished fourth; m. 33, consecutive dissonances (between S. and CT.); m. 39, cross-relation; m. 48, $^6_4$ chord, with anticipation (e') producing the sonority of a seventh.

10. Ph. Vuildre [Wilder], *Pour un plaisir* (fol. 5^v)

Lyrics: For a pleasure, which lasts so little,
  I have endured pain and travail,
  I have suffered sadness too severe over it,
  I have received a hundred thousand evils from it,
  But God owes me good luck,
  Fortune has made her assaults on me.

Parts: S., CT., T., 5^a, Bs.[19]
Musica Ficta: mm. 12 (g♯'), 17 (b♭), 18 (c♯'), 20 (c♯'), 26 (g♯), 30 (g♯'), 32 (c♯'), 35 (g♯'), 40 (g♯, twice, and f♯), 56 (b♭), 58 (b♭), 63 (B♭), 65 (b♭), 68 (g♯), 71 (b♭'), 73 (b♭), 75 (b♭), 76 (g♯), 77 (b♭, c♯'), 79 (b♭), 85 (b♭', c♯'), 87 (b♭), 89 (b♭), 90 (g♯), 91 (b♭, c♯'), 93 (b♭), 97 (f♯), 100 (b♭, twice).
Remarks: mm. 81 and 95, CT., flat only indicated for initial n. affected. At m. 31, an augmented chord is found.

11. Phl. Vuildre [Wilder], *Je me repens* (fol. 6^r)

Lyrics: I repent of having loved,
  Of true love, so loyally,
  Her who is without loyalty,
  And changeable as the wind,
  From now on, I shall be careful,
  Not to love too much suddenly.

Parts: S., CT., T., 5^a, Bs.
Errors: m. 32, CT., "vraye" (not "vray"); mm. 48–9 and 58–9, S., "variaute" (not "variante").
Musica Ficta: mm. 9 (b♭), 19 (c♯'), 21 (b♭), 26 (B♭), 28 (CT., b♭), 30 (c♯'), 31 (B♭), 34 (b♭, c♯'), 37 (b♭), 38 (b♭), 39 (f♯), 50 (G♯), 51 (g♯), 53 (b♭', b♭), 54 (b♭), 57 (b♭), 58 (g♯), 60 (b♭'), 61 (g♯), 63 (b♭'), 64 (g♯', twice, and f♯'), 72 (b♭), 73 (b♭), 83 (c♯'), 85 (b♭), 90 (B♭), 95 (B♭), 98 (c♯'), 100 (b♭, twice).
Remarks: At mm. 27 and 91, a diminished triad in root position occurs; at m. 92, a cross-relation. The bracketted flat, m. 33, is derived from m. 97.

12. Ph. Vuildre [Wilder], *Ma bouche rit* (fol. 6^v)

Lyrics: My mouth laughs and my thoughts weep,
  My eye rejoices and my heart curses the hour,
  That the good fortune was attained, which health perverts,
  And the pleasure, that death so pursues,
  Without encouragement, which aids me or helps,
  My mouth laughs and my thoughts weep,
  My eye rejoices and my heart curses the hour.

Parts: S., CT., T., 5^a, Bs.
Musica Ficta: mm. 6 (b♮), 9 (f♯'), 11 (e♭'), 15 (e♭''), 16 (e♭''), 20 (S., f♯'), 29 (e♭''), 31 (e♭'), 32 (e♭'), 46 (e♭'), 55 (e♭''), 58 (f♯'), 67 (f♯'), 69 (e♭'), 73 (e♭''), 74 (e♭''), 78 (S., f♯'), 84 (e♭''), 85 (e♭''), 89 (S., f♯'), 90 (b♮').
Remarks: At mm. 37 and 54, augmented triads occur; at mm. 39–40 (CT.), the leap of a diminished fourth. The part-writing of the T., mm. 34–6, consists of a descending minor third, followed by a descending perfect fifth.

13. Phl. Vuildre [Wilder], *Je file quand Dieu* (fol. 7^r)[20]

Lyrics: I spin, when God gives me the means,
  I spin my distaff on my way,[21]
  I entered a garden,
  I spin, when God gives me the means,
  I found three flowers of love there,
  I go, I come,
  I turn, I twist, I bind, I trim, I clip, I shave,
  I dance, I leap, I laugh, I sing, I ready myself,[22]
  I guard my sheep from the wolf,
  I spin my distaff on my way,
  I spin, when God gives me the means,
  I spin my distaff on my way.

Parts: S., CT., T., 5^a, Bs.
Concordances: *Le Rossignol musical* (Antwerp, P. Phalèse, 1597; = RISM 1597$_{10}$), fol. 21^r; modern edition: H.M. Brown, ed., *Theatrical Chansons of the Fifteenth and Early Sixteenth Centuries* (1963), 102.[23]
Errors: m. 32, Bs., first n. reads d (not f; correction from concordance). CT., final *custos* (for repeat) lacking; 5^a, final staff, superfluous repeat sign and *custos* given; 5^a and Bs., last n. should be a white sb.
Musica Ficta: mm. 8 (f♯': forms part of the reading of the Phalèse concordance), 13 (f♯'), 18 (B♮), 22 (c♯''), 23 (e♭'), 24 (c♯'), 27 (e♭''), 29 (f♯': indicated in the

reading of the Phalèse concordance), 38 (eb″, twice), 41 (f♯′, thrice), 46 (eb″, twice), 47 (eb″), 49 (b♮).
Remarks: mm. 49 and 50, CT., and 52, S., sharp only indicated for first n. affected. The opening m. should perhaps have been interpreted as a smi. upbeat (i.e., without the rests). A cautionary natural sign is given in the Phalèse concordance for e″ in the S., mm. 15 and 65, to which *musica ficta* presumably might have been applied. Similarly, this concordance reads a (not f) for the second n. of the 5ᵃ, m. 66, obviating the simultaneous cross-relation found in the *Mellange*. Other dissonances found in this work are: mm. 4 and 53, the sonority of an augmented triad; m. 33, S., a leap of a diminished fourth.

14. Ph. de Monte,[24] *Secourez moy ma dame* (fol. 7ᵛ) [C. Marot]

Lyrics: Help me, my lady, by love,
Otherwise, death will come to fetch me,
No other but you can render help,
To my weary heart which is going to die,
Alas, alas, won't you help then,
Him who lives in great distress for you,
Because you are the mistress of his heart.

Parts: S., 5ᵃ, CT., T., Bs.
Concordances: Livre, fol. 15ᵛ;[25] modern edition: *Philippe de Monte, Opera* (ed. C. van den Borren and J. van Nuffel, 1927–   ), XX, 42.[26]
Errors: mm. 58–9, Bs., "vueillez" is syllabified "vueil-lez" (not "vuei-llez").
Musica Ficta: mm. 6 (eb′), 7 (f♯′), 13 (eb′), 16 (f♯′), 20 (f♯′), 28 (f♯′, thrice), 30 (c♯″), 35 (c♯″), 37 (eb′), 40 (b♮), 41 (eb″), 42 (c♯″), 44 (eb), 48 (f♯′), 58 (eb′), 66 (f♯′), 67 (b♮′, twice), 70 (eb″), 85 (b♮′), 86 (eb″), 90 (f♯′), 100 (f♯′), 101 (b♮).
Remarks: At mm. 47–8, the part-writing of the 5ᵃ includes consecutive ascending perfect fifths.

15. Mouton, *Vray Dieu d'amours* (fol. 8ᵣ)

Lyrics: True God of love, cursed be the day,
That ever in my life I was in love,
Because now I am disconsolate,
I am [a woman] all alone and indeed have no friend at all,
Is it necessary that I thus be,
I am all alone and indeed have no friend at all.

Parts: S., CT., T., 5ᵃ, Bs.
Concordances: Livre, fol. 33ᵣ.[27]
Errors: mm. 62ff, "damy" (not "d'amy").[28]

Musica Ficta: mm. 3 (b♮′), 8 (eb′), 9 (eb), 12 (eb′), 15 (eb′), 20 (eb), 21 (eb), 22 (eb′), 27 (eb), 28 (eb, eb′), 29 (eb′), 30 (eb′), 31 (eb″), 35 (eb′), 36 (f♯′), 41 (b♮′), 45 (eb′), 53 (eb′, eb), 54 (eb), 55 (f♯), 57 (eb″), 62 (eb′, f♯′), 70 (eb), 78 (c♯″), 79 (f♯), 81 (eb), 82 (eb), 88 (f♯′), 90 (eb), 91 (eb″), 96 (eb′, f♯′), 99 (eb′, twice), 100 (eb′, twice).

16. Mouton, *La rousée du mois de may* (fol. 8ᵛ)

Lyrics: The dew of the month of May,
Has spoiled my green skirt,
One morning, I was awakened [by],
The dew of the month of May,
[I] gained entry into a garden,
You may say that I am foolish,
The dew of the month of May,
Has spoiled my green skirt.

Parts: S., CT., T., 5ᵃ, Bs.
Concordances: As for No. 6 (RISM [1543]₁₅), fol. 4ᵣ; *Livre,* fol. 34ᵣ.[29]
Errors: mm. 34ff, "my" (not "m'y").
Musica Ficta: mm. 4 (eb′: forms part of the reading of the concordance), 5 (eb′), 6 (f♯′), 7 (eb′), 17 (eb′), 20 (eb), 21 (f♯′), 22 (b♮′, eb′), 29 (f♯′, twice), 33 (eb′), 34 (c♯′), 37 (f♯′), 38 (eb′), 42 (b♮), 46 (eb′), 57 (eb′), 67 (eb), 70 (f♯′), 78 (f♯′), 82 (f♯′), 83 (c♯′), 86 (c♯″), 95 (eb′), 99 (f♯′), 104 (f♯′), 111 (c♯′), 112 (f♯′).
Remarks: The source reads, variously, "gasté" and "gaté," "coste" and "cotte"; the most prevalent forms of each word ("gasté" and "cotte") — found also in the *Livre* — have been employed in the reading of this edition. At m. 35, a simultaneous cross-relation occurs; it does not appear in the concordance, whose 5ᵃ lacks the sharp. At the close of the work, the melodic inflection of the 5ᵃ of the concordance is entirely different from its reading in the *Mellange*; in the former, the 5ᵃ, m. 113, reads bb-eb′.[30]

17. Rousée, *Fortune, laisse moy la vie* (fol. 9ᵣ)

Lyrics: Fortune, permit me life,
You torment me harshly,
Only let me live,
And that I prithee,
Alas, why are you my enemy,
Can't it be otherwise,
Fortune, permit me life.

Parts: S., 5ᵃ, CT., T., Bs.

Concordances: Livre, fol. 36ᵛ.
Errors: m. 52, S., superfluous elision of final letter of "vivre."
Musica Ficta: mm. 6 (e♭″), 8 (f♯′), 12 (e♭′), 13 (f♯′), 14 (e♭″), 26 (e♭″), 28 (e♭″), 32 (e♭′, twice), 36 (f♯′), 37 (c♯″), 41 (e♭″), 49 (e♭″), 53 (b♮′, c♯″), 63 (c♯′), 66 (f♯′), 69 (e♭″), 70 (c♯″), 75 (e♭″), 76 (c♯′, twice, and b♮), 79 (e♭″), 81 (e♭″), 82 (c♯″, thrice, and b♮′), 90 (c♯″), 91 (e♭′), 97 (e♭′), 99 (e♭″), 101 (f♯′), 103 (c♯′), 105 (e♭″), 106 (c♯″, thrice, and b♮′), 113 (e♭″), 115 (f♯′), 119 (c♯″), 120 (e♭′), 121 (e♭′), 127 (c♯″), 128 (e♭′), 129 (e♭′).
Remarks: The following dissonances occur in this composition: m. 58, a simultaneous cross-relation; m. 69, parallel sevenths; m. 98, a free dissonant n. (e′), not regarded as a source error.

18. Ciprian Rore, *Susane un jour* (fol. 9ᵛ) [Guéroult]

Lyrics: Susanne, solicited one day for love,
      By two old men, lusting after her beauty,
      Was sad and distressed in her heart,
      Seeing the effort made on her chastity,
      She said to them, if, through treachery,
      You have [your] pleasure with my body,
      I am finished,
      If I resist,
      You will make me die dishonored,
      But I prefer to perish innocent,
      Than to offend the Lord by sinning.

Parts: S., CT., T., 5ª, Bs.
Concordances: Premier livre des chansons a quatre et cincq parties (P. Phalèse, Louvain, 1570; = RISM 1570₅), p. 22.
Errors: mm. 18ff, "d'eux" (not "deux").
Musica Ficta: mm. 6 (e♭′), 13 (e♭″), 26 (f♯′, twice), 56 (f♯′: forms part of the reading of the concordance), 65 (e♭′), 74 (c♯″), 93 (b♮), 106 (b♮′), 130 (f♯′: found as part of the reading of the concordance), 138 (f♯′).
Remarks: mm. 20–1, CT., "viellars" is syllabified "viel-lars" (not "vie-llars)." The natural signs recommended at mm. 77 and 81 (T.) are found in the reading of the concordance. Cross-relations occur at mm. 25 and 55.[31]

19. Strige,[32] *Pour m'esloigner* (fol. 10ʳ) [St. Gelais]

Lyrics: To take myself away and change my residence,
      No other friendship has entered my heart,
      Yours, so well received, made a conquest there,

So that it can only escape through death,
      And [I] do not at all believe that, after us, it [i.e., our love] will die,
      If anything of us remains, after our death.

Parts: S., CT., T., 5ª, Bs.
Errors: S., 2nd staff, clef misprinted; mm. 24–5, Bs., "reçeue" (not "reçeuë").
Musica Ficta: mm. 6 (e♭″), 7 (f♯′), 10 (b♮, twice, opening nn. of 5ª), 11 (f♯′), 22 (e♭″), 23 (c♯″, twice), 24 (e♭′, twice), 28 (b♮, twice), 36 (b♮), 42 (5ª: b♮), 46 (c♯″), 53 (e♭″), 54 (f♯′), 57 (b♮, twice, opening nn. of T.), 58 (f♯′).
Remarks: mm. 5 and 52, S., sharp only indicated for the first n.; m. 20, CT., ditto; m. 12, T., natural sign only indicated for first n.; mm. 4, 5ª, and 51, T., flat only indicated for initial n.

20. Hauville,[33] *Herbes & fleurs* (fol. 10ᵛ)

Lyrics: Herbs and flowers and you, verdant fields,
      Trees, little bushes, and abundant groves,
      Plains and hills and undulating rivers,
      Pretty birds, who, according to your chirping,
          are weeping, your grief languishing,
      If one of you by chance knows,
      That tiny, tiny god, who makes me sad,
      Tell him of the pain that I endure.

Parts: S., CT., T., 5ª, Bs.
Musica Ficta: mm. 7 (f♯′), 10 (f♯′), 23 (f♯′), 27 (f♯′), 33 (f♯′), 36 (f♯′), 41 (f♯′), 49 (f♯′), 51 (f♯′), 56 (e♭′), 63 (c♯″), 75 (f♯′), 77 (f♯′, twice), 78 (f♯′), 81 (e♭″), 82 (e♭″), 83 (e♭′), 93 (b♮: 5ª, 1st n.), 94 (f♯′), 95 (b♮), 96 (e♭′, b♮′), 101 (f♯′), 107 (b♮), 108 (e♭″), 111 (f♯′).
Remarks: mm. 22 and 48, T., and 71, CT., flat only indicated for the first n.

21. Severin Cornet, *Or me traictiez* (fol. 11ʳ)

Lyrics: But, you thus treat me as it pleases you,
      Enduring, my heart will serve you,
      And love better serving you in sadness,
      Than loving elsewhere in joy and in pleasure.

Parts: S., CT., T., 5ª, Bs.
Errors: mm. 58, Bs., and 61, T. and 5ª, "tri-" (not "tris-").
Musica Ficta: mm. 7 (e♭′), 10 (c♯″), 16 (f♯′, thrice), 20 (c♯′), 21 (e♭″), 31 (e♭″), 34 (5ª: e♭′), 38 (f♯′), 43 (c♯′), 44 (e♭′), 48 (e♭′), 51 (e♭′), 52 (c♯′), 53 (e♭′), 62 (f♯′, twice), 71 (e♭″), 72 (c♯″), 73 (e♭′), 75 (f♯′), 77 (e♭′), 80 (f♯′).

22. Cla. LeJeune, *Allons, allons gay* (fol. 11ᵛ)

Lyrics: Let us go, let us go, gay, gaily, my darling, you and I,
My father has had a castle made,
The battlements are of gold and silver, *gaily, my darling, you and I,*
Let us go, let us go, gay, gaily, my darling, you and I,
The battlements are of gold and silver, gaily, my darling,
The King indeed has nothing so lovely, *gaily, my darling,*
Let us go, let us go, gay, gaily, you and I.

Parts: S., 5ᵃ, CT., T., Bs.
Errors: m. 41, CT., "neanx," (not "neaux,"); m. 110, 5ᵃ, "mennt," (not "ment,").
Musica Ficta: mm. 24 (f♯′, twice), 29 (e♭′), 30 (e♭′), 31 (c♯″), 33 (e♭′), 34 (c♯′), 36 (e♭″), 37 (c♯″), 55 (c♯″), 60 (f♯′), 64 (f♯′, twice), 72 (f♯′, twice), 75 (c♯″), 78 (f♯′, twice), 92 (e♭′), 93 (f♯″), 96 (f♯′), 103 (b♮′), 108, (e♭″, c♯″), 112 (f♯′), 118 (e♭′), 119 (f♯′).
Remarks: The natural sign is only indicated for the initial n. affected in: mm. 25, 5ᵃ; 57, T.; 65 and 70, CT. Ditto, for the sharp in: mm. 28, CT., and 109, 5ᵃ. Ditto, for the flat in: mm. 49, CT.; 51 and 77, S.; and 66, T. At m. 91, note augmented triad.[34]

23. Leschenet, *Puis que j'ay belle amye* (fol. 12ʳ)

Lyrics: Since I have a lovely friend,
Lovely, graceful, and pleasing,
I shall live loyally,
And wish totally,
To chase away melancholy.

Parts: S., CT., T., 5ᵃ, Bs.
Concordances: Livre, fol. 19ᵛ.[35]
Musica Ficta: mm. 6 (c♯′), 7 (b♭), 9 (f♯), 12 (f♯′), 13 (CT., g♯), 14 (g♯), 15 (b♭), 16 (c♯′), 18 (f♯), 20 (e♭), 23 (g♯′), 26 (b♭′), 30 (g♯′), 31 (b♭), 32 (c♯′), 39 (b♭, twice), 45 (b♭, twice), 51 (b♭, twice), 54 (c♯′), 55 (b♭), 57 (f♯), 60 (f♯′), 61 (CT., g♯), 62 (g♯), 63 (b♭), 65 (b♭), 67 (c♯′), 70 (f♯), 71 (b♭), 73 (f♯′), 74 (e♭′, e♭), 76 (b♭, c♯′), 77 (f♯).

24. Cla. LeJeune, *Quand vous seriés* (fol. 12ᵛ)

Lyrics: Though you were some daughter of a Scythian,
Even the love which incites tigers,
You would force relief from my misfortune,

But you [are] too much more than a proud tigress,
Alas for my heart, you are its murderess,
And only live to see it die.

Parts: S., CT., T., 5ᵃ, Bs.
Errors: m. 126, T., "nés" (not "vés").
Musica Ficta: mm. 17 (c♯′?), 24 (g♯′), 47 (g♯′), 59 (g♯′), 62 (c♯′), 68 (b♭′), 71 (g♯), 81 (e♭′), 82 (b♭), 96 (b♭′), 97 (g♯′), 98 (g♯′), 104 (e♭), 118 (f♯, b♭′), 119 (c♯′), 128 (b♭), 129 (e♭′), 130 (c♯′, twice).
Remarks: The flat is only indicated for the first n. affected in: mm. 19, 51, and 115, 5ᵃ; 46, S.; 54, T.; 106 and 125, Bs.; 129, CT. Ditto, for the sharp in: mm. 40, Bs.; 44 and 53, S.; 49 and 56, 5ᵃ; 65, T.[36] At m. 49, a C♯-minor triad occurs. The melodic writing presents arpeggios or otherwise outlines harmonies in mm. 89–93 (Bs.), 105–6 (5ᵃ), and 131–4 (Bs.).

25. Nicolas, *Je m'en vois au vert bois* (fol. 13ʳ)

Lyrics: I see myself in the green wood, hearing the little bird sing,
Telling me, telling you, that it is for Marion,
But shepherd boys and shepherd girls are going there,
And if they make up a bouquet [of flowers] and then they go away,
I see myself in the green wood, hearing the little bird sing, telling me, telling
you, that it is for Marion.

Parts: S., CT., T., 5ᵃ, Bs.
Errors: Throughout the work, all vv. read "loisillon" (not "l'oisillon").
Musica Ficta: mm. 1 (b♮′), 3 (e♭′), 6 (c♯′), 8 (b♮′), 10 (c♯″), 12 (e♭), 14 (e♭″), 19 (b♮), 23 (e♭), 28 (e♭), 30 (f♯′), 35 (f♯′), 40 (f♯′), 41 (b♭), 43 (b♭′), 49 (e♭′), 51 (e♭′), 54 (b♮), 56 (f♯), 66 (f♯′), 67 (e♭″), 71 (e♭′), 72 (e♭′), 74 (f♯′), 76 (e♭′, twice), 78 (f♯′), 81 (e♭), 84 (b♭′), 86 (f♯′), 88 (f♯), 96 (b♮, e♭), 97 (e♭″), 100 (e♭′), 101 (e♭′), 102 (e♭′), 104 (c♯′), 113 (c♯″), 119 (c♯′), 122 (e♭′), 127 (f♯′), 129 (f♯′), 131 (b♮).
Remarks: In mm. 45 and 106, Bs., and 134, 5ᵃ, the flat is indicated only for the initial n. affected. The following dissonance is found in this composition: m. 17, parallel seconds; mm. 52–3 and 107, the sonority of an augmented chord (in the latter case, produced by an anticipation); mm. 91–2, descent of a chromatic semitone (which, in this instance, articulates the end of one phrase and the beginning of the next of this chanson).

26. Nicolas, *Susane un jour* (fol. 13ᵛ) [Guéroult]

Lyrics: (See No. 18).

Parts: S., CT., T., 5ª, Bs.

Errors: m. 106, T., rest for this m. missing.

Musica Ficta: mm. 2 (b♮′), 3 (e♭′), 5 (b♮′), 7 (c♯″), 11 (f♯′, twice), 28 (f♯′), 35 (b♮′), 37 (c♯″), 41 (f♯′, twice), 58 (f♯′, twice), 60 (f♯′), 70 (5ª: b♮, c♯′), 78 (f♯′, twice), 81 (b♮′), 83 (b♮′), 124 (f♯′).

Remarks: In S. and Bs., "viellars" is syllabified "viel-lars" (not "vie-llars"). The sharp is only indicated for the initial n. affected in: mm. 67, T.; 69, 5ª; 94 and 97, CT. Ditto, for the natural sign, m. 95, S. Ditto for the flat in: mm. 113 and 121, S.; 114, T.; 121, 5ª; and 122, Bs. In m. 99, 5ª, the second flat *is* indicated in the source. At mm. 75–6, CT., the leap of a diminished fourth occurs; an accidental recommended by the editor, m. 72, brings about the same leap, also in the CT., at a cognate passage. A cross-relation, repeated, is found at mm. 55–7. At m. 69, an augmented triad is followed by a simultaneous cross-relation. The sonority of an augmented triad also occurs at m. 115. An *appoggiatura* (f′) and the decorated resolution of a suspension (5ª) appear in m. 70. In addition, at mm. 19–20 (CT.) and 49–50 (T.), there is unusual, arpeggio-like melodic writing.

27. Nicolas, *Je ry & si ay larmes* (fol. 14ʳ)

Lyrics: I laugh and, indeed, there are tears in my eyes,
   I sing, without enjoying it,
   I dance to the sound of grief,
   I take my pleasure and if there is only pain,
   I laugh and, indeed, there are tears in my eyes.

Parts: S., CT., T., 5ª, Bs.

Errors: In CT., "larme" or "l'arme" (not "larmes"); also, m. 43, "si" (not "sir"); and, last m., comma (not period). Mm. 90–4, T. and Bs., "l'armes" (not "larmes").

Musica Ficta: mm. 3 (e♭′), 7 (e♭′), 8 (c♯′, twice, and b♮), 13 (e♭″), 14 (c♯″, twice, and b♮′), 22 (f♯′, twice), 26 (e♭′), 28 (e♭′), 36 (e♭″), 37 (e♭′), 48 (e♭), 62 (e♭′), 65 (f♯′), 77 (f♯′), 82 (e♭″), 86 (f♯′, twice).

Remarks: Sharp only indicated for the first n. affected in m. 15, 5ª; ditto, for the flat, m. 42, CT. and Bs. Among the dissonances found in this chanson are: a ⁶₄ triad, mm. 7–8; a simultaneous cross-relation, m. 18; a most unusual escaped-n. (c′), m. 58, possibly illustrating the text, "au son de desplaisir"; a very attractive restruck suspension (c′), m. 95. At mm. 43–5, the 5ª sings only in perfect intervals, including consecutive descending fourths.

28. Nicolas, *Tout ce qu'on peut* (fol. 14ᵛ)

Lyrics: All that one can see in her,

Is only sweetness and affection,
Goodness, beauty, and a willingness,
All full of loving compassion,
But I am not better satisfied by anything,
Because her glance,
Puts me into such pain,
That [I] cannot speak of it by halves,
When I see her, I am tormented,
If I do not see her, I grieve.

[2.ª *pars:*] The sweet is never without the bitter,
   That's the way it is when one loves too much,
   The sweet is never without the bitter,
   That's the way it is when one loves too much.

Parts: S., CT., T., 5ª, Bs.

Errors: mm. 107, 5ª, sbr. (not br.); Bs., comma (not period).

Musica Ficta: mm. 4 (e♭′), 6 (T., last n.: e♭′), 8 (e♭), 11 (e♭′), 13 (c♯′), 17 (f♯′), 18 (f♯′), 19 (f♯′), 22 (f♯′), 25 (e♭′), 27 (e♭″), 29 (e♭′), 31 (e♭), 32 (f♯), 34 (e♭′), 36 (c♯′), 41 (f♯′), 48 (c♯′), 49 (f♯′), 50 (c♯′), 51 (f♯′), 55 (f♯′, twice), 56 (f♯′), 64 (f♯′), 70 (e♭′), 72 (e♭″, c♯″), 78 (c♯′), 82 (c♯′), 102 (e♭′), 103 (c♯′, twice), 114 (e♭′), 120 (e♭′), 121 (c♯′), 123 (e♭), 124 (b♮, e♭″), 125 (e♭″, twice), 131 (e♭′, twice), 142 (e♭′), 147 (b♮), 149 (e♭′), 150 (e♭′), 151 (e♭′), 152 (f♯′).

Remarks: Sharp only indicated for the initial n. affected, m. 95, CT.; ditto, for the flat, mm. 130 and 146, Bs., and 156, T. In m. 119, CT., the second sharp *is* indicated in the source. Simultaneous cross-relations occur, in this chanson, at mm. 40 (cf. m. 16) and 52, a simple cross-relation at m. 92. The sonority of an augmented triad is found at mm. 14 and 107; the latter, preceded by a ⁶₄, is brought about by an anticipation (c♯′) of the major third of the final cadence of the work's *prima pars.* At m. 49, there is a diminished triad in root position. Parallel octaves are twice found at m. 120, parallel seconds at mm. 121 and 126. There are many instances of melodic writing in individual parts atypical for the time: at mm. 115–6, the CT., in effect, leaps a diminished seventh, the Bs., a minor ninth. Elsewhere, voices appear, by progression by perfect intervals or by outlining chords, to function harmonically more than melodically: mm. 78–83 (Bs.), 116–8 (Bs.), 134–6 (5ª), 137–40 (Bs.), 138–140 (T.), and 153–5 (5ª).

29. Nicolas, *A ce matin* (fol. 15ᵛ)

Lyrics: This morning, there will be a real gift,
   Breakfasting on good salted ham,
   And with good wine, a large, full bottle,

For [it] is swallowed tenderly by me,
To have a good fire,
White kneaded bread,
Accompanied by a lovely woman with a graceful form,
But nevertheless having drink and merriment,
The most important thing is to have money.

Parts: S., CT., T., 5ª, Bs.
Musica Ficta: mm. 1 (e♭), 2 (CT.: b♮), 7 (b♮′), 8 (b♮′), 12 (f♯′), 14 (e♭″), 15 (5ª: b♮), 20 (b♮′), 21 (b♮′), 25 (f♯′), 36 (c♯″), 38 (c♯′), 50 (e♭), 51 (e♭′, twice), 62 (e♭″), 65 (b♮), 66 (f♯′).
Remarks: Sharp only indicated for the initial n. affected in mm. 5, S., and 52, CT.; ditto, for the flat, mm. 12 and 64, CT., 32 and 69, 5ª, and 69, Bs. The presence of numerous examples of harmonically derived voice-leading in such a homophonic composition is not surprising, e.g., at mm. 3, 10−11, 23−4, and 70 (5ª); 7 and 20 (CT.), 9−12, 16−17, 22−3, 30−2, 44−6, 52−61 (with the same pattern stated three times), and 67−70 (Bs.); and 68−70 (T.); nor is the S. wholly exempt from the work's prevalent harmonic style. At mm. 19 and 40, passing nn. produce augmented triads.

30. Nicolas, *Pour ton amour* (fol. 16ʳ) [C. Marot]

Lyrics: For your love, I have suffered so much vexation,
For so many days and so many long nights,
That the hope which holds me is warned,
That despair holds back the course of heaven,
To that aim which, not drawing near by day,
Draws near from expectation and desire.

Parts: S., 5ª, CT., T., Bs.
Errors: mm. 22 and 25, S., "longue" (not "longues").
Musica Ficta: mm. 5 (e♭″), 11 (e♭′), 16 (c♯″), 38 (f♯′, twice), 55 (f♯, twice), 59 (e♭′), 60 (c♯′, twice, and b♭), 69 (f♯′), 70 (f♯′), 84 (f♯′, twice).
Remarks: Sharp only indicated for the initial n. affected, m. 17, CT. Ditto, for the flat: mm. 29, S.; 75, 81, and 86, CT.; 78, Bs. Ditto, for the natural sign, m. 85, 5ª. In m. 47, S., the second natural sign *is* indicated in the source. At mm. 26−7, a cross-relation occurs; at m. 37, a simultaneous cross-relation. The unique instance in the *Mellange* of a harmonic diminished tenth is found in this composition, at m. 18. In m. 46, an upper auxiliary n. produces the sonority of an augmented triad.

31. Nicolas, *Il est bon enfant* (fol. 16ᵛ)

Lyrics: He is a good creature, he intends no evil,

In my father's garden,
A white bird, which is there,
Which weeps and sighs, nobody knows what is wrong with it,
He is a good creature, he intends no evil.

Parts: S., 5ª, CT., T., Bs.
Errors: The words, "y a", are presented occasionally, in different vv., as "ya", and once, mm. 65−7, 5ª, as "y-a".
Musica Ficta: mm. 4 (e♭′), 10 (e♭′), 12 (e♭″), 13 (e♭′), 14 (e♭′), 16 (f♯′, twice), 26 (c♯″), 28 (e♭″), 29 (e♭′), 30 (e♭′), 32 (f♯′), 37 (c♯″, twice, and b♮′), 38 (b♮), 46 (f♯′, twice), 47 (e♭′), 49 (e♭″), 51 (c♯″, twice, and b♮′), 53 (e♭′), 60 (c♯″, twice, and b♮′), 66 (c♯″, twice, and b♮′), 70 (c♯″, twice, and b♮), 73 (e♭″), 74 (e♭″), 76 (c♯″, twice, and b♮′), 84 (e♭′), 99 (e♭″), 100 (e♭), 101 (e♭′), 102 (e♭, e♭″), 105 (e♭′), 112 (f♯′), 118 (f♯′), 136 (e♭′), 143 (b♮′), 144 (e♭″), 145 (e♭′), 146 (e♭′), 148 (f♯′).
Remarks: Flat indicated only for the first n. affected in mm. 142, Bs.; 150, CT.; 156, 5ª. Ditto, for the natural sign, m. 82, T. At mm. 148−50, the Bs. ascends in perfect fourths. A cross-relation, repeated, occurs, mm. 155−6.

32. Richaffort, *Sy je m'y plain*[37] (fol. 17ʳ)

Lyrics: If I complain, I have good reason,
Because I have lost the one in the world,
In whom I had the most profound love,
Who has banished me from her house.

Parts: S., CT., T., 5ª, Bs.
Concordances: Livre, fol. 36ʳ.
Errors: Treatment of "j'avoye" as having an elided (i.e., mute) final letter, not indicated by source, is mandated by mm. 31−5, CT., and 33−40, Bs.
Musica Ficta: mm. 3 (f♯), 8 (f♯), 9 (e♭′), 11 (e♭), 12 (f♯), 14 (f♯), 16 (e♭, f♯′), 17 (b♮, twice), 21 (b♮′, twice), 23 (e♭), 32 (e♭′), 35 (e♭), 36 (f♯), 38 (F♯), 40 (f♯′), 46 (f♯′), 47 (e♭), 49 (f♯: cf. m. 3), 54 (f♯), 55 (e♭′), 57 (e♭), 58 (f♯), 62 (f♯′), 66 (f♯), 68 (e♭′), 70 (f♯′).

33. Ad. Vuillart [Willaert], *Sonnez m'y donc*[38] (fol. 17ᵛ)

Lyrics: Ring for me then, when you go,
To lead your flock of lambs,
To pasture,
In the shadow of a green tree,
Near a sweetbriar,
[I] found a shepherdess [there] hidden,

She was my valentine,
Who made a garland,
All of rose and lily,
So nice is my friend,
That he said to me, turn your ewes,
Who are eating my sheaf [of straw],
To pasture,
Ring for me then, when you go,
To lead your flock of lambs,
To pasture.

Parts: S., CT., T., 5ᵃ, Bs.
Concordances: Livre, fol. 5ᵛ.
Errors: mm. 70, T., and 74, 5ᵃ and Bs., "roses" (with elided "e", not "rose" also
with elided "e"); mm. 89ff, "Q'uil" (not "Qu'il").
Musica Ficta: mm. 13 (f♯), 26 (e♭′), 28 (f♯′), 31 (e♭′), 32 (e♭′), 33 (f♯′), 34 (e♭′),
38 (b♮, e♭′), 42 (e♭), 49 (e♭′), 50 (f♯′), 51 (e♭′), 55 (b♮, e♭′), 59 (e♭′), 70 (c♯′), 74
(e♭′), 75 (c♯′), 80 (e♭′), 83 (5ᵃ: f♯), 84 (c♯″), 87 (f♯′), 91 (f♯), 100 (e♭), 101 (e♭′),
103 (5ᵃ: e♭′), 105 (e♭′), 107 (e♭′), 108 (f♯′), 113 (e♭′), 116 (e♭′), 117 (f♯′), 118 (e♭),
124 (e♭′, twice), 125 (e♭′), 132 (f♯′), 145 (e♭′), 147 (f♯′).
Remarks: m. 5, CT., flat only indicated for first n.

34. Ad. Vuillard [Willaert], *Puis que j'ay perdu ma maitresse* (fol. 18ʳ)

Lyrics: Since I have lost my mistress,
Through hard and changeable luck,
For what [reason] do I continue in this world,
Since my heart is full of pain,
Which, from my regret, does not cease.

Parts: S., CT., T., 5ᵃ, Bs.
Concordances: Livre, fol. 3ᵛ.
Musica Ficta: mm. 5 (e♭′), 9 (e♭′), 16 (b♮), 18 (e♭), 19 (f♯′), 21 (e♭), 42 (CT.: c♯′),
61 (e♭), 67 (e♭′), 70 (e♭′), 73 (c♯′), 78 (e♭′), 79 (c♯′), 83 (c♯′), 85 (f♯), 89 (c♯), 93
(e♭′), 103 (5ᵃ: e♭), 104 (e♭), 105 (e♭′).
Remarks: At m. 18, 5ᵃ, the suspension (f) is resolved by leap or exchange of vv.

35. Crequillon, *En languissant* (fol. 18ᵛ)

Lyrics: Languishing, I pass my days,
Night and day, [I] wait for help,
May relief hasten quickly, my friend,
To help me, because I wish for nothing else,

Or I go[39] to death, faster than the flow [of a river].

Parts: S., CT., T., 5ᵃ, Bs.
*Concordances: Le douziesme livre contenant trente chansons amoureuses a cincq
parties* (Antwerp, T. Susato, 1558; = RISM 1558₉), fol. 13ʳ; *Livre,* fol. 24ᵛ.[40]
Musica Ficta: mm. 3 (e♭′), 5 (e♭′), 7 (b♮), 8 (c♯′), 11 (e♭), 14 (e♭′), 15 (e♭′), 18 (f♯,
e♭), 19 (f♯), 21 (e♭), 22 (e♭′), 28 (e♭), 29 (f♯′), 31 (B♭), 33 (f♯), 35 (f♯′), 36 (e♭′),
38 (b♮), 41 (b♮), 42 (CT.: e♭′), 43 (c♯′), 44 (f♯), 46 (b♮′), 47 (f♯′?), 50 (e♭), 51
(Bs.: e♭, twice), 54 (f♯), 56 (e♭′), 57 (e♭′, twice), 58 (f♯′), 61 (f♯′), 63 (e♭), 64
(e♭, twice), 65 (e♭′), 75 (e♭), 80 (f♯′), 82 (e♭), 85 (e♭), 89 (e♭′), 91 (f♯′), 94 (e♭),
95 (f♯′), 96 (b♮, e♭′), 102 (c♯′), 103 (f♯′), 104 (e♭), 109 (e♭), 111 (f♯′), 114 (e♭),
115 (f♯′), 116 (b♮, e♭′), 122 (c♯′), 123 (f♯), 124 (e♭), 128 (f♯′), 130 (e♭′), 131 (b♮),
132 (e♭′), 133 (e♭′, twice).
Remarks: Note parallel sevenths, m. 121 (between CT. and T.).

36. Crequillon, *Vivre en espoir* (fol. 19ʳ)

Lyrics: To live in hope is fitting for me henceforth,
Since [she] doesn't show herself unyielding toward me,
Heart, body, and possessions, all I abandon to her,
Because [I] do not require another love ever after.

Parts: S., CT., T., 5ᵃ, Bs.
Concordances: Livre, fol. 26ʳ.
Errors: m. 86, S., initial n. is a dt. smi. (dt. mi. in source);[41] the interpretation in
this edn. follows m. 108.
Musica Ficta: mm. 5 (e♭′), 6 (e♭′), 10 (e♭′), 12 (c♯′), 14 (f♯′), 16 (e♭), 21 (e♭′), 28
(e♭), 30 (e♭), 33 (c♯′), 39 (Bs.: e♭), 45 (e♭′), 47 (e♭′), 53 (e♭′), 59 (e♭′), 60 (f♯′), 62
(c♯′), 65 (e♭), 75 (e♭), 81 (e♭), 97 (e♭′), 115 (b♮), 116 (e♭′), 118 (e♭).
Remarks: Cf. S., mm. 84 and 106.

37. Ad. Vuillard [Willaert], *Aller m'y faut*[42] (fol. 19ᵛ)

Lyrics: I must go to the verdant countryside,
To look for amusement in some good place,
To be bold,[43] lively, and merry,
Secret pasture is never found,
Friend, I have [no-one] who solicits me,
I must go to the verdant countryside,
Friend, I have [no-one] who solicits me,
From the game of love, alas, I endure too much,
I must go to the verdant countryside,
Friend, I have [no-one] who solicits me,

From the game of love, alas, I endure too much,
If I find a galant,
Of my own volition, I will make [him] an overture,
If I enter this wood, [I] shall meet some creature,
I must go to the verdant countryside.

Parts: S., 5ª, CT., T., Bs.
Concordances: Livre, fol. 47ᵛ.⁴⁴
Errors: mm. 78ff, Bs., and 91ff, other vv., "j'eu" (not "jeu").
Musica Ficta: mm. 5 (e♭'), 8 (f♯', thrice), 12 (e♭'), 14 (e♭'), 15 (f♯', thrice), 18 (f♯', thrice), 30 (e♭), 32 (e♭), 42 (e♭'), 44 (e♭'), 45 (f♯'), 46 (e♭'), 49 (e♭), 52 (f♯, thrice), 58 (c♯''), 63 (c♯'), 68 (c♯''), 78 (e♭'), 80 (b♮), 81 (e♭', twice), 85 (e♭'), 86 (c♯'), 96 (e♭'), 98 (b♮), 100 (b♮), 102 (f♯', b♮'), 114 (T., initial n.: e♭), 122 (e♭'), 126 (e♭'), 133 (e♭'), 136 (f♯', thrice), 140 (e♭'), 142 (e♭'), 143 (f♯', thrice), 146 (f♯', thrice), 150 (e♭).
Remarks: Sharp only indicated for the first n. affected in mm. 56, 5ª, and 77 and 95, CT. Ditto, for the flat, m. 109, S. An augmented triad is produced, m. 56, by a passing n. (b♭').

38. Maillard, *Force d'amour* (fol. 20ᵛ) [Ste. Marthe]

Lyrics: Force of love — often [it] all but compels me,
To declare openly to you my heart,
But your refusal, which always is to be feared,
Until the present has discouraged me,
From which, [I] am compelled to endure patiently,
Concealing my misfortune as much as I can, [and,]
On the other hand, the favor I pursue,
[Whose] remembrance increases my martyrdom,
Alas! Observe the torment to which I have come,
I want to speak and cannot one word say.

Parts: S., CT., T., 5ª, Bs.
Concordances: Livre, fol. 13ʳ.
Errors: m. 124, Bs., point of exclamation omitted.
Musica Ficta: mm. 5 (c♯''), 7 (c♯'), 8 (b♭), 12 (b♭), 13 (f♯'), 14 (b♭', twice), 15 (e♭'), 16 (b♭'), 24 (g♯'), 31 (c♯''), 33 (c♯'), 34 (b♭), 38 (b♭), 39 (f♯'), 40 (b♭', twice), 41 (e♭'), 42 (b♭'), 43 (b♭, twice), 50 (g♯'), 55 (b♭'), 63 (b♭', twice), 67 (b♭'), 68 (b♭', c♯''), 72 (b♭'), 73 (f♯'), 75 (b♭'), 76 (c♯'), 78 (c♯'), 80 (c♯''), 81 (b♭), 86 (c♯'), 87 (c♯'), 89 (c♯'), 100 (b♭, f♯'), 101 (b♭'), 114 (b♭), 115 (c♯''), 127 (b♭, f♯'), 128 (b♭'), 131 (c♯'), 141 (b♭), 142 (c♯''), 145 (b♭, f♯), 146 (b♭).

Remarks: m. 59, 5ª, flat only indicated for first n. Repeat-marks and second-endings in S., CT., and T., for mm. 117 or 118ff in those parts.

39. Nicolas, *N'aurai-je*⁴⁵ *jamais mieux* (fol. 21ʳ)

Lyrics: Will I never have better than I have,
Attending her wherever I dwell,
Will I live always in pain,
Won't you remember me,
That I am yours and will [so] be.

Parts: S., CT., T., 5ª, Bs.
Errors: Second word ("jamais") reads "j'amais"; m. 33, 5ª, initial n. reads a (not c'); mm. 62 and 89, T., elision of "tre" with "&" not indicated.
Musica Ficta: mm. 7 (b♭'), 11 (c♯''), 18 (g♯'), 24 (c♯''), 31 (b♭), 41 (T., second n.: b♭), 45 (b♭'), 51 (c♯''), 53 (b♭), 55 (c♯'), 57 (b♭), 60 (c♯''), 70 (b♭), 71 (b♭'), 77 (c♯''), 80 (f♯), 81 (c♯'), 84 (b♭'), 86 (c♯'').
Remarks: Flat only indicated for initial n. affected in mm. 12, 5ª; 52 and 78, S. Ditto, for the sharp, m. 25, CT. There are simultaneous cross-relations at mm. 13 and 48 (for the latter, cf. m. 74); at m. 21, an *appoggiatura* (B); at m. 28 (bt. 2), a seventh chord; and at mm. 29, 39, 53, and 79, augmented triads. The augmented triad, m. 29, is followed, without interruption, by a harmonic augmented second (between CT. and T.). The T., moving into m. 30, produces a cross-relation (g♮') with the CT. (on g♯'), m. 29.

40. Maillard, *Helas ma fille, il te tuera* (fol. 21ᵛ)

Lyrics: Alas, daughter, he will kill you,
With his big thing, which he wiggles about,
Alas, mother, that won't happen,
Entirely naked, [I] am strong enough,
[I] imbibe, with great endurance, standing up,
[A] woman on the wrong side⁴⁶ bears a great deal,
I don't care if he kills me,
But may I die from a handsome thrust.

Parts: S., 5ª, CT., T., Bs.
Concordances: Livre, fol. 13ᵛ.
Errors: mm. 5, T., and 6, Bs., elision not indicated in source.
Musica Ficta: mm. 1 (e♭''), 2 (e♭''), 3 (c♯''), 6 (c♯''), 11 (c♯'), 12 (b♭, c♯''), 13 (f♯', thrice), 15 (b♭', thrice), 16 (c♯': applied to avoid simultaneous cross-relation and because it ascends, even though it forms part of the leap of a diminished fourth), 17 (e♭''), 18 (c♯''), 21 (c♯''), 23 (c♯'': cf. m. 8), 26 (c♯'), 27 (b♭, c♯''), 28 (f♯', twice),

30 (b♭′), 31 (b♭), 32 (c♯″), 38 (b♭′), 39 (b♭′), 41 (c♯″), 42 (b♭′), 43 (c♯′), 45 (c♯′),
46 (f♯′), 50 (b♭′), 51 (b♭′), 52 (g♯′), 55 (c♯′?, twice), 59 (c♯″, g♯′ — cf. m. 79,
and b♭), 61 (b♭′, twice), 63 (b♭′, twice, and c♯′), 64 (b♭′, twice), 66 (b♭′), 67 (b♭′,
twice), 68 (c♯″, twice — cf. m. 87), 71 (c♯′), 73 (c♯′), 74 (b♭′), 77 (c♯′, twice),
78 (5ª: c♯″), 82 (b♭′, twice, and c♯′), 83 (b♭′, twice), 85 (b♭), 86 (b♭′, twice), 90
(b♭′, twice, and c♯″), 91 (e♭″), 92 (b♭′, twice).
Remarks: Flat only indicated for the initial n. involved in mm. 7, 22, 73, and 80,
Bs.; ditto, for the sharp, mm. 15, 57, and 74, S. The augmented-triad sonority
found in mm. 16, 68, and 87 is further borne out in this composition by the use, at
mm. 16–7, of the leap of a diminished fourth (cf. *musica ficta,* m. 16) and the
unique instance in the *Mellange,* at mm. 79–80, of the interval of an augmented
sixth (cf. *musica ficta,* m. 59): all representative of a type of whole-tone harmony.

41. Roussel, *Content ou non* (fol. 22ʳ)

Lyrics: Content or not, I must endure it,
   Beyond my wish and my sole hope,
   Buf if once it comes into my power,
   I shall end that with which I am putting up too long.

Parts: S., CT., T., 5ª, Bs.
Concordances: Livre, fol. 50ᵛ.[47]
Musica Ficta: mm. 8 (c♯′), 14 (e♭′), 18 (f♯), 22 (e♭′), 27 (e♭), 30 (f♯′), 31 (b♮), 33
(e♭), 42 (c♯′), 44 (e♭′), 45 (e♭), 48 (e♭′), 51 (f♯, twice), 55 (e♭′), 57 (c♯′), 63
(e♭′), 66 (e♭), 71 (f♯′), 72 (b♮), 76 (e♭), 78 (b♮), 93 (f♯′), 95 (b♮), 110 (f♯′), 116
(B♮).
Remarks: Flat only indicated for first n. affected, m. 112, 5ª.

42. Ad. Vuillard [Willaert], *Je l'ay aymée* (fol. 22ᵛ)

Lyrics: I [have] loved [48] her, a good seven and a half years,
   My love, my infatuated one, whom my heart has chosen,
   Presuming that she was my friend,
   But she has lied about it,
   Another, through envy,
   Yes, has banished me from her,
   Alas, I have lost my solace,
   Oh God, Oh Dear, I have lost my friend.

Parts: S., CT., 5ª, T., Bs.
Concordances: Livre, fol. 5ʳ.[49]
Errors: mm. 68, S., final letter of "elle" not elided; 70–3, T., "mamye" (not
"m'amye").

Musica Ficta: mm. 4 (e♭), 6 (e♭′), 8 (e♭′), 11 (e♭), 14 (e♭), 16 (e♭′), 20 (b♭), 30
(e♭′), 36 (e♭′), 39 (e♭′), 40 (e♭′), 43 (b♮), 44 (e♭′), 46 (e♭), 47 (e♭′), 51 (b♮, twice),
53 (e♭′), 55 (e♭′), 56 (c♯′), 58 (e♭), 59 (e♭′), 61 (e♭), 62 (e♭′), 65 (e♭), 66 (b♮), 67
(e♭′), 69 (e♭′), 71 (b♮), 77 (e♭), 78 (e♭′, twice), 82 (e♭′), 84 (e♭′), 85 (CT.: e♭′), 88
(e♭′), 90 (e♭′), 91 (f♯′), 94 (e♭′), 96 (f♯, c♯′), 97 (f♯′), 98 (b♮), 119 (e♭′), 121 (e♭′),
125 (e♭′), 126 (e♭′), 127 (c♯′), 129 (e♭′), 132 (e♭), 133 (f♯′), 136 (e♭′).
Remarks: At m. 17, consecutive dissonances occur; at m. 42, a $\frac{6}{4}$ triad.

43. Phl. Vuildre [Wilder], *Si de beaucoup* (fol. 23ʳ)

Lyrics: If by far I am loved, do not be displeased by it, friend,
   That augments your reputation,
   Which [you] would enjoy from their desire,
   Is it not a great pleasure for you,
   To have in your power alone,
   The entire well-being and the hope,
   Of so many poor lovers,
   Whom your honest pleasure,
   Meanwhile has made unhappy.

Parts: S., CT., T., 5ª, Bs.[50]
Musica Ficta: mm. 4 (e♭′), 6 (e♭), 10 (e♭′), 12 (f♯′, twice), 17 (e♭′), 19 (e♭), 23
(e♭′), 30 (b♮), 35 (e♭), 36 (f♯′), 43 (e♭′), 51 (c♯′), 60 (e♭), 61 (f♯′), 66 (e♭′), 68
(e♭), 72 (e♭′), 79 (e♭′), 81 (e♭), 85 (e♭′).
Remarks: At m. 43, a suspension (a), resolving by leap, produces the sonority of a
chord with a major seventh in it.

44. Roussel, *Banny j'en suis* (fol. 23ᵛ)

Lyrics: By pretence, I am banished,
   But for us to see [each other] again together,
   [You] must be like me,
   In constancy, because it seems to me,
   That when false relations separate,
   Lovers who are together,
   If firm love does not reunite them,
   [They] forever will be separated.

Parts: S., CT., T., 5ª, Bs.
Concordances: Livre, fol. 51ʳ.
Errors: m. 22, 5ª, "ble," (of "ensemble") indicated as elided to the initial syllable
of the word following ("encor'").
Musica Ficta: mm. 9 (e♭′), 26 (e♭′, twice, and f♯), 27 (c♯′), 29 (e♭′), 33 (f♯′), 34

(e♭), 35 (f♯′), 36 (e♭), 37 (e♭), 38 (e♭, B♮), 39 (f♯), 48 (e♭′), 50 (e♭′), 58 (e♭′), 63
(f♯), 65 (e♭), 71 (c♯′), 75 (e♭, twice), 79 (e♭′), 85 (f♯′), 86 (f♯′, e♭), 88 (e♭), 94
(e♭′), 98 (c♯′), 100 (e♭′), 103 (f♯′), 106 (e♭), 110 (e♭′), 112 (e♭′), 116 (c♯′), 118
(e♭′), 121 (f♯′), 122 (b♭), 126 (b♭), 127 (e♭).
Remarks: Flat only indicated for the first n. affected in mm. 12, 5ᵃ, and 64, CT.

45. Nicolas, *Avecques vous mon amour finira* (fol. 24ʳ)

Lyrics: With you, my love will end,
    Since my heart is in you solely,
    May it please you then to be happy,
    Because, [even] with the body dead, the spirit will serve you.

Parts: S., CT., T., 5ᵃ, Bs.
Musica Ficta: mm. 7 (e♭′), 8 (f♯′), 13 (e♭), 18 (e♭, e♭′), 19 (e♭), 20 (f♯′), 36 (c♯″),
41 (c♯′), 50 (e♭), 55 (e♭), 56 (f♯′), 59 (f♯′).
Remarks: Flat only indicated for the initial n. affected in mm. 26, T. and Bs.; 57,
Bs.; 61, CT. Ditto, for the natural sign, m. 21, 5ᵃ. Note diminished triads in root
position at mm. 11, 33.

46. Goudimel, *Amour me tue* (fol. 24ᵛ) [Ronsard]

Lyrics: Love kills me and if I do not want to say,
    The pleasant evil that it is for me to die,
    I am so very afraid, that help would be welcome,
    The evil from which tenderly I sigh,
    It is so true that my languor desires,
    That, with time, I may be able to recover,
    But I do not wish, milady, to request [it],
    By my health,
    So much does my martyrdom please me.

Parts: S., 5ᵃ, CT., T., Bs.
Concordances: Modern editions: *Anthologie de la chanson parisienne au XVIe
siècle* (ed. F. Lesure, et al., 1952), 85; *Claude Goudimel: Oeuvres Complètes* (ed.
P. Pidoux, et al.), XIII (1974), 11.
Errors: mm. 73–4, S., "pensse" (not "puisse").
Musica Ficta: mm. 14 (e♭′), 22 (c♯′, twice, and b♮), 39 (f♯′, twice), 40 (S.: b♮′), 44
(b♮′), 48 (f♯′), 56 (f♯′), 62 (f♯′, twice), 74 (c♯′), 78 (c♯′), 98 (f♯′, twice), 101 (f♯,
twice), 104 (f♯′, twice), 107 (ditto).
Remarks: Natural sign only indicated for the initial n. affected in mm. 49, T., and
76, 5ᵃ; ditto, for the flat, m. 65, S.

47. Crequillon, *Pis ne me peut venir* (fol. 25ʳ)

Lyrics: Worse cannot come to me,
    Than I have until now,
    For your remembrance, I languish in anxiety,
    And am far from mercy,
    Treated too rudely,
    Your callous heart,
    Gives me this torment.

Parts: S., CT., 5ᵃ, T., Bs.
Concordances: Livre, fol. 6ʳ; modern edition: *Antonio Valente: Intavolatura de
Cimbalo (Naples, 1576)* (ed. C. Jacobs, 1973), 152.[51]
Errors: m. 37, S., "loiu" (not "loin").
Musica Ficta: mm. 8 (e♭′), 9 (e♭′), 10 (f♯′), 14 (e♭′), 15 (e♭), 20 (e♭′), 21 (c♯′), 28
(f♯), 30 (e♭), 31 (f♯′), 33 (e♭′), 34 (b♮, e♭′), 36 (e♭″), 40 (e♭′), 41 (b♮, e♭′), 43
(e♭′), 44 (f♯?), 45 (c♯′), 59 (e♭′), 60 (e♭′), 65 (e♭′), 66 (c♯′), 73 (f♯), 75 (e♭), 76
(f♯′), 81 (B♮?, e♭), 82 (e♭).

48. Nicolas, *Sur tous regretz* (fol. 25ᵛ)

Lyrics: Above all regrets, mine most piteously weeps,
    Emitting sighs, piercing through my weary heart,
    Because I have lost the amiable liqueur,
    Which I lament so much and shall lament, for a considerable time,
    Above all regrets.

Parts: S., 5ᵃ, CT., T., Bs.
Musica Ficta: mm. 15 (f♯′), 21 (f♯′), 24 (f♯′, twice), 29 (e♭′), 32 (c♯′, twice, and
b♮), 40 (c♯′), 47 (e♭′), 49 (e♭′), 50 (c♯′), 54 (f♯′), 60 (c♯′, twice, and b♮), 63 (f♯′),
65 (e♭′), 67 (e♭′), 70 (c♯′), 76 (c♯′, twice, and b♮), 79 (f♯′), 81 (e♭′), 83 (e♭′), 86
(c♯′), 88 (e♭).
Remarks: Flat only indicated for the first n., m. 10, Bs. In m. 38, implied parallel
octaves occur (between S. and T.); in mm. 94–5, parallel unisons (S. and 5ᵃ).

49. Alf. Farabosco,[52] *Auprés de vous* (fol. 26ʳ)

Lyrics: Near to you, secretly lives,
    My poor heart, without anything to comfort it,
    And indeed [it] languishes for the pain it bears,
    Since [you] want it to die in this torment.

Parts: S., CT., T., 5ᵃ, Bs.
Errors: mm. 10–11, Bs., "Anprés" (not "Auprés").

Musica Ficta: mm. 8 (b♮), 11 (e♭′), 13 (f♯′), 15 (f♯′), 16 (b♮′; CT., last n.: f♯′), 20 (f♯), 23 (c♯′), 26 (b♮′), 28 (e♭′), 33 (b♮), 44 (c♯′, twice, and b♮), 50 (f♯), 60 (e♭′), 62 (b♮), 79 (f♯′), 92 (f♯′).
Remarks: m. 91, CT., flat only indicated for the first n.

50. Josquin, *Je me complein* (fol. 26ᵛ)

Lyrics: I complain about my friend,
        Who was so much in the habit of coming to see me,
        In the fresh forenoon,
        But it is prime and [then] it is midday,
        And indeed [I] hear no news of him, [as] verpers approach,
        The cudgel, the lovely cudgeling.[53]

Parts: S., CT., T., 5ᵃ, Bs.
Concordances: Modern edition: *Josquin des Prés: Werken: Wereldlijke Werken* (ed. A. Smijers, 1921–), I (1922–5), 26.
Errors: mm. 21–2, Bs., "emy" (not "amy").
Musica Ficta: mm. 3 (e♭′), 6 (e♭), 10 (e♭), 28 (e♭′), 30 (c♯′), 48 (b♮), 52 (e♭′), 54 (e♭′), 66 (e♭), 68 (f♯′, twice), 72 (e♭), 73 (b♮), 76 (b♮), 82 (e♭′), 86 (e♭′), 87 (e♭), 88 (f♯′, twice), 89 (e♭′), 90 (b♮), 93 (e♭′), 94 (c♯′, twice, and b♮), 95 (e♭′), 98 (e♭′), 100 (f♯′, twice), 108 (e♭′), 110 (f♯′).
Remarks: At m. 47, a diminished chord in root position occurs.

51. Josquin, *Parfons regretz* (fol. 27ʳ)

Lyrics: Deep regrets and joy lamented,
        Come to me, wherever I may be,
        And hasten, without dissembling,
        To put my heart to death quickly,
        So that, in pain and tears, it may blacken.

Parts: S., CT., T., 5ᵃ, Bs.
Concordances: Modern edition: *Josquin des Prés: Werken: Wereldlijke Werken* (ed. A. Smijers, 1921–), I (1922–5), 5.
Musica Ficta: mm. 4 (e♭′), 5 (e♭′), 6 (e♭′), 11 (e♭′), 12 (e♭′), 17 (e♭′), 18 (e♭′), 22 (b♮′, twice), 36 (f♯), 42 (b♮′, twice), 62 (f♯), 63 (e♭), 64 (e♭, twice), 70 (c♯″, twice, and b♮′), 72 (f♯′), 78 (f♯), 79 (e♭), 80 (e♭, twice), 86 (c♯″), 92 (c♯″), 101 (e♭′), 102 (c♯′), 105 (e♭′), 106 (e♭′), 108 (f♯′), 111 (e♭′), 117 (e♭′), 118 (f♯′, twice), 120 (b♮′), 121 (e♭′), 122 (e♭′), 125 (e♭′), 126 (e♭′), 128 (e♭′).
Remarks: A cross-relation occurs at mm. 30–1 and 50–1.

52. Ad. Vuillard [Willaert], *Voulez ouir chansonnette* (fol. 27ᵛ)

Lyrics: Do [you] wish to hear a ditty,
        [About] what happened in Paris day before yesterday,
        About three women of Montmartre,
        Who danced in a field,
        The psalter and prayer books of the most beautiful of the three fell to the
                ground, in fact, indeed,
        And my God, remarked the abbess,
        I did not know,
        That the root of teeth,
        Had to be sought so deeply,
        Your lower parts will be stuffed,
        By gripping the crupper,[54] *in fact, indeed.*

Parts: S., CT., T., 5ᵃ, Bs.[55]
Errors: mm. 59–60, T., "psauier" (not "psautier").
Musica Ficta: mm. 6 (c♯′), 10 (c♯′), 11 (c♯′), 13 (b♮), 14 (e♭′), 15 (e♭″), 16 (c♯″), 18 (f♯′), 19 (c♯′), 27 (c♯′, f♯), 31 (c♯′), 32 (c♯′), 33 (f♯′, twice), 34 (b♮′), 35 (e♭′), 36 (f♯′), 37 (b♮, e♭′), 38 (b♮, thrice), 40 (c♯″), 41 (e♭′), 43 (e♭′), 44 (e♭″), 45 (c♯″), 47 (e♭′), 48 (e♭), 50 (e♭″), 52 (b♮), 53 (c♯′), 55 (c♯′, thrice, and b♮), 57 (e♭′), 63 (c♯′), 65 (e♭′), 67 (e♭′), 69 (f♯′), 71 (e♭′), 72 (e♭′), 73 (e♭′), 75 (c♯′), 76 (c♯″), 77 (e♭″), 79 (c♯″, twice, and b♮′), 82 (e♭′), 83 (e♭′), 85 (c♯′), 87 (c♯′), 90 (e♭′), 91 (c♯′), 93 (c♯″), 95 (e♭′, f♯′), 97 (c♯′), 100 (e♭′), 103 (c♯′), 105 (f♯, thrice), 106 (b♮′), 109 (f♯′), 112 (c♯″, b♮′), 116 (e♭″), 117 (c♯″), 120 (e♭′), 121 (c♯′), 122 (e♭′), 124 (e♭″), 128 (c♯′), 132 (f♯′), 137 (c♯″), 138 (e♭″), 140 (e♭′), 142 (e♭′, twice), 146 (e♭′), 148 (f♯′), 150 (e♭′), 151 (c♯′), 152 (e♭′), 153 (c♯″), 154 (f♯′, twice), 155 (f♯), 158 (f♯), 160 (c♯′), 161 (e♭″), 162 (c♯″), 165 (f♯).

53. Josquin, *N'est-ce pas un grand desplaisir* (fol. 28ʳ)

Lyrics: Isn't it a great misfortune,
        When I do not dare, for my pleasure,
        For my well-being, and for my health,
        To make my wish mine,
        And indeed [I] have absolutely no other desire.

Parts: S., CT., T., 5ᵃ, Bs.
Concordances: *Livre,* fol. 29ʳ; modern edition: *Josquin des Prés: Werken: Wereldlijke Werken* (ed. A. Smijers, 1921–), I (1922–5), 17.
Musica Ficta: mm. 4 (b♭′), 8 (b♭), 17 (g♯′), 18 (b♭′), 20 (g♯′), 24 (g♯′), 28 (b♭′), 32 (b♭), 41 (g♯), 42 (b♭′), 44 (g♯′), 48 (g♯′), 52 (b♭), 62 (e♭′), 64 (c♯′), 66 (e♭′), 67 (B♭), 68 (c♯′), 73 (b♭′), 74 (b♭), 76 (e♭′), 77 (b♭′), 78 (g♯′, twice, and f♯′).

Remarks: Note repeated cross-relation, used at the end of the chanson, mm. 79–85.

54. Ad. Vuillard [Willaert], *Mort ou mercy* (fol. 28ᵛ) [J. Marot]

Lyrics: Death or mercy, while languishing, I wait,
  But knowing that in vain I lose my time,
  Reason advises, but prudence [otherwise] exhorts me,
  To leave all, but love is so strong,
  That my spirits are not at all satisifed.

Parts: S., CT., T., 5ᵃ, Bs.
Concordances: Livre, fol. 4ᵛ.
Musica Ficta: mm. 5 (c♯′), 7 (f♯), 8 (b♭), 12 (c♯′, B♭), 13 (c♯′), 17 (b♭), 19 (f♯), 20 (b♭), 21 (e♭), 22 (f♯), 23 (b♭, twice), 26 (b♭′), 30 (b♭), 31 (g♯), 32 (g♯), 37 (c♯′), 39 (b♭), 40 (g♯′), 42 (f♯′), 46 (f♯′), 51 (g♯), 56 (c♯′), 59 (b♭), 60 (c♯′), 62 (c♯′), 63 (c♯′, twice), 64 (b♭), 66 (g♯), 67 (f♯), 69 (g♯′), 71 (f♯′, g♯′), 73 (b♭′), 76 (b♭), 77 (e♭′, b♭), 79 (c♯′), 85 (b♭′), 88 (b♭), 89 (e♭′, b♭), 91 (c♯′), 94 (b♭), 95 (g♯), 97 (g♯), 99 (g♯), 101 (b♮), 102 (c♯′), 103 (B♭), 104 (c♯′, f♯), 107 (b♭), 108 (c♯′), 110 (e♭′), 111 (g♯), 112 (c♯′), 113 (f♯′), 114 (g♯), 116 (g♯), 119 (b♭′), 120 (g♯), 122 (g♯′), 123 (c♯′).

55. Josquin, *Coeur langoureux* (fol. 29ʳ)

Lyrics: Weary heart, whose only act is to reflect,
  To complain, to groan, to weep, and to sigh,
  Rejoice,
  For your beautiful mistress,
  Through her pity, wishes to give you merriment,
  Joy and pleasure, in order to revive you.

Parts: S., CT., T., 5ᵃ, Bs.
Concordances: Modern edition: *Josquin des Prés: Werken: Wereldlijke Werken* (ed. A. Smijers, 1921–), I (1922–5), 1.
Errors: m. 21, T., "que-" (not "que"); mm. 80–2, S., "donver" (not "donner").
Musica Ficta: mm. 16 (f♯′), 19 (b♭), 20 (b♭), 23 (b♭), 36 (f♯′), 39 (b♭), 40 (b♭), 44 (c♯″), 48 (c♯″), 51 (e♭′, b♭), 52 (f♯′), 55 (e♭′, b♭), 56 (f♯′), 61 (Bs.: b♭), 62 (b♭, f♯), 63 (b♭′, b♭), 64 (f♯′), 66 (e♭′, twice), 68 (e♭′), 79 (b♭), 80 (b♭′), 82 (c♯′), 89 (B♭), 90 (f♯, twice), 91 (b♭), 92 (b♭), 97 (b♭′), 98 (g♯′, twice, and f♯′), 101 (b♭′), 102 (g♯′, twice, and f♯′), 103 (c♯′), 105 (c♯′), 106 (c♯′, twice), 109 (c♯′), 110 (c♯′, twice).
Remarks: m. 59, T., flat indicated only for the first n.

56. Nicolas, *Las voulez vous* (fol. 29ᵛ)

Lyrics: Alas, do you want a person to sing,
  Whose heart only can sigh,
  Let someone contented sing,
  And leave me to endure my sole evil.[56]

Parts: S., CT., T., 5ᵃ, Bs.[57]
Musica Ficta: mm. 14 (g♯′?), 20 (g♯′), 32 (e♭, twice), 47 (f♯′), 58 (c♯″), 69 (b♭), 73 (f♯′), 75 (e♭′), 79 (5ᵃ: c♯′), 84 (e♭′, b♭′), 86 (CT.: b♭), 92 (b♭′), 94 (g♯′).
Remarks: Sharp only indicated for the initial n. affected in mm. 36, 60, and 100, T.; 56 and 66, Bs.; 57, 64, 67, and 98, 5ᵃ; 62 and 68, S.; and 70, CT. Among the unusual features of this composition are: extensive use of the sonority of the augmented triad, at mm. 36 and 41 (preceded by $\frac{6}{4}$ chords), 57, 60, 62, 64, and 81 (another $\frac{6}{4}$ chord is found at m. 86); cross-relations, at mm. 41–2 (where the descent of a chromatic semitone is suggested), 72–3, and 102–3; and diminished triads in root position, at mm. 56 and 66.

57. Josquin, *Je ne me puis tenir d'aymer* (fol. 30ʳ)

Lyrics: I cannot keep myself from loving,
  Her who doesn't love me at all,
  I should [be] truly discomfitted,
  Because I have lost my anxiety:
  My sovereign lady,
  Receive your friend,
  With your whole goodness,
  Or death comes by halves.[58]

Parts: S., CT., T., 5ᵃ, Bs.
Concordances: Livre, fol. 30ᵛ; modern edition: *Josquin des Prés: Werken: Wereldlijke Werken* (ed. A. Smijers, 1921–), I (1922–5), 78.[59]
Errors: m. 65, 5ᵃ, last n. (a) given as smi. (not fu.; = sfu. in this edition).
Musica Ficta: mm. 8 (g♯′), 9 (f♯), 13 (e♭′), 14 (c♯′), 21 (b♭′), 22 (g♯′), 28 (b♭), 30 (g♯), 34 (c♯′), 38 (c♯′), 54 (B♭), 64 (b♭′), 65 (b♭), 66 (g♯′), 70 (g♯′), 71 (c♯′), 72 (c♯′, twice), 76 (c♯′), 79 (c♯′), 80 (B♭), 83 (g♯′), 87 (g♯′), 93 (g♯′), 98 (B♭), 100 (g♯′), 102 (b♭), 105 (b♭), 106 (g♯′), 108 (b♭), 111 (g♯′), 113 (b♭′), 116 (g♯′), 123 (g♯′), 131 (b♭), 133 (e♭′), 134 (c♯′), 137 (b♭), 138 (g♯), 142 (g♯), 144 (b♭′), 148 (c♯′: cf. m. 152), 149 (c♯).
Remarks: m. 37, 5ᵃ, flat only indicated for the first n. At m. 28, a seventh chord occurs; at m. 104, an *appoggiatura* (c′) appearing like a seventh; and at mm. 151–2, a cross-relation, involving, in effect, an ascending chromatic semitone.

58. Godard, *Puis qu'ainsi est* (fol. 30ᵛ)

Lyrics: Since thus it is that all those alive,
    Find death in this terrestrial world,
    And that we all forcibly have to be on Earth,
    I abandon love and have no more longing for it.

Parts: S., CT., 5ᵃ, T., Bs.
Concordances: Livre, fol. 27ᵛ.
Errors: Two clefs — Tenor and Alto — are provided on the opening staff of the Tenor. The latter is superfluous: its original, canonic, function is taken by the music given in the 5ᵃ partbook.
Musica Ficta: mm. 5 (g♯'), 20 (g♯'), 22 (b♭), 24 (b♭'), 26 (b♭), 35 (e♭), 39 (b♭), 41 (f♯), 49 (f♯'), 53 (f♯), 57 (f♯'), 59 (e♭), 60 (f♯'), 64 (f♯'), 65 (b♭'), 67 (c♯'), 71 (g♯), 74 (g♯), 81 (b♭'), 82 (g♯'), 90 (f♯'), 97 (b♭'), 111 (b♭'), 112 (g♯'), 113 (c♯', twice), 114 (c♯', twice).

59. Ad. Vuillard [Willaert], *Vous aurez tout ce qui est mien* (fol. 31ʳ)

Lyrics: You will have all that is mine,
    If I can by no [other] means,
    Obtain your good favor,
    Because in this world not to pursue,
    [Is] never to recover something else good.

Parts: S., 5ᵃ, CT., T., Bs.
Concordances: Livre, fol. 4ʳ.
Musica Ficta: mm. 6 (b♭'), 10 (b♭'), 12 (g♯'), 13 (b♭), 14 (b♭), 15 (B♭), 16 (f♯), 18 (g♯'; and 5ᵃ: b♭), 26 (b♭'), 28 (b♭), 31 (b♭'), 32 (g♯', thrice, and f♯'), 36 (g♯, twice, and f♯'), 40 (b♭'), 45 (f♯', twice), 47 (g♯'), 51 (b♭'), 52 (g♯'), 55 (f♯'), 58 (b♭), 60 (b♭; and 5ᵃ: c♯'), 62 (b♭'), 65 (f♯, b♭), 67 (g♯'), 69 (b♭, f♯'), 70 (b♭), 72 (T.: b♭), 73 (b♭'), 74 (b♭), 75 (f♯'), 76 (b♭'), 79 (g♯'?), 81 (b♭'), 82 (b♭), 87 (b♭), 93 (c♯''), 94 (c♯'), 95 (c♯').

60. Crequillon, *A jamais croy* (fol. 31ᵛ)

Lyrics: There will never be, [I] believe, the equal,
    To you, lady, of exceeding beauty,
    [I] think so much of you, that, while sleeping, I awaken,
    In short, without seeing you, it won't be long before [I] die.

Parts: S., CT., T., 5ᵃ, Bs.
Concordances: Livre, fol. 25ʳ.
Musica Ficta: mm. 7 (e♭'), 8 (b♮), 9 (c♯'), 14 (f♯'), 19 (e♭), 21 (c♯'), 23 (f♯'), 24

(f♯), 28 (f♯'), 32 (e♭), 34 (e♭), 35 (b♮), 38 (e♭', f♯), 40 (e♭), 43 (e♭, e♭'), 46 (e♭', e♭), 48 (e♭', twice), 51 (e♭, e♭'), 57 (c♯'), 64 (e♭), 65 (b♭'), 74 (e♭), 75 (f♯'), 76 (e♭), 85 (f♯), 88 (e♭, e♭'), 90 (c♯'), 93 (e♭, twice), 102 (f♯), 105 (e♭, e♭'), 107 (S.: c♯'), 111 (f♯), 113 (f♯).

61. Crequillon, *Content ou non* (fol. 32ʳ)

Lyrics:[60] Content or not, I must endure it,
    By reason of luck, so very perverse and hard,
    Indeed, I must endure so much lassitude,
    From which [I] shall suffer, expecting [it] to last longer.

Parts: S., CT., T., 5ᵃ, Bs.
Concordances: Livre, fol. 25ᵛ.[61]
Musica Ficta: mm. 5 (f♯'), 14 (e♭), 15 (e♭), 16 (B♮), 17 (f♯), 18 (e♭'), 19 (e♭), 20 (e♭', e♭), 22 (f♯), 24 (b♮), 31 (c♯'), 35 (e♭'), 40 (e♭'), 45 (e♭'), 46 (f♯), 49 (e♭), 53 (e♭'), 54 (e♭), 59 (f♯'), 62 (e♭), 63 (f♯), 70 (e♭'), 72 (e♭), 73 (e♭), 74 (b♮), 76 (e♭'), 85 (c♯'), 87 (b♮, e♭'), 89 (b♮), 91 (b♮), 93 (c♯''), 95 (c♯'), 98 (e♭'), 99 (f♯), 106 (c♯''), 110 (e♭'), 112 (c♯'), 114 (e♭'), 115 (f♯), 117 (f♯).
Remarks: Note $^6_4$ triad at m. 66.

62. Josquin, *Faute d'argent* (fol. 32ᵛ)

Lyrics: Lack of money — that's incomparable suffering,
    If I say it, alas, I well know why,
    Without cash, one has to remain silent,
    [A] woman who is sleeping can be awakened for money.

Parts: S., CT., T., 5ᵃ, Bs.
Concordances: Livre, fol. 29ᵛ; modern edition: *Josquin des Prés: Werken: Wereldlijke Werken* (ed. A. Smijers, 1921–), I (1922–5), 38.[62]
Errors: mm. 29–32, CT., "n'om-pareille" (not "nom-pareille").
Musica Ficta: mm. 4 (f♯), 6 (e♭), 9 (f♯), 16 (e♭'), 18 (c♯'), 19 (e♭'), 20 (e♭'), 22 (c♯'), 24 (e♭'), 28 (f♯), 31 (c♯'), 37 (f♯), 38 (e♭'), 40 (c♯'), 42 (f♯), 45 (e♭), 46 (f♯), 49 (f♯'), 52 (f♯'), 55 (e♭', b♮), 58 (e♭', b♮), 76 (c♯'), 90 (f♯), 92 (e♭), 95 (f♯), 97 (b♮), 102 (e♭'), 104 (c♯'), 105 (e♭'), 106 (e♭'), 108 (c♯'), 110 (e♭'), 114 (f♯), 117 (c♯'), 123 (f♯), 124 (e♭'), 126 (c♯'), 128 (f♯), 130 (B♮), 131 (f♯), 132 (f♯), 136 (e♭), 138 (T.: e♭), 139 (e♭'), 140 (c♯').
Remarks: At m. 70, there is a diminished chord in root position.

63. Nicolas, *Grace & Vertu* (fol. 33ʳ)

Lyrics: Grace and virtue, goodness, beauty, and nobility,

Are my friend's, there is no reason to conceal it,
[It] displeases me too much to hear ill said of her,
I detest him who offends her honor.

Parts: S., CT., T., 5ª, Bs.
Errors: mm. 38, S., mi. rest missing; 39, Bs., "m'en" (not "me").
Musica Ficta: mm. 12 (g♯′, twice, and f♯′), 19 (B♭), 40 (c♯′), 52 (b♭′), 54 (B♭), 55 (b♭), 56 (b♭′), 58 (g♯′, twice, and f♯′), 60 (g♯), 68 (b♭′), 70 (B♭), 72 (b♭′), 74 (g♯′, twice, and f♯′), 77 (c♯′, twice).
Remarks: Sharp indicated only for the first n. affected in mm. 26, CT., and 75, 5ª; ditto, for the flat, mm. 30, 5ª, and 35, S. Note the cross-relations in mm. 13–15 and 26–8; also, the leap of a diminished fourth in m. 81 (CT.).

64. Millot, *Le cors*[63] *s'en va* (fol. 33ᵛ)

Lyrics: The body dies, and the heart resides [in] you,
Which wishes to make its lodging with you,
In order to wish to love you so much and [with] such strength,
Which incessantly wishes to undertake the endeavor,
In order to serve you until that [time] in which it dies.[64]

Parts: S., CT., T., 5ª, Bs.
Musica Ficta: mm. 13 (f♯′), 16 (e♭), 17 (e♭′, twice), 19 (f♯), 21 (b♮′), 22 (b♮′), 25 (e♭′), 30 (e♭), 41 (f♯′), 47 (f♯′), 50 (CT.: e♭′), 55 (c♯′), 57 (b♮), 58 (b♮), 62 (c♯′), 66 (e♭′), 77 (c♯′), 79 (e♭′), 83 (f♯′), 84 (b♮′), 88 (f♯′), 91 (b♮), 104 (f♯′), 107 (f♯′, twice).
Remarks: At m. 78, CT., the sharp is indicated only for the initial n. affected; ditto, for the flat, m. 100, 5ª. The natural sign is indicated in the source, however, for both nn. in the S., m. 75. Cross-relations are found at mm. 37, 82, and 98 (note ⁶₄ on the initial half of the opening beat of m. 98); a simultaneous cross-relation at m. 54; and consecutive dissonances at m. 107.

65. Millot, *Douce maitresse touche* (fol. 34ʳ) [Ronsard]

Lyrics: Sweet mistress, be near,
To soothe my misfortune,
From your mouth, redder than coral, my snares.

Parts: S., CT., T., 5ª, Bs.
Musica Ficta: mm. 14 (CT., second note: g♯′), 16 (c♯′), 17 (f♯), 19 (c♯″), 24 (f♯′), 25 (f♯′), 27 (c♯″), 29 (e♭″), 30 (c♯″), 31 (e♭″), 34 (g♯′), 36 (c♯″), 39 (f♯′), 42 (c♯″).
Remarks: Sharp only indicated for the initial n. affected in mm. 2 and 7, 5ª, and 28,

S.; ditto, for the flat, m. 8, CT. At m. 7, there is a cross-relation.

66. Nicolas, *Force d'amour* (fol. 34ᵛ) [Ste. Marthe]

Lyrics: (See No. 38).

Parts: S., CT., T., 5ª, Bs.
Musica Ficta: mm. 4 (f♯′), 6 (c♯″), 14 (c♯″), 21 (e♭″), 22 (b♭′), 25 (g♯′), 26 (c♯″), 30 (f♯′), 32 (c♯″), 40 (c♯″), 47 (e♭″), 48 (b♭′), 51 (g♯′), 55 (b♭′), 68 (c♯″), 72 (b♭′), 98 (b♭), 101 (b♭′), 102 (g♯′), 115 (c♯″), 122 (b♭), 125 (b♭), 128 (b♭), 129 (g♯′), 142 (c♯″).
Remarks: Flat indicated only for the initial n. affected in mm. 17, 46, 105, and 123, T.; 20 and 43, 5ª; and 105, Bs. At m. 52, the descent of a chromatic semitone seems unequivocally required by the music. A simultaneous cross-relation occurs at m. 74; whether *musica ficta* (a sharp) should be applied to f′ in that m. is problematical, as a "double leading-tone" cadence would thereby be suggested. Cross-relations are found in mm. 121 and 130; in the latter, the leap of a diminished fourth (interrupted by a rest) appears in the CT.

67. Nicolas, *Le coeur de vous* (fol. 35ʳ) [C. Marot]

Lyrics: Your heart desires my presence,
But for the best, beautiful, I am withdrawing,
Because, without having another satisfaction,
I could not serve so long,
Let's come to the point [about] which one doesn't dare speak.

Parts: S., CT., T., 5ª, Bs.
Musica Ficta: mm. 2 (e♭′, twice), 6 (e♭′), 10 (f♯′), 19 (e♭), 27 (b♮), 28 (e♭′), 30 (f♯′), 32 (e♭), 36 (f♯), 56 (f♯′), 72 (f♯′).
Remarks: Flat only indicated for the initial n. affected in mm. 13, CT., and 29, 5ª. The homophonic voice-leading of the Bs. is noteworthy here, especially in mm. 1–17, 46–8, 62–7, and 72–9.

68. Benedictus [Appenzeller], *Si je me plein*[65] (fol. 35ᵛ)

Lyrics: If I complain, alas, I am not in the wrong,
Because of false information, indeed, my way is prejudiced,
And without delay, support was removed from me,
And the true haven of my well-being and my life,
Where my life was gratified,
By all solace, by joy, and by comfort,
There is no more comfort, except hard death,
Which I prefer to my doleful life.

Parts: S., CT., T., 5ª, Bs.
Concordances: As No. 1 (RISM 1545₁₄), fol. 9ʳ.
Musica Ficta: mm. 9 (e♭′), 10 (f♯), 13 (e♭′), 17 (c♯′), 18 (f♯′), 19 (b♮), 26 (c♯′), 27 (f♯′), 28 (b♮), 30 (e♭′), 31 (b♮′), 39 (e♭′), 45 (e♭′), 48 (e♭′), 49 (e♭′), 51 (e♭′), 53 (e♭′), 62 (e♭), 63 (e♭′), 65 (e♭′), 70 (e♭), 78 (f♯), 82 (e♭′), 83 (c♯′), 85 (b♭), 92 (e♭′), 93 (e♭), 97 (e♭′), 98 (f♯), 106 (e♭′), 113 (c♯′), 114 (f♯′), 115 (b♭), 122 (c♯′), 123 (f♯′), 124 (b♭), 126 (e♭′), 127 (b♮′), 135 (e♭′), 136 (c♯′), 141 (e♭′), 144 (e♭′), 145 (e♭), 147 (e♭′), 149 (e♭), 150 (f♯′), 152 (e♭′), 154 (e♭).
Remarks: Consecutive sevenths are found at m. 72.

69. Millot, *Revien vers moy* (fol. 36ʳ) [Ronsard][66]

Lyrics: Return to me, [I] who am so aggrieved,
  And you will see, the weariness and the anguish,
  That I have suffered, always waiting,
  Your return, by which [I] shall be consoled,
  Return to me.

Parts: S., 5ª, CT., T., Bs.
Musica Ficta: mm. 3 (e♭′, b♮′), 9 (b♮′), 11 (e♭), 12 (e♭″, b♮′), 17 (f♯′), 29 (e♭″), 30 (e♭′), 33 (f♯′), 34 (b♭), 35 (e♭″), 37 (c♯′), 39 (c♯′), 41 (b♭′), 48 (b♭′), 52 (CT.: f♯′), 56 (f♯′), 64 (f♯′), 69 (f♯′), 75 (f♯), 83 (f♯′), 92 (f♯′), 96 (e♭′, b♮′), 102 (b♮′), 104 (b♮′).
Remarks: Flat only indicated for the first n. affected in mm. 66, 5ª, and 79, S. At mm. 27 and 81, there are simultaneous cross-relations.

70. Gombert, *Le berger & la bergere* (fol. 36ᵛ)

Lyrics: The shepherd and the shepherdess are in the shadow of a bush,
  They are so close, one to the other,
  It is most touching to see them,
  The lady said to her darling, let us catch our breath,
  The wolf is carrying away my sheep, my companion, by God, by God,
    save the wool.

Parts: S., 5ª, CT., T., Bs.
Concordances: Modern edition: *Nicolai Gombert: Opera Omnia* (= *Corpus Mensurabilis Musicae*, 6; ed. J. Schmidt-Görg), XI (1975), 115.
Errors: mm. 41, CT., "grend" (not "grand"); 79, S., "enporte" (not "emporte"); 95–6, Bs., "compagon" (not "compagnon").
Musica Ficta: mm. 11 (c♯′), 12 (e♭′, twice), 13 (e♭), 15 (B♮; e♭′, twice), 20 (e♭′), 26 (f♯′), 33 (f♯′), 35 (f♯′, twice), 37 (c♯′, twice), 38 (e♭′), 39 (f♯′, twice, and c♯′), 41 (c♯′, twice), 43 (c♯″), 44 (c♯″), 45 (CT.: c♯′), 47 (c♯″), 50 (CT.: e♭′, b♮), 51

(c♯′), 52 (b♮), 53 (e♭′), 57 (e♭, e♭′), 60 (e♭′), 63 (e♭′), 68 (e♭′), 69 (e♭), 70 (e♭′), 81 (e♭′), 85 (e♭), 86 (e♭′, twice), 87 (e♭′), 89 (e♭′, f♯′), 95 (e♭′), 99 (e♭′), 100 (e♭′, twice), 101 (e♭′), 103 (e♭′, f♯′), 106 (B♮), 107 (e♭′).
Remarks: Flat only indicated for the initial n. affected in mm. 83, 97, and 105, Bs.; 84 and 98, 5ª.

71. Lupi,[67] *Au joly bois* (fol. 37ʳ)

Lyrics: In the lovely wood, on the grass,
  By my friend I was dispatched,
  I don't care to have any regrets about it,
  By him am [I] well rewarded,
  Because, to let the dew fall,
  Taking with me the lovely sombre plunge,
  He is delightful — [I] am not at all abused,
  As good wine is not at all necessary to him.

Parts: S., CT., 5ª, T., Bs.
Concordances: Le cincquiesme livre contenant trente et deux chansons a cincq et a six parties (Antwerp, T. Susato, 1544; = RISM 1544₁₃), fol. 3ʳ.[68]
Musica Ficta: mm. 3 (e♭′), 6 (e♭), 8 (e♭′), 11 (e♭), 12 (f♯′, twice), 14 (c♯′) 16 (e♭′), 18 (f♯), 24 (c♯′, twice, and b♮), 28 (c♯″, twice, and b♮), 34 (e♭″), 35 (c♯″, b♮), 36 (c♯″, twice), 37 (e♭′), 40 (c♯′), 42 (c♯′), 45 (e♭′), 46 (c♯′), 48 (c♯′), 50 (e♭′), 51 (c♯″), 53 (e♭′), 54 (f♯′), 56 (c♯′), 58 (e♭′), 59 (f♯′), 71 (e♭), 74 (T., last n.: c♯′), 75 (f♯′), 77 (c♯″), 80 (c♯″), 81 (e♭′), 83 (c♯′, twice, and b♮), 84 (e♭′), 88 (c♯′, twice, and b♮), 89 (f♯′, b♮), 90 (f♯′), 93 (e♭), 94 (f♯′, twice), 96 (b♮).
Remarks: At m. 34, there are parallel sevenths.

72. Ad. Vuillard [Willaert], *Sire don dieu* (fol. 37ᵛ)

Lyrics: Lord God, they are so content,
  Our shepherds, when they keep watch over lambs and sheep,
  Do you want me to recite to you,
  The shepherdess's song,
  At a little fire of thorns,
  Which very well heated his brow,
  He has hair on his head, the ugly beast,
  The thing is not right: it is not clean,
  Lord God they are so content,
  Our shepherds, when they keep watch over lambs and sheep.

Parts: S., CT., T., 5ª, Bs.
Concordances: Livre, fol. 52ʳ.[69]

Errors: mm. 88–9, 5ª, "moutos" (not "moutons").
Musica Ficta: mm. 2 (T.: c♯'), 3 (b♮'), 8 (5ª: c♯'), 18 (f♯'), 20 (e♭'), 24 (f♯'), 28 (f♯'), 30 (c♯''), 34 (T.: f♯'; 5ª: e♭'), 35 (f♯', twice), 37 (c♯''), 41 (T.: f♯'), 42 (f♯'), 45 (b♮'), 51 (e♭'', twice), 52 (f♯', twice), 56 (f♯'), 57 (e♭''), 58 (b♮'), 62 (5ª: c♯'), 63 (b♮'), 68 (T.: c♯'), 78 (f♯'), 80 (e♭'), 84 (f♯'), 88 (f♯').
Remarks: Flat only indicated for the first n., m. 36, T.; ditto, for the sharp, m. 49, T.; mm. 85–6, Bs., represent a rhythmically variant reading of mm. 25–6 in the same v.

73.   Arcadet [Arcadelt], *Si la beauté de ma dame* (fol. 38ʳ)

Lyrics: If the beauty of my lady and mistress,
     And her virtue, which is inestimable,
     Make me have unceasing joy,
     To the God of love I should render immortal favor,
     [His] having provided me with so commendable favor,
     And the affection of such a love,
     [As] if she were not mortal.

Parts: S., CT., T., 5ª, Bs.
Concordances: Livre, fol. 47ᵛ;[70] modern edition: *J. Arcadelt: Opera Omnia* (= *Corpus Mensurabilis Musicae,* 31; ed. A. Seay), VIII (1968), 12.
Musica Ficta: mm. 4 (b♮), 6 (e♭'), 10 (e♭'), 14 (f♯'), 16 (e♭), 17 (e♭'), 24 (e♭'), 26 (c♯'), 35 (e♭'), 36 (e♭'), 37 (e♭'), 39 (e♭'), 43 (e♭''), 44 (e♭'), 54 (e♭'), 63 (e♭'), 64 (c♯'), 66 (e♭'), 68 (c♯'), 70 (b♮', e♭''), 71 (f♯'?), 72 (c♯''), 75 (e♭'), 76 (f♯), 79 (e♭'), 80 (f♯'), 82 (e♭'), 83 (e♭'), 84 (b♮), 85 (e♭').
Remarks: Flat only indicated for the first n. in m. 12, T.; ditto, for the sharp, m. 21, CT. At mm. 12–13, there is a cross-relation; at m. 37, a most unusual escaped n.

74.   Millot, *Susane un jour* (fol. 38ᵛ) [Guéroult]

Lyrics: (See No. 18).
Parts: S., CT., T., 5ª, Bs.
Concordances: Modern edition: *Anthologie de la chanson parisienne au XVIe siècle* (ed. F. Lesure, et al., 1952), 90.
Musica Ficta: mm. 2 (b♮'), 4 (b♮), 10 (e♭', twice), 19 (e♭'), 26 (e♭'), 32 (b♮'), 34 (b♮), 40 (e♭', twice), 49 (e♭'), 56 (e♭'), 75 (b♮), 84 (b♮, twice), 97 (b♮), 110 (b♮'), 112 (b♮), 118 (e♭', twice), 127 (e♭').
Remarks: Natural sign only indicated for the initial n. affected in mm. 11, 41, and 81, T.; 27 and 57, S.; 78 and 119, 5ª.

75.   Millot, *Si je trespasse* (fol. 39ʳ) [Ronsard]

Lyrics: If I die in your arms, my lady,
     I am content,
     Because I would not have,
     Greater honor in the world than seeing myself,
     While kissing your breast, render up my soul.

Parts: S., CT., T., 5ª, Bs.
Musica Ficta: mm. 13 (e♭', twice), 17 (e♭', f♯'), 29 (b♮), 34 (e♭), 35 (b♮), 52 (b♮, twice), 53 (e♭'), 57 (e♭').
Remarks: Flat only indicated for the first n., m. 42, 5ª; ditto, for the sharp, m. 54, S.

76.   Millot, *Elle veut donc* (fol. 39ᵛ)

Lyrics: She wishes, then, that [I] content myself with her,
     And that I be aware of her well-being and my great misfortune,
     Without [her] giving me any relief from it,
     And without hope so to accept [her] treatment,
     It behooves me to absent myself from her.

Parts: S., CT., 5ª, T., Bs.
Musica Ficta: mm. 7 (e♭'), 10 (b♮'), 16 (e♭'), 24 (f♯'), 25 (b♮, e♭'), 61 (e♭'), 70 (e♭').

77.   Millot, *Contentement combien* (fol. 40ʳ)

Lyrics: Contentment — how much, how much that [it] may be a great thing,
     [It] lasts not the length of a single day,
     Reason, strength, insatiable love,
     To awaken a heart, when it rests.

Parts: S., CT., 5ª, T., Bs.
Musica Ficta: mm. 9 (b♮'), 17 (b♮'), 25 (e♭'), 35 (b♮), 36 (f♯'), 39 (b♮), 44 (e♭').
Remarks: Flat only indicated for the initial n. affected in mm. 11 and 30, 5ª; and 46, CT. and Bs.

78.   Millot, *Sur la rousée* (fol. 40ᵛ)

Lyrics: Over the dew must I go in the forenoon,
     To listen to the nightingale under the arbor,
     Having his lady in his arms,
     [She] demanding an embrace of him for pleasure,
     And then turning her over beneath [him],

As lovers do for pleasure,
Over the dew.

Parts: S., CT., T., 5ª, Bs.
Errors: All vv., fourth word, "my" (not "m'y": from *table*).
Musica Ficta: mm. 5 (bb'), 6 (f#'), 9 (bb), 11 (eb", f#'), 12 (bb'), 14 (bb), 15 (bb',
twice), 28 (bb'), 30 (bb', twice), 31 (bb', twice), 32 (f#'), 45 (bb', f#'), 46 (f#'),
53 (c#"), 54 (bb'), 55 (c#"), 56 (f#'), 59 (eb", twice), 63 (eb", f#'), 65 (c#', f#'),
69 (bb'), 71 (bb', f#'), 73 (f#'), 74 (eb'), 87 (eb', twice).
Remarks: Sharp only indicated for the initial n. affected in mm. 49 and 51, S., and
53, 5ª. At mm. 32–3, the CT. presents two successive descending perfect fifths.

79. LeBrun,[71] *N'a vous point veu* (fol. 41ʳ)

Lyrics: Have you really not beheld badly struck,
Her about whom they speak so much,
Her mother had sent her,
To watch over the lambs in the fields,
And her friend, who went before, asking her,
Will you be my infatuated one,
Not at all, said she, my friend,
I wouldn't dare, in good faith,
But frolic [with] me on the dew.

Parts: S., CT., T., 5ª, Bs.
Concordances: Vienna, Austrian National Library, Codex 18810, fol. 47ʳ; *Livre*,
fol. 28ʳ.[72]
Errors: m. 46, T., instead of the rest, the n., f, tied from the mi. in m. 45.
Musica Ficta: mm. 4 (eb), 8 (eb'), 14 (eb), 15 (bɦ'), 20 (eb), 21 (bɦ'), 27 (eb), 32
(eb'), 38 (eb), 39 (bɦ'), 45 (bɦ), 46 (eb, twice), 66 (bɦ'), 67 (eb), 68 (bɦ), 79 (eb'),
80 (eb), 83 (eb), 95 (eb'), 97 (f#), 98 (bɦ'), 103 (eb'), 105 (f#), 106 (bɦ).
Remarks: m. 110, Bs., a natural sign unnecessarily indicated here for the second n.,
E. Also noteworthy are the lengthy pedal-like nn. in two vv., mm. 69–78.

80. C. LeJeune, *Rossignol, mon mignon* (fol. 41ᵛ) [Ronsard]

Lyrics: Nightingale, my darling, who, in this willow grove,
Moves alone from branch to branch, flying entirely at inclination,
And sings of my weariness, [I] who go singing, [about]
Her, whom I must always have in my speech,
We sigh, the two of us, thy sweet voice tries,
To toll her friendship, [she] who loves thee so,
And I, sadly I go, regretting the beauty,

[Of her,] who made such a harsh wound in my heart.
[*2.ª pars:*]
Yet, Nightingale, we differ on one point,
It is that you are loved, and I am not at all,
Well may the two of us make similar music,
For you bend your voice to [produce] confusion of your sounds,
But mine, which makes my songs spiteful,
In order not to hear them, [she] stops up her ears.

Parts: S., CT., T., 5ª, Bs.
Concordances: Modern edition: *Anthologie de la chanson parisienne au XVIe siècle*
(ed. F. Lesure, et al., 1952), 95.[73]
Errors: mm. 20, Bs., "branche en" preceded by "de" (omitted); 90, T., second n.
reads f (not e).
Musica Ficta: mm. 3 (T.: f#'), 8 (eb", twice), 14 (f#'), 19 (bb), 28 (bb'), 29 (T.:
c#'), 31 (5ª: f#'), 32 (bb'), 33 (f#', twice), 38 (bb), 50 (c#"), 53 (T.: eb'), 55 (eb",
twice), 62 (f#'), 69 (f#'), 75 (bb), 85 (f#'), 86 (bb), 87 (g#', twice, and f#'), 92
(eb"), 93 (c#'), 94 (eb'), 96 (f#'), 100 (eb"), 104 (eb'), 112 (bb), 113 (f#', twice),
117 (bb), 118 (f#'), 120 (bb), 122 (bb', twice), 123 (bb), 125 (bb), 128 (eb", bb,
f#'), 130 (bb', twice), 132 (bb), 136 (eb", twice), 141 (f#', twice), 146 (f#', twice),
160 (bb), 161 (f#'), 162 (eb", twice, and bb), 163 (bb'), 164 (eb"), 165 (f#', twice),
168 (eb", twice), 172 (f#'), 174 (eb", twice), 176 (f#").
Remarks: Flat indicated only for the initial n. affected in mm. 6, 115, and 153, CT.;
36, Bs. Ditto, for the sharp, mm. 7, 23, 132, and 151, CT.; 24 and 160, T.; 134, 5ª;
154, S. A very rapid cross-relation occurs at m. 18. In mm. 20–1, the CT. moves by
chromatic semitones from f' to a'. At m. 179, a passing-n. creates the sonority of an
augmented chord.

81. Millot, *Le Rossignol sauvage* (fol. 42ᵛ)

Lyrics: The wild nightingale, I always heard him sing,
In a pretty grove concerning our loves,
And what did the handsome darling say,
He said to me, good companion,
Hurl two thunderbolts from your eyes,
To her who loves best.

Parts: S., CT., T., 5ª, Bs.
Errors: m. 5, S., "jé" (not "je"); ditto, mm. 3 and 8, CT.; 9, T.; 7, 5ª; and 14, Bs.
At m. 85, T., "mieuy" (not "mieux").
Musica Ficta: mm. 6 (eb"), 11 (eb"), 15 (eb', twice), 25 (eb"), 30 (eb"), 34 (eb',
twice), 50 (bb'), 59 (c#"), 61 (bb'), 64 (eb'), 66 (eb'), 67 (bb'), 71 (eb', twice, and

bb′), 72 (eb″), 73 (bb′), 80 (bb′), 83 (eb′?).
Remarks: Sharp only indicated for the first n. affected in mm. 52, CT.; 56, S.; and 67, 5ª. At m. 60, the 5ª ascends chromatically. Homophonic v.-leading abounds in this chanson; at mm. 36−7 (T.) and 55−7 (Bs.), there are ascending consecutive leaps of perfect fourths.

82. Phl. Vuildre [Wilder], *Un jeune moyne* (fol. 43ʳ)

Lyrics: A young friar left the monastery,
Met a young nun with a graceful body,
[He] approached to ask her,
If she would like to fool around,
Or dance in small steps.

Hey friar, friar, what do [you] call "to fool around,"
To kiss and embrace, my young lady,
In our religion,
We call "to fool around,"
Nude together between two sheets,

Ha brother, brother, what will your abbots say,
The founders [of the order] are deceived and defrauded,
Instead of chanting well,
You are making the bed rock,
The regulations do not embrace it,

True God, alas, friar, you won't "fool around,"
True God, alas, you won't "fool around."

Parts: S., CT., T., 5ª, Bs.[74]
Musica Ficta: mm. 25 (eb, b♮), 26 (eb′), 28 (b♮), 32 (b♮).

83. Phl. Vuildre [Wilder], *Helas, ma dame* (fol. 43ᵛ)

Lyrics: Alas, my lady, do something good for him,
For this poor blind man, who sees nothing,
Alas, my lady, you will give him nothing,
If [you] wish to do something good for him,
[You] would soon hush his piteous cry,
Alas, my lady, do something good for him,
For this poor blind man, who sees nothing,
Alas, my lady, you will give him nothing,
To this poor blind man, who has nothing of his own, *who sees nothing.*

Parts: S., CT., T., 5ª, Bs.
Errors: m. 30, CT., "na" (not "n'a").
Musica Ficta: mm. 2 (bb), 4 (bb, twice), 8 (bb), 9 (f♯′), 16 (bb), 18 (bb, twice), 20 (eb″, thrice, and bb′), 21 (f♯′, twice), 30 (eb″), 36 (bb), 37 (bb), 38 (f♯′, twice), 46 (eb′, bb), 52 (bb), 54 (bb, twice), 58 (bb), 59 (f♯′), 66 (bb), 68 (bb, twice), 70 (eb″, thrice, and bb′), 71 (f♯′, twice), 78 (eb″), 80 (eb′), 82 (eb″).
Remarks: At m. 83, there are consecutive dissonances between S. and T.

84. Goudimel, *Allez, mes soupirs* (fol. 44ʳ)[75]

Lyrics: Go, my amorous sighs,
Go to that cold heart,
Go and break that ice,
Which forms a rampart around it,
So that, compassion, in turn,
May warm the place with tears.

Parts: S., 5ª, CT., T., Bs.
Concordances: Modern edition: *C. Goudimel: Oeuvres complètes* (ed. P. Pidoux, et al.), XIII (1974), 1.
Errors: All vv., "c'este" (not "ceste") and "l'armes" (not "larmes").
Musica Ficta: mm. 3 (bb′), 11 (bb), 13 (bb), 18 (bb), 21 (bb), 25 (eb″), 29 (f♯″), 32 (bb′), 36 (c♯″), 40 (bb′), 53 (bb′), 56 (bb′), 57 (eb″), 58 (S.: eb″), 60 (bb), 62 (eb″), 65 (eb″, bb′), 70 (bb), 72 (f♯″, twice), 74 (f♯″, twice), 79 (bb′, twice), 80 (f♯″, twice), 82 (T.: eb′), 85 (c♯″, twice), 88 (bb).
Remarks: m. 30, 5ª, flat only indicated for the first n. Note augmented chord in m. 97.

85. Ad. Vuillard [Willaert], *Je ne sçaurois* (fol. 44ᵛ)

Lyrics: I would not know how to sing or laugh,
All my pleasures are only tears,
Since [I] am far from my loves,
That's the reason my poor heart sighs,
My love and my dear friend,
My pretty ninny,
Through love, my lady,
Often I desire you,
All alone in my room,
In order best to play with you.

Parts: S., CT., 5ª, T., Bs.

Concordances: Munich, Bavarian State Library, Music MS 1508, No. 103; *Livre,* fol. 6ᵛ.
Musica Ficta: mm. 7 (e♭), 11 (b♮, twice), 13 (e♭), 18 (e♭′), 21 (e♭), 22 (f♯′), 25 (e♭′), 26 (e♭′, e♭), 28 (e♭), 29 (f♯′), 32 (e♭′), 33 (e♭′), 35 (c♯′), 47 (b♮), 55 (b♮), 57 (e♭′), 59 (b♮, twice), 61 (e♭′), 65 (e♭), 68 (f♯′), 69 (b♮), 70 (b♮), 71 (e♭′), 74 (e♭), 76 (b♮), 80 (e♭′), 81 (e♭), 82 (b♮), 86 (e♭′), 89 (b♮), 90 (e♭), 91 (e♭′), 92 (b♮′, twice), 96 (e♭), 99 (e♭′), 110 (e♭′, b♮), 111 (e♭′), 112 (b♮), 122 (e♭′), 124 (b♮), 128 (e♭′), 129 (e♭′), 130 (b♮), 131 (b♮).
Remarks: Line 4 of the lyrics reads, in all vv. except the S., "Voilà pourquoy mon povre coeur soupire"; in the S., "povre" is omitted (= source error?). Note parallel seconds, m. 37.

86. Mouton, *Du bon du coeur* (fol. 45ʳ)

Lyrics: From the goodness of my heart, my dear lady,
      I shall serve you loyally,
      I beseech you most humbly,
      That [you] retain me sweetly,[76]
      In order to serve you with body and soul,
      And truly [I] swear to you on my soul,
      That *[I] shall serve you loyally.*

Parts: S., CT., T., 5ª, Bs.
Concordances: Livre, fol. 34ᵛ.[77]
Errors: mm. 68–75 (S., CT., T., and 5ª) and 65–6, Bs., "dame" (not "d'ame"; correct in Bs., mm. 73–4, and in *Livre*).
Musica Ficta: mm. 14 (e♭′), 15 (e♭), 16 (b♮), 18 (e♭), 19 (e♭′), 20 (B♮), 21 (e♭), 22 (e♭), 33 (e♭, b♮), 39 (e♭; b♮, twice), 45 (e♭), 46 (b♮), 48 (e♭′), 49 (e♭), 50 (b♮), 53 (e♭), 54 (e♭), 55 (b♮), 61 (e♭′), 65 (e♭), 70 (b♮), 76 (e♭), 78 (b♮), 81 (CT.: b♮), 86 (e♭), 92 (e♭′), 102 (e♭).
Remarks: At mm. 23 and 41, $\frac{6}{4}$ chords are found; at m. 35, a decorative passage in dissonant nn., in the T.; and at m. 98, an *appoggiatura* (d).

87. Phl. Vuildre [Wilder], *Une nonnain refaite* (fol. 45ᵛ) [C. Marot]

Lyrics: A nun, refreshed and at her prime,
      Was sorry to have left the world,
      And I said to her, my friend, there is absolutely no need,
      To have regret over such an unclean thing,
      Haven't you taken Jesus-Christ, pure and clean, in your vows,
         for your spouse,
      To whose name your spirits are together united,

Yes, she said and did not want to drop it [the subject],
But Jesus-Christ is [the] spouse of spirits,
And I need a spouse for the flesh.

Parts: S., CT., T., 5ª, Bs.
Errors: All vv., mm. 21–7, "mamye" (not "m'amye").[78]
Musica Ficta: mm. 4 (e♭′, twice), 11 (e♭′), 12 (e♭′), 24 (e♭), 25 (b♮), 36 (CT.: e♭′), 39 (b♮), 41 (e♭′), 42 (b♮′), 43 (e♭′), 46 (e♭), 51 (e♭′), 52 (e♭′), 54 (e♭), 60 (b♮), 69 (e♭), 70 (b♮), 79 (e♭, e♭), 84 (e♭′, twice), 91 (e♭′), 92 (e♭′), 105 (e♭′), 106 (e♭′).
Remarks: m. 35, S., natural sign only indicated for the first n. The last word of the 5ª (m. 117) is given as "c." (not "chair").

88. Phl. Vuildre, *Amour, partez* (fol. 46ʳ)

Lyrics: Love, depart, I give you chase,
      Not for harm, which my heart procures [for] you,
      But False Pretense, which puts all its effort,
      To deceive, banishes you from my favor.

Parts: S., CT., T., 5ª, Bs.[79]
Musica Ficta: mm. 11 (e♭′), 13 (b♮), 20 (b♮′), 21 (e♭), 22 (e♭′), 25 (e♭′), 26 (b♮, twice), 47 (e♭′), 49 (CT.: b♮).

89. Certon, *Regret, soucy, & peine* (fol. 46ᵛ)

Lyrics: Regret, worry, and pain,
      Make me vile twists,
      If pity is not sudden,
      [I] shall soon end my days,
      Alas, it is loves,
      Which create all this for me.

      [*2.ª pars:*]
      I have fame and renown, [enough]
      To have a new friend.

Parts: S., CT., T., 5ª, Bs.
Concordances: Les Meslanges de Maistre Pierre Certon (Paris, N. DuChemin, 1570; = RISM C-1718), p. 13; *Livre,* fol. 41ʳ.
Errors: mm. 81–2, T. and 5ª, and 82 and 106, S., "n'ouvel" (not "nouvel").
Musica Ficta: mm. 6 (b♮), 7 (f♯′), 8 (b♮), 9 (e♭′), 30 (b♮), 31 (f♯′), 32 (b♮), 33 (e♭′), 51 (e♭), 52 (f♯′), 54 (f♯′), 55 (e♭′), 56 (e♭, b♮), 57 (e♭′, twice), 59 (f♯′), 60 (b♮), 61 (e♭), 62 (e♭, b♮), 77 (b♮), 78 (f♯′), 79 (b♮), 80 (e♭′), 101 (b♮), 102 (f♯′), 103 (b♮), 104 (e♭′).

90. Phl. Vuildre [Wilder], *Je ne fay rien* (fol. 47ʳ) [C. Marot]

Lyrics: I can do nothing other than to request without obtaining,
The gift of amorous pleasure,
Alas, my mistress, say when [it] may be,
That it will please you to succor me,
I can do nothing other than to request without obtaining.

Parts: S., CT., T., 5ᵃ, Bs.
Musica Ficta: mm. 10 (e♭′), 12 (e♭′, e♭), 19 (e♭′), 24 (e♭), 25 (e♭′), 29 (e♭′), 30 (b♮), 33 (b♮), 37 (e♭), 56 (e♭′), 64 (e♭), 72 (c♯′), 74 (e♭′).
Remarks: m. 49, Bs., flat only indicated for the first n.

91. Benedictus [Appenzeller], *Arousez vo vi vo violette* (fol. 47ᵛ)[80]

Lyrics: Water your violet,
Water your wallflower,
The daughter of a gardener,
Was loved as a passing fancy,
Her friend gave her a kiss,
Pretending to do the little thing,
The game of love is most enjoyable for him,
[She] said to him, my dear friend,
Water your violet,
Water your wallflower.

Parts: S., CT., T., 5ᵃ, Bs.
Concordances: As No. 71 (RISM 1544₁₃), fol. 14ᵛ; *Livre,* fol. 39ʳ.[81]
Musica Ficta: mm. 12 (b♭′), 13 (f♯′), 14 (e♭′), 15 (b♭′, twice), 22 (b♭′), 24 (e♭′), 27 (CT., third and fourth nn.: e♭′), 28 (b♭′), 32 (e♭′), 39 (f♯′), 40 (f♯′), 44 (f♯′, twice), 46 (e♭), 47 (e♭, twice), 50 (f♯′), 52 (e♭″), 54 (b♭′), 55 (b♭′, twice), 56 (f♯′), 57 (e♭′), 58 (e♭′), 62 (e♭′), 64 (e♭′, b♭), 66 (b♭), 68 (b♭), 70 (b♭′), 72 (f♯′), 74 (f♯), 78 (b♭), 82 (b♭), 85 (b♭), 90 (b♭), 99 (b♭′), 101 (f♯′), 102 (CT.: e♭′, twice), 110 (b♭′), 112 (CT.: e♭′), 115 (CT., third and fourth nn.: e♭′), 116 (b♭′), 120 (e♭′).

92. Richafort, *D'amour je suis desheritée* (fol. 48ʳ)

Lyrics: Of love am I disinherited,
And [I] don't know to whom to complain,
Alas, I've lost my friend.

[*2.ᵃ pars:*]
[I] am all alone, he has left me.

Parts: S., CT., T., 5ᵃ, Bs.
Concordances: Cambridge University, Magdalene College, MS Pepys 1760, fol. 84ʳ; *Livre,* fol. 36ʳ.[82]
Musica Ficta: mm. 4 (e♭′), 5 (e♭′), 7 (e♭), 8 (b♮), 16 (e♭), 17 (e♭), 23 (e♭′), 27 (e♭′), 28 (b♮), 40 (e♭), 60 (e♭).
Remarks: At mm. 49 and 69, consecutive dissonances occur between S. and 5ᵃ.

93. Ad. Vuillard [Willaert], *Baisés moy tant tant* (fol. 48ᵛ)

Lyrics: Kiss me so very much, frolic [with] me so very much, my friend, I prithee,
Kiss me so very much, frolic [with] me so very much,
If [I] am to be your friend,
In the pretty wood, I met my friend,
When she caught sight of me, she was delighted,
Smiling, she said to me very softly,
Kiss me so very much, frolic [with] me so very much, my friend, I prithee,
Kiss me so very much, frolic [with] me so very much,
If [I] am to be your friend.

Parts: S., CT., T., 5ᵃ, Bs.
Concordances: Livre, fol. 51ᵛ.
Errors: mm. 64–70, all vv., "ma" (not "m'a").
Musica Ficta: mm. 7 (e♭′), 11 (CT., last n.: f♯′), 13 (5ᵃ: e♭′), 18 (e♭′), 22 (e♭′), 26 (b♮′), 39 (b♮′), 41 (b♮), 48 (b♮), 53 (b♮), 59 (b♮′), 62 (b♮′), 66 (b♮), 77 (e♭′), 85 (e♭′), 89 (CT., last n.: f♯′), 91 (5ᵃ: e♭′), 96 (e♭′), 100 (e♭).
Remarks: At m. 74, S., the sharp, not indicated in the *Mellange,* comes from the *Livre.* At mm. 12 and 90, the T. voice-leading comprises consecutive ascending perfect fourths.

94. Crequillon, *Belle, donne*[83] *moy* (fol. 49ʳ)

Lyrics: Beautiful, give me a glance,
Even if only from the corner of your eye,
That will ease my pain,
But may it come from kind concern.

Parts: S., 5ᵃ, CT., T., Bs.
Concordances: As No. 1 (RISM 1545₁₄), fol. 13ʳ.
Musica Ficta: mm. 12 (e♭), 13 (b♮), 14 (e♭″), 16 (e♭′), 17 (b♮), 23 (e♭′), 27 (e♭′), 28 (e♭′), 29 (e♭′), 31 (e♭), 33 (e♭), 36 (e♭), 38 (e♭′, b♮′), 42 (e♭), 43 (e♭″, b♮), 44 (e♭″, b♮), 46 (b♮′), 49 (e♭′), 50 (e♭″), 53 (e♭′), 55 (e♭), 57 (e♭′), 60 (b♮), 62 (e♭′), 63 (e♭′), 64 (e♭), 65 (e♭′), 69 (e♭), 70 (f♯′), 73 (f♯′), 74 (e♭′, e♭), 75 (e♭′, e♭), 76

(e♭), 77 (b♮), 78 (e♭″), 82 (f♯′), 85 (f♯′), 86 (e♭′, e♭), 87 (e♭′, e♭), 88 (e♭), 89 (b♮).
Remarks: CT. and T. are in unison, m. 61.

95. Leschenet, *Est-il douleur cruelle* (fol. 49ᵛ)

Lyrics: Is it cruel suffering,
  Which may be similar to that,
  Which honest love now presents to me,
  Is it necessary that prudent love,
  May have so little advantage,
  That the heart's vision breaks away and absents itself,
  Oh excess of knowledge,
  Oh excess of recollection,
  Of a thing too much esteemed and understood,
  Oh hard and unrighteous law,
  Of chaste and modest love,
  Maintained with too much respect.

Parts: S., CT., T., 5ᵃ, Bs.
Concordances: Livre, fol. 19ᵛ.[84]
Errors: mm. 69–70, 5ᵃ, "cognuë" (not "cogneuë").
Musica Ficta: mm. 4 (g♯, twice, and f♯), 5 (g♯′), 7 (g♯), 9 (c♯′), 10 (g♯′), 12 (g♯), 23 (c♯′), 24 (b♭′, g♯′), 28 (g♯, twice, and f♯), 29 (c♯′?), 31 (g♯), 33 (c♯′), 34 (g♯′), 36 (g♯), 47 (c♯′), 48 (b♭′, g♯′), 49 (b♭′), 54 (CT., last n.: c♯′), 56 (c♯), 60 (f♯, b♭′), 63 (b♭), 64 (c♯′), 68 (b♭, b♭′), 69 (f♯′, b♭), 71 (g♯′), 74 (b♭), 76 (b♭), 78 (g♯), 81 (g♯′), 84 (T.: e♭′, twice), 96 (f♯′), 97 (S., fifth n.: b♭′), 98 (S., third n.: g♯′), 99 (c♯′, thrice).
Remarks: At m. 29, S., the sharp, not indicated in the *Mellange,* comes from the *Livre.* Sharp symbols (here equalling natural signs), whose use is superfluous, are indicated in the *Livre* under the following nn.: mm. 7 and 31, b′ (cf. Plate IX); m. 51, S., sharp only indicated for the third n. The cross-relation at m. 49 signals the end of the repeated section A of the form of the composition and the beginning of section B. In m. 60, the sonorities both of an augmented triad and a seventh chord (in first inversion) are found.

96. Phl. Vuildre [Wilder], *De vous servir* (fol. 50ʳ)

Lyrics: To serve you, above all I try [to do],
    And night and day my heart labors,
    Imagining, according to my understanding,

  How [I] could clearly show,
  The great suffering I endure for you.

Parts: S., CT., T., 5ᵃ, Bs.
Musica Ficta: mm. 4 (b♭), 12 (g♯′), 18 (b♭), 26 (g♯′), 39 (e♭′, twice), 44 (f♯′), 51 (b♭), 56 (e♭′), 57 (c♯″), 62 (g♯′), 63 (b♭), 68 (e♭′), 69 (c♯″), 74 (g♯′).
Remarks: At mm. 14–5, there is a cross-relation including the descent of a chromatic semitone in the CT. and marking the repetition of the initial, A, section of the form of the work.

97. Phi. de Monte, *O triste ennuy* (fol. 50ᵛ)

Lyrics: Oh sad weariness, oh wicked fortune,
  [You] who do not wish to aspire to my wish,
  When misfortune only makes [it] grow worse,
  Alas, do you want [such] a person to sing.

  [2.ᵃ pars:]
  Seeing, in truth, all my luck expire,
  [I] want to leave every pleasant thing,
  And say that joy is not fitting to him,
  Whose heart only causes him to sigh.

  [3.ᵃ pars:]
  But if hope, which guides my waiting,
  Realizes for me success in pulling through to a good haven,
  I will say then, without further martyrizing myself,
  Let him sing, who is happy.

  [4.ᵃ pars:]
  Then, the envious one will not be able more to endure,
  But will set down in a most impetuous voice,
  Be content with the grief which torments me,
  And leave me to endure my misfortune alone.[85]

Parts: S., CT., T., 5ᵃ, Bs.
Concordances: Modern edition: *Philippe de Monte, Opera* (ed. C. van den Borren and J. van Nuffel, 1927–), XX, 49.
Musica Ficta: mm. 9 (e♭′), 10 (b♭′), 12 (b♭), 15 (b♭), 19 (b♭′), 22 (CT.: b♭), 23 (g♯′), 25 (b♭′), 27 (b♭′), 30 (b♭), 33 (e♭′, twice), 34 (b♭′, g♯′), 35 (b♭), 43 (b♭′), 46 (CT.: b♭), 48 (b♭), 50 (b♭), 51 (b♭), 52 (b♭), 54 (b♭′), 56 (g♯), 64 (b♭′), 76 (e♭′?), 79 (b♭′), 80 (g♯′), 91 (b♭), 93 (CT.: f♯′), 96 (b♭, twice), 97 (e♭′), 99 (b♭), 113 (b♭), 120 (b♭′), 128 (b♭), 136 (b♭), 137 (f♯′), 141 (b♭), 145 (B♭), 147 (f♯′), 192

(b♭′), 193 (g♯′), 203 (g♯), 205 (c♯′), 217 (b♭′), 219 (g♯′), 221 (b♭), 224 (b♭), 227 (b♭′), 231 (b♭′, twice), 233 (g♯′).
Remarks: At m. 130, S., "qu'au" (not "qu'a", as in the other vv.; treated as an error). Sharp only indicated for the initial n. affected in mm. 15 and 225, CT.; 82, T.; 211 and 229, Bs. Particularly noteworthy in this chanson are the numerous cross-relations, occurring at mm. 24, 40−1, 77−8, 131−2, and 158−9. At m. 34, a $\frac{6}{4}$ chord appears and, at m. 59, consecutive dissonances (between CT. and T., bt. 1). The voice-leading consists of successive descending perfect fourths, mm. 54−5, Bs., and of ascending ones, mm. 80−1 and 181−2, T. A most unusual dissonance for the *Mellange,* the retardation, appears in m. 118 (5ª: a); (see No. 52, m. 19, for the only other retardation in the collection). At m. 85 (bt. 2), there is a seventh chord (formed by a passing n., e′).

98. Leschenet, *Gris & tanné* (fol. 52ʳ)

Lyrics: Hoary and vexed must I carry myself,
    Because vexed am [I] from hoping,
    And my jaundiced appearance must leave me,
    Which love applies for delight,
    Gloom will be testimony,
    To living in pain and in sadness,
    Since it is expedient that I leave you.

Parts: S., CT., T., 5ª, Bs.
Concordances: Livre, fol. 19ʳ.
Errors: mm. 123, T.; 124, 5ª; 126, S. and Bs.: "qui'l" (not "qu'il").
Musica Ficta: mm. 3 (e♭′), 7 (b♭), 13 (e♭′), 17 (B♭), 20 (CT.: e♭′; Bs.: B♭), 21 (B♭), 22 (c♯′), 27 (b♭′), 37 (b♭), 38 (f♯′), 41 (e♭′), 42 (B♭), 45 (b♭), 51 (e♭′), 55 (B♭), 58 (CT.: e♭′; Bs.: B♭), 59 (B♭), 60 (c♯′), 65 (b♭′), 75 (b♭), 76 (f♯′), 77 (b♭), 87 (B♭), 88 (f♯), 90 (b♭), 91 (b♭), 101 (c♯′), 109 (b♭′), 110 (f♯), 118 (b♭′), 119 (b♭), 120 (b♭), 127 (b♭′), 137 (b♭), 138 (f♯′), 141 (e♭′, b♭), 142 (e♭), 143 (e♭′), 144 (e♭).
Remarks: At mm. 7 and 45, an *appoggiatura* (the last e) produces a seventh chord; at m. 117, a $\frac{6}{4}$ appears.

99. de LaRue, *Incessamment mon povre coeur* (fol. 52ᵛ)

Lyrics: Incessantly, my poor heart laments,
    Without any rest, remembrance torments me,
    Being weary, without any help,
    Banished am I from all diversion,
    And indeed [I] languish near to impetuous death.

Parts: S., CT., T., 5ª, Bs.
Concordances: Livre, fol. 28ᵛ; modern edition in: *Josquin des Prés: Werken: Wereldlijke Werken* (ed. A. Smijers, 1921−), I (1922−5), 70.[86]
Musica Ficta: mm. 12 (c♯′), 14 (b♭), 16 (f♯), 18 (b♭), 20 (B♭), 24 (c♯′), 30 (c♯′), 32 (b♭′, f♯), 34 (f♯′, twice), 36 (e♭′), 45 (b♭), 51 (f♯), 53 (b♭′), 56 (b♭′), 57 (b♭′), 58 (f♯′, twice), 60 (b♭′), 61 (e♭′, e♭), 62 (b♭, twice), 63 (B♭), 64 (f♯), 65 (b♭), 69 (e♭′), 71 (f♯′), 72 (b♭′), 73 (e♭′, f♯′), 75 (c♯′?), 80 (f♯), 82 (b♭′), 84 (c♯′), 86 (b♭, b♭′), 87 (f♯, b♭), 88 (f♯′), 93 (b♭′), 96 (c♯′, twice), 97 (b♭′), 98 (b♭, twice), 99 (b♭), 100 (f♯′, twice), 103 (e♭′, e♭).
Remarks: At mm. 15 and 29, consecutive dissonances are found (last bt. of each m.); at m. 98, parallel sevenths. The sonority of a $\frac{6}{4}$ appears in mm. 67, 87, and 95.

100. Ad. Vuillard [Willaert], *A la fontaine* (fol. 53ᵛ)

Lyrics: At the fountain of the field, Margot bathed herself,
    Her friend passed that way,
    Who watched her, wow,
    Margot, Marguerite, beautiful, what are you doing there,
       Margot, Marguerite,
    I am moistening my parsley,
    And my chick peas, wow.

Parts: S., CT., 6ª (fol. 1ᵛ),[87] 5ª, T., Bs.
Concordances: As No. 1 (RISM 1545₁₄), fol. 4ᵛ; *Livre,* fol. 7ᵛ; modern edition in: *Jacobus Clemens non Papa: Opera Omnia* (=*Corpus Mensurabilis Musicae,* 4; ed. K. P. Bernet−Kempers, 1951−), VII, 43.[88]
Musica Ficta: mm. 2 (b♮), 3 (c♯′), 5 (b♭), 6 (c♯′, f♯), 9 (f♯), 11 (f♯′), 15 (c♯″), 17 (b♮), 22 (f♯), 23 (b♮), 25 (e♭″), 26 (c♯″), 28 (f♯), 30 (b♮), 37 (b♭), 41 (c♯″), 42 (e♭′), 50 (f♯, b♮), 51 (c♯′), 52 (c♯′, twice, and b♮), 56 (c♯′, twice, and b♮), 60 (c♯″, b♮), 61 (c♯′), 62 (b♮, e♭″), 64 (c♯″), 66 (f♯), 67 (b♮, e♭″), 68 (f♯′), 72 (f♯′, twice), 77 (e♭′), 78 (f♯′), 82 (b♭), 84 (f♯′), 85 (b♮), 86 (e♭′), 88 (c♯′), 90 (c♯′), 93 (f♯′), 95 (c♯′), 97 (c♯′), 98 (b♮), 100 (e♭′), 104 (c♯″), 112 (e♭′), 116 (c♯″), 117 (f♯′), 118 (f♯), 119 (b♭), 120 (f♯′, e♭), 122 (c♯″), 124 (b♮), 126 (c♯″), 128 (f♯, b♮), 129 (c♯′), 130 (c♯′), 132 (f♯′), 134 (c♯′, twice, and b♮), 138 (c♯″, b♮), 139 (c♯′), 140 (b♮, e♭″), 142 (c♯″), 144 (f♯), 145 (b♮, e♭′), 146 (f♯′), 150 (f♯′, twice), 155 (e♭′), 156 (f♯′), 158 (b♮′, e♭′).

101. Ad. Vuillard [Willaert], *Puis donc que ma maistresse* (fol. 54ʳ)

Lyrics: Since my mistress, then,
    Has absolutely no pity for me,
    It is proper that I cease,

From loving her, on my faith,
I don't complain at all [about] my pain,
My heart shows that it loves.

Parts: S., CT., 6ª (fol. 2ʳ), T., 5ª, Bs.
Concordances: Livre, fol. 8ʳ.
Musica Ficta: mm. 9 (e♭′), 10 (f♯′), 13 (e♭′), 14 (f♯′), 17 (e♭′), 20 (f♯′), 25 (e♭′, twice), 29 (e♭′), 31 (c♯′), 45 (e♭′), 49 (e♭), 50 (b♭), 53 (e♭), 54 (e♭), 57 (e♭), 58 (f♯), 61 (e♭′), 65 (e♭′), 69 (e♭), 70 (e♭), 77 (b♭), 89 (e♭′), 91 (e♭), 92 (b♮), 95 (5ª: e♭), 96 (b♮), 103 (e♭′), 104 (c♯′), 106 (e♭′), 108 (c♯′), 110 (f♯), 112 (e♭′), 113 (e♭), 114 (f♯′), 115 (e♭′), 116 (f♯), 117 (e♭).
Remarks: The sonority of a $\frac{6}{4}$ chord is suggested at mm. 37 and 66. At m. 120, there is a cross-relation.

102. Ad. Vuillard [Willaert], *Or suis-je bien* (fol. 54ᵛ)

Lyrics: But am I well for the worst,
From my unhappy days,
My situation rather worsens,
And comes to me the wrong way,
And all that [my] loves create for me,
        to endure grievous martyrdom,
If there is no other help from you,
It will be necessary for me to withdraw.

Parts: S., 6ª (fol. 2ᵛ), CT., T., 5ª, Bs.
Concordances: Munich, Bavarian State Library, Music MS 1508, No. 120; *Livre,* fol. 8ᵛ.⁸⁹
Musica Ficta: mm. 9 (b♮), 13 (f♯, twice), 16 (b♮, twice), 19 (e♭′), 22 (e♭′), 25 (f♯), 27 (e♭′), 29 (e♭, twice), 31 (e♭′), 32 (c♯′, twice), 33 (f♯′, twice), 37 (e♭), 39 (b♭), 42 (e♭′), 45 (e♭′), 48 (f♯), 50 (e♭′), 52 (e♭, twice), 55 (f♯ and c♯′, twice), 56 (f♯′, twice), 58 (e♭′), 60 (e♭), 63 (e♭′), 64 (e♭), 65 (b♮), 68 (e♭′), 70 (b♮), 72 (b♮), 73 (e♭), 75 (f♯), 76 (c♯′, twice), 79 (e♭′), 87 (c♯′, twice, and b♮), 92 (c♯″, twice, and b♭′), 94 (B♮), 95 (c♯, f♯), 97 (e♭′), 98 (b♮, twice), 106 (b♮), 109 (B♮), 112 (e♭′), 116 (e♭′), 117 (e♭), 118 (f♯′, twice), 119 (B♮), 122 (e♭′), 126 (e♭′), 127 (e♭′), 128 (f♯′, twice), 129 (b♮, twice), 131 (f♯), 132 (e♭′), 133 (f♯), 134 (b♮, twice), 136 (f♯), 137 (e♭), 138 (f♯′), 139 (b♮, twice), 140 (e♭′), 141 (B♮).
Remarks: At m. 57, T., natural sign indicated only for the initial n. affected. At mm. 34–6, the Bs. moves in successive ascending perfect fourths.

103. Ad. Vuillard [Willaert], *En douleur & tristesse* (fol. 55ʳ)

Lyrics: In pain and sadness,

I shall languish always,
If I lose my mistress,
My lady, by loving,
I gave her my love,
[I] shall never forget it,
And, in melancholy,
I shall finish my days.

Parts: S., CT., T., 5ª, 6ª (fol. 3ʳ), Bs.
Concordances: Livre, fol. 9ᵛ.⁹⁰
Errors: mm. 93 and 108, Bs., "donné" (not "donnée").
Musica Ficta: mm. 16 (e♭′), 22 (e♭), 26 (f♯), 34 (f♯), 56 (e♭′), 62 (e♭), 66 (f♯), 74 (f♯), 86 (c♯′), 88 (e♭′), 91 (e♭), 92 (f♯), 94 (e♭′), 96 (e♭′), 97 (f♯′), 99 (f♯), 101 (e♭, twice), 103 (f♯), 113 (e♭′), 114 (5ª: b♮), 116 (S.: b♮), 117 (e♭), 120 (e♭′, twice), 123 (e♭′, twice), 125 (f♯′), 127 (e♭′), 129 (e♭), 132 (e♭′, b♮), 133 (e♭′), 134 (c♯′), 135 (f♯), 141 (e♭′, twice), 143 (f♯′), 145 (e♭′), 146 (b♮), 147 (e♭), 150 (e♭′, b♮), 151 (e♭′), 152 (S.: c♯′).

104. Ad. Vuillard [Willaert], *Faute d'argent* (fol. 55ᵛ)

Lyrics: Lack of money — that's incomparable suffering,
If I say it, I have good reason why,
Without cash, one has to remain silent,
[A] woman who is sleeping can be awakened for money⁹¹

[*2.ª pars:*]
Whoever is shrewd will drink at the source,
Whoever has money will be the welcome one,
Among very well cared-for ladies,
For you, not sleeping, I am anxious.

Parts: S., CT., 5ª, 6ª (fol. 3ᵛ), T., Bs.
Concordances: As No. 71 (RISM 1544₁₃), fol. 7ᵛ; *Livre,* fol. 9ʳ; modern edition (*1.ª pars* only): H. M. Brown, ed., *Theatrical Chansons of the Fifteenth and Early Sixteenth Centuries* (1963), 70.
Musica Ficta: mm. 6 (B♮), 8 (f♯), 13 (f♯′), 24 (f♯′), 26 (e♭′, twice), 30 (f♯′), 33 (f♯′, b♮), 37 (e♭′), 46 (c♯″), 53 (CT.: c♯′), 54 (f♯, twice), 65 (e♭′), 70 (B♮), 72 (f♯), 75 (e♭′), 77 (f♯′), 96 (f♯′), 99 (b♮), 101 (f♯′?), 102 (b♮), 113 (CT.: e♭′), 124 (c♯″), 128 (b♮′), 131 (f♯′).
Remarks: Flat only indicated for the first n., m. 29, Bs.

105. Ad Vuillard [Willaert], *Mon coeur, mon corps* (fol. 56ʳ)

Lyrics: My heart, my body, my soul, and my possessions,
          Gold and silver — all that [I] may have,
          Nothing held back, [I] present to you good-heartedly,
          But do [you] think, then, how much grief waiting is for me,
          To have a sweet look from your two eyes.

Parts: S., 6ᵃ (fol. 4ʳ), CT., 5ᵃ, T., Bs.
Concordances: As No. 1 (RISM 1545₁₄), fol. 7ʳ; *Livre,* fol. 10ʳ.
Musica Ficta: mm. 2 (f♯), 6 (b♭), 7 (B♭), 8 (c♯′), 10 (c♯′), 14 (b♭′), 16 (g♯′), 18
(f♯, B♭), 19 (b♭), 24 (B♭), 25 (b♭), 27 (b♭), 28 (c♯′), 29 (f♯′), 30 (b♭, twice), 31
(b♭′), 32 (b♭), 33 (g♯), 34 (g♯), 36 (g♯′), 40 (b♭), 41 (f♯), 46 (c♯′), 48 (b♭′), 49
(c♯′), 52 (b♭′), 55 (b♭), 56 (f♯), 64 (e♭′), 76 (b♭′), 77 (f♯′, twice), 86 (b♭′), 87
(b♭′), 90 (f♯′), 91 (b♭, twice), 92 (B♭), 93 (c♯′, thrice), 97 (B♭), 98 (c♯′), 100
(c♯′), 105 (b♭), 106 (b♭, twice), 110 (c♯′).
Remarks: Sharp indicated only for the initial n. affected in mm. 37, 5ᵃ, and 38, S.

106. Ad. Vuillard [Willaert], *Douleur me bat* (fol. 56ᵛ)

Lyrics: Anguish batters me and sadness makes me mad,
          Love hurts me and misfortune consoles me,
          Desire follows me, but [I] cannot help myself,
          [I] cannot take advantage of the good will people
               have toward me,
          Thus to live, by God — rather I be beheaded.

Parts: S., 5ᵃ, CT., 6ᵃ (fol. 4ᵛ), T., Bs.
Concordances: As No. 71 (RISM 1544₁₃), fol. 9ᵛ; *Livre,* fol. 10ᵛ.
Errors: m. 128, 5ᵃ, "Dien" (not "Dieu"). The word "qu'on" occasionally
appears, erroneously, as "q'uon" (in divers vv., in which the correct spelling also is
found).
Musica Ficta: mm. 8 (c♯′), 17 (g♯′), 18 (g♯′), 23 (c♯′), 24 (c♯′), 25 (f♯, b♭), 30
(c♯′), 33 (B♭), 37 (g♯′), 38 (g♯′), 40 (c♯′), 43 (c♯′), 44 (c♯′), 46 (f♯), 50 (b♭), 57
(b♭, twice), 58 (b♭, twice), 68 (e♭′?), 70 (b♭), 75 (b♭), 76 (b♭, twice), 77 (b♭), 82
(b♭′), 91 (c♯′), 96 (g♯′), 100 (b♭), 101 (c♯″), 102 (g♯), 103 (b♭′), 106 (c♯′), 107
(f♯′), 111 (b♭′), 120 (c♯′), 125 (g♯′), 129 (b♭), 130 (c♯′), 131 (g♯), 132 (b♭′), 135
(c♯′), 136 (f♯′), 138 (c♯′), 142 (g♯′), 144 (g♯′), 145 (g♯′), 146 (g♯′), 147 (b♭).

107. Ad. Vuillard [Willaert], *Petite camusette* (fol. 57ʳ)

Lyrics: Little snub-nose,
          [You] have put me to death,
          Robin and Marion,
          They go arm in arm,

They have fallen asleep,
Little snub-nose,
[You] have put me to death.

Parts: S., 6ᵃ (fol. 5ʳ), T., CT., 5ᵃ, Bs.
Concordances: Livre, fol. 11ʳ.⁹²
Musica Ficta: mm. 4 (g♯′), 7 (f♯), 8 (c♯′), 12 (f♯), 18 (b♭′), 20 (g♯′), 24 (c♯′), 26
(f♯), 27 (b♭′), 34 (g♯′), 38 (b♭), 41 (b♭), 42 (B♭), 49 (b♭′), 51 (c♯′, twice), 56
(b♭′), 64 (b♭), 68 (e♭′), 70 (e♭′), 80 (g♯′), 83 (f♯), 84 (c♯′), 88 (f♯), 94 (b♭′,
twice), 96 (g♯′), 100 (c♯′), 102 (f♯), 103 (b♭′), 110 (g♯′), 111 (c♯′), 113 (c♯′), 115
(c♯).
Remarks: Note ⁶₄ at m. 3.

108. Ad. Vuillard [Willaert], *Vous ne l'aurez pas* (fol. 57ᵛ)

Lyrics: You will not have it, if I can [help it],
          That which [you] have demanded to have
               of me,
          Even if you had as much wealth,
          As there could be inside a well.

Parts: S., 5ᵃ, 6ᵃ (fol. 5ᵛ), CT., T., Bs.
Concordances: Livre, fol. 12ᵛ.
Errors: mm. 59–87, all vv. (except Bs.), "davoir" (not "d'avoir"; correct in Bs.).
In mm. 109–10 and 117–8, Bs., "pourṟoi" (not "pourroit"; the underscored letter
is all but non-existent in the present writer's copy of the Bs. partbook). At mm.
117, S., e′ (not d′).
Musica Ficta: mm. 5 (c♯′), 6 (b♭), 14 (g♯), 12 (b♭′), 16 (g♯′), 18 (f♯), 20 (f♯′,
twice), 21 (b♭), 24 (B♭), 25 (c♯′, f♯), 27 (b♭′), 30 (B♭), 31 (b♭′), 32 (g♯′), 33 (b♭),
36 (c♯′), 38 (b♭), 40 (f♯), 42 (b♭′), 45 (B♭), 46 (b♭′), 47 (g♯′), 51 (c♯′), 53 (b♭′),
55 (f♯′), 63 (g♯), 65 (c♯′), 68 (b♭′), 69 (c♯′), 77 (b♭), 79 (c♯′), 83 (c♯′), 85 (c♯′,
twice), 86 (b♭), 87 (f♯′), 88 (b♭), 94 (c♯′, twice), 95 (b♭), 96 (f♯′), 97 (b♭′), 104
(b♭, b♭′), 106 (b♭), 111 (b♭, twice), 114 (c♯′), 115 (c♯′, twice), 117 (b♭), 118 (F♯,
b♭), 119 (f♯), 123 (b♭), 124 (g♯), 125 (c♯′), 127 (c♯′), 128 (c♯′), 129 (f♯, twice),
130 (b♭′), 131 (F♯, b♭), 132 (f♯′).

109. Ad. Vuillard [Willaert], *Qui veut aymer* (fol. 58ʳ)

Lyrics: Whoever wishes to love must be merry,
          And [must] go to see his sovereign lady,
          Two or three times or four weekly,
          In order to have a gracious kiss from her.

Parts: S., CT., T., 6ᵃ (fol. 58ʳ [= 6ʳ]), 5ᵃ, Bs.
Concordances: Le treziesme livre contenant vingt et deux chansons nouvelles a six et a huyt parties (Antwerp, T. Susato, 1550; = RISM 1550₁₄), fol., 13ᵛ; *Livre,* fol. 12ʳ.
Errors: m. 19, CT., "dme" (not "dame"); mm. 23, Bs., 25, 5ᵃ, and 26, T.: "aler" (not "aller"); mm. 73–5, 6ᵃ, the symbol for the commencement of the triple meter ("3") appears after these mm., not (as it should have) before.
Musica Ficta: mm. 8 (b♮, e♭), 13 (e♭'), 15 (b♮', twice), 52 (e♭), 53 (e♭), 54 (B♭), 58 (e♭), 59 (b♮), 60 (e♭'), 68 (b♮, e♭), 74 (e♭), 77 (e♭'), 81 (e♭).
Remarks: At m. 56, an *appoggiatura* (d) produces the sonority of a seventh chord.

110. Ad. Vuillard [Willaert], *De retourner, mon amy* (fol. 58ᵛ)⁹³

Lyrics: To return, my friend, I prithee,
 To make the spirit of your friend happy,
 Because without that, [I] cannot be relaxed,
 [I] shall live sadly, I let you know it,
 If [I] do not see you, because I desire it [your return] greatly.

Parts: S., 6ᵃ (fol. 58ᵛ [= 6ᵛ]), CT., 5ᵃ, T., Bs.
Concordances: As No. 71 (RISM 1544₁₃), fol. 12ᵛ; *Livre,* fol. 11ᵛ.
Musica Ficta: mm. 7 (b♮), 12 (e♭', b♮), 14 (b♮), 17 (e♭), 20 (e♭'), 21 (b♮, e♭), 22 (b♮), 32 (e♭', b♮), 34 (b♮), 37 (e♭), 40 (e♭'), 41 (b♮, e♭), 42 (b♮), 51 (c♯'), 64 (c♯'), 73 (e♭'), 74 (b♮'), 80 (f♯'), 96 (b♮, twice).

111. Leschenet, *Je m'y⁹⁴ plein fort* (fol. 59ʳ)

Lyrics: I complain loudly that love has destroyed me,
 It is a brew more bitter than sour grapes,
 I counsel you all, and [even] if [I] am not wise,
 That to love for love: [you] should avoid the experience.

Parts: S., 5ᵃ, 6ᵃ (fol. 7ʳ), CT., T., Bs.
Concordances: Livre, fol. 22ᵛ.
Musica Ficta: mm. 18 (b♮'), 19 (e♭'), 22 (e♭'), 34 (b♮'), 35 (e♭'), 38 (e♭'), 40 (e♭', b♮), 50 (b♮, e♭), 51 (f♯'), 53 (c♯'), 55 (e♭'), 56 (e♭'), 57 (e♭'), 59 (c♯'), 77 (CT.: e♭'), 78 (e♭', twice), 79 (b♮).
Remarks: Note ⁶₄ sonority, m. 59.

112. Crequillon, *Sy⁹⁵ me tenez tant* (fol. 59ᵛ)

Lyrics: If [you] hold me so indispensable,
 My lady, who will endure,
 Being made to die her servant,⁹⁶

I believe that it may displease you,
At the very least, [to know] he will languish,
For the misfortune he endures,
But your love will cure him,
Because there is no remedy from [any] another love.

Parts: S., CT., 6ᵃ (fol. 7ᵛ), T., 5ᵃ, Bs.
Concordances: As No. 1 (RISM 1545₁₄), fol. 14ʳ; *Livre,* fol. 26ᵛ.⁹⁷
Errors: In the last line of the lyrics, "n'a" is mostly given as "na" (in all the vv.).
Musica Ficta: mm. 1 (e♭'), 5 (e♭'), 10 (b♮'), 11 (e♭), 12 (e♭'), 13 (b♮), 17 (f♯'), 18 (b♮), 21 (e♭), 22 (b♮), 29 (e♭'), 35 (e♭), 38 (e♭), 44 (e♭), 46 (e♭), 54 (b♮'), 55 (e♭), 57 (CT.: b♮), 61 (f♯'), 62 (b♮), 65 (e♭), 66 (b♮), 73 (e♭'), 79 (e♭), 82 (e♭), 83 (b♮), 86 (b♮), 99 (e♭'), 100 (B♮), 101 (e♭), 102 (f♯), 105 (e♭'), 106 (b♮), 108 (f♯), 110 (e♭), 115 (e♭'), 120 (Bs.: e♭), 123 (e♭), 124 (B♮), 129 (b♮), 132 (e♭), 133 (e♭, e♭').
Remarks: Unalterable diminished triads in root position are found at mm. 33 and 77. In very close proximity, at mm. 101 and 105, parallel seconds occur, in the most exposed fashion. And at m. 116, the sonority of a ⁶₄ is suggested.

113. Mouton, *Vray Dieu qu'amoureux* (fol. 60ʳ)

Lyrics: True God, whom lovers have from affliction,
 Certainly I would love better death,
 I have in me neither fortitude nor vanity,
 Which does not feel the effects of remorse,
 I complain loudly, alas, have I [not an] injury,
 What my heart loves was taken away from me,
 Again it can be said that I am wronged.

Parts: S., CT., T., 6ᵃ (fol. 60ʳ [= 8ʳ]), 5ᵃ, Bs.
Concordances: Livre, fol. 35ʳ.
Errors: mm. 13, S., "on" (not "ont"); 21–2, S. and CT., "Cestes" (not "Certes"); 57–72, all vv., "my" (not "m'y").⁹⁸
Musica Ficta: mm. 16 (e♭'), 17 (e♭), 23 (b♮', e♭'), 27 (e♭'), 40 (e♭'), 41 (e♭), 47 (b♮', e♭'), 66 (b♮), 77 (e♭), 82 (f♯'), 86 (e♭), 98 (e♭'), 104 (e♭).
Remarks: Note ⁶₄ chord at m. 25.

114. Nicolas, *Vivés en paix* (fol. 60ᵛ)

Lyrics: Live in peace, all loyal lovers,
 Leave care, all pain, and displeasure,
 Having from love full joy,
 Despite that there may be in it all those false envious
  people [= "all those false envies"?].

Parts: S., CT., 6ª (fol. 60ᵛ [= 8ᵛ]). 5ª, T., Bs.
Concordances: Livre, fol. 58ᵛ.
Musica Ficta: mm. 4 (f♯), 6 (e♭), 8 (e♭′), 10 (b♮), 12 (e♭), 19 (e♭, b♮), 20 (e♭′), 22 (b♮), 24 (b♮), 30 (e♭′), 31 (c♯′), 35 (b♮), 36 (e♭′), 37 (c♯′), 38 (f♯′), 42 (f♯, b♮), 46 (e♭′), 49 (c♯′), 52 (e♭), 53 (e♭), 54 (e♭′), 55 (c♯′), 61 (e♭′), 62 (e♭, b♮), 63 (e♭′), 64 (Bs.: e♭), 65 (b♮), 69 (e♭′), 70 (Bs.: e♭), 71 (b♮), 74 (e♭, b♮), 75 (e♭′), 76 (Bs.: e♭), 77 (b♮).
Remarks: Flat only indicated for the initial n. affected in m. 34, T.

115. Nicolas, *Dieu te gard, bergere* (fol. 61ʳ)

Lyrics: God keep you, shepherdess,
  Watching your sheep, don, don,
  Your lovely manner,
  I give you my love, don, don,
  Haven't you ever seen my wild bird,
  From the morning, he is at the shore,
  My wild bird,
  My pretty falcon, don, don,
  Who catches the woodcock [and] rabbits in season, don, don, don, don.

Parts: S., 5ª, CT., T., 6ª (fol. 9ʳ), Bs.
Concordances: Livre, fol. 58ᵛ.
Musica Ficta: mm. 16 (e♭′, e♭), 46 (e♭′), 49 (b♮), 51 (e♭′), 55 (e♭′), 59 (e♭′), 62 (b♮), 66 (c♯′), 71 (e♭′), 72 (B♮), 73 (B♮).
Remarks: Natural sign indicated only for the first n. affected in mm. 25, 29, 81, and 85, 5ª; m. 90, CT., superfluous natural sign indicated for the single n. in the m. (e′). Striking simultaneous cross-relations occur in mm. 25 and 29 (repeated, mm. 81 and 85). In addition, in m. 24, there are parallel sevenths, while in m. 65, there are consecutive dissonances.

116. Leschenet, *Le coeur est mien* (fol. 61ᵛ)

Lyrics: The heart is mine, which never was conquered,
  Except in one place, where it makes its lodgings,
  And [it] will be there until it dies,
  Because a long time ago, [the place] was thus seized.

Parts: S., 5ª, CT., 6ª (fol. 9ᵛ), T., Bs.
Concordances: Livre, fol. 20ᵛ.
Errors: m. 94, Bs., "loog" (not "long").
Musica Ficta: mm. 5 (c♯′), 8 (c♯′), 9 (f♯′), 10 (g♯′), 11 (b♭), 12 (B♭), 13 (f♯), 16 (b♭), 17 (b♭′, c♯′), 22 (b♭), 24 (c♯′, twice), 26 (b♭), 31 (c♯′), 38 (c♯′), 42 (b♭′,

twice), 46 (b♭′), 47 (g♯′), 51 (b♭), 52 (g♯), 54 (b♭′), 56 (f♯′), 59 (b♭), 74 (b♭′, c♯′), 79 (b♭), 81 (c♯′, twice), 83 (b♭), 88 (c♯′), 90 (b♭), 94 (b♭′, c♯′), 99 (b♭), 101 (c♯′, twice), 103 (b♭), 108 (c♯′), 109 (f♯, twice), 111 (e♭′), 114 (b♭).
Remarks: Flat only indicated for the initial n. affected in mm. 57, CT., and 62, Bs. In mm. 19–20, the T. outlines an arpeggio.

117. Leschenet, *Helas, pourquoy ne suis-je* (fol. 62ʳ)

Lyrics: Alas, why am I [a woman] not married,
  I live in pain, in tears, and in anxiety,
  True lovers, may there be pity on me,
  And some day, you will speak my thoughts.

Parts: S., 6ª (fol. 10ʳ), CT., T., 5ª, Bs.
Concordances: Livre, fol. 21ʳ.
Musica Ficta: mm. 12 (e♭′), 24 (b♮), 26 (b♮), 33 (c♯′), 55 (e♭), 56 (b♮), 61 (e♭), 62 (b♮), 63 (c♯′), 68 (f♯), 74 (f♯), 77 (e♭′, e♭), 82 (f♯), 88 (f♯), 91 (e♭′, e♭), 96 (f♯), 102 (f♯), 108 (b♮′), 109 (e♭).
Remarks: Flat only indicated for the initial n. affected in mm. 27 and 73, 5ª; 67 and 85, Bs. Consecutive dissonances are found in mm. 35 (between S. and Bs., and 6ª and Bs.) and 47 (6ª and Bs.). In m. 41, there are parallel sevenths.

118. Gardane,⁹⁹ *Je cerche autant amour* (fol. 62ᵛ)

Lyrics: I seek love and desire it so much,
  As previously I wanted to flee it,
  I seek so much in desiring to play,
  As previously I would not have dared to say it,
  [I] cannot find another love without saying,
  My foremost and obliged duty,
  Which renders my being happy and content,
  Without seeking further, that one should suffice for me.

Parts: S., 6ª (fol. 10ᵛ), CT., 5ª, T., Bs.
Concordances: Livre, fol. 22ᵛ.
Errors: mm. 23-4, 6ª, "autrefoy" (not "autrefoys").
Musica Ficta: mm. 3 (e♭′), 13 (e♭′), 15 (e♭′), 21 (e♭′), 22 (e♭′), 24 (e♭′), 26 (e♭′), 27 (e♭), 28 (e♭″, e♭′), 30 (e♭′), 31 (CT.: e♭′, c♯′), 32 (f♯′), 34 (T.: e♭′), 36 (e♭′), 37 (5ª: b♮), 38 (e♭′, f♯′), 43 (e♭′), 48 (e♭′), 55 (e♭′), 57 (e♭′), 59 (e♭″), 62 (e♭′), 63 (e♭′), 64 (f♯′), 66 (e♭′), 67 (e♭′), 68 (f♯′), 75 (c♯′), 76 (c♯′), 82 (c♯″), 87 (e♭′), 95 (e♭′), 96 (e♭′), 107 (e♭′), 109 (e♭′), 114 (e♭), 115 (e♭″), 120 (e♭′, f♯′), 122 (e♭′), 124 (f♯′), 131 (e♭′), 132 (e♭′), 138 (S.: e♭″), 140 (e♭′), 141 (e♭′), 142 (f♯′), 144 (e♭″), 146 (e♭′), 147 (e♭′), 148 (S., fourth n.: e♭″), 151 (e♭′, b♮′), 152 (e♭′).

Remarks: There are consecutive dissonances at m. 11 (first between 6ª and CT., then between CT. and 5ª) and parallel sevenths at m. 130. In mm. 31 and 107, $\frac{6}{4}$ chords occur.

119. Rousée, *La rousée du moys de may* (fol. 63^r)

Lyrics: (See No. 16).

Parts: S., 6ª (fol. 11^r), CT., 5ª, T., Bs.
Concordances: Livre, fol. 37^v.
Musica Ficta: mm. 3 (c♯), 4 (B♭), 10 (B♭), 11 (c♯′), 12 (b♭), 17 (B♭), 19 (c♯′), 20 (b♭), 21 (f♯′), 22 (c♯′), 27 (f♯, b♭), 28 (c♯′), 33 (B♭), 34 (c♯′?), 38 (c♯), 42 (c♯′), 43 (c♯′), 44 (B♭), 50 (B♭), 51 (c♯′), 52 (b♭), 57 (B♭), 59 (c♯′), 60 (b♭), 61 (f♯′), 62 (c♯′), 63 (b♭), 64 (c♯), 65 (B♭), 67 (c♯), 71 (B♭), 72 (c♯′), 73 (b♭), 78 (B♭), 80 (c♯′), 81 (b♭), 82 (f♯′), 83 (c♯′), 88 (f♯, b♭), 89 (c♯′).
Remarks: The last word of the lyrics, in 6ª and T., has been broken, to provide text for the isolated n. in mm. 91 and 90, respectively, of these parts.

120. Moulu, *La rousée du moys de may* (fol. 63^v)

Lyrics: (See No. 16).
Parts: S., CT., 5ª, T., 6ª (fol. 11^v), Bs.
Concordances: As in No. 1 (RISM 1545$_{14}$), fol. 7^v; *Livre,* fol. 37^r; modern edition: A. C. Minor, ed., *Music in Medieval and Renaissance Life* (1964), 59.[100]
Musica Ficta: mm. 5 (e♭′), 10 (e♭), 22 (e♭′), 26 (e♭′), 30 (e♭′), 34 (e♭′), 37 (f♯′, twice), 39 (b♮), 44 (e♭′), 50 (b♮), 55 (e♭′), 59 (e♭′), 61 (f♯), 63 (c♯′), 64 (f♯′), 66 (c♯″), 75 (e♭′), 79 (e♭′), 83 (e♭′), 90 (f♯), 92 (c♯′), 93 (f♯′), 95 (c♯″), 104 (e♭′), 108 (e♭′), 112 (e♭′), 116 (e♭′), 121 (e♭′), 125 (e♭).
Remarks: Note $\frac{6}{4}$ in mm. 30, 75, 83, 104, and 112. Consecutive dissonances occur in m. 10. At mm. 67–8 and 96–7, there are parallel octaves (avoided in Susato — cf. Minor edn. — and in the Copenhagen MS concordance).

121. Moulu, *En despit des faux médisans* (fol. 64^r)

Lyrics: In spite of malicious slander,
  I have found a beautiful friend,
  If anyone is speaking ill of it,
  It doesn't matter to me what is said,
  Speaking of it, whoever will wish to speak,
  Loudly and softly in all places,
  That's quite a folly for them,
  Because for that, the love between us two won't be lost.

Parts: S., CT., 6ª (fol. 12^r), T., 5ª, Bs.
Concordances: Livre, fol. 38^r.
Errors: m. 56, T., rest missing.
Musica Ficta: mm. 17 (e♭), 23 (e♭′), 24 (c♯′), 33 (e♭′), 44 (e♭′), 53 (e♭′), 62 (e♭′), 66 (e♭′), 67 (c♯′), 74 (e♭′), 82 (e♭′), 83 (c♯′), 85 (f♯), 87 (f♯), 88 (c♯′), 92 (e♭′), 99 (f♯, twice), 102 (f♯), 104 (f♯′, twice), 107 (e♭′), 108 (c♯′), 109 (f♯′), 112 (e♭′), 113 (c♯′), 114 (f♯′), 115 (b♭), 116 (b♮), 117 (e♭′, e♭), 118 (e♭′).

122. Nicolas, *Je recommence ma douleur* (fol. 64^v)

Lyrics: My suffering begins again,
  And reproaches, and tears, in great melancholy,
  Cursed be desire,
  Through which [I] am in pain,
  It deprived me [of] my darling,
  This is a great misfortune for me,
  My suffering begins again.

Parts: S., CT., 6ª (fol. 12^v), 5ª, T., Bs.
Concordances: Livre, fol. 56^r.
Musica Ficta: mm. 2 (f♯′), 28 (CT.: e♭′), 29 (c♯′), 30 (6ª: e♭′), 32 (e♭), 33 (f♯′), 37 (e♭′), 44 (b♭′), 45 (f♯′), 46 (f♯′), 49 (f♯′), 54 (e♭′), 58 (S.: f♯′), 60 (b♮, e♭′), 62 (f♯′), 66 (e♭′), 68 (c♯″), 83 (c♯′), 86 (f♯, b♮), 87 (c♯′), 96 (c♯′), 98 (f♯′), 99 (e♭′), 103 (e♭′, e♭), 104 (e♭, twice), 109 (e♭′), 117 (e♭′), 120 (f♯, b♭′), 124 (f♯′), 132 (e♭′, twice).
Remarks: Flat only indicated for the initial n. affected, m. 48, T. Superfluous natural sign indicated, m. 76, T., for second n. (e′). Unusual voice-leading is found in this chanson: at m. 46, the T. descends by the leap of a seventh, moreover immediately thereafter descending again; at m. 50, the 6ª ascends by the leap of a tenth. $\frac{6}{4}$ chords occur at mm. 55, 68, and 85. And at m. 57, there is a simultaneous cross-relation.

123. Nicolas, *J'ay contenté ma volonté* (fol. 65^r) [C. Marot]

Lyrics: I have fulfilled my will sufficiently,
  Because I have been treated variously by love,
  I have experienced torment, good treatment,
  I have experienced sweetness and cruelty,
  And [I] complain but solely,
  For having loved so loyally,
  Her who is without loyalty.

Parts: S., 5ª, CT., T., 6ª (fol. 13^r), Bs.

Concordances: Livre, fol. 57ʳ.
Errors: The triple meter signature ("3") is indicated for m. 88 in 6ª and Bs., not for m. 87 (as it should have been). Superfluous accidentals indicated in mm. 78, T. (for c′); 89 and 93, 5ª (for first e″) and CT. (for e′).
Musica Ficta: mm. 2 (e♭′), 8 (b♮), 9 (e♭′), 10 (e♭′), 12 (e♭), 14 (e♭), 20 (f♯′), 26 (e♭), 28 (e♭′), 30 (f♯′), 34 (b♮′), 35 (e♭′), 36 (e♭′), 38 (e♭), 40 (e♭), 46 (f♯′), 48 (e♭), 60 (e♭), 63 (e♭′), 64 (c♯′), 67 (e♭″), 69 (e♭′), 73 (e♭′), 74 (e♭′), 76 (e♭′), 80 (e♭′), 106 (e♭′), 113 (e♭′), 114 (f♯′), 117 (e♭′), 124 (S.: e♭′), 128 (f♯′).
Remarks: Flat indicated only for the initial n. affected in mm. 78, Bs., and 109, T. Noteworthy in this composition are the following: the free dissonant nn., mm. 14 and 40 (the n., a, in both cases), which double the suspension and thereby strengthen the sonority of the seventh in the initial halves of the mm.; an augmented chord, produced by an upper auxiliary, m. 23; $^6_4$ chords, mm. 70 and 77; and a simultaneous cross-relation, m. 73, which may illustrate the text. At mm. 76 and 113, oddly twentieth-century sounding anticipations (on d′ and d″, respectively) occur.

124. Nicolas, *Voz huys sont ilz* (fol. 65ᵛ)

Lyrics: Your doors, they are all closed,
Young girl, you are sleeping,
Open them for me, if [you] care for me,
Are you sleeping, young girl,
Are you sleeping,
Are you sleeping all alone,
Young girl, you are sleeping,
Are you sleeping all alone,
Because for you are consumed,
Young girl, you are sleeping,
My inflamed feelings of love,
Are you sleeping, young girl,
Young girl, you are sleeping,
Are you sleeping all alone.

Parts: S., CT., 5ª, T., 6ª (fol. 13ᵛ), Bs.
Concordances: Livre, fol. 56ᵛ.
Musica Ficta: mm. 4 (f♯), 6 (f♯), 7 (f♯′), 11 (b♮), 12 (f♯, b♮), 14 (b♮), 15 (f♯, b♮), 16 (e♭′), 17 (f♯′), 19 (f♯), 21 (f♯), 23 (f♯′), 28 (f♯′), 31 (f♯′), 32 (b♮), 52 (e♭), 63 (f♯′, twice), 64 (e♭′), 65 (e♭′, twice), 76 (5ª: c♯′?; cf. m. 71), 80 (f♯′), 82 (B♮), 83 (e♭), 84 (b♮), 85 (e♭′), 87 (e♭′), 91 (f♯), 93 (f♯), 95 (f♯′), 97 (f♯′), 99 (f♯′), 101 (f♯′), 103 (b♮), 105 (e♭′), 107 (B♮), 113 (e♭′, b♮), 118 (e♭, B♮), 129 (c♯′), 130 (e♭′), 135 (f♯′), 143 (c♯′), 151 (e♭), 152 (f♯′), 156 (f♯′), 161 (e♭′), 162 (e♭′, twice).

Remarks: Flat indicated only for the initial n. affected in mm. 45, T. and Bs.; 56, T.; 62 and 159, CT. Superfluous accidental (natural sign) indicated, m. 54, 5ª, for e′. At m. 71, there is a simultaneous cross-relation (cf. m. 76). And at m. 79, there are consecutive dissonances involving three vv. (S., CT., and T.).

125. Nicolas, *Puis que j'ay belle amye* (fol. 66ʳ)

Lyrics: Since I have a lovely friend,
She is graceful and pretty,
I shall love loyally,
And wish completely,
To drive away melancholy.

Parts: S., 6ª (fol. 14ʳ), T., 5ª, CT., Bs.
Concordances: Livre, fol. 59ʳ.[101]
Musica Ficta: mm. 7 (c♯′), 8 (B♭), 9 (f♯′), 16 (c♯′), 21 (b♭′), 22 (c♯′), 32 (g♯′), 34 (g♯′), 36 (b♭′), 37 (b♭), 42 (b♭′), 44 (g♯′), 62 (b♭), 65 (c♯′), 66 (B♭), 67 (f♯′), 71 (e♭′, thrice), 74 (c♯′), 80 (c♯′), 87 (c♯′), 88 (B♭), 89 (f♯′), 96 (c♯′), 102 (c♯′), 106 (b♭).
Remarks: At m. 11, there is a $^6_4$. At mm. 18, 76, and 98, a free dissonance (a), creating the sonority of a seventh chord, interrupts parallel octaves between the lowest pair of vv. And at m. 43, there are consecutive dissonances (bt. 1, S. and Bs.).

126. Fourmentin,[102] *Par trop amour* (fol. 66ᵛ)

Lyrics: Through too much love, [she] pursues me intimately,
But power and virtue abandon me,
With her rays, [she] renders me assaults deliberately,
She wounds my heart from too nearby,
And [so] accomplishing, a weakness comes to me,
Which, to be borne, impels me to the pursuit,
Since neither virtue nor nobility are in me,
Adieu, [I] say to you, love, I am running away.

Parts: S., 5ª, CT., T., 6ª (fol. 14ᵛ), Bs.
Concordances: Livre, fol. 27ʳ.
Errors: mm. 52–3, 5ª, 53–4, S., 58–9, T., "axpres" (not "expres"); mm. 55–6, CT., "aussaux" (not "assaux"); mm. 132–5, T., "noblese" (not "noblesse"); m. 164, 5ª, "le" (not "la").
Musica Ficta: mm. 7 (e♭′), 18 (e♭″), 20 (e♭′), 28 (b♮, twice), 30 (c♯′), 32 (c♯″), 34 (c♯′), 35 (c♯′), 36 (f♯′, twice), 41 (f♯′), 46 (f♯′), 53 (e♭′), 64 (e♭″), 66 (e♭′), 74 (b♮, twice), 76 (c♯″), 78 (c♯″), 80 (c♯′), 81 (c♯′), 82 (f♯′, twice), 87 (f♯′), 92 (f♯′),

94 (f♯′), 96 (f♯′), 100 (e♭′), 104 (b♮, e♭′), 106 (c♯′, f♯′), 107 (e♭′), 108 (f♯′), 109 (e♭′), 112 (e♭, e♭′), 114 (e♭′), 118 (e♭″), 119 (e♭″), 120 (c♯″), 121 (f♯′, twice), 122 (b♮′, f♯′), 126 (e♭′), 136 (c♯″), 138 (c♯′), 139 (c♯′), 140 (b♮′), 145 (f♯′), 147 (c♯″), 149 (c♯′), 150 (c♯′), 152 (c♯″), 154 (c♯′), 155 (c♯′), 156 (b♮′), 161 (f♯′), 164 (e♭′).
Remarks: Note the $\frac{6}{4}$ chords at mm. 25 and 71; the *appoggiatura* (d′) in mm. 101 and 134, which suggests a seventh chord; and the cross-relation, m. 163.

127.   Maillard, *Las, je languis* (fol. 67ᵛ)

Lyrics: Alas, I languish and indeed do not know why,
            Living in pain and in melancholy,
            Through which I say and swear on my faith,
            That he is quite mad, who trusts in love.

Parts: S., 6ᵃ (fol. 15ᵛ), CT., 5ᵃ, T., Bs.
Concordances: Livre, fol. 14ʳ.
Musica Ficta: mm. 3 (b♭), 10 (g♯), 12 (b♭), 14 (g♯′), 17 (g♯′), 18 (g♯′), 20 (f♯′), 34 (b♭), 38 (b♭′), 39 (c♯′), 47 (e♭′), 54 (b♭′), 55 (f♯′), 75 (g♯), 79 (g♯′), 82 (g♯′), 89 (b♭′), 91 (b♭′), 93 (b♭′), 94 (c♯′), 95 (g♯′), 98 (g♯′), 102 (g♯′), 105 (g♯′), 112 (b♭′), 114 (b♭), 116 (b♭′), 117 (c♯′), 122 (c♯′).
Remarks: At m. 37, there is a $\frac{6}{4}$ chord.

128.   Josquin, *Tenez moy en voz bras* (fol. 68ʳ)

Lyrics: Hold me in your arms,
            My friend, I am sick,
            Your love will cure me,
            In Paris, or over there,
            There is a clear fountain,
            Hold me in your arms,
            My friend, I am sick,
            Your love will cure me.

Parts: S., CT., T., 5ᵃ, 6ᵃ (fol. 16ʳ), Bs.
Concordances: Livre, fol. 31ᵛ; modern edition: *Josquin des Prés: Werken: Wereldlijke Werken* (ed. A. Smijers, 1921–), I (1922–5), 33.
Musica Ficta: mm. 3 (e♭), 16 (c♯′), 18 (c♯′), 20 (f♯), 25 (e♭), 29 (e♭), 30 (e♭′), 32 (f♯′), 39 (c♯′), 41 (e♭′, e♭), 44 (e♭′), 45 (e♭, f♯′), 46 (e♭), 49 (f♯′), 50 (f♯′), 53 (f♯′, e♭), 54 (f♯′), 56 (e♭′), 57 (e♭), 65 (b♮), 68 (e♭), 76 (e♭), 84 (e♭′), 91 (e♭′), 94 (e♭), 106 (c♯′), 108 (c♯′), 110 (f♯′), 115 (e♭), 119 (e♭), 120 (e♭′), 122 (f♯′), 129 (c♯′), 131 (e♭′, e♭), 134 (e♭′), 135 (e♭, f♯′), 136 (e♭), 139 (f♯′), 140 (f♯′), 143 (f♯′, e♭), 144 (f♯′), 146 (b♮), 147 (e♭), 149 (e♭).

Remarks: There are parallel fifths (involving dissonant nn.) between 5ᵃ and Bs., mm. 69–70.

129.   Josquin, *Allegez moy douce plaisant* (fol. 68ᵛ)[103]

Lyrics: Relieve me, sweet pleasant brunette,
            Under my navel,
            Relieve me of all my pains,
            Your beauty holds me in sweet love,
            Under my navel.

Parts: S., 5ᵃ, T., CT., 6ᵃ (fol. 16ᵛ), Bs.
Concordances: modern edition: *Josquin des Prés: Werken: Wereldlijke Werken* (ed. A. Smijers, 1921–), I (1922–5), 36.[104]
Errors: m. 83, T., accidental placed after the n. affected, not before.
Musica Ficta: mm. 8 (f♯), 10 (f♯), 12 (f♯), 16 (f♯′, twice), 20 (f♯, twice), 24 (f♯′), 25 (b♮), 26 (e♭, twice), 27 (b♮), 28 (f♯), 30 (e♭′, twice), 32 (f♯′), 33 (b♮), 34 (e♭, twice), 35 (b♮), 36 (f♯), 39 (e♭′), 43 (e♭′), 46 (e♭), 47 (c♯), 51 (c♯′), 54 (e♭), 55 (c♯), 58 (f♯), 60 (f♯), 62 (f♯), 64 (f♯, twice), 66 (f♯), 70 (f♯′, twice), 74 (f♯, twice), 78 (f♯′), 79 (b♮), 80 (e♭, twice), 81 (b♮), 82 (f♯), 84 (e♭′).
Remarks: Unusual simultaneous cross-relations occur at mm. 85 and 87–8, perhaps illustrating the text. In addition, at m. 70, there is a $\frac{6}{4}$.

130.   Nicolas, *Tout est vert* (fol. 69ʳ)

Lyrics: Everything is harsh in our house, *gamin, gamine,*
            In returning from Lyon,
            I met a lackey, gamin, gamine,
            Everything is harsh in our house, gamin, gamine,
            He asked me my name,
            Jacqueline, they call me, gamin, gamine,
            Everything is harsh in our house, gamin, gamine.

Parts: S., 6ᵃ (fol. 17ʳ), T., CT., 5ᵃ, Bs.
Concordances: Livre, fol. 58ʳ.
Errors: mm. 47–8, CT., and 49–50, S., "valleton" (not "valeton").
Musica Ficta: mm. 4 (c♯′), 11 (f♯′), 19 (b♭), 21 (e♭′, twice), 26 (f♯′, twice), 27 (e♭′), 30 (e♭), 31 (f♯′, twice), 37 (e♭′), 40 (b♭′), 42 (e♭′), 44 (b♭′), 46 (b♭′), 50 (b♭), 52 (b♭′), 55 (b♭), 61 (b♭), 62 (f♯′), 80 (e♭′), 84 (f♯′), 91 (b♭), 96 (b♭, twice), 97 (b♭, b♭′), 98 (b♭′), 101 (b♭), 102 (b♭′), 111 (f♯′, g♯′), 114 (b♭), 115 (b♭′), 118 (b♭), 123 (b♭), 133 (c♯′), 136 (f♯′), 139 (b♭).
Remarks: Sharp only indicated for the initial n. affected, m. 72, 5ᵃ. In mm. 28–9, the 6ᵃ, moving from one phrase to another, leaps by an ascending seventh; in mm.

154–5, the 5ᵃ line, in effect, is a four-n. arpeggio (other vv. have three-n. arpeggios, as well, at the end of the composition). In m. 52, an *appoggiatura* (c′), effectuates the suggestion (on bt. 1) of a seventh chord in second inversion.

131. C. LeJeune, *O pas en vain perdus* (fol. 68ᵛ) [Bäif]

Lyrics: Oh steps, in vain lost, oh vain hopes,
Oh too powerful desire, oh by too feeble heart,
Oh too flattering love, oh too bitter languor,
Oh my eyes, no longer eyes,
But, from tears, two fountains,
Oh little certain solace,
Sadnesses too certain,
Oh for so costly faith, too blind inclemency,
Oh graces, oh beauty, whose lovely vigor maintains
    vigorously,
My always fresh pains,
Oh wishes, oh sighs, oh thoughts, oh regrets,
Oh fields, countrysides, waters, oh crags, oh forests,
Oh goddesses, oh gods of the earth and of the waves,
Oh heaven, oh earth, oh sea,
Oh god who causes the day to dawn,
Goddess the night [to fall],
Do you see another love,
Who, even in loving,
So abounds in sadness.

Parts: S., 6ᵃ (fol. 17ᵛ), CT., 5ᵃ, T., Bs.
Musica Ficta: mm. 8 (e♭′), 38 (f♯′), 42 (f♯′), 51 (e♭′), 52 (f♯), 56 (c♯′), 58 (e♭), 64 (f♯′), 66 (c♯′), 67 (f♯′), 76 (e♭′), 85 (e♭′), 86 (c♯′), 107 (e♭′), 108 (c♯′), 112 (f♯), 119 (f♯′), 122 (f♯′), 122 (f♯′, twice), 132 (f♯′), 135 (e♭′), 137 (b♮), 138 (c♯′), 145 (f♯′), 156 (f♯′), 159 (e♭′), 161 (b♮), 162 (c♯′), 169 (f♯′), 180 (f♯′).
Remarks: Flat indicated only for the initial n. affected in mm. 12, T., 18, 6ᵃ, and 81, Bs.; ditto, for the sharp, m. 96, S. At mm. 91 and 95, retention of the accidental is queried, since descent of a chromatic semitone may in fact be required by the text. This work is noteworthy for its cross-relations, at mm. 71–2, 91, 101, and 118. Two $\frac{6}{4}$ chords are found, successively, in mm. 60–1; others appear in mm. 66 and 168–9. The CT moves in successive descending perfect fourths, mm. 151–2, repeated by the 5ᵃ, mm. 175–6.

132. C. LeJeune, *Je suis desheritée* (fol. 70ᵛ)

Lyrics: I am disinherited,
Since I have lost my friend,
He left me all alone,
Full of pain and worry,
Nightingale of the lovely wood,
Without further delay,
Go say to my friend,
That, for him, [I] am tormented.

Parts: S., 6ᵃ (fol. 18ᵛ), CT., 5ᵃ, T., Bs.
Musica Ficta: mm. 5 (c♯′, twice), 26 (e♭′), 28 (e♭′), 43 (e♭′), 46 (e♭), 50 (b♮, twice), 52 (e♭′), 54 (e♭″), 56 (f♯), 58 (e♭′), 60 (e♭′), 62 (f♯′), 63 (e♭), 64 (e♭″), 69 (e♭), 70 (e♭′), 76 (c♯″), 78 (e♭), 79 (b♮), 80 (e♭″), 88 (c♯″), 98 (c♯″, b♮′), 99 (c♯″).
Remarks: Note $\frac{6}{4}$ chord, m. 82.

133. Lupi,[105] *Dueil, double dueil* (fol. 71ʳ)

Lyrics: Grief, double grief, strengthened by chagrin,
Sadness, weariness, enemies of pleasure,
From my languor, take care,
And from my misfortune, seeing my affliction,
Do not let me dally living more.

Parts: S., CT., 6ᵃ (fol. 19ʳ), T., 5ᵃ, Bs.
Concordances: As for No. 71 (RISM 1544₁₃), fol. 9ʳ.[106]
Musica Ficta: mm. 4 (b♭), 10 (b♭), 17 (b♭), 20 (b♭), 24 (g♯), 26 (g♯), 30 (g♯), 31 (c♯′), 34 (g♯), 43 (b♭), 44 (b♭′), 47 (b♭), 52 (c♯′), 56 (b♭), 58 (b♭), 59 (b♭), 60 (b♭), 63 (b♭′), 70 (b♭), 73 (B♭), 77 (b♭′), 79 (b♭), 81 (b♭′), 83 (b♭), 86 (c♯′, twice), 88 (b♭), 89 (f♯′), 92 (e♭), 103 (b♭), 104 (b♭′), 107 (b♭), 112 (b♭), 121 (b♭), 122 (b♭′), 125 (b♭), 131 (b♭).
Remarks: Of particular interest is the T. at mm. 43, 103, and 121, which ascends a sixth by leap, only to drop immediately by step; *musica ficta* (a flat to e′) cannot be applied, owing to the presence of e′ simultaneously in the 6ᵃ or CT. Consecutive dissonances occur in the composition, at mm. 4, 67, and 88.

134. C. LeJeune, *C'est une dure departie* (fol. 71ᵛ)

Lyrics: It is a hard departure,
Of him in whom I have placed my heart,
Therefore, [I] shall go to spend my life,
At the hermitage of weariness,
And all my days, in the forenoon,

I shall go to sing in the countryside,
Under the shelter of a little bush, [of]
The suffering I am enduring for him.

Parts: S., 6ᵃ (fol. 19ᵛ), CT., T., 5ᵃ, Bs.
Errors: m. 18, CT., "jay" (not "j'ay").
Musica Ficta: mm. 3 (e♭'), 10 (b♭'), 12 (g♯'), 13 (f♯), 14 (g♯), 17 (B♭, f♯), 18 (b♭), 20 (f♯'), 30 (b♭'), 32 (g♯'), 33 (f♯), 34 (g♯), 37 (B♭, f♯), 38 (b♭'), 40 (f♯'), 44 (b♭'), 46 (e♭'), 49 (g♯'), 57 (f♯), 63 (b♭'), 64 (b♭), 66 (b♭'), 68 (b♭), 71 (c♯'), 74 (c♯'), 79 (f♯'), 82 (b♭'), 84 (f♯'), 88 (f♯', twice), 89 (c♯'), 94 (f♯'), 101 (c♯', twice), 104 (c♯'), 109 (f♯'), 112 (b♭), 117 (c♯'), 118 (e♭).
Remarks: Sharp indicated only for the initial n. affected in mm. 53, T; 73 and 103, Bs. Especially noteworthy, in this chanson, are the cross-relations, mm. 9 and 29, and the ascent of a chromatic semitone, m. 99.

135. Clemens non papa, *C'est à grand tort* (fol. 72ʳ)

Lyrics: It's a great injury that, poor little me, [I] endure,
And that I am so curtly considered,
More unfortunate, there isn't [any woman] under the bare skin,
The pain is too hard for me to endure.

Parts: S., 5ᵃ, CT., T., 6ᵃ (fol. 20ʳ), Bs.[107]
Concordances: Modern edition: *J. Clemens non Papa: Opera Omnia* (= *Corpus Mensurabilis Musicae,* 4; ed. K. P. Bernet–Kempers), X (1962), 134.
Errors: mm. 48, S., "u'y" (not "n'y"); 72–4 and 77–9, S., "lendurer" (not "l'endurer").
Musica Ficta: mm. 18 (b♭), 23 (e♭'), 24 (b♭), 25 (b♭', twice), 33 (b♭), 34 (b♭', twice), 37 (e♭'), 40 (b♭'), 41 (b♭), 42 (f♯'), 46 (b♭'), 48 (b♭'?: use of *musica ficta* here, while eliminating the leap of a tritone in the 5ᵃ, introduces a simultaneous cross-relation between that v. and the T.), 50 (b♭'), 51 (b♭).
Remarks: At m. 4, there is a $^6_4$ triad, followed by a free dissonant n. (g') or, probably better, the 5ᵃ may be interpreted as having a suspension ornamented in resolution; the g' can be viewed, by exchange of vv., as an anticipation to the g' in the S.: cf. m. 56. An *appoggiatura* (a), m. 37, produces the sonority of a seventh chord and, in turn, functions as a retardation to the succeeding harmony. Unique to the *Mellange* and striking in their harshness are the parallel seconds — three pair of seconds in immediate succession — in m. 51. Already mentioned under *Musica Ficta* is the leap of a tritone, m. 48.

136. Don Nicole[108] [Vicentino], *Passa la nave mia* (fol. 72ᵛ) [Petrarch]

Lyrics: (See: R.M. Durling, ed., *Petrarch's Lyric Poems* [1976], No. 189).

Parts: S., 6ᵃ (fol. 20ᵛ), CT., T., 5ᵃ, Bs.
Concordances: Modern edition: *Nicolò Vicentino: Opera Omnia* (= *Corpus Mensurabilis Musicae,* 26; ed. H. Kaufman, 1963), 125.
Errors: In all vv.: "scill'e caribdi" (not "Scill'e Caribdi"); "a ciascun" (not "A ciascun"); "tempest'el" (not "tempest'e'l"); "La vela" (not "la vela"); "humid'atorno" (not "humid'eterno"); "derror" (not "d'error"); "ignorantia torto" (not "ignoranti'atorto"); "celansi" (not "Celans'i"); "Morta" (not "morta"); "Tal ch'inconmincio di sperar" (not "tal ch'i'nconmincio disperar"). Bs., 6ᵃ, and 5ᵃ: "cherno" (not "scherno"); S, "londe" (not "l'onde") and "larte" (not "l'arte"). The following elisions, carried out in this edition, were not indicated in the source (italics represent the elided syllables): "ch'ab*bi a*," "ven*to hu*mid'eterno," "dol*ci u*sati," and "l'on*de e*." In mm. 136–7 and 140–1, 5ᵃ, "Pioggio" (not "Pioggia") and "neblia" (not "nebbia"), respectively; mm. 186–9, 6ᵃ, "scgni" (not "segni"). In mm. 201–2 and 211–12, 6ᵃ; 201–2 and 213–14, T.; 208–9, 5ᵃ; 209–10, Bs.; 213–14, CT.: "region" (not "ragion").
Musica Ficta: mm. 9 (e♭'), 17 (f♯'), 29 (f♯'), 33 (e♭'), 57 (e♭''), 58 (c♯''), 65 (e♭'', twice), 68 (5ᵃ: e♭'), 77 (e♭'), 78 (f♯'), 103 (e♭'), 104 (b♮), 107 (e♭'), 117 (e♭''), 118 (c♯''), 139 (CT.: e♭'), 172 (e♭'), 176 (e♭''), 185 (e♭''), 187 (c♯''), 200 (f♯'), 221 (f♯'), 225 (c♯'').
Remarks: In m. 38, 6ᵃ, the natural sign is indicated only for the first n. affected. Far more common in this composition, undoubtedly owing to its extensive chromaticism, is the indication of the accidentals for every n. affected: S., mm. 160 and 208 (flat), 183 (sharp); 6ᵃ, mm. 173 and 232 (natural sign); CT., mm. 35, 210, and 220 (flat), 55 (natural sign), 119 and 223 (sharp); T., mm. 16 and 117 (natural sign), 26 and 162 (flat), 216 (sharp); 5ᵃ, mm. 181 (sharp), 195 (flat); Bs., mm. 179 (natural sign), 207, 209, and 210 (flat). The unique appearance in the *Mellange* of A♭ and D♭ takes place in this work. As a result of the pronounced use of chromaticism, the following noteworthy details may be cited: at mm. 87–8 (S.), 91–3 (T.), and 122–41 (misc. vv., at the beginning of the 2.ᵃ *pars*), chromatic descents; at mm. 169–71 (CT.), 180–1 (6ᵃ), 208–11 (T.), chromatic ascents; at mm. 191–2, a cross-relation involving an augmented chord. Another cross-relation is found at m. 75 and another augmented chord at m. 132. At m. 169, there is a $^6_4$ chord.

137. C. LeJeune, *Susanne un jour* (fol. 73ᵛ) [Guéroult]

Lyrics: (See No. 18).

Parts: S., S. II (6ᵃ, fol. 22ʳ), CT., 5ᵃ, T., 6ᵃ (fol. 21ᵛ), Bs.[109]
Musica Ficta: mm. 14 (e♭'), 29 (f♯'), 40 (f♯'), 42 (e♭'), 56 (f♯'), 57 (b♮'), 63 (e♭''), 71 (e♭''), 79 (e♭'), 82 (c♯'), 83 (f♯'), 86 (b♮'), 91 (e♭'), 99 (f♯'), 101 (e♭''), 102 (e♭'), 103 (b♮'), 128 (b♮), 130 (e♭''), 135 (e♭'), 136 (f♯'), 137 (b♮'), 142 (e♭'), 144 (f♯'), 148 (e♭').

Remarks: Flat indicated only for the initial n. affected in mm. 8, CT.; 60, 5ª; 77 and 105, 6ª. Ditto, for the sharp, m. 63, CT. At mm. 28 and 55, there are cross-relations, and, at m. 63, a simultaneous cross-relation.

138. Moulu, *J'ay mis mon coeur* (fol. 74ʳ)¹¹⁰

Lyrics: I have put my heart in one place only,
   So well in, that it cannot get out,
   I think about it so much more, and
     there is more worry,
   Alas, I cannot live joyfully.

Parts: S., S. II (6ª, fol. 23ʳ), CT., T., 6ª (fol. 22ᵛ), 5ª, Bs.
Concordances: Livre, fol. 38ᵛ.
Musica Ficta: mm. 3 (e♭), 5 (e♭′), 18 (e♭), 19 (f♯′), 40 (e♭), 53 (e♭′), 55 (e♭′), 56 (e♭), 63 (e♭), 71 (f♯′), 72 (e♭, twice), 74 (e♭, twice), 76 (e♭′), 88 (e♭), 89 (f♯′), 91 (e♭, twice), 93 (e♭, twice), 95 (e♭′), 107 (e♭), 108 (f♯′), 111 (B♮).
Remarks: In m. 31, there are consecutive dissonances (between S. and S.II).

139. Gardane, *Fuyez de moy*¹¹¹ (fol. 74ᵛ)

Lyrics: Flee from me, oh amorous travail,
   And may your well-being be my cruel suffering,
   Beauty, wealth, and harmonious singing,
   And all pleasure, [from] which my heart sparkles,
   I have overcome all, presuming to please her,
   Except that for love, in wanting to serve her,
   [I] have bound myself in immortal contemplation,
   Which will offer me up to sudden death.

Parts: S., 5ª, CT., T., T. II (6ª, fol. 24ʳ), 6ª (fol. 23ᵛ), Bs.
Concordances: Livre, fol. 23ᵛ.
Errors: mm. 115, 119, 126, and 135, T. II; 131 and 133, 6ª: "a" (not "à").
Musica Ficta: mm. 3 (e♭′), 6 (e♭′), 12 (c♯′), 13 (f♯′, twice), 14 (b♮), 15 (e♭, twice), 17 (e♭′), 18 (e♭), 21 (e♭), 22 (e♭, f♯), 26 (f♯′), 27 (T.: b♭), 30 (f♯′, twice), 33 (e♭′), 37 (e♭′), 38 (CT.: f♯′), 40 (c♯″), 42 (c♯″), 43 (f♯′), 44 (c♯′), 54 (b♭′, twice), 59 (b♭′), 63 (f♯), 67 (f♯′), 70 (b♭′), 71 (e♭′), 73 (e♭), 75 (e♭), 76 (c♯″), 78 (c♯′), 84 (e♭′), 85 (e♭′), 105 (f♯′), 110 (b♭), 112 (e♭′), 115 (e♭), 117 (e♭), 119 (e♭′), 121 (e♭), 124 (f♯), 125 (e♭, twice), 128 (f♯), 131 (e♭′), 132 (c♯′), 133 (e♭′), 136 (e♭′, f♯′), 138 (e♭′, f♯′), 140 (e♭′).
Remarks: At m. 34, 5ª, sharp indicated only for the initial n. affected. Unusual voice-leading is found in this chanson: at m. 7, the T. is arpeggiated; at mm. 76–7,

in moving from one phrase to the next, the CT. carries out the leap of a seventh; and at mm. 78–9, the 6ª moves in consecutive fourths.

140. Crequillon, *Petite camusette* (fol. 75ʳ)

Lyrics: (See No. 107).

Parts: S., CT., [CT. II] (6ª, fol. 24ᵛ), 5ª, T., 6ª (fol. 25ʳ), Bs.
Concordances: Livre, fol. 45ʳ.
Errors: mm. 46 and 50, Bs.; 48, 5ª: "a" (not "à"); m. 82, Bs., G (tied from m. 81, not smi. rest).
Musica Ficta: mm. 5 (b♭′), 10 (g♯′), 14 (c♯′), 19 (b♭), 20 (f♯′), 32 (c♯′), 37 (b♭), 38 (b♭), 46 (f♯′), 59 (g♯′), 61 (b♭′), 63 (b♭), 65 (b♭′), 70 (g♯′), 74 (c♯′), 77 (B♭), 79 (b♭), 80 (f♯′), 92 (c♯′), 104 (b♭′), 106 (b♭), 107 (f♯′).
Remarks: At m. 48, an *appoggiatura* (e′), forming the sonority of a seventh chord (in first inversion), is found.

141. Certon, *Revien vers moy* (fol. 75ᵛ) [Ronsard]

Lyrics: (See No. 69).

Parts: S., 6ª (fol. 25ᵛ), CT. II (6ª, fol. 26ʳ), CT., 5ª, T., Bs.
Concordances: Les Meslanges de Maistre Pierre Certon (Paris, N. DuChemin, 1570; = RISM C-1718), p. 138; *Livre,* fol. 43ʳ.
Musica Ficta: mm. 4 (b♭), 17 (g♯′?), 23 (b♭), 30 (b♭), 31 (b♭), 44 (g♯), 45 (b♭′), 47 (b♭′), 48 (b♭′), 49 (g♯′), 50 (c♯′?), 63 (c♯′), 65 (g♯′?, c♯′), 66 (c♯′), 69 (c♯′), 75 (c♯′), 79 (b♭′), 80 (g♯′), 85 (g♯), 88 (b♭′), 89 (g♯′), 91 (g♯), 93 (b♭), 94 (g♯), 95 (b♭′), 96 (g♯′), 98 (b♭), 104 (g♯), 108 (5ª: g♯), 112 (g♯′), 114 (g♯).
Remarks: At mm. 79 and 88, there are consecutive dissonances.

142. Vuildre [Wilder], *Amy, souffrez* (fol. 76ʳ)¹¹²

Lyrics: Friend, tolerate my loving you,
   And do not be unkind to me,
   By telling me that your heart,
   Suffers extreme pain for me.

Parts: S., CT., 6ª (fol. 27ʳ), T., 5ª, [5ª II] (6ª, fol. 26ᵛ), Bs.
Musica Ficta: mm. 6 (e♭), 7 (b♮), 25 (e♭′), 31 (e♭), 32 (b♮, e♭), 36 (b♮′), 39 (e♭), 40 (e♭), 41 (b♮, twice), 53 (b♮), 59 (e♭), 73 (b♮), 79 (e♭).
Remarks: Natural sign indicated only for the initial n. affected, m. 48, 6ª. At mm. 61 and 81, there is an *appoggiatura* (e).

143. Clemens non papa, *Amour au coeur* (fol. 76ᵛ) [C. Marot]

Lyrics: Love stabs me in the heart,
   Whenever I am well loved,
   But I cannot love,
   When I am not loved at all,
   Everyone be advised to do as I,
   Because to love without cause,
   That is anxiety too great.

Parts: S., S. II (T., fol. 77^r), CT., CT. II (Bs., fol. 77^r), T., T. II (S., fol. 77^r), Bs., Bs. II (CT., fol. 77^r).

Concordances: Livre, fols. 46^r (S.) and 45^v (S. II); modern edition: *J. Clemens non Papa: Opera Omnia* (= *Corpus Mensurabilis Musicae,* 4; ed. K. P. Bernet–Kempers), X (1962), 124.

Musica Ficta: mm. 3 (eb′), 6 (eb′), 17 (eb′), 18 (eb′), 20 (eb′), 34 (eb), 38 (eb), 42 (eb), 68 (b♮′), 78 (eb′).

144. Gardane, *Complainte de la Torterelle (Que dis tu, que fais tu)* (fol. 77^v) [Ronsard]

Lyrics: [Ronsard]: What do you say, what are you doing,
    Pensive Turtle-dove, on this gaunt tree,
  [Turtle-dove]: Alas, openly I lament,
  [Ronsard]: Oh why, tell me,
  [Turtle-dove]: For my absent companion, dearer than my life,
  [Ronsard]: Where is she?
  [Turtle-dove]: A cruel bird-catcher, with sticky cunning,
    Caught her and killed her, and night and day, I sing
    [of] her death in this wood, calling death wicked [in]
    that it did not kill me with my faithful one,
  [Ronsard]: Would you really wish to die with your companion,
  [Turtle-dove]: Yes, for I languish, as well, in pain, and the regret of
    her death accompanies me always,
  [Ronsard]: Oh lovely birds, may you be happy,
    From loving so faithfully,
    May your heart be happy,
    Which, without being at all fickle,
    Is always amorous.

Parts: S., S. II (CT., fol. 78^r), CT. II (S., fol. 78^r), CT., T. II (Bs., fol. 78^r), T., Bs., Bs. II (T., fol. 78^r).

Concordances: Livre, fol. 24^r.

Errors: mm. 12, S. and Bs., "c'est" (not "cest"); 30, S. II, "cherc" (not "chere");

57, S. II, "nuic" (not "nuit"); 88–9, CT., "Cuy" (not "Ouy").

Musica Ficta: mm. 2 (eb′), 9 (eb′), 11 (f♯′), 12 (b♮), 17 (b♮), 23 (b♮), 28 (b♮), 34 (b♮), 36 (eb′), 46 (eb′), 49 (eb′), 50 (c♯′), 62 (f♯′, b♮), 64 (b♮′), 66 (eb′), 71 (eb′, twice), 74 (eb′), 85 (eb), 86 (f♯′), 91 (eb′), 92 (eb), 93 (b♮, eb′), 95 (eb′), 97 (eb), 102 (eb), 103 (eb), 118 (eb′), 121 (eb′), 122 (b♮), 124 (eb), 125 (b♮), 126 (eb′), 128 (eb′), 130 (eb), 154 (eb′), 159 (b♮), 161 (eb′).

Remarks: Flat indicated only for the first n. affected in m. 100, CT. The "L.", appearing in the music in the S. and Bs. partbooks (three times[113] in S. and Bs.; four times[114] in CT. II and T. II), evidently represents "L'amant" (the lover) or "Le Poète" (the poet), as in the poem, "R." (representing "Ronsard") appears at the same places. "T." (standing for "Torterelle") also appears in the poem. Both references have been brought forward from the poem to the translation, above, as they clarify the dialogue. Noteworthy in this composition are the parallel seconds, m. 33, and a cross-relation, m. 100. At mm. 11–12, the Bs. moves in consecutive perfect fourths, as, at mm. 52–3, does the S. II; in both cases, the close of one phrase and beginning of another are involved.

145. Phinot, *Vivons m'amye*[115] (fol. 78^v) [after Catullus][116]

Lyrics: Let's live, my friend, and let's pursue love,
   Without paying attention to idle gossip,
   Of those peevish and difficult old people,
   Let's cheat time, holding that we ought [to],
   Considering this little bit that we have to live,
   A lengthy sleep, sound and restful,
   Give me then, my darling, a kiss,
   Then a hundred, then a thousand, and then
    let's start again,
   These sweet kisses in a thousand other ways,
   Doubling them in so sudden a way,
   That these jealous, envious gluttons,
   Will not know at all the tally of our kisses.

Parts: S., S. II (CT., fol. 79^r), CT., CT. II (S., fol. 79^r), T., T. II (Bs., fol. 79^r), Bs., Bs. II (T., fol. 79^r).

Concordances: Livre, fol. 43^v.

Musica Ficta: mm. 4 (b♮), 14 (eb′), 23 (eb), 24 (eb), 28 (eb′), 29 (f♯′), 35 (eb′), 38 (eb′), 39 (b♮), 41 (b♮), 54 (eb′), 66 (eb′), 74 (eb′), 75 (eb′), 76 (b♮), 80 (b♮), 83 (eb′), 90 (eb′), 97 (eb′), 107 (f♯′), 119 (CT. II: eb′), 120 (eb′), 121 (c♯′), 128 (b♮′, twice), 133 (f♯′), 134 (b♮′), 140 (eb′), 141 (f♯′), 146 (eb), 147 (eb′), 155 (T.: eb′?; cf. m. 62), 162 (CT. II: b♮), 174 (eb′), 175 (eb′), 176 (b♮), 177 (T.: eb′?), 184 (f♯′), 188 (CT.: b♮), 192 (eb).

Remarks: Flat indicated only for the first n. affected, m. 6, CT. The cross-relation at mm. 60, 62, and 64 is repeated later at mm. 153 and 157, as well as at m. 179; at mm. 155 and 177, the cross-relation comes about as a result of the *musica ficta* recommended.

146. Phinot, *Qu'est-ce qu'amour (fol. 80ᵛ)*

Lyrics: What is love — nothing but living without life,
   dying without death,
  Rest full of travail, it is voluptousness of
   satiated suffering,
  End of everything good, beginning of evil,
  What is love — voluntary constraint,
  Painful repose, and downright servitude,
  Idle labor, tributary freedom,
  Death without grief, Attention without care,
  What is love, delectable passion —,
  Sweetened rancor, honey pickled in gall,
  Indulgent harshness, and acceptable languor,
  Constant gossip, like waves in [the] sea,
  Love always begins boldly and, through work,
   acquires perseverance,
  Through apprehension and faith, secures its efficacy,
  Discreet conversation keeps it secure.

Parts: S., S. II (CT., fol. 81ʳ), CT., CT. II (S., fol. 81ʳ), T. II (Bs., fol. 81ʳ), T., Bs., Bs. II (T., fol. 81ʳ).
Concordances: Livre, fol. 44ᵛ.
Errors: m. 21, CT., "cest" (not "c'est").
Musica Ficta: mm. 10 (c♯'), 12 (b♭'), 14 (c♯'), 27 (b♭, f♯'), 30 (b♭'), 37 (b♭'), 39 (f♯), 42 (f♯'), 44 (b♭'), 45 (b♭), 46 (f♯'), 48 (b♭'), 50 (f♯'), 54 (e♭''), 55 (e♭), 59 (e♭'), 61 (c♯'), 69 (b♭), 72 (b♭), 74 (e♭', b♭), 75 (c♯'), 81 (b♭'), 85 (b♭'), 91 (b♭), 92 (b♭'), 93 (f♯), 96 (f♯'), 98 (e♭), 99 (f♯'), 105 (b♭, c♯'), 106 (f♯'), 107 (b♭'), 109 (b♭), 110 (CT., first n.: f♯'), 111 (b♭), 113 (e♭', twice, b♭), 116 (b♭), 118 (b♭), 119 (b♭), 121 (e♭', b♭), 122 (c♯'), 130 (b♭), 132 (f♯'), 134 (b♭'), 146 (e♭'), 147 (b♭'), 152 (b♭), 153 (e♭', b♭), 155 (c♯'), 160 (f♯'), 169 (f♯'), 171 (f♯'), 180 (f♯'), 182 (f♯').
Remarks: At mm. 67–71, the Bs. moves in an arpeggiated passage; at mm. 85–6, the T. by consecutive perfect fourths. In mm. 92–4, the CT. outlines a diminished triad, the unique instance of this in the *Mellange.*

147. Phinot, Par un traict d'or (fol. 82ᵛ) [E. Forcadel]

Lyrics: Through a gold shaft, too sharp,
  Which, in spite of myself, I so much wanted,
  Through a good thing, which will make me perish,
  Love makes me live and die,
  Not that god, who has two wings,
  Makes me light up,
  Someone other than he has to move me a bit,
  Love makes me live and die.
  Venus would have her Adonis,
  But that we two were united,
  More handsome [I] would not wish to obtain,
  Love makes me live and die,
  My sad spirit cannot conceive,
  If death, when [it] comes to surprise me,
  Will be able to cure me of this misfortune,
  Love makes me live and die.

Parts: S., S. II (CT., fol. 83ʳ), CT., CT. II (S., fol. 83ʳ), T. II (Bs., fol. 83ʳ), T., Bs., Bs. II (T., fol. 83ʳ).
Concordances: Livre, fol. 44ʳ (S. II).[117]
Errors: mm. 4–14, CT., CT II, T. II, and T.: "dor" (not "d'or").
Musica Ficta: mm. 2 (f♯'), 3 (b♭), 6 (f♯'), 18 (e♭'), 21 (e♭'), 23 (b♭), 25 (e♭'), 28 (e♭), 29 (f♯'), 31 (f♯, b♭), 35 (b♭), 38 (e♭', f♯'), 41 (f♯'), 44 (f♯'), 52 (f♯'), 56 (c♯'), 58 (e♭'), 59 (f♯'), 60 (b♭), 62 (e♭', b♭), 64 (e♭'), 73 (e♭'), 74 (b♭), 78 (e♭'), 79 (e♭), 80 (f♯'), 82 (b♭), 83 (e♭', f♯'), 86 (f♯'), 87 (b♭), 88 (b♭, twice), 94 (e♭'), 95 (c♯'), 108 (f♯'), 109 (b♭), 111 (e♭'), 112 (f♯'), 114 (b♭), 115 (f♯'), 125 (b♭, e♭'), 134 (e♭'), 138 (f♯'), 139 (b♭), 141 (e♭'), 142 (f♯'), 145 (f♯'), 148 (f♯'), 151 (e♭'), 153 (b♭').
Remarks: Flat indicated only for the initial n. affected in mm. 48, 102, and 156, CT. II. Note, at mm. 57–8, the leap of a minor seventh in the CT.

148. Verdelot, *Qui la dira (fol. 83ᵛ)*

Lyrics: (See No. 3).

Parts: S., [S. II], CT., [CT.II], T., [T. II], Bs., [Bs.II].
Concordances: Livre, fol. 40ᵛ.
Errors: The *signa congruentiae* are misplaced in the T.: the first *signum* appears one sbr. too early; the second should have been indicated over the last n. of the T. part.[118]
Musica Ficta: mm. 4 (f♯'), 5 (e♭'), 8 (f♯'), 9 (e♭'), 12 (f♯'), 18 (e♭), 23 (e♭'), 26 (c♯'), 27 (e♭'), 30 (c♯'), 31 (e♭'), 34 (c♯'), 35 (e♭'), 38 (c♯'), 43 (c♯'), 47 (c♯'), 51

(c♯′), 55 (c♯′), 59 (b♮), 63 (b♮), 66 (b♮), 70 (b♮), 74 (e♭′), 75 (e♭), 76 (f♯′), 78 (e♭′), 79 (e♭), 82 (e♭′), 83 (e♭), 86 (e♭′), 88 (e♭′, f♯′).

Remarks: From m. 85 to the end, there is a pedal n. in the T.

Notes

Introduction

1. = RISM 1572_2 (cf. F. Lesure, ed., *Répertoire international des sources musicales.... Recueils imprimés, XVIe-XVIIe siècles,* I [1960], 286). See F. Lesure and G. Thibault, *Bibliographie des Éditions d' Adrian LeRoy et Robert Ballard (1551–1598)* (1955), 156–9; R. Eitner, *Bibliographie der Musik–Sammelwerke des XVI. und XVII. Jahrhunderts* (1877), 184–5. An exact description of the *Mellange,* as to format and size, is given in the Lesure and Thibault *Bibliographie,* 156–7.

2. K. J. Levy, *The Chansons of Claude LeJeune* (unpubl. diss., Princeton University, 1955), 73.

3. Cf. Lesure and Thibault, *Bibliographie,* 91–4.

4. Cf. ibid., 119–21, 129–30, 136, 139–44, 149–51, 156, 166–7, 172–4.

5. Particulars concerning dissemination of the *Mellange* contents are provided with the remarks on individual compositions in the Critical Notes. The present writer first became aware of this source ca. 1958–60, while preparing his unpubl. Ph.D. dissertation, *The Performance Practice of Spanish Renaissance Keyboard Music* (New York University, 1962) — regarding No. 13 (of the *Mellange*), see esp. I, 82, nn. 171 and 172 *et supra*; II, 75–8. The most complete surviving copy of the *Mellange* is owned by the Library of the Royal Conservatory of Music, Madrid. Subsequently, the writer published two *Mellange* chansons (Nos. 3 and 47) in his *Antonio Valente: Intavolatura de Cimbalo (Naples, 1576)* (1973): see pp. xxii–iii, 152, 157. A complete edition of the *Mellange* was already underway and under contract at that time, and autography of the music was carried out in Madrid, beginning Winter, 1974–5.

6. = RISM 1550_5. See D. Heartz, *Pierre Attaingnant, Royal Printer of Music* (1969), 364.

7. The presence of "Nicolas" and "Gombert" simultaneously in the same source, the above-mentioned Attaingnant print, did not prevent Eitner, *Bibliographie,* 112, from regarding them as one and the same composer — Gombert. In his *Biographisch-bibliographisches Quellenlexikon* (1899–1904; repr., 1959), VII, 197, R. Eitner likewise maintained that *"Nicolas* in 16. Jh. ist *Gombert."* In opposition to this interpretation are the following scholars: J. Schmidt–Görg, *Nicolas Gombert, Leben und Werk* (Bonn, 1938), 219, n. 72; D. v. Bartha, "Probleme der Chansongeschichte im 16. Jahrhundert", in *Zeitschrift für Musikwissenschaft,* XIII (1930–1), 522.

8. Gombert for No. 70, Nicolas for Nos. 25–31, 39, 45, 48, 56, 63, 66, 67, 114, 115, 122–5, and 130.

9. By E. Droz, "Les Chansons de Nicolas de la Grotte," in *Revue de Musicologie,* VIII (1927), 133, n. 2. See also F. Lesure and G. Thibault, *Bibliographie,* 303. Identification of

Nicolas with LaGrotte has been argued both ways by K. J. Levy: *contra* in his "'Susanne un jour': The History of a 16th Century Chanson", in *Annales Musicologiques,* I (1953), 379 (n. 2), 395–6; and *pro* in F. Lesure, et al., eds., *L'Anthologie de la Chanson Parisienne au XVIe Siècle* (1953), viii. Cf. Reese, *Music in the Renaissance* (rev. edn., 1959), 305.

10. See H. M. Brown, *Instrumental Music printed before 1600* (2nd printing, 1967), 254–5, 270–2; on p. 490, Brown, like Lesure and Thibault, queries if Nicolas and Nicolas de LaGrotte are identical. Such compositions by LaGrotte as are available in modern edition — see H. Expert, ed., *La Fleur des Musiciens de P. de Ronsard* (1923; repr., 1965), 52–64 (from LeRoy & Ballard's 1572 *Chansons de P. de Ronsard, Ph. Desportes, et autres, mises en musique par N. de la Grotte*); L. de la Laurencie, et al., eds., *Chansons au Luth et Airs de Cour Français du XVIe Siècle* (1934), 133ff (from the above-mentioned 1571 *Livre d'Airs de Cour*) — are characterized by a much tamer use of dissonance than is found in the chansons by Nicolas in the *Mellange*. This restraint in the use of dissonance, however, may have been influenced or even determined by their limited scope and rather surprising simplicity.

11. By v. Bartha, "Probleme," 525; taken over provisionally by Heartz, op. cit., 449, for the three Attaingnant collections in which Nicolas appears. Whether Nicolas in Attaingnant is the same as LeRoy & Ballard's Nicolas is yet another question.

12. Cf. Eitner, *Quellenlexikon,* VII, 197; v. Bartha, "Probleme," 525.

13. It seems most improbable that lesser figures, like Nicolas Champion or Nicole Regnes, would have been referred to by their given names. Concerning Champion, see Reese, *Renaissance,* 338.

14. It is known that DuChemin undertook to study with Regnes; cf. F. Lesure and G. Thibault, "Bibliographie des éditions musicales publiées par Nicolas du Chemin (1549–1576)," in *Annales Musicologiques,* I (1953), 274.

15. Nos. 26–8, 39, 56, 66, 115, 123, 125. No. 40 (by Maillard) is also exceptional in its use of dissonance.

16. See, for example, Levy, *Claude LeJeune,* 73–6, who of course did not have an opportunity to see the *Livre.* The *Livre* is a much simpler looking enterprise than the 1572 *Mellange,* with the music common to them quite differently presented. The 1560 *Livre de Meslanges* opens, fol. [1^r], with its title-page (pr. Lesure and Thibault, *Bibliographie des Éditions d'Adrian LeRoy et Robert Ballard,* 91), which is immediately followed by the Preface to the volume, in two pages, fols. [1^v] and [2^r] (see Plate IVa and b). The music of the *Livre* runs from fol. [2^v] through fol. 59^r. Its *table* is presented after the music, on two pages, fols. 59^v and [60^r]. The colophon of the volume is found on fol. [60^v] (see Plate Va; cf. Lesure and Thibault, op. cit., 207 and plate facing p. 108). (Print-through on the pages of the microfilm support the above description of the *Livre,* the original copy of whose surviving Superius partbook was only seen in microfilm by the present writer.) See also Preface, n. 1.

17. Cf. the Critical Notes of this edition, as well as the translation of the *Mellange* preface, in which detailed examination is made of the relationship between the two anthologies.

18. Information from v. Bartha, "Probleme," 523–4, where other exx. are given. Claudin's setting is pr.: *Claudin de Sermisy: Opera Omnia* (= *Corpus Mensurabilis Musicae,* 52), IV (ed. I. Cazeaux, 1974), 1. Such slight differences as do occur hardly qualify one Superius part to be designated even a variant reading of the other.

19. See P. J. P. Whitehead, "The Lost Berlin Manuscripts," in *Notes,* XXXIII (1976), 7.

Also: *The Sunday Times* [London], 3 April and 10 July 1977 (articles by N. Lewis); D. Henrich, "Beethoven, Hegel and Mozart auf der Reise nach Krakau," in *Neue Rundschau,* LXXXVIII (1977), 165.

20. An empty measure, in any part, represents a measure of rest.

21. A single white ("uncolored") semibreve, interpreted as a dotted minim, occurs in all voices at m. 17.

22. Conflicting rhythms are involved in both places cited, as also at No. 129, m. 68.

23. Three black (colored) minims, against two normal semiminims in the other voices ("two against three") or against a normal dotted semiminim and a normal fusa ("three against four"). This rhythm, in "white" notes, is found at No. 50, m. 71 (Tenor); indeed, it is puzzling why, in No. 54, triplets are indicated in white notation in m. 28, but in coloration in m. 18. In the reading of the concordance for No. 133, mm. 49 and 109 (Tenor), minor coloration is given (not ♩. ♪ in white notation, as in the *Mellange*).

24. The rhythm here is shown as black (colored) dotted minim, semiminim, minim (which, owing to the coloration, appear to be dotted semiminim, fusa, semiminim). This rhythm, with the very same meaning, is expressed in "white" notes at No. 50, m. 19 (Tenor).

25. The three black (colored) semibreves here indicated in the source introduce a "three" against four" pattern with the other voices.

26. At mm. 26 and 40–1 (in four voices), 58 (in two voices), and 59 (Tenor I). See Plate Ia (Tenor I; Tenor partbook, fol. 77^v).

27. See J. Wolf, *Handbuch der Notationskunde,* I (1913; repr., 1963), 394; W. Apel, *The Notation of Polyphonic Music, 900–1600* (5th edn., rev., 1961), 46, 107, 127–9, 136.

28. See J. Wolf, loc. cit.

29. Cf. m. 67, in the same voice, where white notation, not coloration, is used.

30. Cf. mm. 144–5 with mm. 25–6, in the same voice.

31. No. 50 contains triplet rhythms in white notation, mentioned earlier.

32. The reading of the concordance (see p. 604) agrees with the *Mellange* for the first and last of these instances, but not in m. 79, where the concordance has ♩. ♪ in white notation; in addition, there is coloration in the concordance Tenor, mm. 68 and 80–2 (twice), which appears in white notation in the reading of the *Mellange* Tenor. The reading of the concordance Contratenor for No. 35, m. 92, includes coloration not in the *Mellange*.

33. In the reading of the concordance (see p. 612), the former is given, in white notation, as ♩. ♪ , the latter ♩. ♫ (values reduced). Like the *Mellange,* the concordance has a triplet in white notation at m. 96.

34. Preceded, as mentioned above, by two groups (mm. 109–10) of triplets in coloration *with* the signature "3". The reading of the concordance (see p. 619) for this measure is ♩. ♪.

35. The last is given, in white notation, as ♩. ♪ in the concordance. Elsewhere in No. 133 — at mm. 4–5, 6, 11–12, 27–8, 33–4, 40–1, 83–4, 85–6, 98–9 (Contratenor); mm. 12–13, 27, 38–9, 60–1, 69, 70, 77–8, 79–80, 100–1, 111–12, 116–17, 131 (Sexta); mm. 49, 51, 72–3, 90, 103–4, 104–5, 109 (Tenor; mm. 49 and 109 were discussed in fn. 21) — music given as ♩. ♪ (white notation) in the *Mellange* is notated in coloration in the concordance. This information, as similar information in preceding footnotes, serves to show typical notational variance between the *Mellange* and sources of its concordances.

36. See Plate Ib (Tenor, fol. 71^r).

37. There seems no reason for the use of coloration in the Tenor, mm. 10 and 13, and Bassus, mm. 7 and 10.

38. Here, too, there seems no reason for the coloration in the Bassus, mm. 6 and 66.

39. See E. Lowinsky, "A Treatise on Text Underlay by a German Disciple of Francisco de Salinas," in *Festschrift Heinrich Besseler* (1961), 231; D. Harrán, "New Light on the Question of Text Underlay prior to Zarlino," in *Acta Musicologica,* XLV (1973), 24.

40. Cf., for example, the textual repeat signs in No. 37, Bassus, especially the last sign.

41. See Plate II. In Plate IIa (Superius, fol. 48^v; = No. 93, beginning), the elided syllables may be seen in line 2; in Plate IIb (ibid., fol. 55^v; = No. 104), they are in the last line.

42. Cf. Nos. 7, mm. 85–7 (Bassus): "di-re, al-lez" (vs. "di-*re, al*-lez"; italics represent elided syllables); 8, mm. 84 (Quinta), 86–7 (Superius), and 93–4 (Tenor): "fa-ce" (vs. "fa-*ce en*"); 18, mm. 30–1 (Superius) and 35–6 (Tenor): "tris-te" (vs. "tris-*te &*"); 28, m. 10 (Contratenor): "el-*le en*" (vs. "el-le"); 30, mm. 61–3 (Tenor): "l'at-ten-du-e" (vs. "l'at-ten-due"); 31, mm. 106–9 (Contratenor): addition of "&" to text; 36, mm. 67–72 (Contratenor): "j'a-ban-don-*ne à* el-le" (vs. "à el-le"); 39, mm. 47– (all voices): alternatively "vo-tre &" and "vo-*tre &*"; 40, mm. 2–6 (Superius, Tenor, and Bassus): "fi-lle" (vs. "fi-*lle il*"); 44, mm. 20–3 (Contratenor): "en-sem-*ble en*-cor'" (vs. "en-sem-ble en-cor'"); 50, mm. 52– (all voices): alternatively "pri-*me & s*'est" and "& s'est"; 52, m. 142 (Bassus): "voire" (vs. "voi-re"); 71, mm. 14–31 (Bassus): a word of the text, "je", omitted; 75, beginning (all voices, but especially Tenor): "tres-pas-*se en*-tre" (vs. "en-tre"); 86, mm. 12 (Bassus) and 42 (Quinta): separation and repetition, respectively, of "Du" and "Que"; 87, mm. 5–8 (all voices, except Superius): repetition of "bon" and mm. 23–4 (Superius): "m'a-mye" (vs. "m'a-my-e"); 97, mm. 94–6 (all voices, except Contratenor): "joye" (vs. "joy-e"); 120, mm. 92–4 (Sexta): "rou-sé-e" (vs. "rousée"); 133, mm. 27–9 (Contratenor): a separate "en-nuy" (otherwise elided: "tris-tes-*se, en*-nuy" or "tris-tes-s'en-nuy"); 136, mm. 61–4 (Contratenor): "rem' un" (vs. "re-m'un"), mm. 73–4 (Contratenor): "tem-pest' e'l" (vs. "tem-pe-st'e'l"), mm. 223–4 (Bassus): "Tal che" (vs. "Tal ch'i'n-con-min-cio"), and mm. 231–2 (Sexta and Bassus): addition of "a" before "sperar". Cf. remarks to No. 85 (p. 608), regarding omission of the word "povre". See also L. E. Kastner, *A History of French Versification* (1903).

43. Of particular value for attributions of the *Mellange* lyrics was H. Daschner's *Die gedruckten mehrstimmigen Chansons von 1500–1600: Literarische Quellen und Bibliographie* (Bonn, 1962). Concerning the authorship of the lyrics of Nos. 30 and 87 (C. Marot), and 131 (Baïf), see Daschner, 124, 166 (n. 2 *et supra*), and 112, respectively. The poet most represented in the *Mellange* is Clément Marot, with six chansons, besides the two already mentioned: Nos. 1, 14, 67, 90, 123, and 143; literary concordances for these may be found in C. A. Mayer, ed., *Clément Marot: Oeuvres Lyriques* (1964), 177, 174, 191, 189, 188, and 192, respectively. For the lyrics of Nos. 46, 65, 75, 80, and 144, by Ronsard, see G. Cohen, ed., *Pierre de Ronsard: Oeuvres Complètes* (2 vv., 1950), respectively, I, 20, 173, 34; II, 817; I, 162. The attribution of Nos. 69 and 141 (same text) to Ronsard is queried, because neither the edn. of G. Cohen, just cited, nor that of P. Laumonier (18 vv., 1921–68) contains this text. The famous "Susanne un jour" text, by G. Guéroult, is set no fewer than four times in the *Mellange* (Nos. 18, 26, 74, and 137); attribution of the poetry is given in K. Levy,

"'Susanne un jour': The History of a 16th Century Chanson," *Annales Musicologiques,* I (1953), 375. For the text of No. 19, by Mellin de St. Gelais, see P. Blanchemain, ed., *Melin de Sainct-Gelays: Oeuvres Complètes* (2 vv., 1873), I, 210. The lyrics of Nos. 38 and 66 (the same), by C. de Ste. Marthe, are found in C. Ruutz–Rees, *Charles de Ste. Marthe (1512–55),* transl. to French by M. Bonnet [1914], 156. For the poem of No. 54, by Jean Marot, the present writer was able to see an original copy of an early edition in the New York Public Library (Spencer Collection): *Recueil des Oeuvres de Jehan Marot* (Paris, Denys Ianot, 1538); the relevant text is on fols. [D vii^r-vii^v] (cf. Daschner, 106). The text of No. 147, by É. Forcadel, may be found in F. Joukovsky, ed., *Étienne Forcadel: Oeuvres Poétiques* (1977), 226. The predilection of the French Renaissance poets for providing their poems with titles, as well as the absence of indices of incipits from many older editions (and in modern reprints of them), frustrated many attempts to locate further concordances among other significant writers of the time. In concordances found, there were often striking, although seemingly entirely reasonable, variants in the readings of the poems. Nonetheless, the reading of the lyrics provided by the *Mellange* has been retained in this edn. For the translations of the lyrics (see Critical Notes), the editor consulted the monumental dictionaries of F. Godefroy and E. Huguet. Also of very great use was the *Dictionnaire d'Ancien Français* (1947) of R. Grandsaignes d'Hauterive.

44. See No. 136.

45. E.g., see Nos. 14, mm. 52–7 ("Helas"); 15, mm. 64–8 ("Faut-il"); 28, m. 96 ("Si"); 46, mm. 53–62 (rests before "soupire"); 80, mm. 44–50 (a rest interpolated between first and second syllables of "soupirons"); 97, mm. 107–10 (Superius: repeated notes in "soupirer"); 125, mm. 58–63 ("Chasser"). In No. 101, mm. 70–2, "ma peine" is delineated by a lengthy pedal note (bb').

46. The accidentals normal to this source are B$\flat$, E$\flat$, F$\sharp$, C$\sharp$, and G$\sharp$. Inconsistent or problematical passages are cited in the commentary on individual works (Critical Notes). These involve accidentals not indicated in passages where their use is clearly required. Superfluous, i.e., unnecessary, accidentals, found in the *Mellange,* have been cited in the Critical Notes, as well. Those in Nos. 26, 79, 115, and 122 seem wholly superfluous. The others, three (in Nos. 28, 30, and 64) possibly signaling the beginning of a new phrase in the voice involved, one (in No. 124) evidently cautionary to prevent a simultaneous cross-relation, in fact also are superfluous, since accidentals whose function would be identical are omitted from many similar places in the *Mellange.*

47. This includes those formed by an auxiliary note left by leap or a suspension resolved by leap; e.g., Nos. 7, mm. 15 (Bassus), 70 (Superius), 75 (5^a), 98 (Superius); 17, mm. 14, 15, 27, 121, and 129 (in the last two, double escaped notes); 28, mm. 5, 12, 31, 35; 35, mm. 55, 104, 112, and 124; 50, mm. 33, 67; 60, mm. 80–2, 84, 86, 95, 97, 99, 101, 110; 70, m. 52 (Superius); 99, mm. 3, 7, 11, 33, 79; 115, mm. 26, 28, 30, 32, 35; 137, mm. 16, 44, 91, 124, 135.

48. E.g., Nos. 17, mm. 99, 105; 30, mm. 55 (ornamented), 59; 49, m. 49; 62, mm. 30, 116, 131; 102, mm. 28, 51, 91; 113, mm. 19, 43, 55, 99; 115, mm. 71, 72 (ornamented); 116, mm. 24 (ornamented), 30, 81 and 101 (ornamented), 87 and 107; 118, mm. 37, 63, 67, 103, 129, 147; 121, mm. 30 (a'), 81.

49. For example, Nos. 67, m. 21; 79, mm. 99, 102, 107; 115, m. 34; 125, mm. 28, 40, 42.

50. E.g., Nos. 27, m. 7; 35, m. 85; 42, m. 42; 49, m. 55; 54, m. 113; 56, mm. 40, 86; 57, m. 33; 86, mm. 23, 41; 101, mm. 37, 66; 118, mm. 31, 107; 120, mm. 75, 83, 104, 112; 132, m. 82; 142, mm. 51, 55, 71.

51. See Nos. 6, m. 60; 115, m. 72 (f'); 138, mm. 55–6.

52. E.g., Nos. 16, m. 109; 39, mm. 12, 20; 135, mm. 4, 56.

53. For sevenths (whose exact identity may be arguable, as well as those, marked by an asterisk, which are unequivocal), see Nos. 24, m. 118; 25, m. 77; 30, m. 24; 34, m. 96; 35, mm. 46, 66, 77; 37, mm. 33, 38; 39, mm. *28, *33; 55, m. 89; 57, m. 28; 58, m. 41; 61, m. 46; 67, m. 40; 70, mm. 52, 66; 73, m. 26; 78, m. 65; 80, m. 172; 85, mm. 58, 86, 130; 87, mm. 45, 96, 110; 100, mm. 32, 50, *54; 105, m. 96; 113, m. *56; 115, m. 73; 118, m. 129; 123, m. *14; 126, mm. 139, 150, 155; 139, m. *11; 141, mm. 111, 113. Full discussion of problematical passages must await treatment elsewhere; for several examples, see Nos. 25, m. 28 (cf. m. 77); 35, mm. 46–7; 52, m. 19; 115, m. 31; 117, m. 58; 125, mm. 19, 21, 77, 99; 142, m. 45 (beat 2). It would have been easy, of course, to alter some of these passages by presuming notes to be errors and changing them. Considering the fairly high degree of dissonance found in the chansons of the *Mellange* and the general reliability of the source, I preferred, almost without exception, to let the readings given therein stand.

54. See, for example, Nos. 50, mm. 88, 94, 100; 79, m. 87; 85, mm. 11, 39, 53, 59, 92; 100, mm. 52, 134, 150; 102, mm. 13, 87, 92 (see n. 65); 107, m. 106; 117, mm. 18, 24 (?); 129, mm. 64, 68.

55. See Nos. 24, mm. 45–6; 97, mm. 225–6 — the only examples of this cadence found in the *Mellange*.

56. The editor refrained from applying *musica ficta* where "double leading-tone" cadences would thereby result, e.g., at Nos. 3, m. 35; 4, mm. 9, 19–20; 25, m. 124; 38, mm. 13, 39; 41, m. 72 (cf. m. 71, in which f♯ must be used); 59, m. 75; 61, m. 46; 62, m. 46; 68, m. 98; 80, m. 179; 91, mm. 10, 20, 23, 108, 111; 93, m. 59; 100, m. 132 (cf. m. 54); 101, m. 72; 102, m. 13; 103, m. 128; 104, m. 99; 108, mm. 65, 79; 124, m. 95; 129, m. 32; 145, m. 76; 146, m. 62; etc.

57. The principles generally followed are those outlined by E. E. Lowinsky, in his foreword to *Musica Nova*, ed. H. C. Slim (= *Monuments of Renaissance Music*, I, 1964).

58. E.g., Nos. 6, m. 92; 32, mm. 11, 61; 33, m. 61; 34, mm. 62, 88; 37, m. 67; 44, mm. 11, 124; 54, m. 109; 61, m. 72; 69, m. 32; 70, m. 22; 71, m. 15; 80, m. 120; 82, m. 9; 83, m. 36; 90, m. 12; 91, mm. 62–3; 92, m. 4 (just a diminished fifth here); 94, mm. 74–5, 86–7; 103, mm. 15, 55; 104, mm. 32, 78; 106, m. 45; 109, m. 58; 113, m. 83; 115, m. 39; 120, mm. 19, 60, 72, 101; 121, mm. 45, 97–8; 124, mm. 131, 134; 125, m. 30; 126, m. 112; 130, mm. 83, 134; 135, mm. 73, 75; 137, mm. 18, 46; 140, m. 17; etc.

59. Only when a natural sign or sharp could be applied to an ascending note or a flat to a descending note, in stepwise motion, to eliminate the dissonance.

60. As, for example, at Nos. 23, mm. 5–6, 53–4; 84, mm. 36, 67, 73, 94. The rule has been applied, even where *la* is a dissonant note, like a passing- or escaped-note: e.g., see Nos. 135, mm. 25, 34; 137, mm. 91, 135; 138, m. 5.

61. Whether it can do so in the "true" sense of the rule in the Mixolydian or Phrygian modes, for instance, is in fact questionable.

62. See, for example, No. 15, mm. 57–8 (Superius). Questions of mode and tonality in the *Mellange* and related music, beyond the scope of this edition, will be taken up in a future study.

63. Always with a point of interrogation: see Nos. 24, m. 17; 40, m. 55; 95, m. 29; 104, m. 101; 119, m. 34; 141, mm. 17, 50. At No. 60, mm. 10–11, the interchange of voices appears to have been designed to discourage application of *musica ficta*.

64. E.g., at Nos. 17, m. 106; 22, mm. 24, 72, 78; 27, mm. 8, 86; 46, m. 104; 80, m. 165; 102, m. 118; 105, m. 93.

65. See, for example, Nos. 102, m. 92 (harmonic augmented second formed by initial c♯'); 113, mm. 23 and 47 (augmented fifth formed by *musica ficta* notes); 122, m. 29 (harmonic augmented second); 123, m. 73 (harmonic augmented second, following a simultaneous cross-relation); 134, mm. 11 and 31 (harmonic diminished seventh). *Musica ficta* was not recommended at No. 114, m. 41 (for e'), as a dissonance (harmonic diminished seventh) too prolonged, in the editor's view, would have been formed with a note altered by *musica ficta* in the next measure. See also the Critical Notes for No. 40. (In No. 39, m. 29, the source provides a harmonic augmented second, immediately preceded by the sonority of an augmented triad.)

66. See, for example, No. 52, mm. 52–3, 62–3, 65, 132.

67. Cross-relations appearing in the music of the collection are cited, under individual works, in the Critical Notes.

68. These are almost always two-part canons: Nos. 3, 7, 23, 32, 33, 42, 50, 51, 53, 54, 55, 58, 62, 73, 85, 99, 103 (imperfect), 104, 105, 106, 109, 110, 111, 115, 116, 117, 119, 120, 121, 125, 127, 129 (the canon is in the Superius and Contratenor, not in the two lowest voices [6ᵃ and Bassus], which form their own canon, at the unison, through m. 14), 130, 132, 138, and 141. Other two-part canons, involving canon by inversion, are found in Nos. 59 and 137; these canons are accompanied, respectively, by the following rubrics: "Tot capita tot sensus" (As strong as is the intellect, so much so are the feelings [or:] There are as many opinions as there are people [i.e., for every person, a different opinion]) and "Ainsi va le monde" (Thus goes the world), viz., upside-down. Nos. 102, 108, 114, and 140 contain three-part canons; the rubrics for Nos. 108 and 140, respectively, read: "J'ay compagnons comme sensuit [s'ensuit]: L'un va devant, l'autre me suit" (I have companions, as follows: one goes before, the other comes after) and "Trois testés en un chapperon" (Three heads in a hood). Rubrics are also given for two-part canons at the unison: for No. 121, "Te ty te my. Te rogamus audinos" (evidently a reference to a litany sung responsorially); for No. 132, "Et erunt duo in carne una" (And two, in flesh, were one). Other, less fanciful, rubrics are provided in the *Mellange* for the canonic chansons of the collection. All the rubrics, however, in fact are superfluous, since complete readings of the canons are provided by the source. The only exception is No. 148, a quadruple canon at the unison. (Neither the music nor the *table* of the *Mellange* cites the canon in No. 129.)

69. E.g., Nos. 82, 96, 144, 145.

70. There are chansons in the *Mellange* which permit analysis into definite or approximate letter patterns; for example — *ABA* (alternatively, *ABA'* or *ABA* + *coda*): Nos. 6, 11, 12, 43, 62, 68, 83, 90, 93, 107, 128, 140, 142; *AAB*: Nos. 20, 26, 53, 81, 89 (1ᵃ *pars*; 2.ᵃ *pars: AA*), 95, 98, 112, 113; *ABB* (or *ABB* + *coda*): Nos. 47, 78; *AABB*: No. 7; *AABCC* (or *AABCC* + *coda*): Nos. 40, 66, 96, 126.

71. "Tonal" imitation is found, for example, in Nos. 9, 31, 47, 81, and 87; mirror imitation (i.e., by inversion) in Nos. 46 and 93; double imitation in No. 104; triple imitation in Nos. 135 and 147. For excellent general discussion of the Renaissance chanson, see I. Cazeaux, *French Music in the Fifteenth and Sixteenth Centuries* (1975), 197–217; Reese, *Renaissance,* 288–307, 309–11, 380–98.

Preface

1. The Preface to the 1560 *Livre de Meslanges* is directed to Francis II. The identity of the person whose etched or engraved portrait forms fol. [i^v] of the *Mellange* (i.e., the reverse of the title page of the volume — see frontispiece of this edition) is not provided by the source (see Plate III). There is an undeniable resemblance to Francis I, but this writer believes the portrait is rather of Henry II: cf. Clouet's portrait of Henry II at the Musée Condé, Chantilly. Henry II's patronage of the firm (see Lesure and Thibault, *Bibliographie des Éditions d'Adrian LeRoy et Robert Ballard,* 12) encourages interpretation of the portrait as of him; see also n. 15 *et supra*. The *Mellange* portrait cannot represent Charles IX (see portraits of him by Clouet at Chantilly, in the Art History Museum, Vienna, and by the 16th-century engraver, Abraham de Bruyn), Francis II, or Ronsard (see J. J. Boissard, *Icones Virorum Illustrium,* II [Frankfurt, 1598], 104). For portraits of the four kings, see J. de Serres, *A General Inventorie of the History of France* (transl. from French to English by E. Grimeston, pr. G. Eld, London, 1607), II, 419, 555, 574, 584. The Preface of the *Mellange* (see Plate IVc, d, and e) takes up the three pages (fols. [ii^r]–[iii^r]) after the portrait and is followed by the three-page *table* of the volume (fols. [iii^v]–[iv^v]). Unless otherwise noted, all *Mellange* plates included in this edition are from the Superius partbook of the collection.

2. In the 1560 Preface, the phrase "a de coustume d'" (customarily) is included at this point.

3. The 1560 Preface, rather than "un doux accord d'instrumens," reads "l'accord de la Musique" (music's harmony).

4. The *Livre* reads "doner de grade" (not "doner grade") here.

5. Instead of "heureusement né," the 1560 Preface reads "heureusement bien né."

6. This sentence begins "Car comment" (For how) in 1560.

7. The first words of this sentence in 1560 read: "celuy certes n'est pas digne de participer de" (he indeed is not worthy to experience).

8. The object pronoun "luy" is used here in the source.

9. The 1560 Preface reads "travail martial."

10. "Armonique," not "Enarmonique," in 1560.

11. "Armonique," not "diatonique," in 1560.

12. "Chams" ("champs" in 1560).

13. In 1560, the text reads "que Roys" (like kings), not "Princes."

14. The word "tous" (all) is found after "sont" in 1560.

15. Henry II.

16. Followed by an erroneous hyphen (not in 1560) in the source; in 1560, this hyphen correctly follows the succeeding word "bien" (for "bien-naissance").

17. The ampersand has here been translated as "both."

18. "Chose."

19. "Terpende" in 1560.

20. It is unclear to which of several mythical personalities of this name Ronsard is referring.

21. "Advint."

22. In 1572, Charles IX, second son of Henry II and Catherine de' Medici, was twenty-two years old; he became King in 1560, upon the death of his elder brother, Francis II, but actually ruled, 1563–74.

23. The *Mellange* erroneously reads "prinse" (not "prise") here.

24. Also known as the Cyanean Rocks, two cliffs which came together to crush anything attempting passage between them.

25. In the 1560 Preface, the word "apres" (afterward) follows at this point.

26. The *Livre,* omitting the last phrase, reads "de vostre labeur" (for your attention).

27. "Meslanges" in 1560.

28. "Dernier"; perhaps the phrase "dernier age de fer" should be translated simply as "Iron Age."

29. "Songneusement" here.

30. I.e., Willaert.

31. The words "Et de nostre temps" (And in our time) appear here in 1560.

32. I.e., Arcadelt. In 1560, the sentence concludes, as follows: "lequel ne cede en la perfection de cet art, aux anciens, pour estre inspiré de son Apollon Charles Cardinal de Lorraine" (who, in the perfection of this art, does not defer to the old [composers], through being inspired by his Apollo, Charles, Cardinal of Lorraine).

33. I.e., Lassus.

34. This sentence does not appear in the 1560 Preface.

35. Comma, not period, here.

36. In 1560, the word "de" is inserted here.

37. Material from the surviving Superius partbook of the 1560 *Livre de Meslanges* mentioned in the foregoing fns. will make clear shortcomings in the reconstruction of the Preface of the *Livre* in O. Strunk, *Source Readings in Music History* (1950), 286–9.

Critical Notes

1. Also given as "Vuillard" in the *table* of the *Mellange*.

2. Foliation given for sixteenth-century concordances is that of the S. part; foliation of the other parts may differ.

3. I.e., LeRoy & Ballard's 1560 *Livre de Meslanges*; as previously mentioned (p. 18), only the Superius partbook of this source survives. Differences between the *Mellange* and the *Livre* in spelling of individual words, in repetition of words or phrases of the lyrics, or in punctuation, are not cited in these Critical Notes, except for problematical passages.

4. H. M. Brown, *Instrumental Music Printed before 1600* (2nd printing, 1967; hence-

forth abbreviated BrownIM) cites arrangements for lute of this chanson, 223 (and 264), 265, and 436; for instrumental ensemble, 351, and in a sixteenth-century manual on ornamentation, 329. See also H. M. Brown, *Music in the French Secular Theater, 1400–1550* (1963; = BrownM), 245.

5. Concerning a Renaissance lute arrangement, as well as the employment of this composition in a handbook on ornamentation, see BrownIM, 110 and 328, respectively.

6. Information for this concordance and for those to Nos. 79, 85, 102, and 109 from L. Bernstein, "*La Courone et fleur des chansons a troys*: A Mirror of the French Chanson in Italy," in *Journal of the American Musicological Society*, XXVI (1973), 61 ff. (Professor Bernstein has informed me that the Bassus of No. 79, cited in "La Courone," is actually No. [17] in Bologna MS Q 26.)

7. For Valente's harpsichord arrangement of this chanson, see the above-cited edition, 68. A. de Cabezón's *Obras* (Madrid, 1578) contains a *glosa* of this chanson (fol. 153ʳ; to appear in the fifth and final vol. of the present writer's complete edition), as well as a *tiento* based on it (see *Antonio de Cabezón: Collected Works*, ed. C. Jacobs, II [1972], 45), both for keyboard. An arrangement for v. and *vihuela* appears in E. de Valderrábano's *Silva de Sirenas* (Valladolid, 1547), fol. 36ᵛ, where Verdelot is attributed the chanson.

8. A play on words, as *liron* = *lérot* (dormouse).

9. Another play on words: *fourbir* (to polish), Fourbifron (his alleged name).

10. The last word of the text is "*don*" in the *Mellange*; the corrected reading ("*donc*") is taken from the *Livre*.

11. Also given as "Richaffort" in the *Mellange*.

12. Plural in the *Livre*.

13. A sixteenth-century arrangement for lute is cited BrownIM, 145.

14. The reading of "Jusque," with elision of its final letter in the *Mellange*, as "jusques," without elision in the *Livre*, seems erroneous.

15. Attributed to Verdelot in the *Livre*.

16. The flat indicated in the S., m. 95, is included in the reading in the *Livre*; "crain" is spelled "crains" there.

17. Cf. G. Reese, *Music in the Renaissance* (rev. edn., 1959), 322–3, n. 142.

18. Cf. M. Françon, *Poèmes de Transition (XVᵉ–XVIᵉ Siècles)* (1938), I, 687.

19. See BrownIM, 198, for a possible lute arrangement.

20. Cf. p. 625, n. 5. In the *table* of the *Mellange*, the incipit of this chanson reads "Je fille quand dieu m'y donne."

21. Alternative interpretations of "au voy": "in its groove," "in [open] view" (i.e., visibly).

22. = "I heat my oven"?

23. A *glosa* of this chanson, misattributed to Willaert, appears in A. de Cabezón's *Obras* (Madrid, 1578), fol. 136ʳ. See also BrownM, 139, 236.

24. The composer's name is given as "Monté" in the *table*.

25. Attributed therein to "Orlande"; cf. p. 18. The flat in S., m. 72, comes from the *Livre*, as none is provided in the *Mellange* (a bracketed flat would in any case have been provided there, even in the absence of a concordance).

26. Another modern edition of this chanson, with attribution to Lassus, is found in: *O. di Lasso, Sämtliche Werke* (ed. F. X. Haberl and A. Sandberger, 1894–), XVI, 163.

27. For possible lute arrangement, see BrownIM, 92.

28. "Qu'oncq'en" here, oddly, rather than "Qu'oncqu'en."

29. In the latter, a sharp is indicated for m. 29, S., initial n. Another concordance for the work, cited in L. Bernstein, "*La Courone*," 62, is found in Munich, Bavarian State Library, Music MS 1508, No. 96 (attribution to Willaert). Yet another concordance, bearing an attribution to Benedictus, is mentioned, loc. cit. (not seen by present writer).

30. See BrownM, 198.

31. See K. J. Levy, "'Susanne un Jour': The History of a 16th Century Chanson," in *Annales Musicologiques*, I (1953), 375.

32. = Alessandro Striggio?

33. The heading of fol. 10ᵛ actually reads "Havville," while the *table* of the *Mellange* reads "Hauuille." The present writer has been able to find no information concerning this composer.

34. See BrownM, 188.

35. Cf. Bs., mm. 1–4, with S., mm. 8–11; CT., mm. 10–13; Bs., mm. 49–52; CT., mm. 58–61.

36. In the CT. part, the sharp symbol is represented both as a single and double x; (see also No. 25, S., etc.). In No. 22, as is normal in this and many sixteenth-century sources, the double x symbol represents both a sharp and a natural sign, the latter cancelling the flat in the "signature" of the work. ("Signatures" with a single flat, commonplace throughout the *Mellange*, represent no "key", in the modern sense of the term; see p. 21.)

37. The third word reads "me" in the *table*.

38. In the *table*, as at the beginning of each part, the second word reads "my."

39. "Voy" in source.

40. For a possible lute arrangement, see BrownIM, 144, 209.

41. This error also appears in the *Livre*, as does the reading, taken as correct, in m. 108.

42. The second word is given as "my" in the *table* of the *Mellange* and in the *Livre*.

43. The word "joyeux" is inserted between this word ("hardy") and the next ("frisque") in the *Livre*.

44. Attributed to "Arcadet" in the *Livre*, both in the music and in the *table*. A single text variant, between the reading of this chanson in the *Mellange* and its reading in the *Livre*, has been mentioned, n. 43. For a musical variant, cf. mm. 121-2. See Plate VI.

45. Spelled "N'auraige" in music, "N'auray-je" in *table*.

46. "On her back"?

47. For a possible lute arrangement, see BrownIM, 222, 260, 265.

48. This word should read "aymé" (not "aymée").

49. See BrownM, 126, 237.

50. In T. and Bs., "malheureux" twice syllabified "ma-lheureux."

51. In addition to Valente's heavily ornamented harpsichord transcription of this chanson (present writer's edition, 57), there are *glosas* of it by Antonio de Cabezón and his son, Hernando, in the *Obras*, fols. 137ʳ and 151ᵛ, respectively (cf. n. 7). There is a transcription of this chanson, and of Crecquillon's *Si me tenez tant de rigueur*, in a late sixteenth-century manuscript lute tablature, formerly known as Berlin, Deutsche Staatsbibliothek Mus. MS 40598, probably now in Kraków (not available to the present writer; cf. p. 18). BrownIM cites lute arrangements of this composition, pp. 146, 210, 236, 262, 264, 276, and 433 (the first

two, which are identical, are for lute duo); a keyboard arrangement, p. 288; an arrangement for cittern, p. 280. Indeed, from the number of instrumental transcriptions of Crecquillon's *Pis ne me peut venir,* it is clear that this chanson was one of the most popular in the late Renaissance, surpassed only, possibly, by Lassus' *Susanne un jour.*

52. = Alfonso Ferrabosco I, "The Elder" (1543–88)?

53. See BrownM, 251, in which reference is made to "La tricotée" as a dance step; also, A. Curtis, "Josquin and 'La Belle Tricotée'," in *Essays in Musicology in honor of Dragan Plamenac* (ed. G. Reese and R. Snow, 1969), 1, esp. 3.

54. Figuratively, the rump of a horse (i.e., the buttocks). Other interpretations of "in jan voire" are "don't you see," "Hey, Jean, don't you see"; "jan" may have reference to the game, *trictrac.*

55. Concerning the use of this chanson in a manual on ornamentation, see BrownIM, 328.

56. "And leave me to endure my ill [fortune] alone"?

57. An arrangement for instrumental ensemble is cited in BrownIM, 351. See also BrownM, 251.

58. "Or I shall be half dead"?

59. Cf. *Miguel de Fuenllana: Orphénica Lyra (Seville, 1554)* (ed. C. Jacobs, 1978), xlix, lviii, 309. Also: B. J. Blackburn, "Josquin's Chansons, Ignored and Lost Sources," in *Journal of the American Musicological Society,* XXIX (1976), 30–41, 68–76.

60. The opening line of this chanson is the same as that of the lyrics for No. 41.

61. In the *Livre,* the two nn. on g', at mm. 78–9 (S.) in this edition, are given as a single sbr. — a source error. For a possible instrumental ensemble arrangement, see BrownIM, 351.

62. Also, *Historical Anthology of Music* (ed. W. Apel and A. T. Davison, rev. edn., 1966), I, 93–5. Concerning V. Bakfark's transcription for lute of this chanson, see BrownIM, 218, 276; O. Gombosi, *Der Lautenist Valentin Bakfark* (ed. Z. Falvy, 1967), 39. See also BrownM, 118, 125f, 218.

63. Spelled "corps" in the *table* of the *Mellange.*

64. Cf. Françon, op. cit., I, 144.

65. The fourth word of the title reads "pleins" in the *table* of the *Mellange.*

66. Presumed attribution from *Sonetz de P. de Ronsard, mis en Musique a 5. 6. et 7. parties par M. Phil. de Monte* (LeRoy & Ballard, Paris, 1575), fol. 4ᵛ. See F. Lesure and G. Thibault, *Bibliographie des Éditions d'Adrian LeRoy et Robert Ballard (1551–1598),* (1955), 170–1.

67. Spelled "Lupy" in the music; the above reading of the name is from the *table.* Cf. No. 133.

68. Cabezón's *Obras,* fol. 138ᵛ, contains a *glosa* for keyboard of this chanson (cf. n. 7).

69. Cf. BrownIM, 351, which cites a six-part instrumental ensemble arrangement of a composition entitled "Sire."

70. In the *Livre,* line 5 reads: "M'ayant pourveu de dame si louable."

71. The composer's name is given as "LeBrum" in the music of the *Livre,* where the opening words read, "N'aves point veu." F. Lesure and G. Thibault, *Bibliographie des Éditions d'Adrian LeRoy et Robert Ballard* (1955), 92 and 158, give these as "N'avons point veu." In the music of the individual partbooks and the *table* of the *Mellange,* as well as in the *table* of the *Livre,* this text is given as "N'avous point veu," which I have interpreted as "N'a vous point veu" (= "N'avez vous point vue"). Cf. Plate VII.

72. Concerning an arrangement of this chanson for lute, see BrownIM, 162, 202, 276.

73. Cf. related settings of the same text by LeJeune in *Claude LeJeune: Meslanges de la Musique* (LeRoy & Ballard, Paris, 1586; = RISM L-1675), fol. 30ᵛ, and *Le Rossignol musical* (= RISM 1597₁₀; see No. 13), fol. 12ᵛ.

74. In the underlay of "dame" (mm. 8, 5ᵃ, and 11, S.), it seemed best to treat the word as a single syllable, rather than eliding "baiser" and "&" (neither is indicated in the source).

75. Concerning a possible relationship of this text to Petrarch, see I. Cazeaux, ed., *Claudin de Sermisy: Opera Omnia* (= *Corpus Mensurabilis Musicae,* 52), III (1974), xv, 1.

76. = S. reading of this line; in the other vv., it reads "That [you] receive me sweetly."

77. For a possible lute arrangement, cf. BrownIM, 74, 106.

78. Elided in S.: "m'a-mye"; in the other vv., "m'a-my-e."

79. For arrangements of an "Amour, partez" for cittern and lute, see BrownIM, 247, 260, 344.

80. Given as "Arrousés voz violettes" in the *table* of the *Mellange,* "Arousés vo violette" in the *table* of the *Livre.*

81. For an arrangement of this chanson for lute duo, see BrownIM, 146.

82. Information for MS Pepys 1760 from Reese, *Renaissance,* 301, n. 50. See Plate VIII.

83. The second word reads "donnez" in the *table,* as well as in the 5ᵃ and Bs.

84. In the *Livre,* the signature given (probably erroneously) is C (not ₵, as in the *Mellange*). See Plate IX.

85. Another possible interpretation of the last line: "And leave me to endure my sole misfortune."

86. See Plate X. Cf. Reese, *Renaissance,* 273, n. 492a. Concerning arrangements of this chanson for lute solo and for lute and solo voice, see BrownIM, 145, 153, and 199. Fol. 53ʳ of the *Mellange* contains only the colophon of the publisher, with the following text: "By Adrian LeRoy and Robert Ballart [*sic*], printers to the King in Paris/In Montparnasse, Rue S. Jean de Beauvois (in concentric ellipses, within which are representations of Pegasus and a lyre; in two horizontal lines below, the following text:) End of the chansons/in five parts." Except for the last two phrases quoted, this internal colophon is identical to that at the end of the volume; cf. Plate Vb. Cf. also Lesure and Thibault, *Bibliographie des Éditions d'Adrian LeRoy et Robert Ballard,* 154 and plate facing p. 183.

87. Of Sexta partbook.

88. Concerning an arrangement of this composition for instrumental ensemble, see BrownIM, 351; regarding its use in ornamentation manuals, ibid., 328 and 367; cf. also a *branle* for guitar, ibid., 250.

89. Valderrábano arranged this chanson for *vihuela* duo in his *Silva de Sirenas,* fol. 54ᵛ; cf. BrownIM, 102, as well as 146, regarding an arrangement for lute duo.

90. Cf. Reese, *Renaissance,* 338, n. 10c *et supra*; see also BrownM, 126, 212.

91. For another setting of this text (slightly varied), cf. No. 62. Regarding this chanson, see BrownM, 125f, 218.

92. An arrangement of this chanson for *vihuela* duet is included in Valderrábano's *Silva de Sirenas,* fol. 47ᵛ.

93. Concerning François Ier's possible authorship of the lyrics, see A. Champollion—Figeac, ed., *Poésies du Roy François Ier, de Louise de Savoie, Duchesse d'Angoulême, de Marguerite, Reine de Navarre, et Correspondance Intime du Roi* (1847; repr., 1970), 1 (n. 1), 165–6.

94. Given as "me" in *table*; in the *table* of the *Livre,* as "my."

95. "Si" in the *tables* of both the *Mellange* and the *Livre*; in the music of the latter, "Sy" is used.

96. The fifth word of this line reads "your" (*ton*) in the *Livre.*

97. A keyboard arrangement of this chanson appears in E. N. Ammerbach's *Ein New Kunstlich Tabulaturbuch* (Nuremberg, 1575), fol. 48^v; the present writer has in press an edition of Ammerbach's works, which includes selections from the 1575 *Tabulaturbuch.* For another arrangement for keyboard and one for cittern, see BrownIM, 287 and 311, respectively.

98. Concerning this chanson, see BrownM, 282.

99. = Antonio Gardano (1509–69)?

100. Attributed in RISM 1545_{14} (and Minor) to Mouton. For another concordance, see: Copenhagen, Royal Library, MS Gl. Kgl. Samling 1872–4°, fol. 59^v. Concerning this chanson and the preceding one, see BrownM, 198. L. Bernstein, *"La Courone,"* 62, cites yet another concordance in London, British Library, Add. MS 31409, fol. 29^v (not seen by present writer).

101. This is erroneously cited, as a five-part composition on fol. 55, in the *table* of the *Livre*; cf. Lesure and Thibault, *Bibliographie des Editions d'Adrian LeRoy et Robert Ballard,* 92. The lyrics form a variant of those of No. 23.

102. According to F. Lesure, "Some Minor French Composers of the 16th Century," in *Aspects of Medieval and Renaissance Music,* ed. J. LaRue, et al. (1966), 540, the composer's name was actually Philippe Fromentin.

103. Attributed to Willaert in the *table*; cf. B. Blackburn, op. cit., 54. See also BrownM, 125, 186.

104. For an arrangement for lute duo, see BrownIM, 145.

105. "Luppi" in *table*.

106. The lute arrangements, cited at BrownIM, 93, 113, 144, 170, 198, 202, and 209, involve a four-part setting of the same text by Lupi (modern edition in *Das Chorwerk,* XV [1932], 4).

107. Concerning a cittern composition entitled "C'est à grand tort," cf. BrownIM, 295, 310.

108. In the *table*: "Don. nicollo."

109. For an arrangement of this chanson for vocal duo and lute, see BrownIM, 380.

110. See BrownM, 138, 233.

111. The *table* of the *Mellange,* but not that of the *Livre,* gives "Fuyes amans" as the incipit of this work.

112. The 5^a and 6^a partbooks, containing no eight-part music, conclude with No. 142.

113. Before "He," "Voudrois-tu," and "O"; "L." also appears in the same three places in the *Livre.*

114. Before "He," "En," "Voudroys," and "O".

115. The second word is given as "mamye" in the *table*.

116. See V. L. Saulnier, "Dominique Phinot et Didier Lupi, musiciens de Clément Marot et des Marotiques," in *Revue de Musicologie,* XLIII (1959), 80; also, Daschner, op. cit., 169, who makes reference to *Die Musik in Geschichte und Gegenwart* (1949–), II, col. 1064.

117. Oddly, the *Mellange* S. does not appear in the S. partbook of the *Livre* (the music given there, though it should be, is not labelled "S. II"); see Plate XI. Cf. No. 143, for which concordances of both S. and S. II are provided by the *Livre.*

118. Fol. [84^r] of the *Mellange* contains a quotation from the publishers' license, fol. [84^v] (the last page of the volume; see Plate Vb.) the colophon, closing: "End of the great/*Mellange*" (this text is in two horizontal lines; for the other text of the colophon, see n. 86). The text of the "extract of the license" reads:

> By letters patent from the King, issued at Saint Maur the first day of May, 1567, signed by the King. Master Regnault de Beaune, master of requests ordinary of the *hostel* present, marked with hawthorn and sealed on double-label, confirming [without need of] other precedents [that] Adrian le Roy & Robert Ballard, printers in music of his majesty, be permitted and conceded [permission] to print or cause to be printed every sort of music, so vocal as instrumental of any sort and composition by authors, whosoever it may be, especially by Orlande de lassus, Josquin des prez, Mouton, Richaffort, Gascongne, Jaquet, Maillard, Gombert, Arcadelt, and C. Goudimel: without its being lawful for any other [person] to print them, sell, or distribute in the open market or privately, or to take out any part of the said, during the period of ten years; at the same time, it is most amply contained and declared [in the] published letters, on pain of confiscation of the said books, [and payment of] damages, interests, and arbitrated compensation to the said le Roy & Ballard. Which letters his said majesty wishes, without any other formality, and [that] the extract of the said [letters be] placed and inserted at the beginning or end of each of the said books, solely to be considered [as] valid and obligatorily indicated to all printers, so that they may not be able to feign ignorance, without any other indication being necessary.

Bibliography

This Bibliography lists, almost without exception, only items cited in the commentary of the edition. Literary and musical concordances, additional to those mentioned in the Introduction and Critical Notes, were sought in early sources and modern publications; the extensive microfilm resources of the Isham Memorial Library, Harvard, were particularly valuable in this regard.

Manuscripts and Early Prints

Cambridge University, Magdalene College, MS Pepys 1760.
Copenhagen, Royal Library, MS Gl. Kgl. Samling 1872–4⁰.
Munich, Bavarian State Library, Music MS 1508.
Vienna, Austrian National Library, Codex 18810.
Le cincquiesme livre contenant trente et deux chansons a cincq et a six parties (Susato, Antwerp, 1544).
Le douziesme livre contenant trente chansons amoureuses a cincq parties (Susato, Antwerp, 1558).
Le Rossignol musical (Phalèse, Antwerp, 1597).
Le sixiesme livre contenant trente et une chansons nouvelles a cincq et a six parties (Susato, Antwerp, 1545).
Le treziesme livre contenant vingt et deux chansons nouvelles a six et a huyt parties (Susato, Antwerp, 1550).
Livre d'Airs de Cour (LeRoy & Ballard, Paris, 1571).
Livre de Meslanges (LeRoy & Ballard, Paris, 1560).
Musica Nova (Venice, 1540): see H. C. Slim.
Premier livre des chansons a quatre et cincq parties (Phalèse, Louvain, 1570).
Trente cincquiesme livre contenant XXIIII chansons nouvelles a quatre parties (Attaingnant, Paris, 1550).
Vingt et six chansons musicales & nouvelles a cincq parties (Susato, Antwerp, 1543).
Ammerbach, E. N., *Ein New Kunstlich Tabulaturbuch* (Nuremberg, 1575).
Cabezón, A. de, *Obras de Música* (Madrid, 1578).
[Certon, P.:] *Les Meslanges de Maistre Pierre Certon* (DuChemin, Paris, 1570).
Fuenllana, M. de, *Orphénica Lyra* (Seville, 1554): see C. Jacobs.
[LaGrotte, N. de.:] *Chansons de P. de Ronsard, Ph. Desportes, et autres mises en musique par N. de la Grotte* (LeRoy & Ballard, Paris, 1572).
[Lassus, O.:] *Mellange d'Orlande de Lassus* (LeRoy & Ballard, Paris, 1570).
[LeJeune, C.:] *Meslanges de la Musique de Clau. LeJeune* (LeRoy & Ballard, Paris, 1586).
LeRoy, A., *A briefe and plaine Instruction* (J. Rowbothome, London, 1574).

[Marot, J.:] *Recueil des Oeuvres de Jehan Marot* (D. Ianot, Paris, 1538).

[Monte, P. de:] *Sonetz de P. de Ronsard mis en Musique a 5. 6. et 7. parties par M. Phil. de Monte* (LeRoy & Ballard, Paris, 1575).

[Ronsard, P. de:] *Sonetz de P. de Ronsard mis en Musique a 5. 6. et 7. parties par M. Phil. de Monte* (LeRoy & Ballard, Paris, 1575).

Valderrábano, E. de, *Silva de Sirenas* (Valladolid, 1547).

Valente, A., *Intavolatura di Cimbalo* (Naples, 1576): see C. Jacobs.

Modern Source Materials

Adams, C. S. *The Three-Part Chanson During the Sixteenth Century* (unpubl. diss., University of Pennsylvania, 1974).

Allaire, G. *The Theory of Hexachords, Solmization, and the Modal System* (Rome, 1972; = American Institute of Musicology: *Musicological Studies and Documents*, XXIV).

Apel, W. *The Notation of Polyphonic Music, 900–1600* (5th edn., rev., Cambridge [Massachusetts], 1961).

Apel, W., and A. T. Davison, eds. *Historical Anthology of Music* (2 vv., rev. edn., Cambridge [Massachusetts], 1966).

Arcâdelt, J. *Opera Omnia*: see A. Seay.

Bartha, D. v. "Probleme der Chansongeschichte im 16. Jahrhundert," in *Zeitschrift für Musikwissenschaft*, XIII (1930–1), 507.

Bernet–Kempers, K. P., ed. *Jacobus Clemens non papa: Opera Omnia* (= *Corpus Mensurabilis Musicae*, 4; Rome, 1951–).

Bernstein, L. F. *"La Courone et fleur des chansons a troys*: A Mirror of the French Chanson in Italy in the years between Ottaviano Petrucci and Antonio Gardano," in *Journal of the American Musicological Society*, XXVI (1973), 1.

———. "The Cantus–Firmus Chansons of Tylman Susato," in *Journal of the American Musicological Society*, XXII (1969), 197.

———. "The 'Parisian Chanson'; Problems of Style and Terminology," in *Journal of the American Musicological Society*, XXXI (1978), 193.

Blackburn, B. J. "Johannes Lupi and Lupus Hellinck," in *The Musical Quarterly*, LIX (1973), 547.

———. "Josquin's Chansons, Ignored and Lost Sources," in *Journal of the American Musicological Society*, XXIX (1976), 30.

Blanchemain, P., ed. *Melin de Sainct-Gelays: Oeuvres Complètes* (2 vv., 1873).

Borren, C. van den, and J. van Nuffel, eds. *Philippe de Monte, Opera* (1927–).

Brown, H. M. *Instrumental Music printed before 1600* (2nd printing, Cambridge [Massachusetts], 1967).

———. *Music in the French Secular Theater, 1400–1550* (Cambridge [Massachusetts], 1963).

———, ed. *Theatrical Chansons of the Fifteenth and Early Sixteenth Centuries* (Cambridge [Massachusetts], 1963).

Cabezón, A. de. *Collected Works*: see C. Jacobs.

Cazeaux, I., ed. *Claudin de Sermisy: Opera Omnia, Chansons* (= *Corpus Mensurabilis Musicae*, 52), III and IV (Rome, 1974).

———. *French Music in the Fifteenth and Sixteenth Centuries* (Oxford, 1975).

Champollion–Figeac, A., ed. *Poésies du Roy François Ier, de Louise de Savoie, Duchesse d'Angoulême, de Marguerite, Reine de Navarre, et Correspondance Intime du Roi* (Paris, 1847; repr., 1970).

Chapman, J. G. *The Works of Pierre Moulu* (unpub. diss., New York University, 1964).

Clemens non Papa, J. *Opera Omnia*, see K. P. Bernet–Kempers.

Cohen, G., ed. *Pierre de Ronsard: Oeuvres Complètes* (2 vv., Paris, 1950).

Curtis, A. "Josquin and 'La belle Tricotée'," in *Essays in Musicology in Honor of Dragan Plamenac* (ed. G. Reese and R. Snow, Pittsburgh, 1969), 1.

Daschner, H. *Die gedruckten mehrstimmigen Chansons von 1500–1600* (Bonn, 1962).

Droz, E. "Les Chansons de Nicolas de La Grotte," in *Revue de Musicologie*, VIII (1927), 133.

Durling, R. M., ed. *Petrarch's Lyric Poems* (Cambridge [Massachusetts] and London, 1976).

Eitner, R. *Biographisch-bibliographisches Quellenlexikon* (10 vv., 1899–1904; repr., 1959).

Expert, H., ed. *Florilège du Concert Vocal de la Renaissance* (8 vv.; Paris, 1928).

———. *La Fleur des musiciens de Pierre de Ronsard* (Paris, 1923).

———. *Les Maîtres Musiciens de la Renaissance Française* (23 vv. and addenda, Paris, 1894–1908).

———. *Les Monuments de la Musique Française au temps de la Renaissance* (10 vv., Paris, 1924–30).

Forcadel, É. *Oeuvres Poétiques*: see F. Joukovsky.

Françon, M. *Poèmes de Transition (XVe–XVIe Siècles)* (3 vv., Cambridge [Massachusetts] and Paris, 1938).

Godefroy, F. E. *Dictionnaire de l'ancienne langue française* (10 vv.; repr., Vaduz, 1965).

———. *Lexique de l'ancien français* (Paris, 1967).

Gombert, N. *Opera Omnia*: see J. Schmidt–Görg.

Gombosi, O. *Der Lautenist Valentin Bakfark* (ed. Z. Falvy, Budapest, 1967).

Goudimel, C. *Oeuvres Complètes*: see P. Pidoux.

Grandsaignes d'Hauterive, R. *Dictionnaire d'Ancien Français* (Paris, 1947).

Haar, J., ed. *Chanson & Madrigal, 1480–1530* (Cambridge [Massachusetts], 1964).

Haberl, F. X., and A. Sandberger, eds. *O. di Lasso: Sämtliche Werke* (1894–).

Harrán, D. "New Light on the Question of Text Underlay Prior to Zarlino," in *Acta Musicologica*, XLV (1973), 24.

Heartz, D. *Pierre Attaingnant, Royal Printer of Music; a Historical Study and Bibliographical Catalogue* (Berkeley, 1969).

———. "Voix de ville: Between Humanistic Ideals and Musical Realities," in *Words and Music: The Scholar's View* (ed. L. Berman, Cambridge [Massachusetts], 1972), 115 [not seen by present writer].

Henrich, D. "Beethoven, Hegel, and Mozart auf der Reise nach Krakau," in *Neue Rundschau*, LXXXVIII (1977), 165.

Hertzmann, E. *Adrian Willaert in der weltlichen Vokalmusik seiner Zeit* (Leipzig, 1931).

Huber, K. "Die Doppelmeister des 16. Jahrhunderts," in *Festschrift zum 50. Geburtstag*

Adolf Sandberger (Munich, 1918), 170.

Huguet, E. Dictionnaire de la langue française du 16. siècle (7 vv., Paris, 1925–73).

———. L'Évolution du sens des mots depuis le 16e siècle (2nd ed., Geneva, 1967).

———. Mots disparus ou vieillis depuis le XVIe siècle (Geneva, 1967).

Jacobs, C., ed. Antonio de Cabezón: Collected Works (New York, 1967–).

———. Antonio Valente: Intavolatura di Cimbalo (Naples, 1576) (Oxford, 1973).

———. Miguel de Fuenllana: Orphénica Lyra (Seville, 1554) (Oxford, 1978).

———. The Performance Practice of Spanish Renaissance Keyboard Music (unpubl. diss., New York University, 1962).

Jeffery, B., ed. Chanson Verse of the Early Renaissance (2 vv., London, 1971 and 1976).

Joukovsky, F., ed. Étienne Forcadel: Oeuvres Poétiques (1977).

Kastner, L. E. A History of French Versification (Oxford, 1903).

Kaufman, H., ed. Nicolò Vicentino: Opera Omnia (= Corpus Mensurabilis Musicae, 26; Rome, 1963).

———. The Life and Works of Nicolò Vicentino (Rome, 1966; = American Institute of Musicology: Musicological Studies and Documents, XI).

Lachèvre, F. Bibliographie des recueils collectifs de poésies du XVIe siècle (Paris, 1922).

Lasso, O. di. Sämtliche Werke: see F. X. Haberl and A. Sandberger.

Laumonier, P., ed. Pierre de Ronsard: Oeuvres Complètes (18 vv., Paris, 1921–68).

Laurencie, L. de la, A. Mairy, and G. Thibault, eds. Chansons au luth et airs de cour français du XVIe siècle (Paris, 1934).

Lesure, F. "Autour de Clément Marot et de ses musiciens," in Revue de Musicologie (1951), 109.

———. "Some Minor French Composers of the 16th Century," in Aspects of Medieval and Renaissance Music; a Birthday Offering to Gustave Reese (ed. J. La Rue, New York, 1966), 538.

———. Musicians and Poets of the French Renaissance (trans. by E. Gianturco and H. Rosenwald, New York, 1955).

Lesure, F., and G. Thibault. Bibliographie des éditions d'Adrian LeRoy et Robert Ballard (1551–1598) (Paris, 1955); supplement in Revue de Musicologie (1957), 166.

———. "Bibliographie des éditions musicales publiées par Nicolas Du Chemin (1549–1576)," in Annales Musicologiques, I (1953), 269; supplements in ibid., IV (1956), 251; VI (1958–63), 403.

Lesure, F., ed., et al. Anthologie de la chanson parisienne au XVIe siècle (Monaco, 1952).

———. Répertoire international des sources musicales. . . . Recueils imprimés, XVIe–XVIIe siècles, I (1960).

Levy, K. J. The Chansons of Claude LeJeune (unpubl. diss., Princeton University, 1955).

———. "'Susanne un jour': The History of a 16th-Century Chanson," in Annales Musicologiques, I (1953), 375.

———. "Vaudeville, vers mesurés et airs de cour," in Musique et poésie au XVIe siècle (ed. J. Jacquot, Paris, 1954), 185.

Lowinsky, E. E. "A Treatise on Text Underlay by a German Disciple of Francisco de Salinas," in Festschrift Heinrich Besseler (1961), 231.

———. "Early Scores in Manuscript," in Journal of the American Musicological Society, XIII (1960), 126.

———. "On the Use of Scores by Sixteenth-Century Musicians," in Journal of the American Musicological Society, I (1948), 17.

———, ed. The Medici Codex of 1518 (3 vv., Chicago, 1968; = Monuments of Renaissance Music, vv. 3–5).

———. Tonality and Atonality in 16th-Century Music (Berkeley and Los Angeles, 1961; 2nd rev. pr., 1962).

Marot, C. Oeuvres Lyriques: see C. Mayer.

Mayer, C. A., ed. Clément Marot: Oeuvres Lyriques (1964).

Minor, A. C., ed. Music in Medieval and Renaissance Life (Columbia [Missouri], 1964).

Monte, P. de. Opera: see C. van den Borren and J. van Nuffel.

Osthoff, H. Josquin Desprez (2 vv.; Tutzing, 1962–5).

Petrarca, F. Rime, Trionfi, e Poesie Latine (ed. F. Neri, et al., Milan and Naples, 1951; = La Letteratura Italiana, VI).

Pidoux, P., et al., eds. Goudimel: Oeuvres Complètes (New York, 1967–).

Pogue, S., Jacques Moderne: Lyons Music Printer of the Sixteenth Century (Geneva, 1969).

Prés, Josquin des Werken: Wereldlijke Werken: see A. Smijers.

Reese, G. "Maldeghem and His Buried Treasure: a Bibliographical Study," in Notes, VI (1948), 75.

———. Music in the Renaissance (rev. ed., New York, 1959).

Ronsard, P. de. Oeuvres Complètes: See G. Cohen, P. Laumonier.

Ruutz–Rees, C. Charles de Ste. Marthe (1512–55), Fr. transl. by M. Bonnet (Paris, [1914]).

Saulnier, V. L. "Dominique Phinot et Didier Lupi, musiciens de Clément Marot et des Marotiques," in Revue de Musicologie, XLIII (1959), 80.

Schmidt–Görg, J. Nicolas Gombert, Leben und Werk (Bonn, 1938).

———, ed. Nicolai Gombert: Opera Omnia (= Corpus Mensurabilis Musicae, 6; Rome, 1951–).

Seay, A., ed. Jacobus Arcadelt: Opera Omnia (= Corpus Mensurabilis Musicae, 31; Rome, 1965–).

Sermisy, C. de: see I. Cazeaux.

Slim, H. C., ed. Musica Nova (Venice, 1540) (= Monuments of Renaissance Music, I; Chicago, 1964).

Smijers, A., ed. Josquin des Prés: Werken (1921–).

Ste. Marthe, C. de: see C. Ruutz–Rees.

St. Gelais, M. de Oeuvres Complètes: see P. Blanchemain.

Sternfeld, F. W. "Vautrollier's Printing of Lasso's Recueil du Mellange (London, 1570)," in Annales Musicologiques, V (1957), 199.

Strunk, O. Source Readings in Music History (New York, 1950).

Tiersot, J. Ronsard et la Musique de son temps (Leipzig and Paris, 1903).

Trotter, R. M. The Franco–Flemish Chansons of Thomas Crecquillon (unpubl. diss., University of Southern California, 1957).

Vicentino, N. Opera Omnia: see H. Kaufman.

Whitehead, P. J. P. "The Lost Berlin Manuscripts," in Notes, XXXIII (1976), 7.

Wolf, J. Handbuch der Notationskunde (2 vv., Leipzig, 1913 and 1919; = Kleine Handbücher der Musikgeschichte, viii; repr., 1963).

Indexes Incipits

(References are to works in the *Mellange*)

A ce matin (Nicolas): 29
A jamais croy (Crequillon): 60
A la fontaine du pré (Vuillard): 100
Allegez moy douce plaisant (Josquin): 129
Aller m'y faut (Vuillard): 37
Allez, mes soupirs (Goudimel): 84
Allons, allons gay (LeJeune): 22
Amour au coeur me point (Clemens non papa): 143
Amour me tue (Goudimel): 46
Amour, partez (Vuildre): 88
Amy, souffrez (Vuildre): 142
Arrousez vo vi vo violette (Benedictus): 91
Au joli bois (Lupi): 71
Auprés de vous (Farabosco): 49
Avecques vous (Nicolas): 45

Baisés moy tant tant (Vuillard): 93
Banny j'en suis (Roussel): 44
Belle, donne moy (Crequillon): 94

C'est à grand tort (Clemens non papa): 135
C'est une dure departie (LeJeune): 134
Ce que mon coeur pense (Mouton): 4
Complainte de la Torterelle (Que dis tu, que fais tu) (Gardane): 144
Contentement (Millot): 77
Content ou non (Crequillon): 61
Content ou non (Roussel): 41
Coeur langoureux (Josquin): 55
Cuidez vous que Dieu nous (Richafort): 6

D'amour je suis desheritée (Richafort): 92
De retourner, mon amy (Vuillard): 110
De vous servir (Vuildre): 96
Dieu te gard, bergere (Nicolas): 115
Douce maitresse touche (Millot): 65

Douleur me bat (Vuillard): 106
Du bon du coeur (Mouton): 86
Dueil, double dueil (Lupi): 133

Elle veut donc (Millot): 76
En despit des faux médisans (Moulu): 121
En douleur & tristesse (Vuillard): 103
En languissant (Crequillon): 35
Est-il douleur cruelle (Leschenet): 95

Faute d'argent (Josquin): 62
Faute d'argent (Vuillard): 104
Force d'amour (Maillard): 38
Force d'amour (Nicolas): 66
Fortune, laisse moy la vie (Rousée): 17
Fuyez de moy (Gardane): 139

Grace & vertu (Nicolas): 63
Gris & tanné (Leschenet): 98

Helas, ma dame (Vuildre): 83
Helas, ma fille, il te tuera (Maillard): 40
Helas, ma mere (Vuillart): 2
Helas, pourquoy ne suis-je mariée (Leschenet): 117
Herbes & fleurs (Hauville): 20

Il est bon enfant (Nicolas): 31
Incessamment mon povre coeur (LaRue): 99

J'ay contenté ma volonté (Nicolas): 123
J'ay mis mon coeur (Moulu): 138
Je cerche autant amour (Gardane): 118
Je file quand Dieu me donne (Vuildre): 13
Je l'ay aymée (Vuillard): 42
Je me complein (Josquin): 50
Je m'en vois au vert bois (Nicolas): 25
Je me repens d'avoir aymé (Vuildre): 11
Je m'y levay par un matin (Benedictus): 7
Je m'y plein fort (Leschenet): 111
Je ne fay rien que requerir (Vuildre): 90
Je ne me puis tenir d'aymer (Josquin): 57
Je ne sçaurois chanter (Vuillard): 85
Je recommence ma douleur (Nicolas): 122
Je ry & si ay larmes (Nicolas): 27
Je suis desheritée (LeJeune): 132
Jouissance vous donneray (Vuillart): 1

La rousée du mois de may (Mouton): 16

La rousée du mois de may (Moulu): 120
La rousée du mois de may (Rousée): 119
Las, je languis (Maillard): 127
Las voulez vous (Nicolas): 56
Le berger & la bergere (Gombert): 70
Le berger & la bergere (Mouton): 5
Le coeur de vous (Nicolas): 67
Le coeur est mien (Leschenet): 116
Le cors s'en va (Millot): 64
Le Rossignol sauvage (Millot): 81

Ma bouche rit (Vuildre): 12
Mon coeur, mon corps (Vuillard): 105
Mort ou mercy (Vuillard): 54

N'a vous point veu (LeBrun): 79
N'aurai-je jamais mieux (Nicolas): 39
N'est-ce pas un grand desplaisir (Josquin): 53

O pas en vain perdus (LeJeune): 131
Or me traictiez (Cornet): 21
Or suis-je bien au pire (Vuillard): 102
O triste ennuy (Monte): 97

Parfons regretz (Josquin): 51
Par trop amour (Fourmentin): 126
Par un traict d'or (Phinot): 147
Passa la nave mia (Vicentino): 136
Petite camusette (Crequillon): 140
Petite camusette (Vuillard): 107
Pis ne me peut venir (Crequillon): 47
Pour m'esloigner (Strige): 19
Pour ton amour (Nicolas): 30
Pour un plaisir (Vuildre): 10
Pour vous aymer (Vuildre): 9
Puis donc que ma maistresse (Vuillard): 101
Puis qu'ainsi est (Godard): 58
Puis que j'ay belle amye (Leschenet): 23
Puis que j'ay belle amye (Nicolas): 125
Puis que j'ay perdu ma maitresse (Vuillard): 34

Quand je me trouve (Arcadet): 8
Quand vous seriés (LeJeune): 24
Que dis tu, que fais tu (Gardane): 144
Qu'est-ce qu'amour (Phinot): 146
Qui la dira (Verdelot): 148
Qui la dira (Vuillart): 3

Qui veut aymer (Vuillard): 109

Regret, soucy, & peine (Certon): 89
Revien vers moy (Certon): 141
Revien vers moy (Millot): 69
Rossignol, mon mignon (LeJeune): 80

Secourez moy ma dame (Monte): 14
Si de beaucoup je suis (Vuildre): 43
Si je me plein, helas, je n'ay (Benedictus): 68
Si je trespasse (Millot): 75
Si la beauté (Arcadet): 73
Sire don Dieu (Vuillard): 72
Sonnez m'y donc (Vuillart): 33
Sur la rousée m'y faut (Millot): 78
Sur tous regretz (Nicolas): 48
Susanne un jour (LeJeune): 137
Susanne un jour (Millot): 74
Susanne un jour (Nicolas): 26
Susanne un jour (Rore): 18
Sy je m'y plain, j'ay bien raison (Richaffort): 32
Sy me tenez tant (Crequillon): 112

Tenez moy en voz bras (Josquin): 128
Tout ce qu'on peut (Nicolas): 28
Tout est vert en no maison (Nicolas): 130

Une nonnain (Vuildre): 87
Un jeune moyne (Vuildre): 82

Vivés en paix (Nicolas): 114
Vivons m'amye (Phinot): 145
Vivre en espoir (Crequillon): 36
Voulez ouir chansonnette (Vuillard): 52
Vous aurez tout ce qui est mien (Vuillard): 59
Vous ne l'aurez pas (Vuillard): 108
Vray Dieu d'amours (Mouton): 15
Vray Dieu qu'amoureux (Mouton): 113
Voz huys sont ilz (Nicolas): 124

Composers, Poets

(Numerical references are to compositions, not pages)

Appenzeller: see Benedictus
Arcadelt: 8, 73
Arcadet: see Arcadelt

Bäif: 131
Benedictus: 7, 68, 91

Catullus: see 145
Certon: 89, 141
Clemens non Papa: 135, 143
Clement, J.: see Clemens non Papa
Cornet: 21
Crecquillon: 35, 36, 47, 60, 61, 94, 112, 140
Crequillon: see Crecquillon

Farabosco: see Ferrabosco
Ferrabosco: 49
Forcadel: 147
Fourmentin: 126
François I.er: see 110
Fromentin: see Fourmentin

Gardane: 118, 139, 144
Gardano: see Gardane
Godard: 58
Gombert: 70
Goudimel: 46, 84
Guéroult: 18, 26, 74, 137

Hauville: 20

Josquin: see Prez

La Rue: 99
Le Brun: 79
LeJeune: 22, 24, 80, 131, 132, 134, 137
Leschenet: 23, 95, 98, 111, 116, 117
Lupi: 71, 133

Maillard: 38, 40, 127
Marot, C.: 1, 14, 30, 67, 87, 90, 123, 143
Marot, J.: 54
Millot: 64, 65, 69, 74–8, 81
Monte: 14, 97
Moulu: 120, 121, 138
Mouton: 4, 5, 15, 16, 86, 113

Nicolas: 25–31, 39, 45, 48, 56, 63, 66, 67, 114, 115, 122–5, 130
Nicole: see Vicentino

Petrarch: 136; see also 84
Phinot: 145–7
Prez (des Prez): 50, 51, 53, 55, 57, 62, 128, 129

Richafort: 6, 32, 92
Ronsard: 46, 65, 69, 75, 80, 141, 144
Rore: 18
Rousée: 17, 119
Roussel: 41, 44

St. Gelais: 19
Ste. Marthe: 38, 66
Strige: see Striggio

Striggio: 19

Verdelot: 148
Vicentino: 136
Vuildre: see Wilder
Vuillard or Vuillart: see Willaert

Wilder: 9–13, 43, 82, 83, 87, 88, 90, 96, 142
Willaert: 1–3, 33, 34, 37, 42, 52, 54, 59, 72, 85, 93, 100–10